Leg over Leg

Volume Four

Letter from the General Editor

The Library of Arabic Literature is a new series offering Arabic editions and English translations of key works of classical and pre-modern Arabic literature, as well as anthologies and thematic readers. Books in the series are edited and translated by distinguished scholars of Arabic and Islamic studies, and are published in parallel-text format with Arabic and English on facing pages. The Library of Arabic Literature includes texts from the pre-Islamic era to the cusp of the modern period, and encompasses a wide range of genres, including poetry, poetics, fiction, religion, philosophy, law, science, history, and historiography.

Supported by a grant from the New York University Abu Dhabi Institute, and established in partnership with NYU Press, the Library of Arabic Literature produces authoritative Arabic editions and modern, lucid English translations, with the goal of introducing the Arabic literary heritage to scholars and students, as well as to a general audience of readers.

Philip F. Kennedy
General Editor, Library of Arabic Literature

كتاب

الساق على الساق

فى ما هو الفارياق

فارس الشدياق

المجلد الرابع

Leg over Leg

or

The Turtle in the Tree

concerning

The Fāriyāq

What Manner of Creature Might He Be

by

Fāris al-Shidyāq

Volume Four

Edited and translated by
Humphrey Davies

NEW YORK UNIVERSITY PRESS
New York and London

NEW YORK UNIVERSITY PRESS
New York and London

Library of Congress Cataloging-in-Publication Data

Shidyaq, Ahmad Faris, 1804?-1887.
Leg over leg or, : The turtle in the tree / Faris al-Shidyaq ; edited and translated by Humphrey Davies.
volumes cm
Bilingual edition In English and Arabic on facing pages.
Includes bibliographical references and index.
ISBN 978-1-4798-7575-7 (cl : alk. paper) -- ISBN 978-1-4798-8392-9 (e-book) -- ISBN 978-1-4798-7920-5 (e-book) 1. Shidyaq, Ahmad Faris, 1804?-1887. 2. Shidyaq, Ahmad Faris, 1804?-1887--Travel--Middle East. 3. Arabic language--Lexicography. 4. Middle East--Description and travel. I. Davies, Humphrey T. (Humphrey Taman) translator, editor. II. Shidyaq, Ahmad Faris, 1804?-1887. Saq ʿala al-saq. III. Shidyaq, Ahmad Faris, 1804?-1887. Saq ʿala al-saq. English. IV. Title. V. Title: Turtle in the tree.
PJ7862.H48S213 2013
892.7'8503--dc23
2013007540
CIP

New York University Press books are printed on acid-free paper, and their binding materials are chosen for strength and durability.

Series design by Titus Nemeth.

Typeset in Tasmeem, using DecoType Naskh and Emiri.

Typesetting and digitization by Stuart Brown.

Manufactured in the United States of America
c10 9 8 7 6 5 4 3 2 1

Table of Contents

الساق على الساق

المجلّد الرابع

Leg Over Leg

Volume Four

كتاب

الساق على الساق فى ما هو الفارياق

او

ايام وشهور واعوام فى عجم العرب والاعجام

تاليف العبد الفقير الى ربه الرزاق

فارس بن يوسف الشدياق

Leg over Leg

or

The Turtle in the Tree

concerning

The Fāriyāq

What Manner of Creature Might He Be

otherwise entitled

Days, Months, and Years

spent in

Critical Examination

of

The Arabs

and

Their Non-Arab Peers

by

The Humble Dependent on His Lord the Provider

Fāris ibn Yūsuf al-Shidyāq

فهرست الكتاب

Contents of the Book

١ تليها في ١٨٥٥: تصليح ما وقع من الاغلاط فى هذا الكتاب *

الكتاب الرابع

Book Four

الفصل الاول

في اطلاق بحر

من لم يسافر فى البحار ويقاسِ فيه الانوآ والامواج فلا يقدر ترفه المعيشة فى البر ١،١،٤
حق قدرها * فينبغى لك ايها القارى البرّىّ ان تتصور فى بالك كلما اعوزك المآ
القراح واللحم الغضيض والفاكهة الطريّة والبقول الخَضِلة والخبز الليّن ان اخوانك
ركاب البحر محرومون من هذا كله * وان سفينتهم لا تزال تميد بهم وتتقلب وتصعد
وتهبط * فدون كل لقمة يسترطونها غصة * وفى كل رقدة يرقدونها مغصة *
وانه متى وضع بين يديك لون واحد من الطعام فلا تفكر الّا فيه * واعتقد ان غيرك ٢،١،٤
يغتذى بمثله فى تلك الساعة بل باقلّ منه * فبذلك يحصل لك التاسّى والتسلى *
فاما اذا نظرت الى قصور الملوك والامرآ وصروح الوزراء وفكرت فيما ياكلون
ويشربون فانك لا ريب تتعب نفسك وتعنّيها لغير فائدة * ولكن اتحسب أن المعتّقة
التى يشربها الامير الذّ من المآ الذى تشربه انت * حالة كونك عارفا بامور المعاش
والمعاد * مضطلعا بادارة مصلحة لك تكفيك واهلك المؤنة * وحالة كون زوجتك
تجلس قبالتك اوعن يمينك وشمالك * وولدك الصغير على ركبتك * تارة يغنى
لك * وتارة يناولك بيده اللطيفة ما سالت عنه امه * واذا خرجت شيعاك
الى الباب واذا قدمت صعدا معك واجلساك على انظف متكا فى الدار *

Chapter 1

Unleashing a Sea

Only one who has traveled the seas and experienced the misery of their tempests and swells can properly appreciate the ease of life on land. Whenever, then, my dear landlubber of a reader, you feel a need for clean water, tender meat, fresh fruit, succulent greens, or soft bread, you must bear in mind that your seafaring brethren are deprived of all such things, that their vessel never stops moving beneath their feet, tossing them, turning them, and throwing them up and down, that before every mouthful of food they swallow they must first choke, and that before lying down to sleep they must first suffer a bellyache. 4.1.1

Likewise, when food of just one kind is placed before you, think only of that and know well that others too are dining at this hour, and perhaps on something more meager still. If you do so, you will find solace and distraction. If, however, you lift your eyes to the palaces of kings and princes and the mansions of ministers and wonder what they are eating and drinking, you will certainly tire and torment yourself to no avail. Do you really imagine that the aged wine drunk by the prince is more delicious than the water you are drinking, so long as you are informed as to the affairs of this world and the next and are proficient in the management of some business of yours that provides for yourself and your family, so long as your wife sits before you or on your right or left while your small child sits on your knee, singing to you one moment, passing you with his sweet hand anything you may have asked your wife to give you the next, and so long as on your departure, they accompany you to the door and on your arrival, take you upstairs and seat you on the best cushion in the house? 4.1.2

فاما انت ياسيدى الغنى فالاولى لك ان تسافر من مدينتك العامرة حتى ترى ٣،١،٤
بعينيك ما لم تره فى بلدك * وتسمع باذنيك ما لم تسمعه * وتختبر احوال غير
قومك وعاداتهم واطوارهم وتدرى اخلاقهم ومذاهبم وسياستهم * ثم تقابل بعد
ذلك بين الحسن عندهم وغير الحسن عندنا * ومتى دخلت بلادهم وكنت جاهلا
بلغتهم فلا تحرص بحقك على تعلم كلام الخَنَى منهم اوّلا * او تستحلى الاسمآ من
اجل المسمّيات * فان كل لغة فى الكون فيها الطيب والخبيث * اذ اللغة انما هى
عبارة عن حركات الانسان وافعاله وافكاره * ومعلوم ان فى هذه ما يُحمد وما
يذمّ * فأُجلّك عن ان تكون كبعض المسافرين الذين لا يتعلمون من لغات غيرهم
الا اسمآ بعض الاعضآ وعبارات اخرى سخيفة * لا بل ينبغى لك حين تدخل
بلادهم سالما ان تقصد قبل كل شى المدارس والمطابع وخزائن الكتب والمستشفيات
والمخاطب * اى الاماكن التى يخطب فيها العلمآ فى كل الفنون والعلوم * فمنها ما
هو معدّ للخطابة فقط ومنها ما يشتمل على جميع الالات والادوات اللازمة لذلك
العلم * واذا رجعت بحمده تعالى الى بلدك فاجتهد فى ان تولف رحلة تشهرها بين ٤،١،٤
اهل بلادك لينتفعوا بها ولكن من دون قصد التكسّب ببيعها * وياليتك تشارك
بعض اصحابك من الاغنيآ فى انشآ مطبعة تطبع فيها غير ذلك من الكتب المفيدة
للرجال والنسآ والاولاد ولكل صنف من الناس على حدته * حتى يعرفوا ما لهم
وما عليهم من الحقوق * سوآ كانت تلك الكتب عربية او معرّبة * ولكن احذر
من ان تخلط فى نقلك عن العجم الطيب بالخبيث والصحيح بالمعتل * فان المدن الغنآ
تكثر فيها الرذائل كما تكثر الفضائل * نعم ان من هولآ الناس لَمن يابى ان يرى ٥،١،٤
احدا وهو على الطعام * واذا اضطر الى رؤيته وهو على تلك الحالة فلا يدعوه للَوس
شى مما بين يديه * لكن منهم من يدعوك الى صرحه فى الريف فتقيم فيه الاسبوع

As for you, my dear rich gentleman, you would do better to leave your prosperous city to see with your own eyes what you cannot see in your own country and hear with your own ears what you cannot hear there, to experience how other people live and their customs and ways, to discover their morals and modes of thought and how they govern themselves. After that, you may compare the good things in their land with the bad things in ours. And when you enter their country and are ignorant of their language, don't insist on learning the dirty words from them first or delight in words for the sake of the things they denote, for every language in the universe has fair and foul given that language expresses the actions, deeds, and thoughts of men, which encompass, as all will agree, both the praiseworthy and the blameworthy. I hold you in too high esteem to imagine that you will be like those travelers who learn of other people's languages only the names of certain parts of the body and other despicable terms. On the contrary, when you arrive safe and sound in a country you must, before anything else, make for the schools, printing presses, libraries, hospitals, and lecture rooms (by which I mean those places where scholars speak on every art and science; some of these are equipped only for public addresses while others contain every instrument and device required for the science in question). 4.1.3

And when you return, by God's grace, to your own town, exert yourself to write a book about your travels and publicize it among your countrymen so that they may benefit—but without any intention to make money from the sale of it. Would that you might partner too with some of your fellow rich in establishing a printing press on which to print further books that may be useful to men, women, and children and to each category of person so that they may learn what their rights and duties are, whether those books be written originally in Arabic or translated into it. Be careful, though, that in copying from the non-Arabs, you do not confuse the fair with the foul, the sound with the defective. Great cities are as full of vices as they are of virtues. 4.1.4

True, among those people there are some who will refuse to see anyone when they are at table and, if compelled to do so, will not invite him to taste any of what is before them. Others, though, will invite you to their mansions in the countryside, where you may stay for a week, or two weeks, with 4.1.5

والاسبوعين وانت الآمر الناهى * وان منهم لمن يبخل عليك برد التحية * واذا دخلت دار صديق منهم وكان فى المجلس جماعة من اصدقائه لم يعرفوك من قبل فما احد منهم يتحلحل لك فى القيام ولا يعبا بك ولا يلتفت اليك * لكن منهم من اذا عرفك اهتم بامرك فى حضورك وغيابك على حد سوى * واذا ائتمنته على سرّ كتمه لك طول حياته * وان منهم لمن ينبزك بالالقاب اول ما يقع نظره على شاربيك ولحيتك او على عمامتك او يجذبك من ذيلك من ورآ * ولكن منهم من يتهافت على معرفة الغريب ويتراح الى الرفق به والاحسان اليه ويرى اجارته وحمايته فرضا عليه متحتما * وان منهم لمن يسخر منك اذا راك تلحن فى لغته * ولكن منهم من يحرص على ان يعلمك اياها مجانا اما بنفسه او بواسطة زوجته وبناته * وعلى ان يعيرك ما يفيدك من كتب وغيرها ويرشدك الى ما فيه صلاح امرك وتوفيقك *
٦،١،٤ وان منهم لمن يحسبك قد وافيت بلاده تسابقه على رزقه فيكلح فى وجهك وينظر اليك شزرا * لكن منهم من ينزلك فى بلده منزلة ضيف يجب اكرامه واحترامه والذبّ عنه بحيث لا تفصل عنه وفى قلبك ادنى اَلَم من اهله * وان منهم لمن يسخّرك ان تترجم له او تعلمه ثم لا يقول لك احسنت يامترجم او يامعلم * لكن منهم من لا يستحلّ ان يكلمك من دون ان يودّى اليك اجرة فتح فمك وضم شفتيك * وان منهم لمن اذا اضطر الى ان يدعوك الى طعامه ثم راك قد سعلت سعلة او مخطت مخطة او فنخرت فنخرة قال لزوجته اَلَا انّ ضيفنا مريض * فلا ينبغى ان تكثرى له من الطعام * فتقوم عن المائدة متضورا ويمتنّ هو عليك بين معارفه بانه صنع لك وليمة فى عام كذا وشهر كذا ويوم كذا فيجعل تلك الليلة تاريخا * لكن منهم من اذا عرف انك مقيم فى احدى قرى بلاده حيث لا بيع ولا شرآ ولا شى ينال من البقول والاثمار بعث اليك من مباقله وحدائقه ما سدّ فاك عن الشكوى *

everyone at your beck and call. True, some will begrudge a response to your greeting, and if you enter the house of one such who is your friend and his salon is full of friends of his who do not already know you, not one of them will bestir himself to stand and greet you or pay you the slightest attention or even turn toward you. On the other hand, there are those who, once they have gotten to know you, will be as solicitous of your welfare when you are absent as they are when you are present, and if you confide a secret to them, will keep it as long as they live. True, there are those who will call you names as soon as they set eyes on your mustaches, beard, or turban and will tug on the skirt of your robe from behind, but there are also those who have a passionate desire to become acquainted with strangers, are happy to be in their company and to do good to them, and think it a duty to aid and protect them. True, there are those who will mock you when they see you making mistakes in their language, but there are also those who will be intent on teaching it to you without charge, either themselves or via their wives or daughters, and on lending you books and other things that may be of use to you and guide you to whatever may serve your interests and success.

True, there are those who will reckon that you have turned up in their country to compete with them for their livelihoods and therefore scowl in your face and look at you askance, but there are also those who will regard you as a guest in their country to be honored, respected, and defended so that you depart without harboring the slightest hard feeling against their countrymen. True, there are those who will use you as forced labor, to translate for them or teach them, and never say, "Thank you, translator!" or "Thank you, teacher!" but there are also those who will regard it as sinful to speak to you without sending you payment for opening your mouth and closing your lips. True, there are those who, if they are compelled to invite you to eat with them and then notice you coughing, blowing your nose, or flaring your nostrils, will tell their wives, "He must be sick; you don't have to give him a lot of food" so that you rise from the table starving while they make a great show of you among their guests, claiming that in the year so-and-so and month so-and-so, on such and such a day, they held a great banquet for you, treating that night as though it marked the start of some new historical era. On the other hand, there are also those who, on discovering that you are staying in some village in their country where there is no trade 4.1.6

كما كان مستر دراموند يبعث الى الفارياق حين قدر الله عليه بالسكنى فى بعض
تلك القرى فكانت شكواه منها تسمع مع دوى الريح * ليت شعرى اليس وجود مئة ٧،١،٤
كتاب بدارك فى الاقل خيرا من وجود كذا وكذا قصبة للتبغ وكذا وكذا اركيلة * مع
ان ثمن المئة كتاب لا يوازى ثمن ثلث قطع من الكهربا * اليس وجود مطبعة فى
بلادك اولى من هذه الطيالس الكشميرية وتلك الفرآ السمورية وهذه الآنية النفيسة
والحلى الفاخر * فان الغنسان اذا نظر الى الحلى لا يستفيد منه شيا لا لبدنه ولا
لراسه * وغاية فرحه به انما هو الشهر الذى اشتراه فيه فاذا مضت عليه اشهر
استوى عنده وسقط المتاع فلم يبق منه ما يسرّه من وجوده سوى بيعه * فاما
الكتاب فانه كلما مرت عليه السنون زادت قيمته وكثرت منافعه * او ليس اطلاعك
على التاريخ والجغرافية واداب الناس زينة لك بين اخوانك ومعارفك تفوق على زينة
الجواهر * اليس تعليم اهلك وذويك شيا من ذلك ومن قواعد لازمة لحفظ الصحة
من كتب الطب يكسبك عند الله اجرا ويومنك من مضار كثيرة تتطرق اليهم
لجهلهم بها * فان قلت انه ليس عندنا كتب فى العربية تصلح للنسآ * قلت هب ٨،١،٤
ما قلته حقا ولكن اليس عند الافرنج كتب مختصة بالنسآ والاولاد يولّفها الرجال
الفاضلون المهذّبون * فلمَ تشترى من الافرنج الخزّ والمتاع ولا تشترى منهم العلم
والحكمة والاداب * ثم انك مهما بالغت فى ان تبرقع زوجتك عن روية الدنيا فلن
تستطيع ان تخفيها عن قلبها * فان المراة حيثما كانت وكيفما كانت هى بنت الدنيا
وامّها واختها وضرّتها * لا تقل لى ان المراة اذا كانت شريرة لا يصلحها الكتاب بل
يزيدها شرّة * واذا كانت صالحة فما بها من حاجة اليه * فانى اقول ان المراة كانت
اولا بنتا قبل ان صارت امراة * وان الرجل كان من قبل ولداً * ولا ينكر احد
ان التعليم على صغر * كالنقر فى الحجر * وانك اذا ربّيت ولدك فى العلم والمعارف

and nothing to be obtained by way of green vegetables or fruit, will send you, from their own gardens and orchards, enough to stop your mouth against any complaint. Thus it was with Mr. Drummond,[1] when the Fāriyāq found himself fated to reside in one such village and his complaints were carried on the wind to people's ears.

How I wish the presence in your home of a hundred books did not count as less of a witness to good fortune than that of a hundred tobacco pipes or a hundred water pipes, even though the cost of a hundred books is less than that of three pieces of amber![2] Isn't the presence of a printing press in your country more important than all these cashmere shawls, sables, precious vessels, and expensive pieces of jewelry? If a person looks at a piece of jewelry, he derives no benefit from it either for his body or his brain; his pleasure in it lasts no longer than the month in which he bought it, and after a few months have passed it's no more to him than scrap metal, the only pleasure to be derived from it being that of selling it. A book, on the other hand, grows more valuable with each passing year, and its benefits multiply. Are not your readings in history, geography, and the literatures of the world an adornment to you among your brethren and acquaintances that surpasses gemstones? If you teach your family and dependents a portion of such things and, from books of medicine, of the principles necessary for the preservation of their health, will you not win reward from God and protection from many an injury that might befall them as a result of their ignorance? 4.1.7

If you say, "We have no books in Arabic suitable for women," I reply, "Supposing you are right, do not the Franks have books written by refined and virtuous men specially for women and children? Why do you buy fabrics and furnishings from the Franks and not knowledge, wisdom, or literature? Then again, no matter what lengths you may go to in order to shield your wife from seeing the world, you will never be able to hide it from her heart. A woman, wherever and however she be, is this world's daughter and its mother, sister, and co-wife. Do not say to me, 'A book won't set an evil woman to rights but will make her yet more wicked, and if she's righteous, she doesn't need one,' for I will reply that a woman was a girl before she became a woman and a man was once a boy. No one can deny that educating the young is like carving on rock and that if you raise your offspring with 4.1.8

والفضائل والمحامد يربون على ما ربّيتهم عليه * وتكون قد ادّيت ما فرضه الله عليك
من تاديبهم * فتفارقهم بعد العمر الطويل وخاطرك مجبور وبالك رخى مطمئن *
فلم يبق لك الا ان تقول ان ابى لم يعلمنى وكذا جدى لم يعلم ابى وانى بهما اقتدى ٤،١،٩
* فاقول لك ان الدنيا فى عهد المرحومين جدك وابيك لم تكن كما هى الآن * اذ لم
يكن فى عصرهما سفن النار ودروب الحديد التى تقرب البعيد * وتجدد العهيد *
وتصل المقطوع * وتبذل الممنوع * ولم يكن يلزم الانسان فى ذلك الوقت ان يتعلم
لغات كثيرة * فكان كل من يقول خوش كلدى صفا كلدى يقال فيه انه يصلح لان
يكون ترجمانا فى باب همايون * وكل من كان يكتب خطا دون خطى هذا الذى
سودت به هذا الكتاب * لا الذى تقراه الآن فانى برىء من هذه الحروف * كان
يقال عنه انه كاتب ماهر يصلح لان يكون منشى ديوان * فاما الآن فهيهات *
هذا الفارياق حين نوى السفر من الجزيرة الى بلاد الانكليز كان بعض الناس يقول ٤،١،١٠
له انك سائر الى بلاد لا تطلع عليها الشمس * وبعضهم يقول الى ارض لا ينبت
فيه القمح ولا البقول * ولا يوجد فيها من الماكول الا اللحم والقلقاس * وبعضهم
يقول انى اخاف عليك ان تفقد فيها رئتك لعدم الهوآ * وبعضهم يقول امعاك
لعدم الاكل * وبعضهم صدرك اوعضوا آخر غيره * فلما سار اليها وجد الشمس
شمسا والهوآ هوآ * والمآ مآ * والرجال رجالا والنسآ نسآ * والديار ماهولة
والمدن معمورة * والارض محروثة اريضة * كثيرة الصُوَى والاعلام * خضلة
الغياض والرُبُض والاجام * ناضرة المروج * زاهية الحقول * غضة البقول *
فلو انه سمع لاولئك الناس لفاته رؤية ذلك اجمع * فان خشيت ان تفوتك هناك
لذة الاركيلة ولذة تكبيس الرجلين قبل الرقاد * فاعلم ان ما ترى هناك من العجائب

knowledge, general education, virtue, and praiseworthy qualities, they will grow up as you have raised them and you will have performed the duty that God has imposed upon you of making them into decent people, in which case you will leave them (after a long life, God willing) with a clear conscience and a mind at ease and serene."

The only argument left to you is to say, "My father gave me no educa- 4.1.9
tion, just as my grandfather gave my father none, and I have followed in their footsteps," but I tell you, the world in your late grandfather's and father's day was not as it is now. In their day, there were no steamboats or railway *tracks* to bring close far-off *tracts* and create new *pacts*, to connect the *disconnected*, and make accessible what was *once protected*. Then, one didn't have to learn many languages. It could be said of anyone who knew a few words of Turkish—Welcome, my lord! How nice to see you, my lord!—that he'd make a fine interpreter at the imperial court, and of any who could write a hand worse than the hand with which I have penned this book (not the one you're actually reading now, for whose typeface I take no responsibility[3]) that he was a skilled calligrapher who would make a fine secretary to a king's council. Not now!

When our friend the Fāriyāq made his decision to leave the island for 4.1.10
England, someone told him, "You are going to a land over which the sun never rises"; another, " . . . to a land where no wheat or green vegetables grow and the only foods to be had are meat and turnips"[4]; another, "I fear that you may lose your lungs there for lack of air"; another, "or your intestines for lack of food"; and another, "or your chest or some other part of your body." When he got there, though, he found that the sun was the sun, the air air, water water, men men, and women women, that the land was populated and the cities well inhabited, the earth plowed and pleasing to the eye, well signposted and marked, resplendent with woods, mighty trees, and forests, green with meadows, proud in its *fields*, succulent in the green vegetables its soil *yields*; had he listened to those people, he would have missed seeing all of that. Thus, if you're afraid that you would hanker for the pleasures of the water pipe or of having your legs massaged before going to sleep, know that the marvels you will see there will make you forget all such luxuries and distract you from everything to which, in your noble position in society, you have become accustomed.

١١،١،٤ ينسيك هذا النعيم * ويلهيك عمّا الفته فى مقامك الكريم * كيف ترضى لنفسك
ان تفارق هذه الدنيا ولم ترها وانت قادر على ذلك * وقد قال ابو الطيب المتنبى

ولم ارَ فى عيوب الناس شيا   كنقص القادرين على التمام

ام كيف تقتصر على معرفة ربع لغة ولا تتشوق الى علم ما يفكر فيه غيرك * فلعل
تحت قبعته افكارا ومعانى لم تخطر بما تحت طربوشك * بحيث انك اذا استوعبتها
تودّ لو انك عاصرت صاحبها وتشرفت بمعرفته وصنعت له مادبة فاخرة زينتها
بصحاف الرز والبرغل * وكيف تبلغ من عمرك ثلثين سنة ولم تولّف شيا يفيد
اهل بلادك * فما ارى بين يديك الا دفاتر بيع وشرآ وفناديق دخل وخرج *
١٢،١،٤ ورسائل فاسدة المعانى ركيكة الالفاظ تنظر فيها فى كل صباح ومسآ * فاما
اذا قصدت السفر لمجرد التفاخر فقط بان تقول مثلا فى مجلس زارك فيه اصحابك
الكرمآ * واقرانك العظما * قد رايت مدينة كذا وشاهدت شوارعها النظيفة
الواسعة وديارها الرحيبة ومراكبها الحسنة واسواقها البهيجة وخيلها المطهمة
ونساها الرائعة وعساكرها الجرارة * واكلت فيها فى اليوم الاول كذا وشربت فى
اليوم الثانى كذا * ثم ذهبنا بعد ذلك الى بعض الملاهى ثم الى احدى الملهيات *
وبت معها على فراش وطى * وكان قبالة السرير مرآة كبيرة فى طول الفراش
وعرضه فكنت ارى نفسى فيها كما كنت فى الفراش * ثم قمت فى الصباح وجاتنا
خادمة صبيحة بصبوح او فطور * ثم عدت الى محلى فوجدت فيه فلانا ينتظرنى
وكان ذلك نحو الساعة الحادية عشرة اى قبل الظهر بساعة * فتوجهنا معا الى
البستان المسمى بالبتسان السلطانى * وبينما نحن نمشى فيه وننظر الى الشجر الباسقة

How can you allow yourself to leave this world without ever having seen it when you have the means to do so? Abū l-Ṭayyib al-Mutanabbī has said 4.1.11

And no failing have I seen among men
To equal the falling short of those who have means.

How can you limit yourself to knowing a quarter of a language[5] and not yearn to know what others think? Under their hats may be ideas and thoughts that have never occurred to what's under your tarbush—so much so that, did you but comprehend them, you'd wish you could have been their thinker's contemporary, had the honor of his acquaintance, and held a splendid feast for him, decorated with sheaves of rice and wheat. How can you have reached the thirtieth year of your life without composing something of benefit to the people of your country? All I see before you are ledgers of sale and purchase, pages of outgoings and incomings, and letters full of corrupt phrases and lame expressions over which you pore morning and evening.

If, on the other hand, your intention in traveling is simply to be able to boast and say, for example, during some gathering when your noble friends and mighty peers are visiting, "I saw such and such a city and beheld its wide clean streets, spacious homes, fine ships, magnificent markets, beautiful horses, wonderful women, and hosts of soldiers, and ate such and such there on the first day and drank such and such on the second, after which we went to a place of entertainment and from there to a lady who entertains and I spent the night with her on a soft bed, and in front of the bed there was a large mirror as long and wide as the bed itself, so I could see myself in it just as I was in the bed, and then I got up in the morning and a bonny maid brought us breakfast (liquid or otherwise) and then I went back to my lodgings and found so-and-so waiting for me, the time being then eleven o'clock, or about an hour before noon, and we set off together for the park known as the Royal Park and while we were walking there, looking at the towering trees and ornamental flowers, I suddenly caught sight of the girl I'd spent the night with walking with a man who was paying court to her and when she saw me, she smiled and said hello, and her greeting didn't seem to upset the man, for he doffed his hat to me, and I was very much surprised at his lack of jealousy, as, had the girl been mine, I'd have hidden her from the light," then it all amounts to nothing but what's called in chaste Arabic *hadhar* ("prating"), *hurāʾ* ("prattling"), *haft* ("nonsense"), *harj* ("confusion"), *halj* 4.1.12

والزهور المدبجة اذا بالفتاة التى بت عندها تماشى رجلا يغازلها * فلما راتنى تبسمت
وسلمت علىّ * وكانّ سلامها لم يسؤ الرجل فانه نزع لى قبّعته فعجبت جدا من عدم
غيرته * اذ لوكانت الفتاة عندى لحجبتها عن النور * فذلك كله يسمى فى العربية
هَذَرا وهُرآء وهَفْتا وهرَجا وهَلْجا وسَقَطا وهَيْشا ووَتَغا وخَطَلا واِخلآ ولَخى وطَفانين
وهَذَيانا وثرثرة وفرفرة وحذرمة وهبرمة وهثرمة وخزربة وخطلبة وغيذرة وشمرجة
ونفرجة وهمرجة وثغثغة وفقفقة ولقلقلة ووقوقة وهتمنة وفى المتعارف عند العامة
فشارا وعلكا * اذ لا فائدة فيه لاحد من الناس * بخلاف ما اذا قلت لهم ان ١٣،١،٤
الغيسانى من الرجال هناك اذا حضر مجلسا فيه نسآ لا يغمز احداهن بعينه ولا
يتبظرم ولا يبتهر(١) * ولا يقول لها انه يزور النسآ المحصنات
بعلم بعولتهن وبغير علمهم وياكل عندهن ويشرب * ثم يخلو بهن فى
مضاجعهن ويرجع الى منزله مسرورا * وكايّ من مرة وضع يده
فى جيبه فوجد فيه كيسا ملان من الدنانير او كاغد حوالة على بعض الصيارفة *
وانه اذا مرّ فى الاسواق تتهافت على رويته البنات من الرواشن والشبابيك
والكُوَى والسِهآء والاَجلآ * فمنهن من تشير اليه بيدها او براسها * ومنهن من
تهجله بعينها ثم تضع يدها على قلبها * ومنهن من ترميه بوردة * واخرى بباقة
من المنثور او برقعة فيها شعر * او انه يقول بحضرتهن قد انحلّت تكّتى اوحكّنى
رفغى لكون حشو سراويلى غليظا * او يحك استه او يرطل عياره * او يتمطى
ويتمتّى ويتمطّط ويتمدّد ويتمطّل ويتمتأ ويتمتّت ويتمأّى ويتنَطّط ويتمعط ويتمغط ويتبسط
ويتبأّط * بل انما يكلمهن متادبا محتشما غاضّ الطرف خافض الصوت * ويسال
كبيرتهن عما طالعت يومها ذاك من الاخبار والحكايات والنوادر الادبية * وانه
شرع فى تاليف كتاب مفيد يشتمل على ذكر اثار الاقدمين واخبارهم * ثم يلقى

(١) تبظرم اذا كان احمق وعليه خاتم فيتكلم ويشير به فى وجوه الناس وابتهر ادعى كذبا وقال فجرت ولم يفجر *

("making incredible claims"), *saqaṭ* ("false reporting"), *haysh* ("talking too much"), *watagh* ("mindless verbiage"), *khaṭal* ("excessive nonsense"), *ikhlā'* ("vacancy"), *lakhā* ("much ado about nothing"), *ṭafānīn* ("idle talk"), *hadhayān* ("senseless jabber"), *thartharah* ("chattering"), *farfarah* ("chittering"), *ḥadhramah* ("loquacity"), *habramah* ("garrulousness"), *hathramah* ("garrulity"), *khazrabah* ("rambling"), *khaṭlabah* ("ranting"), *ghaydharah* ("raving"), *shamrajah* ("blathering"), *nafrajah* ("blethering"), *hamrajah* ("blabbering"), *thaghthaghah* ("gabbling"), *faqfaqah* ("burbling"), *laqlaqah* ("clattering"), *waqwaqah* ("barking"), and *hatmanah* ("bombast")—and in the ordinary speech of the common people, since it's of no use to anyone, *fashār* ("bragging") and *'alk* ("yakkety-yak").

It would be different were you to tell them that if a handsome young man 4.1.13
there attends a gathering where there are women, he doesn't wink at one of them or flash his costly ring about foolishly in her face as he talks or make false boast of his conquests.(1) He doesn't tell her that he visits women of unblemished reputation with and without the permission of their husbands and eats and drinks in their homes, then stays alone with them in their bedchambers and returns home in good cheer, and that many a time he has put his hand into his pocket and found there a purse full of gold coins or a draft drawn on a moneylender, or that when he walks through the markets, the girls crowd the casements, windows, apertures, peepholes, and skylights to catch sight of him, some making signs to him with their hands or their heads, others making sheep's eyes and putting their hands on their hearts, one throwing him a flower and another a posy of stocks or a scrap of paper bearing a verse. He doesn't say in their presence "My drawstring came undone" or "I've got jock itch because my package is so big" or scratch his anus or weigh his "yardarm" in his hand, or stretch, loll, sprawl, extend his body, lie at full length, elongate himself, protract himself, lounge, drape himself, lie flat on his face, extend his arms to their full length, spread himself out, or flop vacantly around. On the contrary, he speaks to them politely and respectfully, averting his gaze and lowering his voice, and he asks the eldest among them what news, stories, and edifying anecdotes have come her way that day, or he mentions that he has commenced that very day the composition of a beneficial book that

(1) One says of a man that he *tabaẓrama* ["flashed his ring about foolishly"] "if he is stupid and is wearing a signet ring and he talks and waves it about in people's faces" and that he *ibtahara* ["made false boast of his conquests"] if he "makes false claims and says 'I committed adultery' when he did not."

على صغيرتهن احجية ادبية ليلهيها بها وبمثل ذلك يدخل مكرما ويخرج محمودا *
١٤،١،٤ وبخلاف ما اذا قلت لهم ايضا ان التاجر المثرى هناك لا يتختم بخواتم الماس
والزمرّذ * ولا يتحلى بسلاسل الذهب * ولا يقتنى النادر من الاثاث والماعون
والفرش * بل انما ينفق امواله فى سبيل البر واغاثة الملهوفين وامداد الارامل
واليتامى * وفى انشآ المدارس والمستشفيات * وفى تصليح الطرق وتحسين المدينة
وازالة الاوساخ والعفونات منها * وفى ان يربى ولده بالادب والعلم والفضائل *
فترى منهم من سنّه اثنتا عشرة سنة يكلّمك بما يكلّمك به من سنّه منا اثنتا
عشرة سنة بعد العشرين * وبخلاف ما اذا تفضلت بذكره فقلت ان لكل انسان
عندهم ممن لا يعدّ من الاغنيآ والفقرآ خزانة كتب نفيسة فى كل فن وعلم * وما من
بيت الا وفيه اضبارة من صحف * وان الرجل منهم اخبر بالبلاد الاجنبية من
اهلها * وان اكثر فلاحيهم يقراون ويكتبون ويطالعون الوقائع اليومية ويعرفون
الحقوق الرابطة بين المالك والمملوك والحاكم والمحكوم وبين الرجل وامراته * وان
من هذه الوقائع المطبوعة ما تبلغ عدة نسخه اربعة عشر مليونا فى العام * وما يدفع
عليها لخزنة الدولة على طبع اجازتها يبلغ اكثر من خمسين الف ليرة * وانها لو عرّبت
نسخة واحدة منها لجات اكثر من مائتى صفحة * وان صاحب العائلة منهم اذا جلس
صباحا على المائدة مع زوجته واولاده يقبّل كلاّ منهم ويسالهم عن صحتهم *
ويفيدهم بعض نصائح وتنبيهات تكون لهم إماما فى ذلك اليوم * وانهم يكلمونه
وهم مبتهجون فرحون ويرون حضوره فيهم سلوانا * وانهم لا يخالفون له امرا
ولا يستثقلون منه تكليفا * وهم مع ذلك يُدلّون عليه بالبنوّة ويهابونه للابوّة *
١٥،١،٤ فهذا وامثاله اصلحك الله ينبغى ان تشنّف به مسامع اصحابك الكرام * عسى
ان ينشطوا الى انشآ مدرسة او ترجمة كتاب او لارسال ولدهم الى بلد يتادبون فيه

will make comprehensive mention of the antiquities left by the ancients and their histories, and then puts some literary puzzle to the youngest of them to keep her entertained. Such things ensure that he is honored on his arrival and praised on his departure.

It would be different too if you were to tell them that the rich merchant there doesn't wear diamond or emerald rings or adorn himself with gold chains or collect rare furniture, vessels, and carpets but spends his wealth instead on charity, assistance to the hard-pressed, and provision for widows and orphans, on building schools and hospitals, mending roads, and cleaning the city and clearing it of refuse and filth, as well as on educating his children in literature, science, and the virtues, as a result of which you find that from the age of twelve they can talk to you of matters that one of ours would not be able to talk to you about were he twelve plus twenty years of age. And it would be different too if you were to be so good as to mention that any person among them of a middling condition has a case of valuable books on every art and science and that there isn't a house that doesn't have a folder full of newspapers; that any man among them is better informed as to the conditions of foreign countries than are those countries' own inhabitants; that most of their peasants can read and write and peruse the daily newspapers and are aware of the rights and obligations that govern the relationships between owner and owned, ruler and ruled, man and wife; that some of their printed newspapers run to fourteen million copies a year, that the sum paid to the state treasury for the printing of their licenses comes to more than fifty thousand lira, and that if a single issue of such a newspaper were translated into Arabic, it would come to two hundred pages; and that when a head of family there sits down to table in the morning with his wife and children, he kisses each, asks after his health, and provides him with profitable pieces of advice and caution to guide him through the coming day and they talk to him and are full of delight and joy, viewing his presence among them as a comfort, never disobeying his orders or thinking his demands upon them a burden yet acknowledging their status as his children and honoring him as children should a father. 4.1.14

It is with this and its like that you, God set you to rights, should be beguiling the ears of your noble friends in the hope that they may bestir themselves to build a school, translate a book, or send their children to a country where they can learn praiseworthy manners and noble traits. But beware, 4.1.15

بالاداب المحمودة والمناقب الكريمة * واياك ياسيدي من ان تميل قبل هذا كله الى ان تاخذ عن بعضهم الخصال الذميمة كالطيش والنزق والبخل والفسق والكبر ومد الرجلين فى وجه جليسك * فقد ذكرت لك آنفا ان البلاد التى تكثر فيها الفضائل تكثر فيها الرذائل ايضاً * وانه ليس من انسان الا وفيه عيب بل عيوب * غير انه ينبغى لكل منا ان لا يزال يجد ويسعى فى طريق الكمال وفى تهذيب اخلاقه وحواسه الباطنة بكل ما يبدو لحواسه الظاهرة * وكما ان لذة الحواس لا يشعر بها الانسان الا فى مقدَّم جسمه دون موخره كذلك ينبغى لكل ذى جسم من الحيوان الناطق ان يعتمد على التقدّم فى المعارف والدرايه * والمحامد الى الغايه * وكنت اود لو ان احدا من اهل بلادنا نقل فضيلة او ماثرة عن هولآ الناس الى اخوانه ومعارفه كما تنقل الاخبار والروايات * وبودى لو تستحيل اصناف الماس والزمرذ والياقوت والدهنج والثعثع والدر والعقيان والكهربا والمها وقلنسوة الراهب معها حالة كونها معدودة من الجواهر والتحف الى كتب ومدارس ومكاتب ومطابع *

my dear sir, before anything else, of taking over from some of them their ignoble qualities, such as frivolity, impetuosity, stinginess, depravity, and arrogance, or showing the soles of your feet to someone sitting with you, for, as I pointed out to you above, countries with many virtues also have many vices and everyone has some fault, or indeed faults. Each of us, however, must seriously strive to follow the path of perfection and to refine his morals and his inner senses by making the best use of everything that appears to his outer senses. Likewise, given that one experiences sensual pleasure through the front of the body rather than its rear, every rational animal that possesses a body should determine to move in a forward direction in pursuit of knowledge, understanding, and praiseworthy qualities till he can go no farther. I would also wish that even one of our countrymen might pass on to his brethren and acquaintances some virtue or memorable deed taken from those people in the same way that news or accounts of events are passed on, and I wish that all kinds of diamonds, emeralds, rubies, jasper, mother-of-pearl, pearls, gold, amber, and crystal (and monk's hoods too, since they're considered to belong to the category of jewels and treasures) might be turned into
books, upper schools, elementary schools, and printing presses.

الفصل الثانى

في وداع

لما حان سفر الفارياق اخذ يودع زوجته بعد ان اوعى القاموس والاشمونى فى صندوقه ويقول * اذكرى يازوجتى انّا عشنا معا برهة طويلة من الدهر * قالت ما اذكر الا هذا * قال فقلت اَذِكْرُ ناكِرٍ ام شاكرٍ * قالت نصف من هذا ونصف من ذاك * قلت يرجعنا النحت الى الاول * قالت او يرجع الاول الى النحت * قلت اىّ اوّل اضمرتِ * قالت ما لك ولتاويل المضمر * قلت حسبى ان تُبيّنى لى حقيقة ذلك * قالت اذا فكرت فى انك لى ولغيرى كنت من الناكرين والا فمن ١،٢،٤
الشاكرين * قلت انك كنت نهيتِنى عن المعاملة بالقَسْم وها انت الآن تاتينه * ٢،٢،٤
قالت بل هو ياتينى * قلت اَما فى فيك لفظة لا * قالت ان لفظتها كانت نَعَم * قلت ان لا من المراة اِلَى * قالت وان نعم نعم * قلت اجعلت هذا دابك * قالت ودابت فى هذا الجَعل * قلت هذا لا يليق بذات ولد * قالت ولا تلد من لا تليق * قلت من مادة واحدة * قالت ان كانت المادة غير زيادة متصلة احوجت الى اختلاف الصور * قلت وكيف تبقى متصلة على اختلاف الاشكال * قالت لا اشكال فى كيفية الاشكال فان واحدا منها يغنى عن الجميع * وانما الكلام

Chapter 2

A Farewell

When the time for the Fāriyāq to travel was close, and as soon as he had put his copies of the *Qāmūs* and al-Ashmūnī into his trunk, he set about bidding his wife farewell.[6] He said, "Just think, wife—we've lived together a goodly span of time." "That's all I think of," she replied. The Fāriyāq resumed his narrative. "I asked her, 'Hatefully or gratefully?' and she replied, 'Half the latter and half the former.'[7] 'Application of *naḥt* brings us back to the first,'[8] I said, to which she responded, 'or the first brings us back to another meaning of *naḥt*.'[9] 'Which first did you have in mind?' I asked.[10] 'You have no business interpreting my intentions,' she responded. I replied, 'I'd be content if you'd just explain to me what you did mean,' and to this she responded, 'If you think you can belong to both me and others, then it's "hatefully," if not, it's "gratefully."' 4.2.1

"'You forbade me before to deal with you on the basis of suspicion,'[11] I said, 'but now you're the sinner in that regard.' 'On the contrary,' she replied, 'I'm the one sinned against.'[12] I asked her, 'Does the word "no" have no place in your mouth?'[13] She said, 'It used to be pronounced "yes."'[14] I said, 'A no from a woman is a boon,'[15] to which she replied, 'And a yes means pleasure.' I asked, 'Have you made the latter your habit?' to which she replied, 'Indeed—and become habituated to the rewards.' I said, 'That's not fitting for a woman with children,' to which she countered, 'If a woman doesn't fit properly, she'll never give birth.'[16] I said, 'It's the same Matter,' to which she responded, 'If the Matter isn't "copious and inseparable," it must necessarily take different Forms.'[17] I said, 'And how can it remain inseparable if the Forms are different?' 'The individual nature of the Forms is not a problem,' she replied, 'for one may stand for all. What we are discussing here is how 4.2.2

على رسم الكمية * قلت ما الحدّ * قالت فى الجد الهزل وفى الهزل الجد *
قلت ارايتك لو اقمت نائبا عنى فى ذاك مدة غيابى * فضحكت وقالت على ما ٣،٢،٤
احبّ انا ام على ما تحب انت * قلت بل على ما تحبين انت * قالت لا يرضى
الرجل بذلك الا اذا كان غير ذى غيرة ولا يكون غير ذى غيرة الا اذا كره امراته
وكلف بغيرها فانت اذاً كلِف بغيرى * قلت ما انا بالكَلِف ولا بالطَرِف * لكن
الرجل اذا كان شديد الحبّ لامراته ودّ لو انه يرضيها فى كل شى * على ان الغيرة
لا تكون دائما عن المحبة كما نصّوا عليه * فان بعض النسآ يغرن على ازواجهن عن
كراهية لهم واعنات * مثال ذلك اذا منعت المراة زوجها عن الخروج الى بستان
او ملهى او حمّام مع عدة رجال متزوجين * هى تعلم انهم فى هذه المواضع لا
يمكنهم الاجتماع بالنسآ فهى انما تفعل ذلك تحكما عليه ومنعا له من ذكر النسآ مع
اصحابه والتلذذ بما لا يضيرها * وكذا اذا خظرته عن النظر من شباكه الى شارع
او روضة حيث يكثر تردّد النسآ * وكذا الحكم على الرجل لو فعل ذلك بامراته *
فهذا عند الناس يعدّ غيرة لكنه فى الواقع بغضة * او ربما كان آخر الغيرة اول
البغض كما ان افراط الضحك هو اول البكآء * وكيف كان فان الرجل لا يمكن ان
يحب زوجته الا اذا اباح لها التلذذ بما شآت وبمن احبّت * قالت ايفعل ذلك
احد فى الدنيا * قلت نعم يفعله كثير فى بلاد غير بعيدة عنا * قالت بابى هم ولكن
ما شان النسآ ايفعلن ذلك ايضا لازواجهن * قلت لا بدّ حتى يعتدل الميزان *
قالت اما انا فلا ارضى بهذا الاعتدال فالميل عندى احسن * قلت وكذا هو
عندى فى بعض الاحوال * قالت ولاحوال البعض * قلت فلنعد الى السفر انى ٤،٢،٤
اسافر اليوم * قالت نعم الى بلاد فيها البيض الحسان * قلت اتعنيهم ام تعنيهنّ *

to define "quantity."' 'And what are the terms of the argument?' I asked. She said, 'That in seriousness is humor and in humor seriousness.'

"'What would you think,' I asked her, 'if I got someone to deputize for me in that matter while I'm away?' She laughed and said, 'According to my taste or yours?' 'To yours, naturally,' I replied. She said, 'No man would agree to such a thing unless he was devoid of jealousy, and a man can be devoid of jealousy only if he hates his wife and is enamored of someone else, so you must be enamored of someone else.' I said, 'I am neither enamored nor inconstant, but when a man is deeply in love with his wife he hopes to please her in everything, though we must not overlook the fact that jealousy is not always, as people would have it, a product of love: some women's jealousy regarding their husbands comes from hatred of them and a desire to hurt them. An example would be if a woman were to prevent her husband from going out to a park, a place of entertainment, or a bathhouse along with a number of other married men; she knows that they cannot meet up with women in such places and she only does this to exercise control over him and to stop him from talking about women with his friends and enjoying himself in ways that can do her no harm. It's the same if she forbids him to look out of his window at a street or a garden frequented by many women, and the same judgment applies to a man if he behaves the same way with his wife. People call such things "jealousy" but in reality they are a form of hatred, or it may be that hatred begins where jealousy leaves off, just as excessive laughter is the first stage of tears. However that may be, a man cannot truly love his wife if he doesn't allow her to enjoy herself in the way she wants and with whom she wants.' 'Does anyone in the world behave that way?' she asked. 'Indeed,' I responded. 'Many behave so in countries not far from us.' 'Good for them,' she replied, 'but what about their women? Do they behave the same way with their husbands?' 'They have to,' I answered, 'to keep things in balance.' 'Personally,' she said, 'I wouldn't put up with such even-handedness. As far as I'm concerned, a tilt is better.' 'That's my opinion too, in certain circumstances,' I said. 'And where the circumstances of certain people are concerned,' she riposted.[18] 4.2.3

"'Let's get back to traveling,' I said. 'I leave today.' 'Indeed,' she said, '—for the lands of the white-skinned beauties.' 'Do you talk of men or women?' I enquired. 'I talk of one sex,' she replied, 'but what worries me is the other.' 'And why should that sex be a concern,' I asked, 'when it's you women who, 4.2.4

قالت اعنى نوعا ويعنينى آخر * قلت ولمَ يعنيك وانتن المطلوبات فى كل حال ولذلك يقال للمراة غانية * قال فى القاموس الغانية المراة التى تطلَب ولا تطلب * قالت ما احسن كلامه هنا لولا انه قال قبل ذلك العوانى النسآ لانهن يُظلَمن فلا ينتصرن * غير ان هذه النقطة شفعت فى تلك * قلت حبكن التنقيط داب قديم * قالت مثل داب الرجال فى التحريف * وكيف كان فان مطلوبيّتنا هى اصل العنآ * فان المطلوبة لا تكون الا ذات العرض والاحصان * فويل لها ان خانت محصنها * وويل لها ان حرمت طالبها وباتت تلك الليلة مشغولة البال بحرمانه وخيبته وبكونها صارت سببا فى ارقه وجزعه وحسرته * والطالبة تعود غير مطلوبة * قلت ليست اخلاق الرجال فى ذلك سوآ * قالت انما اعنى الرجال الذين يطلبون ويكلفون بمن يطلبونه لا اولئك الطَرِفين الشنقين المسافحين الذين دابهم التذوّق والتنقل من مطلوب الى آخر ونفع انفسهم فقط دون مراعاة نفع سواهم * ولكن هيهات هل فى الرجال من يقيم على الوداد ولا يميل عنه كل يوم * لعمرى لوكانت النسآ تطلب الرجال طلب الرجال للنسآ لما رايت فيهم غير مفتون *
قلت هل فى النسآ من تقيم على الوداد ولا تجنح عنه كل يوم الف مرة * هذه ٥،٢،٤
الكتب كلها تشهد للرجيال بالوفآ وعلى النسآ بالخيدعية * قالت مَن كتب هذه الكتب اليس الرجال هم الذين لفقوها * قلت ولكن من بعد التحرّى والتجربة * قالت مَن يات الحَكَم وحده يفلج * قلت بل اوردوا على ذلك شواهد وكفى بما ورد عن سيدنا سليمن برهانا ودليلا * فانه قال قد وجدت بين الف من الرجال صالحا فاما بين النسآ فلم اجد صالحة * قالت ان سيدنا سليمن وان يكن قد اوتى من الحكمة ما لم يوتَه غيره غير ان افراطه فى النسآ شوش عليه الصالحة منهن من غير الصالحة *

in any circumstances, are the ones pursued, which is why they call a beautiful woman a *ghāniyah*[19]?; as the author of the *Qāmūs* says, "the *ghāniyah* is a woman who is pursued and does not herself need to pursue."' She said, 'Excellent words, but earlier he says, "'*awānī*[20] is a word for women, because they are mistreated and no one takes their side," though the dot on the one ought to put in a good word for the other.'[21] 'Love of "dotting,"' I said, 'is an ancient habit among you women.'[22] 'As "scripting" is among men,'[23] she retorted, 'but be that as it may; our being desired is the root of our worries, for the woman who is desired is by definition a woman whose honor is valued and guarded. Woe betide her then if she betrays her guardian and woe betide her if she denies the one who desires her, for then she will spend the night worrying over having denied him and over his disappointment and the fact that she has become a cause of his sleeplessness, anguish, and sorrow, and the woman who chases men ends up unchased.'[24] I said, 'Men's morals are not all the same where that's concerned,' to which she returned, 'I mean the men who desire, and fall in love with the ones they desire, not those fornicating omnivorous fickle-hearted ones whose custom is to take a nibble here and a nibble there and move from one object of desire to another, taking only what is of use to them without caring about what may be of use to others. How few, though, are the former! Is there a single man who can maintain an affection and not deviate from it every day? I swear, were women to desire men as much as men desire women, you wouldn't find a single man unbewitched.'

"'Is there a single woman who can maintain affection and not deviate 4.2.5
from it each day a thousand times?' I asked her. 'All books bear witness to the trustworthiness of men and the treachery of women.' 'Weren't the ones who wrote those books men?' she countered. 'They're the ones who made up those stories.' 'But only after investigation and experience,' I answered. 'If you go to the arbitrator alone, you win,' she said. 'Quite the reverse,' I said. 'They have provided testimonies. The words of Our Master Sulaymān, who said, "I have found one righteous man among a thousand but I have not found a single righteous woman" may serve as sufficient proof and evidence.' 'Even if Our Master Sulaymān was granted wisdom given to none other,' she said, 'his excessive indulgence in women rendered him incapable of distinguishing the righteous among them from the unrighteous. Have you not observed how the musk-seller's sense of smell weakens from length of

اَلَا ترى ان بائع المسك لطول ائتلافه بالرائحة القوية تضعف منه حاسة الشم
بحيث لا يعود يشم الرائحة اللطيفة * واما ايراد الادلة من الرجال على النسآ دون
٦،٢،٤ ايراد ادلة النسآ على الرجال فمحض ظلم وبطر * قلت نعم كان الاَوَلى مناصفة هذا
الايراد ولكن سبحان الله انتن تتهمن الرجال فى كل شى ثم تتهافتن عليهم * قالت
لولا اضطرار الاحوال * لما شغلن بذلك الابوال * قال فضحكت وقلت اىّ جمع
هذا * قالت قسته على غيره * قلت وهل استوى المقيس بالمقيس عليه * قالت
لا فرق * قلت بل كله فرق فان اللغة لا توخذ بالقياس * ولوصح ذلك لم تكن
مناسبة بين الذكر والانثى ولا بين الاثنى والذكر * ولا بين تذكير حقيقة التانيث
وتانيث ما هو غير مقابل بمثله * قالت وهذا ايضا من بطر الرجال وتشويشهم
٧،٢،٤ فلا يكادون ياتون امرا مستقيما * قلت قد رجعت الى لومهم * قالت والله لقد
حرت فى الرجال * قلت والله لقد حرتُ فى النسآ * ولكن فلنعد الى الوداع انى
اعاهدك على ان لا اخونك * قالت بل تخونني على عهد * قلت ما يحملك على
سوء الظن بى * قالت انى ارى الرجال اذا كانوا فى بلاد لم يُعرفوا بها افحشوا غاية
الافحاش * اَلَا ترى الى هولآ الغربآ الذين ياتون الى هذه الجزيرة كيف يتهتكون
فى العهر والفجور * فاول ما يضع احدهم قدمه على الارض يسال عن الماخور *
ولا سيما هولآ الشاميين ولا سيما النصارى منهم ولا سيما الذين الموّا بعلم شى
من احوال الافرنج ولغاتهم فانهم يخرجون من المراكب كالزنابير اللاسعة من هنا
وهناك * قلت لعلهم كانوا فى بلادهم كذلك * قالت ليس عندهم اسباب الفحش
هناك * قلت او كانوا فاسدين بالطبع * قالت نعم هو عرق فساد كامن فيهم فاول
ما يستنشقون رائحة بلاد الافرنج ينبض فيهم * ولذلك تراهم ابدا يتلمظون بذكر

exposure to its strong odor until he can no longer distinguish any more delicate scent? As far as providing the testimony of men against women without providing that of women against men is concerned, it is patent injustice and high-handedness.'

"'Indeed,' I said, 'evenhandedness in such citations would be preferable but, glory be, you women level every possible charge against men and then fall over one another to make a fuss over them!' She responded, 'Were it not that society works to make them *martyrs*, women wouldn't allow such ideas anywhere near their *medulla oblongarters*.'"[25] "I laughed," continued the Fāriyāq, "and said, 'What kind of a plural is that?' to which she replied, 'I made it by analogy.' 'Are the original word and that formed by analogy to it equal?' I asked. 'There's no difference,' she replied. 'On the contrary,' I said, 'they're entirely different, because lexicon cannot be derived by analogy. If it could, there'd be no conformity between male and female or between female and male,[26] or between the masculinization of the true feminine[27] and the feminization of words that have no equivalent.'[28] 'Another example of men's high-handedness and confusion of the issue!' she said. 'They are virtually incapable of dealing with anything straightforwardly.' 'And there you go again!' I retorted. 4.2.6

"She said, 'I swear I don't know what to do about men' and I said, 'And I swear I don't know what to do about women, but let's get back to saying farewell. I give you my word that I will never be unfaithful to you.' 'On the contrary, you will ever be unfaithful to me,' she said. I said, 'What reason do you have to be suspicious of me?' She replied, 'I observe that men who are in a country where they're unknown perform the worst abominations. Just look at how the foreigners who come to this island give themselves over to whoring and depravity. The moment one of them sets foot on land, he asks where the brothel is, especially the Syrians,[29] and amongst them especially the Christians, and amongst those especially the ones who have acquired a little knowledge of the ways of the Franks and their languages; they come off the ships like hornets, plunging their stingers here, there, and everywhere.' 'Perhaps they were like that in their home countries,' I said. 'They don't have the means to behave abominably there,' she returned. 'Or perhaps they're corrupt by nature,' I said. 'You're right,' she said. 'They have a latent disposition to corruption and the moment they smell the Frankish air, it comes to life, which is why you will find that they always drool as they talk of the lands 4.2.7

بلاد الافرنج وعاداتهم واحوالهم * مع انك اذا سالت احدا منهم عن طعامهم قال لا يستطيبه * اوعن الحانهم قال لا تطربه * اوعن كرمائهم قال لم تادبه * اوعن حمّاماتهم قال لم تعجبه * اوعن هوائهم قال لم يلائمه * اوعن مائهم قال لم يسغ
٨،٢،٤ له * فيكون لهجهم بذكر بلادهم وتنويههم بمحاسنها انما سببه الفحش * وانت من يضمن لى طبعك عن الفساد وقد اسمعك كل يوم تُهَيْنِم بذكر الرجارجة والرضراضة والبضباضة والفضفاضة والرِبَحلة والرعبوب والعطبول * وهى لعمرى الفاظ تسيل لعاب الحصور وتشهّى الناسك * قلت ان هو الا كلام * قالت اول الحرب كلام * قلت اترين اعدّى عن هذه الصنعة الشائقة * والحرفة العائقة * قالت ان لم تتصور ذاتا بعينها عند الوصف فلا باس * قلت ان لم اتصور ذاتا لم يخطر ببالى شى * قالت اذن هو حرام * قلت ما كفّارته * قالت تصورك اياى لا غير * قلت ولكن انت خالية عن بعض الصفات التى لا بدّ من ذكرها * قالت اذا كان الرجل يحب امراته راى فيها الحسن كله ونظر من كل شعرة منها امراة جميلة * كما انه اذا احب امراة غيرها احبّ لاجلها بلادها وهوآها ومآها ولسان قومها وعاداتهم واطوارهم * قلت اوَ كذلك المراة اذا احبت رجلا * قالت هو فى النسآ اكثر لانهن اوفر حبا ووجدا * قلت ما سبب ذلك * قالت لان الرجال يتشاغلون بما ليس يعنيهم * فترى واحدا منهم يطلب الولاية وآخر السيادة وآخر البحث فى الاديان وفى ما غمض من السفليات والعلويات * والنسآ لا شى يشغلهن من ذلك * قلت ليتك تشاغلت مثلهم * قالت ليت لى قلبين فى شغلنا * قلت افتنظرين فىّ الحسن كله كما زعمت * قالت أُحْسِن فيك النظر * قلت فلنعد الى الوداع لا بل فلنعد الى التشاغل * فانى اريد ان انهى هذه المسالة قبل ان افصل من هنا

of the Franks and their customs and conditions. If you were to ask one of them about their food, though, he'd say he didn't like it, or about their music, that it didn't move him, or about their nobility, that they didn't invite him to their banquets, or about their bathhouses, that they didn't appeal to him, or about their weather, that it hadn't suited him, or about their water, that he'd found it hard to swallow. The sole reason for their constant praise of those lands and for their lauding of the good things in them is abomination.

"'And you—who can guarantee me that your nature is not corrupt, 4.2.8
when every day I hear you muttering about women with quivering flesh, women with firm and swelling flesh, women with fleshy flesh, women with masses of plump flesh, women with pretty white flesh, and tall, full-fleshed women with long necks, all of them phrases that would, I swear, make the Baptist salivate and excite a hermit?' I said, 'They're just words,' to which she replied, 'Every war begins with words.' 'Would you have me abandon this craft and its *obsession*, this all-consuming *profession*?' I asked. 'So long as you don't visualize, while describing, a specific person, I have no objection,' she answered. I responded, 'If I don't visualize a person, my mind will remain a blank.' 'In that case,' she said, 'it's a sin.' 'And how,' I asked, 'may I expiate it?' 'By visualizing only me and no one else,' she replied. 'But you,' I responded, 'are devoid of some of the characteristics that have to be mentioned,' to which she responded, 'If a man truly loves his wife, he will find in her everything that is fair and see in each hair of hers a beautiful woman. By the same token, if he loves some other woman, he will, for her sake, love her country, its weather, its water, and the language, customs, and manners of its people.' 'Aren't women the same,' I asked, 'when they love a man?' 'They're worse,' she answered, 'because they have larger reserves of love and passion.' 'And why is that?' I asked. 'Because,' she said, 'men spend time on things that do not concern them. Thus you'll find this one seeking position, that one power, and a third delving into religions and all that is obscure, be it profane or divine. Women pay no attention to any of that.' 'Would that you might busy yourself with the same concerns as men!' I said. 'Would that I had,' she rejoined, 'two hearts to devote to these concerns of ours.'[30] 'Do you, then,' I asked, 'see in me everything that is good, as you claim?' 'I hold you in high regard,' she said. 'In that case,' said I, 'let's get back to saying good-bye—or maybe not: let us, in fact, get back to the matter at hand, for I'd like to settle it before I depart; otherwise, it will preoccupy me throughout my

والّا فتكون لى شاغل الطريق و ربما افسدت شغلى عند القوم فارجع باللوم عليك
٩،٢،٤ وعلى سائر النسآء * قالت اعلم ان المراة تعلم من نفسها انها زينة هذا الكون * كما
ان جميع ما فيه انما خلق لزينتها لا لزينة الرجل * لا لكونه مستغنيا عنها بذاته او
لكونها هى مفتقرة اليها لتحلو بها فى عين الناظر واذن السامع * بل لعدم جدارة
الرجل بها * فان الزينة نوع من الاخذ والتلقّى والاستيعاب والزيادة وهى احوال
انسبُ بامراة منها بالرجل * وبنآء على هذا اى على ان جميع ما فى الكون خُلِق لها
بعضه بالتخصيص وبعضه بالتفضيل والايثار * كان من بعض اعتقادها ان نوع
الرجل ايضا مخلوق لها * لا بمعنى انها تكون زوجة لجميع الرجال فان ذلك محال
من وجهين * احدهما انها لا تطيق ذلك لان سريّة ذلك اليهودى (على ما ذكر
فى الفصل التاسع عشر من سفر القضاة) لم تطق اهل قرية واحدة (هى جبعة) على
قلتهم ليلة واحدة * بل ماتت فى الصباح وسيدها يحسبها نائمة * وهذه الحكاية
ذُكِرت رَدْعًا للنسآ * والثانى انه اذا ثبت لامراة حق فى حكر الرجال والاستدباد
بهم ثبت الحق الباقى * ولكن بمعنى انها اهل لان تعاشر جميع الرجال وتتعرف ما
عندهم * فتتلهّى من واحد بتمليقة ومن آخر باطرآءة ومن غيره بمغازلة ومن آخر
بمطارحة وما اشبه ذلك * مما لا يمنعها من محبة زوجها والكلف به * لا بل –
١٠،٢،٤ قال فقلت اتمّى هذه اللابليّة فانى اراها ترجمة لداهية من دواهى النسآ وعنوانا على
مكيدة من مكايدهن * فضحكت وقالت ربّما دلّك على الراى الظنون * غير انى
اخشى من ان تاخذك لبيانها شفشفة و رعدة فتتاخر عن السفر * او ان تظن ان
هذا دابى معك * معاذ الله * انى لم اخُنك بِضِمْد[١] ولا بغيره * وانما علمت ما

١ ١٨٥٥: بضَمْد.

journey and may spoil my work for those I go to serve. If that happens, I shall pin the blame on you and on women in general.'

"'You should know,' she said, 'that women are aware without having to be 4.2.9
told that they are the adornment of this universe, and similarly that everything in it was created to be an adornment for women, not men; not because men are innately in no need of such adornment or because women are in need of it in order to look and sound attractive to the eyes of the beholder and the ears of the listener, but because men are not suited to it. Adornment is something one takes, receives, and assimilates and which then becomes an embellishment—modes more appropriate to women than to men. Based on this—which is to say, on the fact that everything in the universe was created for women, in part by design and in part through preference and predilection[31]—one of her beliefs is that the male sex too was created for her, albeit not in the sense that she should be wife to all men, for that would be an impossibility, from two perspectives. One is that no woman could survive such a thing, for the concubine of that certain Jew mentioned in Judges, chapter 19[32] could not survive the men of a single village (Gibeah), few though they were, for a single night; on the contrary, she died the next morning and her master believed she was asleep; the story is mentioned there as a caution to women. The other is that, if women's right to the exclusive possession and arbitrary disposal of men is admitted, then their right to everything else must be admitted too—though only in the sense that they're qualified to keep company with all men and be acquainted with what they are up to. Thus they may entertain from one a word of flattery, from another a word of praise, from some other courtship, from yet another conversation, and so on, none of which need stand in the way of her feeling love and affection for her husband. Nay, on the contrary . . .'"

The Fāriyāq continued, "At this I said, 'Go straight to the end of this "nay- 4.2.10
on-the-contrary"—as far as I can see it's just the preface to another example of the cunning ways of women and the introduction to another of their wiles.' She laughed and said, 'Likely your misgivings about women make you say so. Nevertheless, I'm afraid that fear and trembling will overtake you as you try to understand it and you'll find yourself unable to leave on time, or will suppose that that's how I conduct myself where you are concerned. God forbid! Never have I betrayed you, with friend or with foe. Everything I know I have learned from other women, for women hide nothing from one another

علمت من النسآ لا ن النسآ لا يكتم بعضهن عن بعض شيا من امور العشق واحوال
١١،٢،٤ الرجال * قلت اَوجِزنى فقد قلقت وفرقت وعرقت * قالت اعلم ان بعض النسآ لا
يتحرّجن من وصال غير بعولتهن لسببين * الاول لعدم اكتفائهن بالقدر المرتب لهن
منهم * فانهم يعودونهن اوّلا على ما يعجزون عن ادائه اليهن آخرا * ولا يخفى ان
من النسآ المُدقِم وهى التى تلتهم كل شى * ومنهن الشفيرة وهى القانعة من البعال
بايسره * ومنهن الضامد وهى التى تتخذ خليلين * ومنهن المِطماع وهى التى تُطمع
ولا تمكّن * ومنهن المرَيم وهى التى تحب حديث الرجال ولا تفجر وهو خُلقى * قال
١٢،٢،٤ فقلت اللهم امين * قالت واللاعة وهى التى تغازلك ولا تمكنك * والسبب الثانى
لاستطلاع احوال الرجال واختبار الابتع منهم وغير الابتع لمجرد العلم يكلا يفوتهن
حال من احوالهم * ومنهن مَن تعتقد ان زوجها يخونها عند كل فرصة تسنح له *
لما تقرر فى عقول النسآ ان الرجال لا شغل لهم الا مغازلتهن ومباغمتهن * فهى
على هذا لا تجد سبيلا للشطح الا وتزفّ فيه * اعتقاد انها اخذت بثارها جزْما
اى قبل وقته الموقوت * ومع ذلك فلا يحلن عن محبة بعولتهن * بل ربما كان ذلك
١٣،٢،٤ الشطح ادعى لزيادة حبّهن لهم * قلت لا متّعنى الله بحبٍ ناشى عن مدقمِيّة ولا
ضمد * ولكن كيف يكون هذا التخليط ادعى الى زيادة الحبّ والمراة اذا ذاقت
البكبك والعُجارم والقازح والكُباس لم تقتنع بعد ذلك بزوجها حالة كونه لا يحول عن
الصفة التى فُطر عليها * وكذا الرجل ايضا اذا ذاق الرشوف والرصوف والحزنبل
والعَضُوض والاكبس فانه يرى زوجته بعد ذلك ناقصة * فضحكت وقالت لو
كانت هذه الصفات لازمة للمراة وكان عدم وجودها فيها نقصا لما كنت تراها فى

where love and the ways of men are concerned.' 'Be brief, then,' said I, 'for I'm disquieted and *frightened*, and my perspiration level's *heightened*.'

"'Know then,' she said, 'that there are two reasons why some women feel no qualms about making love to men other than their husbands. The first is their failure to get from the latter their established due, for men accustom them at the beginning to what they are incapable of giving them at the end, and it's no secret that there are, among women,[33] the nymphomaniac, who "devours everything," the sworn virgin, who "abstains completely from intercourse,"[34] the two-timer, who "takes two lovers," the prick teaser, who "incites without making herself available," and the bluestocking, who "loves the conversation of men but does not fornicate" (which is the way I am) . . .'" The Fariyāq continued, saying, "'Thank God for that!' said I, and she said, '. . . and the ball-breaker, "who flirts with you but doesn't avail you of herself." 4.2.11

"'The second reason is her desire to find out what men are about and to put them all, sturdy and weak alike, to the test, simply in order to know, so that nothing about them may escape her. There are those too who suppose, given women's firmly established belief that men have no interest in anything but flirting with and sweet-talking women, that their husbands will betray them at the first opportunity. Thinking so, any time she finds a means of leaving the strait and narrow, she hurries to seize it, imagining that she is taking revenge preemptively, which is to say before the time otherwise allotted for it—despite which women never lose their love for their husbands. On the contrary, any such straying may be conducive to an increase in love for them on their part.' 4.2.12

"'May God not send me a love that springs from nymphomania or infidelity!' I said. 'How, though, can this promiscuity be conducive to an increase in love[35] when the woman, once she has sampled the thrusting prick, the strong prick, the hard prick, and the huge, mighty-headed prick, will never thereafter be able to limit herself to her husband, given that he can never escape the particular attribute with which he was created? And the man likewise, having once sampled women who are sweet-mouthed and dry-cunted, narrow-quimmed, high-twatted, tight-tunneled, and bulgy-beavered will find his wife ever after diminished.' She laughed and said, 'Were these attributes essential in order for a woman to be a woman and their diminution a defect, they wouldn't be found only in a small number of individuals, for most women are not like that. The reason why affection 4.2.13

افراد قليلة من النسآء * فان معظمهن على خلاف ذلك * فاما سبب زيادة المحبة فيما زعمن مع التخليط فهو ان الزوج لطول الفته بزوجته وضراوته عليها وحالة كون مسّ احدهما الاخر لا يحدث فى جسم الماسّ والممسوس هزة ولا رعشة ولا ربوخيّة * يمكن له معها المماتنة والامعان والوقوف * بخلاف الغريب فانه لشدة نهمه ودهشته او لفرط مراوحة المراة اياه على العمل * او لكون الحرام لا
١٤،٢،٤ يسوغ دائما مساغ الحلال تفوته الصفتان المذكورتان * فاللذة معه جلّها ناشى عن التصور * اى عن تصور كونه غير زوجها * كما ان نغصها مع زوجها جلّه ناشى عن تصور كونه غير غريب * والّا فالواقع ان اللذة فى الحلال اقوى * غير ان التصور له موقع يقرب من الفعل * وبيانه لو اعتقد رجل مثلا ان امراة غير امراته تبيت معه ثم باتت معه امراته بعينها وهو لا يعلم ذلك كما جرى لسيدنا يعقوب عمّ * لوجد امراته تلك الليلة متصفة بجميع الصفات التى تصورها فى غيرها * وكذا شان المراة * فبنآ على ما تقدم من اعتقاد المراة بان جميع ما فى الكون من الحسن والزينة والبهجه يناسبها كان تصورها صفات الحسن وتشاغلها به مطلقا عاما * غير انه اذا كان لها خاصّ قريبا منها تناولت ذلك الخاصّ متناول العام * حتى انه كثيرا ما يخطى فكرُها واحدا منهم بخصوصه * فيتجاذبه اثنان او ثلثة حتى تذهل عن الشاغل والاشغل * وهو فى الواقع تحوّف من اللذة كمن يريد ان يشرب من ثلث قلل يضعها على فيه فى وقت واحد * وقلت كلامك هذا ينظر الى قول الشاعر

اذا بتّ مشغول الفواد بما ترى   من الغيد عينى والجمال مفرّق
اركّب فى وهمى محيّا يشوقنى   على قامة اولى به ثم اشبق

increases, as women claim, with promiscuity is that the husband, given his long familiarity with and lascivious interest in his wife, and the fact that the touching of one of them by the other no longer produces in the body of either the toucher or the touched any shaking, trembling, or tendency to faint, is able to keep going longer, penetrate more deeply, and maintain a harder erection than the stranger. The two last characteristic abilities[36] will elude the latter, either because of his voracity and discombobulation, or because the woman keeps going back to him after short breaks for more, or because what is forbidden is not always as appealing as what is permitted.

"'The pleasure she gets from him derives largely from her conceptualization[37] (meaning her conceptualization of him as other than her husband) just as her boredom with her husband derives largely from her conceptualization of him as something familiar. This aside, it is a fact that licit pleasure is more powerful. Conceptualization, however, is almost as important as performance. The proof of this is that if a man believes that a woman other than his wife is going to spend the night with him and then his own wife does so without his knowing, as happened with Our Master Yaʿqūb,[38] peace be upon him, he'll find that his wife, that night, possesses all the characteristics that he conceives of as being possessed by other women, and the same is true for a woman. Based then on what has been said above about the woman believing that every kind of beauty, adornment, and delight in the universe is most appropriately hers, she will conceptualize, and preoccupy herself with, the attributes of beauty as though they were a universal absolute. Should there, therefore, be a particular example close by, she will deal with it as she would with the universal, to the degree that her thoughts will often go on beyond any one man in his particularity, two or three men pulling them this way and that until she is reduced to a tizzy in her attempts to decide between the beguiling and the yet more beguiling, which amounts in reality to her being surrounded on all sides by sensual pleasure, like someone who wants to drink from three water pitchers and puts them all to his mouth at the same time.' 'Your words,' I said, 'put one in mind of the lines of the poet that go 4.2.14

If my heart's distracted by the young ladies
My eye beholds, and whose beauty's divided, a little to each,
I mount in my fancy a face that attracts me
On a body that suits it and then feel the itch.

ولكن قد نهيتني آنفا فى التغزل عن تصوّر ذات بخصوصها وقلت انه حرام فهلّا قلت بحرميّة هذا ايضا * قالت انما حرميّة ذاك لكونه ذاهبا فى الكلام سدى وسرفا * على ان الغزل كله كيفما كان لا خير فيه ولا جدوى * فاما فى الفعل من ١٥،٢،٤
قبل النسآ فانه ينشا عنه صباحة الاولاد * ولذلك ترى انف بعضهم كانف زيد وفمه كفم عمرو وعينيه كعيني بكر * وهو ايضا جواب لمن قال ان فى رؤية الرجل نسآ كثيرة مصلحة تعود على امراته لاكتسابه منهن التمشير عند الاياب * بخلاف خروج المراة فان التمشير ملازم لها * فاما هولآ الحمقى الزاعمون ان تصوّر الرجل موثر فى توزيع الولد فيلزمهم ان لا يروا امراة اصلا غير نسآئهم * لئلا تاتى ذريتهم كلها اناثا او فى الاقل خِناثا * وذلك لمناعفة التصوّرين من قبل الاب والام * ألَا وانّ امراة لا تستبدل زوجها الا بالفكر والتخيّل لجديرة بان تكون قِبْلة كل مطرئ * وان لا يفكر زوجها الا فيها * قلت مقتضى كلامك ان النسآ المقصورات عن رؤية العموم لا لذة لهن مع الخصوص * قالت اما بالنسبة الى ناظرة العموم فلا * واما بالنسبة الى العدم فنعم * فان المآء مهما يكن سخنا يطفى النار * قلت وبالعكس اى ان النار مهما كانت باردة تسخن المآ * قالت يصح العكس لكن الطرد اولى *
قلت الى كم قسم تقسم اللذة * قالت الى خمسة اقسام * الاول تصورها قبل ١٦،٢،٤
الوقوع * الثانى ذكرها قبله * الثالث حصولها فعلا بالركنين المذكورين * الرابع تصورها بعد الوقوع * الخامس ذكرها بعده * وكون لذة التصور قبل الوقوع اقوى او بعده اقوالٌ * فذهب بعض الى ان الاولى اقوى * لان الفعل لمّا كان غير حاصل كان الفكر فيه اجول وامعن فلا يقف على حدّ * وزعم آخرون ان الحصول يهيئ للفكر هيئة معلومة وصورة معينة يعتمد عليها فى قياس ما يترقب من الاعادة

"'Earlier, however, you forbade me to visualize any particular woman when celebrating women's bodies in verse and said it was a sin, so wouldn't you agree that what you're suggesting is sinful too?' 'The former,' she replied, 'is sinful because it constitutes a pointless and excessive use of language. Words of dalliance have, in fact, no value and are worthless however used.

"'As far as the act, on the other hand, is concerned, women view it as 4.2.15
determining the comeliness of their children and this explains why you will find a child with a nose like Zayd's, a mouth like 'Amr's, and eyes like Bakr's;[39] this is also a riposte to those who claim that it is in the wife's interest for her husband to see lots of other women because on his return his libido will have been increased by his contact with them.[40] It is different, however, when the woman goes out, for her libido is contained within her. Those idiots who claim that what a man visualizes has an effect on the shaping of the fetus in the womb should look at no women whatsoever other than their wives, lest their offspring turn out to be all females, or at least hermaphrodites, the reason being the discrepancy in the different ways in which the father and the mother visualize.[41] Indeed, a woman who exchanges her husband for another in thought and visualization should be nothing less than all men's object of praise and her husband should think of none but her.' I said, 'The necessary implication of your words is that women who are shielded from seeing the generality of men will find no pleasure in one particular man.' She replied, 'As for the woman who sees the generality of men, that is so. However, it is not so in the case of the woman who sees none at all, for water, no matter how hot, puts out fire.' 'That is true,' I said, 'and so it is if read backward, meaning that fire, no matter how cool, heats water.' 'It *is* true,' she replied, 'if read backward, but frontward is better.'[42]

"'Into how many divisions may pleasure be divided?' I asked. 'Into five,' 4.2.16
she responded. 'The first is visualization of it before its occurrence. The second is discussion of it before the same. The third is its actual realization accompanied by these two essential elements. The fourth is the visualization of it after the act. The fifth is discussion of it afterward. Whether the pleasure of visualizing it is greater before it takes place or afterward is a matter of debate. Some believe the first is greater because when it hasn't yet happened one's thoughts about it roam more widely, delve more deeply, and do not stop at any limit. Others claim that the actual occurrence provides one's thoughts with a known shape and a specific form as a benchmark against

والتكرير * وكما حصل الخلاف فى وقتى التصور حصل ايضا فيه وفى الذكر * والعبرة بحدّة التصوّر وذرب اللسان * فاما اصلح الازمنة لها فالصيف عند النسآ والشتآ عند الرجال * فاما الكمية فمن الناس الموحدون ومنهم المثنوية ومنهم اهل التثليث * قلت ومنهم المعتزلة والمعطِّلون * قالت هولآ لا خير فيهم *
١٧،٢،٤ وما هم جديرون بان يعدّوا مع الناس * قلت ما شان من يتزوج اثنتين وثلاثا * قالت هو امر مغاير للطبع * قلت كيف وقد كانت سنّة الانبيآء * قالت هل نحن نبحث الان فى الاديان او نتكلم فى الطبيعيات * الا ترى ان الذكور من الحيوانات التى قُدِر لها ان تعيش مع اناث كثيرة قُدِّر لها ايضا القدرة على كفايتهن كالديك والعصفور مثلا * وغيرها انما يعيش مع واحدة ويكتفى بها * ولما كان الرجل غير قادر على كفاية ثلث لم يكن اهلا لان يحوزهن * وبعدُ فلاىّ سبب حُظرت المراة عن ان تتزوج ثلثة رجال * قلت ان فى كثرة النسآ للرجل الواحد كثرة النسل التى يتوقف عليها عمران الدنيا * وذلك مفقود فى كثرة الرجال للمراة الواحدة * على انى قرات فى بعض الكتب ان هذه العادة لم تزل مستعملة عند بعض الهمج * قالت مه مه اهولآ هم الهمج وانتم المتمدنون الكيّسون * فاما دعواك بتكاثر النسل فى كثرة النسآ فهل سكان الارض الان قليلون * الم تضق بهم البسيطة وتثقل بهم
١٨،٢،٤ بطونها ويمزّق اديمها * فما الموجب الى هذا الاكثار سوى البطر والنهم * قلت قد عدت الى لوم الرجال فلنعد الى الوداع * انى مسافر عنك اليوم وتارك عندك فوادى حتى اذا زارك احد اُحِسّ به * قالت كيف تحسّ وما فوادك معك * والناس يخصّون القلب بالحسّ والشعور * والحزن والسرور * قلت ان حسى براسى * قالت من اى جهة * قلت من الجانب الاعلى من الراس * قالت نَعَم

which to measure any replay or repetition. Similarly, there is disagreement over the times of its visualization, as also of its discussion, though the crucial point is the clearness of the visualization and the foulness of the tongue. The best time for it is the summer in women's opinion and the winter in men's. As to the number of times, some people are Unitarians, some Dualists, and some Trinitarians.' 'And some,' I said, 'Muʿtazilites and some Muʿaṭṭilites.'[43] 'The last,' she said, 'are without redeeming qualities and are unworthy to be counted among mankind.'[44]

"'What are we to think of men who marry two, or three, wives?' I asked. 4.2.17
'It's against nature,' she replied. 'How can that be,' I asked, 'when it was the custom of the prophets?' 'Is this a discussion about religion,' she responded, 'or about natural phenomena? Do you not observe that those animals, such as the rooster and the sparrow for example, that have been granted the capacity to live with a multiplicity of females have also been granted the capacity to satisfy them all? The others live with only one and are satisfied with her. Given that a man cannot satisfy three, he is not qualified to possess them. To return to the matter in hand—why is a *woman* forbidden to marry three men?' I replied, 'A multiplicity of women for a single man results in the multiplicity of offspring on which the world depends in order to thrive. This wouldn't apply in the case of a multiplicity of men for a single woman, though I have read in some book that such a custom continues to be observed among certain savages.' 'Gently, gently!' she said. 'Are they really the savages while you're the civilized and sagacious ones? As for your claim concerning the multiplication of offspring when there's a multiplicity of wives, are the inhabitants of the earth now so few? Is not its surface already too confined to hold them? Do not its innards groan under their weight and is not its skin ripped open? What motive is there then for this increase other than hubris and greed?'

"'You've reverted to heaping blame on men, so let us revert to saying 4.2.18
farewell. I shall depart from you today and leave my heart in your keeping, so that if anyone visits you I shall sense his presence.' 'How will you sense anything when your heart's not with you?' she asked, 'for people say it is the heart alone that has the capacity to feel and *perceive*, be joyous and *grieve*.' 'My sense of feeling,' I said, 'is in my head.'[45] 'Where in your head?' she asked. 'At the tip-top of my head,' I answered. 'Naturally!' she responded. 'There is sympathy between things that resemble one another. But where

الشى الى جنسه اميل * ولكن اين تتركه * قلت على العتبة كيلا يخطوها احد * قالت فاذا طفر فوقها * قلت فى الفراش * قالت فان يكن فى غيره * قلت فيك * قالت ذلك احسن مقرّا * انى اعاهدك على ما كنا عليه من الحب والوداد من ايام السطح الى الان * ولكن حين احسّ واشعر من هنا بانك تبدلت السطح بالشطح اقابلك بفعل مثل فعلك والبادى اظلم * قلت انك كثيرة الوساوس شديدة الغيرة * فلعل شعورك يكون عن وسواس * قالت بل الاولى ان الوسواس يكون عن الشعور * قلت دار ما بيننا الدور * قالت حاوِلْ اذاً فكّه * قلت هو فرض فلا بدّ من قضائه * قالت وقضاً لا بدّ من فرضه * قلت ايعقَد به العهد * قالت اذا عُهد به العقد * قلت لا ارضى بهذه الصفة * قالت ومن لى بوصف هذا الرضى * قلت هل كان العقد فى الشرط * قالت وهل كان الشرط بلا عقد * قلت مَثَلنا مثل ذلك المجنون * قالت لولا الجنون ما جمعنا الزواج * قلت اكثر الناس على هذا * قالت اكثر الناس مجانين * فقلت الحمد لله رب العالمين *

will you leave it?' 'On the doorstep,' I replied, 'so that no one may set foot on the latter.' 'And what if he jump over it?' she enquired. 'In the bed, then,' I said. 'And what if he's in some other bed?' she went on. 'In you, then,' I said. 'That,' she responded, 'is the best place for it. I promise that I will abide by the love and affection that we have shared from the time of "the roof" till now. The moment, however, that I sense and feel, from here, that you've switched your *roofing* feelings for a *roving* eye, I'll match every deed of yours with one of mine, and "the initiator is the more unjust."' I said, 'You're much given to suspicion and very jealous; what's to make sure that anything you sense isn't generated by suspicion?' 'On the contrary,' she said, 'any suspicions I may have are more likely to be the result of what I sense.' I said, 'We've come full circle,' to which she replied, 'Try then to break it.'[46] 'It is a duty,' I said, 'and must be performed,' to which she replied, 'And it is a performance that must be demanded as a duty.' 'Will it seal our covenant?' I asked. 'If such contracts can ever be sealed,' she replied. 'I reject such a characterization,' [47] I said. 'I wish,' she said, 'that someone would tell me what such a characterization means.' I said, 'Was the contract over the condition?'[48] and she replied, 'And was the condition without a contract?'[49] I said, 'We're as mad as that lunatic,'[50] to which she responded, 'But for madness we would never have married.' I said, 'That is true of most people.'

'Many a person's
off his *head*,'
was her response to this, at which 'Praise be to God, Lord of the Worlds,'
I *said*."

الفصل الثالث

فى استرحامات شتى

١،٣،٤ من كان من طبعه المين والافترآ او من كان جاهلا بالنسآ ارتاب فى هذا الوداع
ونسبه الى ترقيش الشعرآ ومبالغاتهم * ولكن اىّ منكر على من جعلت دابها
وديدنها وشنشنتها ونشنشتها ومهوأنها وهُذَيرياها وأُهجورتها وفَعِلتها ومَطِرتها
المحاضرة والمفاكهة والمسقاطة والمطارحة والمحارزة والمجارزة وسرعة الجواب * بل
كثيرا ما كان يجتمع بالفارياق اثنان او ثلثة من اصحابه فاذا خاضوا فى حديث
انتدبت لهم وجارتهم فيه وعارضتهم وماتنتهم * فكل فصيح ان تعارضه لم يُبِن
وكل بليغ ان تساجله يرتِك * وقد علم بالتجربة ان جواب المراة اسرع من جواب
الرجل * وان المشتغل بالعلم يكون ابطا جوابا من غير المشتغل به * لانه لا يقدم
٢،٣،٤ على ذلك الا بعد الفكر والرويّة * على ان هذه العبارات التى نقلتها عن هذه
المراة المبينة من غير قرآة البيان هى دون الاصل بمراحل * فانى لم اقدر فى نقل
الكلام على نقل الحركات التى كانت تبدو منها * وعلى ان اصوّر للمطالع عيونا
تغازل وحواجب تشير * وانفا يرمع * وشفاها ترمع * وخدودا تورد * وجيدا
يلوى * ويدا تومئ * ونَفَسا يربو ويخفت * وصوتا يخفض وينبر * وزد عليه
مسح الماق اشارة الى الاستعبار * وتوالى الزفرات رمزا الى الحزن والانبهار *
والتبلّد ايذانا بالاسف * والتنقل من جنب الى جنب اعلانا بالجزع واللهف *

Chapter Three

Assorted Pleas for Mercy

Those who are by nature mendacious and given to slander, or who know nothing about women, will be suspicious of this farewell and attribute it to the embroidering and hyperbole of a poet. But who can gainsay one who has made it her habit, practice, custom, convention, utmost goal,[51] wont, way, fashion, and observance to riposte, jest, banter, chaff, rally, sally, and respond with alacrity? Often, indeed, two or three of his friends would gather with the Fāriyāq and take on a topic on which she would rise to their challenge, keep pace with them, oppose them, and out-argue them. No speaker, however persuasive, should she oppose him, could find his tongue, and any master of rhetoric, should she enter the lists against him, would tremble, learning by experience that a woman's answer is faster than a man's and that one who has dedicated himself to scholarship may be slower to answer than one who has not, for the former will only venture to answer after cogitation and deliberation. 4.3.1

That said, the utterances that I have reported above from this woman so persuasive (despite her having read not a word in the art of rhetoric) fall far short of the original, for I was incapable, in reporting her words, of reporting likewise the gestures she made along with them and of picturing for the reader eyes that flirt and eyebrows that hint, a nose *aquiver* and lips that *shiver*, cheeks that flush, a neck that twists and a hand that gestures, breathing that rises and falls, and a voice that dips low and soars high, to which may be added the wiping of the eyeball to indicate incipient tears, a succession of sighs to symbolize sadness and joy, a display of foolishness to give notice of 4.3.2

وغير ذلك مما يزيد الكلام قوة وبلاغة * وهذه ثانى مرة ندّمتنى على جهلى صناعة التصوير * والمرة الاولى كانت فى الفصل الرابع عشر من الكتاب الاول عند ذكرى
٤،٣،٣ الحسان على اختلاف جمالهن * ويمكن انى اندم مرة ثالثة * وهنا ينبغى ان اقف على قدمى منتصبا واستميح الاجازة من ذوى الامر والنهى لان اقول * انه قد جرت عادة جميع الولاة والملوك ما عدا ملك الانكليز بان لا يدعوا احدا يدخل بلادهم او يخرج منا ما لم يدفع لدواوينهم او لوكلائهم المعروفين بالقناصل قدرا من الدراهم بحسب خصب ممالكهم ومحلها * وذلك بدعوى ان المسافر اذا نزل بلادهم ساعة او ساعتين فلا بدّ وان يرى قصورهم الفسيحة وعساكرهم المنصورة او خيلهم النجيبة ومراكبهم الفاخرة * فيكون كمن يدخل ملهى من الملاهى *
٤،٣،٤ اذ ليس يدخلها احد من دون غرامة * فان اعترض احد بقوله انّا فى الملهى نسمع اصوات المغنين والمغنيات وآلات الطرب * ونرى الانوار المزدهرة والاشكال المتنوعة ووجوه الحسان الناضرة وحركاتهن الباهرة * ونضحك حين يضحكن * ونطرب حين يرقصن * ونشغف حبّا حين يغازلن * فاما فى رؤية احدى مدنكم فانّا لا نرى شيا من ذلك * بل انما ندخل لكى يغبننا تجّاركم * فتكون فائدتنا فى الدخول بالنسبة الى فائدتهم فى الدخل قليلة * قالوا قد يتفق وقت قدومكم بلادنا ان تكون عساكرنا قد شرعت فى العزف بآلات الطرب فهذا فى مقابلة الطرب فى الملهى * اما النسآ فانّا ناذن لكم فى التمتّع بكل من اعجبتكم فاجروا ورآء من شئتم بحيث يكون النقد على الحافر * ومع ذلك فلا ينبغى ان تشبّه مدائننا التى تشرفت بحضرتنا ببعض الملاهى * ولا سيما ان هذه سنّة قديمة قد مشت عليها اسلافنا طاب ثراهم * وتقادمت عليها السنون والاحوال حتى لم يعد ممكنا تغييرها * فان الملك اذا امر بشى صار ذلك الشى سنّة وحُكما * ويشهد لذلك قول صاحب

regret, a movement from side to side to announce grief and pain, and other things of that sort that lent power and rhetorical force to her words. This is the second time you've made me regret my ignorance of the craft of photography, the first being in Book One, chapter 14, when fair women in all their diverse beauty were discussed, and I may yet feel the same regret a third time.

Here I have to stand up straight and request permission from the powers 4.3.3
that be to declare that it is the custom of all governors and kings, with the exception of the king of the English, to invite no one to enter or exit their lands who has not first paid to their ministries or their agents known as consuls a sum of money in keeping with the fertility or barrenness of their possessions. They do this on the pretext that if a traveler spends one or two hours in their country he is bound to see their spacious palaces and ever-victorious armies or their thoroughbred horses and luxurious vessels, thus putting him on a par with one who enters some place of entertainment, which no one would do without paying a fee.

If anyone objects, saying, "In a place of entertainment we hear the 4.3.4
voices of the singers, male and female, and the sounds of the musical instruments, see the decorative lights and varied decorations, the shining faces of the lovely ladies and their dazzling displays, laugh with them when they laugh, are transported when they dance, and fall in love with them when they flirt, but we see none of these things when we view one of your cities; indeed, as soon as we enter them we are fleeced by your merchants, meaning that what we gain from our coming in is but little compared to what they gain in terms of their incomings," they will tell you, "Your arrival in our country may coincide with a musical performance by our soldiers, and that can be in lieu of any transports you may experience in that place of entertainment. As far as women are concerned we give you permission to enjoy any of them that takes your fancy and run after any of them you wish, so long as you have ready cash. It's not right, however, for you to liken our cities, graced as they are with our presence, to some place of entertainment, especially as the payment of these fees is an ancient custom followed by our ancestors (God bless the sod!) that has been practiced for so many years and eons that it can no longer be changed. If the king commands something, that thing becomes custom and law, as witness the

الزبور ان يد الرب على قلب الملك * بمعنى ان الملك لا يفكر فی شی الّا ويد الله
عاصمة له فيه * هكذا شرح هذه الاية العلمآ الربانيّون فی بلادنا ومن خالفهم فجزاؤه
٥،٣،٤ الصلب * وبعدُ فان الملك اذا اخذ فی تغيير العادات وتبديل السنن فربما افضى ذلك
الى تغييره * فيكون مَثَله كالديك الذی يبحث فی الارض عن حبة قمح فيثير التراب
على راسه * وصَغُر ذلك تشبيها * فالاولى اذاً اقرار كل شی فی محله * ثم لا فرق
بين ان يكون قاصد بلادنا غنيا او فقيرا * صالحا بارّا او لصا فاجرا * رجلا كان او
امراة * فكلهم ملتزمون باداۤ الغرامة وتحمل الغبن — ولكن ياسيدی ومولای انا امراة
معسرة قد اضطررت الى المرور بمدينتك السعيدة * لان زُويجی المُسيكين كان قد
قدم الى بلادكم الملكية ليدير مصلحة فقضى عليه الله تعالى بالوفاة * فتركت صِبْيَة لی
فی البُيَيت يتضورون جوعا وجئت لاری زويجی المويت حالة كونه لا يرانی * ومع
ذلك فانی أُعدّ من الحسان اللاۤی يحق لهنّ من امثالك العناية والالطاف * فكيف
التزم بالغرامة فضلا عن نفقة السفر وفَقْد زويجی الذی كان لی سندا — ارجعی من
حيث جئت فما هذا وقت الاسترحام * لان القواعد التی تقرر فی دفاتر الملوك لا
٦،٣،٤ تقبل التبديل ولا التحريف ولا يستثنى منها شی — وانا ايضا يامولای رُجَيل فقيّر
قد رمانی الدهر بصروفه لامر شاۤه الله * فوافيت بلادكم طمعا فی تحصيل وُظَيّفة
تقوم بأَوَدی * وما انا من ذوی التغاوی والفتن ولا من الباحثين فی سياسات
الملوك واياالاتهم * فقصاری منيتی تحصيل المعيشة * على انی اعرف شيا لا
يعرفه اهل بلادكم العامرة فربما كان مقامی فيها مفيدا لدولتكم السعيدة * ولو صدر
الامر العالی بامتحانی واختباری فيما ادّعيه لاكرمتم مثوای فضلا عن الرخصة لی فی
الدخول بغير غرامة — ياطائف ياعسس يازِبْنِية ياجلواز ياشرطيّ ياعَون ياذَبّیّ[1]

[1] كذا في القاموس وفي ١٨٥٥: ياذِبِّيّ.

words of the psalmodist when he says, 'The king's heart is in the hand of the Lord,'[52] meaning that whenever the king thinks of something the hand of God renders his judgment infallible with regard to it. This is how the divines in our country explain this verse and the reward of any who disagrees is crucifixion.

"But to return to our argument: if the king starts changing customs and exchanging conventions, this may lead to him too being changed. His situation is comparable to that of the rooster that searches for a grain of wheat on the ground and in so doing stirs up the dust till it covers his head (though this is an unworthy comparison). Better then that everything stay as it is. And again, it makes no difference whether the one bound for our country is rich or poor, pious and righteous, a thief and a libertine, a man or a woman—all are obliged to hand over the fee and put up with the fleecing . . ." 4.3.5

"But my lord and master, I am a woman in straitened circumstances obliged to pass through your happy city because my poor dear hubby came to your royal country to conduct some business and the Almighty determined that he should meet his end there, so I left young children I have writhing with hunger in our little cottage and came to see my poor dead hubby (since he can't see me), not to mention that I'm considered one of those good-looking women who deserve to be looked after and well treated by those in positions such as yours. Why then should I be obliged to bear the fee, not to mention the costs of travel and the loss of my hubby, who was a support to me?"

"Return, woman, to whence you came! This is no time for pleas for mercy, for the rules set down in the ledgers of kings admit of no change or modification and no exceptions can be made . . ."

"And I too, my master, am a poor little fellow whom fate has bombarded with its calamities for reasons known only to God and I have made my way to your country hoping to obtain some minor post that will satisfy my needs. I am no seducer or sower of dissent nor am I one who pokes his nose into the policies of kings and their governance. All that I wish for is to make a living, though I do know something that the inhabitants of your ever-prosperous land do not and my presence here may be of benefit to your happy realm. Should a sublime decree be issued that I be examined and tested as to my claims, you would provide me with a house, to say nothing of issuing the 4.3.6

يا مِسحَل يا فارع يا قِيَلع يا تُؤرور يا ثؤرور يا ثؤثور يا تؤثور يا اترور يا ترتور اودع هذا السجن * ان هو الّا جاسوس قدم يتجسّس بلادنا * فتّشوه عسى ان تجدوا معه
٧،٣،٤ اوراقا تكشف لنا عن خبره - وانا كذلك يا مولاى وسيدى غُلَيّم مُسَيكين قد جئت لانظر ابى اذ بلغنى انه كان قادما من سفره فدخل بلادكم فاصابه هواوها الحميد بمرض شديد منعه من الحركة * فلما علمت امى بمرضه وهى مريضة ايضا مما شملها من الحزن والكرب لطول غيابه بعثتنى اليه لعلى اخدمه وامرّضه فيطيب خاطره برويتى ويخف ما به * فان رؤية الاب ابنه حال مرضه تقوم له مقام الدوآء - ما نحن بمربّى الاولاد ولا بلادنا مكتب لهم حتى ياتوا اليها ويخرجوا منها من دون غرامة * اذهب
٨،٣،٤ وكن رجلا بادائها على الفور - وانا ايضا يا عتادى وملاذى * وثمالى ومعاذى * وملجاى وملتحدى * وسندى ومعتمدى * وركحى وركنى * وعزّى وامنى * رجل من الشعرآ الادبا كنت قد مدحت بعض امرآئنا الكرام بقصيدة فاجازنى عليها مئة دينار * فاشتريت بنصفها موّنة لعيالى * ووفيت بربعها ماكنت استدنته لكسوتهم وبقى معى ربع * واذ سمعت بمحاسن مملكتكم الخصيبة البهية البهيجة وبما فيها من التحف والطُرف التى لا توجد فى بلادنا * رمت ان اسرّح ناظرى وانزه خاطرى فى هذا النعيم اياما قليلة * عسى ان يخطر ببالى عند رويته معان[1] بديعة ما سبقنى اليها احد فاصوغ منها بادئ بدى مديحا بليغا فى جنابك الرفيع * ومقامك السنيع * وانشر الثنآ عليك فى جميع الاقطار * فى الليل والنهار * واجيد وصف مكارمك فى الاسفار - ما اكثر الشعرآ الغاوين العاوين فى بلادنا وما اكثر اقاويلهم واقل رزقهم * اما ان تدفع الغرامة واما ان ترجع على عقبك واما ان نؤويك الى دار المجانين *

١ ١٨٥٥: معانى.

permit for me to enter without a fee . . ." "You there, policeman, watchman, guard, nabber, grunter, rozzer, runner, cop, slop, constable, catchpole, cozzpot, woodentop, nabman, beagle, derrick, nubbing-cove—put that man in prison! He's surely a spy come to spy out our land. Search him. No doubt you'll find papers on him that'll tell us what he's up to."

"And I too, my lord and master, am a poor young laddie. I have come 4.3.7
to see my father because he has told me that, on his way home, he entered your country, where the clement climate afflicted him with a malady that prevents him from moving. When my mother, who is also sick from the grief and care that have consumed her as a result of his long absence, learned of his illness, she sent me to him, in the hope that I might serve him and nurse him and his spirits then revive at the sight of me and recover, for when a sick father sees his son the latter takes the place of medicine." "We're not children's nannies and our country's no schoolhouse that they should come and go without paying a fee. Get on with you and show you're a man by paying it right away . . ."

"And I too—O my shield and my refuge, my succor and my resort, my 4.3.8
haven and my shelter, my support and my prop, my foundation and my stay, my strength and my security—am a poet and man of letters who wrote a poem in praise of a certain emir, for which he granted me a hundred gold coins. With half of these I bought provisions for my family, with a quarter I covered what I needed to clothe them, and I have a quarter left. Having heard of the merits of your magnificent, splendid, fertile kingdom and of the treasures and curiosities that it contains, to be found in no other country, I desired to let my eyes roam and my mind saunter in the midst of this luxury for a few days. Who knows? Maybe on seeing it, brilliant tropes that no one has beaten me to will come to my mind and from them I shall fashion, before anything else, a brilliant eulogy in praise of your elevated *position* and gracious *condition*, broadcast praise of you in every *clime*, at every *time*, skillfully describe your noble qualities in books . . ." "How many a dilettantish and doleful poet we have in our country! How many are their writings and how little their income! Either you pay the fee, or you turn around and go home, or we consign you to the madhouse."

٩،٣،٤ ولكن هيهات ان تشرف مسامع المسترحم الحقير من سيده الجليل الخطير بمثل
هذه الاجوبة السلبية * فان السلب من مقام الكبير منة * وانما الغالب ان يكون
جوابه برغم الانف او بالقفد * او باللكم على الخرطوم * او بهتم سن * او ببقر
بطن * او باطنان ساق * او بانقاض ظهر * ولهذا لما عزم الفارياق على
السفر وكان ممن لا يستغنى عن احد اعضائه التمس من خمسة قناصل ان يشرفوا
جَوازه بختومهم * فختم عليه كل من قنصل نابلى وليكورنه ومدينة اخرى فى مملكة
البابا وقنصل جينوى وفرنسا * لان سفينة النار تمرّ على مراسى هذه المدن كلها
وترسى فيها بعض ساعات * اما مدينة نابلى فهى مشهورة بكثرة ما فيها من العجلات
والمراكب والحدائق والغياض * واما ليكورنه فبطيب هوائها وارتفاع بنائها وكذلك
مدينة جينوى * قال وهى عندى احسن منهما * وانحس ما يكون مدينة البابا اذ
١٠،٣،٤ ليس عليها رونق المُلك ولا الملكوت وما بها شى يقرّ العين * فلما وصل الفارياق
الى مرسيلية أُخذ صندوقه الى ديوان المكس واشير اليه ان يتبعه * ثم طلب
منه المكّاسون ان يفتحوه ليفتشوه فظن انهم يريدون ان يفتشوا فى كراريسه ليعلموا
ما فيها فقال * انا ما هجوت سلطانكم ولا مطرانكم فلمَ تفتشون فى كراريسى * فلم
يفهمه احد منهم وهو لم يفهم احدا * فلما فرغوا اشاروا اليه ان اقفل صندوقك
فثلج صدره * ثم انبرى واحد منهم يمسح بيديه على جنبه فظن انه يتمسح به اى
يتبرك لكونه وجد كراريسه بخط غريب * لكنه علمَ من بعد ذلك انهم كانوا يفتشونه
١١،٣،٤ ليعلموا هل كان مدّخرا شيا من التبغ والمسكر * ثم سافر من مرسيلية الى باريس
ففُتّش ايضا هو وصندوقه فى ديوان مكسها * فكانّ مكّاسى هذه المدينة كانوا
يحسبون ان رفاقهم فى تلك قد ناموا عن قيام الليل * فبال الشيطان فى آذانهم
فعمشت عيونهم عن رؤية ما فى الصندوق * او انهم يرتشون كسائر اصحاب

Rarely, though, does the puissant, magnificent master honor the ears of the wretched pleader with the like of such negative responses, for mere negativity from the great is a boon. Usually it comes with humiliation and a slap to the back of the neck, a punch on the snout, the pulverizing of a tooth, the slitting open of a belly, the slicing off of a leg, or the snapping of a back. For this reason, the Fāriyāq, being one of those who couldn't spare any of his limbs, when he resolved to travel, requested five consuls to honor his passport with their stamps. The consuls of Naples, Leghorn, and another city in the Papal States, as well as the consuls of Genoa and France stamped it, because the steamer passes by the ports of each of those cities and docks in them for a few hours. The city of Naples is famous for its numerous carriages, ships, gardens, and forests, Leghorn for the sweetness of its air and the height of its buildings, and the same holds true for the city of Genoa. The Fāriyāq said, "In my opinion, the last is better than the other two. The papal city is as disagreeable as can be, since it has none of the glamour of sovereignty or royalty and there is nothing in it to please the eye." 4.3.9

When the Fāriyāq reached Marseilles, his trunk was taken to the customs office and he was shown by signs that he was to follow it. The customs officers asked him to open it so that they could search through it, but he thought they wanted to look through his notebooks so that they could know what was in them and said, "I haven't written satires on your sultan or your metropolitan, so why would you look through my notebooks?" but none of them understood him and he understood none of them. When they were done, they gestured to him to close the trunk and he breathed a sigh of relief. Then one of them started feeling his side with his hands, so that the Fāriyāq imagined that he was "rubbing" him,[53] in the sense of seeking blessing from him, because he'd found his notebooks in their strange hand. Afterwards, however, he learned that they were searching him to see if he was carrying any tobacco or intoxicating spirits. 4.3.10

Next he traveled from Marseilles to Paris, where he and his trunk were likewise searched at its customs house. The customs officers of the latter city seemed to believe that their colleagues in the former had gone to sleep while on night duty and the devil had urinated in their ears and as a result their eyes had been made too blurry to see what was in the trunk, or that they'd taken a 4.3.11

الوظائف * فاقام فى باريس ثلثة ايام فى دار سفارة الدولة العلية وفيها حظى
بتقبيل ايدى الوزيرين المعظمين والمشيرين المفخمين رشيد باشا وسامى باشا * ثم
سافر من باريس الى لندن وسياتى الكلام على وصف هاتين المدينتين العظيمتين *
ثم من لندن الى قرية فى بلاد الفلاحين وفيها القى العصا وعندها اقف انا ايضا *

bribe, like other civil servants. He stayed in Paris three days, in the house occupied by the embassy of the Sublime State,[54] where he enjoyed the privilege of kissing the hands of the August Ministers and Honored Marshals Rashīd Pasha and Sāmī Pasha. Then he left Paris for London; these two mighty cities will be described later. From London he went to a village in peasant country, where he hung up his hat and where I too shall now call a halt.

الفصل الرابع

في شروط الرواية

لم يمض على الفارياق فى مدى عمره مدة هى انحس واشق من المدة التى قضاها فى ١،٤،٤
تلك القرية * لان قرى بلاد الانكليز ليس فيها من محل لهو واجتماع وانس وحظّ
البتة * وانما اللهو والحظ فى المدن الكبيرة * وفضلا عن ذلك فليس فى القرى
شى يباع للماكول والمشروب سوى ما لا احتفال به * ومن كان عنده دجاجة او
طرفة بعث بها الى احدى المدن القريبة * فمن شآ ان ينقطع عن الدنيا او يترهّب
فعليه بها * اما النسآ هناك ففيهن من تشفى من القمه بل تمنى بالقرم * الا ان
الغريب محروم منهن * اذكل ذات ظلف ملازمة لفحلها فليس من سائب مبهَل الا
العجائز * ثم بعد مضى شهرين عليه وهو على هذه الحالة المشؤمة انتقل الى مدينة ٢،٤،٤
كمبريج مصدر القسوسة وعلم الكلام * فان جل قسيسى الانكليز يمضون اليها او
الى اكسفورد ليتعلموا فيها الالهيات والمناظرة * وفى هاتين المدينتين ايضا سائر
طلاب العلم على اختلاف طبقاتهم ودرجاتهم * ومن احدى مدارس كمبريج نبغ
نيوطون الفيلسوف المشهور * فاكترى الفارياق فيها مسكنين فى دار كما هى العادة
ومكث يترجم بقية الكتاب الذى مرّت الاشارة اليه سابقا * وكان فى تلك الدار
جارية دعجا كاعب وكذا سائر الوصائف غالبا * فكان الفارياق يراها كل ليلة تطلع

Chapter 4

The Rules for Retelling

In all his life, the Fāriyāq never spent a more unpleasant and arduous time than he did in that village,[55] for the villages of England are altogether without places in which to be entertained, to meet, to enjoy oneself, or to have fun; enjoyment and fun are to be had only in the large cities. In addition, such food and drink as are sold in them are no cause for celebration, for anyone who has a chicken or anything special sends it to one of the nearby towns. Anyone who wishes to cut himself off from the world or feels a calling to be a monk should hie himself to them. As for their women, some of them will cure a loss of appetite or even bestow a raging lust, but the outsider is denied access to them. Every cloven hoof stays close to her bull and the only loose, free-ranging beasts are the old ones. 4.4.1

After two months in these calamitous conditions, he moved to the city of Cambridge, wellspring of the clergy and of the science of theology, since most English clergymen go there or to Oxford to learn divinity and apologetics. These two cities are also home to all other students, in all their diversity of class and standing. The celebrated philosopher Newton was the brilliant son of one of the Cambridge colleges. There the Fāriyāq rented, as is the custom, two sets of rooms in a house, where he stayed, translating the rest of the book referred to earlier.[56] In the same house there was a full-breasted girl with wide black eyes, which is how most of the maids there are. Every night the Fāriyāq would see her going up to the room of one of the lodgers. Then, after a time not longer than it takes to say "Good evening!" he would hear her produce a kineto-penetrative gasp. The mistress of the house used to see her coming down from the man's room at ten or so at night but had no interest 4.4.2

الى غرفة احد السكّان ثم بعد هنيهة ليست باطول من قولك عمت مسآء يسمع لها نغمة ايغافية * وكانت صاحبة المنزل تراها نازلة من عند الرجل فى الساعة العاشرة ونحوها من الليل ولا تكترث بطلوعها ولا بنزولها * فاذا جآت فى الصباح لتصلح فراش الفارياق حملق فيها وحدّق فلم يرَ فيها علامة تدل على انها كانت هى صاحبة النغمة * فيظن ان ذلك كان وهماً منه نشا عن اللهج بالايغاف * فاذا جآ الليل عادت النغمة وعاد اليقين * فاذا كان الصباح عادت الحملقة وعاد التصاون وعاد الشك والحيرة وهلم جرا * حتى كاد ذلك يشوش عقل الفارياق ويفسد عليه
٣،٤،٤ الترجمة التى طالما كان يخشى عليها الخلل والفساد من قضية ما نسائية * وهنا ينبغى ان اقرفص واقول * ان هذه المزيّة السنّورية اى الاكل خفوة وان يكن وجودها ملحوظا فى النسآ على الاعمّ الا انها فى نسآ الانكليز على الاخصّ * فان المتّصفة منهن بما اتصفت به السيدة المدقم فى فصل حذنبدى تتظاهر فى النهار بصفات الورع والتقوى والنفورية والقذورية وتنظر الى تبعها نظر المتجاهل * وتوهم الناقد انها متبتلة معتزلة للرجال * وربما حفظت احاديث دينية وروايات نسكية تلقيها على الناس فيعظمونها ويعتقدون فيها الصلاح * واذا دخلتَ بيتها وجدت على مائدتها التوراة والانجيل وكتبا اخرى فى العبادة والزهد * وربما وسّخت الظاهر من ورقها لتوهم انها كثير الدراسة لها * ولا يمكن للرجل ان يذكر بين يديها اسم عضو من اعضائه * فتكون لذة هولآء على مقتضى قاعدة الفارياقية
٤،٤،٤ غير تامة وذلك لخلوها عن ركن الذكر * وعنها ايضا ان ذكر اللذة لا بد من ان يكون مطابقا للواقع * فان كان الوقوع مثلا من ذى مقام ليلاً ذُكرت فيه لِذات مقام * وان يكن من دونٍ صباحاً ذكرت فيه لدون من النسآ * وقس على ذلك سائر التباين فى الاوقات والاشخاص * اللهمّ الا ان خشى فوات الفرصة *

in her ascents and descents. In the morning, when the girl came to make the Fāriyāq's bed, he would stare at her and observe her closely but could see no sign to indicate that she was the gasper. He therefore assumed that it was a delusion born of his fervent desire for penetration. Then night would come and the gasp would be there again, and so would his certainty. With morning the staring would be repeated as would the pretence of virtue, and the doubt would be there and so would the confusion, and so on and so forth. Things got so bad that the Fāriyāq's mind almost became unhinged and started to spoil the translation, which he had long feared might fall victim to shortcomings and mistakes due to some issue related to women.

Here I have to squat down on my haunches and declare: "This feline characteristic (i.e., the ability to take one's food without being noticed), though its presence may be observed in women in general, is especially pronounced among English women. Such a woman, if distinguished by those features ascribed to the sexually voracious woman in the *ḥadanbadā* chapter,[57] will put on a show during the day of God-fearingness, piety, reticence, and distaste and look at her devotee as though she had no idea who he was, deluding any who are watching her into thinking she is virtuous and has nothing to do with men. She may have memorized religious sayings and devout narrations to fling at people, making them venerate her and believe her to be righteous, and when you enter her home you may find on the table copies of the Old Testament and the Gospels and other books on worship and self-abnegation (the visible edges of whose pages she will sometimes dirty to give the false impression that she studies them frequently) and a man may not be allowed to utter in her presence the name of any of his members. As a result, the pleasure of such women, according to the rule pronounced by the Fāriyāqiyyah, will be incomplete, because it will lack the element of discussion.[58] 4.4.3

"And we have it on her authority too that any talk of pleasure must be congruent with the reality. If it involves a man of high status at night, it must be discussed with a woman of high status at night, if someone of low status in the morning, it must be discussed with a woman of low status in the morning, and so on and so forth for all the various other times and persons—unless there is reason to fear that the opportunity will be lost: in other words, if it happened at night, for example, but cannot be discussed that 4.4.4

اى اذا حصلت مثلاً ليلاً ولم يمكن ذكرها فى الليل فيصح الذكر فى الفجر او الصباح * او ان حصلت من ذى مقام ولم يتهيّا وجود نظيره فيصح ذكرها لدون ولا تفسد لذة الذكر بذلك * فاما على فرض كونها لم تجد احدا من هذه الاصناف فيصح ذكرها لنفسها * وذلك بان تدخل راسها فى زير فارغ او فى بئر اوجبّ او قبوة ونحو ذلك مما له صدى وتنطق بلسان فصيح مبين بما مرّ لها * حتى اذا رجع الصدى قام لها مقام النديم الكليم * فاما اذا بقى الذكر فى صدرها فيخشى عليها من الصِدارة والذُباح * ويشترط ايضا عندها ان تكون الرواية مطابقة للفعل * فللنبرة نبرة * ٥،٤،٤
وللهمز همزة * وللحركة حركة * وللسكون سكون * وللمد مدّ * وللهذّ هذ * وللترخيم ترخيم * وللترسّل ترسل * وان يبلَّغ التشديد على الذال اذا كانت الرواية بلغتنا هذه الشريفة * وان يكون فى العينين مغازلة * وفى اللعم فيضان * وفى اللسان بلّة * وفى اليدين تلغ * وبما تقرّر علمتَ من ان هذه الخلة المذكورة الموجودة فى نسآء الانكليز اخلال بشروط اللذة * ويمكن ان يقال ان لذة التصور عندهن قوية جدا بحيث تقوم مقام لذتين * او انهن يضعن رؤسهن فى خابية ونحوها *
وعن الفارياق ان الجمال فى النسآ على اختلاف انواعه له نطق ونِدآ ودعآ واشارة ٦،٤،٤
ورمز * فمنه ما يقول لناظره لست ابالى بالمراود * ومنه ما يقول الا اغتنم الآن الفرصة - للتاخير آفات - لن ترانى من الكثير ملولا - لا يغرنّك الشفون - هيتَ لك - مَن لى به الساعة - ما ارى كفايتى عند احد - ان دوآء الشقّ ان تحوصه - اين اين المشبع - اين ابن اَلغز - اين ابن بنى اذلغ - لدىّ يذل الصعب - بعد جهدك لا تلام - لكل مجتهد نصيب - من اطعم اشبع - من ذاق عرف - من مسّ هرف - من سبق فقد ربح - العود احمد - من عدّ عاد - من وصل وُصل * ومنه ما يشير انِ استعمل الحيلة - تلطف فى الزيارة - كن من الجار

same night, it is permissible to discuss it at dawn or in the morning, or if it involves a man of high status but none of his kind is available, it is permissible to discuss it with a man of low status; the pleasure derived from talking about it will not be spoiled thereby. If by any chance she cannot find anyone from any of these categories, she can discuss it with herself. She may do this by inserting her head into an empty water jar, well, pit, vault, or anything of the sort that produces an echo, and speaking with clear and eloquent tongue of everything that happened to her; the responding echo can take the place of an intimate interlocutor. If, on the other hand, the memory is kept in her breast, chestiness and diphtheria are to be feared.

"It is also a rule in her view that the retelling be congruent with the act. 4.4.5
Thus, for the pressings, an accentuation of the voice,[59] for the jabs, a catch in the airflow, for the movements, a vocalic motion, for the moments of inertia, an inert letter, for the prolongations, a prolongation of the *a*, for the rushed bits, a gabbling of the recitation, for the softenings of the voice, an apocopation, and for the languorous moments, a slowing of pace. Also, that special attention be given to the doubling of the letter *dhāl*,[60] if the retelling is done in this noble language of ours, and that there be a flirtatious flash to the eyes, floods of saliva, and a moistness to the tongue, and that the hands sketch what the words describe. This being established, you will have gathered that the trait mentioned as present in Englishwomen is an infraction of the rules of pleasure, and it may be said that the pleasure they take in visualization is so strong because it takes the place of two other pleasures, or that they put their heads inside a cask or the like.

"And on the authority of the Fāriyāq, we have it that the beauty that is 4.4.6
in women, in all its disparate forms, has ways of speaking, calling out, inviting, pointing, and signaling. For example, there is the type that says to the one who gazes upon it, 'I'm not interested in little sticks' and the type that says, 'Seize your opportunity now!' or 'Tarrying has its disadvantages' or 'You won't find me wearied by large numbers' or 'Let not the shy-eyed one deceive you!' or 'Come hither!' or 'O who will bring him to me right now?' or 'I see none who can satisfy me' or 'The best way to mend a slit is to sew it up'[61] or 'Where oh where is the one who can satisfy me?' or 'Where is Ibn Alghaz?'[62] or 'Where is a member of the Banū Adhlagh?'[63] or 'Before me the hard man is humbled' or 'After all that effort, who can find fault with you?' or

على حذر – من تانّى نال ما تمنى – بكّر بكور الغراب وغير ذلك * فجمال نسآ ٧،٤،٤
الانكليز هومما عنوانه اين ابن الغز* اين اين المشبع * لدىّ يذل الصعب * فانك
ترى المراة منهن تمشى وهى صَفُوح منزّة سامدة مساندة شاردة معبّدة شامرة
نافرة جافلة جامزة آبزة نافزة ناقزة معتزة سارية عاسجة طامحة جامحة شامخة خانفة
مشمّة شافنة مُهْطعة مُرْشقة متتالعة هابعة متعاطفة متطلقة مخرنطمة مسحنفرة
مجلوّذة مجلوّظة مذلعبّة مجرهدّة مرمئدة مثمعدّة مصمعدّة مبسئرّة مسكبرّة مسمهرّة
مشفترّة مسجئرّة مسجهرّة متمهلّة متمئلّة مشمعلة مصمئلّة مقلهفّة مرئمّة * ومع
انِ القدرة الخالقية قد خصتهن بالآء الايا سابغة ضافية على ما روت الرواة *
فانهن يتخذن لها المرافد ويعظّمنها بها تعظيما يوقف المستوفز بحيث يقف كالجابه
الحيران * فلا يتماسك عن ان تصطك ساقاه تعجبا واعظاما لهذا التعظيم * وان
تحترق اسنانه ويندلع لسانه * وتنضنض لهاته * وتلتوى عنقه *وتنتفخ اوداجه *
ويحمرّ حملاقه * ويُغان على قلبه ويَطّنَى * وتاخذه القشعريرة والرعدة والأَفكل
والهزّة والاضطراب والرجفان والنغشان والغشيان والغميان والفَشْيان والنُحوَآ
والدُوار والمَيدان واللَبَم والاختلاج والترنّح والارتعاج والارتعاش والارتهاش
والرَعْس والارتعاس والترأّد والترجيد والأَصيص والبَصيص والكصيص والأَرْض
والعُسوم والنِفيضَى والقِلّ والإِرْزيز والزَمَع والزقزقة[١] والشفشفة والصَعْفة والقرقفة
والقفقفة * وتهيج به الاخلاط الاربعة فيطلب كلّ خلط عظّامة * وتنهال عليه
الخواطر والوساوس * وتتجاذبه عوامل الامانى * وتحرضه محرضات النِزّة*
وتطفره خوالج الشهوة * ويميل به مميل التشوق والتلهف على حد قول الشاعر .

علمتك الباذل المعروف فانبعثت   اليك بى واجفات الشوق والامل

١ ١٨٥٥: والزقوفة.

'No conscious effort is entirely wasted' or 'Feed and thou shalt be satisfied' or 'To taste is to know' or 'To touch is to praise' or 'The early bird catches the worm' or 'If at first you don't succeed . . .'[64] or 'Always count twice'[65] or 'Keep in touch with others and others will keep in touch with you.' There is also the type that looks at you as though to say, 'Use cunning' or 'Make your visits discreet' or 'Watch out for the neighbors' or 'Slow and steady wins the race' or 'Come early as the crow.'"[66]

The beauty of Englishwomen is of the sort that falls under the heading of "Where is Ibn Alghaz?" "Where oh where is the one who can satisfy me?" and "Before me the hard man is humbled." You see them turning disdainfully to one side,[67] shying, flying, starting, bolting, flinching, fleeing, proudly turning, racing, baulking, jibbing, bounding, leaping, escaping, like a mirage dissipating, while running full tilt, head high, nose in air, chest out, back straight, and even though the divine creative power has uniquely blessed them with buttocks ample and copious (or so it is reported), yet they apply bustles to these, using the latter to make the former large enough to stop any who lies in wait in his tracks, as though dumbfounded by a head-on encounter, after which he cannot stop his knees from knocking together in wonder and awe at such aggrandizement, his teeth from smoking, his tongue from lolling, his uvula from wagging, his neck from twisting, his jugulars from swelling, and his eyelids from reddening, or himself from being overcome by lust and assaulting her, and the said person is taken by an agitation,[68] a trepidation, a commotion, a flutteration, a trembling, a shaking, a quaking, a shuddering, a shivering, a quavering, a rocking, a jolting, a jarring, a jerking, a bobbling, a wobbling, a fainting, a giddiness, a dizziness, a lightheadedness, a twitching, a tottering, a teetering, a staggering, a faltering, a languorous folding, a stiffening of the joints, a chattering of the teeth, and a rattling of the jaw, and the four humors set him ablaze, each mix[69] demanding its own bustle. Ideas and misgivings bombard him, hopes and fears pull him this way and that, choking passions make him splutter, he trembles with lustful emotions, and he doubles over with yearning and desire, in accordance with the words of the poet 4.4.7

I knew you as one celebrated for your generosity,
And the throbbings of longing and hope swept me to you

فيبقى حائرا بائرا مبهوتا مهفوتا سادرا داهلا مدهوشا ذاهلا * بحيث اذا رجع سالما الى منزله يحسب كل شاخص فيه عظّامة او ما عُظّم بها * وكان الفارياق اذا خرج وابصر هذه الروابى الخصيبة عاد الى ما ٨،٤،٤
ماواه وفى راسه الف معنى يشغله * فما انشده فى بعض هذه الفتن.

يا للعجاب وكلّ عُجُب فليقل يا للعجاب
ما ان يرى فى ذا المكان سوى المرافد من روابى
كلا ولا من غوطة من دون ذياك الجناب
كلا ولا قرموطة تشرى سوى كُعب الكعاب
من كل ذات تبهكن تدعو الحصور الى الدعاب
الشوق يقدم بى وخوف العجز من غَلَم ناى بى
ماذا يقول الناس عمّن خار عن مَلْء الوطاب
ام كيف تضعف معدة العربى عن قحف القعاب
مَن لى بصُنبور فأُترعه بمِنزفة الحُباب
من لى بقبّة مرفد فى ليلتى من ذى القباب
من لى بجثّ أُليّة من ذى الالايا فى مآبى
هذا لعمرك شان ذى قَطَمٍ وهذا الداب دابى

and he remains so confused and at a loss, speechless and flabbergasted, perplexed and bewildered, astonished and amazed that, when he returns safely to his house, he believes everything that pops up before him there is a bustle, or that thing that lends the bustle its bulk.

Whenever the Fāriyāq left the house and beheld these well-endowed mounds, he would return to his refuge with a thousand poetical images crowding his head. A poem he recited in honor of one such enchantress went as follows: 4.4.8

Wonder of wonders! Let every man, "Wonder of wonders!"
  Exclaim, of those who love with women to tussle,
"Not a mound's to be seen
  In this place that isn't a bustle!
No indeed! And not a dip
  That isn't accompanied by its own little hump—
No indeed again!—and not a euphorbia fruit[70] to be bought
  That isn't a high-breasted woman's pink bump.
Longing makes me boldly approach each big-bottomed waddler
  Who invites the celibate to play,
Yet fear of impotence induced by too much lust
  Keeps me away.
What must people say of him who
  Roars from a bursting milk skin that absence of opportunity plugs,
Or how can the stomach of an Arab
  Be too weak to drink deep from those great jugs?
O for a spigot that I might fill the cup
  From my counter-levered love pail!
O for a bustle like one of those domes
  Of which I might myself at night avail!
O for a palpation of one of those
  Bummikins in my home!
This, I swear, is the way of those starved
  Of sex and this same practice is my own."

الفصل الخامس

في فضل النسآء

وكما ان نسآ تلك البلاد اختصصن بهذه المزية كذلك اختصت رجالها بالطافهم ١،٥،٤
الغريب بعد معرفتهم له * فاما قبل المعرفة فانه اذا حيَّ احدا منهم فما يكون جوابه الا الشزر والشصر * ولهذا لما سمع احد طلّاب العربية منهم بوجود الفارياق وكان قد قُرِئ عليه حسبه ونشبه اتى ليزوره * وطلب منه ان يذهب معه الى منزله فيقيم عنده مكرما معززا * وكان مقامه بعيدا عن كمبريج * فاجابه الفارياق الى ذلك لان اهل المدينة على كثرة المدارس عندهم والمعالم هم اشدّ الناس نفورا من الغريب * ولا سيما اذا كان مخالفا لهم فى الزيّ * فكانوا يسخرون من قبعته
الحمرآ حتى كان كثيرا ما يقبع فى غرفته ولا يخرج منها الا ليلا * وقال فى ذلك * ٢،٥،٤

رمتنى النوى فى كمبريج ملازما   لبيتى نهارا اَن ترانى اوباش
فتعبثَ بى حتى اذا الليل جنّنى   خرجت على اَمْن كانى خفّاش

ولان الكلاب ايضا كانت تشم فروته وتلازمه * فقال فيها

ولى فروة تاتى الكلاب تشمّها   ولم تندفع عنها اذا ما دفعتها
تهرّ على تمزيق جلدى وجلدها   كانى من ابائها قد صنعتها

Chapter 5

The Superiority of Women

Just as the women of this country are distinguished by this characteristic, so its men are distinguished by that of kindness to the stranger, once they have been introduced to him. Before he's been introduced, however, if he greets one of them, the response will be a sidelong glance or a brisk nod of the head. Thus it was that one of their students of Arabic, having learned of the presence of the Fāriyāq and having been informed as to his noble pedigree and plentiful property, came to visit him and invited him to go with him to his house, which was some distance from Cambridge, and to stay there as an honored guest. The Fāriyāq accepted the invitation because the inhabitants of the city, despite the large number of schools and places of learning there, were exceptionally unwelcoming to the stranger, especially if he differed from them in dress; they made so much fun of his red cap, for example, that he often hid in his room and would leave it only at night. 4.5.1

On this topic, he wrote 4.5.2

Cast by the tempest on Cambridge's shore,
Lest I be seen and mocked by the rabble, I kept to my house.
Then, when night had driven me mad,
I'd go out in safety, like a flittermouse.

Similarly, since the dogs too would sniff at his fur coat and follow him around, he wrote of them

I've got a fur coat that the dogs all come to sniff at
But when I repel them not one retires.
They snarl as they rip into my skin and the coat's—
You'd think I'd had it made from the skins of their sires.

ولان اهل الدار التى نزل فيها كانوا يشاركونه فى طعامه ولا يشركونه فى لحمهم وشحمهم * فقال فيهم

ولى عـيلة فى كمـبريج خفيّـة   تواكلنى من حيث ليس عيان
فعهدى باسم الآكلات فلانة   وعـهدى باسم الآكلين فلان

ولانه لم يقدر على ان يحرّد الى احدى تلك القبب * فقال فيها

ومـا نفع الوثير من الحشـايا   وليس عـليـه وَثـر اذ تهش
ومـا نفع الشِعار بلا شعار   وحسن الحفش ان لم يُلفَ حفش
ومـا نفـع الحيـاة بغـير حىّ   فـنعشك دونه ما عشت نعش

فسارا فى سكة الحديد وبلغا المنزل ليلا وما كاد الفارياق يدخل حجرته التى اعدت له ٣،٥،٤
حتى رقشها بهذين البيتين

لله درب الحديد كم كفـل   ربا به والثدىّ قد رجفت
لو لم يكن غير تلك فـائدة   لنـا بـه دون أتّوه لكفت

الاتو الاستقامة فى السير والسرعة

ثم لما قام فى الغد راى المنزل بعيدا عن الدار * فاستعاذ بالله واسترجع واضبّ على ما نفسه * لان هذه الشكوى ليس لها عند هولآ القوم اذن واعية * حتى انه لما شكا يوما طول غيبته عن زوجته قال له صاحبه بعد ايام قد فرط منك بالامس كلام فقلت انى مشتاق الى امراتى * وكان الاولى ان تقول الى اولادى *

And because the people of the house where he was staying would take a share of his food and not allow him access to their persons, he wrote about them

In Cambridge I've got dependents undisclosed
  Who partake of my food when there's no one there to watch—
All I know of my lady guest is that her name is So-and-so
  And all I know of the man is that his name is Such and such.

Likewise, because he couldn't find a way to be alone with one of those "domes," he wrote of them

What's the use of a comfy mattress
  If there's no sex to be had on it for all its softness?
What use a nightdress without a cunny
  Or a nice bit of quim if you can't find a cubby?
What use is life with no snatch in your bed?
  No matter how long you live, you're better off dead.

They took the railway together and arrived at the house at night, and no sooner had the Fāriyāq entered the room that had been prepared for him than he decorated it with the following: 4.5.3

What an excellent thing is the railway! How many a bottom
  On its seats spreads wide, while breasts there quiver galore!
If that alone were all it did for us—never mind its forward
    dashing—
  One couldn't think to ask for more.

atw ["forward dashing"] is "directness of motion, and speed."

Then when he got up the following morning, it came to him how far still his new abode was from home but he said, "I seek refuge with God!" and "We are God's and to God we return!" and put a brave face on it, because such complaints do not find a sympathetic ear among those people—so much so that a few days after his complaining of how long he'd been separated from his wife, his friend told him, "The other day you spoke extravagantly. You said, 'I long for my wife!' but it would have been more proper to say 'for my children.'" "What," the Fāriyāq asked him, "is wrong with a man speaking of his wife as he might of his children? Without the wife, there wouldn't be any children! Nay more: without women there would be nothing in this world, neither religion nor anything else." "Hush, hush!" said his friend. "You go too far."

فقال له الفارياق ما المانع من ان يذكر الرجل امراته كما يذكر ولده * ولولا المراة لم يكن ٤،٥،٤
الولد بل لولا المراة لم يكن شى فى الدنيا لا دين ولا غيره * قال مه مه قد افحشت *
قال ارغن لما اقول * لولا بنت فرعون لم ينج موسى من الغرق * ولولا موسى لم تكن
التوراة * ولولا المراة لم يمكن ليوشع ان يدخل ارض الموعد ويستولى عليها * ولولا
المراة ما حظى ابرهيم عند ملك مصر ونال منه الصلات والهدايا فتمهّد لليهود
النزول الى مصر من بعده * ولولا المراة لم ينجُ داود من يد شاول حين اضمر قتله
وان كان ذلك قد تمّ بحيلة وضع صنم فى فراشه * ولولا داود لم يكن الزبور * نعم
ولولا المراة اعنى زوجة نابال ما تقوى داود على اعدآئه * ولولا حيلة بت شبع على
داود لم يملك سليمن ابنه ولم يبن هيكل الله باورشليم * ولولا المراة لم يولد سيدنا
عيسى ولم يذع خبر انبعاثه * ولولا المراة لم يستتبّ مذهب الانكليز كما هو اليوم
* هذا وان المصوّرين عندكم يصوّرون الملئكة بصورة النسآء * والشعرآء عندكم ما
زالوا يتغزلون فى المراة ولولاها لم ينبغ شاعر * قال اِن اراك الا هاجيًا على النسآ ٥،٥،٤
وكانّ العرب كلهم على هذه الصفة * قال نعم انا راموزهم وقِطاطهم وكل من ينطق
بالضاد يكلف بالضأد * فاطرق مليًا ثم قال لعلكم ارشد ممن عدل الى الميم * فقد
بلغنى ان فى بلادكم قوما ميميّين يعدلون عن سوآ السبيل الى مضايق ذميمة وهو اقبح
ما يكون * واقبح من ذلك ان بعض المولفين من العرب قد الّفوا فى ذلك كتبا وتمحّلوا
لايراد ادلّة على تفضيل الحرفة الميمية * قال نعم ومن جملتها كتاب عثرت به فى خزانة
كتب كمبريج ورايت مكتوبا عليه عنوانه بالانكليزية كتاب فى حقوق الزواج * فكانّ
شاريه لم يفهم مضمونه * ومن اسخف ما ورد من الادلة على ذلك قول بعضهم

"Listen to what I say!" said the Fāriyāq. "Were it not for Pharaoh's daughter, Moses would not have been saved from drowning and were it not for Moses, there would be no Old Testament. Were it not for a woman, Joshua would not have been able to enter the Promised Land and take possession of it.[71] Were it not for a woman, Abraham would not have found favor with the King of Egypt and obtained from him gifts and presents, thus preparing the way for the descent of the Jews into Egypt after him.[72] Were it not for a woman, David would not have been saved from the hand of Saul when he decided in his breast to kill him, which was achieved by his placing an image in his bed,[73] and were it not for David, there would be no psalms. Nay more, were it not for a woman, meaning the wife of Nabal,[74] David would not have prevailed over his enemies. Were it not for Bathsheba's stratagem against David, [75] Solomon would not have made his son king and the temple of God would not have been built in Jerusalem. Were it not for a woman, Jesus would not have been born and the news of his resurrection would not have been broadcast. Were it not for a woman, the Anglican sect would not be doing as well as it is today.[76] Furthermore, your painters depict angels in the form of women and your poets never cease writing poems to women, without which no poet would ever shine." 4.5.4

"As far as I can see," said the other, "you are merely lusting after a woman—a trait, it seems, that is common to all Arabs." "Indeed," he replied, "I am their epitome and pattern, and every man who utters the *ḍād* has a weakness for the *ḍa'd*."[77] The man hung his head for a moment, then said, "You may be wiser than those who deviate toward the *mīm*,[78] for I have heard that there are many *mīm*-ists, who abandon the broad highway in favor of ignoble back alleys, which is the ugliest thing imaginable. Uglier still, though, is the fact that certain Arab authors have composed books on the subject and deceitfully sought to present arguments that the *mīm*-ist craft is the better." "That is so," said the Fāriyāq. "Among them is a book I came across in the Cambridge library on which I found written in English the title *A Book on the Laws of Marriage*, the one who bought it seemingly having failed to grasp its contents. One of the most scurrilous arguments made in support of such things is the words of a certain poet who said 4.5.5

انا لست اجزم باللواط ولا الزنا   لكن اقول مقال من قد حررا
ان اللذاذة كلها فى اقذر الـ   جارين فاختر ان عرفت الاقذرا

وسبب تاليف هذه الكتب من مثل هولآ العتاولة امّا للعنّينية فان النسا يعرضن عمّن يبتلى بذلك * او للبخل لان النفقة على المراة اكثر * او لقصر اليد عن هصرهن او لفساد آخر * اما سليم الطبع فلا يميل عن هذا المذهب اصلا * ثم ان الفارياق ٤،٥،٦
لبث عند صاحبه مدة فى خلالها أُدب الى مآدب فاخرة عند بعض الاعيان * ومن عادتهم فى الولائم ان تقعد النسآ على المائدة مكشوفات الاذرع والصدور بحيث يمكن للناظر ان يرى المفاهر واللّبان والبادلة والبَهْو * واذا تطالل واشرابّ وكان حسن الاهطاع راى اللَعْوة ايضا اى آية الحلم * وهى من جملة العادات التى تحمد من وجه وتذم من وجه آخر * حيث كان هذا الكشف مطّردا للصبايا والعجائز بل العجائز عند الافرنج ولا سيما الانكليز يكتشفن ويتفتّين ويتعيّلن اكثر من الصبايا * ثم قلّت الدعوات وكثر قلق الفارياق لان من نظر الى سحنته مرة لم يرد ان ينظر اليها مرة اخرى * فراى الرجوع الى كمبريج اوفق * فسافر اليها فوجد القبب قد رَبَت نحو ثلثة قراريط * وذلك اما لبعد عهده بها او لكون زيادة قرصة البرد
اوجبت ذلك * وهنا ينبغى ذكر فائدة وهى ان كمبريج واكسفورد لما كانتا مشهورتين ٤،٥،٧
بمدارس العلم كما ذكرنا آنفا وكان جلّ الطلبة فيها من الاغنيآ وفى كلّ منهما نحو الفى طالب * كانت البنات الحسان من قرى الفلاحين المجاورة ينتبن سوق هاتين المدينتين لترويج ما عندهن من الصبى والجمال * فترى فيهما من الجمال الرائع والحسن الباهر ما لا تراه فى سائر المدن * غير انه لكل ساقطة لاقطة * فلهذا كانت مشايخنا الطلبة ينظرون الى من زاد به عدد اهل البلد نظر الهرّة التى يوخذ

I make no final decision between buggery and mainstream fornication—
I merely follow the words of those who've written,
'Gratification all lies in the dirtier of the two neighbors,
So choose, if you can, the more beshitten.'

"The reason why the likes of these woman-shy authors wrote such books is either their impotence, for women will have nothing to do with anyone who is so afflicted, or their stinginess, because women are more expensive to maintain, or their lack of the means to attract them, or some other defect. Those of sound makeup, however, never leave the straight path in the first place."

The Fāriyāq stayed at his friend's house for a while, during which he was invited to splendid banquets in the homes of certain notables. It is customary at their banquets for the women to sit at the table with their arms and breasts exposed, so that the observer can see the flesh of their chests, their bosoms, their breasts, and their cleavages, and if he stretches his neck and cranes his head and is good at holding his head steady, he can see the dark ring around their nipples (ah, what a dream!). It's one of those customs that is to be praised from one perspective and condemned from another, in that this exposure is a general rule for both young and old; indeed, the old women of the Franks, and especially the English, uncover themselves more and put on more youthful airs than do the young girls. Then the invitations became fewer and the Fāriyāq's disquiet grew stronger, since no one who had looked on his countenance once wanted to look on it a second time, and he decided it was better to return to Cambridge. When he arrived there, he found that that the "domes" had grown by some three inches, this being due either to his having been so long away from them or because the more bitter cold required that.[79] 4.5.6

Here an edifying observation must be made, to wit, that given that Cambridge and Oxford are, as previously mentioned, celebrated as schools of learning, and given that most of the students are rich and that each city has something in the region of two thousand of them, the pretty girls from the surrounding peasant villages return time after time to the markets of these two cities to find buyers for their youth and beauty. As a result, you will see in these cities examples of exquisite beauty and dazzling good looks such as you will not find in any other. But "for everything that falls there's something to pick it up,"[80] as they say, which is why our shaykhs the students would look at every addition to the town's population as might a she-cat being robbed 4.5.7

منها جرآؤها * فمن ثم ترحّل الفارياق عن هولآ السنانير وهرّآتهم * لا سيما وقد ورد فى الامثال اذا دخلتَ ارض الحُصَيب فهرول واقام فى لندن نحو شهر *

وصف لندن او لندرة عن الفارياق ٤،٥،٨

ها هى ذات التيه والدلال * الخاطرة على الفحول من الرجال * تنظر اليهم شزرا * وتجرّ اذيالها وشالها جرا * كما قلت من قصيدة

قامت تجرّ من الدلال ذيولا   جرّا اضاف الى العميد نحولا

وهى لا ترى لها من بينهم كفؤا * وتهلس منهم سخرية وهزؤا * اَلا فاذكرى ان بينم الاقوى الاقدر * الاسرى الايسر * الاسرع الاعسر * الاقرش الاقشر * الاصرع الاعصر * الاسرد الادسر * الارشف الاشفر * الابرز الازبر * الذى اذا ضمّ زفر * واذا شمّ نخر * واذا هيج زأر * او غُمز بدر * واذا راى طبلا زمّر * او ذات تدهكر دهشر * اذكرى ان بينهم عربيا ذا غرام * وهيام ٤،٥،٩
وأوام * ومغازلة وبغام * ومداعبة وكعام * وتمشير وانكماش * واندساس فى الاعشاش * علامَ تملّقك وانت معرضة كبرا * ونعدك فتتخذين كلامنا هِترا * الم تعلمى انّا اليك متودّدون * وعلى مثلك متعوّدون * كم من صعب رُضْناه * ومتحكّم ارضيناه * وأَبِىّ أمَلْناه * وقَرِم اشبعناه * وجامح استوقفناه * وشاكٍ اشكيناه * وعاتب اعتبناه * وكم من متعنّتة آبت وهى شاكره * ثم انثنت زائره * اَلا لا يغوينّك الشطاط الى الشطط * والعيَن الى الشَحَط * والعَيط الى اللغط * وصهوبة الشعر * الى انكار القدر * وتفليج الثنايا * الى اَلْت المزايا *

of her kittens. Consequently, the Fāriyāq left these tomcats and their females behind—a decision whose correctness was confirmed in his view when he came across the proverb that says, "When you enter the land of al-Ḥuṣayb, run!"[81]—and stayed in London for close to a month.

A Description of London, or Londra,[82] according to the Fāriyāq 4.5.8

See the proud and capricious lady in her *duds*, strutting before the manly *studs*! With a furious stare she gives them a *zap*, dragging behind her her skirts and her *wrap*. As I say in a poem of mine

Coquettishly she set off, dragging her train,
Causing the suffering lover yet more pain.

Among them she finds no *match* and mocks them with her smiles—they're not up to *scratch*. Be mindful, fair lady, that among them is to be found the strongest and the ablest, the manliest and the wealthiest, the speediest and the toughest, the strongest and at stripping the quickest, the best at felling and the pressingest, the proddingest and the pokiest, the lippiest and labia-lovingest, the sticky-outy-est and the largest thingy-est, who, when he hugs, *moans*, when he smells, snorts and when aroused, *groans*; who if winked at, responds in a flash and, the moment he sees a drum, plays on his pipe; who on seeing a woman with body *lavish* is quick to *ravish*.

Be mindful that among them is an Arab who with passion *yearns*, with thirst and torment *burns*, one quick to make love and quick to *lay*, to devour with kisses and engage in *play*, energetic in bed and *nimble*, ever ready to hunt the *thimble*. With what can we flatter you, when haughtily you turn aside your *eyes*, with what entice you, when you treat our words as *lies*? Are you not *aware* that not only do we seek your kindnesses but also that of your kind we've known our *share*? How many a headstrong woman we've been able to *pacify*! How many a willful woman we've known how to *gratify*! How many a disdainful one have we bent to our *will*! To how many a love-hungry one have we given her *fill*! How many a bolter have we given reason to *pause*! To how many a love-sick complainer have we given *cause*! How many a *prude* have we, to their satisfaction, *screwed*! How many an obdurate woman has sung our praises while homeward *bound*, returning later for a second *round*! Let not your stately stature seduce you into being *stiff*, your 4.5.9

وتورد الخدين * الى احتقار اللجين * وتفليك الكُعب * الى التيه والعجب *
وبضاضة البشره * الى النهم والشره * وفعومة الساعدين * الى عنجرة الشفتين *
وجدل الساقين * الى الاستنكاف من مِضّ لناقد عين * وعميد غين * يكفتهما
ويتطوق بهما * او يعتمّ بهما على رَتَبَهما * وينزه زغبهما عن الحلت والنتف *
والحصّ والحفّ * وعن مسّ السقف * ألا ولا يضلنّك الجاهض من ورآ *
الى الازدرآ * ولا الناجخ من امام * الى منع التحية والسلام * ان لدينا من ١٠،٥،٤
المِزْر والفُقّاع * ما يروى كل مَقّاع * ويسكر كل ذات قناع * ومن الشِوآ *
ما يزيل الخَوآ * ومن الدينار * ما ينفث فى عقد الازار * فيحلها حلاّ * ويبلّها
بلاّ * فمن البلّ بَلَل * ومن الحَلّ حُلَل * فبحق من اولاك هذه المحاسن * فتنة
كل سامع ومعاين * الاّ ما احسنت فى عشاقك الظنّ * واقللت لهم من
هذا التزليق والفَتْن * فكلهم الى وصالك حنّ * ومن صلفك اَنّ * وبعدُ ١١،٥،٤
فان هى الاّ مرّة * فان احمدت اللقآ فاجعليها عادة وانت على كل حال حرّة *
والا فما اكثر طرق هذه المدينة وما اطولها * وما اوفر القادمين اليها * وما اوسع
حوانيتها وساحاتها * وندحاتها وباحاتها * وحدائقها وغياضها * ومماشيها
ورياضها * وما ابهج ملاهيها وملاعبها * واجرى عجلاتها ومراكبها * وما
ارحب كنائسها * وما احفل مجالسها * وما اعمر مساكنها * وامخر سفائنها *
فاجر[١] فيها حيث يعجبك من هنا ومن هنا * كل امرء يسعى ليدرك الهنا *

١ ١٨٥٥: فاجرى.

wide eyes into staying *aloof*, your swanlike neck into churlish *demurral*, into denying your fate that auburn *curl*, your gap-teeth into a refusal of men's *due*, into contempt for lucre your cheeks' rosy *hue*, your swelling breasts into pride and *vanity*, your firmness of skin into voracity and *avidity*, the curves of your *hips*[83] into a pursing of *lips*! Let not firmness of calf tempt you to haughtiness in the form of an expression of half-hearted *disdain* for a peek-sneaker or love-sick *swain*—an expression that closes said calves *tight* and wraps itself around them to keep them out of *sight*, or envelops them despite their plumpness and spares their down from any shearing or *peeling*, any shaving or plucking, or from touching the *ceiling*! Let not what sticks out *behind* make you to proper respect be *blind*, or what lifts your bosom's *sheeting* into refusing salutation or *greeting*!

We have enough shandy and champagne every thirsty drinker to *inebriate*, every veiled lady to *intoxicate*, enough meat from the *grill* every empty belly to *fill*, enough *coin* to blow the knots of every lady's waist wrapper from off her *groin* and undo them utterly and moisten them mightily—and with moistening comes munificence, with undoing, dresses.[84] By Him who conferred on you a *charm* that all who hear and see you must *disarm*, think kindly of your suitors and give them fewer angry looks and such *disdain*, for each yearns your lover to be and each at your harsh words has moaned *in pain*! 4.5.10

To proceed: I'm talking about just one time, though if you find the encounter *agreeable*, you can make it *habitual*. In any case, you're free to do as you please, and if you don't—how many and long are this city's roads, how many those who make their way *there*, how many a spacious shop it contains, how many a *square*, how many an open space and *lake*, garden and wood, pathway and *park*! How splendid are its places of entertainment and its pleasure *grounds*! What a stream of carriages it has and how its traffic *abounds*! How vast its churches and well-attended its *councils*! How prosperous its dwellings and stately its *vessels*! Run about in it wherever you *wish*: all men strive in pursuit of *bliss*. 4.5.11

الفصل السادس

في محاورة

وبعد ان فرغ الفارياق من عمله فى هذه المدينة الغاصة بالغوانى سافر الى باريس فاقام ١،٦،٤
فيها ثلثة ايام لا تكفى لمعرفة وصفها * فلهذا نضرب هنا عن ذكره فان حق الوصف
ان يكون مستوعبا * ثم سافر منها الى مرسيلية ومنها الى الجزيرة * واتاح له الله
بفضله العميم ان راى زوجته فى نفس الدار التى غادرها فيها * وقد كان يظن
انها طارت مع عنقآ مغرب او مع الغُنجُول وبَنَى بها هذه المرة السادسة * فان
المرة الثانية كانت بعد قدومه من الشام والثالثة بعد رجوعه من تونس والرابعة بعد
خروجه من المعتزل مع سامى باشا المفخم والخامسة بعد رجوعها من مصر * ثم انشد ٢،٦،٤

مَن يُرد فى زوجه ينكح ازواجا عديده
فليَغِب عنها زمانا   يلقها عِرسا جديده

فقالت لكن المراة لا ترى من زوجها بعد ايابه عِرسا جيددا * قال فقلت انما هو من مخالفتهن الرجال فى كل شى * قالت نعم ولولا هذا الخلاف ما حصل الوفاق * قلت كيف يكون عن الخلاف وفاق * قالت كما ان المراة خُلقت مخالفة للرجل فى الخَلق كذلك كان خلافها له فى الخُلق * وكلٌّ من هذين الخلافين باعث له على شدة الكلف بها والحرص عليها * ألا ترى ان المراة اذا كانت تفعل كل

Chapter Six

A Discussion

When the Fāriyāq had finished his work in that city so crammed with beautiful women, he went to Paris, where he stayed for three days, which wasn't enough to allow him to write a description of it. We therefore decline to provide one at this point, for a proper description should be comprehensive. From there he went on to Marseilles and then to the island, where God, of His all-encompassing bounty, granted him the boon of beholding his wife in the very house in which he'd left her, though he'd expected to find that she'd flown off with a phoenix or the chimera, and he re-consummated his marriage with her for this the sixth time (the second time having been after he arrived back from the Syrian lands, the third after his return from Tunis, the fourth after he emerged from quarantine quarters with the Honorable Sāmī Pasha, and the fifth after her return from Egypt). 4.6.1

Then he recited 4.6.2

He who'd like to keep wanting his wife
Should take many a woman to bed.
Then let him leave her for a little while—
And he'll find her like a newlywed

to which she responded, "But the wife won't find a new groom in her husband when he comes back!" The Fāriyāq continued, "I told her, 'That's because she's the contrary of men in everything.' 'Right,' she said, 'and if it weren't for that contrariness, there'd be no harmony.' 'How,' I asked, 'can harmony come from contrariness?' 'Just as woman is created contrary to man physically,' she replied, 'so she is contrary to him in disposition, and each of these contrarieties is an inducement to him to feel affection for her

ما يريد زوجها ان تفعله كانت كالآلة بين يديه فلا يكترث بها ولا يقبل عليها * لاعتقاد انها موقوفة على حركة يده او عينه او لسانه زيادة على حركة يده فى الآلة * بخلاف ما اذا عرف منها المخالفة والاستبداد بامرها فانه ح يعلق بها ويداريها * قلت هذا غير ما عُهد عند الناس * قالت بل هو معهود عند النسآ من القديم *
٣،٦،٤ ولذلك تراهن جميعهن متحليات بهذه الحلية * قلت ولكن اذا كثر الخلاف وطال * اورث التقاطع والملال * قالت ان عينى المراة لا تبرحان ناظرتين او حقهما ان تكونا ناظرتين الى موضعى القطع والوصل * والّا استطال احدهما على الآخر فوقع ما قلت * قلت بل فى دوام الوصل دوام الوفاق * قالت لا بل هو باعث على السآمة والضجر * فان الانسان مطبوع على ذلك * قلت اى سآمة من وصل الحبيب * قالت السآمة غالبة على الانسان فى كل شى بحيث يودّ تبديل حالته الحسنى بحالة سُوأى * قلت اوَ قد سئمتِ من حالتك هذه * قالت ثم حُلت عن السآمة * قلت ما بال الناس كلهم يقولون ياقرة العين * قالت نعم ان العين تقرّ بشى ريثما يعنّ لها آخر فتُطرَف اليه * قلت وما شان القلب قالت هو متقلّب ومتحيّز معها * قلت فما شان العميان * قالت ان لهم فى بصائرهم عيونا اشد حملقة من العين الباصرة * قلت مَن اسرعُ الناسِ تقلّبَ قلبٍ * قالت اكثرهم
٤،٦،٤ فكرا فان العجماوات اثبت واصبر من الناس اذ ليس لها فكر * قلت فاذاً ينشا عن النفع ضرّ * قالت نعم كما انه ينشا عن الضر نفع * قلت اى نفع فى المرض * قالت سكون العقل والدم والفكر عن الهوى والشهوات * قلت اى نفع فى الفقر * قالت الكفّ عن الشراهة والسرف المهلكين * فان الذين يموتون من زيادة الاكل والشرب اكثر من الذين يموتون لقلتهما * قلت اى نفع فى الزواج بامراة دميمة * قالت كفّ رجل جارك عن دارك وصرف عين اميرك عن مراقبة حالك * على انها

and take good care of her. Do you not observe how, when a wife does everything that her husband wants, she is like a tool in his hands, and he neither pays attention to nor approaches her because he believes her to be dependent on the movement of his hand, eye, or tongue, a mere adjunct to the movement of his hand on that tool? The opposite is true if all he meets with from her is contrariness and refusal to compromise; then, he clings to and humors her.' 'This,' I said, 'is not what people are used to thinking.' 'Not at all,' she responded, 'it's what women have been used to thinking all along. It's why you'll find that they're all tricked out with this trait.'[85]

"'But,' I said, 'if disagreement multiplies and goes too long without *settlement*, the upshot will be mutual cutting of relations and *disgruntlement*.' 'A woman's eyes,' she declared, 'are always trained, or ought to be trained, on the loci of cutting and connection. Otherwise, one of these will gain supremacy over the other and the situation I have described will come about.'[86] 'I disagree,' I said. 'Constancy of connection leads to constancy of concord,' to which she replied, 'Not at all. It's an inducement to discontent and restlessness, for that is how people are by nature.' 'What discontent can there be,' I asked, 'in connection with the beloved?' 'Discontent,' she replied, 'is the dominant emotion of humans in all things because of their desire to exchange good situations for worse.' 'Did you then,' I asked her, 'grow discontented with your present situation?' 'I did,' she replied, 'and then I found a way around being discontented.' 'How, then,' I asked, 'do you account for the fact that everyone says, "O delight of my eye!"?'[87] 'The fact is,' she replied, 'that the eye finds delight in one thing only until another comes along and presents itself as something novel.' 'And what of the heart?' I asked. 'It is as fickle and as partial as the eye,' she replied. 'And what of the blind?' I asked. 'Their insights,' she replied, 'are keener than those of people who have eyes that see.' 'And whose hearts,' I asked, 'are the most fickle?' 'Those who think most,' she answered. 'Dumb beasts are steadier and more patient than people because they don't think.' 4.6.3

"'So bad comes of good?' I said. 'Indeed,' she replied, 'just as good comes of bad.' 'What good,' I asked, 'comes of sickness?' 'Relief for mind, blood, and thought from the pain of love and lust,' she replied. 'And what good,' I asked, 'comes of poverty?' 'Abstention from the gluttony and intemperance that lead to perdition,' she said, 'for more people die of too much food and drink than of too little.' 'And what good,' I asked, 'comes of marriage to 4.6.4

لا تعدم طالبا مثلها ولكن بعض الشراهون من بعض * قلت اى نفع فى دمامة الاولاد * قالت اذا علموا ذلك من انفسهم رغبوا عن اللهو الى العلم واقبلوا على تحسين خُلقهم ليشفع فى خَلقهم * قلت واى نفع من مشيب اعلى الانسان قبل اسفله مع ان شعر الاسفل ينبت قبل شعر الاعلى * قالت اشعاره بان الحيوانية المطلقة اقوى فيه من الحيوانية المقيّدة * ولذلك كان اول ما يشيب فيه راسه الذى هو محلّ الناطقية * واقوى ما يحسّ منه باللذة اسفله * قلت وما نتيجة ذلك قالت اقلاله من الفكر * قلت وما الفائدة فى كونه يعوز الى اوقية من اللحم يملأ بها وجهه فيجد رطلا فى عجزه * قالت هو من النوع الاول * قلت كانك تقولين ان الرجل لم يخلق الّا لاجل المراة * قالت نعم كما ان المراة لم تخلق الا للرجل * قلت ٤،٦،٥
اى نفع فى تحتّت الاسنان * قالت الأكل على هينة فيمرؤ الطعام * قلت اى نفع فى تعميش العينين * قالت عدم روية الحسان ليلاً فانهن اروع فيه وافتن * قلت اى نفع فى العَرَج * قالت الراحة من الجرى ورآ القِرصافة الزقزاقة * قلت اى نفع فى السدّة * قالت الذهول عن العَبِقة * قلت وفى الصمم * قالت عن الرُمُ * قلت وفى الجهل * قالت توفر الصحة للبدن والراحة للبال * فان الجاهل لا يفكر فى الامور الدقيقة المتعبة * فاذا نام اهنأه النوم واذا طَعِم شيا امرأه * لا كدابك فى الهينمة انآ الليل واطراف النهار فما اسمع منك الا تعديد قوافى * وذكر نوئٍ واثافى * ودوارس عوافى * وظعائن خوافى * واذا جلست للطعام اتيت بالكتاب معك فجعلت الصفحة تلو الصحفة * فتاكل لقمة * وتقرا فقرة * وتكرع من الشراب كرعة وتتلو اُسطورة * ولذلك — قلت قد فهمت من هذا الاكتفآ عدم الاكتفآ * ولكن كثرة القرآة ينشا عنها كثرة التصوّر الباعثة على كثرة التشوّق * قالت ولكن كثرة التشوق ينشا عنها الترويلية او الزمالقية والمقصود الجّادية اللِحكية * وقد طالما

an ugly woman?' 'Prevention of your neighbor from visiting your house,[88] and abstention of your emir from following your every move, though she will not lack for a suitor of her own type (some evils, however, are lesser than others).' 'What good comes of ugly children?' 'If they discover their situation on their own,' she said, 'they will give up play in favor of study and strive to improve their inner makeup and so compensate for their outer.' 'What good comes of a person's upper parts graying before his lower, when the hair on the lower sprouts before the hair on the upper?'[89] 'It makes him realize that an animal's absolute nature is more powerful than its contingent nature, which is why the first part of him to turn grey is his head, which is the seat of the rational faculty, while the place where he feels the most powerful pleasure is the lower,' she replied. 'And what does it lead to?' I asked. 'A reduction in the capacity to think,' she replied. 'And what is the point of his needing an ounce of meat to fill his face, and finding it's turned into a pound on his buttocks?' 'That,' she said, 'belongs to the first category.'[90] 'You seem to be saying,' I said, 'that men were created to serve the needs of women.' 'Quite so,' she responded, 'just as women were to serve the needs of men.'

"'And what good,' I asked, 'comes of the crumbling of the teeth?' 'Slow eating,' she replied, 'so that the food is well digested.' 'And what good,' I asked, 'comes of the dimming of the eyes?' 'Inability to see the ladies at night,' she replied, 'for that is when they are at their most delightful and captivating.' 'And what good comes,' I asked, 'of being lame?' 'Relief,' she replied, 'from running after quickly tripping women who bowl along like a ball.' 'What good comes,' I asked, 'of a stuffed-up nose?' 'Indifference to sweet-smelling women,' she replied. 'Of deafness?' I asked. 'To smart-talking girls,' she replied. 'And of ignorance?' I asked. 'Abundance of health for the body and rest for the mind,' she replied, 'for the ignorant man gives no thought to minute and tiresome matters. When he sleeps, his slumber makes him happy and when he eats something, it does him good—unlike your habit of muttering day and night, so that all I hear from you is your voice as on it *drones*, counting off rhymes and speaking of trenches and *firestones*,[91] campsites *half-erased* and concealed women in camel litters *raised*; and when you sit down to eat, you bring your book with you and for every plate you consume a page, then eat a morsel and read a paragraph, or drink, belch, and recite a line. That is why . . .' 'I gather from this excellent sufficiency that 4.6.5

احوج وجود الاولى الى البحث عن وجود الثانية * ولكن دعنا من هذه الملاحك والمغامس * كيف وجدت مدينة لندن * قلت رايت فيها النسآ اكثر من الرجال ٦،٦،٤ واجمل * قالت لو ذهبت اليها امراة لرأت بعكس ذلك فان نسآ الانكليز فى هذه الجزيرة لسن حسانا والحسن كله فى الرجال * قلت هولا نخبة البلاد انتقتهم الدولة حسانا ليخيفوا العدو فى الحرب * قالت بل الامر بالعكس فان الجميل لا يخيف وان يكن عدوا وانما القبيح هو الذى يخيف * اَلا ترى انهم يقولون رجل باسل ومتبسّل اى شجاع وهو فى الاصل الكريه المنظر * قلت وقد قالوا ايضا راعه بمعنى اعجبه واخافه * قالت المعنى واحد فانه ماخوذ من الرُوع[1] اى القلب فروية الجميل تصيب القلب بل وسائر الجوارح * ثم قالت وكيف رايت دكاكينها واسواقها * قلت اما الدكاكين فملآنة من الخز والحرير والتحف البديعة * قالت هل مَن هو فيها كما هو فيها * قلت فيها نسآ بيض حسان * قال انا اسالك عن شى وانت تخبرنى عن غيره * قد عرفت انك زائغ البصر فلن اسالك بعدُ عن الناس وما اسال الّا عينى * هذه خصلة فيكم معاشر الرجال انكم لا ترون فى جنسكم حسنا * قلت هى مثل خصلتكن معاشر النسآ فى انكن لا ترين فى جنسكن جمالا قد تكافأنا * قالت كيف تكافأنا وبيننا خلآ * قلت كل آت قريب * قالت وكل قريب آت * قلت لا ارضى بهذه الكلية بل قولى بعض القريب * قالت اذا ساغ البعض لم يُغَصّ بالكل * ثم قالت اخبرنى عن الاسواق * فقلت طويلة عريضة واسعة نظيفة كثيرة الانوار بحيث لا يمكن للرجل ان ينفرد بامراة اصلا * حتى كانّ الضباب ينجلى بها فى الليل ايضا * قالت هو من بعض المنافع الضارّة * اَلا ليت لى جدّا فانظر مرة محاسن هذا المصر من قبل ان اقضى * قلت لا تقنطى فانى ارجوان

[1] كذا بهذا المعنى في القاموس وفي ١٨٥٥: رَوع.

I stand accused of insufficiency, but much reading leads to much visualizing, which gives rise to much desire,' I said. 'But much desire,' she answered, 'gives rise to a state of semi-erection and premature *ejaculation*, when what's called for is piercing *procrastination*, and how often has the presence of the first required a search for the second! But enough of piercing-places and plunging-places. How did you find London?'

"I replied, 'I found the women there outnumbered the men and were bet- **4.6.6**
ter-looking.' 'If a woman were to go there,' she said, 'she'd find the opposite. The English women on this island are not beautiful, and the men have all the looks.' 'These,' I said, 'are the cream of the country, chosen by the state for their good looks, so that they may scare the enemy in battle.' 'Not so,' she said, 'it's the other way around. The beautiful man can never scare, even if he's an enemy. It's only the ugly that are scary. Do you not observe that they speak of a man being *bāsil* or *mutabassil* when they mean "courageous," even though in origin they mean "of unpleasant appearance"?'[92] I responded, 'And they also say *rāʿahu*, meaning both "he delighted him" and "he scared him."' 'The meaning's the same,' she responded. 'It is taken from *rūʿ*, meaning "heart," for the sight of beauty falls on the heart, and indeed all the other organs of the body, like a bolt from above.' Then 'And how did you find its shops and markets?' she went on. 'The shops,' I replied, 'were full of silk-wool, silk, and amazing trinkets.' 'Are the people inside them like the things inside them?' she asked. 'There are beautiful, white women,' I replied. 'I ask you about one thing and you tell me about another!' she responded. 'I knew you had a wandering eye, so I will never ask you again about the people, I will simply consult my own eye. This is one of your traits, you men: you see no comeliness in your own sex.' 'And it's just like your trait, O women, of not seeing any beauty in your own. We go together.' 'How can we go together when there's a gap between us?' she asked. 'All good things come to those who wait,' I said. 'And every good thing should make love,'[93] she answered. 'I cannot accept such a "universal" statement,'[94] I replied—'You should say "*some* good things,"' to which she countered, 'If some goes down easily, the whole will not be choked on.' Then she said, 'Tell me about the markets,' to which I replied, 'They are high-ceilinged, wide, spacious, clean, and so well-lit that it's impossible for a man to be on his own with a woman under any circumstances. So bright are they they even light up the fog at night.' 'Then they belong to the category of the Harmful Public Service,' she said.

نسافر اليها جميعا بعد مدة * قالت حقّق الله لنا هذه الامنية * فلما امسى المسآ ٧،٦،٤
وبات كل منهما ثملا بذكر لندن على ما مال اليه خاطره قامت فى الغداة تقول *
قد رايت لندن فى المنام واذا برجالها اكثر من نسآئها * وطرقها واسعة كما قلت كثيرة
الانوار* ولكن يمكن للرجل فيها ان ينفرد بامراة * وكانك انما تقوّلت هذا لكيلا
اسيّئ فيك الظن * ولكن ماكنت لاصدقك من بعد ان تحققت انك غير امين فى
الرواية الاولى * ثم بعد محاورة طويلة باتا تلك الليلة على اسم لندن * فاصبحت
تقول * قد حلمت انى اشتريت من احسن دكاكينها ثوب ديباج احمر احمر احمر *
قال انك لا تزالين لاهجة بهذا اللون واهل لندن لا يحبّونه لا فى الحرير ولا فى
الآدميين * قالت ما سبب ذلك * قلت لان الحمرة فى الناس تكون عن كثرة الدم *
وكثرة الدم مظنة بكثرة الاكل والشرب * وهى دليل على الرُغب والنَّهَم * وانما
يحبون اليلق الامهق * وكذلك العرب يحبون هذا اللون فقد قال اعظم شعرائهم

كبكر المقاناة البياض بصفرة غذاها نمير الحيّ غير مجلَّل

فقالت ان كان هذا الاستكراه من طرف الرجال فهو لخشية عزة النسآ عليهم[1]
باللون الاحمر الدال على القوة والنشاط والاشر والبَتَع والكَرَع * فيوهمهم ذلك
عجزهم عن كفايتهن * وان يكن من النسآ وقد نطقن به فما هو الا مواربة ومغالطة * فان
الانسان بالطبع يحب اللون الاحمر كما يشاهد ذلك فى الاطفال * وناهيك ان الدم
الذى هو عنصر الحياة احمر * قال فقلت ولكن خلاصة الدم وصفوته هو فى ذلك
اللون الذى يرغب فيه اهل لندن * قالت فهذا هو السبب اذاً * الان قد حصحص
الحق وبان * اما انا فعلى مذهبى لن احول عنه * وللناس فيما يعشقون مذاهب *

---

١ ١٨٥٥: عليهن.

'Ah, if only I might have the good fortune to see the attractions of that cosmopolis just once before I die!' 'Don't despair!' I said. 'I hope we shall all[95] be able to go there together in a while.' 'God grant our wish!' she replied."

Then evening came and each spent the night drunk on such thoughts of London as accorded with his personal wishes and the next morning she got out of bed and said, "I saw London in a dream, and its men outnumbered its women and its streets were wide and full, as you said, of lights (though it would be possible for a woman to be on her own in them with a man and I think you only alleged what you did so that I wouldn't harbor any suspicions about you, and I will never believe you again if I find out for sure that you were deceitful in the first telling)." Then again, after a long discussion, they went to bed the next night with the name of London on their lips and in the morning she said, "I dreamed that I bought a dress of red red red brocade from one of its best shops." "You're still mad about that color," he said, "but the people of London don't like it, either for silk or for humans." "Why is that?" she asked. "Because red in people comes from too much blood, and too much blood implies too much eating and drinking and is a sign of greed and gluttony. What they like is dull white, a color beloved of the Arabs too, for the greatest of their poets has said,[96] 4.6.7

Like the first egg of the ostrich—its white mingled with yellow—
Nurtured on water pure, unsullied by many paddlers."

She said, "If we're talking about men's dislike of that color, it's due to their fear that women will lord it over them in the color red, which indicates strength, energy, liveliness, headstrongness, and love of intercourse. This deludes them into thinking that they are incapable of satisfying them. If, however, it's women's dislike of it that we're talking about (should they in fact ever express such an opinion), it must be simply equivocation and deception, for humans love the color red by nature, as one may observe in children; not to mention that blood, which is the essence of life, is red." The Fāriyāq continued, "Then I said, 'But the quintessence and best part of blood is of that color[97] that the people of London crave.' 'So that's the reason!'[98] she said. '"Now the truth has come to light"[99] and is made plain. As far as I'm concerned, I'll never abandon my position, and "one man's meat is another's poison."'

فقلت بودى لوكنت احمر احمر احمر حتى تحبينى وان كنت احمق احمق احمق * قالت ٨،٦،٤
وما انتفاعك بالمحبة اذا كنت احمق * وانما يعود النفع لى فى تركك اياى مع الاحمر *
قلت اتزعمين ان العلم يمنع المراة عن اجرآ ما تضمره وان الحمق يمكّنها منه * قالت لا
والله بل ربما كان فى الحمق لها اكثر * فان الاحمق يلازم امراته ويظل محملقا فيها والعالم
يحملق فى كراريسه * وكيفما كان فلم ارَ اسفه ممّن يحرّج على امراته ويلازمها * فان
الرجل كلما اعنت المراة ونكنك عليها بالملازمة والكنكنة زادت هى فى تماديها فلا
٩،٦،٤ يردها شى عما ارادته سوى حشمتها وحيائها * واكثر الرجال حمقا وسخافة من اذا
اوجس من زوجته الميل الى شخص قال لها تزهيدا فيه * ان فلانا متهتّك مستهتر
فاحش لا يبالى بما يقول ويفعل * فاذا حضر مجلس ذوى الادب فاول ما يفوه به
قوله قد راودت فلانة وخلبتها وفتنتها * وقد عشقتنى وعشقتها * كانه اى الزوج
يحذّرها من الاسترسال الى هواه مخافة ان تنفضح بين الناس * او ان يقول لها ان
فلانا ورع تقىّ يتقى مغازلة النسآ اتقآ الافاعى * كانه يقول لها انك ان تعرّضت له
فى الهوى جبهك وندهك وفضحك * فقد تقرر فى عقول الرجال ان كل امر من
امور الدنيا والآخرة يشين عرض المراة ويهتك حجابها * مع انه لا شى يدغدغها
مثل سماعها عن رجل انه مسرف مشط فى حال من الاحوال بحيث لا يلحقها منه
اذى * فهى والحالة هذه تزيد حرصا على فتنته لتصرفه عن تلك الحال اليها فيرجع
اسرافه فى محبتها * قال فقلت نعم ان كيد النسآ كان عظيما *

"I said, 'I wish I were red red red that you might love me, even if I were dumb dumb dumb.' 'And what good would love do you if you were dumb?' she asked. 'Any good would redound to *my* benefit, from your leaving me alone with "the red."'[100] 'Are you claiming,' I asked, 'that scholarship in men prevents women from carrying out what they have in mind to do, while stupidity makes it possible for them?' 'Certainly not,' she replied. 'In fact, a woman may get more out of stupidity, for the stupid husband stays close to his wife and never stops staring at her, while the scholar stares at his notebooks. Be that as it may, I know of nothing more idiotic than the man who keeps his wife on a tight leash and sticks close to her, for the more a man angers his wife and annoys her by staying next to her and never leaving the house, the more she will persist in her excesses, for nothing can keep her from doing what she wants to except her own sense of decency and her modesty. **4.6.8**

"'The stupidest and most ridiculous of men is the one who, if he harbors doubts that his wife may have taken a liking to a certain person, tells her, to arouse dislike for him in her, "So-and-so is without honor, irresponsible, a lecher who doesn't care what he says or does. If he attends a gathering of litterateurs, the first thing to come out of his mouth will be, 'I made a pass at (such and such a woman) and beguiled her and charmed her, and she became my mistress and I became her lover'"—as though he (meaning the husband) were warning her against yielding to his advances and scared she might make a scandal of herself in front of everyone; or the one who tells her, "So-and-so is God-fearing and pious. He is as scared of flirting with women as he is of vipers"—as though he were telling her, "If you declare your love to him, he will repulse you, drive you away, and make a scandal of you." Men have got it fixed in their minds that any matter, whether to do with this world or the next, can mar a woman's honor and violate her sanctity, but in fact nothing tickles her imagination so much as hearing it said of a man that he is so excessively far gone in some way or other that he can do her no harm. In such a case, she will go out of her way to make a conquest of him so that she can dissuade him from whatever he is up to in favor of herself and redirect his excesses into love for her.'" **4.6.9**

The Fāriyāq went on, "And I said,
'Quite right. Great indeed
is women's guile.'"[101]

الفصل السابع

في الطباق والتنظير

١،٧،٤ الانسان كما قالت الفارياقية مجبول على السآمة والملل * ومتى ظفر بالغرض * استحوذ عليه الغرض * وما دام الرجل المتزوج حِلْس بيته وسمع من زوجته هات واشترِ وجدِّد واصلح ودَّ لو انه يكون عزبا ولو راهبا فى صومعة * فاذا تغرب عنها ورای الرجال يمشون مع النسآ سوآکن حليلات او خليلات اَنِف من الصومعة * وهاج به الشوق الى ان يكون له امراة يماشيها مثل اولئك وان كان مشيهم وقتئذ للتحاكم والتخاصم لدى جناب القاضى * فينبغى للزوج الملازم لِكِنِّه والحالة هذه ان لا يزال متصوّرا انه غريب فى ارض بعيدة عند اناس يخدعونه ويغبنونه ويهيجونه بمرافدهم * او ان زوجته قد سافرت عنه الى اناس يعاقرونها المدام * ويرقدونها على فرش من ريش النعام * ويغازلونها فتغزلهم * ويباعلونها فتبعلهم * فاذا فعل ذلك هانت عليه نغمات هات واشتر * وهذا جدول عن الفارياق بيّن فيه الاحوال التى يقول فيها المتزوج

ياليت ما عندى امراة	٢،٧،٤ وياليت عندى امراة
اذا تزبرقت وتزبرجت وتزلقت وتبرجت	اذا سار وحده الى المثابة والمحافل

Chapter 7

Compare and Contrast

Humankind, as the Fāriyāqiyyah said, has a predisposition toward discontent and ennui, and no sooner does it gain the object of its desire than a desire for other objects takes over. Likewise, given that the married man is a fixture around the house and hears nothing from his wife but "Fetch!" "Buy!" "Renew!" and "Repair!" he dearly wishes he might be a bachelor again, even if it means being a monk in a cell. Then, if he leaves the latter and sees men walking side by side with women, whether wedded wives or lady loves, he becomes fed up with his cell, and the longing to have a wife with him and to walk with her like those others (even if their promenading is leading them at that very moment to trial and litigation before His Honor the Judge)[102] rises within him. In such cases, the husband who never leaves his nest ought constantly to imagine to himself that he is a stranger in a distant land living with people who dupe him, cheat him, and inflame his senses with their bustles, or that his wife has left him to go to people who will compete to fill her *glass* and lay her down on an ostrich-feather *palliasse*, or who, should they flirt with her, will find she tells them "*Yes!*" and, on making love to her, find that she to them will *acquiesce*. If he does this, the chant of "Fetch!" and "Buy!" will seem less unbearable. Here is a table, composed on the authority of the Fāriyāq, in which he sets out the conditions under which the married man says, 4.7.1

"Would that I had no wife!" and	"Would that I had a wife!"	4.7.2
When she picks out a red or yellow dress, dresses to make herself look *fine*, smoothes her skin and makes	When he goes alone to where the people get together, to the crowded places and crammed places, to the	

وتعطرت وتبغنجت وقالت له قم بنا الى المثابة والمحافل والمحاشد والملاهى والمراقص *

والمحاشد والملاهى والمراقص ورای النسآ فيها متزبرقات * متزبرجات الخ *

اذا خرج معها وقد نفّجت صدرها واحكمت مرفدها ثم طفقت تتبازى وتوكوك وتميس وتزوزك وتميل عنقها وراسها *

اذا سار وحده ورای من قد نفجت صدرها واحكمت مرفدها ثم غدت تتبازى وتوكوك الخ *

اذا مشى معها فرات نقطة مآ فى الطريق فشمّرت عن ساقيها لتبدو حماتاهما *

اذا مشى وحده فراى من شمرت عن ساقيها عند رويتها نقطة مآ فى الطريق الخ *

اذا سار معها فى يوم ذى ريح وعمدت الى كشف الثوب عن صدرها وعجزها *

اذا سار وحده فى يوم ذى ريح وابصر من عمدت الى كشف الثوم عن صدرها *

اذا جعلت دابها ان توقع منديلها او تربط شراك نعليها ثم تكبّ فتبدى عجيزتها *

اذا سار وحده فراى من تكب لتربط شراك نعليها او تلتقط منديلها فتبدى عجيزتها *

اذا جعلت شيا فى فمها تلوكه وهى ماشية توهم من يعجبها من الفتيان انها

اذا ابصر من تلوك شيا وهى ماشية ٣،٧،٤
وحسب ذلك اشارة اليه بقبلة ثم

it *shine*, makes herself look easy to *get*, puts on perfume and plays the *coquette*, and tells him, “Off with us to where the people gather, to the crowded places and the crush, to the night spots and the dance floors!”

night spots and dance floors and sees the women there all wearing red or yellow dresses, dressed up to look fine, etc.

When he goes out with her after she’s plumped out her chest and adjusted her bustle and then she never stops sticking out her bottom, swinging her hips, strutting, swaying from side to side, and bending her neck and head.

When he strikes out alone and sees women who have plumped out their chests, adjusted their bustles and then set off sticking out their bottoms, swinging their hips, etc.

When he’s walking with her and she sees a drop of water on the road and hikes up her dress, exposing her calves so that everyone can see the mud on them.

When he walks alone and sees the women who have hiked up their dresses, exposing their calves, on seeing a drop of water on the road, etc.

When he sets out with her on a windy day and she deliberately lets her dress reveal glimpses of her breast and her backside.

When he sets out alone on a windy day and sees the women who deliberately let their dresses reveal glimpses of their breasts, etc.

When she makes a habit of dropping her handkerchief or tying her sandal strap, so that she has to bend over and show off her backside.

When he sets out alone and sees the women bending over to fasten the straps on their sandals or picking up their handkerchiefs, thus showing off their backsides.

4.7.3

When she puts something in her mouth and chews on it as she walks, making her young male admirers think that she’s mouthing a kiss at

When he observes women chewing something as they walk and thinks they’re mouthing kisses at him and then they start winking, arching

تشير بقبلة او اذا غمزت احدا و رمزت ولمزت *

غدت تغمز وترمز وتلمز وتابز وتنفز وتنقز *

اذا صادفت رجلا من معارفها فى الطريق فطفقت تعاتبه على طول غيابه عنها ثم امسكت بيده وغمزته[1] غمزا شديدا *

اذا راى امراة تعاتب رجلا على طول غيابه عنها ثم اخذت يده وغمزته[2] غمزا شديدا حتى احمر الغامز واصفر المغموز او بالعكس *

اذا لقيت امراة فى الطريق عليها ديباج نفيس فجعلت تسالها عن سعره وعمن يبيعه *

اذا لقى امراتين تمس احداهما الاخرى وتلك الملموسة تشير بيدها اللطيفة الى مكان *

اذا صادفت احدا فى الطريق فاشارت اليه انِ اتبعنا فاخذ يمشى عن يمينها فحولت وجهها عن زوجها وجعلت جلّ الكلام مع الزبون *

اذا وجد رجلا بين امراتين او امراة بين رجلين ففى الحالة الاولى طلبا للمرازمة وفى الثانية ثقة بالكفاية لان طعام اثنين يشبع ثلثة *

اذا رجعا الى البيت وصرّحت له او عرّضت بشرآ الديباج ولم يكن عنده دراهم تكفى *

اذا رجع الى البيت وراى ان عنده مالًا وليس من تلبس الديباج وتجلس الى جانبه *

اذا قالت له وهما على المائدة لتغصّصه ما اجمل فلانا الذى ماشانا وما الطفه

اذا جلس للطعام وحده وجعل يفكر ٤،٧،٤
ويقول فى نفسه ما اجمل فلانة التى

١ ١٨٥٥: غمزتها. ٢ ١٨٥٥: غمزتها.

them, or when she winks at one of them and arches an eyebrow or rolls her eyes.

their eyebrows, rolling their eyes, skipping, hopping, and springing.

When she happens on a male acquaintance of hers in the street and keeps on rebuking him for not having come to see her for so long, then takes hold of his hand and gives him a big wink.

When he sees a woman rebuking a man for not having come to see her for so long and then taking his hand and giving him such a big wink that the winker blushes and the winked-at blanches, or vice versa.

When she encounters a woman in the street who is wearing an expensive brocade and she starts asking her about the price and who sells it.

When he encounters two women one of whom is stroking the other while the one stroked points to some place with her delicate hand.

When she happens on some man in the street and makes a sign to him as though to say, "Follow us!" and he walks along on her right side and she turns her face from her husband and makes most of her conversation with the chump.

When he finds a man between two women or a woman between two men, for in the first case, the man is seeking to "mix the rough with the smooth"[103] while in the second the men are confident of getting enough, for "food for two will satisfy three."[104]

When they return to the house and she plainly states, or hints, that they should buy the brocade and he doesn't have enough money to pay for it.

When he returns to the house and sees that he has plenty of money but there's no one to wear brocade or sit at his side.

4.7.4

When she tells him at table (to make him choke), "How handsome is (such and such a young man) who walked along with us and how amusing and kind and full of

When he sits down to eat alone and sets to thinking, saying to himself, "How beautiful is (such and such a woman) whom I saw walking with (such and such a man) and how

وابرّه واترّه واطرّه واحرّه وادرّه *

رايتها تمشى مع فلان وما الطفها واترّها واطرّها وادرّها *

اذا بات تلك الليلة وهو تعب موجع الراس حتى اذا اغفى قليلا احسّ بحركة منها فى جنبه فقضى دينه متكارها *

اذا بات تلك الليلة وهو مستريح ناشط ثم احسّ بحركة منه فمد يده فجات على الحائط او على مسمار او وتد فدميت *

اذا سكن منزلا وكان جاره الادنى منه فتى جميلا فجعل يتردد عليه بعلة الجاريّة *

اذا سكن منزلا وكانت جارته فتاة جميلة ولم يمكن له ان يمت اليها بوسيلة الجاريّة *

اذا مرض ولزم فراشه وهو يشكو ويئن فلزمت هى الشباك وهى تمكو وتحنّ *

اذا راى جاره مريضا فى الفراش يشكو ويئن وزوجته بجنبه تحنّ وتهنّ *

اذا جآ وقت الصيف ففتر وفدر وجفر وحَصِر واسترخت عروقه فاثر ان يبيت وحده *

اذا جآ وقت الشتآ فاشتدّ واستد وامتد واحتد ونبضت عروقه فاثر ان يبيت مع من تنخ فى وجهه *

اذا عنّ له سفر لا بدّ منه ولم يمكن له مصاحبة زوجته *

اذا راى جاره قد سافر وترك زوجته خبعة طلعة راغية ثاغية * ٥،٧،٤

اذا غاب عن زوجته او غابت هى عنه فجعلت تكتب له ما تغيره به وتكيده وتقهره *

اذا غاب رجل عن زوجته او غابت هى عنه فجعلت تكتب له ما تصبّره به وتسلّيه وتمنّيه

savor, how full of youth and sap and *ardor*!”	amusing she is and full of *savor* and how full of youth and *ardor*!”	
When he goes to bed that night and he’s tired and has a headache and dozes off for a while and then feels her moving against his side and he performs his marital duty with gritted teeth.	When he goes to bed and he’s relaxed and full of beans and then feels himself moving and puts out his hand and it comes up against the wall, or a nail, or a peg, and comes away covered with blood.	
When he lives in a certain house and his closest neighbor is a beautiful youth who keeps dropping by in the name of good-neighborliness.	When he lives in a certain house and his neighbor is a beautiful girl and he cannot use good-neighborliness as a way to get to her.	
When he falls ill and is stuck in bed whining and *moaning* while she’s stuck to the window wolf-whistling and *groaning*.	When he sees his neighbor sick in bed whining and *moaning* while his wife’s at the neighbor’s side *groaning* and *bemoaning*.	
When summer comes and he feels listless and lifeless, unsexed and unmanned, and his sinews go slack and he’d prefer to sleep alone.	When winter comes and he feels shaken and stirred, distended and agitated, and his sinews throb and he’d prefer to spend the night with someone puffing in his face.	
When a journey looms that is unavoidable and on which he cannot take his wife.	When his neighbor goes off on a journey and leaves his wife now appearing, now retreating, now blatting, now bleating.	4.7.5
When he’s away from his wife or she’s away from him and she writes him things that make him jealous, lay snares for him, and leave him a broken man.	When some man’s away from his wife or she’s away from him, and she writes him things that help him endure, comfort him, and give him hope.[105]	

اذا قرا فى الكتب ان النساكلهن خائنات وان عقولهن فى فروجهن *	اذا سمع عن امراة انها لم تخن زوجها وانها ردّت فى حبه هدايا عشاق كثيرين *
اذا ركبه الضَفَف فلم يقدر على كفاية عائلته ولم تكن امراته جميلة لتنفعه *	اذا راى امراة جميلة تماشى ولدا لها صغيرا بزيعًا فيقع فى الارض فتنهضه بيدها فيبكى قليلا حتى يحمر خدّاه *
اذا جآ من محترفه وقابلته امراته بالصخب والمشارزة والنقار والضجيج والجؤار *	اذا راى جاره قد آب من محترفه فسمع له ولزوجته رَتَلا وزَجَلا وهَمْسا ورِكْزا ومباغمة ثم رفثًا *
اذا غاب عن بيته ورجع فوجد فراشه مشوّشا وشعر امراته مشعّثا بعد ان كانت اصلحتهما قبل خروجه *	اذا رجع الى بيته فائزا بوطر ووجد فرشه موضونا وليس من تملاه شحما ولحما ثم راى فى جملة ذخائره خصلة شعر * ٦،٧،٤
اذا رآها تسارّ الخادم او الخادمة وتانس بهما وتتساهل معهما وتحسن اليهما *	اذا راى امراة لا تسارّ الخادم ولا الخادمة ولا تبتسم لهما ولا تخلو باحد منهما *
اذا رآها تتوقف فى المشى كلّما مرّ بها جميل بدعوى ضيق نعليها او غيره *	اذا راى امراة تماشى زوجها وطرفها اليه ولا يزعجها من يمرّ بها كائنا ما كان *

When he reads in books that all women are unfaithful and their brains are in their vaginas.

When he hears of some woman that she has never betrayed her husband and has returned, out of love for him, the gifts of many suitors.

When he finds he has too many children to feed and can't provide for his family and his wife's no longer beautiful enough to be of any use to him.

When he sees a beautiful woman walking with a small child of hers who's cute and bright and he falls down and she pulls him up again and he cries a little, so that his cheeks turn red.

When he comes home from work and his wife meets him with scolding and bad temper, bickering, bellowing, and bawling.

When he sees his neighbor's returned from work and hears him and his wife billing and cooing, whispering and rustling, talking in low, sweet voices, and, finally, talking dirty.

When he's been out of the house and returns only to find his bed in a mess and his wife's hair disheveled even though she had tidied both before he left.

When he returns to his house having 4.7.6
pulled off some triumph only to find his bedding neatly folded and no one to fill it with a nice warm body, and then comes across a lock of hair among his things.

When he sees her sharing confidences with the manservant or maid, enjoying their company, becoming familiar with them, and doing them favors.

When he sees a woman not sharing confidences with her manservant or maid or smiling at them or never spending time on her own with either of them.

When he sees her pausing as she walks whenever a handsome man passes, claiming her shoe is too tight or something of the sort.

When he sees a woman walking with her husband, her eyes fixed on him and paying as little mind to any who passes by as if they didn't exist.

اذا اضطجعت حتى ينظرها من هو اعلى منها او اسفل واشوق ما تكون المراة ما اذا اضطجعت على جنبها *

اذا راى امراة قد اضطرّت الى الاضطجاع وابت ذلك حيآ وحشمة سوآ كان ذلك فى حضور زوجها او فى غيابه *

اذا كانت ذات هوى وضلع مع جيل بخصوصه ولا تزال تلهج بذكره *

اذا كانت المراة غير ذات ميل وحذل مع احد وعندها ان زوجها يغنيها عن غيره *

٧،٧،٤ اذا غاب عن بيته ثم رجع فلم يجد امراته او اذا قرع الباب فلم تفتح له فى الحال *

اذا راى جاره كلما رجع الى منزله وجد امراته مقبلة على الشغل ولا يكاد يطرق الباب الا ويُفتَح له *

اذا سمعت آلات الطرب فغدت تترنح وتترقص وتقول آه اوه ايه *

اذا سمع امراة تقول وقد سمعت آلات الطرب ان صوت ابنها الصغير اشجى منها *

اذا كانت تسهب مع الفتيان فى الكلام وتضحك معهم حتى تقول طيخ طيخ وعيناها اذ ذاك مغازلتان ووجنتاها محمرّتان *

اذا راى امراة تكلم الحاضرين كلاّ بحسب مقامه ولا يسمع منها طيخ طيخ ولا يبدو فى سحنتها احمرار ولا اصفرار *

اذا كتبت على قميصها حروفا انكرها او راى فى شفتيها اثر العض والكعام *

اذا سمع ان امراة تكتب على قميصها اسم زوجها ولم يُرَ فى شفتيها اوخدّيها اثر ما قط *

When she lies down in such a fashion that anyone who is higher or lower than she can see her, and a woman is never more desirable than when she lies down on her side!

When he sees a woman who has been required to lie down but refuses to do so out of modesty and decorum, whether in the presence or absence of her husband.

When she's full of love and attachment for a particular set of people and can't stop talking about them.

When a woman has no special inclination or liking for anyone and thinks she needs no one but her husband.

4.7.7

When he leaves his house and then returns and doesn't find his wife, or knocks on the door and she doesn't open it right away.

When he sees that whenever his neighbor returns to his house he finds his wife about her work and barely has time to knock on the door before it is opened to him.

When she hears musical instruments and starts swaying and undulating and saying, "Ah! Ooh! Aiee!"

When he hears a woman saying, after hearing musical instruments, that her little boy's voice is sweeter.

When she talks and laughs with the young men at such length that in the end she gives a belly laugh, her eyes being at that moment flirtatious, her cheeks flushed.

When he sees a woman talking with each of those present according to his standing and doesn't hear any belly laughs from her and her face is neither flushed nor pale.

When she writes on her shift letters that mean nothing to him or he sees the traces of bites or devouring kisses on her lips or cheeks.

When he hears that a woman has written the letters of her husband's name on her shift and there is no trace of anything to be seen on her lips or cheeks.

اذا سمعها تذكر اسمآ رجال فى المنام او اذا تحالمت فذكرت ما كان يحبه ويرضيه *	اذا بلغه ان جاره يكاعم امراته ويشاعرها فلا تحلم له ولا يحلم لها *
اذا رآها تكره ولدها وتلهى عنه وعن امور البيت بزينتها وتبرجها *	٨،٧،٤ اذا راى امراة تحب ولدها وتحمله ولا تلهى عنه ولا عن بيتها *
اذا قعدت بالشباك لتخيط شيا فجعلت تدرز درزة وتنظر منه نظرة حتى جآ عملها فاسدا فاضطرت الى فتقه واصلاحه *	اذا راى امراة تخيط لزوجها او لولدها شيا من غير ان تتخلل الدرزات نظرات وزفرات فجآ عملها محكما من اول وهلة *
اذا وضعت القدر على النار لتطبخ شيا ثم شرعت فى الغنآ حتى تهوست فنسيت القدر والطبيخ فتشيّط *	اذا راى امراة تضع القدر على النار ولا تلهى عنها فياتى الطعام قديا مشهّيا معينا على الباه والرقاد *
اذا تمنّت ان تكون فى المواضع التى يكثر فيها تردد الرجال كفندق وخان ونحوهما *	اذا كانت تبتعد عن المثابة ولا تشتهى ان تدخل فى زحام ليقرصها واحد ويغمزها آخر *
اذا كانت تصرّح او تعرّض لزوجها بانها تحب السمان الطوال من الرجال مثلا وهو ليس منهم *	اذا كانت المراة تقول امام زوجها او غيره بانها لا تحب الطوال من الرجال حالة كون زوجها قصيرا *

When he hears her saying men's names while she's dreaming or when she pretends to dream just so as to be able to mention things that would please him or give him satisfaction.

When he hears that his neighbor devours his wife's lips and lies with her under her shift, so she neither dreams of him nor he of her.[106]

4.7.8

When he sees that she hates her children and pays more attention to her finery and toilette than she does to them or to the housekeeping.

When he sees a woman who loves her children and carries them about and lets nothing distract her from them or her house.

When she sits at the window sewing something and looks up after every stitch she makes and her work turns out poorly and she's obliged to unpick it and repair it.

When he sees a woman sewing something for her husband or her children without interspersing the stitches with looks and sighs, and her work turns out well-done from the first moment.

When she puts the cooking pot on the fire to cook something and then starts singing and gets so caught up in the song that she forgets about the pot and the cooking and it burns.

When he sees a woman put the cooking pot on the fire and allow nothing to distract her from it, and the food turns out tasty, stimulating of the appetites, and conducive to intercourse and sleep.

When she wants to be in the places where lots of men go, such as a hotel or an inn or the like.

When she stays away from meeting places and has no desire to enter crowds lest some man pinch her or wink at her.

When she states or hints to her husband that she likes, for example, tall, well-fleshed men and he isn't one of them.

When the wife says in front of her husband or anyone else that she doesn't like tall men, because her husband is short.

اذا كانت تعيب على زوجها انه غير متصف بالمِلْثية ولا بالقُمُدّية *

اذا كانت امراة مفسّلة تعفّفا وشكت ٩،٧،٤
من ملثية زوجها وقمّديته[١] *

اذا وافى منزله وقت الغدا او العشآ ساغبا لاغبا فلم يجد شيا ياكله لان زوجته لهيت عن الغدآ بتصليح ثيابها وتغيير زيّها وعن العشآ بلبسها وجلوسها بالشباك لتنظر وينظرها المارّون *
ما اشبه وذلك *

اذا وافى منزله وقت الغدآ او العشآ فوجد على مائدته كل ما تشتهيه النفس فاكل وشرب وطابت نفسه ثم راى من شباكه جارته تلبس ثيابها وتنظر الى ما ورائها لتعلم هل الثوب والعجيزة هما كشنّ وطبقة او لا *
وما اشبه ذلك *

---

١ ١٨٥٥: وقمديته.

When she rebukes her husband for being characterized neither by insatiability nor continence.

When the wife holds herself aloof from her husband out of modesty when having her period and complains of both her husband's insatiability and his continence. 4.7.9

When he turns up at his house at lunch or dinnertime tired and hungry and finds nothing to eat because his wife has been too busy mending her clothes and trying on her dresses to prepare lunch and too busy getting dressed and sitting at the window to see and be seen by the passers-by to prepare dinner.

And so on and so forth.

When he turns up at his house at lunch or dinnertime and finds everything his heart could desire on the table and eats and drinks and feels well content, then looks out of his window and sees the woman next door putting on her dresses and looking over her shoulder to see if they're a nice snug fit.

And so on and so forth.

الفصل الثامن

في سفر معجّل وهَيْنوم عُقمىّ رَهْبل

١،٨،٤ وظل الفارياق معالجا للبخر وقد ضاق بهم ذرعا * اذ لم يحصل من علاجهم فائدة
فاصبح يحاول التملّص من هذه الحرفة ولا سيما انه كان مطبوعا على الملل والجزع *
واتفق فى غضون ذلك ان سافر الى فرنسا المولى المعظم * احمد باشا باى والى ايالة
تونس المفخّم * وفرّق على فقرآ مرسيلية وباريس وغيرهما اموالا جزيلة شاع ذكرها ثم
رجع الى مقامه * فراى الفارياق ان يهنئه بقصيدة فنظم القصيدة وبعث بها على
يد من بلغها لجنابه * فلم يشعر بعد ايام الّا ورُبّان سفينة حربية يطرق بابه * فلما
دخل واستقر به المجلس قال للفارياق قد بلغت قصيدتك لجناب سيدنا الاكرم *
٢،٨،٤ وقد امرنى ان احملك اليه فى البارجة * فلما سمع ذلك استبشر بالفرج من حرفته
وقال لعمرى ما كنت احسب ان الدهر ترك للشعر سوقا ينفق فيه * ولكن اذا اراد الله
بعبد خيرا لم يعقه عنه الشعر ولا غيره * ألا فَاهزقى يافارياقية المِهزاق * واسلُقى
فما يضرنى اليوم اسلاق * ونغّى ما اسطعت ان تنغّى * وضرّجى وضمّجى ودبّجى *
هذا يوم يعبق فيه المكتفَن * ويشبق فيه من وهن * ويشمق منه ذو الددن *
ويفاز بالغدن * هذا يوم تستحسن فيه الرّبوخ * ويُلغ فيه من به مُلوخ * وتتمّ
الجلهوب والسلقلق * وتُنجب الشريم ثم العفَلق * هلمّى فاتخذى مذ اليوم ظيرا *

Chapter 8

A Voyage Festinate and Language Incomprehensibly and Inscrutably Intricate

The Fāriyāq continued to treat the foul of breath but was at his wits' end, for the treatment did no good. He tried, therefore, to wiggle his way out of this trade, and all the more so as he was by nature given to boredom and disquiet. During this period, it so happened that the August Master, Aḥmad Pasha, Honored Bāy of the Autonomous Province of Tunis, made a trip to France and distributed vast sums of money, that were everywhere spoken of, to the poor of Marseilles and Paris. Then he returned to his seat. It therefore occurred to the Fāriyāq to write him a congratulatory ode, which he did, sending it by hand with someone to deliver to His Excellency. Before only a few days had passed the captain of a warship knocked on his door. When he had come in and settled himself, he told the Fāriyāq, "Your ode has reached Our Most Noble Master and he has commanded me to bring you to him in my ship." 4.8.1

When the Fāriyāq heard this, he took it as an omen that he was soon to be freed from his trade and declared, "I swear I thought the days had left no market where poetry might find a buyer, but if God wishes good fortune for His slave not even poetry can get in the way of it. Rictulate, dear risible Fāriyāqiyyah, and vociferate (though not in *alarm*)! Today not even she-wolves could do me *harm*! Dunk yourself in every ounce of unguent you *possess*; dab it and daub it, and take silk brocade for your *dress*! On such a day as this, our copulatorium must be redolent of *musk*—even its limpest occupant must experience *lust*! The giddy-pate, on such a day, must run *amok* and enjoy his *luck*! On such a day as this, the swooning prude[107] faints with *pleasure*, the stud that shies from service gives full *measure*, the wide-wooed 4.8.2

فانى ارى فى الزند اِيرا * فقال الربّان وقد استعجم عليه الكلام ما هذه اللغة التى تتكلمون بها لعمر الله ما فهمت شيا مما قلتم * اهذا اللسان تحمل فى راسك الى تونس * وبهذه الالفاظ تخاطب سيدنا واهل الفضل من رجال دولته * قال لا وانما هذه لغة اصطلحنا عليها فلا نستعملها الا نادرا * فقال الربّان ينبغى ان تتاهّب الى السفر ولك ان تستصحب ايضا عائلتك اذا شئت * فان سيدنا اكرم الناس لا يسوّءه ذلك * فتاهب الفارياق هو وعائلته وركبوا فى السفينة وبعد مسير اثنى عشر يوما والريح مخالفة كما جرت العادة بذلك بلغوا حلق الواد * فامر

٣،٨،٤ المولى المشار اليه بنزولهم فى دار امير البحر * وهنا ينبغى ان نلاحظ مزية الكرم التى خص الله تعالى بها جيل العرب دون سائر الاجيال * وذلك ان استدعآ المولى الموما اليه لم يكن لجميع من دبّ ودرج بمنزل الفارياق بل كان خاصّا به وحده * الا انه لما بلغ مسامعه الكريمة قدوم مادحه باهله لم يستأ من ذلك ولم يقل ما اقلّ ادب هذا المدعو وما اصفق وجهه لقدومه علينا مزويا * ولم يقلْ لربّانه قد خالفت القوانين السياسيّة والاوامر الملوكية فلننزعنّ عن كتفيك هدّاب منصبك حتى تكون عبرة لمن اعتبر * بل بقى الربان متشرفا بهدّابه * والفارياق متمتعا باهدابه * وبوّئ اكرم مبوّأ فى دار امير البحر واجرى عليه الرزق الكريم * والخير العميم * ولو ان احد اعيان الافرنج دعا شخصا واتاه ذلك الشخص ومعه غير نفسه لجبهه عند اللقآ بل لم يكن ليلقاه قط * لا بل نساوهنّ لما كنّ يدعون الفارياقية كنّ يقلن لها انك انت المدعوة فقط اشارة الى عدم ازوائها بخادمتها

٤،٨،٤ وطفلها * وليت شعرى اين من تكرم من ملوكهم بارسال بارجة لاستحضار شاعر ولغمره اياه بالمال والهدايا النفيسة * فلعمرى ان مادح ملوكهم لا جائزة له من عندهم غير تسفيهه وتفنيده * مع انهم اشد الخلق حرصا على ان يشكرهم

woofer and back-passage bleeder[108] bear *twins*, the single-barreled bawd,[109] followed quickly by the termagant, throw pups despite their *sins*! Up with you, woman, and from today play the mooning she-camel that lives its false calf to *lick*, for I see curly shavings on the fire *stick*!"[110] The captain, to whom these words sounded like a foreign tongue, asked, "What language is this that you speak? I swear I didn't understand a word of what you said! Is this the tongue you'll carry in your head to Tunis? Are these the words with which you will address our master and the great men of his realm?" "No," replied the Fāriyāq. "It's just a private language we've agreed on between ourselves and use only rarely." The captain then said, "You must get ready to travel, and you may bring your family with you if you like, for our lord is the most generous of men and such a thing could never upset him." So the Fāriyāq and his family got ready, embarked on the ship, and after a twelve-day voyage (the wind, as usual, being contrary), reached Ḥalq al-Wād, where the aforementioned master commanded that they be put up at the admiral's house.

Here we must draw attention to the propensity for generosity with which 4.8.3
the Almighty has distinguished the Arabs to the exclusion of all other races, for the invitation of the previously mentioned master was not intended for everyone who trod the boards of the Fāriyāq's house: on the contrary, it was peculiar to him alone. However, when news of the arrival of his eulogizer, with family, reached his ears, he was not upset and did not say, "What an ill-mannered guest you are and how deserving of a slap on the face for coming to us and bringing others with you!" Likewise, he didn't say to his captain, "You disobeyed protocol and the orders of your monarch, so we shall strip from your shoulders the epaulettes of your rank that you be a warning to those who take heed!" On the contrary, the captain continued to bear the honor of his epaulettes while the Fāriyāq continued to enjoy his services and was lodged in the most generous style in the admiral's house and supplied with ample goods and plentiful good things. If a Frankish notable invited someone and that person went and brought with him anyone but his own self, the notable would confront him when they met; in fact, he wouldn't even meet with him at all. Indeed, when their womenfolk used to invite the Fāriyāqiyyah, they would tell her, "The invitation is for you only," meaning that she was not to bring her maid and her child with her.

I'd be intrigued to know which of their kings ever sent a warship so that 4.8.4
he might bring a poet into his presence and shower him with money and

الناس ويمدحوهم * ولكنهم يانفون من ان يمدحهم شاعر يريد نوالهم * فلمن
هذا المال الذى يدّخرونه * ولايّة داهية من الدواهى يُعتدونه * وهم الطاعمون
الكاسون * الحاسون اللاسون * ام يخشون ان يلمّ بهم ضفف او قشف * ام
يحسبون ان صلة الشاعر من السرف * ولهذا اى لكون الكرم مزية خاصة بالعرب ٥،٨،٤
لم ينبغ فى امة من الامم شعرآ مجيدون مفلقون كشعرائهم على اختلاف الامكنة
والازمنة * وذلك من زمن الجاهلية الى انقراض الخلفآ والدولة العربية * فان
اليونانيين يفتخرون بشاعر واحد وهو اوميرس (ομηρος) * والرومانيين بڤرجيل
(Virgilius) والطليانيّين بطاسّو (Tasso) والنمساويين بشِلَر (Schiller)
والفرنسيس براسين ومولير (Racine et Molière) والانكليز بشكسبير
وملطون وبيرون (Shakspeare, Milton et Byron) * فاما شعرآ العرب
المبرّزون على جميع هولاء فاكثر من ان يُعدّوا * بل ربما كان ينبغ فى عهد واحد فى
زمن الخلفآ مائتا شاعر كلهم بارع فائق * وذلك لان اللُّها[1] كما قيل تفتح اللَّها *
على انه لا مناسبة بين الشعر العربى وشعرهم * لانهم لا يلتزمون فيه الروىّ
والقافية وليس عندهم قصيدة واحدة على قافية واحدة ولا محسنات بديعية مع
كثرة الضرورات التى يحشّون بها كلامهم * فنظمهم فى الحقيقة اقل كلفة من نثرنا
المسجّع * وما احد من شعرآ الافرنج استحق ان يكون نديما لملكه * فغاية ما يصلون
اليه من السعادة والحظوة عند ملوكهم انما هو ان يرخَّص لهم فى انشاد شعرهم فى
بعض الملاهى * فاىّ هوانٍ يلحق جناب الملك المعظم من اتخاذه الشاعر نديما وكليما *
ام يقال ان شعرآ الافرنج كثيرون بحيث لا يمكن للملك ان يختار واحدا منهم على
غيره * ارونى اين هم هولآ الكثيرون على خزنته السعيدة * كم فى بلاد الانكليز

---

[1] ١٨٥٥: اللهى.

costly gifts. I swear that all anyone who writes eulogies to their kings ever gets by way of reward is patronizing treatment and ridicule. Even though no people are more punctilious in insisting that others thank them and praise them, they turn their noses up at a poet who, in hopes of gaining their favor, eulogizes them.[111] For whom, then, is all that money that they store away? Against what disaster do they set it aside, when they are already well-clothed and *fed*, well-watered and *banqueted*? Are they afraid they'll be laid low by a surfeit of children or by poverty, or do they believe that a gift to a poet is an extravagance?

This fact—that generosity is a trait peculiar to the Arabs—explains why 4.8.5
no truly glorious and distinguished poets equal to theirs have emerged in any other nation at any place or time, reckoning from the Days of Barbarism to the end of the caliphs and the Arab empire. The Greeks boast of a single poet, namely Homer (*Ὅμηρος*), the Romans of Virgil, the Italians of Tasso, the Austrians of Schiller,[112] the French of Racine and Molière, and the English of Shakespeare, Milton, and Byron, while the number of Arab poets who surpass all of these is too large to count. Indeed, over one period during the days of the caliphs there may have been more than two hundred poets, all of them brilliant and outstanding, the reason being that "purses," as they say, "open throats." Moreover, there is no comparison between the poetry of the Arabs and theirs: they do not observe the rules for rhyme-consonants and rhymes[113] and do not have poems with a single rhyme or stylistically exquisite embellishments, despite the large number of metrical infractions with which their verse is stuffed. In fact, their poetry is less demanding than our rhymed prose, and not one of the poets of the Franks would have been good enough to be a boon companion to his king: the highest degree of good fortune and favor any of them may reach is to be licensed to recite some of their verses in certain theaters.[114] And again, what shame would attach to the august person of the king from taking a poet as the companion of his potations and conversations? Or is one to suppose that the poets of the Franks are so numerous that the king couldn't make up his mind which to choose? Tell me, what are they, compared to his auspicious treasury? How many prose writers are there now in England, how many poets in France?

الان من ناثر * وكم فى بلاد فرانسا من ناظم * وهنا ينبغى ايضا ان اضيف ٦،٨،٤
ملاحظة اخرى فاقول * انه قلما ينبغ شاعر عربى او عجمى ويحب الناس جميعا * فان من الشعرآ من يحب الكلام الجزل الفخم دون ابتكار المعنى * وبعضهم يعنى بالمعانى دون الالفاظ * وبعضهم يتحرّى اللفظ الرقيق والعبارات المنسجمة * وبعضهم الغزل وغير ذلك * ولا تكاد تجتمع هذه المزايا كلها فى شاعر واحد او تجتمع عليها اخلاق الناس كلهم * فان من كان من بنى نَظَرى ذَبَّ الرِياد شَحِما لَحِما مُخْضعا متصندلا زِيَر النسآ وخِلْبهن وشِيْعهن ونِسْأَهن وحِدْثهن وطِلْحهن وطِلْبهن وخِدنهنّ وعَلّهن ورَنُوّهن وحُرقوصهن(١) فاقحا اياهن حيث سرن * وكارزا لهن ايان برزن * لا تهمه الحماسة ولا منازلة الاقران * فعنده ان قول امرء القيس

(١) الحرقوص بالضم دويبة كالبرغوث حمتها كحمة الزنبور او القراد تلصق بالناس او اصغر من الجُعَل تنقب الاساقى[١] وتدخل فى فروج الجوارى *

اذا ما بكى من خلفها انصرفت له بشق وتحتى شقّها لم تحوّل

احسن من قول عنترة

فطعنته بالرمح ثم علوته بمهند صافى الحديدة مِخْذم

ومن يكن عِزْوا او عَزِها او حصورا او عِتوَلا مُقَطَعا او متابّدا او عَنكَشا عِثْيَلا او صَيِّقما صمكمكا كيكآ ليس به حمضة الى العَبْهرة العجنجرة * والعياذ بالله من ذلك * صرف ذهنه الى الزهديات والحكميات * انتهى ثم ان الفارياق انتقل الى المدينة ٧،٨،٤
وهناك تعرف بجماعة من اهل الفضل والادب * منهم مَن ادبه ومنهم من اترفه * وهناك حظى بتقبيل يد المولى المعظم ونال منه الصلات الوافرة * وساله وزير

---

١ ١٨٥٥: الاسافى.

And here I must draw attention to a further point: rarely does a poet, Arab or otherwise, come to prominence who pleases all. Some poets like eloquent and ringing words more than innovation in meaning while some concern themselves with meaning more than with words. Some search for the refined word and the harmonious expression, others for amatory or other effect. All these traits are unlikely to consort together in a single poet, just as not everybody's predilections are likely to be in concert regarding them. Any connoisseur of women who is an oryx bull, rubbery and blubbery, a silver-tongued sweet-talker, a lady's man, one who delights in their company, their fervent supporter, their friend and companion, their follower, their soul mate, their constant visitor, who dies to talk with them, a beaver-boring beetle,(1) bruising their bungholes wherever they go, sniffing around wherever they pee, will have no interest in derring-do and snicker-snee. He will believe that the words of Imru' al-Qays that go[115] 4.8.6

(1) The *ḥurqūṣ* ["beaver-boring beetle"] is "a small creature like a flea with a stinger like that of a hornet, or a tick that clings to people, or something smaller than a beetle that bores through waterskins and enters the vaginas of young women."

Whenever he whimpered behind her, she turned to him
With half her body, her other half unshifted under me

are better than those of ʿAntarah that go[116]

So I thrust him with my lance, then I came on top of him
With a trenchant Indian blade of shining steel.

Likewise, anyone who is uninterested in or indifferent to women, or unwilling to have relations with them even though he is able, or who is of no use to and without any predisposition toward them, or is a confirmed bachelor, or is scruffy and takes no interest in his appearance, or wears no perfume and doesn't adorn himself, or smells foul, or breaks wind disgustingly, or is of no value generally, with no pressing desire for the delicate, fine-looking, white-skinned, plump, full-bodied woman or the short, curvaceous, tightly-knit woman (God save us from such things!) will divert his attention to poems of asceticism and sage advice. End.

Next, the Fāriyaq moved to the city, where he became acquainted with a group of persons of virtue and culture, some of whom invited him to their banquets while others assured him of every luxury. There he had the honor of kissing the hand of the August Master,[117] from whom he received 4.8.7

الدولة هل تعرف اللغة الفرنساوية * قال لا ياسيدي ما عُنيت بها * فانى ما
كدت اتعلم لسان الانكليز حتى نسيت من لغتى قدر ما تعلمته منه * فقد قُدّر
٨،٨،٤ على راسى ان يسع قدرا معلوما من العلم فمتى زاد من جهة نقص من اخرى * فلما
اخبر زوجته بذلك قالت له * الم اقل لك غير مرة عَدِّ عن الغزل بالنسآ وتعلم هذه
اللغة المفيدة وماكنت لترعوى عن هواك * ماذا تريد من الغزل وعندك زافنة *
قال فقلت نعم ورافنة * ثم قالت ماذا يفيدك وصف العِين بالحَوَر * ولست
منهن تقضى الدهر من وطر * اليس ورآك منى رقيب قريب * قلت بلى والله انى
ما خلوت قط بامراة فى الحلم الا ورايتك ورآها * حتى كثيرا ما شاهدتك تمزقين
ثوبها وتنتفين شعرها ثم تتبوّاين مكانها وترسلينها فارغة * فقالت الحمد لله على ان
القى رُعبى فى قلبك فى اليقظة والمنام * قلت قد بدا لى ان انتقل من التغزل بالنسآ
الى هجوهن فعسى ان انتقل بذلك الى حال احسن * قالت افعل ما بدا لك ولكن
اياك من ان تدخلنى فى الجملة * ولكن قف قف لا تذكر النسآ لا فى النسيب ولا
فى الهجآ * فانك اول ما تذكر اسمهن يدور راسك وينبض فيك العرق القديم *
٩،٨،٤ كلاّ ثم كلا * قلت ولكن فى مدح سيدنا الامير قد ذكرت اسم امراة * فقالت
وقد اتقدت عيناها من الغيظ مَن هذه الفاعلة الصانعة * قلت هو اسم عربى *
قالت آه هو من ضلالك القديم * ولوكان اسما عجميا لقمت الان واحرقت
ديوانك هذا الذى هو علىّ اشد من الضرة لانك تصرف فيه نصف الليالى *
فقلت لكن هذا النصف ليس بمانع من كله * قالت لكن ذاك الكل حق لى وضعفَى
مثله * قلت صدقت ما خُلق الليل الا للنسآ وما خلقن هن الا للّيل * قالت
سلّمتُ بالاولى ولا اسلّم بالثانية * فان النسآ خلقن للنهار ايضا * قلت نعم ولكل

copious gifts. The minister of state enquired of him whether he knew French, to which he replied, "No, my lord, I have not bothered to learn it, for as soon as I started learning English I found myself forgetting an equivalent amount of my own language. Fate has decreed that my head shall hold only a predetermined amount of knowledge and that when that expands in one direction, it shrinks in another."

When he informed his wife of this, she said to him, "Haven't I told you more than once to have done with writing love poems to women and to learn that useful language? You would not, however, abandon your obsession. What need have you of love poetry when you have someone to take care of your every conjugal *need*?" Said the Fāriyāq, "And I replied, 'True enough, and a wanton strutter *indeed*.' 'What good to you,' she went on, 'are descriptions of beauties as being "dark of pupil, white of eye," when you will never get from them what you want? Do you not have a watchful warden looking over your shoulder, in the shape of my good self?' 'By God, I do!' I replied. 'Every time I find myself alone with a woman in my dreams, I see you right behind her. In fact, I've often seen you ripping her dress and pulling out her hair, then taking up residence in her place and sending her off empty-handed.' 'Thank the Lord,' she said, 'that you're as scared of me asleep as you are awake!' 'It had occurred to me,' I replied, 'to move from writing love poems about women to satirizing them, in the hope of moving into a better situation.' 'Do as you please,' she replied, 'though you must take care not to include me along with the rest—but stop, stop! Don't speak of women in either your erotic or your scurrilous verses, for as soon as you mention their name your head turns and the old Adam throbs within you. No, and again no!' 4.8.8

"I said, 'But in my eulogy of Our Lord the Emir,[118] I mentioned a woman's name.' Eyes flashing with rage, she enquired, 'And who was this blankety-blank woman?' 'It's an Arabic name,' I replied. 'Ah!' she said, 'One of those ancient delusions of yours![119] If it had been a foreign name, I would have gotten up this second and burned that poem collection of yours that is more harmful to me than a co-wife, because you spend half your nights at work on it.' 'But that half,' I said, 'doesn't stop you from getting the whole thing.' 'But I have a right to the whole thing,' she replied, 'plus two more of the same.' 'You're right,' I said. 'Women were created for the night and only for the night.' 'I grant you the first,' she replied, 'but not the second, for women were created for the daylight too.' 'I agree,' I said, 'and for each hour of it, and 4.8.9

ساعة منه وليس للرجل همّ فى الدنيا غير امراته * قالت الاولى ان تقول اهتمام * قلت فى كل اهتمام همّ * قالت هذا عند الرجال من فشلهم وليس كذلك عند النسآ * قلت هو من خفة عقولهن وثقل نهمهنّ فان اللذة تذهلهن عن الدين والدنيا معا * قالت بل هن يجمعن بين الثلثة فى مكان واحد وآن واحد * واما انتم فمتى كلفتم بواحدة منها اغفلتم الاخرى * وهذه من المزايا التى مزّانا بها البارى تعالى عليكم * ألا ترى ان المراة اذا سمعت مثلا خطيبا جميلا يخطب فى الناس ويزهدهم فى الدنيا تلذذت بكلامه وشغفت حبا بجماله وبكت زهدا فى العالم *
قلت بودى لوكانت النسآ يخطبن على المنابر كالرجال * قالت اذا لابكينهم دما * ١٠،٨،٤
ولكن هيهات فان الرجال من اثرتهم استبدّوا بجميع الامور المعاشية والمعادية وبمراتب العزّ والجاه * وحرموا النسآ من ان يشاركهم فيها * فما كان ابهج الكون واعمره لوكانت النسآ تتولى هذه الرتب * وكما ان الدنيا مؤنّثة وكذا السمآ والارض والجنة والحياة والروح والنفس والنبوة والرسالة والسعادة والحظوة والغبطة والعزة والنعمة والرفاهية والأُبَّهة والعظمة والخطابة والفصاحة والبلاغة والسماحة والشجاعة والفضيلة والمروة والحقيقة والملة والشريعة والايالة والولاية والزعامة والرئاسة والحكومة والسياسة والنقابة والنكابة والعرافة والامارة والخلافة والوزارة والمملكة والسلطنة * واخصّ ذلك المحبة واللذة والشهوة * فما كان اجدرها بان تشرف بالنسآ * قلت قد نسيت العفة والحصانة * قالت لم تخطر لى ببال
والّا لذكرتها * قلت ولكن البعال مذكر * قالت اين انت من المباعلة * قلت ١١،٨،٤
والهكهكة * قالت وما الهكهكة * قلت مضاعف هكّ هك اى هَنَى هنى اى طحز طحز اى فعل فعل * قالت هى احسن مما تقدم * قلت فقولى اذا اخيراً

a man has nothing to concern him in this life but his wife.' 'You ought to say "to interest him,"' she replied. 'Every interest is also a concern,' I countered. 'That is the case with men,' she responded, 'because of their failings, but women are not like that.' 'That,' I said, 'is because of the levity of their minds and the gravity of their appetites, for sensual pleasure blinds them to both this world and the next.' 'Not so,' she replied. 'They combine the three[120] in one place and time, whereas whenever you devote yourself to one, you forget the other. This is one of the characteristics that the Almighty Creator has bestowed on us and not on you. Do you not observe that when a woman listens, for example, to a handsome preacher calling on people to turn from the things of this world, she thrills to his words, falls in love with his good looks, and weeps in a paroxysm of renunciation?'

"'I wish,' I said, 'that women would preach from the pulpits as men do.' 4.8.10
'Were they to do so,' she replied, 'they would make them weep blood. But how unlikely it is that that will ever happen, for men, in their selfishness, have taken full control of all affairs, both mundane and spiritual, and all ranks of dignity and honor, and have forbidden women to share in them with them. How joyful and prosperous the universe would be if women were to take control of these positions! And, just as the word *dunyā* ("world") is feminine in gender, as are the words for heaven, earth, paradise, life, spirit, soul, prophecy, prophetic mission, happiness, grace, joy, renown, comfort, ease of life, splendor, greatness, eloquence, chasteness of speech, rhetoric, tolerance, courage, virtue, manliness, truth, the community of believers, the law of God, national territory, sovereign power, leadership, presidency, government, authority, intendancy, syndicship, chieftainship, monitorship, princedom, caliphate, ministry, kingdom, sultanate, and, most especially, affection, pleasure, and sexual desire, how appropriate it would be for that world to be overseen by women!' 'You forgot chastity and inviolability,' I said. 'They never occurred to me or I would have mentioned them,' she replied.

"'Anyway,' I said, '"intercourse" is masculine.' 'And what would you know 4.8.11
about intercourse?' she said. 'Not to mention,' I said, '*hakhakah*.'[121] 'And what is *hakhakah*?' she asked. 'It's a reduplicative formed from *hakka hakka*,[122] meaning "jiggy-jiggy," meaning "sheeka-beeka," meaning "bonky-bonky."' 'It's better than the ones that preceded it,'[123] she said. I said, 'So say, "At last!" Otherwise it'll lead to corruption[124] and *disbelief*.' 'That would be no fault of

والا فهوكفر وخمج * قالت على النسآ لا حرج فان منهن الفرج * قلت نَعَم الفَرَج
اذا ابصرن ذا فرج * قالت والارج * قلت والمَرَج * قالت وهن احقّ بذى
بَرَج * قلت وبمن نيرج * قالت الجمع بينهما بلج * قلت والثانى عند تعذر الاول

هو الافلج * قالت وبه اللسان الهج * ثم عزما على

الرجوع فسفّرهما المولى المشار

اليه فى سفينة

النار

*

women, for in them lies *relief*.' 'Yes indeed,' I said, 'relief (*faraj*)—and if they look well, they'll see that *farj* ("vagina") resembles *faraj*,' to which she said, 'As it does *araj* ("the sudden blazing of a scent")' and I, 'And *maraj* ("chaos"),' and she, 'And women have the better right to the boy with *baraj* ("comeliness of face"),' and I, 'And to him who performs *nayraj* (i.e., who "screws"),' and she, 'And when you combine the two, you get *balaj* ("joy"),' and I, 'And the one who comes back with a second strike after the first has cried,

"Quarter!" is *aflaj* ("the more victorious"),' and she,
'And has the tongue that is the more *alhaj* ("silver").'"

Then they decided to return
and the aforementioned *lord*
had them sent back
on steamer-*board*.

الفصل التاسع

في الهيئة والاشكال

وبعد ان وصل الفارياق الى منزله جآه بعض معارفه وساله عن سفره * فاسرّ اليه ١،٩،٤
وعينه ناظرة الى باب غرفة زوجته ان نسآ اليهود فى تونس ما زلن حسانا * وانه
ان يكن قد أُنزل بهذا الجيل مسخ كما تزعم النصارى فانه انما نزل بالرجال فقط *
فقالت امراته من ورآ الباب قد سمعت ما تقول بل المسخ وقع على النسآء * قال
حيث قد سمعت نجوانا ولا يخفى عليك منى خافية فضمى نفسك الينا لنخوض فى
هذا الحديث المستحب * قالت اجل انه ما يخفى عن اذنى همهمة * ولا عن ٢،٩،٤
عينى سمسمة * ثم انها تصدرت فى المجلس وقالت * قد اعجبنى من زىّ الرجال فى
تونس ان سراويلهم قصيرة بحيث تظهر سيقانهم * قال فقلت بل زى النسآ
اعجب واشوق * فان الرجال قد يكسون سيقانهم من الجوارب ما يغطيها ومع
ذلك فالسراويل تخفى خصورهم وما يليها * فاما النسآ فسوقهن بادية ولا شى يستر
حقائبهن * فترى المراة تمشى فى اوان الحرّ وثوبها يشف عما تحته من مكبّب
ومقبّب * ومقعب ومقوّب * ومكعّب ومكعثب * فقالت بودى لو كان زىّ
النسا كهيئة اجسامهن * قلت هذا يكون فاحشا من وجهين * لان المتزيية به ان
كانت ركراكة عندلة لفّا كانت فتنة للناس وعطّلت عباد الله عن اعمالهم * وان
كانت دردحة او رسحا كانت وبآء على الناس واجرتهم فى بيوتهم تطيّرا منها *

Chapter 9

Form and Shapes

After the Fāriyāq returned home, an acquaintance came and asked him why he was leaving, so he took him aside and said, his eye trained on the door to his wife's room, that the Jewesses of Tunis were still beautiful and that their race hadn't yet been turned into monkeys, as the Christians pretend—that only applied to the men. From behind the door his wife said, "I heard what you said. You're wrong—it's the women who were turned into monkeys," to which he replied, "Since you heard our private conversation and none of my secrets are hidden from you, come and join us, so that we may continue this pleasant discourse." 4.9.1

"You're quite right," she declared, "not the softest whisper escapes my ears, nor the tiniest speck my eyes" and she came out into the middle of the parlor and said, "What I like about the dress of the Tunisian men is that their pantaloons are short, which makes their calves visible." The Fāriyāq continued, "Then I said, 'You're wrong. The dress of the women is more pleasing and alluring; the men's calves may be covered by socks, not to mention that their pantaloons cover their midriffs and adjacent parts. The calves of the women, on the other hand, are in plain sight and nothing hides their posteriors. You will see a woman walking during the hot weather and everything that's rounded and domed, concave and coned, well-turned and tumescent may be seen through her mantle.' She responded, 'I wish women's clothes could take the shape of their bodies.' I said, 'That would be an abomination, from two perspectives: if the woman wearing them were big-buttocked, big-breasted, and big-thighed, she'd be a source of strife among the people and keep God's servants from their work, but if she were as wide as she was tall, 4.9.2

قالت ما سبب كون الرجال فى هذا البلد يتزيّون بزى كهيئة اجسامهم ولا لوم ٤،٩،٣
عليهم ولا محظور من رؤيتهم * افكل ما تفعله الرجال يسوغ وما تفعله النسآ
يغضّ به * لعمرى ان هذا الزى احسن من زى رجال بلادنا * فانك ترى من له
سراويل منهم يمشى ويفج كالشاة للحلب * وكثيرا ما تلتف عليه من قدام ومن خلف
فتعوقه عن المشى فضلا عن الجرى * ولو انه كان مثلا فى محترفه وقال له قائل قد
زارك اليوم فى منزلك فتى غسّانى فزهد * ولمّا لم يجدك لبث ينتظرك وها هو الان
هناك * وقد احتفلت به زوجتك وهشّت اليه وبشت وهى التى ثبّطته وامرت
الخادمة بان تمرض او تمارض حتى تنفى عنك الشبهة * اذ لو بعثتها اليك وخلا
لهما المكان لرابك امرهما واعتقدت ان زيارته لها انما كانت عن موعد * وانها هى
المقصود بهذه الزيارة لا التشوق الى رؤية سحنتك * وغير ذلك من الكلام الذى
يفور به الدم وينتفخ منه الحملاق * فكيف يمكن له والحالة هذه ان يحفد الى منزله وبين
فخذيه ما يذهب به هنا وهناك * ثم ضحكت وقالت نعم وترى منهم من له جبة يمشى ٤،٩،٤
ويكنس الارض باذيالها فيلصق بها كل ما فى الارض من النجاسة والقذر * حتى
اذا وافى بيته ملأه بالرائحة الخبيثة فعلق بزوجته منها ما يرد الطرف عنها وان كانت
عَبِقة * لان الرائحة الخبيثة تغلب على الرائحة الطيبة كما يقال * وفضلا عن ذلك
فان جبة واحدة يعمل منها كثير من هذه التى تلبسها الافرنج الى خصورهم * وليس
للرجل اذا لبسها من هيئة ولا شارة فانها تخفى قوامه كله فلا يرى له خصر ولا
غيره * وما خلق الله الانسان على هذه الصورة الا واراد ان تكون ظاهرة كما هى *
قلت قد رايت الافرنج فى بلادهم صيفا وشتآء فاذا هم يسترون ادبارهم بهذه الجبب
المزنقة * ولا يمشى احد منهم فى الخارج ظاهر الدبر كما يمشى هولآ القوم القليلو
الحيآ فى هذه الجزيرة * قالت والبطون والافخاذ * قلت ظاهرة * قالت قد شفع

or ugly, she'd be a plague upon people and force them to take refuge in their houses lest she bring them bad luck.'

"'Tell me why,' she said, 'the men in this country dress in form-fitting garments and no one reproaches them and there's nothing forbidden about looking at them. Does this mean that everything men do is to be swallowed with ease and everything women do choked on? I swear this dress is better than that worn by men in our country: there you find men who wear pantaloons and walk with their legs held far apart like ewes waiting to be milked, and sometimes these pantaloons get wrapped around them, in front or in back, and prevent them from walking, to say nothing of running. Let us suppose, for example, that a man wearing such pantaloons were at his place of work and someone came and told him, "A bonny, strapping young man came to visit you today at your house, and when he didn't find you, he stayed to wait for you and he's still there, right now, and your wife gave him a warm welcome and made him feel right at home, and it was she who insisted he stay and ordered the maid to be sick, or to pretend to be sick, so that you wouldn't have any misgivings, because if she'd sent her to you and they'd been left alone together, you'd have been suspicious and thought that his visit to her must have been prearranged and that she, and not a longing to see your ugly face, was the object of the visit," and other things to make the blood boil and the eyelids swell. Under circumstances such as these, how can he rush home with the thing between his thighs knocking him this way and that?' 4.9.3

"Then she laughed and went on, 'Indeed, and you'll see a man walking along wearing a *jubbah* with its skirts sweeping the ground so that everything on it that's polluting and filthy sticks to them, and when he reaches his house, he fills it with a bad smell, enough of which clings to his wife to make one avert one's eye from her even if she be a sweet-scented woman, for, as they say, "bad smells drive out good." Furthermore, out of one *jubbah* many of those things the Franks wear down to their waists[125] may be made and a man who wears one is left with no shape or style, for it hides his whole figure and neither his midriff nor any other part of him may be seen. God would not have created humans in the form that they have unless He had wanted it to be visible the way it is.' I replied, 'I have seen the Franks in their own countries in summer and in winter and, behold, they cover their buttocks with those tight *jubbah*s of theirs and do not walk around outside with their backsides 4.9.4

هذا فى ذاك فاما سترهما معا فشنيع * لعمرى ان الناس لم يهتدوا الى الان الى زىّ
حسن يوافق هيئة الجسم ويلائم للعمل وبه شارة * فان هذه البرنيطة لا تعجبنى وليست
ملائمة للوجه لا فى النسآ ولا فى الرجال * لانها اشبه بالقفة او الزنبيل او القِرْطالة
او السلّة او العَيْبَة او العِكْم او المرجونة او الجوالق او الحُزْبة او اللَّبيد او الجُرُجة او الغَفْر
او الجُفّ او القَفْعة او الجُلّة او القَشْع او المُدارة او القَلْع او الكِنْف او القُنْبع او المِخْرف
او القِنْع او الزكيبة او الجِوآ او القَوْصَرّة او الفَوْد او التلّيسة او الوَفيعة او الجِلْف او
الخَصَفة او الدَوْخلّة او السَفَط او الحَفْص او المِيْضَنة او الصَنُّوت * وهذه العمائم
دونها فى القبح * وهذه الحِبَر التى تلبسها نسآ مصر لا حسن فيها فضلا عن غلائها * ٥،٩،٤
واقبح من ذلك كله هذا الحزام الذى تتحزّم به الرجال فانه يملا الخصر والصدر ويمنع
الطعام عن الهضم * واقبح منه هذا الشريط الذى يربطون به سراويلاتهم من تحت
ركبهم فانه يوقف الدم عن سريانه فى الارجل * وليس فى زى نسآ الافرنج حسن
الا كونه ملائما للمرافد * وقد طالما بتّ مشغولة البال بهذا وحاولت ان اخترع زيا
يكون فيه حسن وتشويق وخفة وطلاوة وجلالة مع موافقة هيئة الجسم ما امكن
فلم يفتح الله علىّ الى الان * وعسى ان يتّجه لى ذلك عن قريب فاكون معدودة من
جملة المستبنطين فى هذا العصر * قلت وهل لم يخطر ببالك الاقتصاد قط فى ٦،٩،٤
استنباطك * قالت لا فان خير المال ما انفق على المراة * قلت بل على هذه الخزانة
واشرت الى سهوة الكتب * قالت اوَ تعانق الكتاب فى ليلك وتشاعره * قلت
ان الرجل حين يشاعر زوجته ليلاً لا تكون متزينة باللباس والحلى بل تكون عريانة
عند قوم * وفُرُجا أو متفضّلة او هِلاّ عند اخرين * فيصدق عليها ما قيل شعر

يتخمّل الانسان جل نهاره حتى يفوز بغادة فى ليله
فاذا استقرا فى الفراش بدت له جهوآ مثل التيس تحت ذُيَيلهِ

showing the way the shameless folk on this island do.' 'And what of their bellies and thighs?' she asked. 'Exposed,' I said. 'So that makes up for the other,' she said, 'but when both are covered, it's horrible. I swear, people have yet, to this day, to arrive at a good-looking form of dress that goes with the shape of the body, is suitable for work, and has some style. I don't like that hat they wear and it's ill-suited to the face, whether on a woman or a man, because it looks like nothing so much as a bin,[126] basket, caddy, swad, punnet, molly, scuttle, trug, frail, haskie, peck, prog, pancheon, bag, barge, sack, barrel, box, bran-tub, wash-tub, poke, cawl, pandan, vat, piss-pot, chamber-pot, jam-jar, firkin, cask, hamper, pannier, satchel, gunny-bag, leather bottle, leathern pottle, tun, or platter, and all those turbans are even uglier.

"'And those cloaks that the women of Egypt wear have nothing attractive 4.9.5
about them, as well as being expensive. Uglier than all the foregoing is that waistband that the men tie around themselves, for it fills up the midriff and the chest and prevents food from being digested. Uglier still is the tape with which they tie their pantaloons below the knee, because it stops the blood from running properly through the legs. The only good thing about the dress of Frankish women is that it is adapted to the bustle. I have spent many a night puzzling over this and trying to invent attire that looks good and is alluring, graceful, elegant, dignified, and as in harmony with the shape of the body as possible, and so far God has failed to inspire me. Maybe it'll come to me soon, and I'll be awarded a place among the creative minds of the age.'

"'In all this creativity of yours,' I asked, 'do you never give a thought to 4.9.6
economy?' 'Never,' she replied, 'because money is never better spent than on a woman.' 'Quite the contrary,' I said. 'It is never better spent than on a closet such as this,' and I indicated the bookcase. 'Can you hug a book at night,' she answered, 'and sleep with it under a single blanket?' 'When a man sleeps with his wife under a blanket at night,' I responded, 'she isn't bedecked with garments and ornaments. Quite the contrary, she's naked among some groups, and wears a single shift or is wrapped in a single sheet or blanket among others, thus fulfilling the promise of the verses that go

One dresses his best for most of the day
  So that at night of a damsel he may take advantage.
Then, when they're settled in bed, his ass may be seen,
  Bare as a billy goat's under its little appendage.'

قالت بل فى تبرّج المراة وزينتها نهارا تشويق وتهييج لزوجها ليلاً * قلت نعم ٧،٩،٤
ولجارها ايضا * قالت بل ولنفسها كذلك * قلت ما فهمت هذا المعنى البديع هل
المراة اذا نظرت الى زينتها تكرع * قالت لا شك فان الزينة حُسْن وكل حُسن
فانما يُذكِّر بالحَسَن * حتى لو نظرتْ جوادا مطهّما او متاعا نفيسا او شيا آخر
من زينة السماوات والارض لكان اول ما يخطر ببالها شخصا متصفا بالجمال *
قلت فهو اذاً تصور مطلق غير معيّن * قالت ان كان الاشوق فى العيان * فهو
الاسبق الى الاذهان * والا فاى كائن كان * قلت وعلى فرض حضور الزوج
وشرط كونه عليه مسحة من الجمال * فهل له خطور بالبال * قالت اذا وُفّق الى
التمليق والتعريب فقد يخطر ولكن لا بالصفة العينية بل بالصفة المطلقة * قلت ٨،٩،٤
قد لمحت الى هذا المعنى سابقا وفهمته حق فهمه * ولكن اسالك سوال متحرّ غير
ذى ضَلع ولا صَغا * هلّا يجب على المراة ان تقدم زوجها فى الذكر والتصوّر
من حيث ان له المزية والقفيّة * وحالة كونه شيخها واباها وحليلها ونفّاحها وكميعها
وكفيحها وضجيعها وعقيدها وعهيدها واكيلها وشريبها وجليسها وسميرها وحليفها
وعشيرها واليفها ونجيّها وضمينها ووليّها وكفيلها وكليمها وعنيقها ونديمها وخليطها
وعميلها وشريكها وخليلها * قالت نعم ورقيبها وسبيبها وشغيبها وعقيبها وغضيبها
وكليبها ولتيبها ووثيبها ونحيصها وخصيمها ولزيمها وزحيمها ونبيزها ولقيسها وفقيسها
وقفيسها وجاسوسها وعاسوسها وجاروسها وناقوسها وفانوسها وكابوسها وناطورها
وناقورها * قلت قد قال مولانا صاحب القاموس دَلّ المراة ودَلالها تدللها على ٩،٩،٤
زوجها تريه جِرآة عليه فى تغنّج وتشكّل كانها تخالفه وما بها خلاف * وقال ايضا

"'You're wrong,' she said. 'A woman who decks herself out and wears her adornments is alluring by day and arousing for her husband by night.' 'Indeed,' I said, 'and for her neighbor too.' 'Say rather,' she responded, '"and for herself too."' 'I didn't grasp that final scintillating point,' I said. 'Does a woman feel a desire to make love when she sees her own adornments?' 'Without a doubt,' she replied. 'For adornment is a form (and what a form!) of pulchritude and everything pulchritudinous puts her in mind of a handsome man. Even if she sees a perfect horse, or a precious object, or any of the adornments of earth or sky, the first thing to enter her mind will be a male distinguished by beauty.' 'Pulchritude, then,' I said, 'is the visualization of something absolute rather than something specific?' 'If it's the thing most attractive to the eye, then it'll be the thing most readily seized on by the mind,' she replied. 'Otherwise, any old thing would do.' 'And if we were to suppose that the husband was present and assuming that he was not without at least a touch of beauty, would the thought of him cross her mind?' I asked. 'If he could be accommodated within the terms of intercourse and copulation, he might cross it, though not in terms of his specific attributes but as an example of the attributes of the absolute.'[127] 4.9.7

"'I have already noted that point,' I said, 'and understood its true meaning. But let me ask you a question, purely heuristically and with no ulterior motive or parti pris: should not a wife put her husband before all others in terms of recall and visualization, given that he has a right to certain prerogatives and privileges, and in view of the fact that he is her shaykh and father, her lawful mate and conjugal benefactor, her bedmate,[128] her playmate, her copemate, her messmate, her tentmate, her roommate, her classmate, her pewmate, her bunkmate, her waymate, her cupmate, her tablemate, her couchmate, her watchmate, her clubmate, her intimate?' 'Indeed,' she replied, 'as well as being her watcher, her insulter, her disturber, her pursuer, her angerer, her attacker, her pesterer, her pouncer, her scrutinizer, her opposer, her clutcher, her jostler, her name-caller, her needler, her hair puller, her tress-tugger, not to mention the one who spies on her, stalks her, raises the alarm against her, beats the clapper-board[129] to raise the hue and cry against her, tells tales on her, and is her nightmare, not to mention her guard and whistle-blower.' 4.9.8

"I went on, 'Our master, the author of the *Qāmūs*, says, "A woman's *dall* or *dalāl* ('coquettishness') with her husband is when she shows boldness 4.9.9

تبعّلت المراة اطاعت بعلها او تزينت له * وفى موضع آخر تقيّأت تعرضت لبعلها
والقت نفسها عليه (انتهى) فهذا دليل على ان حركات المراة كلها ينبغى ان يكون
مقصودا بها الزوج لا غير * قالت لا غرو ان يكون صاحبك قد قيّد هذه الحركات
بالزواج تفرّدا بها من عنده * او انه تابع بعض اهل اللغة المشفشفين على ذلك *
فان الرجال دابهم ان يدّعوا ان المراة لم تخلق الّا لا رضآ زوجها وتعليله وتمليقه *
وان اللغة انما وضعوها استبدادا منهم عن النسآ وافتئاتا كما هو دابهم فى غير ذلك *
مع ان اللغة انثى ولو كانت من وضع النسآ وهو الاولى اذ كل انتاج ووضع لا بدّ
له من ماهية انثوية لكُنَّ وضعن الفاظا تدل على من لا يفكر فى غير امراته * وعلى
قصر طرف الرجال عن النظر الى سواها * وعلى مرضه لمرضها وزحيره لزحيرها *
وعلى الباسه اياها ونضوها من ثيابها * وعلى تمشيطه شعرها واحراز مُراطة منه
للنظر اليها اذا غاب عنها ساعة ما * وعلى بذل جميع ما تحت يده لرضاها * وعلى
من يرى زوجته احسن النسآ * ومن يزيد حبه لها بازدياد رويته لغيرها * او
على من يغمض عينيه اذا تعرضت له اخرى او يُغشَى عليه او يكبّ على وجهه او
ياخذه الدُوار او الهيضة * وعلى من يتخذ صورتها فيعمّ بها حيطانه وكتبه ومتاعه *
فتكون مرة قائمة ومرة مضطجعة ومرة مستلقية واخرى مكبّة * وبعد فقد تركنا لكم ١٠،٩،٤
اللغة تتصرفون فيها كيفما شئتم فلِمَ لا تتركون لنا خواطرنا وافكارنا وهى ليست من
الحركة ولا السكون * فاما دعواك بالمزية والقفية فانى اخبرك خبر من لا يجمجم عليك
رئاءً او حيآ * انه لا مزية للرجل على المراة فى شى * اذ ليس من قفية للرجل الا
وللمراة مثلها * فاما كفالته اياها فينبغى ان اقول لك هنا دقيقةً قلَّ من تنبه لها *

toward him in terms of flirtatiousness and dressing up, as though she were quarreling with him when there is no quarrel."[130] He says too, "*taba''alat* means 'the woman obeyed her *ba'l* ("husband")' or 'she put on her finery for him,'" and elsewhere "*taqayya'at* means 'she displayed herself to her husband and threw herself upon him' (End)." This goes to show that her husband and none other should be the object of every action a woman takes.' She replied, 'Your friend's[131] linking of these actions exclusively to marriage can be only his personal interpretation, or he was following the lead of some particularly jealous and jaundiced philologists. It is men's habit to claim that women were created only to please, entertain, and flatter their husbands, and they have created the language in such a way as to serve their exercise of tyrannical power over and violence against women. This is despite the fact that language is a female,[132] and had women created it (which would have been more proper, given that all generation and creation must be female in nature), they would have created words denoting men who think only of their wives, and how men should avert their glances from all but these, sicken when they sicken, groan when they groan, dress them and divest them of their clothes, comb their hair and obtain some sweepings from it to gaze on if they are ever away from her, and spend everything they have to keep them happy, as well as denoting men who think their wives are the best of women, whose love for their wives increases the more they contemplate other women or who close their eyes whenever another woman appears before them or faint or fall flat on their faces or are taken by dizzy spells or acute diarrhea, and men who get hold of her picture and put it everywhere on their walls, in their books, and among their possessions, with her shown sometimes standing, sometimes lying down, sometimes stretched out on her back, and sometimes flat out on her front.

"'Anyway, we have left the language to you and you can do with it as 4.9.10
you like, so why can't you leave us our thoughts and ideas, which are neither voweled nor unvoweled?[133] And as to your claim to prerogatives and privilege, let me tell you, as one who feels no need to mumble at you out of hypocrisy or prudishness, that the man has no prerogative over the woman in anything whatsoever, for there is no prerogative belonging to the man the like of which does not also belong to the woman. As to men's wardship of their wives, I have to draw your attention here to a nice point with which few have engaged, namely that two individuals may be involved in a commercial

وهى انه قد يجتمع مثلا شخصان فى شركة او دعوة او زواج ويكون قد تقرر فى
بال احدهما ان له منّة على صاحبه * وذاك الممنون عليه يعتقد باطنا وظاهرا انه
مظلوم * مثال الزواج ما اذا كانت البنت قبل زواجها تهوى شابا ولم يمكنها ان
تتزوج به فتزوجت آخر * فرات من افعاله واطواره ما انكرته * فيخطر ببالها
ذلك الذى فاتها فتقول فى نفسها لعله كان مستثنى من هذه الاخلاق * فلو انى
تزوجت به لكنت الان فى اهنا عيش * وزوجها يظن اذ ذاك انه اسدى اليها
منة عظيمة بكونه تزوجها بعد ان فاتها خليلها الاول * فكان ينبغى للرجال والنسآ
ان يمعنوا النظر فى احوال الزواج قبل ان يرتبقوا فيه * وعلى الرجل ان لا يتزوج
من كانت تهوى آخر قبله * وعلى المراة ان لا تتزوج بمن كان يعاف الزواج خوف
الانفاق والاملاق * اومن كان يهوى اخرى وهو عزب * ومثال الشركة ما اذا ١١،٩،٤
كان احد الشريكين هو الذى قدّم راس المال من عنده والقى عبء المصلحة على
رفيقه * فكل منهما يحسب انه ذو منة على شريكه * ومثال الدعوة ما اذا دعاك
احد الى الغدآ فى العصر وكانت عادتك ان تتغدى فى الظهر * او اذا قدّم لك
من الطعام ما تعافه * فقد ركز فى طبع كل انسان ان يحسب ما يستحسنه هو
حسنا عند غيره * او اذا تكرم عليك وقت الغدآ بقُدَيرة وكُسَيرة وجُرَيعة غير عالم
ان المادوب تكبر معدته عند الآدب وتتسع امعآوه * او اذا دعاك الى منزله وكان
بعيدا عن المدينة فلزمك ان تكترى مركبا بما يساوى غدائين وعشائين عنده * او
اذا كنت مثلا عند احد اكابر الافرنج لمصلحة له وعلم انه قد مضى عليك عدة ساعات
من غير اكل فامر خادمه بان يقدم لك لهنة من الخبز ومن هذا الجبن اللَخَنّ *
وبك اذ ذاك قَرَمٌ الى اكل دماغه * فايّكما والحالة هذه الممتنّ والممتن عليه *

partnership, for example, or an invitation, or a marriage, with one of the two believing privately that he is doing his partner a favor, while the other, to whom the favor supposedly has been done, inwardly believes and outwardly proclaims that he is hard done by. An example of a marriage of this sort would be if the girl has been in love, before marriage, with a young man but has been unable to marry him, so she marries someone else, from whom she witnesses deeds and habits that she finds unacceptable, and then she happens to think of the other, whom she failed to marry, and says to herself, "He was perhaps innocent of such conduct, and if I'd married him, I'd now be living the happiest of lives," while at the same time her husband believes that he has done her a great favor in marrying her after she'd failed to marry her first beloved. Men and women must pay close attention to the conditions surrounding a marriage before they insert their heads into its noose. A man should not marry a woman who was in love with another man before him and a woman should not marry a man who avoided marriage out of fear of expenses and impoverishment, or who was in love with another woman when a bachelor.

"'An example of a commercial partnership of this sort would be if one of 4.9.11
the two partners is the one who advances the capital out of his own pocket and puts the burden of responsibility for managing things on his comrade's shoulders; each of them then believes that he is doing the other a favor. An example of an invitation of this sort would be if someone invites you to lunch in the afternoon while it is your custom to take lunch at noon, or he offers food you find unpalatable (for the belief that what he finds agreeable must be agreeable to others is an entrenched part of everyone's nature) or a tiny piece of meat, or a mere crust of bread, or the smallest sip of something to drink, unaware that the stomach of a person invited to a feast grows larger at the house of the host and his guts more capacious, or if he invites you to his house and the latter is so far from the city that you are obliged to hire a boat at a cost equivalent to him to that of two lunches and two dinners, or if you are at the house, for example, of some Frankish notable engaged in some business of his, and he is aware that you have gone for a number of hours without eating and he orders his servant to bring you a morsel consisting of bread and of that smegma-like cheese of theirs, at which moment you are hungry enough to eat his brains. Which of you, in cases such as these, is the doer of the favor and which the one to whom the favor is done?

او ان يكون احد فى خدمة امير فالمخدوم يعتقد ان خادمه ممنون له لكونه ياخذ ماله ١٢،٩،٤
* والخادم يرى ان مخدومه هو الممنون لكونه ياخذ من شبابه وصحته * او ان
يكون احد قد زار صديقا له ليسامره وبالمزور همّ وقلق * فكل من الزائر والمزور
يحسب انه متفضل على صاحبه وقس على ذلك المعلّم والمتعلم والمادح والممدوح
والمغنّى والمغنَّى له * فمن ثم لا ينبغى للرجال ان يحسب ان مجرّد اطعامه المراة ١٣،٩،٤
والباسه اياها منة منه عليها * فان حقوق المراة اكثر من ان تذكر * قلت قد لحنت
ذلك على طوله وعرضه فقولى لى اى الرجال احب الى النسا * قالت ان اقل لك
تعربد * قلت قولى لا باس فانما هو بساط حديث نُشر فلا يطوى حتى نصل الى
آخره * قالت يوم النشر اذاً * فاعلم ان الكاعب من النسآ تحب الغلمان والاحداث
بشرط كونهم حسانا * والمُعصر تحب الشبّان بالشرط المذكور * وقد تانس بالكهل
اعتقاد انه يكون بها ارفق واعشق * ولكن ذلك لا يسمَّى محبة لانه يؤول الى نفع
نفسها * ومن شرط المحبة ان تكون مجردة عن الاستنفاع * ولكن هيهات فان
كل محبّ اذا تحقق دوام حرمانه من محبوبه وعدم الانتفاع به ملّه بل ربما كرهه
فعلى هذا فالمحبة عندى لفظ يرادفه الفائدة * فقول القائل انا احب فلانة حقيقة
معناه انا استفيد منها * فاما العانس فتحب الصنفين المذكورين ومن جاوزهما فى
السنّ قليلا بالشرط المذكور * واما النَصَف فتحب الثلثة والكهل ايضا بذلك
الشرط * واما العجوز فتحب الجميع * قلت ما قولك فى الشوارب * قالت هى زينة ١٤،٩،٤
الفم كما ان الحواجب هى زينة العيون * قلت وفى اللحى * قالت حلى الشيوخ *
قلت وفى العارضين * قالت بخ بخ هما زينة الناظر والمنظور اليه * قلت اى
حسن فيهما وخصوصا مع حلق الشاربين * قالت هما بمنزلة الاكمام للزهر *

"'Or it might be that someone is in the service of the emir and the master believes that his servant is indebted to him because he takes his money while the servant believes that his master is indebted to him because he is taking from him his youth and his health, or that someone visits a friend of his to spend the evening in idle chatter while the one visited is suffering from worry and anxiety, so both the visitor and the one visited think that he is the one who is conferring a benefit on his companion—and the same, by analogy, is true of the teacher and the taught, the eulogizer and the eulogized, the singer and the one sung to. 4.9.12

"'It follows that a man shouldn't think he is doing his wife a favor just because he is feeding and clothing her. The rights of women are too many to list.' 'I have taken that in,' I said, 'lock, stock, and barrel. But tell me, what sort of men do women love most?' 'If I tell you,' she replied, 'you'll kick up a row.' 'Speak,' I said, 'and don't worry! Conversation's carpet has been unrolled and will not be rolled back up until we reach its end.' 'At the End of Days,[134] then!' she replied. 'So, you must know that the perky-breasted young female loves adolescent boys and juveniles, on condition that they're good-looking. The young woman loves young men, the same condition pertaining, and may become intimate with an older man in the belief that he will be kinder and more loving. This, however, is not to be called love because it has its origin in self-interest, it being a condition of love that it be devoid of any advantage-seeking—though, sad to say, any lover, should continued lack of access to his beloved and absence of any good from him become a reality, will grow tired of him and may even come to hate him; thus "love," in my opinion, is synonymous with "benefit." The young woman who has moved beyond the age of marriage loves both the two previously mentioned sorts and those who are a little older, the same condition pertaining, and the middle-aged woman loves all three plus the older man, the same condition pertaining. The old woman loves the lot.' 4.9.13

"'What do you think of mustaches?' I asked. 'They are an adornment to the mouth in the same way that eyebrows are to the eyes,' she said. 'And beards?' I asked. 'Old men's embellishments,' she said. 'Side-whiskers?' I asked. 'Squeal! An adornment for the looker and the looked-upon alike,' she answered. 'What element of beauty do they possess,' I asked, 'especially when the mustaches have been shaved off?' 'They are,' she said, 'what calyxes 4.9.14

او الورق للغصن * او القطيفة للثوب * او السياج للحديقة * او الهالة للقمر *
وبينما هما فى الكلام واذا بطارق يطرق الباب * ففتح له واذا برجل معه كتاب من ١٥،٩،٤
اللجنة المذكورة سابقا يتضمن استدعآ الفارياق واهله اليهم * فلما طالع زوجته بذلك كادت تطير فرحا وسرورا * وقالت ما ابرك صباح هذا اليوم وما ايمن شمسه * ثم قامت الى الصندوق فاوعت فيه لوازم السفر ما عدا القاموس * فقال لها الفارياق رُوَيدك فان دون هذا السفر امورا كثيرة * فاقعنفزت وقالت اذكرها لى جُملةً حتى اَلِى بنفسى جُلّها * قال اطمئنى واصبرى فانك قد شوّشت عقلى بكلامك الاخير * واعوذ بالله من ان يكون سببا فى فساد ترجمة الكتاب * فتركته واشتغلت بامرها * وانا كذلك اتركه الى وسواسه فى العارضين اذ ليس علىّ ان اشاركه فيه *

are to a flower, leaves to a bough, a velvet edging to a robe, a hedge to a garden, a halo to the moon!'"

While they were talking, someone knocked on the door. He opened it and there stood a man with a letter from the aforementioned committee containing an invitation asking both the Fāriyāq and his family to come to them. When he acquainted his wife with this, she almost took flight out of joy and pleasure and said, "How blessed a morning is today's, how full of promise its sun!" Then she went over to the trunk and packed everything needed for the journey except the *Qāmūs*. "Not so fast!" said the Fāriyāq. "There is still much to be done before our departure." She crouched then, like one waiting to pounce, and said, "Tell me what, all at one go, so that I can take care of the greater part myself!" "Calm down and be patient," he said. "Your recent statements have put my mind in a spin—pray God the translation of the book isn't spoiled as a result!" Then she left him and busied herself with her own affairs, and I too shall leave him to his obsessing over side-whiskers, for I am not obliged to participate with him in that. 4.9.15

الفصل العاشر

في سفر وتفسير

من جملة ما لزم لهذا السفر ما عدا القاموس كان هذا الشرط * وهو ان يغيب ١،١٠،٤
الفارياق عن الجزيرة عامين واذا رجع يُوَظَّف فى وظيفته الاولى * فمن ثم كتب عرضا للحاكم واقام ينتظر الجواب * وبعد ايام ورد الجواب بقبول هذا الشرط * فوجد كل شى ناجزا للسفر لان زوجته لم تكن فى تلك المدة تهمل شيا * فلم يبق عليهما الا تشريف الجواز بختم القناصل واداء الغرامة الختمية الحتمية * الا انه بقى غير مختوم عليه من قنصل ليكورنه * فلما بلغوا مرساها اراد الفارياق ان يدخل البلد فاعترضه صاحب ديوان المكس * فقال له انا اعطيك هنا ما كان يحق ان اعطيه للقنصل فى الجزيرة * قال لا بل تعطى هنا ضعفين فابى وعزم على الرجوع الى السفينة * فرآه وزوجته رجل يدير زورقا فلما علم بقضيتهما قال لهما انا ادخل بكما البلد بنصف ما طلب منكما هذا المكّاس الحرامى * فركبا فى زورقه وعرج بهما من مكان خفىّ حتى دخلا البلد * ثم رجعا الى السفينة فسارت بهما الى جينوى ثم الى مرسيلية ثم سافرا الى باريس * وفيها اجتمع بمسيو دُ لامرتين الشاعر المشهور فى اللغة الفرنساوية * واقاما فيها اياما تحوّفت من الكيس جانبا * (فائدة اذا كنت فى بلاد فرنسا فلا تنزل خانًا للانكليز واذا

Chapter 10

A Passage and an Explanation

Among the baggage needed for this journey was, over and above the *Qāmūs*, 4.10.1 the following precondition: that if the Fāriyāq were to absent himself from the island for two years, he would, on his return, be reappointed to his original position. He therefore wrote a petition to the ruler and settled down to await the answer. After a few days, the answer arrived accepting the condition. Everything was, he found, prepared for their departure, for his wife had neglected nothing in the interval, and all that was needed was for their passport to be honored by the consul's stamp and for the final stamping fee to be paid. It remained unstamped, however, by the consul of Leghorn. When, therefore, they reached that port and the Fāriyāq wanted to enter the country, the head of the customs authority prevented him. The Fāriyāq told him, "I will give you here what I should have given the consul on the island." "No," said the man. "Here you must give twice as much." The Fāriyāq refused and decided to return to the ship but a man with a skiff caught sight of him and his wife and when informed of their situation told them, "I'll get you into the country for half of what that thief of a customs officer demanded from you." They got into his skiff and he took them by a secret route till they were inside the country. Then they returned to the ship, which took them on to Genoa and then Marseilles, from which they departed for Paris. There the Fāriyāq met Monsieur de Lamartine, the famous poet of the French language, and they stayed for a few days, which considerably trimmed their purse. (Tip: in France, don't stay at a hotel for the English, and in the latter's country, don't stay in a hotel for the former.) Then they departed for London, of which they had dreamed.

كنت فى بلاد هولآ فلا تنزل خانًا لا ولئك) ثم سافرا الى لندن المحلوم بها * فلما رات ٢،١٠،٤
المدينة وما فيها من التحف العجيبة * والرغائب الغريبة * ومن الانوار المزدهرة *
والحوانيت النضرة * قالت ايه ايه لقد قصرت الاحلام عن اليقظة * نعمَ الدار هى
مقاما * وحبذا العيش فيها دواما * غير انى رايت من نسآئها امرا بِدْعا * قال
فقلت الحمد لله على انك بدأت بالنسآ فهو من جدّ طالع الكتاب الذى يراد ترجمته *
ولكن اىّ بدع هو * قالت كنت اسمعك تحكى عن بعض الائمة ان عقول النسآ فى
فروجهن * وقد ارى نسآ هذه الدنيا الصغرى عقولهن فى ادبارهن * قلت فسّرى
فانى لم افهم ما اردت * قالت اذا كانت المراة توقع نفسها بين تهاتر الصنعة والفطرة ٣،١٠،٤
مع الاستهتار * اى انها تفخم شيا بالصنعة وهو فى الخلقة غير عظيم المقدار *
وتهيج الناس على اكباره والفضل كله للجار * اى اذا كانت تقول بلسان الحال ان
لدىّ عنصر عِصار كالاِعصار * لا يجدى معه الاعتصار * وطبلا فيه زمّارة
لكل زمّار * وصفّارة فى حالتى الشبع والصُفار * ودنًّا مِقعارا * يحتاج الى
صِمام اذ قد ملئ الى الاَصمار * وزَوْرآ تستدعى بالزيار* وخَرتًا حريًا بالدِسار *
وجَحْرا او دَحْلا ينجحر فيه الخاذر اىّ انجحار * وحشّة ذات اكوار واوكار * ووَرْبًا
ياوى اليه من ليس له وجار * وواُبّة موئِبة فى الليل والنهار * ونُقرة ذات تنقير
ونقر على ابتدار * وصرّة فرث ذات صرير وصِرار * وانقوعة اشتملت على صلّة
ولا سيما عند الاِهجار * وعَزْلآ لو انحلّ وكاؤها لمنّت بالدمار * ووَطبا لو فُشّ
لاكفهرّ منه الجو اىّ اكفهرار * وكِيرًا يتطاير من نفخه الشِرار * وهَيْفًا اذا هبّت فى
الصيف قال الناس الفرار الفرار * اى اذا كانت خلقت وما تارَبَها احد فاتخذت
لها تِرْبا ورآها * ليغنى غنآها * اى اذا جعلت دابها كله فى تسنيم المسطح *

When the Fāriyāqiyyah beheld the city with its marvelous curios and exotic, desirable *delights*, resplendent shops and splendid *lights*, she said, "My oh my! My dreams fell short of the waking reality! What a wonderful place in which to *live*, and how nice it would be if we never had to *leave*! Albeit I note among its women something strange and new." The Fāriyāq resumed: "I said, 'Thank God you started with the women, for that augurs well for the book that they want me to translate! But to what novelty do you refer?' 'I have heard you declare, on the authority of some leading figure, that "women's brains are in their vaginas" but I observe that the brains of the women of this microcosm of the world are in their backsides.' 'Explain,' I said. 'I didn't catch your drift.' 4.10.2

"She said, 'If a woman throws herself, recklessly, between the contradictory witnesses of craft and nature, i.e., if she makes, through craft, a great *amount* out of something which, in the form in which God bestowed it, was of little *account*, and provokes people to have the *vapors* (the benefit here going all to the *neighbors*) or, to put it differently, were she to say, using the wordless language of her body, "I own a source of wind like a *twister* that sorts ill with the tight-*fister*, a drum inside which there's a pipe for every piper to *finger*, a whistle that whistles in both satiety and *hunger*, a deep-bottomed *tun* in need, when it brims, of a *bung*, a cup that for a cover *begs*, a hole just right for *pegs*, a deep cave or narrow but spreading *ravine* fit to protect a fleeing sultan (he'd never be *seen!*), a dome with a mighty *frieze* and nests for both birds and *bees*, a refuge for the lair-less in the form of a *burrow*, a shameless, ever-ready, water-holding rock *furrow*, a hollow pecked out in the *dirt* where eggs may be laid in one big *spurt*, a puling purseful of *dung* kept closed with a *thong*, a dip like that for the dripping in a mound of crumbled bread and *meats* that foully fumes (especially when intercourse is foregone in the days before a *feast*), a waterskin with a tied-up *spout* whose string, if undone, will bring destruction *about*, a milkskin which, if it suffer a *prick*, will turn the air *thick* (and oh how thick!), a bellows at whose puffing sparks rise *high*, a scorching wind which, when it blows in the summer, makes men shout, 'Fly! *Fly!*'"; i.e., if she is born and finds no coeval with whom to *consort* and therefore obtains one and puts it behind her to lend her *support*; i.e., if she makes it her sole custom to turn what's flat into *humps* and what's squashed into *bumps*; i.e., if she takes those who look at her for 4.10.3

وتقبيب المفلطح * اى اذا استحمقت الناظرين اليها * واشارت اليهم ان عندى قعيدة او نضيدة يقعد عليها * اى اذا رمزت اليهم ان الرِكاز * تحت الجَراز * اى اذا استحقبت المصادغ ثم جعلت تمشى وتنظر الى حقيبتها وتعجب منها وتزهى بها وتنافس فيها وتحرص عليها وترتاح لها وتشوّق اليها * فوجدت اخرى تفخرها فى ذلك ثم وجدت هذه ايضا من غلبتها فى الاستحقاب فاجدر ان يقال ان عقولهن فى الحقائب * هذا معنى ما قالته والجراز عبرت عنه بالقرع * والترب بالردف
٤،١٠،٤ والحقيبة بالعِدل * ولفظة اى فى الاصل * قلت هذه عادة لهن فلا تشاحنى فى العادات فان لنسآئنا ايضا عادات كثيرة مكروهة فى هذه البلاد * وذلك كالتحيل والترجيج والتخضيب والتحنئة واليرنئة والثمّغ والتسيير والتوقيف والاغتماس والترقّن والترثّن والتقفّز والتطريف والوشم والتنوّر والامتهاش والجَمش والتحفّف والنَمص والحَلت والاستعانة والتفريب والضِياق والفرَم والاِلهاط والاستطابة والتصنيع والتسمين وعقص الشعر وتقليم الاظفار وتدريمها * وكشف الصدر وتحريك الخصر لمن قُرصت او قرزت او مُرصت او مرزت اوغمزت * والحق به ايضا العُقَر
٥،١٠،٤ وبيضة العقر والاختفاض والاهتجان وغير ذلك * قال فما كدت اتمّ كلامى هذا الوجيز حتى استشاطت غيظا واحرنفشت * ثم قالت لقد اَبسلك الى التهلكة مقولك * وفضحك عندى وعند الناس فضولك * من اين علمت انهن لا يغنجن * اذا خُلجن * ولا يرقصن * اذا قُرصن * ولا يستعملن الضياق والفرم * اذا كان الفَلْهم ذا لَهم * او اذا كان قوَأبا * ذا بقبقة مقبقبا * او اذا كان العفلق * يسمع له جَلنبَلَق * والخُفُق * احب الى الهُقَق * لولا انك جرّبت منهن ذلك * قلت هذا امر شائع مستفيض نبَهٌ مشهور منوّه به ذو دالة وبُثلة وتشرير لا يخفى على احد *

fools and signals to them, "I have a *fellow* on which you may sit, or a *pillow*"; i.e., if she winks at them as though to say, "Beneath where sprouts the desert rose[135] on the desert *floor*, there lies the precious *ore*"; i.e., if she stuffs her backside with cushions, then sets off, gazing at it, admiring it, flaunting it, showing it off, coveting it, feeling good about it, and using it to allure, then finds another woman who outdoes her in this regard, and then this other in turn finds another who beats her too in terms of stuffing, it would be more proper to say that their brains are in their backsides.' (Thus the gist of what she said, though for 'desert rose' she said 'pumpkin,' for 'coeval with whom to consort' she said 'back-hugger,' and for 'backside' she said 'booty.' 'I.e.' is as per the original.)

"I replied, 'It's a custom with them, and you shouldn't quarrel with 4.10.4
custom. Our women too have many customs that are disliked in this country, such as painting the eyelids with antimony, penciling in eyebrows, coloring, dyeing, tingeing, staining, striping, dotting, plain-staining, or staining with designs the hands, hair, or fingertips with henna or sometimes with saffron, tattooing, depilation, shaving the face or the head with a razor, removing facial hair using a thread,[136] plucking out or uprooting the hair, shaving the head, removing the pubic hair, using medicaments to narrow the vulva or using a bung made of perfumed rags for the same purpose or the same using a different verb, douching, cleaning the anus after defecation with water or a stone, cosseting slave girls to make them salable and fattening them up, braiding the hair and intertwining the braids with ribbons, and paring and rounding the fingernails, or the exposing of the breast and wiggling of the hips by those who have been pinched or palpated, had their nipples brushed by someone's hand or gently tweaked or pawed. To these you may add payment of compensation for rape, the "pelvic egg,"[137] circumcision of girls, intercourse with young girls, and other such things.'

"I had barely reached the end of this brief speech before she flew into 4.10.5
a rage and bristled her feathers ready for a fight, saying, 'Your words have sealed your *doom*, your meddling exposed you for what you are, to me and to everyone in this *room*. How do you know that they should not moan and sigh if winked at, or pirouette if pinched, or use the scented rag or the raisin pits if the well's so wide it swallows everything in gulps, or is too deep to fill and gurgles and glups, or if it's large and flabby and groans like

فهو كقول القائل السمآ فوقنا والارض تحتنا وهو عند النحاة ليس بكلام افتغضبين مما لا يصح ان يسمى كلاما * قالت ما لى وللكلام انما غضبى عن الفعل * انك عندى قوّال * وعند غيرى فعّال * ما هذه صفة المتزوجين * ما هذا شان المحصنين * ياللعجب انت لا تستحى ان تطلب * وانا استحى ان اُطلَب * الا ليت قاضيا يقضى بين الرجل وامراته حتى يبين للناس كافّة مَن الظالم والمظلوم منا * قلت فقولى اذاً ليت قاضية * لان القاضى من حيث كونه والحمد لله ذكرا يحكم للرجل على المراة * قالت بل الامر بعكس ذلك فان القاضى لا يرى الحق الا للمراة على الرجل ولا سيما اذا جأشت اليه واجهشت وكذاكل رجل الا امراة نفسه * قلت لله درك من امراة خبيرة بامور الرجال ومن رجل خبير باحوال النسآ * انى على مذهب سيدنا القاضى * فانى حين كنت احضر خصام رجل وامراة وارى الرجل منتوف اللحية مخرّق الجيب ماكنت لانظر الى المراة الا نظر المبرّى * ولا سيما اذا اجهشت فكنت اودّ لو افديها بروحى * ولكن رويدك لا تزبئرّى ولا تزمخرّى * ولا تجذئرّى ولا تجظئرّى * ولا تحزئرّى ولا تقدحرّى * انى لم يبق لى الان الا
النظر فاما التفدية فلا حكم لى اليوم على نفسى * ولكن اخبرينى ما هذه الخصلة ٦،١٠،٤
الغريزية فيكن معاشر النسآ * انكن تبكين وتضحكين ايان شئتن من اى شى كان * ونحن معاشر الرجال لا نبكى الا منكن ولا نضحك الا لكنّ ومن اجلكن * قالت سبب ذلك هو كون النسآ ارق طبعا * واكرم خلقا * وادق فهما والطف تخيّلا * وارأف قلبا واحنى فوادا * والين جانبا واسرع سمعا ونظرا * وانفذ فكرا واعجل تاثرا * واخف يدا واعلق بالدنيا والدين * واقبل للتلقين * وابدر الى الرسيس * والقف للعلق النفيس * قلت مهلا مهلا * قالت واروق بالا * قلت وبعالا *

a large door swinging open—tight tunnels being preferred by frequent fuckers—unless you yourself have had experience of them in this regard?' 'It's a widely bruited matter,' I replied, 'thoroughly documented, much noted, celebrated, often alluded to, famous—a scandal hidden from none. It's as though one were to say, "The sky's above us," or "The ground's beneath us," such things not being considered speech by the grammarians.[138] Are you going to get angry over something that can't even be called speech?' 'I don't care,' she said, 'about the speech, my anger is at the deeds. With me you're all talk, with others all do. This isn't how married men are supposed to be. It is not with this that the respectable wife is *tasked*. It's amazing—you feel no shame in asking, while I feel ashamed at being *asked*! Would that there were a judge to decide between a man and his wife, so that everyone might know which of the two is the oppressor and which the oppressed!' 'Say rather,' I responded, '"Would that there were a woman to judge!" for a male judge, by virtue of his being, thank God, a male, will find for the man over the woman.' 'Quite the contrary!' she said. 'The male judge will always find the woman to be in the right over the man, especially if she breaks down before him and blubbers, and so will all men, unless it's their own wives.' 'Hats off to you, as a woman expert in the affairs of men, and a man expert in the ways of women! I belong to the school of His Honor, for if I was ever present at a dispute between a man and a woman and saw the man to have a clean-plucked beard and a pocket with a hole in it,[139] I'd decide the woman was innocent, especially if she burst into tears, in which case I'd be ready to die for her. But hold on! Don't raise your hackles or *growl*, or stand tall the better to hurl abuse, strike out, make ready for a fight, or *scowl*! These days I can do no more than look; where dying for women's concerned, it's out of my hands.

"'Tell me, though, what is this inborn trait of yours, you women, 4.10.6
that lets you weep and laugh at the drop of a hat and for any reason? We men weep only for you and laugh only because of you and for your sake.' 'The reason,' she said, 'is that women are finer by nature, nobler by *creation*, nicer in understanding, more refined of *imagination*, softer of heart and more tender, faster to hear and see and more *kind*, quicker to be moved and more penetrating of *mind*, lighter of touch, deriving from both this world and the next more *pleasure*, more eager to learn, bolder to fall in love,

قالت وابلغ حِيَلا * قلت وتململا * قالت واوفى صلة * قلت وغربلة * قالت واعجل الطافا * قلت وايغافا * قالت واكثر ترفقا * قلت وشبقا * قالت واوفر كرما * قلت وغلما * قالت واطول حبّا * قلت وقنبا * قالت وابقى وجدا * قلت وزردا وعصدا * قالت واشهى عتابا * قلت وقرابا * قالت وابدع شمظا * قلت ولمظا * قالت وارخم منطقا * قلت وحَمَقا * قالت واسبق شعورا * قلت وشغورا * قالت واحلى تحدثا * قلت ورفثا * قالت واغرب رَتَلا * قلت
وعَفَلا * ثم قلت قدكان حديثك اولا فى الحقائب بما يذهب بصبر ايوب * ويزّى ٧،١٠،٤
المثمود والمنجوف والمنجوب * والان اخذت فى تفضيل النسآ على عادتك وفى تعداد محاسنهن وستنتهين الى كشف المغطّى منهن * فهل تريدين ان اقدم على صاحبنا مجنونا او ذا لمم فتفسد ترجمة الكتاب * قالت ان كنت تجنّ هنا فلا يكون لك فى البيت قرصعة كما فى الشام * فان المجانين الذين هم فى بيوتهم هناك اكثر من الذين هم فى اديار الرهبان * قلت لعل ذلك هو الذى اغراك بهذا التشويق المعذّب * فكفّى عن هذا الحديث الملهب المُحَرِب * بحق من اعطاك هذا اللسان الذَرِب * وتاهّبى للاشخاص الى من يكون عنده شغلى * قالت اليس هو بلندن * قلت لا بل هو فى الريف * قالت ويلى على الريف وعلى الفلاحين * من يطيق السفر من هذه المدينة ليسكن بين الهمج * فان الفلاحين فى جميع البلاد سوآ * قلت ثم ننتقل من هنالك الى مدينة غاصّة بالرجال * قالت فيها رجال بلا نسآ * قلت بل فيها نسآ
وانما هن قليلات بالنسبة الى كثرة الرجال * قالت ان القليل من النسا كثير * ثم ٨،١٠،٤
انهما سافرا فى غد ذلك اليوم واذ كانا سائرين فى درب الحديد ذكر المنبّه اسم القرية التى كانا يقصدانها فلم ينتبه الفارياق لاشتغال باله بتلك المساجلة * حتى اذا سارا

greedier to snatch up every precious *treasure*. . .'—'Stop! Stop!' I said—'. . . more serene of *thought*,' she said—'and more ready for conjugal *sport*,' I responded—'. . . more effective at getting her *way*'—'and at saying *nay*'—'as a friend more *loyal*'—'and more willing the wheels of gossip to *oil*'—'. . . readier to hand out charitable *grants*'—'and do the horizontal *dance*'—'. . . more *trustful*'—'and more *lustful*'—'. . . more likely to provide the needy with a *treat*'—'and more often in *heat*'—'. . . longer of *love*'—'and of clitoral *glove*'—'. . . more steadfast in *passion*'—'and in swallowing and *coition*'—'. . . more agreeable a *scold*'—'and to raise a leg more *bold*'—'. . . more inventive at finding acceptable ways to pass on thoughtful *tips*'—'and to lick the leftovers off your *lips*'—'. . . with a voice more *melodious*'—'and a beaver less *commodious*'—'. . . quicker to *empathize*'—'and to let your legs *rise*'—'. . . sweeter of *discourse*'—'and in talking dirty during *intercourse*'—'. . . with teeth yet *pearlier*'—'not to mention,' I said, 'your vaginal *hernia*.'

"Then said I, 'Your first discourse, on backsides, was enough to give Job the *hump* and make every wrung, strung, and unhung member *jump*, and now you've started praising the virtues of women, as is your wont, and recounting their charms, and you'll end up by giving away all their secrets. Do you want me to present myself to our friend[140] in a state of insanity or imbecility and have the translation of the book go badly?' 'If you go mad here,' she replied, 'you won't be able to hide away at home as one can in the Levant (for there are more madmen in the houses there than there are in the monasteries).' 'Perhaps that's what seduced you with such tormenting excitement,[141] so desist from this provoking, inflaming *discourse*, by Him who gave you that tongue so *coarse*, and prepare yourself to set off for the one for whom I'll be working.' 'Isn't he in London?' she asked. 'No,' I replied, 'in the countryside.' 'Woe is me! The countryside and peasants?' she cried. 'Who could bear to leave this city to live among savages—for peasants are the same in every country.' 'Afterward,' I told her, 'we shall move to a city thronging with men.'[142] 'Are there men there who don't have women?' she asked. 'There are women,' I answered, 'but they're few in comparison to the men.' 'A few women are a lot,' she said." 4.10.7

The next day they set off. When they were on the train, however, and the guard called out the name of the village for which they were bound,[143] the Fāriyāq was so preoccupied with their earlier duel of wits that he failed to pay 4.10.8

طويلا وسال احد السكوت عن رُحلته قال له قد فاتتك *فخرج ح وهو آسف على غفلته عن تذكير المنبّه * وما بلغوا القرية الا بعد مشى مسافة طويلة وتعب كثير *

تنبيه دروب الحديد فى بلاد الانكليز مثل خطوط الكف يسير فيها
المسافر الى اى موضع شا طولا وعرضا
شرقا وغربا
*

attention and they went for a long way before he asked one of the silent passengers about his destination and the man told him, "You missed it." Then he got off, regretting his negligence in having failed to remind the guard, and they reached the village only after walking a long way and becoming very tired.

Note: The railway tracks in England
are like the lines on the palm of your hand:
via them the traveler can go wherever he wants—
up or down, east or west.

الفصل الحادى عشر

في ترجمة ونصيحة

ثم لبثا فى تلك القرية وشرعت الفارياقية فى تعلم لسان القوم * فقال لها زوجها ٤،١١،١ ذات يوم انى اريد ان انصح لك فى امر يختص بتعلم هذه اللغة الجليلة * قالت هات ما عندك فهى لعمرى اول نصيحة خرجت من فمك الى مسمعى * قال ومن قلبى ايضا * قالت قل * قال من شان المبتدئين بعلم اللغات الاجنبية ان يتعلموا بادئ بدءٍ ما يؤول الى جسم الانسان من العروق والعضلات والربلات الى اخره *
قالت قد لحنت ما تعنيه فما هذه بنصيحة * قال فقلت سبحان الله خُلق الانسان ٤،١١،٢ من عَجَل * انما اريد ان اقول لك ان من شآء ان يتعلم هذه اللغة ينبغى له اولا ان يبتدى باسمآء من فى السماوات لا بمن على الارض * فان القوم يتظاهرون بالتقوى والصلاح * حتى ان البغىّ منهم تجأر وهى مستلقية بالدعآ مرة وبالرَفَث اخرى * قالت وقد قلقت اَوَ هنا بغايا * قلت لا فان اهل القرى الصغيرة فى هذه البلاد يتزوجون كسائر الناس ولا يمكنهم السفاح * ولكن المراد ان اقول انهم جميعا يبدون التورّع * فلا ينبغى الان والحالة هذه ان تسالى عن اسمآ الربلات * وستعرفين ذلك كله بعد قليل * بل لا ريب عندى فى انك تعرفينه دون معرّف وتحفظينه دون محفّظ وذلك بطريق الافتحار او الالهام * فان لقَنَك وحدّة ذهنك وقوة قريحتك يسهّل عليك كل امر عسير * قالت لعمرى لوكان مثل هذا الكلام

Chapter 11

A Translation and Some Advice

They now took up residence in that village and the Fāriyāqiyyah began to learn the language of the people. One day her husband said to her, "I want to give you a piece of advice on a matter related to the learning of that magnificent language." "Out with it!" she replied. "It will be the first piece of advice destined for my ears to have left your mouth." "And my heart too," he said. "Speak!" she said. "It is typical of beginners in the science of foreign languages," he said, "to learn at the very first words relating to the human body, such as sinews, muscles, fleshy parts, and so on." "I already knew that," she responded, "so it doesn't count as advice." 4.11.1

The Fāriyāq resumed, "I said, 'Glory be to God, "Man is a creature of haste"![144] I simply wanted to tell you that anyone who wishes to learn this language should begin with the names of things divine, not earthly. The people put on a show of piety and righteousness. Even their prostitutes, flat on their backs, bellow now a prayer, now an obscenity.' 'So there are prostitutes here?' she asked, anxiously. 'Not at all,' I replied. 'The people of the small villages in this country get married just like everyone else and have no opportunity for debauchery. The point is, I'm telling you that they all put on a show of godliness, so, that being the case, you shouldn't right now be learning the names for the fleshy parts. You'll learn all that soon enough. In fact, I have no doubt you will learn it without an instructor and memorize it without a prompter, through your own inquiries and inspiration, for your quickness of understanding, acuteness of mind, and genius make everything difficult 4.11.2

نصيحة لكانت الحكمة ارخص ما يكون * اناشدك الله كم بلغت من السنين * قلت ما هذا الاستفهام عقب هذا الكلام * قالت اى فصل هذا الذى نحن فيه * قلت فصل الخريف * قالت فالذنب اذاً على الفصل * قلت اتزعميننى قد خرفت * قالت والّا فما هذا القول الذى زحرت به وتحسبه نصيحة * قلت فافعلى ما بدا لك
فلقد وعظت من لم يتّعظ وزجرت من لم ينزجر * ثم لما مضت ايام جآت ذات ٣،١١،٤
غداة تقول للفارياق * اَلَا ما احسن هذه اللغة موقعا فى السمع والخاطر وما اخفّها على اللسان * فلقد حفظت اليوم منها بيتى شعر من دون تكلف غير انى لم افهم معناهما * فهل لك ان توقفنى عليه * قال اهلا بك اليه ان شئت الان فابرق حتى امطر * قالت اى لُقَعة انت ما عنيت الا المعنى قال فقلت وما المعنى الّا ما عنيت فانى اعلم عين اليقين انك لم تضمرى غيره * ولكن انشدينى ما حفظت فقالت

Up up up thou art wanted,
She is weary and tormented,
Do her justice she is hunted
By her husband, she has fainted.

اَپ اپ اپ ظاوَ آرت وانتِد شِى ازِ وِيَرى اَند طُرمانتِد
دُوهَرْ جسْتِس شِى ازِ هَنْتِد بَىْ هر هَزْبَنْد شِى هَز فانتِد

فقلت ان الشاعر هنا يشكو من شطط امراة عليه * ولكن لست ادرى اية امراة هى فيقول ما معناه

تبغى لكاعى سَدّ سمّيها معا اذ يفتح الثانى لسدّ الاول
كالاذن ان حكت تهيّج اختها وتظل هائجة اذا لم تفعل

easy to you.' 'I swear,' she responded, 'if such words were advice, wisdom would be the cheapest thing there is. Pray tell me, how old are you?' 'What has this question to do with what I just said?' I asked. 'Which season are we in?' she asked. 'Autumn,' I answered. 'So it's the fault of the time of year,' she said. 'Are you trying to tell me I've reached the autumn of my mind?' I asked. 'If you haven't,' she answered, 'how is one to explain this nonsense you're voiding onto me and calling advice?' 'Do what you like, then,' I said. 'I'm preaching to the wind and talking to the deaf.'"

One morning, after a few days had gone by, she came to the Fāriyāq and 4.11.3
said, "How wonderfully this language falls on the ear and the mind, and how light it is on the tongue! Today I learned by heart a few lines of verse without any difficulty, except that I didn't understand what they mean. Would you be kind enough to explain them to me?"[145] "By all means," he said. "Right now, if you'd like. Show me your lightning so I can give you my rain!" "How full of nonsense you are!" she said. "All I meant was, 'Tell me what they mean.'" The Fāriyāq continued, "'And all I meant was the meaning,' I said, 'for I know very well that you didn't have anything else in mind. But recite to me what you've learned.' So she said

Up up up thou art wanted,
She is weary and tormented,
Do her justice she is hunted
By her husband, she has fainted.

"I said, 'The poet complains here of some woman who has gone too far with him—I don't know who the woman is though—for it's in the same vein as

My silly wife wants me to plug both holes at once,
  But as the second opens up the first shuts down.
It's like the ear: if scratched, its twin starts itching
  And will continue to do so till you give it its turn.'

فتمعّر وجهها غيظا وقالت ما هو الّا تقوّل منك * فانكم معاشر الرجال ابدا لهجون ٤،١١،٤
بالسدّ * فقلت كما انكن معاشر النسآ ابدا لهجات بالفتح * قالت ان القوم لا يقولون
هذا الكلام وليس فى اشعارهم هُجر وفحش كما فى اشعار العرب * قلت اليست
اجسامنا واجسامهم سوآ * قالت الكلام هنا على الكلام لا على الاجسام *
قلت من اين ياتى الفحش الا من الاجسام * فحيثما وجد الجسم وجد منه الفعل
* وحيثما وجد الفعل وجد عنه القول * هذا دِين سويفت مع انه كان فى درجة
هى دون درجة الاسقف فقد الّف مقالة طويلة فى الاست * وكذا استرن فانه
كان قسيسا والّف فى المجون * فاما جون كليلاند فانه الّف كتابا فى اخبارِ فاجرة
اسمها فَنِى هِل جآء فيه من الفحش والمجون بما فاق به ابن حجّاج وابن ابى عتيق وابن
صريع الدلآ ومولف كتاب الف ليلة وليلة * فمّما ذكره عن فحش اهل لندن ان
زمرة من اعيانها كانوا قد انشأوا ماخوراً جمعوا فيه عدة زوانى * وكان بعضهم
يفجر ببعضهن بمراى من الباقى مناوبة * واول من نهج طريقة المجون فيما اظن كان
ربلى الفرنساوى المشهور وهو ايضا من اهل الكنيسة * قالت الم تقل لى آنفا انهم ٥،١١،٤
متلبّسون بالورع والتقوى * قلت بلى ولم ازل اقول غير ان هذا التلبس قد جرى
عندهم مجرى العادة * فان الملبَّس عليه يعلم ما انطوى عليه الملبِّس* ليت شعرى
لو ان احدا لبس مثلاً عشرة اثواب ليوهم الناس ان ليس له قُبُل ولا دبر افيخفى علم ذلك
عن الناظر * قالت لا فاذاً هم مدهونون بالدِهان * قلت نعم هذا النوع ينمى فى
هذه الارض كثيرا * فتاوّهت وقالت ويلى على المداهنين * كيف اطيق عشرتهم
وانا كسائر اهل البلاد المشرقية منبسطة النفس واللسان * لا اكتم ما فى صدرى
عن عشيرى * قلت اياك وذلك * وانما ينبغى لك التكتم والتحرز دائما * واياك
ايضا والاهزاق فان ضحك القوم اِهّمات وغَتّ وِاهلاس وِاهناف وِارْتاء وانتداغ

"At this, her face flushed with anger and she said, 'That's just lies you're making up. You men are obsessed with "plugging."' 'Just as you women,' I responded, 'are obsessed with "opening."' 'These people don't say such things,' she said, 'and their poetry doesn't contain the sort of obscenities and indecent language that are found in the poetry of the Arabs.' 'Aren't their bodies and ours the same?' I asked. 'We're talking about words here, not bodies,' she replied. 'Where does indecent language come from if not the body?' I asked, 'for wherever the body is found, so will the act, and wherever the act is found, so will talk about it. The celebrated Dean Swift, though only one rank below a bishop, wrote a long essay on the anus. Sterne is a similar case, for he too was a priest but he wrote bawdy stuff. John Cleland wrote a book recounting the doings of a harlot named Fanny Hill in which he outdid in obscenity and bawdiness Ibn Ḥajjāj, Ibn Abī 'Atīq, Ibn Ṣarī' al-Dilā', and the author of *Alf laylah wa-laylah* (*The Thousand and One Nights*). He writes, for instance, speaking of the licentiousness of the people of London, that a coterie of notables there, having set up a brothel, gathered together a number of whores and would perform depraved acts with them in front of the others, taking turns. The first to follow the path of bawdiness was, I believe, the celebrated Frenchman Rabelais, who was also a man of the church.' 4.11.4

"'Didn't you just tell me that they put on a show of godliness and piety?' 4.11.5
she asked. 'I did,' I replied, 'and they do, but this show has become second nature to them and the audience knows well what is in the hearts of the performers. I'd like to know: if someone puts on, say, ten garments, to fool people into thinking that he has neither front nor back, is the onlooker really taken in?' 'No,' she said, 'and such people are but whited sepulchers.' 'Indeed,' I responded, 'and that's a species that grows rampant in this soil.' 'Woe to the hypocrites!' said the Fariyaqiyyah with a sigh. 'How am I to put up with their company when I, like most Levantines, am an open book, both in how I am and what I say? I don't hide what is in my heart from those around me.' 'That won't do!' I said. 'You must be ever reticent and on your guard, and beware too of laughing too much, for these people express their mirth through stifled giggles with mouths covered, tepid titters, sarcastic simpers, lukewarm laughs, sniggers, smirks, snickers, wan smiles, laughing

وارتاك وزقزقة وهرنفة وانتاغ وهنبصة * والّا فكونى من التاغيات * قالت كيف تامرنى ان اكون من الطاغيات * وانت لا تزال تشكو من النسآ طرًّا حتى من العادلات * قلت بل المراد ان تغالبى الضحك يقال تغت الجارية - فابتدرتنى
وقالت يكفى يكفى ما اريد ان تذكر لى الجارية ولا الجارة * قلت نعم واكلهم نأج ٤،١١،٦
وتدلّس وتوجّس وهَمْس ومَدْش وتبرّض وهرمزة ومَطْع وتذوّق وتطعّم وتغذّم * وشربهم غنثرة ولَماظ وترشّف وتزحّن وترنّخ وترنّح وتقنح وترمق وتمقق وتمزّز وتمزّز وتمصص * ومتى تكلمت يجب ان تغضى طرفك وتخفضى صوتك وتبدى غاية ما يكون من الترزّن والتوقر * والتحرز والتحذر * والتظرّف والتكيّس * والتلطف والتنطس * والتادب والتخضع * والتعزف والتخشع * والتخفر والتقرز * والتعوّذ والتعزز * والتنزه والتقرش * والتمنع والتجهّش * والتنسك والتنقع * والتاوّه والتنطع * والتحوّب والتذمم * والتحرج والتأثّم * والتحنث والتحشم * والتدلس والتكتم * والتخنث والتانق * والتودد والتملق * والتحسب والتحرى * والتوقى والتحشى * والتوخى والتخشى * والتبرّى والتذكى * والتحذلق والتحصى * والتوقف والتحمى * والتصلف والتكلف * والتاسف والتلهف * والتحشف والتحنف *
والتعفف والتانف * والتخيف والتخوف * والتنطّف والتنظف * فقالت ويك ٤،١١،٧
ويك ما هذا اَلعلك اتيت بى الى هذه البلاد لتسبكنى وتصوغ منى امراة اخرى * قلت فديتك فاسمعى ولا يكن كلامى فى هذا الفصل من السنة الا اِخفاسا اى قليلا * وفى الفصل القابل تزيدين عشرين فى المئة * وان حدّثك رجل او امراة وجب عليك ان تستحسنى المحدّث وتحبّذيه عند ختام كل جملة * وتومّنى له وتهيمنى اى تقولى له آمين آمين بَسَلا بسلا * وتنعّميه اى تقولى نعم نعم* وتبجّليه اى تقول بَجَل بجل * وتوجّليه اى تقولى اَجَل اجل * وتبسّليه اى تقولى بَسَل

behind their hands, and hidden chortles. If you don't, you'll be counted among the cheap girls who laugh till they're fit to *bust*.' 'How can you tell me to be one of the *unjust*,'[146] she said, 'when you're always complaining of women, even those who are the opposite?' 'Not at all,' I said. 'The idea is that you should master your laughter. One says, *taghat al-jāriyah* ("the slave girl tried and failed to suppress her laughter") . . .' but she interrupted me and said, 'Enough, enough! I don't want to hear any more from you about slave girls or girls next door.'

"'And that's not all,' I said: 'Their way of eating consists of snacking,[147] 4.11.6
picking, pecking, nibbling, tasting, testing, and chewing over and over again, while their way of drinking consists of sipping little by little, bit by bit, drop by drop, slowly slowly, listlessly and unenthusiastically. Whenever you say something, you must lower your eyes and your voice and display the utmost possible sedateness[148] and solemnity, equanimity and dignity, pleasantness and wariness, courtesy and good manners, finickiness and fastidiousness, modesty and self-deprecation, caution and apprehension, abstemiousness and affectedness, ingratiation and flattery, quick thinking and wit, reticence and confidentiality, deference and acquiescence, scrupulosity and persnicketiness, canniness and costiveness, squeamishness and priggishness, sheepishness and embarrassment, timidity and bashfulness, mawwormism and sanctimoniousness.'

"'My my!' she said. 'What's this? Could it be that you've brought me to 4.11.7
this country to recast me and fashion me into another woman?' 'I'd rather die!' I said, 'so, at this season of the year, speak pauciloquently, meaning only a little, and in the next increase the amount by twenty percent. Should a man or a woman address you, you must show the speaker how pleased you are and express your appreciation at the end of each sentence. Likewise, you must assent and consent (meaning, say "Amen, amen! Quite so, quite so!"), agree (meaning, say "Yes, yes!"), show respect (meaning, say "Certainly, certainly!"), concur (meaning, say "Absolutely, absolutely!") and go along (meaning, say "How true, how true!"). Also, you must cook nothing on a Sunday, just eat the leftovers from Saturday cold, as do the Jews, because hot food heats the blood and excites the hot humors and also because Our

بسل * ولا ينبغى لك فى يوم الاحد ان تطبخى شيا وانما ناكل مما فضل من يوم
السبت باردا كما تفعل اليهود * لان الطعام السخن يسخن الدم ويهيج الحرارة *
ولان سيدنا موسى رجم رجلا وُجد يجمع حطبا فى السبت * ولا ينبغى لك الحركة
فى يوم الاحد ايّة حركة كانت اَلحنت ذلك * قالت لحنت * قلت ولا ترفعى فيه
الستائر عن الشبابيك لئلاّ يراك الناس فيكون ذلك باعثا ايضا على الحركة *
الحنت هذا ايضا * قالت قد لحنته وزكنته * وفهمته ولقنته * وعلمته ودريته *
وادركته ووعيته * ولكن ما سببه وهذا اليوم عندنا يوم الفرح والسرور * والتزاور
والحبور * قلت انهم يموتون فيه لكون سيدنا عيسى أُنشر فيه من الموت * ثم ان
عليك ان لا تفترى من ذكر يوم السبت اى الاحد * فان المسمّى قد يتغيّر بتغيير
اسمه * وذلك بان تقولى مثلا ما كان اشرف السبت الماضى وما اجلّه * من لى
بالسبت القابل حتى اخلو فيه مع ربّى * ياليت كل يوم فيه ساعة من ساعات
السبت * اَلَا ان يوم السبت ليوم عظيم * مهيب كريم * جليل وسيم * كيف
كان الناس يعيشون ولا سبت لهم * كم من سبت فى السنة * وكم فى ساعات
السبت من دقائق * وكم فى دقائق السبت من ثوانى * اَلَا ما ابهى شمس السبت
وقمره * وغلسه وسحره * وازهاره واطياره * وحره وازمهراره * واذا انكرت فَعِلة ٨،١١،٤
من فعلاتهم فاياك وان تذكريها لهم * واطرئ ما امكن على عاداتهم واطوارهم
ومعالمهم ومشاعرهم ومآكلهم ومشاربهم ومآدبهم وملابسهم * وعلى طول
اظفارهم واظفارهنّ وعلى عظم مرافدهن وعلى تفتيل سوالفهن * وعلى المنفش من
شعرهن اعنى على قُذُلهن * وعلى كشف ادبارهم للاصطلآ * وكلما رايت شيا
فى بيوتهم من اثاث وغيره فاستحسنيه واعجبى به فقولى وانت مدهوشة * آه ما
احسن هذا * آه ما اجمل ذاك * آه ما ابهى هولآ * اه ما املح تلك * اَلا ما

Master Mūsā stoned a man whom he found gathering firewood on the Sabbath; neither can you make any other kind of movement on a Sunday. Have you got that?' 'I have,' she said. 'And don't draw the curtains back from the windows on that day,' I said, 'in case anyone sees you and that too leads to movement. Have you got that too?' 'I've got it,' she said, 'and grasped it and understood it and assimilated it and absorbed it and digested it and am seized of it and have perceived it. But what is the reason for it, when the same day, among us, is a day of pleasure and *exultation*, exchange of visits and *jubilation*?' 'They behave on that day like the dead,' I said, 'because that is the day on which Our Master 'Īsā rose from the dead. Furthermore, you must not take the name of the Sabbath, meaning Sunday (for the thing named may change with the changing of its name), in vain. Thus you should say for example, "What a noble and sublime Sabbath day that last one was, and when oh when will the next Sabbath come that I may again be alone with my Lord? Would that every day had a Sabbath hour! The Sabbath day is truly mighty and *awe-inspiring*, sublime and *beguiling*. How did people survive when they had no Sabbath? How many Sabbaths are there in a year? How many minutes in their hours, how many seconds in their minutes? How lovely are the Sabbath sun and moon, its predawn dark and *hours*, its heat and cold, its birds and *flowers*!"

"'Should you disapprove of any of their doings, be careful not to say so. 4.11.8
Praise what you can of their customs and conditions, their landmarks and sites, their dishes and drinks, their banquets and clothing, the length of the nails of both their men and their women, the size of the latter's bustles and the braiding of their side locks, as of their "frights" of hair (by which I mean where it's drawn together at the backs of their heads), and how they expose their backsides to warm them up.[149] When you see any piece of furniture or the like in their houses, say how well it looks and express your admiration, saying, in astonishment, "Oh how lovely is this! Oh how beautiful is that! Oh how pretty are these! Oh how charming are those! How sweet-smelling are your latrines! How aromatic your drains! How spotless your other household offices! How elegant your sewers! How clean your lintels and doorsteps! How cheerful your underground tubes and tunnels!" This is

اذكى مراحيضكم * واشذى بواليعكم * وانقى مرافقكم * وآنق مثاعبكم * وانظف اعتابكم وصُدكم * وابهج نَفَقكم وسَرَبكم * فهذه هى الذريعة التى يتذرع بها الغربآ هنا لاستجلاب مودتهم وكسب رضاهم * واعرف كثيرين قد استعملوها ونجحوا بها *

٩،١١،٤ ثم ينبغى لك اذا دعينا الى وليمة عند احد اكابرهم ان تاكلى هنا من قبل ان تذهبى * فان المدعوّين لا ياكلون عند آدبهم حتى يشبعوا ولكن يشبعون حتى ياكلوا * وكما ان ادب الآدب عندنا ان يغصب ضيفه على الاكل ويحلفه براسه ولحيته وشواربه ان ياكل فخذ دجاجة او ست كُبَيبات او يلقمه اياها فى فمه * كذلك كان ادب الآدب عندهم ان يراعى حركات فم الآكل ويديه ليعلم هل هو سرطم او ذو لَقَف ونقف * وكلما تحرك فم او يد على المائدة — قال فابتدرتنى وقالت وخصر * قلت وكفل بل اى عضو كان * وجب عليك ان تقولى لذى العضو المتحرك انت مشكور على ذلك * انت ممدوح * انت محمود * انت مفضل * انت محسن * انت برّ * انت ذو منّة وما اشبه ذلك مما يوذن بضعة المادوب ولَمْده وحقارته وهَوانه وذلّه وخساسته وهَطْرته وكَفْره(١) وتسكسكه * فى مقابلة رفعة الآدب وعظمته وجلاله وابّهته وشرفه وكرمه وبذخه وعزّته *

(١) الهَطْرة تذلّل الفقير للغنى والكَفر تعظيم الفارسى ملكه *

١٠،١١،٤ والحذر الحذر من ان تمدّى يدك الى زجاجة الخمر او الى جفنة الطعام فتاخذى منهما ما شئت * فان ذلك يكون انتهاكاً لحرمة المائدة والمجلس والقرية بل وللمملكة بأسرها * وانما ينبغى ان تنتظرى من كرم الآدب ان يوعز اليك فى ذلك * واذا قُدّم لك بُضيعة من ارنب قد خنق مذ شهر وعلّق فى الهوآ حتى انتن فاثنى على الارض التى نشا فيها جنس هذا الحيوان النفيس وعلى خانقه وطابخه * واذا رايت شيخا ذا وقار وهيبة يخدم عجوزه فلا تنكرى ذلك كما انكره بعض الشعرآ المفرّكين بقوله

the expedient that strangers here make use of to gain their affection and win their goodwill; I know many who have used it to their advantage.

"'Next, if we are invited to a banquet at the home of one of their great **4.11.9**
men, you must take care to eat here before you go, for the guests don't eat their fill in the homes of their hosts but fill themselves up before they eat. And just as it is considered good manners on the part of the host in our country to force his guest to eat and to swear on his head, his beard, and his mustache that his guest must eat a chicken thigh or six meatballs or to stuff the same into his mouth, so, among them, it is considered good manners for the host to keep a watch on every movement of the guest's jaw and hands so as to know whether he's a wolfer or a pouncer and a pecker, and whenever at table a mouth moves, or a hand'—here she interrupted me and said, 'or a waist' to which I responded, 'or a rump, or indeed any part of the body whatsoever'—'you must say to the owner of the moving part, "You are to be thanked for that! You are to be praised! You are to be lauded! You are to be commended! You have done well! You are too kind! You are most gracious!" and other stuff designed to proclaim the lowly status, humility, despicableness, insignificance, abjection, baseness, obsequiousness to and exaltation of the other,(1) and the self-abasement, of or by the guest, in comparison to the elevated status, might, sublimity, grandiosity, nobility, generosity, and pride of the host.

(1) "'*haṭrah* is "the obsequiousness of the poor man toward the rich" and *kafr* is the adulation by the Persian of his king.

"'Also, never, ever, extend your hand to a bottle of wine or bowl of food to **4.11.10**
take what you want from them, for to do so would be a violation of the sanctity of the table, the gathering, and the village, nay, of the whole kingdom. You have to wait for the host to be generous enough to urge you to do so, and should he offer you a fragment of meat from a rabbit that was strangled a month ago and has been hanging in the air till it has gone rotten, praise the soil on which such a precious animal and its species was raised, as well as the one who strangled it and the one who cooked it. Should you behold a dignified and venerable old man serving an old woman, do not condemn this, as a certain misogynistic poet did when he said

ورُبَّ عجوزٍ تحاكى السَّعالِى   تُشيرُ وتنهَى وتامر امرا
يقابلها شيخها بأمتثال   ويسعى لخدمتها مستمرّا
وتقعد تحكى كلاما سخيفا   ومستمعوها يقولون سحرا
تقول بدارى كلب وهرّ   وللهرّ ذعر اذا الكلب هَرّا
ويرقبنى الهرّ ان كنت اكل يُمنَى ليمنى ويُسرى ليسرى
وبنتىَ ليزَى تؤاسيه مما   لديها فمنها يلازم حجرا
وقدكان عندى من قبلُ جروٌ   تلوّن بطنا وصدرا وظهرا
وكنت عليه لفى غاية الحر   ص اسقيه ملء كؤوسىَ دَرّا
فجآت عزيزة قوم الينا   فرامته منى والعين شَكْرَى
وكان ينام على فخذىّ   ويلحس رُفغى اذا ما استبطرّا
وكان فلان اتانىَ عام كذا بجُرَىّ فما عاش شهرا
وتسأل ان تنسَ تاريخ ذاك النهار المعظم زيدا وعمرا
الى ان قال * فاما النسآ فمما اختصصن به اكل ما اشبه التين نحرا ١١،١١،٤
وياكلن والراح منهن بالجلد مستترات ويمضغن سرّا
وتسمع للشاى قرقرة من   معاهن تحكى هنا قرَّ قرّا
وتأخذ فى صحنها بالمشكّة قدرا من اللحم يشبه ظفرا
فتعلكه برهة من زمان   ليمرأ من بعد ان يتهرّا

Many an old woman who looks like a demon
   Gestures to, forbids, and commands
Her old man, who stands before her submissively
   And strives without ceasing to fulfill her demands.
She sits talking nonsense
   And her listeners say, "Enchanting!"
She says, "At home I have a dog and a cat.
   The cat panics if the dog starts snarling.
He watches me as I eat—
   Eyes right if I use my right hand, eyes left if I use the other,
And he sticks to my daughter Liza's lap
   Because she shares with him from her portion what's left over
And once I had—with different colors
   On belly, chest, and back—a pup
And took the greatest care of him
   And gave him milk in a cup.
Then the Dear Queen came to me
   And though my eyes were full of tears she begged him from me—
He would sleep on my thighs
   And lick my armpit when he stretched out his body[150]
And in such and such a year so-and-so brought me a little whelp
   But it died and for only a month did it tarry"
And if she's forgotten the date of that momentous day
   She'll ask every Tom, Dick, and Harry . . .

"'and so on until he gets to 4.11.11

Women have made an art, among other things,
   Of eating things like figs by slicing them in cross section
And they eat, their hands concealed
   In skins,[151] and chew with circumspection,
And the tea emits burbling sounds,
   Like hens cluck-clucking, from their bowels
And she spears[152] on her plate portions
   Of meat the size of parings of fingernails
And champs on them for a while
   So that they will slip down after disintegrating,

وزوج المضيف تقول له خذ   عـزيزى مـما امـامك وَذْرا
فيشكرهـا ويقول لقـد كثر الفضـل مـنك عـلىّ ودرّا
وتجلس تقسم اكل الضيوف   فتعطيك من ذاك نزرا فنزرا
وفى كل نزر تنال تطاطى   ءراسك رغما وتشكر شكرا
وان يك لونان قالت لك اختر   نصـيبك مـما هنّـا وتحرّا
كان لم يجز بين ذينك جمع   كانك ناكح اختـين تَتْـرى

فقالت هذا تكليف فوق الطاقة فما انا بالذائقة عندهم شيا ولوكان المنّ والسلوى *
قلت ومع ذلك فهم ذوو محامد شهيرة * وفضائل كثيرة * ليست فى غيرهم من ١٢،١١،٤
الافرنج * منها انجاز الوعد وصدق الوفآ فى الحضرة والغيبة * وتوفية اجر من يعمل لهم ومراعاة حرمته اى اكرامه لا انهم يعفّون عن زوجته * قالت لا تتكلف التفسير فما ذلك بشذوذ عن القاعدة * قلت ومنها انهم قليلو الكلام كثيرو الفعل * حسنو المعاطاة للامور بالترتيب والسياسة * والرشد والكياسة * ومن ياتِ الى بلادهم فلا يسال عن جَواز ولا اجازة * ولا يهمّه ان كان جاره قاضى القضاة او وزير الوزرآ او شرطيا او جلوازا * ولا يخاف ان يسكن دارا او يدخل مثابة فيها بعض الشرطة فيرهقوه بكلام ونحوه مما يكون سببا فى سجنه او
غرامته * فكل الناس فى الحقوق البشرية عندهم متساوون * هذا وانهم يحبّون ١٣،١١،٤
الغريب ما خلا اوباشهم * ويشفقون على الفقير ويغيثون المحتاج * ويكرمون ذوى السيادة والمجد ويعرفون قدر ذوى العلم * ويعينون على ادراك العلوم والمعارف فى البلاد الاجنبية * وعندهم جمعيات منعقدة لاجرآ كل نفع وخير * وازالة كل شر وضير * وكثير من الاطبآ هنا يداوون المرضى مجانا ما عدا المستشفيات المبثوثة فى

And the host's wife says to him, "Take, my dear,
A morsel from what's before you waiting"
And he thanks her and says, "I owe you so much
For your generosity and being so clever!"
And she sits and divides up the food for the guests
And hands it out, sliver by sliver,
And with each sliver you get you must bob
Your head and say "Thank you!" without protest
And if there are two kinds, she'll tell you, "Take
Your due of what you find tastiest and choose the one you like the best"
As though it weren't allowed to combine the two—
As though if you did so, you'd be screwing two sisters in a row.'

"Said the Fāriyāqiyyah, 'That's too much to cope with. I'm never going to put anything in my mouth in their homes, even if they're having manna and quails.'

"I said, 'Despite this, they have many qualities *well-known* and virtues 4.11.12
to which they may *own*, ones not to be found among the other Franks. Among these are the honoring of promises and punctuality in both arriving and departing, payment in full of the wages of any who works for them and respect for his privacy (meaning, treating him decently, not sparing his wife their attentions).'[153] 'Don't bother to explain,' she said. 'There's nothing exceptional in that.' 'Another virtue of theirs,' I said, 'is that they say little but do a lot, and are good at dealing with matters with order and *diplomacy*, good sense and *sagacity*. One who comes to their country is not asked whether he has a passport or a permit and it will not worry him if his neighbor is the chief judge or the prime minister or a police officer or a constable; he will not fear that, should he live in a house or enter a place frequented by policemen, they will wear him out with questions and suchlike that may lead to his going to prison or paying a fine, for in their country everyone enjoys the same rights inasmuch as they are all human beings.

"'Moreover, the rabble aside, they love strangers, are compassionate to 4.11.13
the poor, and go to the aid of those in need. They honor the eminent and the celebrated and know the value of the scholar. They support the acquisition of the sciences and general knowledge in foreign countries and have societies that have been formed for the putting into practice of all that is useful and beneficial and the eradication of all that is evil and injurious. Many physicians

كل قطر وصقع من بلادهم * ومن ينزل نزلا لديهم او يستاجر غرفة فى منازلهم فان صاحبة المنزل تؤانسه وترفق به وتحفّه وترفّه وتمرّضه * وتدعوه الى مسامرتها ومجالستها من غير ان يستآء زوجها لذلك * واذا اتفق وقتئذ ان زارها بعض معارفها تعرّفهم به وتنوّه باسمه * وانه اذا قدم الى بلادهم احد بكتاب توصية احتفل به الموصَّى ودعاه الى منزله وجعل اسمه نَبَها عند اخوانه ومعارفه * ولا يدع شيا فى وسعه الا ويبذله لراحته ورفاهيته ونخله له الود والنصح حاضرا وغائبا * فرُقعة وَصاةٍ بيد صاحبها تفيزه عندهم باب وام واهل واخوان * وفى الجملة فان كفّة محامدهم ترجح كفّة مذامّهم * وليس الكامل الا الله وحده سبحانه وتعالى * وليس شى من هذه المزايا الحميدة موجودا فى غيرهم من الافرنج لان غيرهم محّاحون ملثّون مراوغون * ذوو ايادى مغلولة والسنة مطلقة * فهم ليسوا كاصحابنا فى الرشد
والاستقامة ولا مثلنا فى الانس والكرم * قالت قد فهمت هذا كله فينبغى ان نعود ١٤،١١،٤
الى تفسير البيتين بشرط ان لا تاتى بشى من عندك فانى اعرف تزيّدك فى الكلام * قلت كانك تقولين انى ذو فضول غير فعول كما ذكرت ذلك غير مرة * قالت اذا كنت قد الفته فما يضرك الان والّا فعدّها فلتة * قلت دونك تفسيرهما من دون تزبّب

قم عجلا قم سؤلى عندك وابلغ اربا منها جهدك
فلقد ضجرت ولها بعل يبغى ان يعسلها بعدك

فقالت انت قلت ان الشاعر يشكو من امراة وها هو يشكو من نفسه * وليس المراة بملومة على ضجرها فى مثل هذه الحال * قلت لمثلك تلقى مقاليد الشرح * قالت ومنه يرجى تخفيف البَرْح *

here treat the sick without charge, and that's to say nothing of the hospitals that have been set up in every region and district of their country. If a person stays at one of their hotels, or rents a room in one of their houses, the landlady treats him as a friend, keeps him company, coddles and cossets him, nurses him, and invites him to sit with her of an evening and keep her company without her husband thinking there is anything wrong with that. Should some of her acquaintances visit her at such a time, she introduces them to him and sings his praises. If anyone arrives in their country with a letter of recommendation, the addressee makes a fuss over him and invites him to his home and makes his name known to his brethren and acquaintances, sparing no effort to secure his ease and comfort and providing him with disinterested friendship and advice both in his presence and in his absence. A scrap of paper with a commendation in the commender's hand thus gains him a father, mother, family, and brothers. In sum, then, their virtues balance out their vices, and none is perfect but God alone, the Glorious, the Almighty. None of these good points is to be found among the rest of the Franks because the others are disobliging, insincere, and shifty, with hands that are closed and tongues that are loosened, for they are neither like our friends[154] in their good sense and uprightness nor like us in our bonhomie and generosity.'

"'I've grasped all that,' said the Fāriyāqiyyah, 'so let's get back to explaining the two verses above, on condition that you not make anything up, for I know how you love to go to great lengths when talking.' 'You seem to be implying, as you so often have before,' I said, 'that I'm a talker, not a walker.' 'If you've grown used to hearing it,' she retorted, 'it won't do you any harm. If you haven't, consider it a slip of the tongue.' 'Here's the interpretation of them,' I said, 'without further beating about the bush: 4.11.14

Have at it, quickly, have at it! My needs you know,
  So do your best to have your fun!
She is bored and has a husband
  Who wants to screw her once you're done.'[155]

"'You said,' she said, 'that the poet was complaining of a woman but look, he's complaining of himself,[156] and the woman's not to be blamed for being annoyed under such circumstances.' 'To the likes of you,' I said, 'should be tossed the keys of linguistic *interpretation*!' 'From which,' she replied,

'may be expected relief
after *tribulation*.'"

الفصل الثانى عشر

فى خواطر فلسفية

١،١٢،٤ ثم لما مضت مدة على الفارياقية فى بلاد الفلاحين حيث لا انس للغريب ولا حظ غير خضرة الارض عيل صبرها وضاق صدرها وعرتها السآمة والقلق * فقالت لزوجها ذات يوم * ياللعجب من هذه الدنيا ومن احوالها * واعجب ما فيها هذا الحيوان الناطق الماشى على ظهرها * كيف تمر عليه الليالى والايام والامانى تغره * والامال تشغله وتعلله * وكلما جرى ورآها ليدركها تقدمته وبعدت عنه كظله * وكل يوم يحسب انه فى يومه اعقل منه فى امسه * وان غده يكون خيرا من يومه * قد كنت احسب ونحن فى الجزيرة ان الانكليز احسن الناس حالا * وانعم بالا * فلما قدمنا بلادهم وعاشرناهم اذا فلاّحوهم اشقى خلق الله * انظر الى اهل هذه القرى التى حولنا وامعن النظر فيهم تجدهم لا فرق بينهم وبين الهمج * يذهب الفلاح منهم فى الغداة الى الكد والتعب ثم ياتى بيته مسآء فلا يرى احدا من خلق الله ولا يراه احد * فيرقد فى العشآ ثم يبكر لما كان فيه وهلم جرا * فهو كالآلة التى تدور مدارا محتتنا فلا فى دورانها لها حظّ وفوز ولا فى وقفها راحة * فاذا جا يوم الاحد وهو يوم الفرح واللهو فى جميع الاقطار لم يكن له حظّ سوى الذهاب الى الكنيسة * فيمكث فيها ساعتين كالصنم يتثاب ساعة ويرقد اخرى ثم يعود الى بيته * فليس عندهم مثابة ولا موضع للسَمَر والطرب *

Chapter 12

Philosophical Reflections

After the Fāriyāqiyyah had stayed a while in the land of the peasants, where there was no solace for the stranger and nothing pleasant but the greenery, her patience wore thin, her heart became oppressed, and she was overcome by ennui and anxiety. One day, she said to her husband, "How strange is this world and its ways, the strangest thing in it being this rational beast that walks upon its surface! How strange that no matter how many nights and days pass over him, his desires delude him, while his hopes beguile and distract him in vain, and no matter how hard he runs to catch up with them, they stay ahead of him and keep the same distance from him as his shadow! Each day he believes that he is smarter than he was the day before and that the next day will be better than this. I used to think, when we were on the island, that the English were the happiest of people and enjoyed the greatest peace of mind. But when we came to their country and lived among them, lo and behold, their peasants turned out to be the most wretched of God's creatures. Look at the inhabitants of the villages around us and scrutinize them well and you will see that they are no different from savages. A peasant of theirs sets off in the morning to toil and travail, then returns to his house in the evening without having seen any other human being and without any having seen him. At night he lies down to sleep and the next day he gets up early to more of the same, and so it continues. He is like a machine that turns at an even pace: it has neither gain nor pleasure in its turning nor rest when it comes to a stop, for when Sunday—the day for joy and recreation in all parts of the world—comes, the only pleasure the peasant may enjoy is to go to church, where he sits for a couple of hours like a booby, yawning for 4.12.1

وليست ايضا عيشة المتمولين فى الريف بانعم من عيشة الفلاحين اذ لا يعرفون من ٢،١٢،٤
المطاعم غير الشِوآ وهذا القلقاس * ولكن هيهات اين المتمولون فى القرى * فانك
لا ترى فيها مثريا الا القسيس وخولىّ الارض وهو الذى يضمن المزارع والحقول
من مالكها * وهما ايضا بمثابة الفلاحين * ومع ذلك فاذا دخلت قصور الملوك
وطفت فى اسواق المدن وعاينت ما فيها من الصنائع البديعة والتحف العجيبة
والالات الظريفة والفرش النفيس والثياب الفاخرة والاوانى المحكمة ولا سيما
مدينة لندن * علمت ان صناعها هم القائمون بالدنيا وهم منها محرومون * فان
داب الصانع كداب الفلاح من جهة انه يشقى ويكدّ النهار كله ولا حظّ له فى الليل
سوى اغماض عينيه * فكيف يزين هذا الصنف من الناس هذه الدنيا ويبهجونها
ويعمرونها وهم عطل عنها ومحدودون منها * والمترفون فيها لا يحسنون عمل شى ٣،١٢،٤
وربما لم يكونوا ايضا يحسنون الكلام * واذا كان الناس عباد الله فى ارضه على
اختلاف احوالهم ومراتبهم هم كالجسم الواحد باختلاف ما فيه من الاعضآ
الجليلة والحقيرة فلمَ لا يجرى العدل بينهم كما يجرى بين الاعضآ * فان الانسان
اذا اكل شيا او لبس شيا فانما يفعل ذلك لاصلاح الجسم كله * ام يزعم المثرون
اذا وسّعوا على هولآ الضِناك الصعاليك * ونفّسوا عنهم الكرب الذى يكابدونه
من جهد المعيشة ومن عدم قدرتهم على تربية اولادهم انهم يحملونهم على اهمال
شغلهم وعلى تركهم الارض بورا فتتعطل وتمحل فيهلكون جوعا * فما بال ذى الدولة
اذاً يولى المبالغ الجسيمة والجوائز الجزيلة لمن يقلّده عملا ويرقيه مرتبة ولا يخاف ان
يفسد عمله بكثرة ما يعطيه * لا بل ان الفقير اذا كفاه واليِه او سيّده المونة وهو شى
بالنسبة اليه هيّن فانه يودى ما[1] يجب عليه من الخدمة والعمل عن طيب نفس *

---

١ ١٨٥٥: ما ما.

an hour and sleeping for the rest; then he goes home. They have no places of entertainment or spots where they can pass the evening in conversation and good cheer.

“Nor is the life of the better-off in the countryside any better than that of 4.12.2
the peasants, because the only dishes they know are roast meat and those turnips[157] that are everywhere. But where, in fact, are the better-off in the villages? The only rich people you see are the priest and the stewards who look after the farms and fields on behalf of their owners. They too are no different from the peasants. Despite this, if you enter the palaces of their kings and make a tour of the markets in their cities and see with your own eyes the amazing products, marvelous works of art, stylish machines, valuable stuffs, luxurious clothes, and well-made vessels that are there, especially in London, you will realize that the ones who manufacture these things are the ones who make the world go round while they themselves are deprived of them, for the daily life of the worker is no different from that of the peasant in that he goes and labors all day and has nothing to look forward to at night other than the closing of his eyes. How can it be that this sort of person creates the adornments of this world, makes it a delight to live in, and creates its prosperity, while they themselves are excluded from it and have but little share in it?

“Meanwhile, the cosseted rich do nothing well and sometimes cannot 4.12.3
even express themselves properly. If people—God’s creatures on His Earth in all their disparate states and statuses—are like one body with all its different members, noble and lowly, then why does justice not apply among them as it does among the members, given that, if a person eats something or dresses in something, he does so for the good of the body as a whole? Or would the rich claim that, by being more generous to those good-for-nothing weaklings and relieving them of the distress they suffer from the effort of making a living and their inability to raise their children, they would cause them to neglect their work and leave the land uncultivated, so that it become unworkable and turn to desert and they perish of hunger? If that is the case, why do rulers allocate vast sums and magnificent rewards to those whom they appoint to office and promote in rank without fearing that they will spoil their work with their largesse? In fact, if the poor man is compensated by his ruler or master with his provisions—which are a trifle to the

ويدعو له بزيادة الخيرات والبركات بدل ما انه يبيت الليالى شابحا يديه بالدعآ عليه * لتيقّنه ان حقه ضائع عنده وان هزاله وضواه ذاهب فى تسمين غيره * وفى حمله على البطر والعتو واقتنآ ما لا تلزم قنيته من الخيول المطهمة والمراكب النفيسة والاثاث المنضد * فياكل الغنى لقمته والحالة هذه مغموسة بدعآ الفقير
٤،١٢،٤ عليه * ام يحسبون ان الله تعالى انما خلق الفقرآ لخدمتهم فقط * لعمرى ان حاجة الغنى الى الفقير اشد من حاجة الفقير الى الغنىّ * ام يانفون من النظر من مقامهم الرفيع السامى الى ذوى الضعة والخمول خشية ان يسرى اليهم من بؤسهم ما يسوءهم * كمن ارتقى شرفا باذخا وتحته هوّة عظيمة فهو يابى من ان يتطاطا وينظر اليها لئلاّ يلحقه من ذلك دوار او غشيان فيهبط من شرفه * ليت شعرى هل جرّب الاغنيآ حينا من الدهر ان يسعدوا الشقى بمالهم وينعشوه برفدهم * ثم وجدوه مقابلا نعمتهم عليه بالكفران والبطالة وباهمال ما فرض عليه من قِبَل الله والطبيعة * وانما هو محض وَهْم دخل فى رؤسهم مع الرحيق فخرج هذا ولم يخرج ذاك * اَلَا فليمكّنوه من ان يذوق لذة العيش ويرى الدنيا كما هى عليه شهرا واحدا فى عمره فى الاقل او يوما فى العام حتى يموت راضيا قرير العين * واذا كانوا يخشون منه الفساد لكسله وتعطّله فخوفهم من فساد نيته لفقره ومن كراهته اياهم اَوْلَى * لان الشقاوة ادعى الى الفساد من السعادة * اَلا ترى الى هولآ الالوف من البنات اللاى يجرين فى اسواق لندن وجميع المدن العامرة باخلاق من الثياب * كيف يتهافتن على الرائح والغادى رجآ ان ينلن ما يتقوّتن به ويتجمّلن به من الثياب * ولا سيما هولآ النواشى اللاى لم يبلغن بعدُ من العمر خمس عشرة سنة * فهذا لعمرى الاهتجان بعينه * فكيف يعيبون علينا هذه العادة فى بلادنا وهى مستعملة عندنا على وجه الحلال وعندهم بالحرام * فلو كنّ مكفيات

latter—he will perform whatever service or work he has to with enthusiasm. He will pray God grant the latter more good fortune and blessings rather than spend his nights, arms raised to heaven, calling down curses on him because of his certainty that he will never give him his due and that what has been taken from him to make him thin and scrawny has gone to others to make them fat and encourage them in their wantonness and arrogance and in the acquisition of purebred horses, fine carriages, and stacks of furniture such as no man should own. Under such circumstances, the rich man eats his food dipped in the curses of the poor.

"Or do they imagine that the Almighty created the poor just to serve 4.12.4
them? I swear, the rich need the poor more than the poor need the rich. Or do they refuse to look down, from their sublime and elevated station, on the humble and the obscure for fear lest something of the latter's misery touch them and do them harm—like one who achieves some lofty height while at his feet lies a vast chasm, which he refuses to bend over and look into lest it make him feel dizzy or nauseous and he fall from his pedestal? Would that I knew whether the rich have ever attempted to make the wretched happy by giving them something of their wealth or reviving them with their aid and then found that they rewarded their kindness with ingratitude, refusal to work, and neglect of their duties before God and nature. Such an idea is simply a delusion that has entered their heads with their wine, the former remaining when the latter departs. Let the rich give the poor the opportunity to taste the sweetness of life and see the world as it really is for just one month out of their lives, or for one day in the year, so that they may die happy and gratified! The rich, rather than fearing that some evildoing may result from the leisure or unemployment of the poor, would do better to fear the evil intentions that they may harbor as a result of their poverty and their hatred of them, for wretchedness is more conducive to evil than happiness. Have you not seen the thousands of girls who run around the markets of London and other prosperous cities in rags? How they crowd around those who come and go hoping to obtain the means to buy food or clothes to make themselves pretty, especially the young ones who are still not fifteen? This, I swear, is no more or less than exploitation of children for sex! How can they blame us for this custom in our countries when it is practiced among us in the form of legitimate marriage and among

المؤنة لما فعلن ذلك * لان البنت فى هذا الحدّ من السنّ لا تكرع الى الرجال * ولا تضبع للبعال * ولا سيما فى البلاد الباردة * ولَسَلِم من كيدهن وتهافتهن[١] جشعا الى المال اناس كثيرون جلب عليهم شرههم اليهن مضارّ كثيرة * وما عدا ذلك فان هولآ البنات الحسان لوكانت الدولة واهل الكنيسة يُعنَون بتجهيزهن بما يقدرهن على الزواج الشرعى بعد تربيتهن وتهذيبهن * لكُنَّ يلدن الاولاد الصباح فيزيّنّ المملكة باثمار ارحامهن كما تقول التوراة * بخلاف ما اذا بقين على حالة السفاح فما يتولد منهن الا الخبائث والرذائل * فهن كالشجرة الناضرة التى فضلا عن كونها لا تثمر تَلْثَى بالسمّ الناقع لمن تذوّقها * وكم لعمرى من بنت حبلت اوّل مرّة من مبادى شوطها فى ميدان العهر * ثم اسقطت جنينها خوف الفقر * وان منهن لمن تلد فى طرق المدينة فى ليالى الشتآ الباردة لعدم ماوًى لها * او انها تبيت مع بنت اخرى على فراش واحد وهى عادة مستفيضة فى لندن * وذلك لعدم قدرتها على ان تستقلّ بفراش وِكِنٍّ خاصّ بها * فلا تامن والحالة

٥،١٢،٤ هذه من ان يلحقها اذى من ضجيعتها ليلاً * نعم ان اولاد الزنا ياتون فى الغالب شياطمة جبابرة كيفتاح الجلعادى الذى حلّ عليه روح الرب فانقذ اسرائيل من بنى عمون * وكولِّيم الفاتح الذى فتح هذه البلاد اى بلاد الانكليز * الا ان النفع الاكثرى مع الاقتصاد والاعتدال * احق بالمراعاة والتقديم من النفع الاندرىّ مع الاسراف والإِرْغال(١) اليس يعاب صاحب ارض اريضة يغادرها بورا ومتمرغا للوحوش * او صاحب اشجار مثمرة يتركها دون سياج ولا ناطور عرضة لنهم كل متفكّه * نعم لا ينكران وجود الغنى والفقير فى الدنيا لا بدّ منه كوجود الجميل والقبيح * ولولا ذلك لوقف الكون عن الحركة

(١) الإِرغال وضع الشي فى غير موضعه وهى لعمرى جديرة بالاشتهار والاستعمال

١ ١٨٥٥: وتهافتن.

them in the form of illicit relations? If these girls had sufficient sustenance they would not behave so, because a girl at that age has no desire for a man and no craving for intercourse, especially in cold countries, and many men whose lust for them has brought them great harm would be saved from their wiles and their greedy pursuit of money. Moreover, were the state and the clergy to take it upon themselves to set them up with enough money for them to equip themselves for a legitimate marriage—after first giving them some education and polish—they would bear bonny children and adorn the kingdom with the fruit of their wombs, as it says in the Old Testament.[158] Contrarily, if they continue to practice fornication, they will give birth only to rascals and scoundrels and will be like green saplings that not only do not bear fruit but also ooze a poison that puts an end to the thirst of any who taste it. How many a girl, I swear, has become pregnant the moment she set foot in the arena of whoredom and has then aborted the fetus from fear of poverty! Some of them, for lack of any shelter, give birth on the city's streets during the cold nights of winter or spend the night on a single bed with another girl—a custom widespread in London—for lack of means to acquire a bed and a cubbyhole of her own. Under such circumstances, she may fall victim to some harm from her bedmate.

“True, illegitimate children usually grow up to be mighty men and giants, 4.12.5
like Jephthah the Gileadite, upon whom the spirit of the Lord descended and who saved Israel from the children of Ammon,[159] or William the Conqueror, who conquered these lands (meaning England); yet it is more right and proper to heed and advance the common good with thrift and *moderation* than that of the individual with extravagance and *misallocation*.(1) Should not the owner of fine productive lands who leaves them uncultivated and a place for wild animals to wallow be censured and likewise the owner of fruit-bearing trees who leaves them unfenced, unguarded, and prey to the depredations of every passing fruit fancier? True, it cannot be denied that the existence of rich and poor in this world is as unavoidable as the existence of beauty and ugliness; were it not so, the universe would cease to move and men's affairs would come to a standstill, or so the theologians assert.[160] However, we speak here of that

(1) *irghāl* [“misallocation”] is “the placing of something in other than its correct place,” and is, I swear, a word that deserves to become well-known and much used.

وتعطلت المصالح كما افاده المتكلمون * الا ان الكلام هنا فى الفقر الذى لا يقال
فيه انه عيش مؤدٍّ الى الشره والبطر * لا فى الفقر المدقع الذى يلقى الهموم والاحزان
الدائمة فى قلب صاحبه * فيفضى به مرة الى الانتحار ومرة الى الاغراق او الخنق
كما شاع فعل ذلك فى هذه البلاد * اليس من العار على الرجال فى هذه الارض ٦،١٢،٤
ارض العلوم والصنائع والتمدن والتحضّر انهم لا يتزوجون المراة الا اذا كان عندها
الجهازان * واقبح من ذلك ان الكبرآ هنا لا يتزوجون عن حبّ بل عن طمع فى زيادة
المال * فان من كان دَخْله مثلاً مائة دينار فى كل يوم يريد ان يتزوج من دخلها
مائة دينار ايضا تماما * ولو كان تسعة وتسعين لم يصح * ولذلك فكثيرا ما ترى
شابا جميلا قد تزوج نَصَفاً شوهآ * وهيهات فان الرجال هنا اكثرهم مصاييف *
اى لا يتزوجون الّا اذا دخلوا فى حيّز الكهول * فيقضون شبابهم فى السفاح
ومن حدّ الثلثين الى الاربعين فى البحث عمن عندها جِدَة وغنى * وتبقى الجميلة
الفقيرة كاسدة وما عليهم من الاِصافة من عار * مع ان مراعاة الولد فى حق
الزوجة من اعظم الاسباب الباعثة على الزواج على ما ذهب اليه الربانيون *
وان يكن توزيغ الولديتمّ بمرة واحدة فى مدة تسعة اشهر * اعنى ان اولاد النَصَف
الشوهآ لا ياتون صباحا اصحّآ كاولاد الفتيّة الجميلة * وفضلا عن ذلك فان من
تزوج وهو فى سن ثلثين سنة مثلا امراة فى سن ثمانى عشرة فمتى بلغ الخمسين
وكانت امراته بعدُ لَفُوتا متلجة كان له من ولده رقيب عليها * فلاى شى زيادة
المال لمن اغناه الله بفضله * ومن يكن له فى كل يوم مائة دينار فما الفرق بينه وبين
من له خمسون او عشرون * فان من لم يكتف بهذا القدر لم يكفه ملء الارض
ذهبا * هذا وان المراة اذا كانت غنية فلا بدّ وان يتبع غناها عنآ * لانها تتعمّدِ
الولائم والمآدب والمحافل وان تزور وان تزار * وان تتخذ لها من الخدّام من تقر

poverty that cannot be described as conducive to savagery and wantonness, not of the abject poverty that creates constant worries and sorrows in its sufferer's heart and that leads him in some instances to cut his own throat or in others to drown or hang himself, as has become commonplace in these countries.

“Is it not a shame upon the men in this land—the land of science, industry, urbanization, and civilization—that they will marry a woman only if she is well-endowed in both senses?[161] Uglier still is the fact that the great men here do not marry for love but out of greed for more money: a man whose income is one hundred guineas a day will want to marry a woman whose income is also precisely one hundred guineas; if it's ninety-nine it won't do. This is why you often see handsome young men married to ugly middle-aged women. Unfortunately, most of the men here are late marriers, meaning that they don't marry until they've reached later middle age. Thus they spend their youth in fornication and their thirties in looking for a woman possessed of position and wealth while the poor but beautiful woman is left on the shelf, and the men feel no shame at having children when they are old—this despite the fact that the raising of children under a wife's care is one of the most important reasons for marriage according to the divines and that conception takes place only once every nine months. What I'm getting at is that the children of raddled middle-aged women will not turn out bonny and healthy like those of beautiful young girls. In addition, when a man who gets married at the age of, say, thirty, to a woman aged eighteen, reaches fifty and his wife still has a roving eye and is randy, he will have his children to keep an eye on her. What use is more money to one whom God through His bounty has already made rich? What difference is there between a person who has a hundred guineas a day and one who has fifty, or twenty? Anyone who isn't satisfied with such an amount will not be satisfied with all the gold in the world. Furthermore, if a woman be rich, trouble is bound to follow on her wealth, because she will resolve to throw banquets, feasts, and parties, to visit and be visited, and to hire servants whose lustiness and blooming good looks appeal to her eye, and the moment she feels an ache or a pain in any of her limbs, she'll make out that she feels ill and conceive a notion to go abroad, or to the country, and there, while her husband is preoccupied with 4.12.6

عينها بترارته وبضاضته * وكلما اختلج منها عضو تمارضت وتوحّمت على السفر او
الارافة * وهناك حالة كون زوجها فائر الدماغ بالامور السياسية او البواعث
المالية فى مقره تخلو بمن تخلو* وتلهو بمن تلهو * وبيد خادمها من الدينار ما
يعمى عينه ويصمّ اذنه ويقطع لسانه * اليس هولآ الاغنيآ يُمنَون بالامراض والادوآ ٤،١٢،٧
كالفقرآ * اليس الموت يفاجئهم وهم فى غمرة لذاتهم منهمكون * وان كثيرا منهم
لسرفهم ورُغبهم ونهمهم وفسادهم واستهتارهم فى الشهوات يموت عن غير
ولد * او انه اذا رزق ولدا يعيش ما عاش ضاويا نحيفا شقوة له وكمدا على ابويه *
وقد قال احد مولّفيهم ان من ترى من اولاد الاعيان والامرآ هنا تارّا قويا فانما
هو من القاح بعض الحشم * وترى اولاد الفلاحين صباحا اقويآ يلهمون الرطب
واليابس * ولعمرى لولم يكن لهم هذا الجزآء من الله تعالى اى رؤية اولادهم حولهم
معافين محبّبين لكانوا فى عداد الموتى * كيف بُنى هذا العالم على الفساد * كيف ٤،١٢،٨
يشقى فيه الف رجل بل الفان ليسعد رجل واحد * وایّ رجل * فقد يكون له
قلب ولا رحمة * ويدان ولا عمل * وراس ولا رشد ولا نهية * وكيف يقع
هذا فى هذه البلاد التى ضربت بعدلها الامثال * لا جرم ان فلاحى بلادنا اسعد
من هولا الناس * بل التجار هنا اشقيآ على غناهم وثروتهم * فان احدهم يقضى
النهار كله وهزيعاً من الليل واقفا على قدميه * وقد سالت واحدا مرة فقلت له لمَ لا
تقعد على كرسى وعندك كراسى كثيرة * فقال لى انها للذين يشرفوننا بالزيارة ليشتروا
من عندنا * فاذا قعدت مثلهم صرت منهم * فاما فى يوم الاحد فيلبثون خَدِرى
الابدان والافكار * سَدرى البصائر والابصار * فاين هذا من التاجر عندنا
يعقف احدى رجليه على الاخرى بعض ساعات على اريكته * ثم اذا حان العصر
كبَّب جبته ورآه وذهب الى بعض المنازه وهو يمشى الخُيَلآء * فان كان التمدّن

political affairs or economic issues in his town house, she will closet herself with whomever she wishes and disport herself with whomever she likes, her manservant finding in his hand enough gold coins to shut his eyes, close his ears, and seal his lips.

"Do not these rich persons suffer the same diseases and illnesses as the poor? Does not death surprise them while they are engrossed in their pleasures? Do not many of them die childless as a result of their intemperance, their desires, their avarice, their corruption, and the recklessness with which they pursue their lusts? Or, if they be blessed with children, do not these live out their short lives thin and famished with hunger, a misery to themselves and an inconvenience to their parents? An English writer has said that any vigorous, strong child of their great men or princes one may come across is the result of impregnation by one of their retainers. The children of the peasants, on the other hand, you will find to be bonny and strong, with the appetites of horses, and I swear, if their parents didn't have this reward from the Almighty, namely the sight of their children around them, in lively good health and full of affection, they would be no better than dead. 4.12.7

"How did this world come to be built on immorality? How is it that a thousand, or two thousand, men must suffer here for one man to be happy? And what a man! He may have a heart but no mercy, two hands but no work, a head but no sense or brains. And how did this come about in this country whose justice is the stuff of proverbs? There can be no denying that the peasants of our country are better off than these people. Indeed, even the shopkeepers here are in a miserable state despite their wealth, for one will spend the entire day and part of the night on his feet. I asked one once and said, 'Why don't you sit on a chair, of which you have many?' and he told me, 'Those are for the people who honor us by visiting us in order to buy from us. If I were to sit like them, I would become one of them.' They pass their Sundays benumbed of body and mind, brains and eyes alike in a daze. What a contrast with a shopkeeper at home, who crooks one leg over another for a few hours on his bench, then, towards the end of the afternoon, casts his mantle in a heap behind him, and goes to some pleasure garden, walking proudly. If civilization and knowledge are the cause of these things, then ignorance is bliss. 4.12.8

والعلم قد سبّب هذا فالجهل اذاً سعادة * غير ان الفلاحين هنا فى غاية الجهل ٩،١٢،٤
زيادة على بؤسهم * ومن اين ياتيهم العلم وهم ملازمون للكدّ والترّح وليس عندهم
مدارس * قد كنت اظن انهم جميعا يحسنون القرآة والكتابة فاذا هم لا يحسنون
النطق بلغتهم * فانى اقرا فى الكتاب شيا واسمعه منهم مخالفا لحقيقة استعماله *
وناهيك ان اكثرهم لا يعرف اسم بلادنا ولا جنسنا * وقد قيل لاحدهم مرّة ان الملك
امر بتسفير خيل فى سفن لحرب العدو * فقال انى اعجب كيف يقاتل الناس فى
البحر على الخيل * وكانّى بهم لجهلهم يحسبون ان سكان الارض باسرها دونهم *
او يظنون ان الرجال فى غير البلاد يبيعون نساهم او ياكلونهن اكلا * او انهم
يتقوّتون بالجذور والبقول * ولو انهم عرفوا احوال الامم وخصائص البلدان لعلموا
انه لو كان لهم من لذات العيش اضعاف ما لنا مع شدة بردهم ومنكر هوائهم
ودكنة جوّهم لما وفى ذلك لهم * وان غَنآ الصنعة عندهم لا يقوم مقام غنآ الطبيعة
عندنا من طيب الهوآ والمآء وصفآ الجوّ وزكآ الارض وعَذْوها ومرائتها ولذة المطعوم
والمشروب والتنزه فى الرياض والحدائق * والاكل عند المياه الجارية تحت الاشجار
الناضرة * والتردّد على الحمامات والسهر فى السَمَر واستماع الات الطرب * يعرف
ذلك منهم من زار بلادنا والِف حظّنا ونعيمنا * غير ان اللبيب مَن استخرج من ١٠،١٢،٤
كل ضرّ نفعا * واعتبر بكل ما جرى عليه فاستفاد وارعوى * قد تعلمت الان
مما لقيت من الوحشة والتقشف فى بلادهم كيف اعيش فى بلادنا ان رجعت اليها
سالمة * وكيف ان الطخطخة والقرقرة والهزر والكركرة والتجلق والهرهرة والاغراب
والكدكدة والاَهى والهزرقة والانزاق والزغربة وطيخ طيخ وعِيط عيط وتِغ تغ وهاه
هاه لاَفَرَج للهمّ عن القلب من اوانى موضونة ومبانى مرصونة * فخير البلاد ما
الفت هوآها والفيت فيها مخلصا لك ودّه * وكيف يكون خلوص الود من دون

"Not to mention that the peasants here are not only wretched but also extremely ignorant—though how are they to acquire knowledge when they spend all their time toiling to provide for their families and there are no schools where they live? I used to think that they could all read and write well, but it turns out that they do not even speak their own language well. I read something in a book and hear it from them in a form that contravenes its proper usage, not to mention that most of them have never heard the name of our country or our race. One of them once heard that the king had ordered horses to be sent overseas on ships to make war against his enemy and he said, 'I'm amazed that people can fight on horses at sea'! It seems to me that in their ignorance they believe everyone else in the world to be less than they, or they think that men in other countries sell their womenfolk, or eat them, or that they live on a diet of roots and greens. If they knew the conditions of other nations and the peculiarities of other lands, they would be aware that even if they had many times what we do, their cold, the unwholesomeness of their air, and the darkness of their skies mean that it would profit them little and that the wealth that they have from manufacturing cannot take the place of the natural wealth that we enjoy by way of sweetness of air and water, clearness of air, sweet-scentedness, healthiness, and wholesomeness of soil, tastiness of food and drink, picnicking in the meadows and gardens, eating next to running waters beneath verdant trees, visits to the bathhouses, and evenings spent in pleasant conversation and listening to musical instruments. Those of them who have visited our country and become familiar with our good fortune and comforts know this. 4.12.9

"The wise person, however, is he who knows how to extract from every reverse some good and, giving thought to all that has befallen him, how to benefit and find lessons for life. I have now learned, from all the loneliness and hardship that I have met with in their country, how to live in ours, should I return to it safely, and how belly laughing, splitting one's sides, laughing like a horse, laughing for no reason, laughing immoderately, laughing oneself silly, peeing oneself with laughter, chuckling, chortling, checkling, kenching, fleering, cackling, cachinnating, and 'ho-ho!' and 'hee-hee!' and 'ha-ha!' and 'tee-hee!' bring the heart greater relief from worry than unbreakable vessels or unshakable buildings. The best of countries, then, is that to whose airs you've become accustomed and in which you've found someone who 4.12.10

كشف السرائر * وكيف تتكشف السرائر وتعلن الضمائر من دون اطلاق اللسان
فى ميدان الكلام * والقوم هنا يتكتّمون ويرون ان فى ذكر الانسان ما يحسّ به
وما يحبه وما يكرهه طيشا وهوجا * انما مَثَلى كمثل الثعلب الذى كان يسمع لطبل
تضربه اغصان شجرة صوتا عظيما * فلما اتاه وعالجه حتى شقه وجده فارغا * لا
جَرَم لا عدت املّك خاطرى سمعى * او كراكب البحر وهو ظمآن يرى المآ حوله
ولا يمكنه ان يروى غليله منه * انى ارى وجه الارض هنا اخضر ولكن لا شى
من هذه الخضرة يبيّض الوجه عند الاكل * اذ ما به من الطَعْب شى * لان كل
ما ينبت عندهم فانما تغصب الارض تنبيته غصبا من افراط التدميل * فلو كان
احد هنا من اللاّطة لسالناه عن طعم بقولهم ما هو * هذا ما عدا خلطهم الماكول ١١،١٢،٤
والمشروب وغشّهم وافسادهم ما منّ الله تعالى به عليهم سائغا طيبا * وناهيك ان
الخبز الذى هو قوام هذا البدن لا طعم له * فانهم يخمّرونه برغوة نبات ويخلطونه
بهذه البطاطة ثم يخفقونه بعد الاختمار خفقا * فماذا يفيد القائل قوله انى كنت فى
بلاد الافرنج وهو لم يجد فيها الا الوحشة والنكد * بل ذكر ذلك له فيما بعد غصّة *
الى مصر الى الشام * الى تونس ذا العام * فهناك تلقى من يزورك او تزوره *
وهناك تلقى البِشْر دون تصلّف والفضل دون توقّف وتكلّف * الى آخر ما ذكرت
لى من التانّف والتافف * لا يطيب العيش للانسان الا اذا كان يتكلم بلغته *
ليس العيش بطول الليالى ولا بكثرة الايام ولا برؤية ارض خضرآ ولا بمشاهدة
ادوات وآلات * وانما هو باغتنام انس الاحباب * وعشرة ذوى الآداب *
الذين تصفو منهم السرائر فى الحضرة والغياب * وتخلص لك مودتهم فى الابتعاد
والاقتراب * انما الدنيا مفاكهه * قال فقلت ومناكهه * قالت ومنادمه * قلت ١٢،١٢،٤
ومشامّه * قالت وملآمه * قلت ومطاعمه * قالت وملاينه * قلت وملاسنه *

is sincere in his love for you—and how can there be sincere love without a baring of secrets and how can secrets be bared and innermost thoughts declared if the tongue isn't let off its leash to run free in the field of speech? Here people keep everything secret and think that for a person to talk of what he feels, loves, and hates is frivolity and folly. I, though, am like the fox who heard a loud noise coming from a drum that was being beaten by the branches of a tree; when he got to it and went to work on it and tore it open, he found it was empty. No wonder then that I no longer surrender my judgment to my hearing. Or, like one at sea who is thirsty and sees water all around him but cannot use it to quench his thirst, I see that the face of the earth here is green but that nothing of that greenness brings a flush of good cheer[162] when eaten because it has nothing appetizing about it, which is because everything that grows in their country is forced out of the soil by over-manuring. If there were a sodomite here, we should ask him what their greens taste like.

"All this is aside from their habit of mixing up solid with liquid food and **4.12.11**
their adulteration and corruption of the palatable foods with which the Almighty has blessed them. Given this, it is only to be expected that the bread, which is the main support of our bodies, has no taste, for they leaven it with a vegetal scum and mix it with those potatoes of theirs, and then, following the leavening, they pat it down. What good is it to one to say, 'I was in the land of the Franks' if all he found there was loneliness and adversity? Quite the opposite: recalling it later may cause him to choke in distress. To Cairo! To Damascus! To Tunis this very year! There you will find people to visit you or whom you can visit. There you will find cheerful faces devoid of flattery, and generosity devoid of restraint or artificiality—and any other words for scorn and contumely you've mentioned to me. A person cannot live happily if he cannot talk in his own language. Life is not to be valued according to the length of its nights or the number of its days, by views of green land, or by observing instruments and machines. Rather, its value lies in seizing the convivial moment with those who are *dear*, keeping company with persons of culture of whom one thinks with pleasure whether they be elsewhere or *here* and whose affection's *sincere* whether they're far or *near*. This world's worth lies in exchanging bon *mots*."

The Fāriyāq went on, "And I said, 'And in breathing on your *nose*!'— **4.12.12**
and she, 'In companionable *carousal*'—'And olfactory *arousal*!'—'In

قالت ومطايبه * قلت ومراضبه * قالت ومخادنه * قلت ومحاضنه * قالت ومرآمه * قلت ومفاغمه * قالت وملاطفه * قلت وملاغفه * قالت ومخالقه * قلت ومعانقه * قالت ومحاضره * قلت ومخاصره * قالت ومباغمه * قلت ومكاعمه * قالت ومعاشره * قلت ومشاعره * قالت ومؤانسه * قلت وملامسه * قالت ومساجله * قلت ومباعله * قالت ومخالطه * قلت ومخارطه * قالت ومطارحه * قلت ومشارحه * قالت ومجارزة * قلت ومراهزة * قالت ومداعبه * قلت ومزاعبه * وهنا كان ختام الملاعبه *

mutual *delectation*'—'And *degustation*!'—'In shared *affection*'—'And lingual *refection*!'—'In having *fun*'—'And letting saliva *run*!'—'In friendship's *charms*'—'And taking you in my *arms*!'—'In granting each other's *wishes*'—'And giving you *kisses*!'—'In kind *consideration*'—'And *osculation*!'—'In talking face-to-*face*'—'And mutual *embrace*!'—'In discussion and *debates*'—'And arms around *waists*!'—'In talking in tones that are *soothing*'—'And lying together in one set of *clothing*!'—'In close *associations*'—'And sleeping together in a single pair of *combinations*!'—'In mutual *stimulation*'—'And *exploration*!'—'In witty *contestations*'—'And conjugal *relations*!'—'In *jesting*'—'And *besting*!'—'In *conversation*'—'And *copulation*!'—'In *banter*'—'And going for a *canter*!'—

'In *joking*'—'And *poking*!'—
and that concluded
our *merrymaking*."

الفصل الثالث عشر

في مقامة ممشية

حدس الهارس بن هشام قال * كنت سمعت كثيرا عن النِسا * حتى كدت أُمنَى ١،١٣،٤
بالنَّسا * فمن قائل ان المحصن اطيب عيشا من العزب * واسلم عاقبة من المزاحمة على منهل دونه مِذَب * او المكابدة لِلَّوب واللهب * او التعرّض للتجبيه والعطب * وانه كلما صدى قلبه من الكُرَب * جلاه بابتسامة من زوجه عن شنب * وارتشافة من رضاب كالضَرَب * وسماع نامة تغنى عن آلات الطرب * ومدام ذات حبب * فان مما خصّ الله تعالى به المراة من المزايا * وفضلها به من السجايا * ان صوتها الرخيم لا يمرد عليه نكد * ولا يبدو معه همّ وكمد * فاول ما تحرك شفتيها * تسكن القلوب اليها * وعند مغازلة عينيها * تنهال المسرات على من هو بين يديها * فيحنبش ويمحّش * ويحفّش وينتعش * ويدركل ويدرقل * ويسجّل ويدوقل * ويحشل ويدربل(١) وحين تمشى فى بيتها متبدّحة * تقول لها الاقدار فديناك من مغناج مرحه * ان شئت رفعنا زوجك الى قرن الغزالة * لينعم بالك باحسن حاله * وان شئت بقاه عندك الليله * لم تُعينا فى ذاك حُوَيلة * وان شئت ان نزيّن له السفر * عاما او اكثر * الى طَرَح ذى اَمْن او خطر *

(١) حنبش رقص ووثب وصفق ونزا ومشى ولعب وحدث وضحك * والمحش شدة النكاح وشدة الأكل * والتحفيش لزوم البيت الصغير * ودرقل رقص وتفحج وتبختر ونحوه دركل وبحشل رقص رقص الزنج *

Chapter 13

A *Maqāmah* to Make You Walk

Al-Ḥāwif ibn Hifām faid in lifping tones,[163] "I'd heard so much about women I almost ended up with *sciatica*, for some say that the life of the married man is better than that of the *bachelor*, one safer in all it *entails* than that of shouldering one's way up to water holes guarded by jealous *males*, or enduring the pangs of thirst and *fire*, or exposing oneself to public disgrace and *ire*; and that, should life's worries coat one's heart with *rust*, a smile from one's spouse revealing pearly teeth in a *line*, a sip of saliva like honey, a voice so sweet it obviates the need for musical instruments or sparkling *wine* will polish off the *dust*. For among the things with which the Almighty has singled out woman by way of *merit*, and virtues that He has seen fit to have her *inherit*, is that no ill temper her sweet voice *resists*, no anxiety or heartsickness with it *coexists*. The moment her lips are *moved*, the heart is *soothed*, and when with flirtatiousness her eyes are *lowered*, whoever's in her presence with pleasures is *showered*, so that he *frolics* and *rollicks*, confines himself to the '*little nest*'[164] and is *refreshed*, *capers* and *caracoles*, stiffens and *comes*, dances like a Negro and bangs on *drums*(1). When she walks through her house in a willowy *fashion*, the fates declare (with *passion*), 'Our lives we'd give for you, you merry coquette! If you'd like us to place your husband on high, like a sun at its highest *position*, so he can keep you in the most pampered *condition*, or you'd like him to stay tonight at your *side*, no stratagem could turn us *aside*. If you'd like us to seduce him with the notion of travel (for a year or *more*) to some place (safe or dangerous) far from this *shore*, all that's needed from 4.13.1

(1) *ḥanbasha* means "to dance, jump, clap, leap, talk, and laugh"; *maḥsh* is "vehemence of intercourse, or of eating"; *taḥfīsh* means "confining oneself to a small chamber"; *darqala* means "to dance, spread one's legs, and strut" and *darkala* something similar; *baḥshala* means "to dance the dance of the Negroes."

فانت لدينا اكرم من نهى وامر * فما عليك الّا نضنضة لسان * او اشارة بنان *
وحسبنا بطرفة عين من بيان * قال وان الزوج متّعه الله باحصانه * وهنّاه ٢،١٣،٤
بنضرة بستانه * وجنى تفاحه ورمانه * وزاده من الآئه واحسانه * يعبث
بحضرة زوجه باللذات كما شا * ان توخّى مسّاً مسّ وان اشتهى نشوة نشا *
وان شآ داعب ولاعب * وان اَبَى الا الجِدّ فالجَدّ طوع له كما احبّ * وان له
منها منزها (ولكن غير بعيد عن المآ) تغيب فيه الاتراح * وتطلع منه الافراح *
وبشائر النجاح * وسِرا تُزَفّ به الدنيا اليه بمعرض بشر * ومِهْدَى كَشَر * ان
التوى عليه امر قوّمته بمهارتها * وسددته باشارتها * وانها اذا تدعّبت عليه ٣،١٣،٤
وتقيّأت * وتبعّلت له وفيّأت * زاده الله نضرة ونعيما * وزادك صبرا وجموما *
خُيّل له انه مَلَك الدنيا بحذافيرها * وفاز بجميع لذاتها وحبورها * وانه قد قام
مقام العاهل الاعظم * خليفة بارى الامم * فلو راى وقتئذ قاضى القضاة مارّا
على بغلته * حسبه من اتباعه وخدمته * ولو راى كاهنا[١] او وافها * لانف
من ان يكلمهما مشافها * فبعث مكانه الى جناب الاول وصيفا والى حضرة
الثانى وصيفة * وقال لهما ان لدىّ لكل فاتح قاهر ولاية شريفة * ولكل سائل
شاكر وظيفة * ولو ان امرءًا اغلظ له وحاشاه فى الكلام * وسفه فبادره بالتقريع
والملام * او راى والعياذ بالله ان يمس له قذالا * ويسومه عليه قَفْدا واذلالا *
فزع الى زوجته اعزّها الله فنفت عنه كل كرب * وامّنته من كل رعب * وردّت
عليه حجْره من حجرها * وصدارته من صدرها * وقالت له لا تخش من كيده
وغِلّه * فانما يدفع كل استحصاف بمثله * فرجع الى ما كان عليه من الانفة
والفخار * والعِزّ والذرار * حتى لو راى قَيْلا او ردفا * لهآءَ بنفسه عن ان ينظر

١ ١٨٥٥: كافها.

you (you being to us the noblest of those who forbid and *command*) is a hiss with your tongue or a sign with your *hand*; a mere wink from your *eye* would make us *comply*.'"

He went on, "Likewise I've heard it said that a husband—God grant him protection from all that's *unchaste*, let him in the greenery of His orchard and the plucking of its apples and pomegranates, and with ever more of His charity and bounty make him *blest*!—can enjoy with his spouse whatever pleasures he likes. If he wants, he can *touch*. If he craves intoxication, that too is not too *much*. If he wishes, he can *fondle* and *trifle*, and if he refuses to be *unserious*, wealth and social standing are at his command *imperious*. Also, that he has in her a fastness *high* (but not *dry*)[165] in which she may his cares *dispel*, from which joy and happiness augur *well*, and a fruitful meadow to which the world beats a *path* with glad tidings on display and offerings fit to make him *laugh*. If some affair of his should go awry, with her skill she'll set it *straight* and with a gesture she'll make it *right*. 4.13.2

"I've heard too that if she flirts with him and throws herself upon his neck, dresses up for him and tosses her *hair*—may God increase him in ease and *opulence* and you in patience and *indulgence*!—he'll think he's gained the world and all that's in it, carried off every pleasure and joy that's *there*, and that he's reached the most elevated of *stations*, that of that most mighty monarch, viceroy to the Creator of *Nations*.[166] Should he at that moment the chief judge, passing on his hinny, *observe*, he'll suppose him one of those employed by him to follow and *serve*, and should he a priest or churchwarden *behold*, the honor of any direct communication he'll *withhold* and send in his stead, to the honored first, a male *flunky*, to the respected second, a lady *lackey* and tell them, 'For any who can conquer and subdue, I have a noble *commission*, for any who inquires as to my well-being or expresses their thanks, a *position*.' Should any man bark at him, cut him dead, or call him a *name*, he'll come right back at him with rough words and *blame*, and should anyone—perish the thought!—cuff his occiput, deal his nape a *thwack*, or subject his feelings to *attack*, he can run to his wife—God grant her strength!—and she'll relieve him of all grief, give him from every terror *rest*, restore his impregnability with her private parts, his prominence with the promontories on her *chest*, and tell him, 'Fear not his wiles and his *spite*: every show of force can be repelled by an equal display of *might*.' He then returns to his former haughtiness and *pride*, his overweeningness and being 4.13.3

اليهما نظر الاكفآ * فهو الراتع المفنَّق * المترف المتملَّق * الآكل وتلقاءه من درر
الثنايا ومرجان الفم * ما يخيّل اليه ان الكامخ خير مطعم * والمسيخ اهنأ مغنم *
وان الاجاج والزعاق * اشهى من مدام الاغتباق * اَلَا ولو انه بات معها على
فرش حشوه شظايا * وماسّ منها زغابة لكان له من اوطأ الحشايا * فكل ضرّ
معها يستحيل الى فَنَع ونفع * وكل شَظَف بقربها فهو قصوف ورَتع * ومن قائل ٤،١٣،٤
لا بل عيش العزب اهنا * وللّذات اجنى * فان السيدات يحسبنه فى كل وقت
ذا جموم * وعندهن ان نبّة واحدة منه تنفى جميع الهموم * اذ ليس له من تلزّه
كل ليلة للعظال * وتؤرّقه هزيعا من الليل على مثل ذى الحال * ليتذكر دائما انه
محصن ذات قُرطق وخلخال * فهو على هذا محبّب عند البنات * محروص عليه من
السيدات المتزوجات * مشار اليه بالبنان من الارامل الهائجات * وانه اذا
رجع الى منزله رجع ويده خفيفة * ورانفته نظيفة * فلا من تقول له هات *
او تلومه على ما فات * ولا من تستوحيه عن المستقبل * وتستفتيه فى مصالح
المَهْبل * ولا من تزجره عند قَيْق غيرها له وحلجه اليها بحَفْ حَفْ * اوتنجفه قبل
مفارقته اياها اىّ نجف * او تقول له نَزاف نزاف * والّا فالازهاف(١) * ولا
من يبكى بين يديه * وهو عاجز عن كفالته كما يحق عليه * فتراه ابد الدهر ميّاحا
مفراحا * متعرضا للنسآ متياحا * شرّاحا سدّاحا *
رفيقا بالمُجّ منهن مساحا * وقد قيل فى الامثال السائرة
سير العَجاج * فى كل فُجاج * من لم يكن ذا زوجة
كان ذا ازواج * قيل فمن ثم كانت خطوات العزب
اوسع * وحركته اسرع * وكلامه انجع * واناؤه اترع *
ونغمته ارخم * ونهمته اضرم * ونهزته اقوى *

(١) القَيْق صوت الدجاجة اذا دعت للسفاد وحلج الديك نشر جناحيه ومشى الى انثاه للسفاد وحف حف زجر للديك والدجاج والنجف منع التيس حتى لا يقدر على السفاد وذلك بان يشد جلد بين بطنه وقضيبه وذلك الجلد يسمى النجاف ونزف مآء البئر نزحه كله وازهف القى شرّا ـــ وعليه اجهز وبالشر اغرى ـــ والخبر زاد فيه وكذب ونمّ *

snide. Even should he see a princeling or king's *vizier*, he'll think himself too fine to treat him as his *peer*—for he's the one in clover and luxuriating in a life of *relaxation*, coddled and gazed at with *adulation*. He eats with such pearly teeth and coral lips before him that he thinks pickles are the best of *fare*, that the most blessed of possessions is a shirt of *hair*, that water that's brackish and *briny* is tastier than the wine at any evening *party*. And oh! should he spend the night with her on a mattress stuffed with wooden *shavings* and touch her downy skin—he'll think them the most luxurious of *stuffings*, for any injury suffered along with her is transformed into bounty and *gain*, into revelry and carousal any *pain*.

"From another, though, I've heard it said that the bachelor's life is the happier, the one in which pleasures are more likely to *bloom*, for the ladies view him as ever roaming free, and think one rutting bleat from him will dispel all *gloom*, given that he has none to tie him up each night in order to *tup* or half the night to keep him *up* lest he forget he's now the sheltered *spouse* of one who wears anklet and *blouse*. For this he's beloved of the girls, a prize to which matrons *aspire*, pointed out by randy widows as an object of *desire*. When he goes home, his hands are free, his cuffs *unsoiled*,[167] there being none to tell him, 'Hand over!' or blame him for what's past, quiz him on things to come, seek to have him in matters vaginal *embroiled*, tell him 'Shoo! Shoo! (*ḥaf ḥaf*!)' at every amorous *clucking* (*qayq*) from some other woman and his every roosterous wing *flapping* (*ḥalj*), tie—and how *tie*!—the piece of skin between his belly and his willy (*najf*) before he bids her *good-bye*, or tell him 'Quaff! To the dregs, the water *quaff* (*nazāfi nazāfi*), or else I'll finish you *off*!'(1) nor any to weep before him in *supplication* when he's powerless to support her, even though to do so be his *obligation*. You'll see him ever with a happy, rolling *gait*, full of joy, throwing himself in women's way and never walking *straight*, *laying* and *splaying*, keeping company with women who're ready to *pup* and feeling them *up*. As says a proverb that's making the rounds like a bad *penny*,[168] 4.13.4

(1) *Qayq* is the sound made by a hen when it demands to be trodden; when you say that a rooster *ḥalaja*, you mean that it spread its wings and went to its female to tread her; *ḥaf ḥaf* is a call made to drive away a cock or chickens; *najf* is making it impossible for a buck to mount, which is done by tying a piece of skin between its belly and its member, this piece of skin being called the *nijāf*; when you say that a man *nazafa* the water of the well, it means "he drained it dry"; *azhafa* means "to revile . . ." or, followed by *ʿalā*, "to finish off (a wounded man)" or by *bi-l-sharr* "to lure to evil," or by *al-khabar* ("report") "to exaggerate [the report], to lie, or to slander."

ومَرّته اروى * وسنانه اذلق * وسهمه اخسق * ونشره اعبق * وحبه اعلق * وُطعمته اطيب واوفر * ومادته اسكب واغزر * وقد نسوا ان تبعّق حوضه فى غير سِقّى واحد هو عين السبب فى تنكيز نزّه ونِزّته * وتفتير شَرزه ولزّته * الى غير ذلك مما لا يليق ان تقابل به مومسة ولا حَصان * ولا يوصف به دالف
ولا تيَّقان * قال الهارس فلما تراجح المذهبان * وتكافح المطلبان * قلت فى ٤،١٣،٥
نفسى من لنا اليوم بالفارياق * فيفتينا فى هذا الامر الربّاق * فانه اعلق بالنسآ من الريبة * واعرف باحوالهن من ذى شيبة وشبيبة * فلقد ذاق منهن الحلو والمرّ * ولقى من حبهن النفع والضر * فلو كان حاضرا لدينا * لجلَا عنّا ما التبس علينا * فسرت الى بعض اصحابى * لاطلعه على ما بى * فما كدت اقرع الباب * حتى هوى الىّ وبيده كتاب * ثم قال بشرى بشرى * فهذا كتاب من
الفارياق بلغنى امس ولم يحوِ الا شعرا * فتلقفته من يده فاذا فيه * اما بعد فان ٤،١٣،٦

القرطبان هو الذى يقرو البلاد بعِرسه
وبها الحسان الغيد يستنشين نفحة فلسه
من كل ذات تدهكر شحاذ نابى ضرسه
شدّاد رخو فقاره نعّاشه من تعسه
وبها الفحول الهائجو ن الى تسدّى عَنْسه
والى اشتفاف جميع ما فى قعبه او عُسّه

'He who has no wife has *many*.' The result, it is claimed, is that the bachelor's stride is *vaster*, his movement *faster*, his words less *trimming*, his cup more *brimming*, his intonation more *melodious*, his cravings more *imperious*, his thrusts more *pressing*, his delicious wine more *refreshing*, his lance's blade of keener *bite*, his arrow truer in *flight*, his breath more *sugarcoated*, his love more *devoted*, his food tastier and more *plenteous*, his vital juices more fluid and *copious*. They forget that the emptying of his basin into more than one plot is the very cause of the dropping of his water table and *lust*, the weakening of his vigor and *thrust*—and so on and so forth by way of phrases that shouldn't be used to describe whore or honest *matron*, or characterize a man, whether he run or trudge to his *damnation*."

Said al-Hāwif, "The two schools being thus equally balanced, the two claims in *contention*, I said to myself, 'If only the Fāriyāq were with us today so that to this thorny question he might turn his *attention*, for he cleaves more closely to women than does even *doubt* and better knows their ways than any graybeard or youthful *gadabout*. Of them he's tasted both sweet and *bitter*, and of their love he's been both victim and *benefitter*. Were he present with us now, all this confusion that we've *endured* would straightaway be *cured*.' I went then to one of my friends to apprise him of my *dilemma* and, no sooner had I knocked upon the door than he fell upon me, in his hand a *letter*. 'Good news!' he said, 'Good news! Here's a letter from the Fāriyāq that reached me in yesterday's *mail*, written in verse, down to the smallest *detail*.' I snatched it from his hand and here's what it contained:[169] 4.13.5

"'After salutations, be informed that 4.13.6

A procurer's one who goes
  With his bride from one land to another
Where the long-necked lovelies
  Swoon to the scent of his money,[170]
One who, on every beauty shaking with fat,
  Sharpens the two fangs with which he bites,
And stiffens the slackness of his spine,
  His resuscitator from misery.[171]
There too are bull camels,
  Aroused to mount his recalcitrant she-camel
And to drink up everything
  In his trough or his tumbler,

ولربما نبزوه بالاد   ساف اقبح رجسه
حتى يعود وما له   آسٍ لمعضل اَلْسه
ان اللبيب من استشا   رمنجّذا فى لَبْسه ٧،١٣،٤
لا سيّما شان الزوا   ج وحمل فادح وَقسه
من شاقه تمويهه   ومذاق لذة رَغسه
فليبعلن فى قَسّة   كى يستبد بحلسه
حيث السفاح مغصّص   من يشرئبّ لحسه
ان الغريب اضرّ من   متهتك فى جنسه ٨،١٣،٤
اَوَلا ففى حال العزو   بة وهو مالك رأسه
صون لدرهمه وحر   مته وراحة نفسه
بل من تزوج يومه   خير له من امسه
اذكان فى حال التعزّ   ب موحَشا من انسه
لكن بشرط نفوره   عن ريبة فى حَدسه
فالبضعَ ثم البضعَ لا   تتشاغلن عن قَسّه
ما ان يضر ختام ما   قد طاب نافع رَسّه
لكنما يجب التحرّ   ز من بواعث نحسه

قال الهارس فلما تصفحت الابيات * وزكنت ما فيها من الاشارات * قلت لله ٩،١٣،٤
دره ما افصله لامور النسآ ناظما وناثرا * وما احوجنا الى استفتائه فيهن غائبا

And sometimes they nickname him "pander,"
  The ugliest of his evil vocations.
In the end he returns, no
  Physician left to him to treat his incurable treachery.
The wise man is he who consults 4.13.7
  One well tried in adversities when bewildered,
Especially in the matter of marriage
  And how to bear its crushing atrocity.
He who is attracted by its deceptive coloration
  And the pleasant taste of its comforts
Let him marry in a small village
  That he may deal as he wishes with the contract
For depravity chokes
  Any who cranes his neck to lick it.
The stranger[172] is more harmful than 4.13.8
  One indifferent to his reputation among his own folk—
Or perhaps it is not so, for in the state of bachelorhood,
  While he is his own master,
Lies protection for his money, his privacy, and his peace of mind.
Again though, the present of him who marries
  Augurs better for him than his past
Since, in his state of bachelorhood,
  He missed having someone to keep him company.
He must, though, avoid
  The harboring of doubts.
Marriage, then, and more marriage! Be not
  Distracted from practicing it again and again
So long as the advantages of starting over at it
  Do not damage the ending of what was good.[173]
One must, however, be alert
  To whatever may turn it into catastrophe.'"

Said al-Hāwif, "Once these lines I'd *scrutinized* and, with a fair degree of certainty, the truths at which they hinted had *surmised*, I said, 'What a paragon! How much insight into women's affairs he *shows*, in verse as much as in *prose*! And how greatly we need from him, concerning these creatures, a *fatwah*, be it delivered in person or in *absentia*! Except, 4.13.9

وحاضرا * لكنه لم ينبس عن حاله الا فيما هو من مشكل الزواج * فكانه راى كل امر دونه فانما صوانه الاعفاج * ثم انصرفت مثنيا عليه * وقد زاد تشوقى اليه *

(حاشية صغا الهارس مع الفارياق فلذلك لم يعب عليه بعض ابياته فانها مضطربة العبارة * وليس من شانى التدليس على القارى فقد صار بيننا صحبة طويلة من اول هذا الكتاب * فليتنبّه لذلك)

though, where he speaks of marriage, of his own state he nothing *vouches*, as though he thought all else of lesser purport and best consigned to that place where, after passing through the stomach, the food *debouches*.' Then I departed singing his *praise*, all the more desirous of seeing his *face*."

(Note: because he was fond of the Fāriyāq, al-Hāwif didn't take him to task over some of these lines of his, which are awkwardly expressed. It is not my way, however, to pull the wool over the eyes of the reader, with whom I share an old friendship going back to the beginning of this work. Let him, therefore, take note of that fact.)

الفصل الرابع عشر

في رثاء ولد

قد غُرس فى طبع كل والد ان يحب ولده كلهم على كثرتهم وبرحتهم وعيوبهم * ١،١٤،٤
وان يراهم احسن الناس * وان يحسد كل من يفوقه فى المحامد والمكارم الا اباه
وابنه * ومتى شاخ الرجل وضعف عن التمتع بلذات الدنيا فحسبه ان يرى ابنه
متمتعا بها * ولا لذة للمتزوج اعظم من ان يبيت مع امراته على فراش واحد وبينهما
ولد له صغير لا يورّقه ببكائه وصراخه ولا يبلّه ببلبله * كما انه لا شى اوجع لقلبه
من ان يراه مريضا غير قادر على الشكوى بلسانه ليعلم ما ينبغى ان يداوى به * بل
الاطبآ انفسهم يحارون فى مداواة الاطفال وقلّما يصيبون الغرض * وكان الاولى
ان يعيّن لعلاجهم اطبّآ اختصوا بمزاولة ذلك عهدا طويلا * وان ينوَّه بمن نبغ منهم
فيه فى كل كلام مستطر ومطبوع * ويجب على الوالد اول ما يرى ولده قد مرض
ان يتعهده ويراعى احواله وما يطرا عليه ويقيد ذلك فى كتاب ليخبر الطبيب به اخبارا
مبينا * فربما اغنى ذلك عن كثير من الدوآ الذى يجازف به الاطبآ احيانا لامتحان
حال المريض * ومن اهمّ ما يستنهض عناية الوالدين فى حق ولدهما امر الطعام * ٢،١٤،٤
لان الطفل لما كان لا يدرى حدّ الشبع الذى يقف عنده الراشد كان اكثر اسباب
مرضه من الاكل * فليس من الحنوّ والشفقة ان تطعم الام ولدها كل ما يشتهيه *
وانما الاولى ان يلهَّى عنه باشيآ من اللعب والصور المنقشة والالات المزوقة

Chapter Fourteen

Elegy for a Son

It is ingrained in the nature of every father to love all his offspring, no matter how many, ugly, or vicious they may be, to think each of them the best of persons, and to envy anyone, other than his own father or son, who is superior to him in praiseworthy qualities and virtues; and when a man grows old and too weak to enjoy the pleasures of this world, it is enough for him to watch his son enjoy them. Likewise, there is no greater pleasure for a married man than to spend the night with his wife on a single bed with, between them, a small child of his who neither keeps him awake with his weeping and crying nor wets him with his little willy. By the same token, nothing pains his heart more than to see that same child sick but unable to give tongue to a complaint so that he may know how to treat him. The physicians themselves are at a loss when it comes to treating small children and rarely find the right cure. It would be better if specialized doctors were to be appointed who could devote themselves to their treatment long-term and that those who excel at it be extolled wherever words are written or printed. It is the father's duty, as soon as he sees that his child has fallen sick, to pay him close attention, observe his condition and any new developments, and write everything down in a book so that he may be able to give the doctor a clear account of it. Doing so may avoid the need for many a medicine that the doctors will sometimes try out as a way of probing the patient's condition. 4.14.1

Food is one of the most important matters that should engage the parents' concern where their offspring are concerned, for, given the child's lack of awareness of the limits to intake, at which the mature person stops, the most frequent cause of his falling ill is food. It is not a form of tenderness or solicitude for the mother to feed her child whatever he wants; it is better to 4.14.2

وما اشبه ذلك * وما احلى الولد يطلب شيا من ابيه وقد حمّر الخجل وجنته او غض الوجل طرفه * وما احبّه وهو مطوق عنق والده او والدته بيديه اللطيفتين ويقول انى اريد هذا الشى لآكله * ومن سوء التدبير ايضا ان يحرم ما يشتهيه * ويبكى لاجل ما لا ضرر فيه * ولعمرى ان من اغفل رضى ابنه حتى ابكاه واجرى دموعه لغير تاديب كان بمعزل عن الابوة * وينبغى ان يدرّب الطفل على الخفيف من الطعام بعد ولادته بستة اشهر مع بقآء الارضاع قليلا * فان الطعام يغذيه ويقوّيه فضلا عن انه يحفظ صحة والدته * بل ربما مناها طول ارضاعها اياه بمرض ولم يفده شيا كما هو مذهب الافرنج وهم اكثر الناس ذرّية * ولا ينبغى ان ترضعه
٣،١٤،٤ وهى غضبى او مذعورة مضطربة او مريضة * ثم انه ما دام الرجل عزبا او كان لم يربّ ولدا قط لم يشعر حق الشعور بالحنو على اولاد غيره * بل لم يقدر والديه اللذين ربّياه حق قدرهما الا بعد ان يصير هو والدًا مربّيا * والامّهات اللاى يرضعن اولادهن يكُنّ بالضرورة احنّ فوادا عليهم من اللاى يستاجرن لهم المراضع * ولا جرم ان من كان له ولد وقرأ قول الشاعر * وربّ امّ وطفل حيل بينهما كما تفرّق ارواح وابدان * لم يتمالك ان يذرف الدمع لوعة وتحسّرا * وكذا لو قرا قصصا فيها فجع الآبآء بقتل اولادهم الصغار الابرئآ كقتل اطفال مدين بامر موسى على ما ذكر فى الفصل الحادى والثلثين من سفر العدد * سوآء كان ابوا الطفل مومنين او كافرين * ومن لم يكن قد تحلّى بصفة الابوة كالراهب وامثاله ودعاك يابُنىّ او ياولدى فلا تثق بكلامه ولا تعول على دعائه * لانه لا يعلم معزة البنوّة
٤،١٤،٤ الا من كان ذا ابوّة * وكان الفارياق ممن اذاقه الله حلوآء البنين ثم تجرع مع ذلك مرارة الثكل * فقد كان له ولد بلغ سنتين وكانّه كان قد سُبك فى قالب الحسن والجمال فجآء لم يَعْدُه شى مما تقر به العين * وكان على صغر سنه ينظر نظر المميز

distract him from it with things such as toys, painted pictures, ornamented devices, and so on—though how pretty the child when he asks his father for something, his cheeks blushing with shyness or timorousness forcing him to lower his gaze, and how lovable he is as he throws his delicate arms around his father's or his mother's neck and says, "I want that to eat"! It is equally bad management to deny him what he wants and make him cry over something that can do no harm. I swear that anyone who pays so little attention to keeping his child content that the child cries and his tears flow for any reason other than his being disciplined has no right to be called a parent! The child has to be trained to take light foods six months after birth, breastfeeding continuing for a short while. Solid food nourishes and strengthens him, not to mention that this preserves his mother's health; indeed, extended breastfeeding of the child will sometimes result in her falling ill and benefit her nothing. This is the method followed by the Franks, who are the people with the most offspring. She should never breastfeed the child if she is choleric, or upset and disturbed, or sick.

Moreover, so long as a man is a bachelor or has never raised a child, he 4.14.3
will never feel proper feelings of tenderness for the children of others. Yet more, he will never fully appreciate his own parents who raised him until he became a father and a raiser of children himself. Mothers who breastfeed their children are of necessity more tenderhearted toward them than those who hire wet nurses. Without a doubt, any who have children and read the words of the poet, "And many a mother and child have been torn asunder as are soul and body when they part,"[174] will not be able to prevent themselves from shedding tears of heartfelt agony and sorrow, and the same if they should read stories in which fathers are stricken by the killing of their innocent little children, such as the killing of the children of Midian at Moses's command, as recounted in Chapter 31 of the Book of Numbers,[175] whether the children's parents are believers or unbelievers. As to those who have not been graced with fatherhood, such as a monk or his like, should they address you as "My dear son" or "My child," put no trust in their words or faith in their blessings, because only one who has experienced fatherhood can know the affection that goes with filiation.

The Fāriyāq was one of those whom God had given sons as sweet to the 4.14.4
taste as candy only for him thereafter to sip the bitterness of parental bereavement. He had a child who reached two years of age and was as though cast

بين المؤنس والموحش ويالف من تملق له ولو باشارة * فكان ابوه اذا رنا اليه ينسى
فى الحال جميع اشجانه وهمومه * ولكن لم يلبث ان يغشاه عارض من الكابة اذكان
يوجس انه لا يدوم له على عين الدهر اللامّة * ويرى نفسه انه غير جدير بان
يتملى بتلك الطلعة الناضرة * وكان يحمله على ساعديه مسافة ساعة وهو يناغيه
ويغنى له * حتى اَلِفه الطفل بحيث لم يعد يشا ان احدا غيره يحمله او يلهيه او
انه ياكل وحده على انفراد * الى ان قدر الله ربّ الموت والحياة ان اخذ الصبىّ ٥،١٤،٤
سعال فى تلك القرية * ولما كانت قرى الانكليز الصغيرة كغيرها من قرى البلاد من
انه لا يوجد فيها اطبآء مهرة وكان لا بدّ من مشاورة طبيب على اية صفة كان *
استشار ابواه احد المتطببين هناك * فاشار عليهما بان يتداركاه بالاستحمام بالمآء
السخن الا راسه * فعملا بوصيته اياما * ولم يزدد الصبى الا سقاما * حتى
كان اذا انزل فى المآ بعدها يُغشَى عليه ويُرَى فوق قلبه لطخة حمرآ كالدم على شكل
القلب * ثم اشتد به الدآء حتى احتبس السعال فى صدره وخفت صوته *
وكان يعاوده مع ذلك الرعدة والهزّة * وبقى فى حالة النزع ستة ايام بلياليها وهو
يئن انينا ضعيفا وينظر الى والديه كالشاكى لهما مما يقاسيه * فاستحال الورد من
خديه عبهرا * وغارت عيناه النجلاوان * ولم يعد شى من الغذآ والدوآ يسوغ فى
حلقه الّا تكلّفا * وكان الفارياق فى خلال ذلك يذرف العبرات ويجأر بالدعآ الى
الله ويقول * ربّ اصرف هذا العذاب عن ابنى الىّ ان كان ذلك يرضيك * انى
لا مأربَ لى فى الحياة من بعده ولا طاقة لى على مشاهدته فى هذا النزع الاليم *
فاَمِتْنى قبله ولو بساعة حتى لا اراه يجود بنفسه * آه عظمت ساعةً * وان
كان لا بدّ من نفوذ قضائك به فتوفّه الان * ولعل الفارياق هو اوّل والد دعا على
ابنه بالموت عن شفق وحنوّ * فان رؤية الطفل يغرغر ستة ايام مما لا يطاق *

from the very mold of comeliness and beauty, having arrived lacking nothing of what is needed to bring refreshment to the eye. Despite his young age, he had the look of one capable of distinguishing those who cheer from those who oppress and would make friends with any who treated him kindly, be it but by a gesture. When his father gazed at him, he would straightaway forget every sorrow and concern, though there would quickly descend upon him then a touch of melancholy since he had a foreboding that the child would not last long before Fate's dread eye, and he would decide to himself that he was unworthy to enjoy for long that radiant countenance. He would carry him in his arms by the hour, talking to him tenderly and singing to him, until the child became so comfortable with him that he would no longer want anyone else to carry him or entertain him or to eat on his own.

Things went on this way until God, Lord of Death and Life, decreed that 4.14.5
the child should be taken by a cough in that village of which we have spoken and, given that the smaller villages of England, like those in other countries, are without skilled doctors and it was essential to seek the advice of some doctor, of no matter what kind, his parents consulted a quack there who advised them to bathe him repeatedly up to the neck in hot water. They followed his advice for some days, the child only growing worse until it eventually reached the point that, when he was put into the water, he would pass out and a heart-shaped blotch as red as blood would appear over his heart. Then the sickness grew worse until the cough settled in his chest and his voice became weak, though at the same time he was overcome by repeated tremors and shakes. He continued to struggle for life for six days and nights, moaning weakly and looking at his parents as though complaining to them of his sufferings. The roses of his cheeks were transformed into jasmine, his eyes, with their startling contrast of black and white, became sunken, and no food or medicine any longer went down his throat without difficulty. While this was going on, the Fāriyāq shed copious tears and prayed fervently to God, saying, "O Lord, turn this torment from my son onto me, if that should please Thee! I have no desire to live without him or strength to watch him in this painful struggle. Let me die before him, though by a single hour, so that I do not see him give up the ghost. Ah, how terrible an hour! But if Your decree must be carried out, let him die now!" It may be that the Fāriyāq was the first father who ever prayed for his son to die, out of pity and tenderness, for the sight of the child dying over a period of six days was too much to bear.

وبعد ان تُوفّى الولد * وابقى فى قلوب والديه الحسرة والكمد * استوحشا من مقامهما اذكان كل شى فيه يذكرهما فقده ويزيد فى لوعتهما * ففصلا منه الى لندرة على حين غفلة وقد وضعاه فى صندوق فلما دفناه واستقرا فى منزل قال ابوه يرثيه

الدمع بعدك ما ذكرتك جارٍ   والذكر ما واراك تربٌ وارِ   ٦،١٤،٤
يا راحلا عن مهجة غادرتها   تصلى من الحسرات كل اوار
خطأً وهمتُ فاين بعدك مهجتى   ما فى حشاى سوى لهيب النار
رَمَقًا اقلّ الجسمَ منى فادحا   فكأنّه وِقر من الاوقار
ما كان ضرّ الدهر لوابقاك لى   عينا على الآثار والاذكار
ما بعد فقدك رائعى او رائقى   شى من الظلمات والانوار
سيان ان جنّ الظلام علىّ او   طلع الصباح وانت عنى سار
يابئس ذاك الليل اذ لم يبقَ لى   من مطمع فيه الى الاسحار
ارّقتنى من قبله ستًا وفيه حُرِمْت خمسى واستطبتُ شِعارى
أَبُنىَّ ما يجدى التصبّر قولهم   حكم المنيّة فى البرية جار
كلّا ولا بى قرّ بعدك من حمى   ما هذه الدنيا بدار قرار   ٧،١٤،٤
كم قد حملتك فوق راحى اذغدو   ت ورحت ثُمّتَ حُزتُ خير محار
ولكم سهرت الليل من جزع فما   اغنى بكاى عليك او اسهارى
ولكم جأرت لبرء دائك ضارعا   ولغير نفع كان طول جُؤارى

After the child died and only sorrow and grief remained in their hearts, they could no longer bear the place where they were living because everything in it reminded them that they had lost him, adding to their distress. They left it therefore and departed suddenly for London, having placed him in a casket; and when they had buried him and had settled in a house, his father recited, in lamentation for his death

You gone, the tears, when I recall you, run 4.14.6
And memory, now that dust conceals you, festers like a wound,
O forsaker of a heart that you have left
Exposed to sorrow's every flame
(Or so I wrongly thought, but, after you, where is my heart?
Naught's in my chest but fire—
A meager diet, hard to bear, that has reduced my body
That even so constrains).
What harm to Fate should it have left you to me
As reality and not mere memory?
You lost, nothing more affrights me or delights,
Not of shadows nor of lights.
All one it is to me if night o'ertake me
Or morning come, now you are gone.
Ah how evil was that night, for no desire did it leave me
To see another dawn!
Six nights till then you had me sleepless kept
And on that last, longing for my bed, of a fifth of myself I was
deprived.
O little son, they cannot help me to endure,
Those words of theirs "Death's rule on Man's imposed."[176]
No indeed—now you are gone, no consolation's left to cool my heat: 4.14.7
"This world for permanence can furnish no abode."
How oft did I cradle you before I departed of a morning
Or left at night, to return to the best homecoming!
How many a night was I kept awake by fear, though
My tears and lack of sleep availed you nothing!
How often did I pray for a cure to your disease, beseeching,
Though unavailing were my prayers!

ولكم حضنتك فى الحنادس خوف ان　　يطرا عليك من الحوادث طارى
وجمال وجهك لى يخيّل اننى　　فى روضة أُنُف ضحا نهار
ان لم يصوّرك المصوّر لى فقد　　صُوّرتَ بالماثور من اشعارى
او ان يكن واراك لحد ضيّق　　فالارض عندى اليوم اضيق دار
او ان تكن عنى حُجِبتَ فانما　　بَقِيتْ حِلاك خوالج الافكار
٨،١٤،٤ لا انسينّك او احين فما اتى　　حين علىّ خلا مِن استذكار
ولا رثينّك ما بقيت وان اَمُت　　فليتلونّ رثاك عنى القارى
ياحسرةً عُدم التصبّرُ بعدها　　عَدَمَ التبصّر فى احتمال خَسارى
كثر المعاين لى وقلّ معاونى　　وكوت حشاى شماتة الزوّار
فرويتُ بيتا قاله من ذاق ما　　قد ذقت من ثكل ووحشة جار
جاورت اعدآى وجاور ربّه　　شتان بين جواره وجوارى
يافجعة نزلت فحطّم كاهلى　　تأويقها وابان قصم فَقارى
فى ليلة فارقت فيها ناظرى　　ابدا وفارقنى على اجبار
لا غرو ان يك قد سرى جنح الدجى　　عن ناظرىّ فكل نجم سار
قدكنت اطمع ان يعيش مهنّاً　　بعدى ويبلغ اطول الاعمار
وودت لو ان ذقت حتفى قبله　　لكن خيار الله غير خيارى

How many a dark night did I embrace you lest sudden mishap should
you befall—
Such were my fears—
The beauty of your face transporting me
To some fresh forenoon garden.
No painter mayhap your portrait for me painted, yet
In these my verses you are portrayed; they are your guardian—
Or if a narrow grave-shelf has hid you,
For me the Earth today is the narrowest of spaces,
Or if from me you have been hidden, yet still
Nothing in my troubled thoughts remembrance of your charms
displaces.
Ne'er shall I forget you—or should I do so, I shall be dead, for never have 4.14.8
I known
A time when upon your memory I did not dwell;
Your elegy I'll declaim so long as I remain, and if I die,
Then let the reader my place fill!
What grief! My capacity for patience thereafter was as little as
My ability to conceive of how to bear my loss.
Many gazed upon me, few helped,
And the gloating of my visitors seared my guts,
Leading me to recite a verse uttered by one who'd tasted
The same bereavement and alienation from neighbors as had I:
"I kept company with my neighbors, he with His Lord—
And how different his neighbors from mine!"
What a disaster! It descended, its weight crushing
My shoulders and announcing the snapping of my spine,
On a night when I parted company with the light of my eyes
Forever and he was of me perforce bereft—
Small wonder that, when the darkness of night had passed
From before my eyes, every star had also left.
I would have hoped that happily
He'd outlive me and reach a ripe old age
And wished I might taste my own end before he did his,
But God's choice and mine were not the same

وِوسّدته بيدىَ رغمًا ليته هو كان وسّدنى على ايثارى 9،14،4
عينى اليه رنت وما لى حيلة ياليت من نَظَرٍ مُنَى اِنظارِ
قصرت يدى عن كف ما اَوْدَى به ان القصور مظنّة الإقصار
لهفى عليه وطرفه لى يشتكى اذكان لم يقدر على الإخبار
لهفى عليه على السرير موسّدًا ولواستطعت لكان فوق يسارى
لكنّ ادنى اللمس كان يزيده المًا فكان يؤوّه من اشعارى
ويئن انّة مستجير واجفا كالطير قُرّ فبات دون قرار
حتى خشيت الدمع يولم جسمه لمّا عليه همى كوَدْق جار
يارعشة اودت به قد اورثت قلبى الوجوب ولوعة التذكار
ليت النفوض اقرّعينى بعد ان سخنت بنفض فيه ذى اقرار
لهفى عليه فى الظلام معانق وكراىَ من شفق اليم غِرار 10،14،4
لهفى عليه والغنآء ينيمه واذا سكتّ صبا الى الاكثار
لهفى عليه وهو ياخذ من يدى ويعيد ما يعطوه لاستغزار
لهفى عليه وهولا ئكُ رُدْنه بلآلئٍ وضّاحة ودرارى
يايومَ انشبت المنيّةُ فيه طفلًا لا يطيق عوالق الاظفار

And 'twas I who laid his head to rest with my own hands, by greater force compelled. Would that 4.14.9
He'd laid my head down in keeping with my hopes!
My eye gazed at him and there was nothing I could do.
O for a look that could have brought about my wishes for delay!
My hand fell short of unhanding from him that which brought about his end;
Verily, incapacity is born of a conviction of inability!
How I grieved for him as his eye complained to me
For he could not himself inform me.
How I grieved for him, laid down upon his bed,
And had I been able, he would have lain on my left arm
But the slightest touch added
To his pain and he would wail at the touch of my hairs
And moan the moan of one who seeks aid, heart throbbing
Like a bird that feels the cold yet passes the night with nowhere to alight,
Till I feared my tears might hurt his body,
When they flowed down over him like falling rain.
What a shudder it was that took him off! It left my
Heart to palpitate and suffer memory's desolation.
Would that recuperation had then cooled my eye, after
It had heated, with a shaking off that contained consolation.
How I grieved for him, as he embraced me in the darkness 4.14.10
And my sleep, for painful pity, was cut short!
How I grieved for him as my singing lulled him
Though, if I stopped, he craved for more!
How I grieved for him when he took from my hand
And returned what he had taken in his, hoping for more!
How I grieved for him as he gummed my cuff,
Leaving shining pearls and fiery stars!
Ah, what a day, on which death fastened its talons into
Soft clay not made to withstand the hooks of its claws!
What a dire affair! It oppressed me, making death and
Life to me as one until my fated end!

ياخطّةً عالت فسوّت بين حتفى والحياة الى مدى مقدار
قدكان يحلو العيش حين يلوح لى   والآن مرَّ فصار ذا امرار
لا البعد يسلينى ولا طول المدى   وتخالف الاعصار والامصار
ما تنقضى الحسرات او اقضى اسىً   فبذا علىَّ جرى قضآ البارى
كلّا ولا تطفى اوارى عبرتى   ولئن هَمَت فى الصبّ كالامطار ١١،١٤،٤
فالنار الّا نار ثكل تنطفى   والمآء الا الدّمع ضدّ النار
ياليت راهى العيش يوما راجعٌ   وفدآء مربوب ابوه الهارى
فاكون فادىَ عمر نجلىَ لاقيا   حتفى لقآء القانع المختار
داريتُ ما لا ضير فيه لاجله   فاليوم لست لما يضير ادارى
ان المنية والامانى بعده   سيّان مستويان فى استئثارى
فلتفعل الايام بى ما تشتهى   ما بعد هذا الخطب من اضرار
ولتذهب الامال عنى اننى   لم يبق لى فى العيش من اوطار
من ذاق ثكلا مثل ثكلى فاجعا   فليُقصرنَّ اليوم عن اِصبارى
وليبكينَّ معى ويحملنى على   فرط البكآء بمدمع مِدرار
ما هَدَّ ركنَ الصبر مثلُ الثكل او   حَسَم المطا لحسامه البتّار
الطفل يقضى مرة لكنما   يقضى ابوه قبله بمرار ١٢،١٤،٤
تعروه فى نزع ابنه وخفوته   ادوار حيَنٍ ايّما ادوار
هيهات مَن قد اشبهت اطواره   فى فقده اوطاره اطوارى

Living was sweet to me when he would wave to me
  But now that he has gone is naught but gall.
Neither distance can console me nor length of time
  Nor change of days and cities.
My sorrows will never end nor can I die of grief
  For thus the Creator's decree with me must take its course.
Nay, nor shall my tears extinguish my burning fire **4.14.11**
  Though they pour forth like rain,
For any fire but the fire of a parent's loss may be extinguished
  And any water but that of tears will douse a fire.
Would that tranquillity of life might one day return
  And a child, reared by a father sore beset who'd give his life for him!
I would pay with my life for that of my son, facing
  My death as one content, freely choosing.
For his sake I would hide away things that could do no harm
  But today I do not hide even that which may do harm.
Death and my aspirations, after him,
  Are one and the same in terms of what I prefer
So let the days do with me as they will—
  After this calamity no further injuries can come.
Let hopes forsake me—
  No aims in life are left to me.
Let he who has tasted a bereavement as devastating as mine
  Be incapable today of making me endure patiently
But let him weep with me and bear
  The excess of my tears from a tear duct overflowing.
Naught demolishes the underpinnings of patience like a child's loss or
  Slices through the back so brutally as its severing sword.
The child dies but once, but **4.14.12**
  His father dies before him many times.
The wresting from him of his child and his disappearance bring down
    upon him
  Repeated episodes of demise, and what episodes!
How unlikely that any man's experiences of the loss
  Of his desires will resemble mine

او انّ فى سوء الاسى لى اسوة اوان فى طول الحياة قُصارى
لن ينفع الانسان شيا حرصه كلٌّ الى اَجَل على مقدار
الموت غاية كل حىّ يستوى فيه ذوو الايسار والاعسار
والسابقون يضمهم يوم مع المتاخرين الى ثرًى منهار
لكن يوم الطفل افجع حيث لم يعرف له مضمار سعى دار
ما لذَّ طعمَ العيش الّا من عدا ه الثكل لا من كان ذا ايسار
فالرزء فى الاموال مثل الشَعرتر زأه فينبت خِلفة الاطوار
فليَهْنِ من عاشت بنوه عيشه وليَصفُ مورده عن الاكدار
بعض الرزايا قد يساغ وبعضها يبقى شجا يشجى مدى الاعصار

Or that in the violence of others' grief I might find a model
    Or in length of life an end deserving of my pursuit!
A person's care will avail him nothing.
    All are headed to an end that's been measured out.
Death is the end of every living thing—in this
    The well-off and the poor are all as one.
Those who went before one day with those
    Who followed after will be gathered in one crumbling clay.
The death of a child, however, is a day more dread, for he has known
    No space in which to run and strive.
The one who knows the sweet taste of life is he whom
    Loss of a child has passed by, not he who is possessed of riches.
Loss of wealth is like loss of hair—you
    Lose it and then it sprouts anew, time after time.
Let him be happy then whose children live as long as he does
    And may his well remain of what may muddy it ever free!
Some catastrophes may be easily swallowed but some
    Leave a lump in the throat on which to choke until the end of time.

الفصل الخامس عشر

في الحِداد

ثم لمّا لم يكن بدّ للفارياق من السكنى بالقرب من تلك القرية المشؤمة سافر باهله ٤،١٥،١ الى كمبريج * وبقوا مدة طويلة يمشون وجفونهم ما بين منطبقة ومنفتحة * لان شدة الحزن تصرف القلب عن الشهوات او بالعكس * ثم تراخت عقدة الحزن قليلا عن العيون لا عن القلوب * لان العينين لا تطاوعان القلب دائما * كيف وقد قيل وضعيفان يغلبان قويا * فاستحلّ كل منهما اوّلا الصأصأة والوصوصة والتيصيص والتيضيض والتجصيص والتبصيص والوَبْص والتبصير والتفقيح * ثم اللوح واللمح والنَقد والخزر والتخازر والشُطور والمخاوتة والمخاوصة والملاوصة والتحشيف والعِرَضْنة والرَمْق والحَدَل والزَرّ والايماض واللحظ والالتفات والدنقسة والتشاوس والمغاضنة والمخاوتة * ثم الايشام والنظر والبَغْو والصَرْو والاجتلآ والتجلية والرَنْء والبصر والمعاينة والمشاهدة والرؤية والبَغى والبَقاوة والبَقّ * ثم الرأرأة واللألأة والتبريق والبَشْق والتحديج والتحديق والتحيط والتبجيم والتحجيم والتحميج والحملقة والعسجرة[1] واللتء والضَبْز والتبخّص والإِسفاف والارغاف والورورة والحتر والطنفشة والإِتآر والحدقلة والطرفسة والزنهرة والبندقة والبنق

---

١ ١٨٥٥: والعسحرة.

Chapter 15

Mourning

Since the Fāriyāq had no choice but to live close to that ill-fated village,[177] 4.15.1
he left with his wife and went to Cambridge. For a long time, they walked around with eyelids half closed and half open, for extreme grief distracts the heart from the natural appetites, or vice versa. Then the knot of sorrow loosened a little from the eyes, though not from the heart because the eyes do not always obey the latter—and how can they when it has been said, "Two weak things will conquer a stronger"?[178] Each permitted himself first to peer,[179] peek, and peep like a puppy opening its eyes for the first time, then to snatch stolen, furtive glances through narrowed eyes that looked askance, then to watch and observe, then to stare and scrutinize, then to crane the neck, cover one eye the better to see, and to contemplate and meditate.

والتجنيص والتفصيص والتهصيص والإرشاق والرَّعام والبرشمة والبرهمة والجرسمة * ثم الشُخوص والطمس والجم والإِشصآ والتطاول والتطالل والاشرئباب والاسلنطآء والاشتياف والاستيضاح والاستشراف والإِهطاع والتدنيق والترنيق والحثء والحتش والصَذء والإِسجاد والتامّل والتكلئة والتفرّس والتطلّع والرنوّ والترنّى * ثم تصالحت العيون والقلوب * فغدت تلك تترجم عن هذه والكمد مع ذلك مخيم
٤،١٥،٢ فى اطرافها * غير ان الانسان خُلق من نطفة امشاج وركّب من عدة اخلاط وجواهر واعراض مختلفة * فهو لا يزال ابد الدهر ماشجًا هذا فى ذاك وخالطا جدّا بهزل وفرحا بترح * فتراه ساعة قانعا[1] واخرى كأشعب * وآونة مفراحا واخرى مبتئسا * ويوما طربا شنِقا ويوما او بعض يوم عَزِها * فهو بشر خَلقا وغول خُلقا * واكثر ما ترى منه غَمَلَجيَّته هذه فى امر النسآ * فانه ان تزوج بمليحة قال ليتنى كنت تزوجت بقبيحة وسلمت من ضيزنية معارفى وجيرانى * وان تزوج قبيحة قال ليتنى تملّحت بمليحة لاكون ذا وجاهة ونباهة * وان كانت امراته بيضآ قال ليتها كانت سمرآ * فان السمر اخف حركة واسخن فى الشتآ * وان كانت سمرآ قال ليتها بيضآء فان البيض ارطب ابدانا فى الصيف * وان كانت كمكامة مكتنزة قال ليتها كانت ممشوقة هيفآ * فان الهيف اقل موّنة * وان سافر عنها قال ليتها هى التى سافرت وبالعكس * الّا فى مدة وضعها فانه لا يتمنى ان يكون فى موضعها وقس على ذلك من الاحوال النسائية ما لا يمكن حصره * اذ اخفى شى
٤،١٥،٣ من المراة انما هو بحر لا يمكن البلوغ الى قعره * والحاصل ان للقلب شؤونا كثيرة واحوالا متباينة لا يزال يتقلب بها * او لا تزال هى تتقلب به * وعلى كلٍّ فتسميته قلبا دالّة عليه * ويستثنى من هذه القاعدة شى واحد وهو ثبات الانسان فى كل

---

١ ١٨٥٥: قانطا.

Finally, eyes and hearts made peace and the former began to speak on behalf of the latter, though heartbreak still ruled their depths.

Humans, though, were created "from a drop of mingled fluid,"[180] com- 4.15.2
posed of a number of varied humors, essences, and contingent characteristics, and they will continue as long as time shall last to combine this with that and mix the serious with the humorous, joy with grief. On one occasion, then, you will find a man content with his lot, on another as greedy as Ash'ab,[181] at times joyful, at others miserable, one day rapturous and blithe of heart, on another, or part of it, too despondent to sport or play. He is human in form but a ghoul by nature and this unsteadiness of his is nowhere more visible than in his dealings with women. Thus, if he marries a pretty woman, he says, "Would that I'd married an ugly one and saved myself the attempts of my acquaintances and neighbors to muscle in!" and if he marries an ugly one, he says, "Would that I'd been acute enough to marry a cutie and gain prestige and renown!" If his wife is fair, he says, "Would that she were dark-skinned, for the dark-skinned are livelier and warmer in winter!" and if his wife is dark-skinned, he says, "Would that she were white, for white-skinned women have cooler bodies in summer!" If she is short and generously proportioned, he says, "Would that she were svelte and narrow-waisted, for the narrow-waisted are less expensive to feed!" If he leaves her to go on a journey, he says, "Would that it were she who had traveled!" and vice versa. Only when she is pregnant does he have no desire to be in her place. The same rule applies to too many matters concerning women to count, for even the most seemingly obvious matters relating to them are an unplumbable ocean.

In sum, the heart has many contrasting states and conditions among which 4.15.3
it constantly changes, or which keep it in a constant state of change, and, when all's said and done, its very name—*qalb*—points to what it is.[182] One thing only is an exception to this rule and that is man's unshakable insistence, in every state and under every condition, in every place and at all times, on preferring himself over others. If he leads a dissolute life, he believes that no one is more pious in God's sight than he. If he is crass and crude, he thinks every elegant wit his inferior. If he's a miser, he supposes that every letter he utters is the most generous gift and if he is ugly and mean-spirited, he thinks

حال وشان * واصراره فى كل زمان ومكان * على تفضيل نفسه على غيره * فلو كان فاجرا حسب ان لا برّعند الله الا برّه * وان كان فظّا غليظا راى كل كيّس ربيز دونه * وان كان بخيلا ظن ان كل حرف يفوه به هو منّة كبرى * وان كان دميما ذميما لم ير اللوم الا على نظر الناظرين له * وكما ان عين الانسان تنظر كل ما واجهها ولا ترى نفسها كذلك كانت بصيرته مبصرة بعيوب الخلق كافة الا عيب نفسه * ولو طاف الدنيا باسرها لما راى فيها من المحاسن ما فى مدينته او قريته * ثم ليس من المحاسن فى بلدته ما فى بيته * ولكن ليست هى فى احد من اهله كما هى فيه * فتحصّل من ذلك انه افضل من العالم كله * ولو انه كان شاعرا او بالحرى شعرورا لا يحسن الا الاطرآ على بخيل او التغزل بهند ودعد * ثم راى علمآء الرياضة والهندسة يخترعون من الادوات مثلا ما يطوى شقة خمسمائة فرسخ فى يوم واحد *لحسب ان شعره انفع من ذلك والزم * ولوكان مغنّيا او لاعبا بآلة من آلات الطرب وراى جارا له طبيبا نطاسيا يداوى فى كل يوم خمسين عليلا ويبرئهم باذن الله لاعتقد ان صنعته اشفى وانفع * ولم يخطر بباله قط ان الانسان يمكنه ان يعمّر فى الارض دهرا طويلا من دون سماع غنآ او عزف
٤،١٥،٤ بآلة * فمتى يتعلم الانسان ان يعرف نفسه * وان يفرق بين الحق والباطل * وان لا يخلط الحزن الكامن فى القلب بالتحديق والحملقة * واقبح من ذلك ان كل واحد من الناس يظن ان غيره ايضا يفعل كذلك فهو معذور عند نفسه بكونه حاذيا حذو غيره * ومثله قباحةً شان من تلبس الحداد على ميّت لها وهى فى خلال ذلك يزدهيها الرِنآ ويستخفها ذكر الذكران * وترتاح الى رؤية غير اللون الاسود وتطربها نغمة القائل لها ان فلانا مشغوف بحبك * وانك جديرة بان تقعدى على منصّة

the blame attaches only to those who view him as such. Likewise, just as a man's eye sees only what is in front of it and not itself, so his mental faculties apprehend all the faults of mankind except his own. Should he travel all the way around the world, he won't find anywhere the good qualities that are to be found in his city or village, and the good qualities of his town fall short of those of his own house, though none of them are to be found among his family to the same degree as they are in him, from which it may be gathered that he is the best thing in the entire world. If he be a poet, or more accurately a poetaster, the only thing he'll do well is to sing the praises of misers or write love verses to Hind and Daʿd,[183] and if he should see scientists and engineers inventing, for example, devices that make it possible to travel five hundred miles in a single day, he'll reckon that his poetry is more useful and necessary than any of those. If he's a singer or a player of a musical instrument and sees that a neighbor of his is an experienced physician who treats and, God willing, cures five hundred patients each day, he'll believe that his trade is more conducive to health and more beneficial and the thought will never occur to him that a person may exist on this earth for a lengthy period without hearing a song or the playing of an instrument.

When, then, will men learn to know themselves and to distinguish 4.15.4
between right and wrong? Not to combine the sorrow buried in the heart with peering and staring? Uglier still than these traits is the fact that everyone imagines that everyone else is doing the same and that he is to be excused because all he is doing is keeping pace with them. Exemplary of such ugliness is the woman who wears mourning dress for a dead relative and over the same period flaunts her bold looks and thinks nothing of talking about males, who finds comfort in looking at colors other than black and finds it as music to her ears when someone tells her, "So-and-so is in love with you, and you should be seated on a dais and telling the ladies- (or more accurately, gentlemen-)in-waiting around you what to do and what not to do, and you should never handle anything with this soft hand of yours and never leave your house on this delicate foot of yours, and you have so many suitors in every place and you will never, at any time, be without people to surround you, serve you, indulge you, and make you forget your sadness"

وتامرى وتنهى الوصائف من حولك او بالحرى الوُصفآ * وان لا تتناولى شيا بيدك هذه الرخصة * وان لا تخرجى من دارك ماشية على رجلك هذه اللطيفة * وان لك فى كل مكان عشاقا كثيرين بحيث لا تعدمين فى كل وقت من يحوطك ويخدمك ويلاطفك وينسيك حزنك * وغير ذلك من الكلام الذى هو انتهاك لحرمة كلّ من الموت والميّت * قال الفارياق قد رايت كثيرا من النسآ الحوادّ فى بلاد ٤،١٥،٥
الانكليز وغيرها وهن اكثر خفة وطربا وازدهآ وضحكا من العروس وامّها * ولم ارَ بينهن من كانت تنظر الى ثيابها السود اذا ضحكت لتتذكر ان كركرتها فى غير محلها * اما فى امر الزوج فربما يطلب لهن الحليم عذرا بان يقول مثلا * لعل زوجها كان يخونها فى الليالى الحالكة فترديها بالسواد انما هو لتتذكر سوء افعاله معها فى سواد تلك الليالى * او ان ايامها معه كانت كلها سودا كالليالى * فاما فى امر الولد والاب وغيره فلا عذر لمن احدّت وهى مرائية[1] مهزقة * ثم ان المحدّ عند الافرنج مطلوبة للرجال مرغوب فيها بمنزلة العروس * اذ الفحول يتزاحمون على تسليتها وتلهيتها لعلمهم بما تحت ذلك السواد * وبان هذه العادة هى من جملة العادات التى خالف استعمالُها وضعها * والظاهر ان لفظة المُحدّ فى لغتنا هذه الشريفة مشتقة من حدَّ ٤،١٥،٦
السكين واحدّها وحددها اى مسحها بحجر او مبرد فحدّت تحدّ * فكانّ لابسة الحداد تحدّ شهوة الناظر اليها اذ يرى عليها آثار الحزن والكآبة والانكسار وهو اشوق ما يكون فى النسآء * ويويّده ان صنفا من الثياب السود يسمى اِسْبادا * وهذا الحرف يجى ايضا بمعنى حلق الشعر كالسَبْد وانت بتمام المعنى ادرى * وتسمى ايضا سِلابا والسليب هو المستلب العقل * فكانّ المراة اذا تسلّبت اى

[1] ١٨٥٥: مرارئة.

as well as other things that are a violation of the respect owed to both death and the dead.

The Fāriyāq resumed,[184] "In England and elsewhere I have seen many women dressed in mourning garb who were more cheerful, rapturous, blooming, and mirthful than a bride and her mother and I never saw one of them, on laughing, look at her black garments and think to herself that her cackling was out of place. If it is the death of a husband that is involved, however, one inclined to clemency may seek to excuse a woman by saying, for example, 'Maybe her husband used to betray her on dark nights, and her dislike for black simply reflects her memories of his evildoings toward her in the blackness of those nights,' or that the days she spent with him were all as black as night. When it comes to offspring or fathers or others of that sort, no woman who wears mourning while showing off and laughing hard can be excused. Moreover, among the Franks a woman wearing mourning dress is as much in demand among and desired by men as a bride, because the studs among them jostle one another to entertain and distract her, well aware of what lies beneath that black and that this is one of those customs whose practice contradicts its theory. 4.15.5

"It appears that the word *muḥidd* ('woman dressed in mourning') in this noble language of ours derives from the *hadd* ('edge') of the knife and from '*aḥaddahā* or *ḥaddadahā*, meaning "He rubbed it with a stone or a file and it thus became sharp (*ḥaddat, taḥiddu*)."'[185] Thus it is as though the lust of the one looking at a woman who is wearing mourning clothes (*ḥidād*) were sharpened by his seeing upon her the traces of sorrow, melancholy, and dejection, this being the most attractive state a woman can be in. It also helps him that a certain kind of black cloth is called *isbād*, a word that also occurs in the sense of 'shaving of the hair,' which is also called *sabd* (and you know better than I the full sense of that word).[186] The *isbād* is also called a *silāb*, while the *salīb* is a person whose mind has been stolen (*mustalab*). Thus it seems that if a woman *tasallabat*, i.e., puts on mourning and dresses in a *silāb*, she steals (*salabat*) the mind of any who looks on her, for the moment his glance falls upon her, his heart falls with it and he says to her, or to himself, 'I would give my life in ransom for yours! I would sell my father and my mother for you! 4.15.6

احدّت ولبست السِلاب سلبت عقل ناظرها * فاول ما يقع نظره عليها يقع قلبه معه فيقول لها او فى نفسه * فديتك * بابى انت وامى * لله انت * وقاك الله * وهبنى الله فداك * ان شئت ان اكون اول من توسّل لمحو هذا الحزن من صدرك فعلت * فانى انا اَقْدَر منك على تحمل المكاره * فالقِ علىّ هذا الهمّ القادح وكونى انت مهنّاة مسرورة * ان لدى آلة طرب عظيمة وخزعبيلات كثيرة تفرّج عنك هذا الكرب * فلو زرتنى مرة اوسمحت لى بان ازورك لم يَعُد يخطر ببالك شى من الاشجان * انك رخصة رعبوبة وارى هذا الخطب قاسحا عليك فلا يزول الّا بقاسح مثله * ليتك تعلمين ما عندى من الاَسَى والوجد لاجلك * وانى عتيد لان احرم نفسى من جميع المسرّات بحيث اراك تفترّين عن ذلك الشنب الاشهى * وتبدين فى خديك عند الضحك تلك النقرة التى طالما نقرت قلوب العشاق * اىّ قلب لا يذوب لهذا الانكسار * واية عين لا تنزف الدمع على هذا الازار * قَدْنى حزنا لحزنك وحسبى ان اجلو عنك صدا هذا الهم * وكذلك المراة المحدّ فانها ٧،١٥،٤
تعلم وهى ماشية ما يخطر ببال ذلك المشفق عليها فتقول له او فى نفسها * نعم والله انى محتاجة اليك لتخفف عنى ما اجده اليوم من الوحشة والسدم * وقد بت البارحة وانا غريقة فى بحر الافكار والاكدار * واراك جديرا بان تعاقرنى وتسامرنى وتعاشرنى وتبادرنى وتباكرنى وتجاورنى وتحاضرنى وتخاصرنى وتذاكرنى وتسارّنى وتسايرنى وتداورنى وتشاعرنى * فالحمد لله الذى هدانى اليوم اليك وهداك الىّ وقيّضك لى * لانى امراة منكسرة الخاطر ولا بدّ لى ممَّن ينفّس عنى ويونسنى * حتى اذا نسيت ما اكابده والمّ بك كرب كان علىّ ان افرّج عنك فان عندى مصدر اشتقاق الفَرَج * ومنى تنال اتمّ الحبور * واعمّ السرور * فهلمّ اذاً الى المخالطة

What a wonder you are! God protect you! God grant me a chance to give my life as a ransom for you! If you wish me to be the first to implore you to allow him to wipe this sadness from your breast, I will do so, for I am more able than you to bear adversities. Throw then this piercing pain upon me and be you happy and joyful! I have a large musical instrument[187] and many entertaining stories with which to release you from this care. If you would visit me once, or allow me to visit you, none of these sorrows would ever cross your mind again. You are soft and plump, and I can see how hard this loss is for you; it can be removed then only by something equally hard. Would that you knew how I grieve and suffer for your sake! I am prepared to deny myself every pleasure to see you part your lips and reveal those delicious glistening teeth of yours and display on your cheeks, when you laugh, that dimple that has so often dented the hearts of your suitors. What heart could forbear to melt before such dejection? What eye would not shed tears onto this black wrap? Sufficient reward it would be for me to take your sorrow upon myself, enough for me that I lift from you the rust of this care!'

"The woman wearing the mourning is the same, for she is conscious, as 4.15.7
she walks, of what is going on in the mind of the man who feels such pity for her and so says, to him, or to herself, 'Indeed, I swear I need you to lift from me the loneliness and sadness that I feel today! I spent last night drowning in the ocean of cogitations and perturbations, and you look to me to be qualified to pick quarrels with me, to spend the evenings chatting with me, to keep me company, to take me by surprise, to come to me early of a morning, to come and live near to me, to engage in give-and-take with me, to walk hand in hand with me, to discuss with me, to share secrets with me, to travel with me, to ramble here and there with me, and to vie with me in quoting poetry.[188] Praise, then, to God who today has guided me to you and you to me, and decreed that you be mine—for I am a poor dejected woman and must have someone to dispel my grief and cheer me, until, when I have forgotten my sufferings and some disaster falls upon you, it becomes my duty to provide relief (*ufarriju*) to you, for I possess the very source from which relief (*faraj*) is derived[189] and through me you will obtain joys most *sweet*, pleasures most *complete*. Off with us then to social intercourse and evening *prattle*, to repartee and to doing *battle*!'

والمراوحة * والمساجلة والمكالحة * فهذا ما ينشا عن لبس الحِداد * ولذلك كان ٨،١٥،٤
كثير من النسآ يوثرن الثياب السود ثقة بانها تقوم فى تشويق من يلاقينهُ من الرجال
مقام الحِداد * ولذلك كانت الافرنج ايضا يحبّون اللون
الاسود فى الملابس ولا يتجاوزونه *
ولذلك كان لباس القسيسين
والائمّة
اسود
*

"This is what comes of wearing mourning and this is why many women prefer to wear black garments—being confident that they will have the same effect of attracting any men they may run across as does mourning dress. 4.15.8

This is also why the Franks love the color black for clothes
and never go beyond it
and why priests' and imams' robes
are
black."

الفصل السادس عشر

في جور الانكليز

١،١٦،٤ لما فرغ الفارياق من عمله فى كمبريج سافر الى لندرة على عزم ان يرجع الى الجزيرة واستصحب معه حمّى نافضا * غير ان احد الاطبآء الخيّرين فى هذه المدينة نفضها عن ظهره ولم يتقاضه شيا * ثم اصيبت الفارياقية بخفقانى القلب واللسان * فانها كانت وقتئذ مهرت فى لغة القوم * ثم اصيب هو بخفقانى العقل والراى * وذلك انه لما تصرمت مدة غيابه عن الجزيرة وازف وقت رجوعه راى ان العود اليها غير احمد * لان احوالها تغيرت عما كانت عليه من الخصب والصحة فى المساكن * وتلك عادة للفارياق انه لا يدخل بلدا خصيبا الا ويفارقه محلا كما تقدمت الاشارة اليه * ولانه فاته فيها بعض فوائد فحرم منها لطول غيابه *

٢،١٦،٤ فمن ثم قصد مدينة اكسفورد ومعه كتاب توصية الى احد اعيانها وعلمائها وهو من اهل الكنيسة * فراى الوصول اليه متعذّرا فان العلمآء فى هذه المدينة ليسوا كعلمآ مصر فى رقة الجانب وبشاشة اللقآ * بل هم اشد فظاظة من العامة * وعندهم ان الغريب لا ياتى الى بلادهم الّا والشلّاق على عاتقه * ولذلك لما ذهب الفارياق ذات ليلة ليرى بعض هولآ العلمآ صادفه احدهم بباب المدرسة فقال له من تقصد * قال فلانا * قال اين تسكن * قال فى محل كذا * قال اعندك دراهم لتفى اجرة المسكن * قال ما انا بمطران ولا راهب حتى تزعمنى انى قدمت اليكم متسوّلا *

Chapter 16

The Tyrannical Behavior of the English

When the Fāriyāq had finished his work in Cambridge, he went to London intending to return to the island and a shaking fever went with him. One of the kind doctors of that city, however, shook that shaking fever off his back and charged him nothing. Next, the Fāriyāqiyyah came down with palpitations of the heart and tongue, for she had by now become skilled in the language of those people. Then he in turn was afflicted with palpitations of mind and thought, the reason being that, his leave of absence from the island over and the time for him to return nigh, he had decided that if he hadn't at first succeeded, he wouldn't if he tried again.[190] This was because the easy living and comfortable housing conditions that had formerly prevailed there had changed, and this was usual for the Fāriyāq: he never entered a land of plenty that he didn't leave a barren waste, as noted earlier. Also, he had missed out on certain benefits there which he was now denied in view of the length of his absence. 4.16.1

Taking this into account, he made his way to the city of Oxford, taking with him a letter of introduction to one of its notables and scholars, a clergyman. He believed it would be difficult to make contact with him, for the scholars of that city are not like those of Cairo in their graciousness and warmth of welcome; on the contrary, they are ruder than the common people and think no stranger comes to their country without a beggar's bag over his shoulder. Thus it was that when the Fāriyāq went one evening to see one of these scholars, someone confronted him at the door to the college and said, "Whom do you want?" "So-and-so," he replied. "Where do you live?" asked the other. "In such and such a place," he said. "Do you have money enough to pay the rent?" the man asked. "I'm no metropolitan or monk[191] that you should suppose that I come to you as a beggar," he answered. 4.16.2

ثم لما تعذّر عليه الوصول الى جناب ذلك القسيس المعظم ولم يجد فيها اهلا للخير
سوى رجل من الطلبة يسمى وليم سكولتك (Williams Scoltock) وآخر من
التجار كان الفارياق اشترى منه قطعة حبل ليربط بها صندوقه فابى التاجر ان ٤،١٦،٣
ياخذ منه ثمنها فكانه ظن ان الفارياق لم يشترها الا بعد ان استخار الله فى ان
يخنق بها نفسه * رجع الى لندرة وفاوض زوجته فى ذلك * فقالت له ان الجزيرة
اقل خيرا من اكسفورد وانى مللت منها كل الملل * فقد اضعنا فيها زهرة عمرنا ولم
نحصل منها على ثمرة * فما الراى ان نعود اليها * فقرّ رايه ح على ان يستعفى
من خدمته فيها وكتب كتابا الى كاتب سر الحاكم يوذن بذلك * ثم اشتد بالفارياقية
الخفقان فرأى ان مقامهما بباريس خير لهما * وذلك لما شاع عند الناس ان
هوآ باريس اصح من هوآ لندرة * وان المعيشة فيها ارخص والحظ اوفر * وان
الفرنسيس ابشّ بالغريب من الانكليز وابر * وان لغة العرب عندهم اكثر نفعا
واشهر * وغير ذلك من الاوهام التى تدخل احيانا فى رؤس الناس ولا تعود
تخرج الا مع خروج الروح * ولكن ينبغى قبل سفر الفارياق من هذه المدينة ان
نعيد عليك بعبارة وجيزة وصف ما فيها من المحاسن والجور على اهلها اى على اهل
الجمال * لتعلم هل رحيل الفارياق منها حلال او حرام * وليكون لك ذلك وداعا من
الانكليز * فان الكتاب قارب ان يتمّ ولم يبق من مجال للاسهاب * لانى اخشى
من ان ياتى هذا الكتاب الاخير اكبر من الاول فيكون ذلك موجبا للقدح فى من ٤،١٦،٤
وجهين * احدهما ان مطالعيه يقولون ان المولف كان يولف الفصول فى اوله
قصيرة والان ينشئها طويلة * فكانّه كان اوّلا غير ذى دربة بالتاليف او انه يريد
ان ينسب اليه مضمون قولهم جرى المذكّيات غِلآ * والثانى انه كاد ان يلحق نفسه
بالطرّادين وهو لم يشعر ولم يدر * فلقد مللنا من كلامه واعادة قوله قيل وقال وكان

After this, when he experienced such difficulty in reaching that honorable and mighty clergyman, and found no one there disposed to be kind—with the exception of a student called William Scoltock[192] and a shopkeeper from whom the Fāriyāq bought a piece of rope to tie his trunk but who refused to take payment for it, imagining, seemingly, that the Fāriyāq had only wanted to purchase it after consulting God by divination as to whether he shouldn't use it to hang himself—he returned to London and opened negotiations on the matter with his wife. She told him that the island was less likely to provide a living than Oxford and that "I have become utterly bored with it. We wasted the flower of our youth there and acquired not a single fruit. What then is the point of going back?" At this, he decided to resign from his government position there and wrote a letter to the governor's private secretary informing him of this. **4.16.3**

Then the Fāriyāqiyyah's palpitations grew worse and he decided that it would be better for them to live in Paris, because of the popular idea that the air of Paris was healthier than that of London, that living there was cheaper and opportunities were more abundant, that the Parisians were more welcoming to the stranger than the English and more charitable, that the Arabic language was more useful there and more widely known, and other delusions of the kind that sometimes enter people's heads never again to leave them until the soul does so too. Before, however, the Fāriyāq departs that city, we must repeat to you, in compressed form, a description of the good qualities that it contains and of the injustice meted out to its inhabitants—which is to say its *fair* inhabitants—so that you may decide whether the Fāriyāq's departure was right or wrong. Let this be too your farewell to the English, for the book is drawing to a close and there is no space left for expatiation since I'm afraid that this last book may come out longer than the first and that that would require my censure, from two perspectives. One is that its readers might say that the author had made the chapters at the beginning short and now was making them long, as though at first he'd been unschooled in writing or he now wanted the saying "mature horses run ever longer heats" to be applied to him.[193] The second is that they might say, "He's come close to joining the ranks of those who drive away their listeners by the length of their readings but remains oblivious and unaware, and we've grown bored with his words and his saying again and again 'this is claimed and so is that' and 'once it was and now it is not.' He has taken the reins of debate between **4.16.4**

وصار * فهو قد تبوّا صهوة الجَدَل منه واليه * ولم يغادرنا نراجعه ونعترض عليه *
٤،١٦،٥ فما جزآ الثرثار من المولفين * الّا القاء كآبه فى القمين * قال الفارياق تصوّر فى
عقلك انك ساكن فى حارة من حارات لندرة ذات صفين متوازيين * متصاقبين
متناوحين * فى كل صف عشرون دارا * ولكل دار باب * ولكل باب عتبة *
وامام كل عتبة درج او وصيد مبلّط * ثمّ مثّل لعينك هداك الله اربعين بنتا
من الرُمُم النواهد * والجُشُم الخرائد * والعُبُن المواغد * والرُجُح الثوامد * ذوات
التبهكن والمرافد * والمراضب والمشانب * والصلوته والسجاحة * والاسولة
والصباحة * واللباقة والملاحة * والكلثمة والترارة * والوثامة والنضارة *
والوضآة والبشارة * والقسامة والشارة * والطلاوة والوثارة * والوسامة
والبضاضة * والطراوة والغضاضة * والغِرَض والمَسالة * والمَلَد والعبالة * ومن
الزُهْر والغُرّ والفُرّ والصهب والصُبح والصُحّ والعُفر والفُضح والمُغْر والأُدم والخُلس
والبُره والوده والعِين والنُجل والشُهل والبُرج * والشُكل والدُعج والجُود والبُج والفُرق
والزُجّ والجُبه والبُلج والبُلد والذُلْف والخُنس والشُمّ واللُعس والحُوّ واللُمى * ومن كلّ
٤،١٦،٦ رُعبوبة شطبة تارّة او بيضآ حسنة رطبة حلوة او ناعمة * وكان حق هذا الحرف ان يوضع فى جدول الكتاب الثانى لكن رايت الحكاكات اولى به لتحقق معناه فيهن *
ولَبّة لطيفة *
وذات وجه مُصفَح المصفح من الوجوه السهل الحسن *
وبُهْصُلة شديدة البياض *

his teeth, argued both sides of the issue, and left us no room to review his arguments or object. The reward for a writer who's a *chatterbox* is to have his book cast into the *tinderbox*."

Said the Fāriyāq, "Picture in your mind that you are living in one of London's residential quarters, with two rows of houses, parallel, face-to-face, façade to façade, twenty houses to a row, a door to each house, a lintel to each door, and in front of each lintel a step or tiled threshold. Then conjure up before your eye, God guide you right, forty girls, each of them smart and perky-breasted, fat and virginal, corpulent and compliant, big-buttocked and buxom with a twitch to her backside and bustle, with saliva sweet and teeth that glisten, clearness of brow, length of back, and evenness of cheek and possessed of loveliness, wit, and fun, plumpness and facial chubbiness, good looks and tubbiness, freshness and beauty, pulchritude and handsomeness, goodliness and comfiness, tenderness of skin and attractiveness, succulence and juiciness, pretty length of face and dewiness, well-roundedness and willowiness, each of them being white and comely, bright-complexioned, beaming, blonde, strawberry blonde, near-strawberry blonde, chestnut, ash-blonde, dirty blonde, dusky blonde, or dusky chestnut blonde, of a healthy whiteness and white prettiness, the white and the black of her eyes clearly defined and as large as oryxes', her pupils blue but as though mixed with red, her whites suffused with black, or her pupils blue but as though streaked with red, or wide and black, swan-necked,[194] her eye sockets wide, her eyes widely spaced, her eyebrows delicate, broad and uncreased of brow, mighty-bodied, fine-bridged, snub-nosed, high-bridged, beautifully black-lipped, or with lips between black and red, or brown-lipped, and each of whom is 4.16.5

ruʿbūba,	"tall and languid, or white, comely, soft, and sweet, or smooth"; this word should have been included in the table in Volume Two but I thought that the scrubbers[195] deserved it more, because its meaning is made real in them 4.16.6
labbah,	"refined"
with a face that is *muṣfaḥ*,	"even and comely"
buhṣulah,	"of extreme whiteness"

ورَبِلة	عظيمة الرَبَلات والرَبَلة ويُحرِّك كل لحمة غليظة والربالة كثرة اللحم *
ورِبَحلة	ضخمة جيدة الخلق طويلة *
ورَيْبل	ناعمة لحيمة *
وذات شعر رَجِل	بين السبوطة والجعودة *
ورَفِلة	اى تجرّ ذيلها جرًا حسنا *
وزَوْلة	خفيفة ظريفة فطنة *
وذات عين سَبْلاَ	طويلة الهدب *
وذات صوت خريد	لين عليه اثر الحيآ *
وسِجَلّ	ضخمة كالسجلل * ٤،١٦،٧
واسْحلانيّة	المراة الرائعة الطويلة الجميلة *
وطَفْلة	رخصة ناعمة *
وعَبْلة عَثِلة	ضخمة فخمة *
وعَيْطل	طويلة العنق فى حسن جسم *
وعُطْبول	فتيّة جميلة ممتلئة طويلة العنق *
وعَيْطَبول	طويلة القدّ *
وعَمَيْثلة	البطيئة لعظمها وترهّلها ومن تسبل ثيابها دلالا *
ومكّلة	مدورة مجتمعة *
وهَيْضَلة	الضخمة الطويلة *
وهيكلة	عظيمة * ٤،١٦،٨
وهُوْلة	المراة تهوّل بحسنها *

rabilah,	"mightily fleshed; *rablah,* also pronounced *rabalah,* is any thick piece of meat . . . and *rabālah* is copiousness of flesh"
ribaḥlah,	"large, well-formed, and tall"
raybal,	"smooth and fleshy"
and has hair that is *rajil,*	"between straightness and curliness"
[and each of whom is] *rafilah,*	meaning "she drags her train behind her in a comely fashion"
zawlah,	"light, witty, and intelligent"
and has an eye that is *sablā',*	"long-lashed"
and a voice that is *kharīd,*	"soft, with a trace of shyness"
[and each of whom is] *sibaḥl,*	"large; synonym *sabaḥlal*" 4.16.7
isḥilāniyyah,	"a beautiful, tall, splendid woman"
ṭaflah,	"soft and smooth"
'ablah 'athilah,	"large and stately"
'ayṭal,	"long-necked and with comeliness of body"
'uṭbūl,	"a beautiful young woman, full-figured and with a long neck"
'ayṭabūl,	"tall"
'amaythalah,	"slow, because of her largeness and the wobbliness of her flesh, and a woman who drapes her clothes coquettishly"
mukattalah,	"rounded and compact"
hayḍalah,	"huge and tall"
haykalah,	"large" 4.16.8
hūlah,	"a woman who stuns with her beauty"

وَعَيْهل — طويلة ومثلها العَيْطبول والغِلْفاق والعنشطة والغَنَطْنطة والعَلْهبة والسَلْهبة *

وعَنْدَلة — ضخمة الثديين وهى ايضا الطويلة *

وعَرَطويلة — حسنة الشباب والقدّ *

وعَرَنْدَلة — طويلة صُلبة شديدة *

ومَجْدولة — لطيفة القصب محكمة الفتل *

وخَثْلة — ضخمة البطن *

وهِرَكْل — حسنة الجسم والخلق والمشية كالهِرَكَولة *

ومأرومة — حسنة الخلق مجدولته *

وجريمة — عظيمة الجسد ونحوها الجسيمة * ٩،١٦،٤

وجمّآ العظام — كثيرة اللحم *

وحَمامة — جميلة *

ودَرْمآ — لا تستبين كعوبها ومرافقها (من تغطية اللحم لها)

ورُعْموم — ناعمة *

وسَلِمة — ناعمة الاطراف *

وشُغْموم — طويلة مليحة كالشغمومة *

وضِخَمّة — عريضة اريضة ناعمة *

ومطهّمة — السمينة والبارعة الجمال والمدوّرة الوجه المجتمعته *

وفَعْمة — استوى خلقها وغلظ ساقها *

وقسيمة — جميلة وكذا الوسيمة * ١٠،١٦،٤

وكَثِمة — ريّا من شراب وغيره *

ʿayhal,	"tall; synonyms *ʿayṭabūl, ghilfāq, ʿanshaṭah, ghanaṭnaṭah, ʿalhabah, salhabah*"
ʿandalah,	"huge-breasted and also tall"
ʿarṭawīlah,	"comely in her youth and of figure"
ʿarandalah,	"tall, firm, and strong"
majdūlah,	"slender-boned and compactly built"
khathlah,	"huge-bellied"
hirkīl,	"comely of body, form, and gait; synonym *hirkawlah*"
maʾmūrah,	"comely and compactly formed"
jarīmah,	"large-bodied; synonym *jasīmah*" 4.16.9
jammāʾ al-ʿiẓām,	"abundantly fleshed"
ḥamāmah,	"beautiful"
darmāʾ,	"whose elbows and wrists cannot be seen" (because they are covered by flesh)
ruʿmūm,	"smooth"
salimah,	"smooth-limbed"
shughmūm,	"tall and pretty; synonym *shughmūmah*"
ḍikhammah,	"wide, pleasant-looking, smooth"
muṭahhamah,	"fat, outstandingly beautiful, with a round, compact face"
faʿmah,	"a woman whose figure has ripened and whose legs have thickened"
qasīmah,	"beautiful; synonym *wasīmah*" 4.16.10
kathamah,	"plump as a result of drinking or other cause"

ومكلثمة مجتمعة لحم الخدين بلا جهومة *

وكمكامة قصيرة مجتمعة الخلق *

ووثيمة مكتنزة لحما *

ومُوشِم اوشمت المراة بدا ثديها *

وهَضِيم الهَضَم خمص البطن ولطف الكشح *

وبَثْنَة حسناَ بضّة *

وبَخْدن ناعمة.

وبادن معروف كبادنة *

وبَهْنانة الطيبة النفس والريح او اللينة فى عملها ومنطقها ٤،١٦،١١
والضحّاكة الخفيفة الروح *

وبَهْكَنة شابة غضة ويقال للعجزآ تبهكنت فى مشيتها *

وجُهانة شابة *

وحَبْنآ ضخمة البطن.

وذات شعر جَجِن متسلسل مسترسل *

وخَلِيف المراة التى اسبلت شعرها خلفها *

وراقنة حسنة اللون *

ومسنونة الوجه حسنته سهلته او فى وجهها وانفها طول *

ومَشْدونة العاتق من الجوارى *

وذات عَسَن الطول مع حسن الشعر *

وعَكْنآء تعكّن بطنها * ٤،١٦،١٢

وغَيْسانة ناعمة *

mukalthamah,	"having the flesh of the cheeks firm but not coarse and ugly"	
kamkāmah,	"short and of compact physique"	
wathīmah,	"bulging with flesh"	
mūshim,	"with budding breasts"	
haḍīm,	"*haḍam* is concavity of the belly and delicacy of the haunch"	
bathnah,	"a plump young beauty"	
bakhdan,	"smooth"	
bādin,	[stout] "too well-known to require definition; synonym *bādinah*"	
bahnānah,	"having sweet breath and smell, or tractable in her work and her speaking and full of laughter and good company"	
bahkanah,	"a succulent young woman . . . and one says of a big-buttocked woman *tabahkanat fī mishyatihā* ('she walked with a swaying gait')"	4.16.11
juhānah,	"young (of a woman)"	
ḥabnā',	"huge-bellied"	
possessed of hair that is *ḥajin*,	"flowing and loose"	
khalīf,	"a woman who wears her hair loose down her back"	
rāqinah,	"attractively colored"	
with a face that is *masnūnah*,	"comely and even, or with length to her face and nose"	
mashdūnah,	"a barely pubescent girl"	
possessed of *'asan*,	"[possessed of] height, with attractiveness of the hair"	
'aknā',	"one whose belly has developed folds of flesh"	4.16.12
ghaysānah,	"smooth"	

وفَينانة	كثيرة الشعر *
وقِتين	جميلة *
وملَسَّنة القدمين	الملسَّنة من الاقدام والنعال ما فيها طول ولطافة كهيئة اللسان *
ووَهْنانة	بها فتور عند القيام *
وبَرَهْرَهة	البيضآء الشابة والناعمة او التى تُرعَد رطوبة ونعومة والبره الترارة
وذات رَهْرَهة	الرهرهة حسن بصيص لون البشرة ونحوه وترهره جسمه (والاحرى جسمها) ابيض من النَعمة وجسم رَهْراه ورُهروه ورَهْره ناعم ابيض *
وفارهة	الجارية المليحة والفتيّة *
ووَدهآ	المراة الحسنة اللون فى بياض *
ومُوَهْوهة	التى ترعد من الامتلا *
وسَجوْآ الطرف	ساجيته اى ساكنته *
وعابية	حسنآ من عبا يعبو اى اضآ وجهه *
وحسنة العُرْية	اى المجرد والمعارى حيث يُرَى كالوجه واليدين والرجلين *

تاخذ بيديها اللطيفتين مكشطا وصابونة ودلوا فيها مآء حميم * ثم تجثو على ركبتيها المدملجتين وتطفق تحك عتبة الدار ووصيدها وهى تذبذب وتضطرب وتتحثحث وتتعثعث وتتمثمث وتتبع وتتجلج وتتخلج وتترجرج وتتمخ وتتمع وتتنجنج وترتج وتتضحضح وتتاوّد وتتخضد وتترعد وتميد وتتأطر وتتدهكر وتتزرزر وتسجهرّ وتتمرمر وتتململ

faynānah, “having abundant hair”

qaṭīn, “beautiful”

with feet that are *mulassanah,* “feet and soles that are *mulassanah* are those that have length and delicacy and are shaped like a tongue [*lisān*]”

wahnānah, “languorous on rising”

barahrahah, “a smooth, white young woman, or one who quivers with softness and smoothness and with glowing good health”

possessed of *rahrahah,* “*rahrahah* is the attractive glow of the complexion and the like, and when you say ‘his body’” (though it would be better to say “her body”) “*tarahraha,* it means ‘it grew white with ease’ and *rahrāh* and *ruhrūh* and *rahrah,* said of the body, mean ‘white and smooth’”

fārihah, “a young, pretty girl”

wadhā’, “a woman of comely coloring, toward the white”

muwahwahah, “one who quivers with fullness of flesh”

sajwā’ of glance, “calm, i.e., tranquil, of glance”

‘ābiyah, “comely,” from “*‘abā, ya‘bū,* meaning ‘his face beamed with light’”

and comely of *‘uryah,* i.e., “the exposed and naked parts that may be seen, such as the face, the hands, and the feet”

“and each of whom has taken in her delicate hands a scrubbing brush, a cake of soap, and a bucket of hot water and gone down on her rounded knees and set about scrubbing the threshold and doorstep of the house, all the while vibrating,[196] shaking, quivering, quaking, shimmering, quavering,

وتمور وتحيّز وتترجّز وتتلزلز وتمزمز وتهزز وتحسحس وترهّس وتمخس وترخش
وتنغش وترتعص وترقّص وتلصلص وتنصنص وتُوخِص وتخضخض وتلضلض
وتمخض وتنغض وتريّع وتريّه وتسيع وتنوّع وتغضف وترقرق وتريق وتركرك
وتروه وتريه وتلوّه وتلوّى وتَصّرى * وربما اتفق مع رؤية ذلك سماع آلات
١٣،١٦،٤ الطرب يعزف بها فى الشوارع فياحسن ذلك منظرا ومسمعا * ولكن يااغنيآ
لندن واعيانها الم يكن لكم من وسيلة لمشاهدة هذه الشواخص والجواهض الا
باذالة عزة الحسن المصون * ايحل لكم انتهاك حرمة الجمال وامجال ايدى هولآ
الحسان وركبهن لتملاسّ اعتابكم * ما بال جيرانكم الفرنساوية لا يفعلون ذلك وانما
يسومون خدمتهم تنظيف درج الديار من داخل فقط * فيضع الخادم شيا
كالقبقاب او النعل فى رجله ويكشط به ما قدر عليه وما لم يقدر عليه يتركه الى
المرة الثانية او الثالثة * ونحن كذلك لا نكلف نسآنا هذا التنطّس الذى لا معنى
له * وانما نَكِل اليهنّ ما آل الى القفش والرفش اى الطعام والفراش * ومع
ذلك فتزعمون انكم تحترمون النسآ وتعرفون قدرهن اكثر منا * لقد كَبُر ذلك قولا *
فاما تسريحهن فى الليالى الحالكة ليطفن فى كل زقاق وشارع وتسفيرهن الى البلاد
الشاسعة وحدهن فلا يعدّ عندنا من الاكرام لهن فى شى * بل هو احرى ان
يكون دَيْبوبيّه وقَرْطَبانية وقلطبانية وكلتبانية ودُؤثية وديوّثية وقُمعوثية وقوّادية وتَوَريّة
وسَقّرية وصَقّرية وعَزْورية ولِياسيّة وطَرِعية وطَسِعية وقُنْدعية وقنذعية ودُسْفانية
١٤،١٦،٤ واِدّسافية واِمذائية ومُمانويّة وشَغْنبيّة وشَحطبيّة وادفائية وارخيّة * ليت شعرى
كيف يكون قلب الخادمة حين تامرها مخدومتها فى كل يوم قائلة حكّى العتبة * او
حين تسالها رفيقتها هل حككت اليوم عتبة سيدتك * نعم لوكانت العتبة وردت
عندكم بمعنى المرأة كما هى فى لغتنا هذه الشريفة لكان لا يبعد ان يسبق وهمها عند

shuddering, shivering, shimmying, wobbling, bobbling, jouncing, bouncing, fluttering, flickering, turning, twisting, jerking, twitching, trembling, jiggling, swinging, swaying, tossing, tumbling, jolting, and scudding, the sight of this perhaps coinciding with the hearing of musical instruments being played in the streets, producing oh what a lovely sight and sound!

“But, O rich men and burghers of London, have you not at your disposal 4.16.13
any means to contemplate these humps and bumps without demeaning the dignity of respectable good looks? Do you believe it right that beauty’s decency be violated and the hands and knees of these fair ladies blistered to make your doorsteps smooth? How is it that your neighbors the French don’t do the same but force their servants only to clean the stairs of the house on the inside? There, the servants put something like pattens or sandals on their feet and scrub what they can, and what they can’t they leave to the next time, or the one after that. Nor do we charge our women with acquiring this meaningless skill: we just entrust to them things involving board and bed, meaning eating and sleeping arrangements. Yet despite this, you pretend that you respect women and know their value better than us! What a monstrous thing to say![197] And when it comes to sending them out into the dark nights to roam the alleys and streets and dispatching them to distant lands unaccompanied, it wouldn’t be considered among us as showing any kind of respect for them. On the contrary, it would more likely be considered panderation,[198] wittolism, whoremongery, pimpism, poncification, hornism, and cuckolderation.

“I wish I knew how a maidservant’s heart feels when her mistress 4.16.14
orders her each day to ‘Scrub the threshold!’ or when her colleague asks her, ‘Did you scrub your mistress’s threshold today?’ For sure, did the word ‘threshold’ occur among you in the sense of ‘woman,’ as it does in this noble language of ours,[199] her imagination would likely have raced to

السوال الى ذلك * الا ان لغتكم يابسة قاسحة لا تحتمل التاويل ولا التخريج * ولست ارى لهذه العادة المشطة من سبب سوى ان احد كبرائكم كان قد اتخذ خادمة رعبوبة والله اعلم منذ ثلثمائة وخمسين سنة * وكانت امراته دميمة فغارت السيدة منها فكلّفتها حك العتبة والوصيد فى كل يوم اذلالاً لها فى عين سيدها * كانّ القلب لا يعلق بهوى الجميلة المسكينة كما يعلق بهوى الفُنُق * او كأنّ الشى المبجج يحتاج الى مرفد * اوالشى المتدملك الى وشيعة من القطن * اوالغَيْل الى غلالة من الخز * او المكّرة الى جوارب من حرير * فسرت هذه العادة الذميمة فى جميع كبرائكم الى عصرنا هذا عصر التمدّن والرفق بالنسآ * وانتم اسارى العادات والتقليد * فمتى الفتم فِعلة لم يمكنكم ان تنتقلوا عنها * وذلك كتكليف الفتيان من خدمتكم ذرّ رماد ابيض على رؤسهم حتى يكونوا كالشيوخ من فوق * وككشف عجائزكم فى الولائم عن ترائبهن واذرعهن * مع انه لا مناسبة بين اوقات القصوف والحظ ورؤية ترائب منجردة تمنى القوم بالقَمَه * فاما مواطاة الناس على ما اخترعه الامرآء والاعيان على اجرآء العادات السيّئة فهو غير خاصّ بكم * بل هو عام ايضا عند سائر الامم الافرنجية *

that conclusion as soon as she was asked. Your language, though, is stiff and hard and cannot accommodate interpretation or extrapolation. I can see no reason for this outrageous custom other than (though God alone knows the truth) that one of your great men acquired a white, comely, soft, and sweet maidservant some three hundred and fifty years ago, and his wife was ugly, and, the mistress being jealous of the girl, she told her to scrub the threshold and the doorstep every day to make her look abject in the eyes of her master—as though the heart doesn't fall as easily for a pretty but pitiable girl as it does for one in easy circumstances, or as though the thing that quivers has to have a bustle, or the thing that is rounded a cotton wrapper, or the full plump arm a silk-wool padding, or a fine fat leg a stocking of silk. This vile custom then remained something natural to all your great men up to this day of ours, the day of civilization and kindness to women. You are slaves to customs and tradition. Once you've become used to a certain way of doing things, you are incapable of abandoning it. By way of example, you make your young male servants sprinkle white ashes on their heads[200] till they look like old men on top and your old women expose their chests and arms at dinner parties, though to do so is ill-fitted to times of revelry and good cheer and the sight of their naked chests puts everyone off their food. The complicity of people in the imposition of bad customs thought up by princes and notables is not something special to you. On the contrary, it's widespread among all the other nations of the Franks as well.

الفصل السابع عشر

في وصف باريس

كان وصول الفارياق الى هذه المدينة الشهيرة فى ليلة ذات ضباب فكانت ١،١٧،٤
عيناه معمشتين عن رؤية ما فيها من الخصائص * فلما اصبح اخذ يطوف فى شوارعها كالمتفرّغ المتبطّل فاذا بها ملآنة من المزالج والمزالق والرواج والروامق(١) والجرآءى والاَطْناء والرَبّاى والمَلْمُوآت والجَذّابات والرُجَب والرُوَب والغُوت والحِراج واللُبَج والبيّاحات والنِصاحات والمصايد والفخاخ والشواصر والنوامير والقُحّازات والدّحاحيس والمفاقيس والشصوص والبيضاوات والقُفّاعات والمجازف والخواطيف والعواطيف والكُفَف والرِبَق والطِبَق والعوادق والنُشَق والعلائق والاوهاق والشباك والاَشراك والشَوْدَكانات والاحابيل والكوابيل والشهوم والمصالى * فظهر له ان قوام كل شى وعتاده وملاكه وقطبه فى هذه العاصمة متوقف على وجود امراة * فجميع الصُوَب والكُلَب والحوانيت والكُفَت والقرابج والكرابج والكناديج والمفاتح والمحاسب والمثابر والانبار والمخازن والمحارف والمصانع والفناتق والفنادق والدكاكين والقرابق والبلّانات والمنامات والحانات والخانات والافدية والمطاعم والمشارب تديرها نسآ واى نسآء * وما من كَعْب او تأريج او اَوارجة او اَنْجيدج او بُرْجان او جُذاء(٢) او بَرْنامج او عهدة او محضر او جَذْر او وِصْر او قِطّ او فُنْداق او صَكّ او فذلكة او سَيّال

(١) الرامج مِلواح يصطاد به الجوارح وكذا الرامق *

Chapter Seventeen

A Description of Paris

The Fāriyāq arrived in that celebrated city on a foggy night and was too bleary-eyed to be able to see its distinguishing features. Then, in the morning, he set off to roam its streets as though he were unemployed and had all the time in the world. He found them to be full of slipways[201] and slides, snares, decoys and baits,(1) traps, lures, ropes, nooses, lassos, nets, hooks, and hunters' hides. It occurred to him then that the mainstay, working gear, support, and central pole of everything in this capital was the presence of a woman. All the eating houses, drinking houses, shops, warehouses, marts, groceries, godowns, depots, countinghouses, butcheries, showrooms, storehouses, workshops, factories, hostels, hotels, boutiques, corner stores, bathhouses, dosshouses, brasseries, bars, magazines, granaries, restaurants, and watering holes were run by women—and what women!—and there wasn't a stub, a daybook, a tax-book, a list of accounts due, or any calculation involving multiplication (*burjān*(2)), any jottings sheet, invoice, certificate, product, entry book, accounts ledger, record of charges, deed, abstract, liquid account,[202] or precautionary blank-filling[203] that wasn't handled by a woman. He noted too that the clever man 4.17.1

(1) A *rāmij* ["decoy"] is "an owl used to lure predatory birds" and a *rāmiq* ["bait"] is the same.

(2) The *Qāmūs* gives the following definition of *burjān*: "calculation by *burjān* is when you say, 'How much does such and such times such and such make (*mā judhā'u kadhā fī kadhā*) and what is the square root of such and such times such and such (*mā jidhru kadhā fī kadhā*)?' In other words, the *judhā'* is the product, the *jidhr* is the square root by which two things are multiplied with one another, and the whole thing is called *burjān* [i.e., 'multiplication']." However, under the letter *yā'*[204] he speaks only of *judā'*, with *dāl*, providing the following definition: "*judā'*, of the pattern of *ghurāb*: the amount produced by multiplication, e.g., the *judā'* of three times three is nine"; likewise, he fails to mention the use of *al-ḍarb* in this sense [i.e., in the sense of "multiplication"] in the entry for *ḍ-r-b*.

او ترقيم او ترقين او جُداَء الا وتتعاطاه المراة هنا * واللبيب من الرجال مَن اتّخذ فى حانوته او محترفه راجما مليحا يلوّح به للشارين والمجتازين فى السبيل * ولا فرق بين ان يكون ذلك الراج من اهل بيته او غريبا وانما العبرة بانفقاس الفخ على اعناقهم * هذا وقد اختصت نسآ باريس بصفات لا يشاركهن فيها احد ٢،١٧،٤
من نسآء الافرنج * فمن ذلك انهن يتكلمن بالغنّة والخنّة والنشيج والهَزَج والهُزامج والترنج والتطريب والسَكْت والخبْرة والنبرة والاجَشّ والتعثيث والترجيع والاضجاع والقُطَعة والتغريد والتهويد والمدّ والترسيل والترتيل والفصل والوصل والزَجَل والهلهلة والادغام والترخيم والتدنيم والترنيم والرَوْم والاشباع والتفخيم والامالة والتنعيم والتنغيم والتحزين والحنين والجَدَن والتلحين والطَنْ والشجو والترنية * حتى ينتشى السامع فلا يعلم بعد ذلك هل هن يفككن ازراره او فقاره * ومن ذلك تغيير الزى فى كل برهة وبهن تقتدى سائر النسآ * فلو لبست احداهن مثلا عَبْعبا او حرّقت ثوبها لعبّ الناس حبّ ذلك العبعب وصار التحزيق سنة فيهم * وعنهن يوخذ ايضا تقصيب الشعر وسَبْته وتسريجه وتسريحه وتسميده وتجميره وضفره وتطريره وتنفيشه وعقصه وتصفيفه وزرقلته وتشكيله وفرقه وكَدْحه وكدهه وادّرآؤه وجدله وتفتيله وتغبيته ومشطه الكُعَكُبَة والمُقدِمة واتخاذ قُصّة منه او قزّعة او قُنْزعة وجعله مكرهفًا او مسبلا * ومن ذلك انه لطول ترددهن على مواضع الرقص يحسبن كل مكان يطأنه مرقصا * فترى المراة منهن تمشى فى الاسواق والشوارع وهى تميد وتميل وتخلع وتتفكك * وياليت مولانا صاحب القاموس كان يعرف البُلْكَى والمازُرْكَى والسُوتِشكَى والكدريل والرِيدُوقَى

(٢) عبارة القاموس فى ب ر ج وحساب البُرجان قولك ما جُذاَكذا فى كذا وما جذر كذا فى كذا فجذاوه مبلغه وجذره اصله الذى يضرب بعضه فى بعض وجملته البرجان انتهى غير انه لم يحك فى باب اليآ غير الجدآ بالدال المهملة وعبارة الجدآ كغراب مبلغ حساب الضرب ثلاثة فى ثلاثة جداؤه تسعة * واضرب عن ذكر الضرب بهذا المعنى فى موضعه *

among them placed in his store or workplace a pretty decoy that he could wave at the shoppers and those passing on the street. It made no difference whether the said decoy was a member of his family or a stranger; all that mattered was to slip the noose around their necks.

Furthermore, the women of Paris are distinguished by characteristics shared by no other women among the Franks. For example, they speak with such nasality[205] and huskiness, such a catch in the throat, so thrillingly, so tunefully, with such vibrato and tremolo, such resonance, such bravura, such lyricism, such intonation, inflection, and modulation, such melodiousness, such tunefulness, such musicality, such mellifluousness, such sweetness, such a lilt and a swing, so excitingly and so movingly that the listener is intoxicated and loses all awareness of whether they are undoing his buttons or his vertebrae. Another aspect of their appeal is that they change their costumes every little while and all the other women imitate them in this. Thus should one of them don, for example, a cloak, or wear her clothes skintight, everyone straightaway cleaves to a love of cloaks, while skintight dressing becomes a custom. From them too is taken the curling of the hair,[206] its braiding, plaiting, coiling, cutting, gathering, loosening, parting, combing, currying, twisting, tousling, and rumpling, as well as the grooming of the *kuʿkubbah* and the *muqaddimah*.[207] Another thing is that, from their long frequentation of places where people dance, they think that everywhere they set their feet is a dance hall, and you may observe one of these women walking in the markets and streets swaying and bending, loose-limbed and leggy, and how I wish Our Master, the author of the *Qāmūs*, had known the *polka, mazurka, schottische, quadrille, rigadoon,*[208] *valse*, and other kinds of 4.17.2

والقلس وغيرها من ضروب الرقص حتى كنت ارويها عنه هنا فى حق الماشيات
فى باريس * ومن ذلك تحكّمهن على الرجال وتعزّزهن عليهم فى كل حال وبال * ٤،١٧،٣
فترى الرجل يماشى المراة وقلبه بين رجليها * واذا خلا معها فى البيت فهى الآمرة الناهية المستعلية القاضية * وهو المُصحِب المِصحاب المُدَرج المُدَلبح المدمّح المكبوح المكفوح المعنوج المصوَّب المدبَخ المتزنّخ المحتضَد المُسجد المعتسَر المشروس المتَّضَع * ولا يزلن طول الدهر وِحاماً ولا حَبَل * ويرمن ان يكون لهن كل شى صِهابيّا مؤرّبا مرفّلا موفّرا موفّلا مسبغا ضافيا مرتبزا وافيا تامّا كاملا * حتى ان اللغة الفرنساوية مبنيّة على هذا الوحم * وذلك انهم يحذفون فى اللفظ اواخر جميع الالفاظ المذكرة وينطقون بها فى المونثة * وعلى ذلك قول الفارياق

عند الفرنسيس المونّث واجب تبليغ آخره الى الاسماعِ
وهو الدليل على تؤوق نسآئهم طبعا على التبليغ والاشباع
او انه صفة الكمال لهن ان يك ممكنا يوما لذات قناع

وكانّ احد التيتائيّين من نحاتهم غاظه ذلك فجعل من بعض قواعد لغتهم تغليب المذكر على المونث * ولكن هيهات فان امراة واحدة هنا تقوى على عشرين
ذكرا * ومن ذلك ان عنوان جمالهن مكتوب على جباههن نظما ونثرا * فمن النظم ٤،١٧،٤

مَلِكُ الجمال اعزّ من ملك له جند واعوان وعرش ارفع
ذو المُلك تتبعه الجنود تكلفا ولذى الجمال الناس طوعا تتبع

ومنه

من حارب العِيْن خانته مضاربه وليس يجديه شحذ السيف عن جَلَده

dance that I might relay the words for them here, to the credit of the walking women of Paris!

A further aspect of their appeal is the sway they hold over the men and the power they have over them in every situation. You'll find the man walking next to the woman in abject submission[209] and when he's alone with her at home, she it is who forbids and *commands*, reigns and *remands*, while he is servile, bowed, *licked*, reined in, *whipped*, checked, humbled, *ill-used*, cringing, domesticated, ill-treated, *abused*. They, on the other hand, never cease to crave special foods even when not pregnant and to demand that everything be in full measure, in full supply, shaken down and running over, abundant, *complete*, full, perfect, *replete*. Even the French language is built upon these female cravings, for in speaking they drop the ends of all the masculine words and pronounce them in the feminine[210]—on which topic the Fāriyāq said, 4.17.3

Among the French, the feminine ending
 To listening ears must be conveyed.
This points to their women's desire, by nature,
 To make it to the end and obtain satisfaction when getting laid.
Or perhaps it's a sign of their complete consummation
 (If, among veil-wearers, claim to any such thing may be made).

Some impotent grammarian of theirs, seemingly annoyed by this, made it a rule of their language that the masculine should take precedence over the feminine.[211] It didn't do him much good, though: a single woman here can take on and get the better of twenty men.

Another thing about them is that an epitome of their beauty is written on their foreheads, in verse and in prose. An example of the verse: 4.17.4

A king of beauty is mightier than any king
 Of army, ministers, and lofty throne.
Soldiers follow the ruler at his command
 But men follow beauty on their own.

and

Who fights the black-of-pupil, white-of-eye by his weapons must be betrayed
 And the whetting of his sword will avail him naught for all his pluck,

فمضرب السيف مشحوذ على حجر ومضرب الطرف مشحوذ على كبده

ومن النثر * الكلام بالغُنّة * شفاء من العُنّة * فرط التنهيد * ابلغ فى التهنيد * الخَدَل * جلآ المقل * ضخم الحماة * يفتح اللهاة * صغر الاقدام * يقرح الإدام * كم صريع فى السوق * من كشف السوق * ان ابراز الترائب * كاشف غمّ النوائب * ان العبَعَب * املا للعين واحبّ * ان الاعجان * داعى الافتتان * ان النَوَق * اصل الشَنَق * لا تفكّن * الا ويزيله التبهكن * التهيّم * ادعى للتهييم والتيّم * المغاضنة * دليل المحاضنة * غلائل الصيف * امضى من السيف * لا فرار* بعد الافترار * لا عاصم * بعد كشف المعاصم * توهج الطيب * اشوق للحبيب * ربّ ابتسامه * جلبت غرامة * العين غزّالة * والقامة فتالة * الحسن معبود * والدينار منقود * الدينار* فكّاك الازرار * من اكثر من الصلة * نال ما امله * البضع لذى الدنيا * والدنيا لذى البضع * من ذاق عرف * ومن غازل هرف * الى الملهى الى الملهى * فبادر ثمّ لا تلهى * وعللها بكاس ثم عما شئت فاسالها * والحاصل ان الفرق بين عنوان جمال الفرانساويات وجمال الانكليزيات هو ان الاول من قبيل التداوى من الشى بضده * والثانى من قبيل التداوى منه بجنسه * وذلك ان العنوان الاول هو ناطق عن الونى والفتور والترهّل والتربّخ والاسترسال والاسترخآ والاسترخاخ والاسترخاف والرشرشة والنشنشة والانخرار والثملطة والثلمطة والختَت والهنبتة واللُوثة والهُلاث والابثجاج والطرشحة والامرخداد والترترة والتخثّر والفيشوشة والتّعة والخراعة واللَخع والطِرّيقة والرهوكة والثرطلة والغَدَن والانثطآ المستدعية لنقائضها من الاشتداد والتصلّب والاتمئرار والتاتّب والتقسّح والتقسّب والتوتّر والتعلّب والتعرّد والتعلّد والانزاز والتادّد والعَصّ والاستعراز والتأيّد والكأن

For the eye is a weapon sharpened on his liver
While the sword's merely sharpened on a rock.

An example of the prose:

> That nasal *twang* makes of the impotent a *man*. Strong mammary *development* is the most effective form of *blandishment*. The well-fleshed *thigh* brightens the *eye*. Largeness of *leg* makes a man open his throat and *beg*. Small *feet* make your food *sweet*. How many a one in the market has fallen to the *ground* on catching sight of a calf that was *round*! A display of the *chest* brings, after trouble, *rest*. Nothing's more lovable or pleasant to the *eye* than a little miss, pretty as *pie*. Plump girls encourage *infatuation*; whiteness with a rosy flush can be a cause of *dissension*. There's no *regret* that a wagging behind won't make you *forget*. There's no gloomy *thought* that a buttock-rolling walk can't *thwart*. Nothing's as likely as an attractive *gait* to induce abject love and *humiliate*. *Winking* of *eyes* points the way to *linking* of *thighs*. The bustle-pins of *summer* are sharper than any *saber*. No *flight* after a smile *bright*. After exposure of the *wrist*, none can *resist*. A burst of scent! There's nothing more attractive to the *desirer*. Many a smile has won an *admirer*. The eye spins *webs*, the figure spins *threads*. Good looks make a *splash*, gold coins are *cash*. A golden *guinea* unties many a *pinny*. He who gives presents *galore* wins what he's hoping *for*. Sex is for those endowed with worldly goods and the world is for sex. To know her, *taste her*, the rest's *conjecture*. To the play, to the *play*, there to make your move without *delay*! Pour her a second drink from the *flask*, then for whate'er you desire *ask*.

In sum, the difference between the epitome of the beauty of Frenchwomen and that of Englishwomen is that the first belongs to the class of things that cure using opposites and the second to the class of things that cure using things of the same sort. Thus the first epitome speaks of languorousness,[212] lassitude, lethargy, lounging, lolling, lissomenesss, litheness, indolence, inanimation, drooping, draping, pliancy, pliability, and flexibility, and calls out to their opposites such as stiffness, solidity, turgidity, rigidity, hardness, firmness, unbendingness, unyieldingness, tautness, and tensile strength,

والاتّكاع والتكلّد * وجمال اولئك عنوان على هذه الصفات المستدعية لنظائرها
وكلاهما فى المراة حسن * ومن ذلك انهن يرين التقليد فى الحبّ والزىّ معرّة * ٥،١٧،٤
فكل واحدة منهن تجتهد فى فنّها حتى تصير قدوة لغيرها * اما فى الزى فمنهن من
تقبّب صدرها بقدر ما تقبب نساَ الانكليز بتائلهن * ومنهن من تتّخذ لها قبّتين
من قبل ومن دبر * حتى تكون اذا مشت عائقة لساتهها ومواجهها * وكشف
الساق لابراز الحماة ونظافة الجوارب مطّرد لهنّ * فاما فى الحبّ فمنهن من تزيد على
صفات المدقم الصفة التى ذكرها ابو نواس فى الهمزية * ومنهن من توثر التجضّم
الكمرى او الامتلاج القنبى * واكثر الناس حرصا على هذا الشيوخ المحنكون *
فاِمّصاصهم وتبظيرهم ليس من السب فى شى * ومنهن من تجمع بين اللذتين
الخزنوفية والفنقورية ولها سعران * ومنهن من تزيد على ذلك ما اراده الشيخ جمال
الدين بن نباتة من شوص الفرخ وله ثلثة اسعار * ومنهن من تزيد عليه الشوص
بالاخمصين وله اربعة * ومنهن من تمكن من قفط النَوْدلين وثغرما بينهما مجردا *
ومنهن من تضيفه الى اللذتين المذكورتين مع شوص الفرخ بانامل واخامص وهو
اغلى ما يكون * ومنهن من تتقاحل وتتقمّد على اخرى مثلها * وهذا النوع عزيز لا
يراه الا الموسرون * ومنهن من تتعاطى الحرفة الترّسية وهو قرع الترس بالترس *
ومن اغرب ما يكون ان بعض شيوخ الفرنساوية الذين يشب فكرهم وتخيلهم لهرم
اجسامهم ووهن حركتهم يوثرون على جميع الانواع المذكورة التلمّظ بالعَذِرة *
وذلك بان يضطجع احدهم وهو عريان ويامر من تستوى فوقه وتملأ فمه * ومنهم
من يستغنى عنه بشرب الزغرب من مشخبه زُغلةً زُغلةً او بمص القنب * وقد يجتمع
رجال بواحدة فيقيمونها بين ايديهم عريانة ويقعد لدى قبلها ودبرها اثنان * وياخذ
آخر فى صبّ الشراب من فوق صدرها وظهرها * فيبادر اليه الرجلان وهما

while the beauty of the others is an epitome of the same qualities that calls out to their likes. Both in a woman are attractive.

Another thing about them is that they regard imitation in love and dress as shameful. Each of them works hard at her art, so as to become a model for others. As far as dress is concerned, some pad out their busts as much as Englishwomen do their backsides and some make two domes, one in front and one in back, so that when she walks she impedes the progress of both those approaching her from behind and those approaching her from in front. Exposure of the calf to make a show of the fleshiness of the leg and the cleanliness of the stockings are usual among them. As far as love is concerned, some add to the quality of the all-devouring vagina that other quality mentioned by Abū Nuwās in his poem rhyming in the glottal stop.[213] Some prefer to take the head of the man's penis into their mouths or to have their clitorises sucked. Those most avid to oblige them regarding the latter are the old experienced men, and telling these "Go get sucked!" or "Go cunnilinger!" is no insult.[214] Some of them offer a combination of the pleasures of the vagina and the anus, each having its price. Some add to this working the little fellow up and down, as requested by Shaykh Jamāl al-Dīn ibn Nubātah, and this has three prices. Some further add to this working it up and down with the hollows of the feet, making four charges. Some are capable of servicing two men at the same time and inserting themselves between them naked. Some add this to the two abovementioned pleasures *plus* working it up and down with the fingertips *and* the soles of the feet, and this is the most expensive of all. Some of them will act like stud bull camels and mount another woman like them, necks astretch, but this type is in short supply and only to be seen by the well-off. Some of them practice the craft of the shield bearer and bang shield on shield. One of the strangest things is that some old Frenchmen, the decrepitude of whose bodies and the feebleness of whose physical motion have inflamed their thoughts and imaginations, favor over all the aforesaid activities the slurping down of feces; one such will lie down, naked, and call for a woman to sit down on top of him and fill his mouth. Others substitute for this the drinking of the copious stream from its point of emergence, gush after gush, or sucking on the clitoris. Sometimes men meet up with a woman and make her stand in front of them naked; two of them then sit down, one in front of her and the other behind, and another 4.17.5

فاغران افواهما ويشربانه عند مروره على السَّمَّين * والنسآ المثريات المغتلمات يستعملن رجالا يقودون اليهن كل من راوه ابتع من الرجال ولا سيما من اهل الريف * فيدخلون عليهن فى بعض الديار وهن متبرقعات كيلا يُعرَفن ثم ياجرنهم على ذلك * وفى الجملة فان كل ما يخطر ببال النحرير من امور الفسق يراه الانسان فى باريس
٦،١٧،٤ بعينه بالعَيْن * واعلم ان اهل باريس قد اصطلحوا على امور فى المعاش والنسآ تميزوا بها عمن سواهم * اما فى امر المعاش فان من ياكل منهم فى المطاعم الشائعة فانه يشارط صاحب المحل او بالحرى صاحبته على ان يعطيها فى الشهر قدرا معلوما وياكل عندها شيا معلوما * فتعطيه تذاكر توذن بعدد المرات فيدفع ثمنها ثم يعيدها عليها فيودّى اليها عن كل غدآ او عشآ تذكرة * فيتوفر عليه فى ذلك ربع المصروف * وقس عليه الحمامات والملاهى وما اشبهها * فاما فى امر النسآ فان اصحاب البيع والشرآ لمّا كانوا قد اتخذوا لادارة اشغالهم نسآ حسانا كما سبقت الاشارة اليه * فاذا خرجن فى الليل بعد انقضآ اشغالهن ترصدتهن الرجال ودعوهن الى مواضع الاكل والقهوة والرقص واللعب * فتذهب كل واحدة مع من تحب * فمتى رافقته الى احد هذه المواضع علم ان حقه عليها صار ضربة لازب * فاما ان يستوفيه منها تلك الليلة فقط او يوافقها على اعادة الوصل فى كل اسبوع مثلا مرتين او ثلاثا وان يعطيها فى آخر الشهر اجرة معلومة * وما بقى لها من الساعات فانها توجره لآخرين باجرة معينة * فترى للواحدة منهن عدّة عشاق تواصلهم فى اوقات مختلفة من الليل والنهار * ومع ذلك فلا تزال تلقب بدُمّوازل وهى كلمة تطلق على الابكار على وجه التعظيم * ومعناها سيّدة غير ذات بعل * ومنهم من يتصدى لمعرفة هولآ البنات من المراقص * فيعمد الرجل الى بنت ويدعوها للرقص * فاذا اعجبته واعجبها دعاها للشراب فى موضع مخصوص فى المرقص وعقد عليها عقد

starts pouring wine over her chest and back. The two men set to it, opening their mouths wide and drinking the wine as it passes over the two holes. Lustful rich women use men to bring them any men who look to them well-endowed, especially those from the countryside. These go to them in certain houses, where the women's faces are veiled so that they cannot be known, and the women pay them for that purpose. In general, any kind of depravity that might occur to the mind of the most learned scholar may be seen in Paris in the barest detail and by the naked eye.

You must know that the people of Paris have adopted certain conven- 4.17.6
tions regarding matters of daily life and women that distinguish them from all others. Where daily living is concerned, those that eat in the restaurants that are everywhere agree with the master—or, to be more accurate, the mistress—of the establishment to pay her a set amount each month and eat there a set meal, and she gives such a one tickets that display the number of times and he pays her the price for them, then returns the tickets to her, handing over a ticket for each lunch or dinner. This saves him a quarter of the cost. The same thing applies to baths, theaters, and other places of that sort. Where women are concerned, given that the men who buy and sell have taken good-looking women to manage their affairs, as explained above, the latter, on leaving in the evening after finishing their work, are watched out for by men, who invite them to places where they can eat, have coffee, dance, or play. Each then goes with whomever she likes. When the man has accompanied her to one of these places, he knows that his possession of her is only a matter of time. He will either have his fill of her that very night or make an arrangement with her to repeat the contact twice or three times every week, for example, or to give her a set amount at the end of the month. Any remaining hours she then rents out to others for a certain fee. You'll find that one of them has a number of lovers that she makes love to at different times of the day and night. This does not prevent such women from being addressed as *demoiselle,* which is a word applied to virgins as a sign of respect and means an unmarried lady. Some men spend their time getting to know these girls via the dance halls. The man goes up to a girl and invites her to dance. If he likes her, and she likes him, he invites her to take a drink in a private part of the dance hall and contracts with her for a monthly visit. A man who makes a monthly arrangement with one of them

الزيارة الشهرى * ومن عامل واحدة منهن مشاهرة لم ينفق عليها نصف ما ينفقه لو قضاها على كل مرة على حدتها * وللنسآ رخصة فى باريس ان يدخلن جميع المراقص العمومية من دون ان يدفعن شيا اجتذابا للرجال بكثرتهن * ولكن عليهن ان يرقصن معهم اذا استرقصوهنّ * الا اذا اعتذرن لهم بعذر يقبلونه كاَنْ تقول المدعوة مثلا قد دعانى آخر من قبلك فلا بد لى من ان ارقص معه او نحو ذلك * ثم انه لا حرج ايضا على من اكترى فى منزل بيتا مفروشا كان او غير مفروش ان تزوره صاحبته فى مسكنه * سوآ كانت من النوع الذى ذكرناه اعنى من النسآ اللآى بمنزلةٍ بين الحرائر والزوانى او من غيره * وان تبيت عنده على علم من الجيران والسكان * فان منزلة هذا عند اهل باريس كمنزلة المتزوج * ولا فرق عند اهل باريس بين امراة متزوجة لها سبعة بنين وسبع بنات تربيهم فى تقوى الله وطاعة الملك وبين قحبية تبيع عرضها لكل ابن سبيل وتتفنشخ لكل مجتاز فى الطريق كما تقول

٧،١٧،٤ التوراة * وهناك اسباب اخر كثيرة للفساد فى الديار * وذلك انه لما كانت جميع الاشغال فى باريس تديرها النسآ وكان منهن غسّالات وخدامات لهنّ ياخذن ثياب السكان وخياطات وفرّاشات وبياعات للماكول والمشروب والملبوس * امكن للرجل ان يصاحب واحدة منهن فتاتيه مياومة اذا شآء بحجة انها تقضيه شيا او تبيع له حاجة * او ملايلة او مشاهرة او مساوعة او محاينة وذلك ممنوع فى لندرة * بل ربما صاحب الرجل امراة من نفس الدار التى يسكنها * لان ديار هذه المدينة العامرة لما كانت تشتمل على عدة طبقات وكان اصغرها يحوى فى الاقل عشرين نفسا ما بين رجال ونسآ * امكن للرجل ان يعاشر احدى جاراته * بل المتزوجون المقيمون فى هذه الديار لا يامنون على نسائهم وبناتهم * لان الرجل اذا خرج من بيته وخالفه فيه جاره الى زوجته مئة مرة فى اليوم لم يمكنه ان يعلم ذلك لقرب ما

will pay less than half for her what he would if he settled with her separately each time. Women in Paris are permitted to enter any public dance hall without paying a thing, as a way of attracting, by their large numbers, the men. They must, however, dance with them if they ask them to do so, unless they refuse them with an acceptable excuse, such as if the invitee were to say, for instance, "Someone else invited me before you, so I have to dance with him" and so on. Nor is there any objection to a man who has rented a room, furnished or unfurnished, in a house having his mistress visit him in his residence—be she one of the kind to which we have alluded, meaning one of those women whose status is somewhere between that of a respectable woman and a prostitute, or of any other kind—and spend the night with him with the knowledge of the neighbors and residents. Such a man, in the eyes of the people of Paris, has the same status as if he were married, and there is no difference in the eyes of the people of Paris between a married woman who has seven sons and seven daughters whom she raises to fear God and obey the king and some little whore who sells her virtue to every passerby and who spreads her legs to any "that passeth by" on the road, as the Old Testament has it.[215]

There are many other occasions for corruption inside the houses. As all 4.17.7
businesses in Paris are run by women and among these women are washerwomen and their female employees who take the inhabitants' clothes, and seamstresses, cleaners, and sales girls for food, drink, and clothing, a man may take one of these as his mistress and she may come to him, daily if he wants, on the excuse that she's going to do some work for him or sell him something—or nightly or monthly or hourly or every now and then; this is prohibited in London. Indeed, sometimes a man will take as his mistress a woman from the same house that he's living in, for the houses in this flourishing city, given that they consist of a number of stories and the smallest of them holds at least twenty souls, men and women, allow a man to keep company with his neighbors. In fact, the married men living in these houses cannot ensure the safety of their wives and daughters because if a man leaves his apartment and his neighbor takes his place there with his wife a hundred times a day, the man will have no way of knowing given that the two residences are so close to one another. This is why the people of Paris are the

بين المسكنين * ولهذا كان اهل باريس اقلّ غيرة على نسائهم من جميع الناس *
لانهم ربوا على هذا ولا مناص لهم منه * ولا يمكنهم ان يربوا اطفالهم عندهم ٨،١٧،٤
خوفا من تضجر الجيران منهم * وانما يبعثونهم الى الريف من اول اسبوع ميلادهم
فيربون فى اجار المراضع * وهى عادة حميدة من جهة ان الاطفال يتقوّون هناك
بطيب الهوآ * وهناك سبب آخر وهو ان المُطفل بترشيحها ولدها وتربيته تخسر
من نفع حرفتها اكثر مما تعطيه للظئر * لان نسآ باريس يباشرن جميع الحرف ولا
يرين فى التكسب عارا باىّ وجه كان * وهنّ فى البيع والشرآء اشط من الرجال *
ومن تكن جميلة تتقاضَ على النظر الى جمالها شيا زائدا على الثمن * ثم ان حالة
الرجال مع النسآ على المنوال الذى ذكرناه تعدّ عند هولآ الناس من المصالح المهمّة
المرتّبة المطردة * بمعنى انه ليس من دار الّا ويحصل فيها وصال بين الرجال والنسآ
مع مراعاة حرمة كل من الزائر والمزور * ومع عدم الاخلال بالوقت الموقوت لئلا
يحصل تعطيل للمزور فى شغله * ومع مجانبة ما يسوء الجيران من لغط وعربدة *
ولا تكاد ترى فى باريس كلها فقيرة او مومسة تطوف فى الليل وهى سكرى كما ٩،١٧،٤
ترى فى لندرة * وندر وجود احداهنّ فى متاخر الليل * وقلّ من آذت زائرها
او قاصدها * وهناك فرق آخر بين نسآ الفرنسيس والانكليز من جهة الخُلق لا
الخَلق * فالظاهر من نسآ الانكليز فى الغالب الكِبر والاَنَفَة والصَلَف * والظاهر
من نسآ الفرنسيس اللين والبشاشة * الا ان نسآ الانكليز لا يتدللن على الرجال
ولا يجشّمنهم التُرَف والتحف والولائم والملاهى والمنازه والفرج * فاكلة من الكباب
وكرعة من المزر تكفيان فى استجلاب رضاهن * وليس عندهن من الرَّوم والمِحال *
والخَلب والاختتال * والدها والنكر والاحتيال ما عند نسآ باريس * فامّا ان
تحب احداهن مثلا شخصا وترضى معه بالكثير والقليل واما ان تصرمه * فاما نسآ

least jealous of their womenfolk of any people in the world: they were raised to it and they have no alternative.

They cannot raise their children at home with them for fear the neighbors will find them annoying, so they send them to the countryside the first week after they are born and there they are raised in the laps of wet nurses, which is a praiseworthy custom from the perspective that the children grow strong there on the good air. There is another reason, which is that the woman who has a child loses more, in terms of what she would make from her trade, through the raising and upbringing of her child than she would pay to the wet nurse, for the women of Paris personally direct all the trades there and see no shame whatsoever in making money. Buying and selling, they ask for more than the men, and the good-looking ones add something as the price of gazing on their beauty. These people consider the regulation of relationships between men and women in the fashion we have described to be important, well-established, and normal, meaning that there isn't a single house in which liaisons between the men and the women do not occur, the respectability of both the visitor and the visited being maintained, the appointed time being strictly observed so that the person visited is not inconvenienced in his work and any annoyance or disturbance to the neighbors' peace and quiet is avoided. 4.17.8

In Paris you hardly ever see a poor woman or a prostitute wandering around drunk at night as you do in London; it's rare to find a woman out late at night and seldom does one of them do harm to a man who visits or solicits her. And there is another difference between the women of the French and of the English, from the moral rather than the physical perspective. Generally, Englishwomen appear proud, disdainful, and self-important while Frenchwomen appear easygoing and cheerful. On the other hand, Englishwomen do not play the coquette with their men and do not put them to the expense of presents, trinkets, dinner parties, theaters, parks, and outings; a serving of grilled meat and a swig of beer are enough to make them happy. Nor do they have the same avarice and *underhandedness*, wheedling ways and *pryingness*, cunning, deceit, and *deviousness* as the women of Paris; an Englishwoman will either fall in love with a person and be happy with him through thick and thin or cut off relations with him. A Parisienne, though, no matter what show she may put on of being pliable, 4.17.9

باريس فمما يظهر منهن من الملاينة والمباغمة * والملاطفة والملآمة * فاذا عاشرت واحدة منهن وشعرتَ بانك ارتبقت فى هواها و رُقبت تبغنجت عليك وتدللت * وتصلّفت وتمحّلت * واوهمتك ان مجرد كلامها معك منّة * وان ارضآها والخضوع لها سنّة * وان كثيرا فى عشقها متيمون ناحلون * هائمون ناسمون * حتى تستقلّ عليها كل كثير من الصِلات والهدايا فتقبل منك ما تقبل وانت لها من الشاكرين * واذا دعوتها لوليمة فلا بدّ من اروائها من الرحيق المختوم * وتوحيمها بافخر المطعوم * فتلتهم ما تلتهم وتشتفّ ما تشتفّ وهى متشبعة متعففة * متمنعة متظرفة * فاذا ضَحِكَتْ حَسِبتَ ان ليس لضحكها من نظير * واذا مشت ودت لو كان خطوها على الديباج والحرير * حتى ان هذا التصلّف ايضا صفة ملازمة ١٠،١٧،٤
للمتزوجات * فان المراة المتزوّجة فى باريس تغرّم زوجها على كسوتها فقط ما ينفقه المتزوج من الانكليز على جميع اهله * فداب الرجل فى باريس وهمّه وشغله ارضاء زوجته وهيهات ان ترضى وما احسن ما قيل فى هذا المعنى

لا يعجب الزوج الا ان تكون بمن   تحبّ محفوفةً او لا فاعنات
وكيف يرضى امرء يحمى حقيقته   بالقِرن والقَرن افتوا ايها الناتُ

وقال

وداخلة الانسان تفسد كلها   اذا اصبحت زوج له امّ خارجَه
ويخرج عنه الحلم لو قيل مرة   له هى فى البيت الفلانى والِجَه

ولهذا يقال فى المثل السائر عند الفرنساوية ان باريس نعيم النسآ ومطهر الرجال وجحيم الخيل * ولما كانت حالة الرجال مع النسآ هكذا كان ثلثة ارباع سكان باريس

of voice *melodious,* kindly, and with your inclinations *harmonious,* will, if you keep company with her and she senses that you've become ensnared by her love and caught by the *neck,* take liberties and act the *coquette,* be devious and play hard to *get.* She'll give you to think that just by talking to you she's doing you a *favor,* that keeping her happy and submitting to her wishes is required *behavior,* that so many are dying for her love and in condition *dire,* wandering like lost souls and about to *expire,* that you end up believing that all your many gifts and presents are of little worth, at which point she accepts what she accepts and "thou art among those thankful to her."[216] If you invite her to *dine,* you must tempt her palate with the finest food and give her to drink of your vintage *wine,* while she deigns to devour what she may and quaff what she will, pretending the while to have no appetite and wrinkling her *nose,* making a show of refusing and striking a *pose.* When she laughs, she thinks no other has a laugh of her *ilk,* and when she walks, thinks she should be treading on brocade or *silk.*

This disdainfulness is a characteristic even of married women, for a married woman in Paris will make her husband pay for her outfits alone what an English husband spends on his entire family. Thus all the effort, concern, and worry of a man in Paris go toward keeping his wife happy, but how unlikely it is that she will be so! How excellent the words of the poet on this matter when he says 4.17.10

A wife's ne'er happy unless by those she loves
  Surrounded; if not, expect feathers to fly!
Yet how can a man agree to protect his dependents
  With both hanger and horn?[217] Good people, do edify!

and

A man's inner state will go all to pot
  If a wife of his as Umm Khārijah's[218] viewed,
And he'll lose all sense of proportion if one day told,
  "She's in so-and-so's house, being screwed."

This is why the proverb current among the French has it that "Paris is heaven for women, purgatory for men, and hell for horses."[219] Relations between men and women being as they are, three quarters of the inhabitants of Paris

مسافحين * ونصف الربع الاخر متزوجين زواجا شرعيا والباقى منقطعون عن النكاح * كذا اخبرنى من يوثق بكلامه * ثم ان المومسة من الانكليز تعرف نفسها انها غير حرّة وتعرف ايضا ان الناس يعرفونها كذلك * فلا تكلفهم احترامها * ولا تسومهم اعظامها * فاما البغىّ من الفرنسيس فعندها ان مجرّد استبضاعها للبضع يؤهّلها لان يكرمها الناس ويداروها * ويجلّوها ويسانوها * وذلك لعدم
١١،١٧،٤ استغنائهم عنها * وجرّهم النفع منها * وقد تقدّم ان الفرنساوية لا يفرقون بين
الحرة والبغىّ وبقى هنا ان نقول انهم اشد الناس شبقا الى البعال * واقرمهم الى السفاح * وناهيك انهم فى الفتنة الكبيرة التى حدثت فى سنة ١٧٩٣ اقاموا امراة عريانة على مذبح احدى الكنائس وسجدوا لها * فصوّر لخاطرك ايها القارى كيف تكون الرجال والنسآ فى هذه المدينة فى ليالى الشتآء الباردة الطويلة * وكم من ملهى يغصّ بهم وبهن وكم من مآب * وكم من مائدة تميد لهم بالطعام والشراب * وكم من سرر تهتزّ * ومضاجع تأزّ * واجناب تلزّ * واوطاب تمزّ * واوتار تنزّ * انشدنى الفارياق لنفسه فى وصف باريس واجازنى روايته

وفى باريس لذات كما فى   جنان الخُلد حَيْرٍ وحور عِيْن
ولكن شانهن دوام طمث   لكلٍ اربعون من القرين

وقال فى الراقصات

لله درّ الراقصات لنا على   نغم المثانى حيث تُجلَى الكوبُ
لوكان يوما وطؤهن علىّ لم   تثقل لدىّ من الزمان خطوب

وقال فى راجح

are fornicators, half the remaining quarter are legally married, and the rest are celibates; I was told this by someone whose word is to be trusted. It's also the case that the English prostitute knows she is not a respectable woman and she knows everyone else knows it, so they don't bother to respect her and she doesn't demand that they glorify her. The French harlot, on the other hand, thinks that the mere fact that she sells sex qualifies her to be honored and *adulated*, made much of and *appreciated*, because they can't do without her and they make a profit from her.

I have already noted that the French make no distinction between the respectable woman and the harlot and all that remains to be said is that no people are more lascivious then they in their desire for intercourse or more lickerish in their desire for fornication. It is enough to mention that, during the great schism that arose in 1793, they put a naked woman on the altar of a church and bowed down to her. Only imagine, then, dear reader, how the men and women of this city are during the long, cold nights of winter, and how many a place of entertainment and resort becomes packed with them, how many a table is set for them with food and drink, how many a bed shakes, how many a couch creaks, how many a flank is pressed to flank, how many a milk skin gushes, how many a bowstring buzzes! The Fāriyāq recited to me the following description of Paris, of his own composition, and licensed me to transmit it: 4.17.11

The pleasures of Paris, I swear, are as those of Paradise—
Yes indeedy!—and it holds as many houris too.
Here, though, they're forever being touched,[220]
And there are forty consorts for each man to woo.

On dancers he said

How fine the sight of them dancing for us
To the notes of the lute where e'er the cup's displayed!
Should their feet e'er happen to tread upon me,
Of time's misadventures I'll ne'er feel the weight.

And on a decoy, he said

ذی البارىزية طلعتها كالصبح بها قلبی مغرم
فی الليل اريد تحيتها فاقول لها بُن جور مادم

قال وكما ان الغريب المسكين ينشرح صدره وينجلى بصره بمشاهدة تلكم الحكاكات ١٢،١٧،٤
للاعتاب فی لندرة على الصفة التى تقدم ذكرها * كذلك تقرّعينه برؤية امثالهن فی باريس طائفات فی الشوارع والاسواق من دون غطآ على روسهن ولا ساتر لخصورهن وما يليها * بخلاف عادة النسآ فی لندرة فانهن لا يخرجن الا ملتحفات * قال وعندى ان هاتين الخلتين وهما حك الاعتاب والخروج من دون التحاف هما السبب فی قلة وجود العميان فی هاتين المدينتين السعيدتين * وقلما ترى فی رجالها احول او ازور او احوص او اخوض او ارمص او اكمس او اعشى او اخفش او اعفش او اعمش او اغبش او اغمش او ارمش او امتش او ذا دَوَش او مدش او طَخَش اوغطش اوغفش او طَفَنْشَأً او غَطَمَّشا او مغطرشا او مطغمشا او مطرفشا او مطفرشا او مطنفشا او مدنفشا او مدنقشا * فعلى كل من كان فی بلادنا اعمش ذا عين ان يقصد هذه البلاد ليجلو بصره بهذه المناظر الانيقة * وليستصحب معه ايضا لهذا الجلآ[١] جِلآ اى لقباً ينبى عن شرف وسيادة * فان القوم يعظمون هذه الزَنَمة ولا يرون للانسان فضلا بغيرها * وعلى فرض تحرّجه من الانتحال والتزوير فان غناه يكسبه اياها من عندهم * لانه متى كان غنيا وجعل دابه ان يتردد على مواضع اللهو والحظ لم يلبث ان يتعرف بزمرة من الكبرآ السعدآ وان يزورهم فی مغانيهم * وح يسمونه بسمة شرف تشريفا له وتشرّفا به اذ لا يزورهم الّا الشريف مثلهم * فاما حرص النسآ على هذه الزنمة وخصوصا نسآء الانكليز فهو اوسع من ان يحصر فی هذا الكتاب *

١ ١٨٥٥: الجِلاء.

This Parisienne has a face
 Like the morn—I'm smitten with her, I am.
I'd like to greet her of an evening
 And tell her, "Bonjour, madame!"

And another time he said, "And just as the pitiful stranger's chest is relieved of everything that crushes it and his eyes brighten at the sight of all those women scrubbing steps in London in the manner described above, so his eye finds relief at the sight of their like in Paris roaming the streets and the markets with no covering on their heads and no impediment to the sight of their haunches and adjoining parts (in which they differ from the habits of the women of London, who never go out without being well bundled up)." I am of the opinion that these two propensities—namely, to scrub doorsteps and to go out without being tightly bundled—explain why there are so few men with eye disorders in these two happy cities. Rarely does one see among their men any who are squint-eyed,[221] cross-eyed, sunken-eyed, rheumy-eyed, purblind, night-blind, bleary-eyed, sand-blind, red-eyed, or walleyed, or who suffer from astigmia, nystagmus, amblyopia, myopia, presbyopia, esotropia, hyperopia, exotropia, anoopsia, or pinguecula. Every man in our country who suffers from rheum and has the means should make for this land so that his sight may be polished back to brightness by these elegant scenes. Let him bring with him too on this emigration an eminent title (which is to say a title that proclaims his nobility and authority), for the people there think highly of such "skin flaps"[222] and believe a man without one to be of no worth. If he's embarrassed to claim one falsely or make one up, his wealth will obtain him one, because if he's rich and makes it his habit to visit places of entertainment and good cheer, he will soon become acquainted with a band of their great and fortunate men and visit them in their homes. When this happens, they will bestow on him some title of nobility so as to honor him and be themselves honored by him, for no one who is not noble like them can ever visit them. Women, and especially Englishwomen, have an interest in such skin flaps that is too extensive to document in this book. 4.17.12

الفصل الثامن عشر

في شكاة وشكوى

١،١٨،٤ ثم رام الفارياق ان يستاجر شقة دار ليسكنها هو واهله فراوا عدة اماكن لم تخل من عيوب * وكانت الفارياقية فى خلال ذلك تتمعّص من ارتقآ الدرج فان بعضها كان يشتمل على مئة وعشرين درجة فاكثر * حتى اذا تبواوا محلا وجدوا موقده رديئا * فلم يمض على ذلك ايام حتى طفقت تشكو وتقول * ياللعجب كيف تنخدع الناس احيانا بشى وتنوّه به دون تحقق معرفة حاله * ومتى يستقر ببالهم وجوده على حال من الاحوال يَعُد تغيير وهمهم عنه محالا * حتى ان تغيير الوهم من الخاطر يكون اصعب من تغيير اليقين * لان من تيقّن شيا فانما يتيقّنه عن علم * ومن طبع العالم ان ينظر دائما فى الحقائق واضدادها ولا يزال باحثا عن الصحيح والاصحّ * فاما الوهم فلا يدخل الا راس الجاهل * ومتى دخل فلا يكاد يخرج منه *

٢،١٨،٤ مثال ذلك وَهْم الناس ان مدينة باريس هى اجمل مدينة فى الدنيا * مع انى رايت فيها من العيوب ما لم اره فى غيرها * انظر الى طرقها والى ما يجرى فيها من الدم والنجاسة ومن المياه المتنوعة الالوان * فمن بين اخضر كماء الطحلب واصفر كمآ الكركم واسود كمآ الفحم * ويتلاحق بها جميع اقذار المطابخ والمرافق * ورائحتها ولا سيما فى الصيف اشدّ اذى من رويتها * فهلاّ جُعل لها مثاعب تحت الارض او ابياب تنفذ منها الى نهر او غيره كما فى لندن * وانظر الى مبلّط هذه الطرق حيث

Chapter 18

A Complaint and Complaints[223]

The Fāriyāq then decided to rent an apartment to live in with his family and they saw a number of places, each of which had its drawbacks. During this process the Fāriyāqiyyah got sore feet from climbing staircases, some of which comprised a hundred and twenty steps or more. In the end, they moved into a place but found that the stove didn't work properly and it was only a few days before she began complaining, saying, "It surprises me how sometimes people are deceived about something and extol it without first making sure they know what condition it's in, and once they've made up their minds about something, it becomes impossible to get them to abandon their delusion. It reaches the point that to change a delusion is more difficult than to change what is known to be true, for when someone knows something to be true he does so because he has determined its truth through scholarship, and scholars by nature always look at the evidence and the counterevidence and never stop searching for what is correct and what is more correct. Delusion, however, enters only the head of the ignoramus, and after it has entered it's almost impossible for it to exit. 4.18.1

"We may cite by way of example the popular delusion that Paris is the most beautiful city in the world, though I've observed here faults I have seen nowhere else. Look at its roads and the blood, filth, and waters of varied colors that flow along them, part green like pond scum, part yellow like turmeric, and part black like coal! All the unclean wastes of the kitchens and sanitary facilities gather there and the smell of them, especially in summer, is even more harmful than the sight. Have no drains or conduits been made underground for them to pass through into a river or something of the sort as in London? Look at the pavement of these same roads, where the carriages 4.18.2

تجرى المراكب والعجلات * فانك ترى حجارته قد اختلت وتباعد بعضها عن بعض حتى عاد سير العجلات عليها كطلوع عقبة او درج فهى لا تزال تهتز وتضطرب * وسبب ذلك ان البلاط هنا يفرش فرشا غير مرصوص ولا منضم بعضه الى بعض فاذا اتت عليه سنون زاد تباعداً وتخللا * فاما فى لندن فانه يرص بعضه الى بعض قائما فتسير عليه العجلات سيرا سريعا سهلا بلا قرقعة ولا اضطراب * وانظر ايضا الى برازيق الطرق هنا اى حيث تمشى الناس * فما اضيقها واقذرها واقل جدواها * ففى كثير من الحارات لا يمكن لاثنين ان يمشيا معا على حافّة واحدة منها * بل هى لا توجد راسا فى كثير من الطرق او توجد غير كاملة من الاول الى الاخر فتراها قد تعطلت فى موضع واختلّت فى آخر * وانظر الى هذه الانوار القليلة فى الاسواق والى فوانيسها البارزة من الحيطان والى بعد المسافة ما بينها * فقد يمشى الانسان فى اكثر الطرق من فانوس الى اخر اكثر من مئة وعشرين خطوة * وانظر الى صغر هذه الحوانيت وقلة انوارها وبؤس اهلها وشحّهم * فقلما ٣،١٨،٤ تجد عند احدهم نارا * مع ان هذا الشهر هو من ابرد الشهور * وتامل هذه الديار وعلو طبقاتها وكثرة درجها ووسخها وفساد ترتيب مرافقها ومراحيضها * فقد تجد فى الدار الواحدة عدة مراحيض بجانب المساكن وعدّة مصاب للمآ والاقذار * وناهيك ما يخرج منها صباحا من الروائح الخبيثة * ومع كون هذه المراحيض قذرة نجسة خالية عن لوالب الماء فليس لها مزالج من داخل ليامن الانسان فى حال خلوته من انبعاق احد عليه * فكثيرا ما يدمق عليه دامق ولمّا يكن اتى على اخر ما عنده فيلحقه بالبِدْغ والاَمْدر او الماصِع او الجازم او الراطم او المزرَم(١) وقد سالت عن سبب ذلك فقيل لى ان صاحب الدار اذا

(١) البِدغ الخارى فى ثيابه ونحوه الامدر ومصع بسلحه على عقبَيه اذا سبقه من فرق او عجله وجزم بسلحه اخرج بعضه وبقى بعضه ورطم السلح حبسه وازرمه قطع عليه بوله

and carts have to pass, and you'll see that its stones have been shaken loose and pushed apart so that when a cart moves over them it seems to be climbing a mountain pass or a flight of steps and it keeps rocking and shaking, the reason being that the cobblestones here are not laid in rows or set snugly next to each other and they grow further apart and looser as the years go by. In London, on the other hand, they're laid flush with one another and upright and the carts move over them quickly without rattling or shaking. Look too at the pathways alongside the roads here, meaning where people walk: how narrow and dirty they are, and what little purpose they serve! In many of the side streets, it's impossible for two to walk side by side along one edge of the street; indeed, they're not to be found at all in many roads or do not go the whole way from the beginning to the end, for you'll find they're obstructed in one place, disintegrating in another. Look at how few lights there are in the marketplaces and at how far apart are the lanterns that stick out of the walls! In most streets, one has to walk more than a hundred and twenty paces between one lantern and the next.

"Look at how small the shops are and how poorly lit, and at the wretchedness and hardscrabble existence of the city's inhabitants! Rarely does one of them have a fire, even though this is the coldest month. Look well at these houses and how high their stories rise and how many steps they have and how dirty and badly arranged are their sanitary facilities and latrines—for in a single house, you may find a number of latrines next to apartments along with a number of outlets for water and sewage, and you may well imagine the disgusting smells that issue from them in the morning! In addition to the fact that these latrines are dirty, squalid, and without water supply, they have no bolts on the inside to prevent anyone from bursting in on a person in his privacy. As a result, someone will often intrude upon another before he has finished his business and he will find himself joined by one whose clothes are beshitten and befouled, or whose shit falls on his heels because he's in such a hurry, or whose turd gets stuck half in and half out, or who can't get it out, or who was interrupted while pissing.(1) I asked about the reason for this and was told that if the landlord was 4.18.3

(1) "A *bidgh* is 'someone who defecates on his clothes,' synonym *amdar*; to say of a man that he *maṣaʿa* his ordure on his heels means that 'he did so before he could stop himself, by reason of fright or haste'; to say that he *jazama* his ordure means 'he got some of it out and some of it stayed where it was'; to say that he *raṭama* his ordure means 'he retained it'; *azramahu* means 'he interrupted him while he was urinating.'

كان متورّعا يتحرج من وضع المزالج خيفة ان يدخل بعض الساكنين والسكانات معا ويتحصنوا بها * ومن اقذر ما يرى فى حيطانها آثار اصابع مختلفة فكاّن الفرنساوية يستطيبون الاستطابة باصابعهم * وحين ينظّفونها ليلاً تخرج رائحتها الخبيثة وتنتشر فى الحارة كلها * فلا يمكن للانسان ان يبيت الا مسدود المنخرين *
٤،١٨،٤ ثم ان هذه الديار ما عدا كونها تشتمل على ست طبقات فاكثر * وعن ذلك وعن فساد التبليط يسمع لمرور العجلات قرقعة زائدة كما لا يخفى * وما عدا كونها تحوى سكّاناكثيرين ما بين فاجر وفاجرة ومستهتَر ومستهترة * فان كثيرا من مساكنها لا يصلح للسكنى لخلوه من النور والهوآ * ولا يكاد الانسان يستريح فى محل منها * فانه اما ان يجده قريبا من المرحاض * او يجد موقده رديّئا * او يجد فيه فارا او جرذانا * او يجد جاره ذا صَخب ووقاحة يغنّى النهار والليل او يعزف بآلة طرب * او يخلو بالمومسات على هَرَج ومرج وقرقرة وكركرة * وان من داخلها ما يضحك ويبكى * فالمضحك ما يرى من الخلل فى هندمة الابواب والشبابيك وفرش المبلّط بالآجُرّ واتصال بعض المساكن ببعض * والمبكى رؤية هذه المواقد فانها مبنية على شبه القبور وذلك اول ما يخطر ببال الداخل الى مسكنه * فهى جديرة والحالة هذه بان تكون صوامع للرهبان المتبتّلين لا مضاجع للناس المتزوجين * واغرب من ذلك ان ابواب الديار لا تزال مفتوحة * وان البوابين يتعاطون الحرف والصنائع فى كنّ لهم يلزمونه ليلا ونهارا * فمنهم من يشتغل بالخياطة ومنهم بحذو النعال ونقلها وغير ذلك * بحيث ان كل انسان يمكنه ارتقآ الدرج بلا مانع * وقلّ ان يبصر البواب من كنّه احداً لان عينيه ابدا ملازمتان للابرة او الإشْفى * ولذلك كانت دواعى الفساد فى باريس اكثر منها فى لندن * وما يرى هنا من الديار البهية والطرق الواسعة الحسنة فانما هو حديث عهد * فكيف كان لباريس شهرة

a God-fearing man, he'd be uneasy at the thought of installing bolts lest certain of the male and female residents go in together and barricade themselves inside. Nothing filthier is to be seen than the various finger marks on their walls, as though the French liked to wipe their anuses with their fingers. When they clean these latrines at night, they give off a horrible smell that spreads throughout the quarter, and a person has no choice but to sleep with his nostrils plugged.

"In addition, many of these houses—despite the fact that they comprise **4.18.4**
six or more stories (which, along with the poor paving of streets, produces an undeniably excessive rumbling because of the passing of the carts) and despite the fact that they hold numerous residents (some of whom are lechers, male and female, others doting lovers, male and female)—are unfit for habitation because of their lack of light and air, and it's difficult to find an apartment in them in which one can relax, for one finds either that it's close to the latrine, or that the stove doesn't work properly, or that it has a mouse or a rat, or that one's neighbor is noisy and rude, singing day and night or playing a musical instrument or closeting himself with prostitutes with hurly-burly, loud laughter, and hilarity. Inside the apartment itself, there are things to make you laugh and things to make you cry. The crudeness with which the doors and windows are made, the paving of the floor with brick, and the way that some of the apartments interconnect with others will make you laugh. Those stoves of theirs that are built in the shape of tombs, the first thing to strike a person when he enters his apartment, will make you cry. As they are, they're better suited to be cells for hermits than sleeping quarters for married couples. Stranger still is the fact that the doors to the buildings are always open and that the doorkeepers carry on trades and crafts in a closet of their own which they stick to, night and day. Some work as tailors and some make or mend shoes and other things, which means that anyone can go up the stairs with nothing to stop him. Rarely does the doorkeeper take note of anyone from his closet because his eyes are glued to his needle or his awl. This is why there are more incitements to sin in Paris than in London. The only fine houses and wide, handsome streets are of recent date. How can Paris have

فى الزمن القديم وديارها العتيقة وطرقها العهيدة مما ينبو عنه الطرف وتقذره النفس * فاين هذا من شوارع لندن الرحيبة الوضيئة ومن دكاكينها الواسعة
٤،١٨،٥ الظريفة المزجّجة باحسن الزجاج وانفسه * ومن ديارها النظيفة المهندمة * قال فقلت ومن حكّاكات اعتابها * فقالت ومن اِعتاب حكّاكاتها * ثم استمرت تقول ومن مساكنها الانيقة ومن درجاتها الحسنة التى لا تزال مكسوة بالزرابى الفاخرة * اَيم الله ان صعود خمسين درجة منها لاهون علىّ من صعود عشر درجات هنا * واين تلك المواقد البهية المصفّحة بالحديد اللمّاع المجلو فى صباح كل يوم * وتلك الشبابيك والطيقان المحكمة الترجيج * واين تلك المطابخ التى لا يزال فيها نور الغاز متوقّدا والمآء السخن عتيداً للسكّان * وكم فيها من وصائف خُرَّد يتمنّى اعظم المخدومين عندنا ان يكون لاحداهن خادما او طبّاخا * قلت بل لامجاً * قالت او لاحساً * اَلَا واين حسن نهر تامس وما فيه من سفن النار التى تسير الى ضواحى لندن فى الصيف وفيها الآت الطرب * فتراها ملآنة من الرجال والنسآ والاولاد فكانما هى رياض مزيّنة بالازهار * واين تلك الحدائق الكثير وجودها فى كل جهة فى المدينة وهى التى يسمونها ترابيع * ومن يسكن فى غرفة مطلة عليها يخيّل له انه مُريف * فاذا مشى بعض خطوات وراءها راى الناس وازدحامهم اقبالا وادبارا * ثم اين تلك الانوار المتوقدة فى كل من الطرق والدكاكين * بحيث انك اذاكنت فى اول الشارع وسرّحت نظرك الى اخره ادهشك حسنها وازدهارها * وظننت انها نسق كواكب قد نظمت فى سلك واحد * وانما يمدح باريس من لم يكن قد راى لندن او من راها بعض ايام ولم يعرف لسان
٤،١٨،٦ اهلها * ثم اين ملاطفة مكريات المساكن ورفقهن بالنازل عندهنّ غريبا كان اَوْ لا * فان الغريب اذا تبوّا منزلا عندهن يصبح وقد صار واحدا من اهل البيت *

had any fame in the past when its historic houses and age-old streets repel the eye and made the gorge rise? How can this be compared to the broad, well-lit streets of London and its attractive, spacious shops, glazed with the finest and most expensive glass, or its clean, well-proportioned houses?"

Said the Fāriyāq: "I told her, 'Or its scrubbers of doorsteps' to which she replied, 'Or the pleasuring of its scrubbers.' Then she continued, 'Or their elegant apartments or their attractive staircases, ever draped with fine carpets. I swear to God, climbing fifty of their steps is easier on me than climbing ten here. Where too are those polished, shiny, iron-clad, wonderful stoves of theirs every morning and the well-glazed windows and transoms? Those kitchens where the gas light burns forever and the hot water is ready and waiting for the residents? And all those charming young maids for whom the mightiest of employers at home would want to work as a manservant or cook?' 'Or taster,' I said. 'Or licker,' she said. 'And where oh where is the beauty of the River Thames and its steamboats that go to the outskirts of London in summer and have music on board? Filled with men, women, and children, they look like meadows adorned with flowers. Where are those gardens they call "squares" of which there are so many in every part of the city and which make anyone living in a room overlooking them feel he has moved to the countryside, though should he take a few steps beyond them he would see crowds of people coming and going? Where are those lights that burn on every street and in every shop, so that if you are at the beginning of the street and you set your eyes on its far end, you wonder at its beauty and radiance and imagine that they must be an array of planets strung on a single string? Only those who haven't seen London, or who have spent only a few days in it without knowing the language, praise Paris. 4.18.5

"'And where is the kindly fussing of the landladies and the companionship they show their lodgers, be they foreigners or not? There, if a foreigner takes up residence in a house, he joins the family because all of them, from the mistress of the house to the maid (and what shall teach thee what is "the Maid"?)[224] make a fuss of him, keep him company, serve him, cook for him, buy him what he needs from the market, bring him hot water every 4.18.6

لان كلاّ من صاحبة المنزل ومن الخادمة * وما ادراك ما الخادمة * تلاطفه
وتوانسه وتقوم بخدمته وتطبخ له وتشترى له ما شآء من السوق * وتطلع اليه كل
يوم بالمآء السخن وتضرم له النار وتمسح نعاله * لعمرى ان النازل عندهن يمكنه ان
يتعلم اللغة الانكليزية بمجاورته معهن فى اقصر مدة * فاما فى باريس فان النازل فى
احد هذه المساكن قد يموت فى ليلته ولا يعلم به احد * فان بينه وبين البواب بُعَدا
٧،١٨،٤ باعدا * وفى اكثر المساكن هنا لا يجد الانسان جرسا ليطنّه فيتحرك له البواب * ثم
اين استقامة تجار لندن وصدقهم فى البيع والشرآ وتودّدهم الى الشارى واناتهم
معه من تجار باريس الذين لو قدروا على سلخ جلد المشترى ولا سيما اذا كان غريبا
لما تاخروا * وانهم قد حاكوا تجار لندن فى وضعهم بطاقة الثمن على البياعات *
ولكن هيهات * فان مَن سعَّر حاجة بمئة افرنك مثلا يبيعها بثمانين * وقد يضعون
فى وجوه الحوانيت اصنافا من البضاعة مسعّرة فاذا اردت ان تشترى شيا من ذلك
الصنف جاءك بصنف دونه فى الجودة * وحلف لك انه من عين ذلك الراموز
* ولا يزال بك مبربرا ومثرثرا وحالفا وحانثا حتى تشتريه حيآء او خصما للنزاع *
٨،١٨،٤ وغير مرة يعطون الشارى فلوسا او دراهم زائفة * فاما باعة الماكولات والمشروبات
فانهم اكثر غشا وشططا فى هذه المدينة من سائر الناس * ولهم فى الوزن لباقة
لم ارَها عند غيرهم * وذلك ان من باعك شيا موزونا يطرحه فى كفّة الميزان بعجلة
وهوج كالغضبان من رؤية سحنتك او على الميزان * واول ما تميل به الكفّة يرفعه
بلباقة ويسلمه لك * ولو ارسلت اليه خادمك او ابنك لباعه نفاية ما عنده وكان
على السَّنجة اشدّ غضبا * هذا ما عدا غشّهم الماكول والمشروب وتغييرهم الاسعار
بتغيير الاوقات والاحوال * وهذه اللباقة معروفة ايضا عند باعة الاصناف
٩،١٨،٤ كَيْلًا وذَرْعًا * فاما ما يقال فى مواضع التنزه والحظ فى باريس وذلك كحديقة

morning, light his fire, and polish his shoes. I swear, one who stays with them can learn the English language in no time at all by talking to them. Someone lodging in a house in Paris could die overnight and no one would be any the wiser, for there is an unbridgeable gulf between him and the doorkeeper and in most of the houses here one cannot find a bell to ring to make the doorkeeper come to him.

"'And how can the shopkeepers of Paris, who, if they had the means to strip a customer, and especially a foreigner, of his skin wouldn't hesitate to do so, be compared to those of London, with their straight dealing, their honesty in selling and buying, and their friendliness toward and patience with their customers? They have imitated the London shopkeepers by putting price tags on the goods but what difference does it make? A shopkeeper who puts a price of, say, a hundred francs on something will sell it for eighty. They also put in the fronts of their shops types of goods bearing a certain price, but if you want to buy something of that type, they'll bring you something of inferior quality and swear that it's the same as the sample and keep prattling and chattering and swearing oaths and perjuring themselves till you buy it, out of embarrassment or to avoid a quarrel. Often they even give the buyer forged coin. 4.18.7

"'The purveyors of food and drink in this city are even worse cheats and violators than the rest of its inhabitants, for they display a sleight of hand at weighing that I have seen nowhere else, meaning that someone selling you something that has to be weighed will throw it into the pan of the scales swiftly and carelessly, as though he were furious at seeing your face or at the scales, and the second the pan starts to dip will whip it off and hand it to you, and if you send him your servant or your son, he'll sell him leftovers, showing even greater fury at the scales-pan; and this is over and above their adulteration of foodstuffs and drinks and the way they change prices according to the time of day and the weather. The same sleight of hand is well-known too among those who sell goods by volume and by length. 4.18.8

"'Concerning what they say about places for promenading and having fun in Paris, such as the gardens of the Palais Royal and surroundings, I swear that 4.18.9

قصر الملك وما يليها فلعمرى ان من راى حدائق كريمون وڤكس هال وروجڤيل (CRÉMORNE GARDENS, VAUXHALL, ROSHERVILLE) التى فى ضواحى لندن ما عدا حدائق كثيرة فى حاراتها فلا يطاوعه لسانه بعدها على ذكر غيرها * نعم ان حديقة القصر هنا حسنة على صغرها لكونها فى قلب البلد وتلك منحازة عن الوسط * ولكن آه من قلب هذا البلد * كم من فاسدين وفاسدات تجمع هذه الحديقة فى كل يوم فهى عبارة عن حابور * لان النسآ ينتبنها ليتصيّدن منها الرجال * اذ تجلس المراة على كرسىّ بجنب رجل ممّن اعجبها وهى لا تعرفه * ويكون بيده كتاب يطالعه وبيدها منديل تخيطه او نحو ذلك * فيطفق هو يقرا فى الكتاب كلمة وينظر اليها نظرة وهى كذلك تمل ملّة وتهجل هجلة فلا يقومان الّا وهما متعاشقان * حتى اذا كان اليوم القابل تبدّل كل منهما مقامه وعشقه * اما الجمال فليس من مناسبة بين جمال نسآء باريس ونسآء لندن فالذأبة ١٠،١٨،٤
او الخَفُوت هناك تعدّ هنا عَبْهرا(١) ولعزة الجمال هنا صار عزيزا فان الشى متى عزّ عزّ فكان كلف الناس به اكثر وتنافسهم فيه اشد * ومن اعجب العجب عندى ان الجميلة الرائعة فى لندن تطوف باخلاق من الثياب * والدميمة الشوهآ فى باريس ترفل بالحرير والكشميرى * فاما مواضع الرقص فانها فى لندن تفتح كل ليلة وفى باريس ثلث مرات فى الجمعة لا غير * وفى اكثر شوارع لندن تسمع الغنآ من جوارى حسان والات الطرب ليلا ونهارا من دون غرامة ولا كلفة * وليس كذلك فى باريس الا ما ندر * وغاية ما يقال فى التنويه بباريس وفى تفضيلها ان فيها مواضع للشراب والقهوة ظريفة يجلس داخلها وخارجها الرجال والنسآ متقابلين ومتدابرين * فهل لمجرد القعود على كرسى يحكم لها بالفضل وتشهر عند الخاصة والعامة من اعصر متعددة بانها

(١) الخَفُوت المراة تستحسن وحدها لا بين النسآ *

no one who has seen the gardens at Cremorne, Vauxhall, or Rosherville[225] in the suburbs of London, not to mention the numerous gardens in its various quarters, will thereafter find it in him to speak of any others. True, the gardens of the Palais Royal here are attractive, despite their small size, which is due to their being in the heart of the city, while the former are at a distance from the center; but what is one to say of the heart of this city? How many reprobates, male and female, does that garden bring together each day! It is in essence a meeting place for fornicators, because women frequent it to hunt for men: the woman sits down on a bench next to a man whom she fancies but doesn't know; he will have in his hand a book that he's reading and she will have in hers a handkerchief that she's embroidering or something else of the sort; he reads a word from the book and for each word gives her a look; she likewise sews a stitch and for every stitch throws him an amorous glance, and by the time they get up, they're lovers (even if the next day each of them changes his bench and his affections).

"'As far as beauty is concerned, there is no comparison between that of **4.18.10**
the women of Paris and that of the women of London. In the first, a woman with lupus[226] and one who might be considered handsome only when there were no others about (*al-khafūt*)(1) would be regarded here as combining every possible beauty of body and disposition since the short supply of beauty here renders it much esteemed, for when something is in short supply, it comes to be regarded highly and people become more intent on it and their competition over it becomes more intense. The most amazing thing to me is that women of outstanding beauty in London go around in rags while in Paris ugly and misshapen women strut about in silk and cashmere. Dance halls in London open every evening and in Paris three nights a week only, and in most streets in London you can hear singing coming from pretty serving-girls, and musical instruments, night and day, without penalty or fine; in Paris, this is rarely to be found. The most one can say in praise of Paris and its claims to precedence is that it contains elegant places to drink alcohol and coffee where men and women sit inside and out, face to face and back to

(1) The *khafūt* is "the woman who is considered comely on her own but not among other women."

اجمل مدينة فى العالم * ثم اين حشمة فتيان الانكليز وتادبهم مع النسآ سوآ كانوا فى البيوت والشوارع من فتيان الفرنساوية هولآ الهصاهيص الذين يهصهصون ويهصّصون(١) فى وجوه النسآ حرائر كن او بغايا * ومتى ينظروا امراة مكبّة لربط شراك نعلها يطيفوا بها فيصيروا لحَلْقتها حلقة ولِحتارها حتارا * ولا سيما حين ياتون الى هذه المناصع ويبدون فيها منادفهم – قال فقلت استمرى فى الحديث وقولى ما شئت بحيث لا تقفين على المنادف * قالت اتغار علىّ ايضا من الوقوف بالكلام * وانما وقفت بُهرا من هذه الدنيا المبنية على النادفية والمندوفية * لا جرم لو انى كنت فى مقام ملك او امير لما اكلت ممّا مسّته ايدى الرجال شيا * وبينما هما فى الكلام اذا برجل يطرق الباب * ففتح له الفارياق وهو مستعيذ من دخوله على ذكر المنادف * واذا به يقول * قد سمعت بقدومك فاتيتك رغبة فى ان اقرا عليك فى العربية شيا واعطيك فى مقابلة ذلك خمسة عشر افرنكا فى الشهر * فلما سمعت الفارياقية اغربت فى الضحك على عادتها وقالت لزوجها * دونك اوّل دليل على كرم اصحابنا هولآء الذين طبّل بذكرهم العالَم و زمّر * فقال له الفارياق ما اريد منك مالاً وانما تبادلنى الدرس فى لغتك عن لغتى * فرضى بذلك * ثم زاره احد علمآء باريس بعد ايام وقال له قد بلغنى قدومك وانك مُوَلَع بالنظم * فلو نظمت ابياتا على باريس وذكرت ما فيها من المحاسن لقام ذلك عند اهلها مقام توصية بك * لان الناس هنا يحبّون الاطرآء والتمليق اى يحبون ان الدخيل فيهم يطريّهم بالاطرآء * واذا كانوا هم دخلآ فى غير بلادهم اطرأوا على حكام تلك البلاد ونالوا عندهم الوجاهة والمكانة * فاجابه الفارياق الى ذلك ونظم قصيدة طويلة فى مدح باريس واهلها

(١) الهصهاص البرّاق العينين وهصهصه[١] غمزه *

١١،١٨،٤

---

١ ١٨٥٥: هصهه.

back. Are a few people sitting on chairs enough to make one judge in its favor or for it to have had over the ages the reputation among both elite and commons of being the most beautiful city in the world? How too can the modest decency of the young Englishmen and their good manners with women, whether indoors or on the streets, be compared to those French youths with their bold eyes who glare and stare(1) into women's faces, be they respectable ladies or prostitutes, and who when they see a woman bend over to tie her shoelace, surround her, making an annulus around her anus and a ring around her rectum, especially when they go to the *pissoirs* here and pull out their tent pegs . . .'"[227] The Fāriyāq: "I said, 'Keep on talking and say what you want, just don't stop and stare at the tent pegs.' 'You become jealous,' she asked me, 'even when I'm only talking? I only paused out of amazement at a world built upon pegging and being pegged. For sure, were I a king or an emir, I would eat nothing that had been touched by the hands of men.'"

(1) The *haṣhāṣ* is one with bold eyes and *haṣhaṣahu* means "he made eyes at him."

While they were thus engaged in conversation, a man knocked suddenly on the door. The Fāriyāq opened it to him, chagrined at his entering to find them talking of tent pegs. The man spoke and said, "I heard of your arrival and am come to you in the hope that I might be able to study with you some text in Arabic. In return, I'll give you fifteen francs a month." When the Fāriyāqiyyah heard this, she laughed excessively, as was her wont, and said to her husband, "Here's your first evidence of the generosity of these friends of ours over whom the world has made such a hullabaloo!" The Fāriyāq told the man, "I don't want any money from you. Just give me lessons in your language in exchange for lessons in mine." The man agreed. Some days later, one of Paris's learned men came to him and said, "I heard of your arrival, and that you're passionate about poetry. If you were to write a few verses about Paris and speak in them of its charms, it would serve as a recommendation to its people, for people here love praise and flattery, meaning that they love the outsider in their midst to butter them up with praise, just as, if they're outsiders in countries other than their own, they write in praise of the rulers of that country and gain from them respect and status." The Fāriyāq did as **4.18.11**

سمّاها الهرفية لانه مدحهم مجازفة من قبل ان يعرفهم * وستاتى مع نقيضتها الحرفية ومع نبذة مما نظمه بباريس فى الفصل العشرين * فلما وقف العالم المومأ اليه على معانيها استحسنها جدا وترجمها الى لغته * وتوصل فى ان طبع الترجمة فى احدى الصحف الاخبارية وجآ بنسخة منها الى الفارياق وهو يقول * قد طبعت ترجمة قصيدتك فى هذه الصحيفة وقد وعدتنى جمعيّة العلم الآسياوية (نسبة لاسيا) بان تطبع الاصل العربى فى صحفهم العلمية * لكونك اول شاعر مدح باريس باللغة العربية * فشكره الفارياق على ذلك وقال له انى اريد نسخة من هذه الترجمة * قال انها تباع فى مكان كذا بنحو ثلثى افرنك فسار واشترى نسخة * ثم قدم عليه بعد ايام بعض من قرا تلك الصحيفة وهو يقول * قد قرات ترجمة قصيدتك واعجبتنى * فهل لك فى ان تبادلنى الدرس * قال هو كما اريد * فاستمرّ يتردد عليه اياما فى خلالها عرّفه بالعالم المشهور مسيو كترمير (Quatremère) وهذا العالم عرّفه بمدرّس اللغة العربية مسيو كُسّان دُ پرسُڤال (Caussin De Perceval) ثم تعرف ايضا بالمدرّس الثاني مسيو رينو (Reineaud) ولكن كانت معرفته بهم كاداة التعريف فى قولك اذهب الى السوق واشترِ اللحم * ثم زاره ايضا احد ١٢،١٨،٤
الاعيان الذين يتقدم اسمآهم اداة دُ وهى علامة النبالة والشرف * وهو مسيو دُ بوفورت (De Beaufort) وكان له اخت فى دارها مدرسة تعلم فيها بعض بنات الكبرآ * فلما حان وقت امتحانهن فى العلم صنعت مادبة فى بعض الليالى وادبت اليها الفارياقية وزوجها * فقال الفارياق لزوجته * هآءك مثالا على كرم القوم فقد مضى عليك مدة وانت تشكين من الوحدة ومن بخل من تعرّفتُ بهم وتقولين انهم لم يادبوك قط * وقد كان يادبك فى بلاد الانكليز من كان يعرفك ومن لم يعرفك * حتى انك كثيرا ما كنت تضجر من ذلك * لما انه كان يلزمك له

he advised and wrote a long poem in praise of Paris and its inhabitants that he named "the Presumptive" since for him to praise them before he got to know them was speculation; it will appear later, in Chapter 20, along with its counter-poem, "the Prescriptive," and a selection of other verses he wrote in Paris. When the learned man examined its tropes, he admired them greatly and translated them into his own language and went on to have the translation published in a newspaper, a copy of which he brought to the Fāriyāq, saying, "I have had the translation of your poem printed in this newspaper, and the Société Asiatique[228] (the adjective means 'pertaining to Asia') has promised to have the Arabic original printed among its scientific papers, as you are the first poet to write in praise of Paris in Arabic." The Fāriyāq thanked the man and told him, "I would like a copy of the translation." The man told him, "It's sold at such and such a place for around two-thirds of a franc." So he went and bought a copy himself. A few days later, someone who had read the paper came to him and said, "I read the translation of your poem and I liked it. Would you be willing to exchange lessons with me?" "That's exactly what I want," said the Fāriyāq, and the man continued to visit him for a number of days, during which he introduced him to the well-known scholar Monsieur Quatremère,[229] and that scholar introduced him to Monsieur Caussin de Perceval,[230] the teacher of Arabic. Subsequently, he also became acquainted with the other teacher of Arabic, Monsieur Reinaud.[231] However, his acquaintance with them was like the definite article in the sentence "Go to the market and buy meat!"[232]

Then he was visited by one of those notables whose names are preceded 4.18.12
by the article "de," which is a mark of nobility and honor. This was Monsieur de Beaufort, whose sister had a house in which she gave schooling to a number of the daughters of the leading members of society. One night, when it was time for them to be examined, she held a banquet to which she invited the Fāriyāqiyyah and her husband. The Fāriyāq said to his wife, "Here's an example for you of the generosity of these people. For a while now you've complained of being lonely and of the tightfistedness of the people I've come to know, saying, 'They never invite you, and in England everyone invited

تغيير زيّك ووقت غدائك وحرمانك من الدخان * فابشرى الان ان اصحابنا بالخير قمينون حريّون * قالت نعم كل منهم قَمِين حِرىّ * ثم سهرا تلك الليلة عند اخت الدُّ الموما اليه على احسن حال واصفى بال * فرجعت الفارياقية الى منزلها بقلب آخر وهى تقول * نعم لقد تفضل بوفورت واحسن كل الاحسان * وقد رايت من نسآ الفرنساوية من البشاشة والطلاقة ما لم اكن اصدّقه * نعم ويعجبنى منهن هذه الغنّة والخنّة التى تكثر فى كلامهن وهذا هو الذى جعل اللغة الفرنساوية فيما اظن مستحبة * وهى من الاولاد اشجى واطرب * قال فقلت الظاهر ان العرب ايضا تحبّ هذه الخنخنة * فقد قال سيدى صاحب القاموس نَخِم وتَنَخَّمَ دفع بشى من صدره او انفه * ونَخَمَ لعب وغنَّى اجود الغنآ * فضحكت وقالت اظن صاحبك كان يهوى مخنخنة وانى اشفق من انك لا تلبث ان تسرى اليك عَدْواه * سلّمتُ بان الغنّة بل اللُثغة بل اللدغة تستحبّ من الغلمان والجوارى * ولكن هل يطيق فتى ان يسمع عجوزا خفافة تخنخن عليه فى انفه * وهل تطيق شابة خُنَّةَ شيخ هرم فى خياشيمها * نعم ويعجبنى من العامّة فى باريس انهم لا يسخرون من الغريب اذا راوه مخالفا لهم فى زيه واطواره * بخلاف سفلة لندن فانهم يسلقونه بالكلام * بل ربما تكلف الواحد منهم ان يناديه من مكان بعيد حتى يبحّ * وما ذلك الّا ليقول له انك ياغريب دمويّ ملعون * ولعلى فى ذلك مخطئة * قال فقلت بل مصيبة فان جميع الناس يثنون على ادب الفعلة وسائر العامة فى باريس وعلى حسن كلامهم *
١٣،١٨،٤ ثم لبثا مدة وهما يقابلان محاسن باريس بمحاسن لندن * فمما كرهت الفارياقية فى باريس غاية الكراهة هو ان النسآ يرخّص لهن فى دخول الديار مهما يكن من تخالف انواعهما * وزعمت ان ترتيب الديار فى لندن بهذا الاعتبار احسن * فقال لها الفارياق لا ينكر ان ديار لندن احسن ترتيبا باعتبار ان درجها قليل وان

you, whether they knew you or not, to the point that it often irritated you since it meant you had to change your clothes and the hour at which you ate lunch and deprive yourself of tobacco!' So be happy now that our friends are with virtue furnished." "Indeed," she replied, "every one of them's a vaginal furnace."[233] They spent that evening at the house of the sister of the aforementioned "de" under the most felicitous *conditions* and with the most serene of *dispositions*, and the Fāriyāqiyyah went home in an altogether different mood, saying, "Beaufort was most gracious and kind, and the Frenchwomen showed me a degree of friendliness and informality I would never have believed! And I liked too all that speaking through their noses and snorting that occurs so much in their speech and to which the French language must owe, in my opinion, its appeal and which is even sweeter and more captivating from the children." The Fāriyāq went on, "I said, 'It seems the ancient Arabs liked that kind of twang too, because my Master the author of the *Qāmūs* says, "*nakhima* or *tanakhkhama* means 'he expelled something from his chest or his nose'" while "*nakhama* means 'he sported, or he sang most excellently.'"' She laughed and said, 'I think your friend must have been in love with a woman who spoke through her nose, and I'm worried you may catch the same infection. I grant that nasality, or even drawling, or even a sharp tongue may be attractive in young boys and girls, but can a young man really stand a sterterous old woman snorting up his nose or a young woman a senile old man wheezing into her nostrils? And I like the way the common people in Paris don't make fun of a foreigner when they see that he's different from them in dress and manners, unlike the London rabble, who lacerate him with their words, one of them sometimes going to the trouble of calling out to him from some distance away till his voice is hoarse just so that he can tell him, "Foreigner, you're a bloody bastard!" though perhaps I'm mistaken in this.' 'On the contrary,' I said, 'you're quite right, for everyone praises the manners of the laborers and other poor people in Paris and their well-spokenness.'"

They went on for a while comparing the good qualities of Paris with those 4.18.13
of London. One of the things that the Fāriyāqiyyah hated most about Paris was that the women[234] were licensed to enter houses of whatever kind,[235]

سكانها قليلون ملازمون للسكون * وان اعتابها تحك فى كل يوم * وان فى مطابخها ربلات قَدِية * وان داخلها مهندم مفروش بالبسط الجيّدة الا انها بَلْو النار * فاما ديار باريس فانها ابقى على الاحوال ومنظرها فى الخارج ازهى * فاما منع المومسات عن دخول تلك وترخيصهن فى دخول هذه فهو فى ظنّى دليل على اتصاف المومسات فى باريس بالادب * بخلاف موسمات لندرة فانهن يتهتكن فى الشرب والومس * ولذلك منعن من الدخول الى السكان * وهناك سبب آخر وهو ان بغايا باريس معروفات فى ديوان البوليس واسماوهن مقيدة فيه * فلا يتجرأن على التفاحش والتهتك وان كن فواحش * فاما بغايا لندرة فقد
١٤،١٨،٤ خُلّين وطباعهن * ثم مضت مدة على الفاريقاية وهى تقاسى من الخفقان المًا مبرّحا * فكان يلازمها اياما متوالية ثم يخف عنها * وفى خلال ذلك اُدبت مرة اخرى عند اخت الدُّ * فسارت مع زوجها وهما متعجبان من هذا التكرم الذى لم يجدا له فى باريس نظيرا * ثم اشتد بالفارياقية المرض ولزمت الفراش فاحضر لها طبيبين من النمساوية فعالجاها مدة حتى افاقت قليلا * وكانت اخت الدُّ قد تزوجت برجل اسمه (LEDOS) فلما جآ اخوها ذات يوم الى الفارياق على عادته وجد الفارياقية تئنّ وتشكو من بلوغ الالم منها * فقال لزوجها لو استوصفت صهرى دواء لزوجتك فانه خبير بخصائص النبات وقد ابرا كثيرين من هذا الدآء * فسار اليه الفارياق وساله ان ياتى معه ليرى زوجته * فقال له انى غير مرخَّص لى من الديوان فى مداواة المرضى ولكنى لا آبى ان آتى معك رجآء ان يحصل شفا امراتك على يدى * ثم اتى ووصف للفارياقية ان تشرب مآ بعض اعشاب تغلَى وبعث لها من ذلك بستة قراطيس * فلما فرغت وطلب الفارياق غيرها جآت اخت الدُّاعنى زوجة المتطبّب تقول * ان زوجى يتقاضاكم

and she claimed that the arrangement for houses in London was better in this respect. The Fāriyāq told her, "It cannot be denied that the houses of London are better arranged from the perspective that their stairs and their inhabitants are few and maintain peace and quiet, that their doorsteps are scrubbed every day and that their kitchens hold tasty cuts of meat, that their interiors are well-proportioned and spread with fine carpets, but they are firetraps [?].[236] The houses of Paris, on the other hand, withstand the weather better and look finer on the outside. As for prostitutes being forbidden to enter the former and permitted to enter the latter, this, in my opinion, is evidence of how well-behaved the prostitutes of Paris are, in contrast to those of London, who drink and prostitute themselves shamelessly, which is why they are forbidden to go in to visit the residents. And there is another reason too, which is that the prostitutes of Paris are known to the police stations, where their names are written down. As a result, they don't dare to behave in a depraved or shameless way, even if they are depraved. The prostitutes of London, on the other hand, are left to their own devices."

The Fāriyāqiyyah now went through a period during which she suffered 4.18.14
from extremely painful palpitations, which would stay with her for several consecutive days before settling. While this continued, she was invited several times to the house of the "de"'s sister and she'd go with her husband, the two of them being most pleased at this generosity, the like of which they had not met with in Paris. Then the Fāriyāqiyah's sickness took a turn for the worse and she took to her bed, and he brought her two Austrian physicians who treated her for a while, until she got a little better. The "de"'s sister had married a man called Ledos, and when her brother came to visit the Fāriyāq, as he often did, and found the Fāriyāqiyyah moaning and complaining of the pain, he asked her husband, "Have you consulted my brother-in-law about medicine for your wife? He is an expert in the qualities of plants and has cured many of this disease." So the Fāriyāq went to see the man and asked him to go with him to see his wife. The man told him, "I'm not licensed by the Board to treat patients but I won't refuse to go with you, in the hope that your wife may be cured at my hands." Then he went and advised the Fāriyāqiyyah to drink the water of certain herbs, boiled, and sent her six

خمسين افرنكا ثمن القراطيس * فلما سمعت الفارياقية ذلك تراجع اليها نشاطها وبادرتها اجمع وقالت لها * اما تستحيين ان تطلبى هذا المبلغ على ستة قراطيس من العشب وزوجك ليس بطبيب * فقال لها زوجها ولكن اذكرى ان المراة اَدَبَتنا الى شرب القهوة والشاى مرتين وقد تخلّلناهما باشيآ من الحلوآ والكعك فلا ينبغى مقابحتها * ثم بعد جدال طويل ونزاع وبيل رضيت اخت الدُّ بان تاخذ نصف المبلغ المذكور فاقبضها اياه الفارياق فولّت وهى مدمدمة وانقطع اخوها عن الزيارة * ومن هولآ المتطببين من اذا راى غريبا بشّ فى وجهه واحتفى به ودعاه الى منزله وواصل زيارته الى ان يراه يشكو من سعال او غيره فيصف له دوآ * ثم يتقاضاه غرامة رابية على كل زيارة جرت بينهما من اول تعارفهما * وياتى بجيرة المحل شهودا على الرجل فى انه كان كثير التردّد على منزله وادعى ان مرضه كان مزمنا * وحامل لوآ هذه الزمرة اللئيمة هو دَلِكْس (D'Alex)
المتطبب المقيم فى لندرة فى Berner's street, n° 61, Oxford street ثم ١٥،١٨،٤
رجع الطبيب النمساوى الى مداواة الفارياقية * فلما نقهت اشار عليها بالسفر من باريس فاستقر الراى على تسفيرها الى مرسيلية * فقالت لزوجها قد طاب الان لى السير * من ارض ما فيها خير * هولآ معارفك الذين اتيتهم بكتب توصية من لندن والذين تعرفت بهم بعد ذلك هنا بوسيلة علمك لم يدعُك احد منهم الى الجلوس على كرسى فى بيته * وهذا لا مرتين الذى ابلغته كتاب توصية من الشيخ مرعى الدحداح فى مرسيلية كتبت اليه تساله عن امر فلم يجبك * مع انكَ لو كتبت الى الصدر الاعظم فى دولة الانكليز لاجابك لا محالة سواء بالسلب او الايجاب * وهذا المتطبّب صهر الدُّ غرّمنا على ستة قراطيس خمسة وعشرين افرنكا * مع ان هذا الطبيب النمساوى وصاحبه قد عالجانى مدّة

packets of these. When these were used up and the Fāriyāq asked for more, the "de"'s sister, meaning the fake doctor's wife, came and said, "My husband is charging you fifty francs for the packets." When the Fāriyāqiyyah heard this, her energy returned to her all at once and she asked her, "Aren't you ashamed to ask for such a sum for six packets of herbs when your husband isn't even a doctor?" Her husband then said to her, "But remember that she invited us to drink coffee and tea twice, and provided us, between the one and the other, with confections and cakes, so you mustn't be rude to her." After prolonged discussion and punishing struggle, the "de"'s sister agreed to take half the sum mentioned, which the Fāriyāq paid her, and she left, muttering to herself. After this her brother stopped visiting. A quack of this sort on seeing a foreigner will show him a smiling face, make a fuss of him, invite him to his house, and keep on visiting him until such time as he sees him complaining of a cough or anything of the sort, at which point he prescribes medicine for him. Then he'll charge him an excessive amount for each time they visited one another from the start of their acquaintance, bring neighbors as witnesses that the man used to frequent the man's house, and claim that his disease is chronic. The standard-bearer for this vile regiment was the quack D'Alex, who lived at 61 Berner's Street, Oxford Street, in London.

After this the Austrian doctor resumed his treatment of the Fāriyāqiyyah. 4.18.15
When she was convalescing, he recommended that she leave Paris, and they decided to send her to Marseilles. At this, she said to her husband, "I would like now to leave this land in which there is no good to be found. Not one of those acquaintances of yours to whom you brought letters of recommendation from London and whom you then came to know here by virtue of your learning has invited you to sit on a chair in his house. You wrote to that Lamartine, to whom you had transmitted a letter of recommendation from Shaykh Marʿī al-Daḥdāḥ in Marseilles, asking him about something, and he never answered you, though if you were to write to the prime minister of England, he'd certainly give you an answer, whether negative or positive. And that quack, the 'de''s brother-in-law, made us pay twenty-five francs for six packets of herbs, while this Austrian doctor and his friend have treated me

وعُنيا بى ولم يتقاضياك شيا * وكذلك تفعل اطبآء لندن جزاهم الله خيرا *
افكل الناس يكرمون الغريب ويرفقون به الا اهل باريس * لقد كنت اسمع انه ٤،١٨،١٦
يوجد فى الدنيا جيل ملاّذون ملاّثون ملاّقون ولاّذون ولثيّون محّاحون مُرامقون
ذَملَّقيّون مماذقون غَمَلَّجيّون مبذلخون مطرطرون مطرمذون خَيْتَعوريون مُبَهلقون
مُرامقون مذّاعون طَرِفون خَيْدعيّون قِشعون مِقْطاعيّون اَعْفكيّون مِجْذاميّون
جُذامِريّون كُموصيّون هَمَلَّعيون مَنْبجيّون تِلِمّاَظِيّون بَذْلاخيّون وماكنت ادرى اىّ
جيل هم * فالان اغنى الخُبْر عن الخَبَر * وتحققت ان هذه الصفات التى كنت
استكثرها ان هى الّا بعض ما يقال فى اهل هذه المدينة * فان مودتهم يقطينية
اى تنبت سريعا كاليقطين ولا تلبث ان تذوى * ومواعيدهم عرقوبية طالما
وعدوا فاخلفوا * ومنّوا فازهفوا * وحالفوا فحنثوا * وعاهدوا فنكثوا * يبشّون
بالمغترّ بهم ويهشون * ثم هو ان لازمهم ملّوه * وان غاب عنهم نسوه * وما
ينجزه غيرهم بنعم ولا فهم يرتكبون فيه اياما وليالى * يبداونه باساطير طويلة *
ويختمونه بتهاتر وبيلة * فاما بخلهم على غير المراقص فيضرب به المثل * وناهيك ٤،١٨،١٧
ان نارهم فى الشتآء كنار الحباحب * ولو انهم اوقدوا نارا كنار الانكليز لرايت
جوّهم اكثر دُجُنة ودُكْنة من جوّ اولئك * وانهم فى الصيف لا يستسرجون *
وما عندهم غير هذين الفصلين من فصول السنة * فاما برد عارم * واما غَتْم
ملازم * اَلَا وان احدهم لينزّل الافرنك اجرة من يعمل له منزلة الدينار عند
الانكليز * على ان بلدهم اغلى اسعارا من لندن فى لوازم المعيشة او مثلها *
ارايت انكليزيا يعمل حسابه بالفلس كما يعمل اهل باريس حسابهم بالصنتيم * بل
ان كثيرا من الانكليز لا يعلمون كم فى صلديّهم من فلس * نعم وان احدهم (اى
اهل باريس) ليكتب اليك مكتوبا فى شان مصلحة تقضيها له ولا يدفع جُعْله *

for a long time, have taken a lot of trouble with me, and haven't charged you a thing, which is how the doctors of London are, may God reward them well.

"Does everyone except the people of Paris treat the foreigner well and 4.18.16
show him kindness? I used to hear that there existed somewhere in this world a tribe of people who were full of artifice,[237] insincere, double-dealing, doublehearted, two-tongued, two-faced, falsehearted, faithless, fickle, hollow-hearted, glib, inconstant, mealy-mouthed, tongue-in-cheek, capricious, hypocritical, treacherous, shifty, sneaky, and backstabbing, but I didn't know which tribe they were. Now, direct experience has taken the place of hearsay and I have discovered that these adjectives that I have listed at such length above are but a few of those that may be applied to the people of this city, for their affection is 'squashy,' meaning that like squash it grows fast and withers quickly, and their engagements are like those of 'Urqūb:[238] How often have they promised and not come *through*, raised false hopes and dashed them, sworn oaths and broken them, given undertakings and proven *untrue*! They're all 'hail-fellow-well-met' to any who's new to them but when he keeps them company they grow *bored* and when he's not among them he's *ignored*. What others settle with a 'yes' or a 'no,' they dither over for days and nights, starting with long *confabulations* and ending with gross *self-contradictions*.

"Their tightfistedness where everything but the dance hall's concerned is 4.18.17
proverbial: the fires they light in winter are weaker by far than those of the glowworm (though if they were to light fires like those of the English, you'd find their weather turning darker and grayer than theirs) and in summer they don't light lamps. These are the only seasons they have, so it's either freezing cold or burning hot. Note too that a Frenchman will set the pay of anyone who works for him at the same rate in francs as the English would pay in guineas even though their country has higher prices for staples and so on than London. Did you ever see an Englishman counting his pennies the way the French do their centimes? Many English don't even know how many pennies they have amongst their small change. Yes indeed—not to mention that one of them (i.e., the Parisians) will write you a letter asking you to do something for him and then not pay you for doing it.

ولقد يضحكنى من فخرهم انهم ياكلون ابشع الماكول ولا تزال امعآوهم ملأى من ٤،١٨،١٨
شحم الخنزير * ثم هم اذا خرجوا الى المحافل والمثابات بالغوا فى التخلل والزَّفلان غاية ما يمكن * وان كثيرا منهم يغلقون فى الصيف كواهم وشبابيكهم ولا يفتحونها ابدا * يوهمون الناس انهم قد ساروا الى بعض منازه الريف ليصيفوا فيه كما تفعل كبرآوهم * وان كثيرا منهم ليتقوتون بالخبز والجبن نهارا ليبدوا فى الملاهى والملاعب ليلاً * وان اشرافهم وذوى الدُّ منهم ياكلون مرتين فى اليوم ويفطرون على محار البحر * والناس كلهم ياكلون ثلث مرات والانكليز اربع مرات * ولكن معاذ الله ان تكون الفرنساوية كلهم كاهل باريس * والّا فياخُسْرَما ضاع الثنآء عليهم كما ضاع مآء
الورد فى غسل مرحاض * فاما نسآ باريس المضروب بادبهن وظرافتهن المثل فلعمرى ٤،١٨،١٩
انهن بُخْرٌ مجخرات(١) واكثرهن لا يستوغلن ولا يتلجّمن ولا يعتركن ولا يشمذن ولا يستنجين ولا يتخذن الفِرام ولا المعابئ ولا الفِراص ولا الثَّمَل ولا الجدائل ولا المماحى ولا الرِبَذ * وليس لهن من نظافة الا على ما ظهر منهن من نحو قميص ومنديل وجورب * ولذلك تراهنّ ابدا يكشفن عن سيقانهنّ وهن ماشيات فى الاسواق صيفا وشتآء * بدعوى رفع اذيالهن عن ان تمس النجاسة فى الارض * فمن تكن منهن سوقآ افتخرت بساقها وبجوربها معا * ومن تكن نَقْوآء افتخرت بالثانى * وليس فى نسآ الارض كلها اكثر منهن تيها وعُجبا و زهوا وإِرَبًا وتعنفصا وخداعا ومجابّة وغطرفة وتبغنجا * سوآكن قباحا او ملاحا * طوالا او قصارا وهو الغالب فيهن * عجائز او صبايا * حرائر او بغايا * ذوات لحًى وشوارب او نقيات الخدّ * مذكّرات الطلعة

(١) الجَخَر محركة رائحة مكروهة فى قُبُل المراة وهى بجزآ واجخر غسل دبره ولم ينقَ فبقى نتنه واستوغل غسل مغابنه واللجام ما تشده الحائض وقد تلجمت واعتركت احتشت بخرقة وشمذت المراة فرجها حشته بخرقة خشية خروج رحمها والفرام دوآ تضيق به والمعباة خرقة الحائض والفراص جمع فرْصة وهى خرقة اوقطنة تمسح بها المراة من الحيض ونحوها الثمل جمع ثملة والربذ والجدائل جمع جديلة وهى شبه اتب من ادم تاتزر به الحيّض والمماحى جمع ممحاة وهى خرقة يزال بها المنىّ ونحوه *

"Among the things that make me laugh at their complacent self-regard is that they eat the most revolting of foods and their stomachs are always full of pig fat. Then, when they attend parties or public places, they go to great lengths to dress up and strut about looking as fine as they can. Also, that many of them close up every chink and window in the summer and never open them, to deceive people into thinking that they've gone to spend that season on some estate in the countryside as do their aristocrats, that many sustain themselves on bread and cheese by day so that they may appear in the theaters and places of entertainment by night, and that their nobility and those with a 'de' before their names eat twice a day and breakfast on shellfish, while everybody else eats three times and the English four. God forbid that all the French are like those of Paris—what a waste it would be if all the praise that has been lavished upon them were to end up like rosewater used to clean a latrine! 4.18.18

"As for the women of Paris and their reputation as examplars of good manners and sophistication, I swear that their front parts stink and they don't wipe themselves properly(1) and most of them don't wash under their arms or use sanitary towels or stuff in a piece of cloth or block it with a rag or wash their bottoms or use vulva-tightening preparations or menstrual cloths or cloths or rags to wipe off the menses or remove semen or menstrual bandages. Based on what one can see of them, the only cleanliness they know is that of the blouse, the handkerchief, and the stockings. That is why you see them forever exposing their legs as they walk in the markets, summer and winter, on the excuse of raising their skirts so that any filth there may be on the ground won't touch them. Those who have good legs show off their legs and their stockings together, and those that have thin shanks show off the second. There are no women in the entire world 4.18.19

(1) *jakhar* is "a foul smell in a woman's front parts, adjective *jakhrā'*"; *ajkhara* means "he washed his back parts and did not clean them well so they continued to stink"; *istawghala* means "he washed his armpits"; the *lijām* is "what a menstruating woman straps on, verb *talajjamat*"; *iʿtarakat* means "she stuffed herself with a piece of cloth"; *shamadhat* means "the woman stuffed her vagina with a piece of cloth lest her womb come out"; *firām* is "a medical preparation" that they use "to make themselves tighter"; the *miʿba'ah* is "the cloth used by the menstruating woman"; *firāṣ* is the plural of *firṣah*, which means "a cloth or piece of cotton with which a woman wipes off the menses" and *thuml*, plural *thamalah*, means the same, as does *rabadhah*; *khadā'il* is the plural of *khadīlah*, which is "something like the *itb* ('a kind of shift open at the sides') made of hide with which menstruating women . . . cover themselves"; *mamāḥī* is the plural of *mimḥāh*, which is "a piece of cloth with which semen and the like are removed."

والسحنة اَوْ لا * على انى لم ارَ فى جيمع النسآ تذكيرًا الا فى نسآ باريس ولندرة[1] غير ان هولآء لسن مزهوّات مغانيج كالباريسيّات * وانما الذى صيّرهن الى ذلك هو شدة شبق الرجال عليهن * وقرمهم اليهن * فترى الفرهد الغسانى مخاصرا لسعلاة منهن ومتذللا ومطيعًا لها * فلقد اصاب الذين يتزوجون منهم فى بلادنا الجوارى السود تخلّصا من اسرهنّ وسرفهن * وقد رايت عامتهن لطّاعات اى يمصصن اصابعهن بعد الاكل ويلحسن ما عليها * فاما ذوات الشرف فانهن يغلسن ايديهن فى فنجانة على المائدة بحضرة المدعوّين ويتمضمضن بالمآ ثم يقذفنه فيها * فهل ذلك يعد من الظرافة والادب * اليس فعلهن هذا افظع من التجشّؤ[2] عندنا * وانما يمدح محاسنهن ويهيم بهن من الفت عينه النظر اليهن بعد مدة * وهب ان نسآ باريس ظريفات كيّسات ولكن ما شان هولآ النسآ اللاى يقدمن ٤، ١٨، ٢٠
من السواد والبراغيل والراذانات والرساتيق والمَذارع والدساكر والفلاليج * فمنهن من تغطى راسها بمنديل فلا يبين منه الّا شُعَيرات من عند فَوديها * ومنهن من تلبس طرطورا من القماش على راسها * حتى ان اهل باريس لا يتمالكون ان يضحكوا حين يرون واحدة من هولآ الباديات * واقبح من ذلك لهجتهن * وفى باريس كثير من النسآ يكنسن الطرق ويتعاطين اعمال الرجال * وفى بولون وكالى ودياب وهافر وغيرها من الفرض تجد النسا يحملن اثقال المسافرين على ظهورهن ورؤسهن * وليس فى بلاد الانكليز كلها من حمّالات الّا لاصحاب الاثقال * وزيّهن كلهن سواء * فكيف يزعم الفرنساويون انهم جميعا متمدنون * ولعمرى لوكانت النسآ فى بلادنا يخرجن فى الاسواق سوافر ويبدين قوامهن وخصورهن وسوقهن كنسآء باريس * لما تركن لهن ان يذكرن معهن بالجمال والظرافة اصلا *

---

١ ١٨٥٥: وارلندة.   ٢ ١٨٥٥: التجشّئ.

more haughty, self-admiring, proud, cunning, arrogant, perfidious, competitive, vain, or vainglorious than they, be they ugly or pretty, tall or short (as the majority of them are), old or young, respectable or harlots, bearded and mustached or smooth-cheeked, mannish of aspect and countenance or not (though I have never seen mannish-looking women anywhere but among the women of Paris and London, albeit the latter are not proud and coquettish like Parisian women). They have been driven to this by the extreme lecherousness and lustfulness toward them of the men. You'll see an upstanding young buck walking with his arm around the waist of some hideous she-ghoul and obeying her abjectly. Men of theirs who take wives in our country target black slave girls, as a way of escaping the imperiousness and profligacy of their own women. I have seen women of the common people among them performing *laṭʿ*, which means sucking their fingers after eating, and licking off what is on them.[239] Their noblewomen wash their hands in a cup placed on the table, in the presence of their guests, and rinse their mouths out with water and then spit it into the cup. Is this to be considered a form of good manners or sophistication? Isn't their doing so more disgusting than the belching that happens among us? Only someone whose eye has accustomed itself to them over time could praise their charms or become infatuated with them.

"But even if we suppose, for argument's sake, that the women of Paris **4.18.20**
are sophisticated and smart, what are we to make of the women who come from the provinces, from the small towns by the river, from the villages and hamlets, from the small rural towns, the country estates, the countryside? Some of these countrywomen cover their heads with a kerchief so that all that can be seen is a few hairs at the temples, while others wear a dunce's cap made of cloth on their heads, with the result that the Parisians can scarcely restrain themselves from laughing when they see one of them, and their accents are uglier still. Many women in Paris sweep the streets and take on men's work. In Boulogne, Calais, Dieppe, Le Havre, and other port cities, you'll find women carrying travelers' baggage on their backs and heads, but there are no female porters to be found anywhere in England except those who carry for men with heavy loads.[240] Their clothes, too, are all the same. How, then, can the French claim that they are all civilized? I swear, were the women in our country to go out into the markets unveiled and show off their feet and waists and legs like the women of Paris, no one would think of mentioning the latter in the same breath when beauty and sophistication

الى مصر الى مصر بلاد الحظّ والأرَب * الى الشام الى الشام معان الفضل والادب * الى تونس نعم الدار فيها اكرم العرب * كفانى من الافرنج ما قد لقيته وعندى ان اليوم فى قربهم عام * اَلَا دعنى اسافر من بلاد اسقمت بدنى * بماكلها ومشربها وبرد هوائها العَفِن * فقال لها الفارياق ان كنت تطيقين السفر فشانك * فقالت لَموتى فى الطريق الىّ اشهى من التخليد فى دار اللئام * فمن ثم تاهبّت له * غير انه حصل لها فى غد ذلك اليوم من الضعف والالم ما منعها عن الحركة * وتفصيل ذلك ياتى فى الفصل التالى

*

were the topic of conversation! To Cairo, to Cairo—the land of fun and *aspiration*! To Syria,[241] to Syria—where virtue and literature are exemplified in *combination*! To Tunis—the best of abodes, where dwells the most generous of the Arab *nation*![242] I have had enough of the treatment I've met with from the Franks, and feel that a day spent with them is like a year. Let me leave these countries that have sickened my body with their food and drink and the chill of their putrid airs!" The Fāriyāq told her, "If you can stand the journey, then let it be as you wish." "Death on the road," she replied, "would be better than staying on forever in the land of the ignoble!" From that moment then, she prepared herself to travel, though the next day she was so weak and in such pain that she could not move—

details to follow
in the coming
chapter.

الفصل التاسع عشر

في سرقة مطرانية و وقائع مختلفة

لمّا نُكبت نصارى حلب وجرى عليهم من نهب المال وهتك العرض ما جرى * ١،١٩،٤
اجتمعت روسآؤهم فى الدّين وارتأوا ان يبعثوا من طرفهم وكلآء الى بلاد الافرنج ليجمعوا لهم من دولها وكنائسها ومن اهلها الخيّرين مدداً يقوم باودهم * فاختارت الكنيسة الرومية الارثودكسية الخواجا فتح الله مرّاش * واختارت الكنيسة الرومية الملكية المطران اتناسيوس التتونجى مولف كتاب الحكاكه فى الركاكه * ورجلا آخر معه يقال له الخواجا شكرى عبود * فاقبلوا يجولون فى البلاد حتى انتهوا الى مملكة اوستريا فجمعوا منها مبلغا * وكان معهم منشور من مطرانى الكنيستين المذكورتين فى حلب يوذن بوكالتهم من الطائفتين فى هذه المصلحة * فلما فرغوا من بلاد النمسا قدم الخواجا فتح الله المزبور ورفيقه الخواجا شكرى عبود الى باريس ومعهما ذلك المنشور * وبقى المطران هناك على عزم ان يجتمع بهما فى بلاد الانكليز * وانما لم يقدم معهما الى فرنسا مع انه هو وكيل الكنيسة الملكيّة وهى على مذهب الكنيسة الفرنساوية * لما انه كان سابقا ارتكب فيها من اسآءة الادب وتعدّى طور امثاله ما اوجب حبسه ثم طرده منها مدحورا * فخشى والحالة هذه ان يشهر امره هذه المرة فيها فيحيق به سوء عمله * فلما ابرز رفيقاه

Chapter 19

A Metropolitan Theft and Miscellaneous Events

When the Christians of Aleppo suffered their calamity[243] and were subjected to that pillaging of their wealth and property and that rapine, their religious leaders met and took the decision to send agents on their behalf to the lands of the Franks to collect aid from the governments and churches there to assure their survival. The Greek Orthodox Church chose Khawājā Fatḥallāh Marrāsh[244] and the Greek Melkite Church chose Metropolitan Atanāsiyūs al-Tutūnjī, author of *Al-Ḥakākah fī l-rakākah* (*The Leavings Pile Concerning Lame Style*),[245] and with him another man, called Khawājā Shukrī ʿAbbūd. These then set off on a tour of the various countries, ending up in the Austrian Empire, from which they collected a significant sum. They had with them a proclamation from the metropolitans of the two aforementioned churches in Aleppo announcing that they were commissioned by the two sects to act in this matter. When they had finished with Austria, the abovementioned Khawājā Fatḥallāh Marrāsh and his colleague Khawājā Shukrī ʿAbbūd went to Paris, taking the proclamation with them, while the metropolitan stayed behind, intending to meet up with them in England. He did not go with them to France, despite his being the delegate of the Melkite church, which is in communion with the French church, because he had committed there, on a former occasion, such breaches of etiquette and oversteppings of the bounds set for such as him that he had had to be imprisoned and subsequently expelled from the country. He was therefore afraid, things being as they were, that he would be exposed there this time and his bad behavior come back to haunt him. Now, when his colleagues 4.19.1

منشور الوصاة لمطران باريس والتمسا منه المعونة عجب من رؤيته اسم المطران
التونجي مذكورا فيه دون رؤية سحنته * فقال لهما ما بال وكيل الكنيسة الملكية لم
يحضر معكما * فاعتذرا عن غيابه باعذار لم يقبلها منهما المشار اليه * وتذكر ما
٢،١٩،٤ كان فعله التونجي من قبل فردّهما خائبين * وكان الخواجا فتح الله مراش ورفيقه
يترددان على الفارياق مدة مكثهما فى باريس * لكن تردد الاول اكثر * وانما انس
به الفارياق مع علمه بانه رفيق التونجي لكونه رآه من ذوى المعارف والدراية ما
عدا كونه متزوجا وله عيال * وقلّ من كان على مثل ذى الحال وانطوى على غش
ودَخَل * لان العلم يلطف العقل والعيال ترقق القلب * ثم ارتبك المطران فى
رُطْمة فى بلد من بلاد اوستريا وهو فيما اظن بولونيا * ففصل منه على نكظ وخزيٍ
وسار الى بلاد الانكليز مجتديا * ويومئذ ارسل الى رفيقيه المذكورين ان يلحقا به *
فما مضت بعد سفرهما ايّام قليلة حتى ورد الى الفارياق كتاب من كاتب اللجنة (اى
جمعية اخويّة) وفى ضمنه كراسة من كتاب كان قد عربه الفارياق من كتب العجم
وفيها ما يسوء اللجنة * فايقن حينئذ بان احد رفيقى المطران عند ترددهما عليه سرقها
من مخدعه باشارة المطران * وانه لما اجتمع به فى لندن سلمها له فاهداها المطران
الى اللجنة طمعا فى ايصال الضرر من جانبهم الى الفارياق * غير ان اللجنة المذكورة
لما كانت منطوية على اخلاق كريمة ردّت الكراسة على الفارياق * اذ لم يكن لهم
بحفظها من مصلحة * وكان ورود الكراسة يوم عزمت الفارياقية على السفر *
فبلغ منها الغيظ والحزن كلّ مبلغ حتى لزمت الفراش * فاما المطران فانه تصدّى
له فى لنذرة بعض رؤسآء الكنيسة البابوية ومنعوه من تعاطى الحرفة الساسانية *

produced their sponsors' proclamation for the Bishop of Paris and asked him for assistance, the latter was surprised to see the name of Metropolitan al-Tutūnjī mentioned therein but not to see his face, and he asked them, "How is it that the delegate of the Melkite church is not in attendance with you?" The two men made excuses for his absence that the aforementioned did not accept and, recalling what al-Tutūnjī had done before, he sent them away empty-handed.

Khawājā Fatḥallāh Marrāsh and his colleague had been paying visits to the Fāriyāq throughout their stay in Paris, the first, however, visiting the more frequently. The Fāriyāq gave him a warm welcome, even though he knew him to be al-Tutūnjī's colleague, because he believed him to be a man of learning and insight, not to mention that he was a married man with children and these rarely resort to cheating and skulduggery, for learning refines the mind and children soften the heart. Then the metropolitan became involved in some shady affair in some town belonging to Austria—Bologna, I think[246]—and was expelled from it at speed and in disgrace and went to England seeking further funds. On the same day, he sent to his two colleagues to join him there. A few days after they had left, the Fāriyāq received a letter from the secretary of the Committee ("committee" meaning "fraternal association"), included with which was a quire from a foreign book that the Fāriyāq had translated into Arabic and which included something displeasing to the Committee. He then realized that one of the metropolitan's two colleagues must have stolen it from his room during one of their visits at the metropolitan's behest, that when he met with him in London he had handed it over to him, and that the metropolitan had given it to the Committee in the hope that its members would inflict some injury on the Fāriyāq. The said Committee, however, being committed to a high standard of conduct, had returned the quire to the Fāriyāq, as they had no reason to keep it. The quire arrived on the same day that the Fāriyāqiyyah had determined to travel, and she became so angry and upset that she took to her bed. As for the metropolitan, he was accosted in London by certain leaders of the Roman church, who forbade him to practice the Sassanian trade.[247] Things got to such a point that his disgrace and notoriety there created difficulties for the others with those whom they were importuning on church business, 4.19.2

حتى ان شنعته وشهرته هناك عطّلت ايضا على غيره ممن كان يجتديهم لمصلحة
من مصالح الكنيسة * فحسبوا كل قادم اليهم من بلاد الشرق منافقا * امّا ٣،١٩،٤
الفارياقية فانها نقهت بعد ايام وصممت على السفر * فكتب لها زوجها كتاب
توصية الى المولى المعظم سامى باشا المفخم فى مدينة القسطنطينية * ثم شيّعها
وسفّر معها اصغر اولاده تسلية لها * ولما حان الفراق توادعا وتباكيا وتواجدا
حتى اذا لم تَعُدِ العين تجيبهما بالدمع وهى العَسْقفة والعَسْقبة والتغبيض رجع الى
منزله مستوحشا مكتئبا * وسافرت هى الى مرسيلية فزال ما كان بها وشفيت
اتمّ الشفآء * لكنها لم تغيّر نيّتها عن السفر الى اسلامبول * ثقة بان هذا الفراق
يكون سببا فى وشك اللقآء * فلما بلغت مقام المولى المشار اليه وادّت كتاب
التوصية لولده النجيب الحسيب صبحى بيك اذ كان والده حينئذ غائبا * اكرم
مثواها واحسن اليها غاية الاحسان * وهذا مثال آخر على الكرم الشرقىّ ينبغى
ان يبلّغ مسامع الامرآء الغربيّين من الافرنج * وفى غضون ذلك نظم الفارياق
للمومى اليه قصيدة يمدحه بها على كرمه ومعروفه * ولزوجته ابياتا اودعها ذكر
ما لقى من وحشة النوى وستاتى كلها فى الفصل التالى الذى هو خاتمة هذا
الكتاب * ثم انتقل من منزله ذاك الى غرفة وجعل دابه فى كل يوم نظم بيتين ٤،١٩،٤
على بابها * ثم بلغه قدوم السيد الاكرم الامير عبد القادر الى باريس فاهداه
ايضا قصيدة وتشرف بمجلسه * ثم عيل صبره من الوحدة فاستماله بعض معارفه
الى اللعب بهذه الاوراق المزوّقة فضار من زمرة المقامرين * لكن جهله بها
كان غير مرّة يبعث شريكه على العربدة عليه * فكان يرضى بان يكون حُرْضة
فقط * (الحرضة امين المقامرين) ثم تعرّف برئيس تراجم الدولة وهو الكونت

for these now reckoned that anyone coming to them from the lands of the East must be a hypocrite.

The Fāriyāqiyyah recovered after a few days and insisted on traveling. Her husband therefore wrote her a letter of recommendation to the August Lord Sāmī Pasha the Grand in Constantinople. Then he sent her off, accompanied by the youngest of their children to keep her company. When the time came for them to part, they bade each other farewell and wept and expressed their emotions until, when their eyes ceased to respond with tears—a state known as "dry eye" or "dry cry" or "the unresponsive eye"—he returned home feeling lonely and downcast. She traveled to Marseilles, where her illness left her and she recovered completely, but she did not abandon her intention of going to Islāmbūl,[248] confident that their parting could lead only to their imminent reunion. When she made contact with the aforementioned lord and presented her letter of recommendation to his son, Ṣubḥī Bayk,[249] of noble lineage and line (his father being at that moment absent), he honored her lodgings with a visit and showed her every kindness—and this is another example of Eastern generosity that ought to be conveyed to the ears of the Western, Frankish, princes. While this was going on, the Fāriyāq composed a poem dedicated to the aforementioned person in which he praised him for his generosity and friendship. He also composed verses into which he poured all the loneliness he felt at being so far from her. All of these will be presented in the next chapter, which forms the conclusion to the book.[250] 4.19.3

Next he moved from that house to a room, where he made it his habit to write each day two lines of verse, which he inscribed on its door. Then the Most Noble Master ʿAbd al-Qādir came to Paris, so he dedicated a poem to him too, and was honored by being invited to attend a gathering in his presence. Then his patience wore out due to loneliness, and some acquaintances persuaded him to play at those decorated pieces of paper,[251] and he joined the gambling fraternity. More than once, however, his ignorance of the game drove his partner to lose his temper with him, so he made do with just being the *ḥurḍah* (the *ḥurḍah* is "the gamblers' record keeper").[252] Then he made the acquaintance of the chief state translator, Conte Desgranges; however, he never crossed the doorstep of any of the other translators, scholars, or teachers 4.19.4

ديكرانج فاما غيره من التراجمين وشيوخ العلم ومدرّسى اللغات الشرقية فلم يطأ لهم عتبة * لانهم نَفِسوا عليه بمآئهم وبَضَيْحهم وبودّهم وكلامهم ولقآئهم حتى انهم ابوا ان يطبعوا له قصيدته التى مدح بها

باريس بعد ان وعدوا بذلك *

وما كان خُلْفهم

الّا حسداً

ولؤما

*

of oriental languages because they so begrudged him a share of their milk and honey, their affection, their words, and their meetings that they refused to print his poem in praise of Paris even after they had promised to do so,

and their empty promises
were made of nothing
but
envy
and
bad faith.

الفصل العشرون

فى نبذة مما نظمه الفارياق من القصائد والابيات فى باريس على ما سبقت الاشارة اليه

آى فارياق * قد حان الفراق * فان ذا آخر فصل من كتابى الذى اودعته من ٤،٢٠،١
اخبارك ما املّنى والقارئين معى * ولوكنتُ علمت من قبل الاخذ فيه بانك تكلفنى
ان ابلّغ عنك جميع اقوالك وافعالك لما ادخلت راسى فى هذه الربقة * وتجشمت
هذه المشقة * فقدكنت اظن ان صغر جثتك لا يكون موجبا لانشآء تاليفٍ كبير
الجِرم مثل هذا * واقسم انك لو تابّطته ومشيت به خُطًى على قدر صفحاته لنبذته
وراك وشكوت منه ومن نفسك ايضا اذكنت انت السبب فيه * وما تمنعنى
صداقتى لك اذا وقفت على احوالك بعد الان ان اولّف عليك كتابا آخر * ولكن
اياك وكثرة الاسفار * والتحرش بالقسيسين والنسآ فى الليل والنهار * فقد مللت
من ذكر ذلك جدّا * ولقيت منه عنآ وجهدا * والان قد بقى علىّ ان اروى عنك ٤،٢٠،٢
بعض قصائدك وابياتك * ولكن قبل الشروع فيه ينبغى ان اذكرحكاية حالى * وهى
انى لما كنت فى هذه السنة بمدينة لندرة وشاعت اراجيف الحرب بين الدولة
العلية ودولة روسية نظمت قصيدة فى مدح مولانا المعظم * وسلطاننا المفخم *
السلطان عبد المجيد ادام الله نصره * وخلد مجده وفخره * وقدّمتها لجناب سفيره
المكرم الامير موسورس * فبعث بها الى جناب فخر الوزرآء سيدى رشيد باشا

Chapter 20

A Selection of Poems and Verses Written by the Fāriyāq in Paris as Previously Alluded To

All hail, the *Fāriyāq*! The time has come to *part*! This is the last chapter of this book of mine, into which I have put enough of your doings to bore me and the readers alike. Had I known before embarking on it that you'd task me with transmitting everything you said and did, I would never have inserted my neck into this noose or taken upon myself such a heavy load. I thought at first that the exiguousness of your body would obviate the need to put together a composition of any great size, such as this, and I swear if you were to tuck it under your arm and walk with it as many steps as it has pages, you'd toss it over your shoulder, complaining of it and of yourself as well since you're the cause of its existence. My friendship for you will not prevent me, should I examine your situation at some later time, from writing another book about you—but mind you don't go in for lots more journeys, or nightly and daily molestation of priests and women, for I have grown very weary of talking about such stuff and all I have gotten in return are trouble and toil. 4.20.1

It remains for me now to transmit, on your authority, some of your poems and verses. Before I start, however, I must say something about my own situation. This year,[253] when I was in London and malign rumors spread of war between the Sublime State and the Russian Empire, I wrote a poem in praise of Our August Lord and Honored Sultan, Sultan ʿAbd al-Majīd—may God remain forever on his *side* and immortalize his glory and his *pride*!—and presented it to his honorable and ennobled ambassador, Prince Musurus, who sent it on to His Honor, the Pride of Ministers, Rashīd Pasha, may God grant his every desire. Only a few days had passed before the latter sent to the 4.20.2

بلغه الله ما شا * فلم تمض ايام حتى بعث المشار اليه الى الامير السفير يخبره بانه قدّم القصيدة للحضرة السلطانية فى وقت رضى وقبول ووقعت لديها موقعا حسنا * وانه صدر الامر العالى بتوظيفى فى ديوان الترجمة السلطانى * فكان هذا الخبر عندى اسرّ ما طرق مسمعى * فينبغى لى الان ان اتاهّب للسفر لاتشرف بهذه الوظيفة * ولكن اعلم ايها القارى العزيز انه لما كان همى وقصارى مرامى ٣،٢٠،٤
كله انجاز طبع هذا الكتاب قبل سفرى الى القسطنطينية وكان مكثى فى لندرة موجبا لتاخيره * لان اجزآءه المطبوعة كانت ترسل الىّ فيها لاصححها آخر مرة قبل الطبع * اشار الىّ الخواجا رافائيل كحلا الذى وَلِى طبع الكتاب بنفقته ان اسافر الى باريس تعجيلا لطبعه فاجبت الى ذلك * وكان وقتئذ فى مرسى لندرة سفينة نار للدولة العلية يراد تسفيرها بعد مدة * فالتمست من صاحبى الخواجا نينه الذى قدم مع الخواجا ميخائيل مخلع فى مصلحة متجرية بان يراقب وقت سفر السفينة ويخبرنى بذلك لئلا تفوتنى فرصة السفر معها * وكان للخواجا نينه المذكور بعض حاجات ومآرب فى باريس جُلّها يختص بامراته فوكّل بشرآئها بعض معارفه هناك * حتى اذا اشتراها له اوعز اليه فى ان يسلّمها لى وكتب الىّ كتابا يقول فيه ان السفينة لا تلبث ان تسافر فالاولى سرعة رجوعك الى لندرة * فصدقت قوله واقبلت اسعى الى الندرة وانا موجس من ان تكون السفينة قد سافرت دونى * وتركت التصليح على عهدة الخواجا رافائيل المومأ اليه * فلما وصلت الى لندرة تبيّن لى ان نصح صاحبى لم يكن مقصودا به حاجة حضورى ولكن احضار حاجته معى ليتوفر عليه بذلك جُعلها ومكسها ولتتزيّن بها زوجته قبل انقضآ اوانها * فان السفينة بقيت فى المرسى مدة طويلة لتصليح آلاتها على علم من ناصحى * فكان قدومى الى لندرة هذه المرة الثانية سببا فى تاخير الطبع ايضا لاجل لزوم ارسال

prince-ambassador to inform him that he had presented the poem to the Sultan's Presence at a propitious moment and that it had made a favorable impression, and that a Sublime Command had been issued appointing me to the Imperial Translation Bureau. This was the sweetest news that could come to my ears. I must now therefore make ready to travel and assume the honor of that post.

You must know, however, dear reader, that, since my concern and only desire was to see the book printed before I left for Constantinople and since my sojourn in London required the delaying of my departure (for the parts of the book that had been printed were being sent to me there to make final corrections), Khawājā Rāfā'īl Kaḥlā, who had undertaken to print the book at his expense, suggested that the printing would go faster if I went to Paris myself, and I did so. At that time there was a steamship belonging to the Sublime State in the Port of London that was supposed to set sail soon. I therefore entreated my friend Khawājā Nīnah, who had come with Khawājā Mīkhā'īl Mikhalla' to take care of some business, to let me know when the date of the ship's departure was announced and inform me of that, so that I didn't miss the chance of leaving on it. This Khawājā Nīnah had certain things that he needed and wanted from Paris, most of them related to his wife, and he had commissioned an acquaintance there to buy them. Once that person had bought them, he instructed him to give them to me and wrote me a letter in which he said that the ship was about to leave, so it would be better if I were to return to London quickly. I believed what he said and set off in a hurry for London, worried that the ship might have departed without me, and I left the proofreading I was doing to Khawājā Rāfā'īl to see to. When I reached London, I realized that my friend's advice had not been given because of any need for me to be there but in order to ensure that I would bring his things with me and so save him the usual costs and customs charges and also so that he could adorn his wife with them before they had time to go out of fashion—for the ship remained in the port for a long while to repair its engines, as the one who gave me that advice had known it would. My coming to London this second time resulted, therefore, in a further delay in the printing, since the sheets had to be sent to me to look at before they were printed, as explained above. Were it not for this, the book would have been produced quickly. 4.20.3

الصحائف التى لا نظرها قبل الطبع كما سبقت الاشارة اليه * ولولا ذلك لنجز
الكتاب سريعا * غير انى احمد الله تعالى على انه لم يعرض له من الامور النسائية ٤،٢٠،٤
الا ما اوجب تاخير طبعه فقط دون ابطاله ونسخه بالكلية * فقد طالما اشفقت
عليه من ذلك كما كان الفارياق يشفق على فساد ترجمته من امثال هذه العوارض *
وهذه القضية مصداق على ما قالته الفارياقية فى الفصل التاسع من الكتاب
الرابع من انه قد يجتمع اثنان فى زواج او شركة او غير ذلك ويكون قد تقرر فى
بال احدهما ان له منّة على صاحبه * فمتى وردت على سمعك ياصاحبى نصيحة
من احد فانشر طيّها واسبر غورها لتعلم هل الغرض منها نفعك خاصة او نفع
ناصحك وحده او نفعكما معا * ولكن لا تبتدئ بنصيحتى هذه فانى لم اقصد بها
الّا مجرّد نفعك فقط * واعلم يافارياق انه قبل تشرّف قصائدك وابياتك بادماجها ٥،٢٠،٤
فى هذا الكتاب يجب علىّ ان اشرّفه والقارئين ايضا بالقصيدة المشار اليها وهى

الحق يعلو والصلاح يعمّرُ   والزور يمحق والفساد يدمّرُ
والبغى مصرعه ذميم لم يزل   آتيه عرضة كل سوء يثبر
والوغد تبطره من النعم التى   يغنَى بها الحرّ الكريم ويشكر
طغت الطغاة الرُّوس لما غرّهم   فى الارض كثر سوادهم وتجبّروا
كادوا ويرجع كيدهم فى نحرهم   فطُلاهم دون القواضب ينحر
المعتدون ولا نُهًى تنهاهم   الظالمون القاسطون الفجّر
نقضوا العهود وكان ذلك دأبهم   لؤما وللعدوان بغيا اضمروا
حتى راى بعضَ المآثر راسُهم   بخس الحقوق وسآء مَن يستاثر
ايظنّ ان الدولة العليا السويد وانّه هو بطرس المتاخّر

Nevertheless, I thank the Almighty that the womanish matters to which He subjected the book were only such as to delay its printing and not to result in its total cancellation or abrogation, which is something I often worried about, just as the Fāriyāq worried over the misrepresentation of his life story because of similar obstacles. The case lends credence to the Fāriyāqiyyah's statement in chapter 9 of Book Four[254] to the effect that two people may be involved in a marriage, a commercial partnership, or something similar, with one of the two believing privately that he is doing his partner a favor; so whenever, my friend, you are given a piece of advice to listen to by someone, pick it apart and probe its depths to discover whether its goal is to help you specifically, or to help the one who is giving you the advice and only him, or to help the two of you equally (but don't start with this advice of mine since my sole intention in giving it to you is to help you and you alone). 4.20.4

And know, O Fāriyāq, that before your poems and verses are honored by incorporation into this book, I must honor it and its readers too with the aforementioned poem,[255] which goes 4.20.5

Truth prevails and Right builds.
Falsehood nullifies and Evil destroys.
Injustice comes to an ugly end, its perpetrator
To every ruinous iniquity being ever exposed.
The knave's discontent springs from those same blessings with which
The noble freeborn man's enriched and for which he offers thanks.
The Russian tyrants went too far when their large numbers made them feel hubris and they acted haughtily.
They laid plots, but their scheming has come back to cut their own throats
For their necks will be slit by sharp swords.
The aggressors, whom no reason can restrain,
The oppressors, the wrongdoers, the debauched,
Violated the agreements (and so was ever their way)
Out of bad faith, and nursed a baseless grudge,
To the point that their leader deemed that violation of rights
Should be counted a glorious deed, but they do wrong who prefer their own interests.
Does he take the Sublime State to be Sweden
And himself some latter-day Peter?[256]

كلّا لَيرتدعنَّ ثم لَيعلمنْ   آن ربّها من يبتغيها يثأر

يامسلمون تثبّتوا ان جاءكم   نبأ عن الروس العدى وتبصّروا ٦،٢٠،٤

لا يغررنّكم كثير جموعهم   فالحق ليس يضيره المستكثر

يامؤمنون هو الجهاد فبادروا   متطوعين اليه حتى تؤجروا

هذا جهاد الله يحمى عرضكم   فاسخوا عليه بكلّ علق يُذخَر

فى لَنْ تَنالُوا ٱلبِرَّ حَتَّى تُنْفِقُوا   مِمَّا تُحِبُّونَ الدليل الاظهر

وتمسّكوا بالعروة الوثقى من الصبر الجميل على القتال وذمّروا

يغنيكم التكبير والتهليل عن   ان تعملوا فيهم سلاحا يبتر

فالقَوْهُمُ بهما كفاحا تظفروا   وعليهم صولوا وطولوا وانفروا

واغزوهمُ بحرا وبرّا واحشدوا   ركبا وفرسانا ونسرهمُ آنسروا

لو لم يكن منكم سوى نفر لما   غُلبوا فكيف بكم وانتم اكثر

من كل فتّاك اذا اعترضت له   يوما شُعوبٌ بل شَعوبُ يدسّر

انتم عباد الله حقا فاعبَدوا   للدّين فهو بكم يعزّ ويجبر ٧،٢٠،٤

واحموا حقيقتكم لحفظ ذماركم   فرض عليكم ليس عنه تأخُّر

غاروا على الاسلام حتى ترفعوا   اعلامه فلكم به ان تفخروا

لا تُسمِعِ الاجراس فى اوطانكم   بدل النداء ولا ينجّس منبر

It is not so! Let him then be deterred and let him know
That its sovereign takes his revenge on whomever he desires!
Muslims, check well,[257] should you hear 4.20.6
A report about the aggressive Russians, and reflect!
Let not the size of their hordes deceive you:
Great armies cannot harm the Truth.
Believers, this is the struggle to which God calls you, so make haste
To volunteer, that you may receive your divine reward!
This is God's struggle, which protects your honor.
Contribute to it with every precious thing you have saved up—
In the words "You will not attain piety until you expend
Of what you love"[258] is the clearest guide—
And hold fast to "the most firm handle"[259] of
Goodly patience in combat and be advised.
"God is greater!" and "There is no god but He!" will relieve you
Of the need to set to against them with trenchant blade.
Meet them, then, with these two cries in struggle and you will triumph
And fall upon them, take the fight to them, and charge against them!
Attack them by sea and by land. Mass against them
In companies and troops of horsemen and peck the feathers off their eagle.[260]
Were you but a small band of soldiers,
They would not be overcome[261]—so how can you fail when you are more?
From any bloody tyrant whole nations, nay, fate itself, will be defended
On the day you, O Sultan, bar his path.
You are those who worship God aright, so cleave to 4.20.7
The True Religion, for through you it gains in strength and is restored to its former state.
Protect your households, for the safekeeping of your family
Is a religious duty incumbent upon you that may not be shirked!
Defend your Islam jealously until you raise
Its banners! You must show your pride in it.
Let not the bells be heard in your territories
In place of the call to prayer, and let no mosque pulpit be desecrated!

وليُسمعنَّ اليوم فى ارجائكم   قرع القوانس بالظُبَى او تخدروا
فَلَذاك اشجى من غناء مطرّب   بمسامع القوم الذين به ضَرُوا
لكن يد الله القوية معكمُ   توليكم أيدًا فلن تتقهقروا
ما ان يقاويكم بهم من عسكر   لو ان ملءَ الارض طرًا عسكر
قد قال فى الذكر المفصَّل ربكم   حقًا علينا نصرهم فتذكروا
ما الله مخلف وعده لعباده   ان هم بعصمته اتّقوا واستنصروا
قدكان مولاكم وها هو لم يزل   وَزَرًا لكم ايّانَ كنتم يخفر ٨،٢٠،٤
ولربما شرعوا الرماح عليكم   لكن على انفاذها لن يقدروا
لن يعمل البتّار الا ان يشا   ءَ الله ما شيءٌ سواه مؤثّر
والنار منهم ان يُرد اطفآها   برد فلا تلظى ولا تتسعّر
واذا يشآ يثلّ عرشهم فلن   يستقدموا عنه ولن يستاخروا
غاروا على حُرَم مخدَّرة لكم   قد طالما اُحصِنّ عمن يعهر
ايقودهن اليوم علج فاجر   وسيوفكم بدمائهم لا تقطر
ولئن يكن نجما ورجسا مَسَّها   فنخوضها قد حلّ ان تتطهروا
الصبر محمود ولكن حين تُنتَهك المحارم لا اَرى ان تصبروا
لا خير فى عيش يقارف ذلّة   حاشاكم ان تفشلوا او تدبروا
شهد الاله بانه مولاكم   ونصيركم فبمجده فاستظهروا ٩،٢٠،٤

Let there be heard today in your lands
The cracking of pates by sword blades—or would you be paralyzed?—
For that is sweeter than the song of any singer who entrances
The ears of the people, and they are greedy to hear it.
But God's strong hand that is with you
Will bring you strength, so you will never retreat
No matter how many soldiers of theirs try your strength,
Even should soldiers fill the entire earth.
In the Portioned Narration,[262] your Lord has told you,
"It was ever a duty upon us to help" them,[263] so be reminded!
God will not break his promise to his servants—
They shall remain in his safekeeping, and be victorious.
He was your Lord and has never ceased to be 4.20.8
A stronghold for you. Wherever you may be, He guards.
They may point their lances at you
But never will be able to drive them home.
The cutting sword can do no harm, unless God
Wills. None but Him can induce effect.
Any fire from them, should He wish to extinguish it,
Will turn cold, never to catch again or flare back up.
When He wishes, he will brush aside their throne, and they cannot
Advance that day or delay it.[264]
They attacked protected women of yours
Who for so long had been kept inviolate from any who might
debauch them.
Shall some lecherous unbeliever lead them away today in chains
And your swords not drip with blood?
If the touch of it be polluting and filthy,
Then by wading into it, says the law, you may be made clean.
Patience is praiseworthy, but when what is sacrosanct
Is violated, I see no reason for you to be patient.
There is no good in a life that is mingled with humiliation—
Shame on you should you fail or turn your backs!
God has borne witness that He is your Lord 4.20.9
And your supporter, so while praising him, vanquish!

والله قد وعد المجاهد منكم   فتحًا مبينًا فى الكتاب فأبشروا

ويبوّء الشهدآء خير مبوّأ   جنات عدن ملكها لا يغبر

الحرب بينكم سِجال فاثبتوا   والنصر عقبَى امركم فاستبشروا

فى اهل بدر عبرة لكم ألَا   ياقوم فليتذكّر المتذكّر

أَبلُوا ليرضى ربكم عنكم فمن   أَبلَى فعند اللائميه يُعذَر

كم بين مَن ياتى القتال تطوّعا   ومسخّر كُرْهًا عليه يُجبَر

يقتاده ويسوقه مولًى له   فظّ زنيم غاشم متغشمر

ويبيعه لو شآء للنخّاس مع   ولدٍ له وبزوجه يتسرّر

لا عرض يمنعهم ولا كرم لهم   يثنيهم فى الناس عن ان يفجروا

١٠،٢٠،٤ يتترّعون الى الفواحش حيث مع   اهل المحامد فاتهم ان يُذكَروا

وكذا الطغام اذا عَدَتْهم مِدحةً   ودّوا بايّة شهرة ان يُشهَروا

سعدوا ولكن ربَّ سعد ذابح   للفائزين به اذا لم يشكروا

ولعل نسرهم المدوِّم واقع   فمن الهلال علاه ضوء يبهر

لن يفلح العاثون ما عاشوا ولا العاتون ما رغدوا ولن يتيسّروا

أَوَ لم يَعُوا ما جآهم عمن طغى   من قبلهم بطرًا وانّى دُمّروا

ام يعجزون الله اذ يُملِي لهم   عن ان يغار لقومه أَن يُنصَروا

God has promised those of you who struggle on His behalf
"A manifest victory,"[265] in the Book, so be joyful!
He provides the martyrs with the best of abodes—
Gardens of Eternity[266] whose dominion is never eclipsed.
The war between you is an ongoing battle, so stand firm,
And victory is the outcome, so be glad!
In the fighters of Badr[267] is a lesson for you.
O People, let him who would remember remember!
Fight bravely that your Lord may be pleased with you
For he who fights bravely by his detractors is excused.
What a difference between him who comes to the combat as a volunteer
And the one impressed against his will, compelled!
He is led and driven by a master,
Who is coarse, ignoble, tyrannical, unjust
And who can sell him, should he wish, to the slaver,
Along with his son, and take his wife as his concubine.
No honor restrains them nor does any magnanimity
Turn them aside from the debaucheries they inflict on people.
They hasten to commit abominations because 4.20.10
No hope remains that they might be remembered along with men of virtue.
Likewise, the vilest of people, if a praiseworthy deed is beyond them,
Would like to become known by any notorious act.
They have gained fortune, but how often has fortune cut the throat
Of those who win it when they give not thanks.
Maybe their circling eagle[268] will fall
And a light from the crescent moon[269] will rise over it and dazzle.
The wicked shall not flourish so long as they shall live
Nor shall the arrogant so long as they live in luxury, and never shall God ease their way.
Have they not noted what has come down to them concerning those who oppressed men
Before them out of arrogance, and how they were destroyed,
Or do they think God incapable, since He has left them so long to their own devices,
Of taking His people's side that they be victorious,

او اَن يُمِدَّهمُ بجند لا تُرَى   وبمنشئات مُخَّرٍ لا تُجِر
او ان تخرِّمهم[1] وهم مرحون فى   أمْن رخيّو البال ريح صَرْصَر
او يرسل الطير الابابيل التى   قد اهلكت امثالهم لاكُثّرِ وا
ما كان عبّاد البعيم ليغلبوا   قوما على اياك نعبد يُحشَر ١١،٢٠،٤
من كان يُرضى اللهَ خالص سعيه   فى الناس فهو بكل خير يجدر
من لم يصخ اذنا لنصح وليّه   ركب الضلال ولم يُفدّه المنذر
من ابطرته نعمة المولى عتا   عَسْفا وغشمرة يمين ويغدر
من لم تكن تقنية قسمة رزقه   فاذا اشرأبّ الى الزيادة يخسر
من يتكل سفها على جند له   دون الاله يَحِقّ به ما يحذر
من ظن ان يقوى بقوة باسه   وسلاحه وذويه فهو مغرَّر
من غالب القهّار عاد مخيَّسا   مستضعفا وَكِلاً يُذلّ ويقهر
من سرّه فى يومه كفرانه   وافاه فى غده العذاب الاكبر
من كان يوما راغبًا فى عاجل   عن آجل اَوْدَى به ما يوثر
من كان من بين الورى سلطانه   عَبْدُ المَجِيدِ فانه لمظفّر ١٢،٢٠،٤
سلطاننا الاسمى الذى سعدت به   ايامنا وزهت فدته الاعصر
نشر العدالة فى البلاد فكلنا   مستأمن فى ظله مستبشر

[1] ١٨٥٥: تخرّمهم.

Or of providing against them an army that may not be seen
Or running galleons that cleave no waves,
Or a wailing wind to uproot them
As they sport in security, their minds oblivious,
Or of loosing against them the "birds in flights"[270] that
Caused their like—may they not be increased!—to perish?
Those who worship the idol can never overcome 4.20.11
A people who are marshaled to the sound of "You we worship."[271]
He among mankind whose sincerity of effort pleases God
Deserves all good.
He who does not lend an ear to the advice of his friend
Is guilty of error, and no warner will be of use to him.
He whom the Lord's gifts have made proud turns violent
In injustice, and out of obstinacy lies and betrays.
He whose God-given allotment of daily bread is not enough to make him rich
And so cranes his neck to look for more loses.
He who foolishly places his trust in an army he has
And not in God will be seized by that against which he was warned.
He who thinks he will be made strong by the force of his intrepidity
And of his weapons and his followers—he is the one who has been duped.
He who challenges the All-Conquering will end up humiliated,
Weakened, and impotent, made abject and defeated.
He who is happy in his day with his disbelief,
The next will receive full measure of the Great Torment.
He who ever should wish for the things of this world
Before those of the next will be carried off by what he prefers.
He whose king among men 4.20.12
Is ʿAbd al-Majīd is the one to whom God grants victory.
Our Most Exalted Sultan, through whom our days
Have been rendered happy and bright—may the ages be his ransom!—
Has spread justice throughout the land. Thus all of us,
In his shadow, feel confidence and joy.

ولكلّ جيل فى ممالكه يدٌ   منه وآلاء تعمّ وتغمر

ما ان عداهم عدله وامانه   سيان ان هم اعسروا او ايسروا

انّا اذا اتّخذ العدى طاغوتهم   ربًّا لنأتمر الذى هو يامر

لسنا نروم بغير طاعته الى الرحمن من زلفى ولا نتخير

كلّا ولا فى غير خدمتنا له   عِرْض واخلاص لنا وتبرّر

كفر المبايعُ غيرَه والمعتدى   بغيا وطغيانا عليه اكفر

من ذا يحاكيه عُلًى ومناقبا   ومن الذى فُضْلَى حِلاه ينكر   ١٣،٢٠،٤

لو انه اقترح الوجود تحكّما   ما زاد فيها غير ما نتنظر

من جوهر الاخلاص صوّر ذاته   رب قدير كيف شا يصوّر

ولّاه امر الدين والدنيا معا   فهو الامام الحاكم المتامّر

وهو الذى بين الملوك مقامه الاعلى يكرّم هيبةً ويوقر

وهو الذى بين العباد محبّب   ومعظم ومبجّل ومعزّر

يستدفعون الضر فيهم باسمه   وعلى المنابر حمده المتكرّر

ان قال لم يستثنَ مما قاله   احد وان يفعله فهو مخيَّر

ليس الفرنج مشايعى اعدائه   ما هم لهم حزب ولا هم معشر

افمن يكون على هدى من ربّه   كغويّ استهواه جِبْتٌ منكر   ١٤،٢٠،٤

Each nation within his possessions receives aid
From him and gifts that include and embrace all.
His justice and his guarantee of safety never fail them,
Whether they are in hard straits or at ease.
If our enemies take their idol
As master, let us carry out whatever our sultan commands.
We do not hope for proximity to the Merciful
By any means except obedience to him, nor do we pick and choose [which divine commands to obey].
No indeed, nor will we find in anything but service to him
Honor, purity of intention, and justification.
He who pledges allegiance to any but him is an unbeliever, and the aggressor
Against him out of injustice and tyranny is yet more so.
Who is that man who would claim to be like him in exaltedness and glorious feats 4.20.13
And who is it that would deny his most excellent adornments?
Had he demanded [more virtues] from Creation,
He would not have added aught to what we already expect of him.
From the essence of purity was his person shaped
By an All-Capable Lord, who shapes the world according to His wishes.
He put under his charge the affairs of religion and this world together,
For he is imam, ruler, and commander
And he it is whose higher status among other kings
Is honored out of awe and venerated,
And he it is who is beloved among mortals
And exalted and revered and esteemed.
With his name they ward off harm amongst them
And from the pulpits his praise is repeated.
If he speaks, none are exempted from what he says,
And when he acts, he does so as his own master.
The Franks are not partisans of his enemies.
They are not their supporters nor are they their kinsfolk.
Is one who follows the guidance of his Lord 4.20.14
Like one misled, whom an evil sorcerer has seduced?

ام من له الخلق الكريم يقاس بالنكد اللئيم جِبلّةً وينظّر
ام يستوى فى العرف والامكان من يهب الجزيل ومن يشح ويصمر
ايهٍ امير المومنين ومن دعا ايه امير المؤمنين فقد سرُوا
سُدْ بالمعالى فائقا كل الورى مجدا وشانئك البغيض الابتر
وَسِعَت عوارفك العميمة سولنا الاقصى وما بالبال منا يخطر
حتى لقد كلّت خواطرنا بما اقترحت وانت منفّل لا تضجر
نطق العييّ بفرض مدحكم مفصحا حتى الجماد يكاد عنه يعبّر
ولقد اضآ الكون مجدك كلّه حتى استوى فى ذا العِمِى والمبصر
نظر الطغاة اليك نظرة حاسد فتجرّعوا مَضَضًا بها وتحسَّروا
ان يُجلبوا فالله ماحق جيشهم او يمكروا فلَمكرُ ربك اكبر ١٥،٢٠،٤
ان المِحال من المُحال اذا جرى بخلاف طِيّته وحقّ مقدّر
ماكان جمعهم سوى كِسَف هَبَت والشمس ليست بالهبآء تستّر
ليست فَرُوقُ لغير عرشك وهى ما بقيت على[١] الفرقان ليست تقفر لقب قسطنطينية
انت الذى بمديح وصفك تنجلى عنا الهموم وافقنا يتعطر
وتصحّ احلام الامانى فى غد اللاّهى بها والدهر انكد اعسر
ما ان يفى نظم اللآلئ مدحةً لك باللهى من سحب كفك تنثر

١ ١٨٥٥: عن.

Or one who possesses a noble character to be compared
To a base pest in nature and to him likened?
Or is one who gives with open hand on the same plane
In beneficence and capability as one who gives grudgingly and is a miser?
More, O Commander of the Believers!—And all who call,
"More, O Commander of the Believers!" are made princes!
Rule in your nobility, excelling in glory all mankind
And any spiteful gelding who hates you![272]
Your all-encompassing rewards have encompassed our most extreme
Requests and all that we could ever think of,
Until our imaginations have become exhausted from
Asking so much, while you still hand out booty and do not grow angry.
The stammerer, when obliged to speak your praise, speaks fluently;
Even the inanimate comes close to being able to express it.
Your glory has illumined the entire universe
To the point that it is as one to the blind and to the sighted.
The tyrants directed at you an envious look,
Then reluctantly retracted it and grieved.
Their army has no right, by God, to menace **4.20.15**
Or to devise plots. Verily your Lord's devising is greater!
Craft is impossible if it runs
Contrary to His design, and what is fated will be.
Their horde was but fragments blowing in the wind
And the sun is not hidden by motes.
Farūq belongs to no throne but yours; so long as it lives by
The Furqān,[273] it will not become desolate.

An epithet of Constantinople.

You are he the eulogizing of whose form causes cares
To be lifted from us and our horizon to exude perfume,
And dreams of hopes come true on the morrow of the one
Who diverts himself with them, though the times be contrary and harsh.
The stringing of the pearls in praise
Of you cannot match the precious gifts that are scattered from the clouds of your palm.[274]

لم يبقَ ما بين الورى من ناطق الّا وعن آلآء فضلك يخبر
حرس الاله جنابك الاعلى ولا زالت عبادك فى حماه تخفر
وادام دولتك العلية ما سرى نجم وما زخرت لجودك ابحر
انشدت تاريخين هجريّين فى ختمى مديحك وهوحظى الاوفر
عَبْدُ المَجِيْدِ الله اَرْگى ضده سلطاننا خير بجدٍّ يُنصَر

سنة ١٢٧٠ سنة ١٢٧٠

القصيدة الهرفية فى مدح باريس

اذى جنّة فى الارض ام هى باريس
ملائكة سكّانها ام فرنسيس
وهل حُور عِين فى منازهها تُرَى
والّا فكل حين تخطر بلقيس
وهل ذى نجوم ترجم الهمّ فى الدُجَى
عن البال ان يخطر به ام نباريسُ
وهل زهرة الدنيا ترى فى هوادج
تمرّ كبرق خاطف ام طواويسُ
نعم انها خُلْدُ النعيم وشاهدى
رياض وحوض دافق وفراديس

القصيدة الحرفية فى ذمها ١٦،٢٠،٤

اذى عَبْقَرٌ فى الارض ام هى باريس
زبانيةٌ سكّانها ام فرنسيس
وهل ذى نسآء فى مواحلها ترى
والّا فكلّ حين تخطر جاموس
وهل ذا شرار يجلب الهمّ فى الدجى
الى البال ان نبصر به ام نباريس
وهل زفرة الدنيا ترى فى هوادج
تمرّ كعير ظالع ام مطافيس
نعم انها ماوى الجحيم وشاهدى
شقيّون فى ساحاتها ومناحيس

No speaker is left among mankind
Who does not tell of the gifts of your beneficence.
God protect Your Sublime Excellence and may
Your slaves forever be safe in His protection,
And may He preserve your Sublime State so long as
Stars travel by night and seas, like your liberality, swell!
I have declaimed two Hijri dates[275] in
Concluding my praise of you, which is in itself my best reward:
ʿAbd al-Majīd, may God curse his enemy— In the Year 1270
Our sultan is the best of those who by fortune are assisted. In the Year 1270

The Presumptive Poem[276] in Praise of Paris

Is this Paradise on earth or is it Paris?
Is it angels its inhabitants are, or French?
Are these houris in its pure fastnesses one sees
Or is it that every little while Bilqīs comes sauntering by?

Are these stars that in the darkness of the night chase care
From the mind, should it ever occur, or are they streetlamps?

Is it the flower of this world that one sees in litters[277]
That pass like lightning flickering, or are they peacocks?
Indeed, it is the promised paradise of ease, and my evidence for this
Is meadows, a gushing basin, gardens,

The Prescriptive Poem in Dispraise of Paris 4.20.16

Is this an abode of the jinn on earth or is it Paris?
Is it rebellious jinn its inhabitants are, or French?
Are these women in its mires one sees
Or is it that every little while a water buffalo comes sauntering by?

Are these sparks that in the darkness of the night attract care
To the mind, should we be able to distinguish them, or are they streetlamps?

Is it the effluvia of this world that one sees in litters
That pass like wild donkeys limping, or are they gobs of filth?
Indeed, it is an infernal abode, and my evidence for this
Is villains in its squares, wretches,

ونهر وعلّيون فيها كواعب
على سرر مرفوعة واعاريس
وفاكهة مع لحم طير ونضرة
وراح وريحان وروح وترغيس
واعمدة تحبو السحائب دونها
كان لها فوق السماكَين تاسيس
هنيّئا لمن منها تبوّأَ منزلا
وطوبى لمن فيها له تاح تعريس
اذا شدّة او كربة بك برّحت
فَجِّ اليها فهى للكرب تنفيس
فتونس منها وهى تونس غبطةً
فبين المقامين اتحاد وتجنيس
وان تكُ يوما قانطا من لُبانة
فرؤيتها اطلاب ما منه ميئوس
بها ما يقرّ العين من كل اربة
وما تشتهى نفس وما تالف التوس

وفسق وعلّيون فيها فواجر
على سرر مرصوعة وتناجيس
واكل من الزقّوم يخبث طعمه
وشرب من الغِسْلين يسقيه ابليس
واعمدة تلقى الشياطين عندها
كان لها فوق الخبائث تاسيس
شقآء لمن منها تبوا منزلا ١٧،٢٠،٤
وتعسا لمن فيها له تاح تعريس
اذا شدة او كربة بك برّحت
بها فانأ عنها فهو للكرب تنفيس
وبرّز عليها ان يفتك مبرّز
فبين المقامين اتحاد وتجنيس
وان تك يوما طامعا فى لُبانة
فرؤيتها ياس لما هو محدوس
بها ما يسوء العين من كل اربة
وما تجتوى نفس وما تكره التُوس

A river, and a *ʿIlliyyūn*[278] in which
are women with jutting breasts
On "raised couches,"[279] and
cotton mattresses [?][280]

Evildoers, and a *ʿIlliyyūn* in which
are debauched women
On perfume-bedaubed couches,
and menstrual rags

And fruit with flesh of fowl and
plenty
And wine and sweet-smelling
herbs and perfume and ease
of life

And food from the *zaqqūm* tree
whose taste is foul
And drink of foul pus adminis-
tered by Satan

And pillars below which crawl the
clouds
And whose foundations have
been laid atop the Uplifted
Ones.[281]

And pillars where you will find
devils
And whose foundations have
been laid on top of filth.

Good health to him who takes
therein a dwelling!
Blessing to him to whom it is
given to take a bride there!

Toil and trouble to him who takes 4.20.17
therein a dwelling!
Misery to him to whom it is given
to take a bride there!

Should adversity or trouble beset
you,
Make pilgrimage to it, for it is the
comforter of troubles,

Should adversity or trouble beset
you
There, go far from it for it is an
outlet for troubles,

And be delighted by it, it being like
Tunis[282] in bliss
For the two places are as one in
their similarity of form.

And defecate upon it if you should
fail to find a latrine
For the two places are as one in
their similarity of form.

And should you some day feel
hopeless over anything,
The sight of it is an answer to
prayers, from which none are
turned away in despair.

And should you some day feel
greedy for a thing,
The sight of it will breed despair
of ever obtaining what was
envisioned.

In it are objects of desire of every
sort that's pleasing to the eye
And that the soul might desire
or inborn disposition find
sympathetic.

In it is dross of every sort that's
offensive to the eye
And that the soul might hate
or inborn nature find
antipathetic.

وفى ذكر ما فيها تلَذّ لذاذةٌ　　وفى ذكر ما فيها يسوء اساءة
تطيب بها عن غيرها وهو محسوس　　تفوق على ما خفته وهو محسوس
هى المنهل المورود من كل ظامئ　　هى المنهل المسموم حتف لظامئ
وللزائريها الخير اجمع مبجوس　　وللزائريها الشرّ اجمع مبجوس
هى الامن من جور الخطوب فما على　　هى الخوف من كل الخطوب فما على
عزيز بها ضيم يُحاذَر او بوس　　عزيز بها الا المخاطر والبوس
نعم هى من عين الزمان تميمة　　نعم هى فى عين الزمان قذًى فما
فما امّها ذو عسرة وغدا فى سو　　اتاها امرؤٌ الا ومنها غدا فى سو
فما نعمة فيها تشان بحاسد　　فما نعمة فيها خلت عن محسّد
ولا صفو لذات يقانيه تسجيس　　ولا وطر الّا وقاناه تسجيس
ولا بخس ذى حقٍّ من الناس حقه　　وبخس ذا حق من الناس حقه
فيا حسن دار حيث لا حقَّ مبخوس　　فيا قبحها دارا بها الحق مبخوس
فلا ذأم فيها يستبين لعائب　　فلا رَوح منها يستبين لناصب　　١٨،٢٠،٤
سوى هادم اللذات ما دونه طُوس　　سوى هادم اللذات ما دونه طوس

At the mention of it you will feel a true pleasure
That will lead you to abandon all other, a pleasure palpable.
It is the well-filled spring that everyone who thirsts must come upon,
All that is good to those who visit it, ever gushing.
It is security from the tyranny of adversities and no stranger there
Has call to be on guard against injustice or distress.
Yea, it is an amulet against the envy of the age—
No one in straits has ever made his way there and found himself facing calamity.
No comfort there is marred by any envious person
Nor has the purity of its pleasures been mixed with any turbidity
Nor is any right taken from any right-holder among the people unjustly.
How beautiful then an abode where no right is infringed!
Nothing diminishing there is manifest for the faultfinder [to seize on]
Other than the Destroyer of All Pleasures,[283] against whom there is no potion.

At the mention of it one will feel something vexatious
That will surpass what you feared, a displeasure palpable.
It is the poisoned spring that spells death for the thirsty
All that is evil for those who visit it, ever gushing.
It is fear of every adversity and no stranger there
Finds anything but dangers and misery.
Yea, it is a mote in the eye of the age—
No man has ever gone there who did not find himself facing calamity.
No comfort is there but someone wishes to take it for himself
And nothing desirable that is not mixed with turbidity
And it takes from every right-holder his rights.
How ugly then an abode where rights are infringed!
No rest there is manifest for the one who is weary 4.20.18
Other than the Destroyer of All Pleasures, against whom there is no potion.

عليها بهآء المُلك والعز والعُلَى
ومنها سناَ المجد والفخر مقبوس
الى مثلها يُنْضى الرشيد مطيَّه
اذا كان يُلفَى مثلها وتجى العيس
هو العيش فاغنم طيبه فى ربوعها
فانك فيها ما اقمت لمرغوس
وانك منها لست يوما بواجد
بديلا ولو امسى وراك برجيس
وانك فيها ضارب كُرَة الاَسَى
بمجن بشر ليس يتلوه تعبيس
وانك منها مجتن ثمر المنى
فان بها اصل الفوائد مغروس
اذا رثَّ ثوب العمر منك فانّ من
قشيب حِظاها ريّق العيش ملبوس
فبِتْ آمنا فيها وقم باكرا الى
مراتع لَهْوٍ لم تشبه وساويس

عليها ظلام الكفر والظلم والخنى
ومنها اُوار الفسق والفحش مقبوس
وعن مثلها ينضى الرشيد مطيّه
اذا كان يُلفَى مثلها وتجى العيس
هو العيش فاغنم طيبه فى سوآئها
فانك فيها ما اقمت لمنحوس
وانك لا تلقى لها من مُشابه
برجْسٍ ولو امسى وراك برجيس
وانك فيها ضارب كرة المنى
بمجن ياس تلوه الدهر تعبيس
وانك منها مجتن ثمر الاسى
فان بها اصل المحارم مغروس
اذا كان ثوب العزّ عندك معلما
فمن نغص فى عيشها هو مطلوس
فبت صابرا فيها وقم باكرا الى
نعيم سواها لم تشبه وساويس

Over it are the splendor of sovereignty and might and sublimity.
From it the resplendence of glory and pride may be acquired.
To reach such a city—if its like is to be found—
The wise traveler wears out his steed and to it come the well-bred camels.
We speak of life, so savor its perfume in its quarters to the full
For so long as you shall reside there you will be at ease!

And never will you find for it
A substitute, even should you travel so far that Jupiter lies behind you in the sky.[284]
There you will strike the ball of grief
With a mallet of joy, after which there need never again be frowns.
From it you will garner the fruits of hope
For there the root of all useful things is implanted.
Should the garment of life become too tattered for you to mend,
In the new clothes of its favors, in the bloom of life, you will be clothed.
Spend your night there secure and set off early for
Pastures of diversion unspoiled by misgivings.

Over it are the darkness of unbelief and injustice and fornication.
From it the flames of evildoing and debauchery may be acquired.
To escape such a city—if its like is to be found—
The wise traveler wears out his steed and from it flee the well-bred camels.
We speak of life, so savor its perfume in some other city
For, so long as you shall reside there, you will suffer ill fortune!

And never will you find a city like it
In filth, even should you travel so far that Jupiter lies behind you in the sky.
There you will strike the ball of fate
With a mallet of despair, after which there must always be frowns.
From it you will garner the fruits of grief
For there the root of all forbidden things is implanted.
Should the garment of greatness that you possess be distinctive,
From the loathsomeness of life there, it will end up drab.
Endure the night there and set off early for
The comforts of some other city unspoiled by misgivings.

ولا ترغبنْ عنها الى غيره تكن
كمن شاقه بعد السعادة انكيس
فدهرك فيها ما اقمت مسالم
وقدرك مرفوع وشملك محروس
فآثرْ بها ليلاً على عام غيرها
على فرض ان الليل اذ ذاك ادموس
ولا غرو ان تزداد فى العمر حقبة
ففى الصفر للفرد العقيم تخاميس
لقدكنت اخشى الحَيْنَ فى غير منشأى
فقدنى بها بشرى اذا انا مرموس
وقد طالما عللت نفسى برغدها
فبتّ ولى احلام خير وتغليس
فالفيتا يربو على الوصف حسنها
فما ثمَّ اشباه لها ومقاييس

ولا ترغبن فيها ولو ليلة تكن
كمن شاقه بعد السعادة انكيس
فدهرك فى دار سواها مسالم ١٩،٢٠،٤
وقدرك مرفوع وشملك محروس
فآثر بها ليلا على عمر بذى
على فرض ان الليل اذ ذاك ادموس
ولا غرو ان تزداد فى العمر حقبة
ففى الصفر للفرد العقيم تخاميس
لقدكنت اخشى الحَين فى غير منشاى
فياشقوتى فيها اذا انا مرموس
وقد طالما حذّرت نفسى فسادها
فبت ولى احلام سوء وكابوس
فالفيتا يربو على الوصف قبحها
فما ثمَّ اشباه له ومقاييس

Do not yearn for other than it, or you will be
Like one afflicted, after happiness, by a geomancer's spell.[285]
For your days, as long as you reside there, will be peaceful,
Your worth upheld, your right to be together with your family preserved.

Better a night there than a year in any other city
Even should the night then be dark as pitch
And there can be no doubt that you will grow older by an age
For if you add a zero to it even an odd number becomes divisible by five.[286]
I used to fear death if not in my birthplace
But now it would be good tidings enough for me if I were to be buried there.
How often have I distracted my soul with promise of its ease,
Then spent the night dreaming good dreams, arriving there in the last hours of darkness
And found it too beautiful to describe
For it has no likes and is beyond compare.

Do not yearn for it even for one night, or you will be
Like one afflicted, after happiness, by a geomancer's spell.
For your days, as long as you reside in some other abode, will be peaceful, 4.20.19
Your worth upheld, your right to be together with your family preserved.
Better a night in that other abode than a lifetime in this
Even should the night then be dark as pitch
And there can be no doubt that you will grow older by an age
For if you add a zero to it even an odd number becomes divisible by five.
I used to fear death if not in my birthplace
And ah what distress for me should I be buried there!

How often have I warned my soul against its corruption,
Then spent the night dreaming bad dreams and nightmares

And found it too ugly to describe
For it has no likes and is beyond compare.

وفيها من الغرّ الكرام اعزّة
جَحاجحُ ضرّابون يوم الوغى شوش
لقد فُطروا طبعا على الودّ والوفا
جميعا فما يعروهما عوضُ تلبيس
لئن سُبقوا سَبْقَ الوجود فانه
لَيسبقُ جسمًا ظلُّه وهو مدعوس
لهم في سمآء العلم شمس براعة
وفي الادب الطامي العباب قواميس
فكم فيهم من عالم متقن له
لتطليس آثار المعارف تطريس
اذا اغطشت آفاق امر فانما
يجلّيه لفظ موجز منه مهموس
وكم فيهم من فاضل ذي استقامة
تقيم قوام الدهر اذ هو منكوس
وتمسكه ان لا يجور كانما
تُعدَّل في كلتا يديه قساطيس

وفيها من القوم اللئام ثعالب
ولكنهم ان يؤدَبوا اسد شوس
لقد فطروا طبعا على الغدر والجفا
جميعا فلا يغررك في ذاك تلبيس
لئن سَبَقوا سبق الوجود فانه
ليسبق جسما ظلُّه وهو مدعوس
٢٠،٢٠،٤ لهم في بحور الشك خوض وطالما
تغشّتهم منه ضلالا قواميس
فكم فيهم من مدّع صَلِف له
لتطريس آثار المعارف تطليس
اذا ما انجلت آفاق امر فانه
ليخفيه لفظ موجز منه مهموس
وكم فيهم من فاضل من فضوله آع
تدال قوام الدهر احدب منكوس
يحاول لؤمًا ان يميل به فلا
تعدّل في كلتا يديه قساطيس

Notable men, generous and honorable, are there,
Lords, mighty smiters on the day of battle, of imperious looks.
Affection and loyalty are natural gifts
Among them all; no duplicity shall ever mar them.
Verily, if they were preceded by aught,
It was as a shadow precedes a body, foreshortened.
In the heavens of scholarship they possess a shining sun
And in their billow-filled literature oceans,[287]
For how many a scholar do they have, perfectly qualified,
Who has obliterated, by overwriting, the knowledge of former generations
And a concise word from whom illumines any matter whose horizons
May be dark, be it merely whispered
And how many a virtuous, upright man there is among them
To set fate straight again should it be reversed

And hold it so that it cannot stray, like balances
Made even between his two hands!

Base men are there, foxes,
Though if invited to dine, lions, of imperious looks.

Treachery and coldness are natural gifts
Among them all; let no duplicity on this point deceive you.
Verily, if they precede aught,
It is as a shadow precedes a body, foreshortened.

Into the seas of doubt they have waded, and how often 4.20.20
Have its ocean waves covered them in error—
For how many an arrogant claimant to scholarship do they have
Whose knowledge, from former generations, has been obliterated by overwriting
And a concise word from whom darkens any matter whose horizons
May be bright, be it merely whispered
And how many a meddler there is among them by whose meddling
The straight back of fate is bent and inversed
And who tries, falsely, to make it bend though never
Can balances be even between his two hands!

وربَّ خطيب لفظه فوق منبر وربَّ عَيِيٍّ لفظه فوق منبر
يُبين ولو بُلّغته وهو معكوس يسوء ولو بلّغته وهو معكوس
يشف خفيّ الغيب عما يقوله يشفّ خفيّ العيب عما يقوله
فيبصره مَن طرفه بعدُ مطموس فيبصره مَن طرفه بعدُ مطموس
وكم فيهم من خيّرٍ صالح له وكم فيهم من فاسق عاهر له
انآ الليل تسبيح طويل وتقديس انا الليل تجديف طويل وتنجيس
وكم فاتح منهم وما بارح الحمى وكم طامع فى الملك منهم سفاهة
كتائبه اقلامه والقراطيس كتائبه اقلامه والقراطيس
وكم بينهم من ليث حرب اذا سطا وكم من طفيليّ لكل وليمة
جريّءٍ له فيها احتناك وتضريس جريّ له فيها احتناك وتضريس
حِمام اذا هيجوا حياة اذا اتُّقوا حمام اذا زِيْروا حياة اذا اجتدوا ٢١،٢٠،٤
اسود اذا صالوا جبابرة هيس اسود اذا لاسوا جبابرة هيس
اذا سمحوا لانوا وان حَمِسوا قسَوا اذا سألوا لانوا وان سُئلوا قسَوا
ويَرْبُون فضلاً ان بغيرهم قيسوا ويربون شحّا ان بغيرهم قيسوا

And how many a preacher they have whose pronouncements from atop the pulpit
Bring clarity, even if they are conveyed to you back to front.

And how many a stammerer they have whose pronouncements from atop the pulpit
Are evil, even if they are conveyed to you back to front.

Hidden mysteries are glimpsed as a result of what he says,
So that he whose eye is yet unseeing may see them.

Hidden vices are glimpsed as a result of what he says,
So that he whose eye is yet unseeing may see them.

How many a good and righteous man there is among them who
Throughout the night says long glorias and hallelujahs

How many a lecherous fornicator there is among them who
Throughout the night complains of his lot at length and in impurity

And how many a conqueror there is among them, who never left his home pastures,
His pens and papers being his battalions!

And how many a one foolishly greedy for dominion there is among them,
His pens and papers being his battalions!

And how many a lion of war among them, when he pounces,
Is bold and has battle-won experience therein—

And how many a scrounger among them at every banquet
Is bold and has battle-won experience therein—

Death to his enemies if they rise up, life if they fear God;
Lions if their enemies attack—courageous colossi!

Death [to their visitors] if they are visited, the soul of liveliness if the latter are handing out gifts; 4.20.21
Lions if they taste food—courageous colossi!

When they forgive, they are gentle; when they become zealous, they are cruel.
To compare them with others is to understand how gracious they are.

When they beg, they are gentle; when others beg from them, they are cruel.
To compare them with others is to understand how miserly they are.

اولو همّة دانت لها هِمَم الورى
وفخرهم فى ذاك كالدهر قُدموس
بشاشتهم للضيف خير من القِرَى
وما لقراهم لو تاخّر تبنيس
واكرامهم مثوى الغريب سجية
فيغدو وقد اقناه اهل وتانيس
مديحهم يشدو به كلّ رائح
وغاد ويرويه رئيس ومرؤوس
لقد اكرموا هذا اللسان واهله
فما زال يحظى عندهم وهو مدروس
وقد الّفوا فيه تآليف جمّة
وجلّت لهم فيه شيوخ وتدريس
يعزّ الفتى بالمال عندهم سواهم
وعندهم تغنيك عنه الكراريس

اولو جَشَع من دونه جشع الورى
وصيتهم فى ذاك كالدهر قدموس
بشاشتهم للضيف فى زعمهم قرى
وفى وعدهم مَيْنٌ ومطل وتبنيس
واكرامهم مثوى الغريب سجية
اذا كان ذا زوج وبالزوج تانيس
هجاؤهم يشدو به كل رائح
وغاد ويرويه رئيس ومرؤوس
لقد جهلوا هذا اللسان واهله
فما زال يخفى عنهم وهو مدروس
وقد لفّقوا فيه اساطير جمّة
وشطّت لهم فيه شيوخ وتدريس
يعزّ الفتى بالعلم عند سواهم
وعندهم ليست تفيد الكراريس

They possess a vaulting ambition before which that of all mankind falls short.
Their pride in this is as ancient as the days.

The friendly face they show their guest is better than a meal of welcome
And their welcoming meal, even should their guest be late, is provided without delay.

Their hospitality to the stranger is an inborn trait
And he wakes up to find that [a new] family and the comforts [of family support] have made him wealthy.

All who come to them, evening and morning, sing their praises,
And these are passed on by master and by servant.

They have brought honor to this language and its speakers
And it continues to gain favor among them and be studied.

They have written a large number of books on it
And their shaykhs and their teaching have achieved illustriousness.

In other cities, the young man takes pride in wealth;
Among them, his exercise books render wealth unnecessary.

They possess a greed before which that of all mankind falls short.
Their reputation for this is as ancient as the days.

The friendly face they show their guest is, they claim, as good as a welcoming meal
And their engagements are full of lying, procrastination, and delay.

Their hospitality to the stranger is an inborn trait,
Provided he has a wife and the wife is friendly.

All who come to them, evening and morning, declaim invectives against them,
And these are passed on by master and by servant.

They have no knowledge of this language and its speakers
And it continues to disappear among them, though it is studied.[288]

They have fabricated a large number of myths about it
And their shaykhs and their teaching have strayed far from it.

In other cities, the young man takes pride in scholarship;
Among them, exercise books are of no value.

فقل للمباريهم تحدّوا لغيرهم	فقل لذوى الدعوى المبارين منهم	
فان مجاراة المجلّين تهويس	لعمرى مجاراة المجلّين تَهْوِيس	
شِعارهم حرّية واُخوّة	شعارهم حرّية واخوّة	٢٢،٢٠،٤
وتسوية كلٍّ بذلك ناموس	وتسوية لكن عدا ذاك ناموس	
فلا فرق بين الدون والدون فى القضا	فلا فرق بين الدون والدون فى القضا	
وارِئيسهم فى اليُسر والرَفه ارّيس	وارّيسهم فى الامر والنهى ارّيس	
ترى كلَّ فرد منهم كيّسا له	ترى كل فرد عاتيا طاغيا له	
مشاركة فى العلم والفضل ما كيسوا	مشاركة فى الحكم مع انهم خيسوا	
وان لهم من سيمياً وجوههم	وان لهم من سيمياً وجوههم	
دلائل ان الخير منهم مانوس	دلائل ان الشرّ منهم مانوس	
وان لهم رزقا كريما رضوا به	وان لهم رزقا حراما رضوا به	
فما هم مسفّ مارب فيه تدنيس	فشانهم اِسفاف ما فيه تدنيس	
فتحسب كُلّا حلّ صرحا ممرّدا	فتحسب كلّا حلّ ماخور ريبة	
تحيّته فيه سلام وتقليس	تحيّته فيها سِلام وتلقيس	

Say then to those who would engage them to a duel, “Challenge others,
For to seek to compete with the highest is madness!”

Their motto is Liberty, Equality,
Fraternity, and all are entrusted with upholding these.

Thus there is no difference between two lowly opponents before the courts
And their prince in wealth and affluence is treated like any ploughman.

You will find that each of them is shrewd
And dabbles in scholarship and learning, and they cannot be outwitted.

From the cast of their countenances
Evidence may be drawn that goodness to them is no stranger

And that they have a noble way of earning their daily bread, with which they are satisfied
And they do not stoop to any purpose that is demeaning.

You would think that each must dwell in a well-plastered edifice
Where the greeting he gives is a salute and a bow with hands on heart.

Say then to those of them who issue challenges to duels,
“I swear, to compete with the highest is madness!”

Their motto is Liberty, Equality, 4.20.22
Fraternity, but that’s become a lie.

Thus there is no difference between two lowly opponents before the courts
And their prince in commanding and forbidding is like any ploughman.

You will find that each of them is arrogant, tyrannical,
And dabbles in government, even though they have been betrayed.

From the cast of their countenances
Evidence may be drawn that evil to them is no stranger

And that they have a sinful way of earning their daily bread, with which they are satisfied.
They stoop to all that is demeaning.

You would think that each must dwell in a house of ill repute
Where the greeting he gives is scorpions’ bites and insults.

فما نظرت عيناى فيهم صاغرا   فما نظرت عيناى فيهم فاضلا
ولا من عن الخيرات والرشد مرجوس   ولا من عن الآثام والرجس مرجوس
ارانى سعيدا مُحْبَرا فى جوارهم   ارانى كئيبا نادما فى جوارهم
ومن لم يزر هذا الحمى فهو منحوس   ومَن زار يوماً ارضهم فهو منحوس
عفوت عن الايام سالف ذنبها   وجدت على الايام عتبا بعيشها
فقد شفعت فيها وفى الناس باريس   فقد اخبثته والبريةَ باريس
وقد كنت فى مدحى لها قبلُ مخطئا
فهذا له كفّارة وهو مركوس

القصيدة التى امتدح بها الجناب المكرم الامير عبد القادر بن محيى الدين المشهور بالعلم والجهاد ٢٣،٢٠،٤

ما دام شخصك غائبا عن ناظرى   ليس السرور بخاطر فى خاطرى
يامن على قرب المزار وبُعده   حبّى له والشوق ملء سرائرى
ان كنتُ لى يوما فديتك وافيا   ما ضرّنى ان كان غيرك غادرى
فاذا رضيت فكلّ سُخط هيّنٌ   واذا وصلت فلم ابال بهاجر
واذا بقربك كنت يوما نافعى   لم اخشَ شيا بعد ذلك ضائرى
يافاتنى بدلاله وشِماله   وكماله وجماله ذا الزاهر

Never have I seen among them one who was servile Nor one who did not share in their good things and good conduct.	Never have I seen among them one who was virtuous Nor one who did not share in their sins and filth.
I find myself happy and joyful in their company And any who has not visited this sanctuary is unlucky.	I find myself gloomy and regretful in their company And any who has ever visited their land is unlucky.
I have excused the days whatever sins they may commit, For Paris has interceded on their behalf and that of all people.	I am angry with the days, rebuking them for what I have lived through For Paris has rendered it, and all creation, repugnant.
	In my earlier eulogizing of it I was mistaken: This, then, is atonement for that and is its reverse.

The Poem in Which He Eulogized the Honorable and Ennobled Emir ʿAbd Al-Qādir Ibn Muḥyī Al-Dīn, Celebrated for His Scholarship as for His Struggle on God's Behalf:[289] 4.20.23

So long as your person is absent from my sight,
My mind can pay no mind to pleasure,
O you, love for whom, whether you be close enough to visit or too far,
And longing, fills my heart!
If you—may I be your ransom!—be true to me but once,
Others' treachery can harm me not.
If you are content with me, then all other discontents are paltry,
And if you come to me, I shall ignore any other who may abandon me.
If you should ever benefit me through closeness to you,
I shall never thereafter fear anything that may injure me.
O you who have entranced me with your sweet appeal, your disposition,
Your perfection, and your radiant beauty,

عقلى سلبتَ ومهجتى فارددْهما لا جيد مدح شمائل لك باهرى
وليعلمَ العذّال انى صادق فى وصف حسن حلاك وصفة شاعر
يامحرقى شوقا بفاتر جفنه ارايت قبلى مُحرقًا بالفاتر
يابدر تمٍّ لاع قلبى حبُّه ياشمس حسن قد تملّك سائرى
ياظبى انس شاق عينى شكله لكن له طبع الغزال النافر ٢٤،٢٠.٤
هلاّ رثيت لحالتى ورفقت بى ووعدتنى عدةً ولو فى الظاهر
كَلَمَ الحشا منى وعيدك قَسْوةً قبل الفراق بان تكون معاسرى
وفطرت قلبى بالجفا عَمْدًا فلا عجب اذا ما قلت انك فاطرى
افهكذا فعل الحبيب بحبّه ام صرت بعدى عاذلى لا عاذرى
لوكنت تدرى ما لقيتُ من النوى لرحمتنى وودت[1] انك زائرى
مذ غبتُ عنك ارتدَّ عن طرفى الكرى من بعد ما هُدى آرتدادَ الكافر
وازداد سقمى واستُثيرت لوعتى وبدا بحبّك ما تكنّ ضمائرى
انى وحقِّ هواك غاية مطلبى وسنا محيّاك الصبيح الناضر
من يوم لُحتَ لناظرى ما لاقنى شيءٌ ولم يملأ جمال ناظرى
ما كان حسن سواك يوما شائقى كلا ولا لحظ لغيرك ساحرى ٢٥،٢٠.٤

١ ١٨٥٥: وودت.

You have carried off my mind and heart! Return them to me
That I may eulogize well qualities in you that bring me joy
And let the disapproving know that I am sincere
In describing the beauty of your sweetness as a poet would.
O you the drowsiness of whose eyelid has made me burn with longing,
Have you before seen anyone burned by what is lukewarm?[290]
O moon of perfection, your love has wracked my heart;
O sun of beauty, you have taken possession of my soul.
O dorcas of companionability, your form has made my eye yearn, 4.20.24
But you have the nature of the shy gazelle.
Did you not feel pity for my state and want to be kind to me
And did you not promise me a tryst, even if in public?
My innards were wounded by the cruelty of your threat
Before we parted that you would treat me harshly
And you split my heart in two with your coldness, deliberately,
So no wonder I said you were my creator.[291]
Is it thus that the beloved should act with his lover,
Or is it that after loving me you have become my rebuker instead of my excuser?
Had you but known what I suffered from your distance,
You would have taken mercy on me and wanted to visit me.
Since I have been separated from you, sleep has turned its back on my eye
Like an apostate who, after finding guidance, renounces his commitment.
My illness has grown worse and my agony has been stirred up,
And all that was hidden in my heart has been revealed through your love.
I swear by your love, which is the thing I most hope for,
And by the resplendence of your blooming, effulgent countenance,
Since the day you first appeared to my eye, nothing has seemed worthy to me
And no beauty has filled my eye.
The beauty of others has never made me yearn— 4.20.25
No indeed, nor has another's look bewitched me.

اَهْوَى لاجلك مَن حكاك بِشكله　　لا شَكله اذ ذاك دون النادر
كيف اصطبارى اليوم والاجل انقضى　　وابيت ارضاى بطيف زائر
وبمهجتى انّى اراه ساعة　　قبل الممات معانقى ومسامرى
هَبْه اتى فلقد يرانى ساهرا　　والطيف ليس براقد مع ساهر
انسيتَ عهدى حيث ملت مع الهوى　　ولقد عهدتك ما ذكرتك ذاكرى
اما انا فكما علمت على النوى　　والقرب صبّ فيك غير مغاير
شيآنِ لست اطيق صبرا عنهما　　ذكرى هواك ومدح عبد القادر
هو ذلك الشهم الذى شهدت له　　كل البرية بالفَعال الفاخر
ومناقب محمودة وشمائل　　مرضية ومحامد ومآثر
هو ذلك المولى الممدَّح سعيُه　　عند الاله وعند كل مفاخر ٢٦،٢٠،٤
هو ذلك الفرد الذى افعاله　　اُمْدوحة البادى وفخر الحاضر
وهو المهيب لدى الملوك نزاهةً　　والنازح الصيت الكريم الطاهر
من معشر العرب العريق نجارُهم　　اهل المكارم كابرا عن كابر
العاملين بحكم التنزيل فى　　التحريم والتحليل حزب الحاشر
الناحرين اذا دَعَوا واذا دُعوا　　ياللبراز فنحرهم للناحر
المؤثرين على خَصاصتهم وقد　　نظروا الى الدنيا كشى غابر

I love for your sake any who resembles you in his coquettishness—
Not in his outward form, since any such resemblance would be too rare to imagine.
How can I remain patient today, when the set time has passed
And you refused to make me content by visiting me as a night phantom?[292]
My heart I would give to behold him for an hour
Before I die, embracing me and keeping me company of an evening.
Suppose he were to come, he would find me unsleeping—
And the phantom does not sleep with one who is awake.
You forgot your pledge to me when other love made you turn aside
When, for as long as I have known you, you have borne me in mind.
As for me, as you know, whether distant
Or close I am your impassioned lover, never changing.
Two things I cannot endure to be separated from:
The memory of your love and praise for ʿAbd al-Qādir.
He is that gallant man, to whose proud good works
All creation bears witness
As well as to his praiseworthy virtues, pleasing traits,
Good qualities and deeds.
He is that lord whose efforts are praised **4.20.26**
By God and by every praise-sayer.
He is that individual whose deeds
Are the object of the eulogies of the desert-dweller and the pride of the city-dweller.
He is the one who inspires awe among kings for his integrity
And the one of far-reaching, pure, and noble reputation,
Descended from the nation of the Arabs, ancient of lineage,
The people of noble deeds, one proud man following another,
Who act according to the precise rules of the Revelation regarding what
Is permitted and what forbidden—the party of the Assembler,[293]
Men who place their hands on their breasts when they pray and, when they hear the call
"To battle!", cut the throats of all those who would cut theirs,
Men who prefer their poverty and
Look on this world as something evanescent—

ولَرُبَّ قوم يحسبون خَلاقهم فيها وغابرَ لهوها كالغابر
ولديهم ردّ التحية مِنّةً[1] كبرى بها احياء عظم ناخر
يُحْيِي الليالى بالدعاء تهجدا فيميت فى الاعداء اى جماهر
٢٧،٢٠،٤ ويروع افئدة الرجال لقاؤه حتى يخوروا عن نداء الناصر
فى قلب كلّ محنّك من رُعْبه ما عنه يحجم كلّ ليث زائر
وبكل حرف من بليغ كلامه حرف يفلّهم كحرف الباتر
الفضل شيمته وسيمته التقى لله واسترباح اجر الصابر
يولى الندى قبل السوال وبِشْره للزائريه موذنٌ ببشائر
يغنيهم عن ان يمتّوا عنده بضرورة وَخَتّهم واَواصر
جهد الزمانَ غِلاآؤُه فكبا ولم يبرح لديه وفيه سَوْرة آفر
ولقد يكون النسر يوما واقعا ويعود بعدُ الى مطير الطائر
فالله ينصر مَنْ يغارُ لدينه والله يخذل كل عات فاجر
والله عزَّ يداول الايام ما بين العباد لسابق ولقاصر
٢٨،٢٠،٤ سكن الاميرُ وطار فى الدنيا اسمه ورَوَى المعالىَ عنه كل معاصر
فالعجم بين موقّر ومبجّل والعرب بين مُفاخر ومنافر
ياناصر الدين العزيز وحزبه ياخير صبّار واعظم شاكر
ياخير ناهٍ عن تعاطى مُنكَر وبخطّة المعروف افضل آمر

١ ١٨٥٥: مِنّة.

And how many a people have attached importance to their lot
Therein only to see their pleasure pass like ages receding.
In their eyes, to return a greeting is to do a favor
Most great, one great enough to return life to a worm-eaten bone.
He brings his nights to life with prayerful vigil
Then brings death to great masses of his enemies.
An encounter with him strikes such terror into the hearts of men 4.20.27
That they grow too weak to call for help.
In the heart of each hardened warrior is enough fear
To cause every roaring lion to retreat
And in each word of his eloquent speech
Is a consonant to make them flee, like a severing sword-edge.[294]
Virtue is his trait, his mark the fear
Of God and his gaining the wages of those who are patient.
He distributes largesse before he is asked and his joy
At the appearance of visitors is announced with gifts.
He relieves them of the need to ask, when with him,
For some necessity that has led them to him, or for favors.
His long bow-shots put fate to the test and it faltered, while he
Still possessed and had within him the liveliness of a sprightly man.
The eagle may one day fall
And yet afterward return to where birds fly
For God supports those who are zealous on behalf of His religion
And God forsakes every debauched tyrant
And God, may He be exalted, divides the days among mortals
So as to fit both front-runner and laggard.
As the emir became still,[295] his fame flew throughout the world, 4.20.28
And every contemporary related his high deeds.
The non-Arabs are divided among those who venerate and those who revere,
The Arabs among those who boast of him and those who vie in singing his praises.
O you who came to the aid of the Dear Religion and its followers,
O you most patient man most grateful to your Lord,
O best of those who forbid the consumption of what is forbidden
And best of those who command to the path of the good,

لا تخشَ من بأس فربّك قاهر　　بدعائك الميمون جيش الجائر
كن كيف شئت فانّ اجرك ثابت　　فى اللوح وهواجل ذخر الذاخر
لك حيث شئت عناية صمديّة　　ترعى حماك ونصر ربّ قادر
فاذا مدنت فانت اعظم خادر　　واذا ظعنت فانت اكرم سافر

٢٩،٢٠،٤ القصيدة التى امتدح بها الجناب المكرم النجيب
الحسيب صبحى بيك فى اسلامبول

ارى الدهر صافانى ومال الى الصُلحِ　　ومن بعد حِرمانى اتانى بالنُجحِ
واصغى الىّ الجدّ حين دعوته　　ولاحت تباشير المُنَى لى من صُبْحى
اتانى على الابحار والبرّ بِرّه　　باسرع من شكوى احتياجى الى سَمْحِ
فلم تكُ الّا دعوة فاجابنى　　اجابةَ صِنْوٍ وهو لى سيّدٌ لَحِ
ولو لم يُجِرْنى من زمانى بفضله　　لاصبحت فى بؤس وامسيت فى بَرْحِ
وحِنْتُ باشجآء التمنّى فان لى　　لجرحا مُمِضًا دونه اَلَمُ الجُرحِ
فلى فى نهارى جهد سَبْحٍ وحرفةٍ　　وفى ليلتى حبس وحُرْف عن السَبْحِ
اذا كنت لا اشكو اليه فمن عسى　　يكون اليه مشتكى الضرّ والتَرْحِ
ومن ذا الذى تلقاه فى الناس مُسْجِحا　　سواه اذا اضطُرَّ المضيم الى السَجْحِ
خلائق لا يوفى الثنآء بوصفها　　ولو كنت حسّان البلاغة والفَصْحِ
٣٠،٢٠،٤ اغار على اوصافه الغر انها　　تشاركها اوصاف آخر فى المدحِ

Fear not calamity, for your Lord will crush,
At your blessed prayer, the tyrant's army.
Be as you will, for your reward
Is recorded on the Tablet,[296] the most glorious store for any who lay up stores.
You will have, whenever you wish, the care of an Eternal God
That will assure your protection, and the support of an All-capable Lord.
If you settle, you will be the mightiest of lions in their lairs
And if you depart, you will be the most noble of those who travel.

The Poem in Which He Eulogized the Honorable and Ennobled Ṣubḥī Bayk, of Noble Lineage and Line, in Islāmbūl 4.20.29

Methinks Time has dealt kindly with me and is disposed toward a truce
And after keeping me in deprivation has offered me success,
And that Fortune hearkened to me when I called upon it
And Fate's dawn glimmerings appeared before me, from Ṣubḥī.[297]
Across sea and land his kindness reached me
Faster than my petition could reach any magnanimous man.
That was but a prayer, yet he responded to me
As would a twin, when he is to me a master who yet is close.
Had he not taken my side with his bounty against the days in which I live,
I would have risen in misery and spent the evenings in pain
And would have perished from the sorrows of desire, for I have
Been wounded painfully, with a wound more painful than a physical wound.
Thus by day I have the toil of business and a trade
And by night I am imprisoned and deprived of aught to do.
If I am not to complain to him, then to whom, perchance,
Should he who complains of injury and sorrow complain
And whom will you encounter among men who is forbearing
If not he, when the wronged is forced to express his grief?
Virtues [he has] whose praise no description can adequately fulfill
Even should you be the Ḥassān[298] of rhetoric and eloquence.
I feel jealousy on behalf of his brilliant traits that 4.20.30
The traits of any other should have a share in praise alongside them.

هدانى له جَدّى وقد كنت غاوِيًا مع الشعرآء البائرين ذوى الكسح
وكان زمانى مازحا فمزحته فلمّا تعاطى الجِدَّ ملت عن المزح
فصار لشعرى رونق وطلاوةٌ وحُقَّ له الإملآء فى ملأ فُصح
وقد كان فى سوق الاعاجم كاسدا مقالى واطرآى عليهم بلا ربح
فكم بتُ أُنضى خاطرى لمديحهم فقمت وبى رَنْح واعييت كالطِلح
ولم يُغنِ عنى ما مدحتهم به فتيلاً وما ازدادوا سوى البخل والشح
ولم ينقدوا كفّارة الكذب الذى علىّ باعلى اللوح ما هو بالممّحى
اعظم شعراء الفرنساوية ولو اننى راسِيْن عصرى فيهم ومِلْطن ما استسقيت منهم سوى النشح اعظم شعراء الانكليز
فها انا ذو ربح ولست بمفترٍ ثنآءً واطرآء وكنت بذا أُلحى ٣١،٢٠،٤
فحُلّ يا زمانى بين فوزى ومطلبى ان آسطعتَ واستعِدِ الخطوب على فدحى
فلى باسمه استفتاح كلّ قضية ويمناه اقليد السعادة والفتح
ألا فَلْيزرنى اليوم من كان مزريًا بشانى يجد كوخى اعزَّ من الصرح
علا بمعاليه مقامى ورتبتى وصرت الى اقصى الامانى ذا طمح
اذا ابصرت عيناى مَن هو مُخفَق كدأبى من قبل انتخلت له نصحى
وقلت له ابشر بما انت طالبٌ فمن يدعُ يوما باسمه فاز بالسنح
هو الماجد النآى مدى الدهر صيتُهُ قريبٌ من الداعى على القرب والنزح
فليس على بُعد يوخّر رفده وليس على قرب يملّ من المنح

My fate guided me to him when I had gone astray
 With unprofitable poets, weaklings.
The days made jest with me so I made jest with them.
 Then, when they assumed seriousness, I turned away from jest
And my verse acquired élan and polish
 And became worthy to be recited in the assembly of the eloquent.
In the market of the non-Arabs my words and my praises
 Of them found no buyers and were without profit.
How many a night I spent exhausting myself in writing their praise
 Then arose, dizzy, and fell like an exhausted camel
And all my eulogies of them enriched me by not so much as
 A lampwick and they merely grew more miserly and stingy.
They paid no expiatory gift for my lies—what I owe is [written] at the top of the board and cannot be erased[299]—
And were I the Racine of my age among them — The greatest poet of the French.
 And its Milton, I would get out of them barely enough sustaining water to quench my thirst. — The greatest poet of the English.
But see me now—profited, and no liar 4.20.31
 In my praise and commendation, when once I was insulted for it!
Come then, my days, between my triumph and my demands,
 If you can, and bring disasters down, once more, upon me and crush me
For I have, with his name, entrée to any affair
 And his right hand is the key to happiness and victory.
Should any visit me today who once ridiculed
 My state, he'd find my cottage grander than any mansion.
My status and my rank have risen through his noble acts
 And I am now ambitious for the furthest prizes.
Should my eyes light upon one whose hopes are thwarted
 As mine once were, I'd sift my advice down to the essential
And tell him, "Rejoice that you are a petitioner,
 For he who ever calls his name gains wealth!"
He is the glorious, whose repute shall last as long as time,
 Ever close to his petitioner, be he near or far.
When distant, his succor is not delayed
 And when he is close, he feels no distaste at giving.

٣٢،٢٠،٤ هو الحازم النحرير طلّاع اَنْجُد   كريم نزيه النفس ذو خلق سُجح
سليل اجلّ الخلق سامى الذرى الذى   مناقبه الغرآء تغنى عن الشرح
اميرى ومولاى الكريم وسيّدى   ومَن هو بعد الله لى سند الرُكح
تظنّيت فيك الخير والفضل كلّه   فحقّقت ظنّى فهودونى فى صحّ
اتانىَ وعدٌ عنك انّك منزلى   لديك كما انزلت اهلى فى نَدْح
ولا ريب عندى ان وعدك مُنجَز   وانى لا احتاج معه الى فَسْح
فهآك منى المدح خدمة مخلص   فجُدْ بالرضى عنه فديتك والصفح
ودم كهدف عزّ للذليل وملجا   لقاصده ما انجاب ليل من الصبح

شبه الجواز يقال فسح له الامير فى السفر كتب له الفسح

٣٣،٢٠،٤ وكتب الى الفاضل اللبيب الخورى غبرائيل جباره ارسلها
اليه من باريس الى مرسيلية وهواول شعر مدح به قسّيسا

قِفْ بالطلول ان استطعتَ قليلا   واسال عن الركب المغذّ رحيلا
ساروا وابقوا وحشة لك دونها   غصص المنون وحسرة ونحولا
طللٌ عهدت به الخلاعة والصبى   وشربت فيه سلسلا مشمولا
وجررت اذيالى وتهت على المُنَى   واقتدت منها ما استعزّ ذليلا
وخلعت من نعم ولذّات على   اهل الهوى ما كنت منه مَلولا

He is the resolute, the learned scholar, bold, efficient, 4.20.32
Generous, full of integrity, with the morals of lenient men,
Scion of the greatest of creation, Sāmī of the summits,[300]
Whose brilliant feats need no introduction—
My emir, my noble lord and master,
And he who, after God, is my mountain-like support.
I expected that in you I would find all that is good and generous
And I found what I expected to be true; the soundness of my expectation is before my eyes.
A promise from you reached me that you would host me
In your house, as you were hosting my family, in spacious quarters.
There is no doubt in my mind that your promise will be carried out
And that I shall need, beyond that, no further leave to travel (*fasḥ*).
Here then is a eulogy from me, the service of an honest man.
Be gracious in accepting it, may I be your ransom, and in overlooking its flaws
And remain forever a cave of strength[301] for the abject and a refuge
For those who seek it, so long as night shall fade to morn.

[*fasḥ*:] "A kind of permit." One says, "The emir *fasaḥa lahu* for travel," meaning "The emir wrote him a permit."

And he wrote a eulogy to the Virtuous and Wise Priest Ghubrā'īl Jubārah and sent it to him in Marseilles from Paris, this being the first time he had written verse in praise of a priest. 4.20.33

Halt by the orts,[302] if you can, a little while
And enquire after the company that departed at such fast pace.
They left, and left behind them a loneliness
That made you choke as though in death, and grief, and emaciation.
A camping place where I knew riotousness and passionate love
And drank sweet water, cool to the taste,
And dragged the skirts of my robes and cocked a snook at the fates
And led by the nose those of them that put on airs
And conferred such comforts and pleasures upon
Love's followers as I myself had tired of!

واحسرتاه متى يعود العيش فى   عرصاته والذّ فيه مقيلا
لم يبقَ الّا ذكر افراحى به   ومضى كامسِ نعيمُه مبتولا
ان غيّرت آثاره الايام او   ان عطّلت اعلامه تعطيلا
فبخاطرى تذكاره متجدّد   ولقد يظلّ بانسهم مأهولا
من بعض حسّادى عليه الريحُ قد   حامت لديه بكرة واصيلا
تبدى الحنين به وانّةَ ثاكل   فازيد فيه زفرة وعويلا ٣٤،٢٠،٤
تسفى تراب فنائه وكانما   تهفو به لتحلّه الاكليلا
عجبا وقد بلّته منى عبرة   أن صار فوق عِنانها محمولا
ام قد درت نكب الرياح بانه   اوَلَى بان يثوى السمآ مقيلا
ام مثل عينى اعين الجوزآء قد   رمدت فتستشفى به تكحيلا
ما كدت ادرى رسمه لولا شذا   عرْف اليه كان منه دليلا
نؤى الحبائب للمحبّ اعزّ من   صرح لديه لا يصيب خليلا
وسُوَيعة مع من تحب اجلّ من   دهر به تلقى اخاك عذولا
قلبى السَمَندل يصطلى نار الهوى   وسلوّه العنقآ عزّ وصولا
لله كم منه يعذّب عاشق   ولكم به يمسى البرىّ قتيلا
لو رقّ من عشقٍ كلامٌ رتّل   القرآءُ قولى فى الدجى ترتيلا ٣٥،٢٠،٤
او لو تداوَى الناس منه بالبكا   لشفيتُ كلّ شجٍ يبيت عليلا

Alas! When will life return to
Its courtyards and I take my pleasure there as a resting-place?
Naught remains but the memories of my joys there
And its life of ease has departed like a bygone day, irretrievable.
Even should time have changed its traces or
Utterly stripped it of its markers,
Its memory is ever renewed in my mind
And it remains by their kind company inhabited.
The wind, occasioned by some of those who envy me it,
Has blown upon it in the morning and at day's end.
It displays tenderness for it, and the moaning of a mother who has lost her child, 4.20.34
To which I add wails and sighs.
It raises the dust in its empty spaces and seems
To whirl it high in the air only to deposit it at the Crown.[303]
Strange that, after a tear of mine had wetted it,[304]
It should appear as though borne upon the reins of the wind,
Or is it that the shifting winds have realized that
Its best use is to provide the sky with a place to rest,
Or that, like mine, the eyes of Gemini
Have become rheumy and are seeking a collyrium there?
I would barely have made out its vestiges, were it not for a trace
Of perfume that acted as a guide to where it was.
The tent-trench of the beloved is to the lover dearer than
A mansion in his own land to which no friend makes his way
And a brief while with the one you love is longer than
An age in which you find your brother full of reproof.
My salamander heart burns with the fire of love
And it is hard for it to forget the phoenix.
By God, how many a suitor is tormented by love
And how many an innocent killed!
If words could assuage passion, my readers 4.20.35
Would chant my words in the darkness
Or if it were possible to use weeping to cure people of it,
I would have cured every head wound that remains uncured.

حاولتُ قلب القلب عن علل الهوى   فاجاب انك قد ضللت سبيلا
منى ابتدآ الشوق كان وختمه   بى لست عن دابى احول حؤولا
قد قاننى المولى عليه كما على   حبّ المكارم قان غبرائيلا
هو ذلك الحبر المهذّب خُلقه   وعليه يبدو خَلقه دِلّيلىٰ
الطيّب الاصل الكريم الفعل لن   تلقاه الّا مرشدا ومنيلا
يهب الجزيل وعنده كالجزل ما   يجوه جزلا غيره منفولا
المرتدى ثوب العفاف مطرّزا   بتقًى يقى التحريم والتحليلا
طلق المحيا واللسان طلاقة   تَدَع الاسى من قيده محلولا
يستدرك الاشكال فصل خطابه   وبعلمه يستخرج المجهولا ٣٦،٢٠،٤
فلكل ريب قضية ما زال مسئولا   وللراجى ندًى مامولا
صافى السريرة حيث آىُ وفائه   لن تقبل التحريف والتبديلا
ما ان يزال اذا دنا واذا نأى   بَرًّا نصوحا واصلا مسئولا
كانت مشورته هدى وسعادة   للمستشير ونصحه منخولا
ودعاؤه فى الضرّ اعظم عاصم   لك فاطمئنّ به وكن مكفولا
ليس المنيخ ببابه قَنِطا ولا   من يستغيث بجاهه مخذولا
مولى تحرّى الزهد فى الدنيا وقد   دانت له لو شآها تبتيلا
فنجاره ما زال ملجأ لاجئ   يلقى الامانى عنده والسولا

I tried to turn my heart from the maladies of love,
But it answered, "You have lost your path.
With me the longing began and with me is
Its conclusion. It is not my way to shift and turn.
The Lord endowed me with this way, as he endowed
Ghubrāʾīl with love of noble qualities."
He is that sage of refined moral character
To which his beauteous form is a sure guide,
Of good stock and noble deeds, whom you will never
Find anything but a guide and facilitator.
He gives largesse openhandedly and to him
What others keep largely to themselves is as dry brushwood.[305]
He wears the mantle of continence embroidered
With a godliness that obviates the need to declare things sinful or allowed—
Of cheerful countenance, with a tongue so fluent
It frees sorrow from its shackles and sets it free to leave.
The clarity of his discourse sets right what is confused 4.20.36
And with his scholarship he extracts what was unknown.
Men never cease to ask him about every puzzling matter
And any who seeks finds a hoped-for reward.
Clear of conscience, for the solemn assurances of his loyalty
Will never accept either distortion or substitution,
He was always there if close, and if far
Was kindly, full of advice, loving, available to ask.
His counsel was guidance and felicity
For whomever sought counsel, his advice well-chosen.
His prayer in times of hurt is the greatest guardian
You can have, so take comfort from it and be reassured.
Neither he who kneels his camel at his door, despairing, nor
He who solicits his help is disappointed by what he gives.
A lord he is who has pursued abstinence in this world,
Which, had he wanted it, would have come to him without restraint.
Thus his stock is ever a refuge for many a refuge-seeker
Who will find with him what he hopes and requests.

جبر الخواطر من جبارة يرتجى وبفرعه كل الفخار انيلا
٣٧،٢٠،٤ سمح الزمان بقربه لى سبّةً ما كان احلاها وعاد بخيلا
حتى ارى قِصَر الايادى بعده ومَن آستطال بفضله مفضولا
ولقد علمتُ اوانَ كان الطرف مق صورا عليه ذلك التاويلا
مارست دهرى واختبرت صروفه فاذا به لا يستفيق غفولا
هلّا اتانى سائلا من قبل ان يقضى الفراق وكان فيه عجولا
هل من ممارٍ ان شخصا واحدا يحوى الفضائل كلّها تكميلا
ام منكر ان ليس يُذكَر سيدٌ مع ذكره الا وكان ضئيلا
ولئن أُفِض فى ذكر الآءٍ له فاضت علىّ أُمِلّ عنه طويلا
ادب واحسان وبشر دائم وسماحة تستغرق التمثيلا
٣٨،٢٠،٤ ما كنت فى مدحى له بمبالغ ما قلت الّا بعض ما قد قيلا
ولو استطعت لكنت انظم كل درّىّ له مدحا او التنزيلا
من حاول الاسهاب فيه فانما هو موقد وقت الضحى قنديلا
بشرى لمن يحظى بقرب جنابه ولمن يقبّل ذيله تقبيلا
ولمن له يهدى التحية والثنا والحمد والتعظيم والتبجيلا

The mending of broken hearts may be requested of any Jubārah[306]
And through his offspring every glory may be gained.
The days allowed me closeness to him for a long while; 4.20.37
They decided that was not good and became miserly once more.
Now, after him, I meet only with stinginess
And those who have achieved great things through his bounty are lesser men than he;
I learned to make this interpretation in the days when eyes were trained on him alone.
I put the age to the test and experienced its adversities
And behold, it is sleeping still, unheeding.
Should it not have come to me and asked before
Departure was decreed, and urgently too?
Can any doubt that a single person
May contain within himself all virtues in fullest form
Or deny that no prominent man may be mentioned
In the same breath with him other than in terms of exiguity?
If I expatiate in mentioning gifts of his
That have poured down upon me, I shall dictate at length—
Good manners, charitableness, constant good cheer,
And a magnanimity that exhausts any analogizing.
I have not exaggerated in my eulogy for him: 4.20.38
I have said but little of what has been said [by others]
And if I could I would string for him every shining star
To sing his praises, or the Scriptures.
Any who tries to speak long about him is
Like one who lights a candle in the forenoon.
Good tidings are his who enjoys proximity to his honorable person
And who kisses, repeatedly, the hem of his garment
And who addresses to him a salutation, and commendation,
And praise and adulation and veneration.

٣٩،٢٠،٤

القصيدة القمارية

جمعتنا الشيوخ ما بين اصّ   وكولّ وفرشخ هو شِقصى
فى مقام جيرانه لا يبيحو   ن هُتاف المغلوب او بعض نبض
بعضنا شاطر وآخر غِرّ   خصمىّ اثنين غابن ثم لصّ
لم اقم قطّ غالبا غير ليل   بات فيه للاصّ ظفرى كَشِصّ
ظل سعدى يقوى على النحس حتى   خلتنى فى القمار شيخ ابن بعص
وشريكى له نشاط الى قنص   ملوك يدينها اىّ قنص
فانثنى ساحر المزوق حيرا   ن عليه تاليفه متعصّى
وبه من سماته ما يحاكى   بعضه خاتما وبعض كفصّ
بلغ اللعب منه ما يبلغ الجِدّ   والهاه عن مداراة خِلْص
فغدا بالكلام يقرص والاصبع   مَن جاد رميه كل قرص
لم يبت ليله واصبح يشكو   من دُوار امضّه مع مغص
٤٠،٢٠،٤ جاره ذو الزلّات وهو انا لم   يبدُ منه فى الرمى خطة نقص
بعد ست واربعين ولم يبلغه عن بندة احتجاج بنصّ
ما عليه ان كان يَغلب او   يُغلَب او لزّه الشريك بشِرص
فكره فى اختلاق اكذوبة عن   ذى علآء ما ان يجود بجص
يسهر الليل مطرئا فاذا ما   اصبح الصبح خار من فرط خَمَص

A Poem on Gambling[307] 4.20.39

It brought us[308]—the old men: "the Ace," Cavell, and Farshakh[309] (my partner)— together
In a place where there are no neighbors
To reveal the loser's cries or even a whimper.
One of us[310] was a clever fellow, the other a greenhorn.
My two opponents, a cheat plus a thief.
I never got up from the table a winner, except one night
When my fingernail became like a fishhook for the ace.
My good luck kept getting the better of my bad till
I fancied myself, at gambling, an old hand, a bit of a dog.[311]
And my partner with a will set about hunting louis d'ors[312] he owed[313]—and how he hunted them!
So the wizard of the pack[314] withdrew, at a loss
As to what to do about him, his hand[315] unhelpful,
His features imitating
In part a seal ring, in part a bezel.[316]
The "game" made him[317] turn serious
And distracted him from covering for a true friend,[318]
So the one who was playing well
Took to stinging[319] him with words and pinching him with fingers.
He didn't sleep that night and got up in the morning complaining
Of a nausea that burned his throat, as well as an upset stomach.
His neighbor, he of the slipups, meaning me, had never 4.20.40
Made a show, in the cards he played, of a plan to get any poorer
After forty-six[320] and he'd not served him in writing notice of any protest.[321]
He didn't care if he won or was beaten
Or his partner gave him a jab on the temple.
All he thought about was how to fabricate lies concerning
Some exalted person who wasn't even good for the price of whitewash.[322]
He'd spend the night writing eulogies and, when morning
Came, bellow from the pain of an empty stomach.

لو اطاق المسير من هذه الار   ض لما حلّ غير بلدة حمص
ربما ينفع التغفّل يوما   ويضرّ الانسان زائد حرص
ليس يدرى ما اللعب الا بِشِعر   عنه ما عاش ليس بالمتقصّى
وبشعر من شاربيه اذا حا   ول شعرا ينحى عليها بنمص
واذا سامه امرؤ سهرَ الليل   اتاها من غيظه بالمقصّ
لم يدعها تطول حتى تحاكى   نصّة الخود ذات ضفر وعقص ٤١،٢٠،٤
عن قريب يخضّب البيض منها   بمدادٍ او زعفران وحُصّ
ليس ينفكّ ذا ملال وشكوى   وعلى كل نعمة ذا غمص
وشريك له تربَّع فى الدَست كشيخ مسائل العلم يُحصى
او كمن ينقد الدراهم للسلطان من شانه تمام التقصّى
ان يجدْ هفوة يصحْ ويولول   ويُقم للجدال قيّم فحص
يبذل الاصّ بذلة المال لكن   ثمّ فرق فى بذل هذين اَصّى اصلی
حيث فى الاول اضطرارًا وفى الثا   نى اختيارا لغير كسب ورَبص
اخذ العلم عن شيوخ مشاهير ذوى حكمة ومَحص ولحص
لا كبعض الغواة خرّيج بصّا   قين كلّ اعتمالهم عن خَرص
ليس يدرى سوى الخديعة والمكر وما يجمُل الخداع بشخص ٤٢،٢٠،٤
يفرز الغالبات فى اللعب لكن   يتعاطى جدّ الامور بخبص
ليس فى حارة اليهود سواه   من يُجيز الحرام والحقّ يعصى

If he had been able to leave this
  Land, he wouldn't have stopped till he got to the town of Homs.
Perhaps one day, gullibility[323] will prove to be of benefit
  And excessive caution will do harm to a person.
All he knows about gaming is what he's read in poetry
  About it; all his life long he's been bad at getting out of situations.
Whenever he tried to write poetry with hairs from his mustache[324]
  He'd turn against them and pluck them out
And if someone demanded that he stay up all night [writing eulogies],
  He'd set upon the same hairs in a fury with the scissors.
He hasn't let them grow so long that they're like 4.20.41
  The lick of hair of a pretty young girl with braids and plaits;
Soon their white parts will be dyed[325]
  With ink, or saffron and Indian yellow.
He never stops fretting and complaining
  And refusing to be grateful for any blessing.
A partner of his[326] has squatted in the midst of the game[327]
  Like a shaykh enumerating the topics of scholarship
Or like one who assays coins for the sultan
  Whose job it is to examine closely.
If he finds even a tiny mistake, he cries out and wails
  And sets in motion a thorough examination of the give-and-take.
He gives away the ace as though he were spending money but
  There's a basic difference between these two ways of spending [*aṣṣī* ("basic")
Inasmuch as in the first case it is under compulsion and in the means] "original"
  Second by choice, not to win or in expectation of gain.
He acquired his knowledge from famous shaykhs
  Possessed of sagacity and depth of insight and understanding.
He is not like a certain misleader, graduate of the school of spitters[328]
  Who all rely on guesswork.
All [the latter] knows is trickery and cunning 4.20.42
  And deceit ill becomes a person.
He picks out the winning cards when "in play" but
  Deals with serious matters by shuffling.
Even in Jews' Alley there's none but he
  Who permits what is sinful and defies the truth.

قد حكاهم فى اكله ذات ظِلْف   فوق ساق وفى الدهآء الاخصّ
ان يكن غالبا تجده طروبًا   ضاحكا ذا غمز وقرص و رقص
واذا فاز خصمه ودّ لو كلّ   خبير سواه باللعب مخصى
ولذات الثلث يعطو بكلتا   راحتيه وللثمانى بقبص
فاغرا فاه كالذى لاح ماءً   ثم لم يروَ منه غُلاّ بمصّ
ما لعمرى دهآؤك اليوم مُنجٍ   لك ان كدتَّ شيخنا او محصّى
قد حباك المزوّقات ولكن   ليس يعفيك من نكال مغصّ
انَّ بعض العطآء حلو شهىّ   ثم من دونه مرارة عفص ٤،٢٠،٤٣
يالها زهرةً قماريّةً ما   عابها جهبذ ولا حبر قص
غير كون اجتماعها خارجا عن   غرفتى فالحرام فيها بقفص
شكلها شكل بيضة ولهذا   فالمعاصى من جوفها ذات فقّص
مَن بناها اوصى بهذا وشانى   كل حين امضاء عهد الموصّى

الغرفيّات ٤،٢٠،٤٤

انا الولىّ على كل المفاليس   وغرفتى ذى مزار للمناحيس
ياتى بهم زُحَل القوّاد سدّتها   وثمّ تصرعهم ريح الكراريس

He has imitated them in his eating of animals whose legs have cloven
hoofs[329]
And in their distinctive cunning.
If he's winning, you'll find he's overjoyed,
Laughing, given to winking, pinching, and dancing.
If his opponent triumphs, he wishes
Every expert player other than he were castrated.
To the one with three, he gives with
Open palms and to the one with eight with his fingertips,
Leaving his mouth agape from raging thirst like one who finds water
But fails to be quenched by it through sucking.
Your cunning today, I swear, will not save
You if you trick our shaykh, or protect you!
Your cunning may have gained you the cards but
Will not save you from an exemplary, choking, punishment.
Some gifts seem sweet and appetizing, 4.20.43
Only to be followed by the bitterness of gall.
What a gang of gamblers! No great critic or master
Of storytelling has found fault with them
Except for the fact that their meeting takes place outside of
My room[330]—for sinfulness looks lively there.
Its shape[331] is that of an egg, which is why
Sins are hatched in its belly.
He who built it made that his testament and all I have to do
Is, every little while, apply the testator's will.

Room Poems[332] 4.20.44

I am the bankrupts' benefactor,
This room of mine a Mecca for the luckless.
Saturn,[333] that pimp, brings them to its door.
Once they're there, the smell of notebooks renders them senseless.

ومنها لا يدخلنّ مقامى ذو حجى ابدا فانما هو منتاب المآفيك
يلفون فيه اكاذيب المديح على زمّارة او على نذل من النُوَك

ومنها ياطالعا درجات قدرها مئةٌ الىّ ماذا ترجّى بعد ذا الدرج
ان كنت من حركات طالبا فَرَجا فاننى بسكون طالب الفرج

ومنها ما زارنى الّا خليع ماجن فدع الحيآء اذا حضرت حصيرى
ان الحيآء اخو النفاق وما صفت دون المجون سريرة لعشير

ومنها يازائرى راسَك اَحفظ من ضرب زيد وعمرو
فما بِكسرى هذا يصاب جابر كسر

ومنها ايها الزائرى لفائدة لا ترم المستحيل ما ذاك عندى
راح علمى فى طلب الجدّ والجد شرود فضاع علمى وجدّى

ومنها للناس نار بلا دخان ولى دخان بغير نار
فها انا اليوم منه قار ضيفى وفيه ابيت قارى

And

Let no one with brains ever enter my dwelling
For it's naught but a haunt for the weak of mind.
Inside, the lies of the panegyric, accompanied by
A female piper or a base and stupid scoundrel, is all they'll find.

And

O you who've climbed steps one hundred in number
To reach me, what would you after such a stunt?
You may want relief after all that action,
But I'm here, quite quiescent, just hoping for cunt.[334]

And

None visit me but the depraved and the bawdy
So abandon modesty, all ye who enter my place!
Modesty is hypocrisy's brother, and no two friends can relax
Without some breathing space.

And

Visitor, watch your head—
From the onslaught of grammar![335]
This apartment of mine
Hosts no bonesetter.

And

O you who visit me to acquire some knowledge beneficial,
Don't expect the impossible: I have none left!
My scholarship got lost in my search for Fortune,
But Fortune's fickle; now of both I'm bereft.

And

People have fire without smoke[336]
And I have smokes but no fire.
See me offer them today with open hand
To my guest and chew the cud when I retire.[337]

ومنها ان للصالحين معجزةً ان يجعلوا ان شآوا الضرير بصيرا

عكسُ ذا اليومَ معجزاتُ دخانى انه يجعل البصير ضريرا

ومنها تجود علىَّ زوارى ولكن اكافئهم بوآءً وهو شانى

تُقِلّ نعالهم لى ترب كُحْل فاكحلهم بشىءٍ من دخانى

ومنها نَعَمْ لى غرفة عُلْيا ولكن باسفل سافلين هبوط نجمى

فكيف اطيق اصعد مرتقاها واحمل حمل اشجانى وهمى

ومنها من يكن مثلى رفيع الدرجات فهو اولى بمفاعيل السّراة

من معاطاة فضول الشعر فى فاعلات فاعلات فاعلات

ومنها كل زوّارى ذكور ليس فيهم من اِناث ٤٥،٢٠،٤

افما فى الكون من انثى ولا جنس الخِناث

ومنها قُصِرت عن الورى وامنت منهم سَبّة غَدْرا

فلا عجب اذا ما قلت صارت غرفتى قصرا

And

It's a miracle of the righteous that,
Should they wish to, they can grant vision to the unsighted.
My tobacco's miracles today do the opposite:
They leave the seeing benighted.

And

My visitors are generous to me but
I reward them with something equal—it's my way to do so:
Their shoes bring me dust from kohl-painted eyes
And I blacken their eyes with a bit of my tobacco.

And

It's true I've a room at the top, but
My star's the lowest of the low.[338]
How then can I bear to climb to its heights
When I carry such a burden of woe?

And

One like me who's of exalted standing[339]
Is best qualified to describe the feats of an elite
By furnishing the gifts of poesy
In the form of feet, feet, feet.

And **4.20.45**

All my visitors are males,
Among them there isn't a single female.
Isn't there one female left in the universe
Or even a single she-male?

And

I kept myself from fellow men aloof
And spared myself their falseness through days of darkness.
No wonder then that I should say,
"My room's become a fastness."

ومنها اذا زارنى مُلْوٍ نظيرى امنته وان يك ذو جَدّ حذرتُ مِحاله
فانى اَدْرَى بالمناحيس كلهم وما فيهم مَن اجهل اليوم حاله

ومنها من آوَى الى بيت مثل بيتى الحَرَج
ضاق صدره سدما وانزوى مع الهمج

ومنها ولى داخل البيت جثة قطّ وخارجه صيت فيل عظيم
وقد كنت احسب اَن بالعظام تكون العظام واهل العلوم

ومنها تعالوا وافقهوا عنى ثلثا تعلّمكم مراعاة النظير
خَلاقى ثم جسمى ثم بيتى صغير فى صغير فى صغير

ومنها امسى بيتى قبرا حرجًا لكن زوارى احياء
مع انى لست ارى فيهم حيًا لى منه اِحياء

ومنها اذا عصفت ريح وثارت زوابع وهدّت رعود والغيوم مواطر
ومادت زوايا غرفتى وتزلزلت علمت بان عندى يشرّف زائر

And

If I'm visited by some debt-dodger like myself, I feel quite safe
But if he be in fortune's way, his trickiness I fear
For I'm well-versed in the ways of each unlucky wretch
And there's not a one of whose state I'm unaware.

And

He who returns
To an abode as cramped as mine
Will feel chagrin grip his breast
And hunger round his empty stomach twine.

And

Inside the house I've a dead cat's body,
Outside, a mighty elephant's renown.
I used to think 'twas by their bones
Great men and scholars were known.

And

Come, learn from me three things
That'll teach you to distribute a predicate.[340]
My allotted portion of good things, my body, and my house—
Each is exiguate, exiguate, exiguate.

And

My house has become a narrow grave
Though my visitors remain alive—
Despite which I don't find a living soul
Among them to make me revive.

And

When a gale blows and dust storms rise,
Heavens thunder and rain bedecks the skies,
When my room's walls shudder and shake—
I'm about to be honored by a visitor, make no mistake.

ومنها ارفعوا لى حاجاتكم فانا اليو | مَ رفيع المقام والدرجات
ان يكون مُفْلسون فليستعيروا | مُدْيتى لانتحارهم او دَواتى

ومنها يقولون انى لضنك وجارىَ | قد رقّ شعرى وصار ركيّا
واجدر بشى اذا ما تبعَّث | من ضيّق ان يكون قويّا

ومنها مُقامى بذى الغرفة | لحرمان ذى الحِرفه ٤٦،٢٠،٤
فمن زارنى فيها | فلا يرجُونْ تُرْفه

ومنها اصبحت فى غرفتى رهن الهموم فما | يعتادنى غير اشجانى واوطارى
ارى لكل امرء انثى تؤانسه | وليس عندى من انثى سوى النار

ومنها الا لا يطمعن احد | لكونى صاحب الغرفه
بانَّ لدىَّ مادبةً | له من فيضها غرفه

ومنها حقّ المَزُور على الزوّار انهم | يُؤَمّنون له فى الصدق والكذب
وما عليه لهم حقّ ولو جلبوا | اليه من سبأ وسقا من الذهب

And

Bring me your requests, for today
 I'm exalted of status and of staircase!
(If they're broke, they can borrow
 My razor to slit their throats, or my pen case.)

And

They say we're in straits, me and my anus—
 My verse is now lame and its strength is gone.
Yet anything that flows through so narrow a space
 Ought, by rights, to be strong!

And **4.20.46**

I live in this room
 As I can't practice my trade
So any who visits me in it
 Should expect no aid.

And

In my room I became a hostage to my cares
 For all that came to see me were my griefs and my desire.
I see every man has a female to keep him company
 But I have nothing feminine except for my fire.[341]

And

Let none out of greed suppose that
 Because of this room I'm the owner—
That I sit here at a banquet
 And he's due a scoop of what's left over!

And

The host's due from those who visit
 Is that they say "Amen" to whatever truth or lies are told,
But he owes them nothing, even if they bring him
 A camel from Sheba loaded with gold.

ومنها ولى حرفتان فلا احذر البطالة عندى ان ترسخا
اصوغ القوافى فى ليلتى وفى الصبح استقبل المطبخا

ومنها طبخ المحاشى رائج فى عصرنا لكنما طبخ القوافى كاسد
من اجل ذلك صرت طباخا فما انا شاعر فالشعر شى فاسد

ومنها حوت غرفتى كتبى ورزقى كله فرثطتى فيها عزآء وسلوان
اذا غبت عنها خلتنى افقر الورى وان جئتها أُوهمت انى سلطان

ومنها يفوح من حجرتى عرف الشوآء على عرف القريض ومعه عرف مَيّان
فمن يكن جائعا ينعشه اوّلها ومن يكن كاذبا ينعش من الثانى

ومنها ارى فى الحلم انى ساقط من مهدَّم طاقتى فى مثل غار
فاصبح فى الفراش ولا قوىً لى فلست الى المعبّر ذا اضطرار

ومنها بينى وبين دخانى أُلفة ثبتت ان نمت نام والا فهو لم ينم
وان يزرنى امرؤ غطّى على بصرى اذ عنده رؤية الزوّار كالسقم

And

I've got two trades and am unafraid
Of having no work while they remain stable:
By night I fashion rhymes,
In the morning set off to cook for another's table.

And

Cooking stuffed dishes these days is quite common
While cooking up rhymes is a trade unprofitable.
That's why I'm a cook and I'll not be a poet
For poetry's something unconscionable.

And

My room holds all my books and my daily bread
So not to go out is a comfort and a consolation.
When I'm away from it, I think I'm the poorest of men.
When I come back to it, I'm the king of creation.

And

From my chamber wafts the scent of the grill, plus
That of poetry and that of the liar[342] bare-faced.
If any's hungry, the first will revive him,
And if any's a fibber by the second he's braced.

And

In my dreams I see myself fall,
So exhausted am I, into the like of a cave,
Then wake in my bed but with no strength left.
No need for a seer—it must be my grave.

And

Between me and my tobacco there's a friendship firm—
When I sleep, it does; when I don't, it too takes no ease,
And if any come to see me, its smoke covers my eyes
For it reckons the sight of men a disease.

ومنها　لى غرفة ملأى من الكذب الذى　　انفقته فى مدح كل بخيل　٤٧،٢٠،٤

لم يبق فيها من محلّ فارغ　　للزائرىّ ولا مقيل خليل

ومنها　قالوا نزورك حيث كنت خليلنا　　فاجبتهم لا ريب فيه زور

قد محّص العرفان عن اخلاقكم　　وخلاقكم فلكم بذا التعزير

ومنها　اقول لزائرىّ قفوا قليلا　　الى ان البس الثوب القشيبا

فانى فى الخليع ارى خليعا　　وفى لبس القشيب أُرَى اديبا

ومنها　لبابى صريفٌ حين يفتح هائل　　يقول لزوّارى دعونى مغلقا

فهذه عَدْوَى كفّكم فىّ قد سرت　　ولم يُعْدِكم داب افتتاحى مطلقا

ومنها　كانت مقاما للكواعب غرفتى　　والآن صارت معدن التشبيب

ما زال فيها من عبير العشق ما　　هاج المحبّ الى عناق حبيب

ومنها　يرانى الناس فى كِرِح حقير　　فيحتقرون منزلتى احتقارا

فهل ياقوم عندكم المعالى　　علوّ مباءة تحوى حمارا

And 4.20.47

I've a room that's full of the lies that
In praise of each and every miser I did coin.
There's not an empty spot left inside it
Where a visitor or a friend may recline.

And

They said, "We'll visit you: you were our good friend once."
I answered, "For sure, there's a lie here somewhere.
Gratitude's been trimmed from your natures like fat,
As from your natural share of virtue, so no censure."

And

I tell my guests, "Wait a little
While I put on clothes without tatters:
In rags I look debauched
But in new clothes like a man of letters."

And

My door when opened gives a squeak that's quite terrifying.
It says to my visitors, "Let me stay shut!
This, the infection of your hand, has passed into me
But the habit of opening me hasn't infected you a jot!"[343]

And

'Twas once the home of perky-breasted girls, my room.
Now it's become a mother lode of amorous verse.
Enough of love's perfume still lingers on
To stir the lover a beloved to embrace.

And

People see me in a wretched cell
And despise my status frankly.
Do you, good folk, live in grand houses?
The grandest of dwellings may still house a donkey!

ومنها من زارنى ورأى مكانى ضيقا   فلبِرّه صدرى يكون رحيبا
اهلا به للنار والاصلآء مع   كِسَف الدخان ونعم ذاك نصيبا

ومنها طوّقت بابى بابيات منمّقة   لمّا بدا عُطُلا من خير زوّارى
فصار كنز علوم غير ذى رصد   تنقير اظفاره فى نقر اظفار

ومنها الا ياداخلين الىّ مهلا   لا سالكم سوالا عن مزارى
اأعجبكم له شكل فجئتم   لتبنوا مثله دار القِمار

ومنها نعمَ المهندس مَن بنى   كوخى باشكال وهندس
هو كالمثلث والمربَّع والمخمس والمسدس

ومنها من جآنى تَعِبا وابصر سدَّتى   نسى الذى قاساه من اتعابه   ٤٨،٢٠،٤
فالناس تعرف من تزور اذا هم   نظروا ولو لمحا الى اعتابه

ومنها لا يطلعنّ الىّ اليوم مشئوم   فطالعى بضروب الشؤم موسوم
ومن يكن واحدا مثلى فليس له   لطالعين احتياج قاله البوم

And

He who visits and thinks my place small,
For his kindness I'll make my welcome grand.
Welcome be he to the fire and the roasting
Plus the tobacco crumbs! What better lot could he demand?

And

I ringed my door with verses closely written
When it was innocent of any visitor of worth.
Thus what's been scratched through the wrinkled paint by the scraping
of nails [?] [344]
Has become a treasury of scholarship with none to observe.

And

Steady on, you who come in here to see me
Till I ask you a question about this place where you so often consort!
Has something about it so caught your fancy you've come
To build something like it as a gambling resort?

And

How great an architect, the one who built my cell
Of different shapes and made it geometric!
It's like a triangle plus a rectangle
Plus a pentagon plus a hexagon—extremely symmetric!

And 4.20.48

If any comes to me tired and sees my front door,
He forgets whatever ails him by way of ills.
People know whom they should visit simply
By directing a glance at its sills.

And

Let no ill-fortuned person come up to see me today
For my ascendant is branded with every form of luck most foul.
Any who's like me has
Of such visitors no need—thus saith the owl.[345]

ومنها يحسدنى الناس على غرفتى لشبهها اعينهم ضيقا
مع انها تحوى جهازا له طول وعرض بلغا الشيقا

ومنها قرَوْتُ المصر بيتا ثم بيتا فلم ارَ مثل مجلسى الشريف
يردّ الشمس اِنْ تدخُله كبرا لرؤيته لها فوق الكنيف

ومنها ولى فى غرفتى ادوات طبخ على مقدار اسنانى جميعا
وان يُكسَرْ من الادوات شى اصاب الكسر اسنانى سريعا

ومنها ليس بالرفس فتح بابى ولا بالقرع فاعلم لكن بنقر خفيف
فهو من جوهر الزجاج لطيف لا يسنّى الا لكل لطيف

ومنها مقامى اوّل فى القدر لكن اتى فى الصفّ عن خطأ اخيرا
فلا تلووا على شى سواه اذا جئتم اليه ولو كبيرا

ومنها اذا صعّدت فى درجات كوخى وجاوزت الاخيرة وهى اعسر
يخيّل لى بانى طالع كى اوذّن صارخا الله اكبر

And

People envy me my room
For it, like their eyes, is mean.
Despite this, it contains a tool
With the length and breadth of a peen.[346]

And

I've gone through the city house by house
And found none like my own noble abode.
It repels the sun, should it enter, disdaining
To see it atop the commode.

And

I have in my room utensils for cooking
Equal to all my teeth in number
And if one of these utensils ever is broken
The break passes on to my teeth instanter.

And

Not with a kick may my door be opened, mayhap,
Nor by pounding, but rather with a gentle tap.
Made of purest glass refined,
It opens only to those who are kind.

And

My residence is first in station
But due to some error came last in the strand.
Turn not, then, away to someplace else
Should you come here, no matter how grand.

And

When I've mounted the stairs to my cell
And passed the top step, the hardest,
Methinks I've been climbing
To cry out, muezzin-like, "God is the greatest!"

ومنها لا يرانى الناس فى غرفتى … لا ارى من غرفتى الناسا
ربّنا يعلم مَن لذَّ من … بيننا البَيْنَ ومَن قاسىٰ

ومنها سموّا على منزلى قبل الدخول ولا … تستعجلوا بعد فتح الباب واحتشموا
فانه حرَم ذو حُرمة ولئن … لم يُلفَ لى حرمة فيه ولا حُرَم

ومنها ان قلت سموّا على مقامى … فلست اعنى سمّا يميته ٤٩،٢٠،٤
وانما القصد ان تقولوا … تبارك الله عزّ صيته

ومنها لا تنظرنّ ملاوصا يا زائرى … من ثقْب مفتاحى الى اَعراضى
كالعِرض لى عَرَضى ومن ينظر الى الاَعراض لم يامن من الإِعراض

ومنها بشرى لمن ينظر المفتاح فى بابى … دليل انى موجود باثوابى
او لا فانى فى فرشى اغطّط او … انى خرجت وامن الله اشعى بى

ومنها انا ساكن فى غرفتى متحرّك … لزلازل العجلات تجرى تحتها
لكن بحمد الله ليس بواطئ … من فوق راسى مَن يحاول نحتها

And

People can't see me up in my chamber
And I can't see them from up in my room.
The Lord alone knows which finds the separation between us
To his liking and which one suffers from gloom.

And

Sammū before entering my home[347]
And don't hasten, after opening the door, to push your way inside.
It's a sanctuary, and holy, even if
You'll find I have there neither one wife nor wives.

And **4.20.49**

When I said, "*Sammū* before entering my place,"
It wasn't a *samm*[348] that will destroy it that I had in mind.
All I meant you to say was
"Blessed be God, mighty His name among mankind!"

And

Don't peep, visitor,
Through my keyhole and look at my stuff!
My stuff's like my honor. If you ogle
My stuff, you won't escape a rebuff!

And

Glad tidings to him who sees the key in my door—
A sign that I'm at home and wearing my clothes!
If not, then I'm in bed snoring or
I've gone out, God protect me from woes!

And

I live in my room in a state of commotion[349]
From the shaking of carriages running beneath it.
Thank God, though, there's none tramping
Over my head and trying to screw it.[350]

ومنها الى الله اشكو ما ارى تحت طاقتى امورا غدا تكليفها فوق طاقتى
ارى كل يوم الف ماش مخاصرا لانثى على انى مخاصر فاقتى

ومنها لى غرفة ما شانها شى سوى ان ليس تجرى تحتها الانهار
وغنيت عن هذا بما يجرى من العجلات تحسد مَن بها الاقمار

ومنها عجبت لكم يا قوم مع ضعف دينكم وشدة برد كف لم تعبدوا النارا
كانى بكم تلهون عنها بحرّ من تذيقكم فى حبّها النار والعارا

ومنها شرط الزيارة من بعد الطعام على حكم المزور وان لا تمنع الشغلا
ومن يزرنى صباحا فهو فى خطر ان لا اقول له اهلا ولا سَهْلا

ومنها راوا دخان قمينى صاعدا فجرى بالمآء قوم ليطفوا سورة اللهب
فقال بعض اَقَينٌ انت قلت نعم اقين شعرا وعندى معمل الكذب

And

To God I complain of what I see beneath my window—
  Things it's no longer in my power to bear.
Each day I see a thousand men walking while embracing
  A female, while I embrace nothing but care.

And

The room I have's just fine
  Except that beneath it run no rivers.[351]
The carriages, though, that run below
  Make up for that—the very moons are their passengers' jealous
    admirers.[352]

And

I wonder at you, good people—that, being such heathens
  And given the cold, you don't worship fire.
It must be that you distract yourselves with the heat from those who,
  Though they feed you both fire and shame, you admire.

And

The visitor, after eating, should think of
  His host and not impede his income
And any who comes of a morning is in danger:
  I'll not tell him either "Come in!" or "Welcome!"

And

They saw smoke from my stove ascending, so ran
  With water to extinguish the conflagration.
"Are you a blacksmith?" asked one. "Indeed!" said I.
  "I forge verses and have a workshop for prevarication."

٥٠،٢٠،٤ الفراقيات

خليلىّ لا تستنكرا عائل الوجد　　اذا كنتما ممن درى لائع البعد
ولا تعذلانى فى الغرام فاننى　　على غير ما اهوى غريم له وحدى
ومن ذا الذى يرضى البلآء لنفسه　　وتركوا له حال مع الحزن والسهد
وهل ينعمَنْ عيشًا مكابدُ وحشةٍ　　مشتَّت شمل ضائع السعى والقصد
نأى سَكَنى عنى وعوّضت عنهم　　بجيرة مقت ليس قربهم يجدى
كانَّ زمانى شآء فى كل حالة　　يرانى فردا يالشانى من فرد
فماضى نعيمى لم يكن من مضارع　　له حيث هم فى الحسن جلّوا عن الندّ
فماذا دهانى بعد حظّ غنمته　　وقد كنت فى عيش بقربهم رغد
وماذا على الايام لوكان طُولها　　له لا سواد من مطالعها يُعدى
افى الناس مثلى فى مقامٍ فؤادُهُ　　وفى غيره جُثمانه واجدَ الفقد
وغيرى اراه فاقدَ الوجد وهو فى　　نعيمٍ له جدّ مُعين بلا جِدّ
٥١،٢٠،٤ وهل فى سبيل الله راحم لوعة　　تعاودنى لا بل غرتنى كالجِلد
وهل مبلغ عنى النسيم تحية　　اليهم وما بى من غرام لهم يبدى
اهيم بما كانت تراه احبّتى　　وان يكُ من بعض الجماد او الضد
والهج بالقول الذى لهجوا به　　فتذكاره ذكرى وايراده وِردى
يحقّ لى التشبيب ما دمت شاعرا　　بهم لا بهند او بميّة او دعد
ولو لم يكن لى مطمع فى لقآئهم　　لآثرت توسيدى مذ اليوم فى لحدى

Poems of Separation[353] 4.20.50

My two friends! Disparage not one needy for love
 If you be among those who have known the agony of separation,
And do not reproach me for my passion, for I,
 Against my desire, love him without requital.
Who is content that tribulation befall him
 Or that he thrive, but with sorrow and insomnia,
And does anyone suffering loneliness enjoy life
 When sundered from his own and lacking energy and intention?
The people of my house have gone far from me and in their place I have
 Hateful neighbors whose proximity is of no value,
As though my times wished to see me, in every situation,
 Alone—and lonely I am indeed!
My past felicity had no like:[354]
 In beauty those people surpassed any peer.
What then afflicted me after this good fortune that I had won
 When, being close to them, I lived a life of ease?
Why, what would it have harmed my days if
 No darkness from their beginnings had infected them to the end?[355]
Is there among men one like me—heart in one place,
 Body in another—suffering the pangs of absence?
Others I see *sans* pangs of love, yet living
 At ease; his good fortune aids him without effort on his part.
Is there someone who, for the sake of God, will take mercy on an agony 4.20.51
 That keeps coming back to me, nay adheres to me like skin?
Is there one who will inform the breeze of me and send this as a greeting
 To them, and show them how I long for them?
I am in love with what the ones I love used to see
 Even if it be certain inanimate objects or an enemy.
I constantly repeat the words they used to repeat
 For to recall them is my *dhikr* and to utter them my *wird*.
Since I am a poet, it is my right to celebrate in verse my love—
 For them, not for Hind or Mayyah or Daʿd.[356]
Did I not harbor a hope of meeting them,
 I would rather lay my head down, from today, in my grave

ولكننى ارجو زمانا يسرنى بهم عن قريب وهواشهى المنى عندى
يقولون لى صبراً وكيف تصبّرى ولست الى نور التبصّر استهدى
لعمرك سلطان الهوى قاهرٌ فما نجا من مغاويه الرشيد ولا المهدى
الا ليت دمعى حيث هم واقفون قد جرى ولدى اقدامهم قام كالحد
فيمنعهم عن ان يسيروا ويبعدوا فحسبى من سير وحسبى من بُعد
ااحبابنا هل ودّكم بعدُ سالمٌ وهل انتم باقون مثلى على العهد ٥٢،٢٠،٤
ارى بكم الدنيا ولست اراكمُ بها انّ شانى اليومَ حَيْرة ذى الرشد
اتى العيد بالافراح للناس كلهم وما اعتادنى فيه سوى الهمّ والنكد
وما لى لا اشكو وقد طال بُعدكم وما بيننا ما ليس يُبلَغ بالوخد
وماذا الذى ارجوه بعد فراقكم وعندى استوى شأنا الترفّه والجَهد
فياحبذا عيد انبعاثى اليكم كما يُبعَث الطيرُ الغليل الى الوِرد
ولو زارنى قبل اللقآء خيالكم وعانقته ليلاً فذلك من جدّى
اذا نظرت عينى البريد فانّ لى لَقلبًا من الايجاس يخفق كالبند
فان كان لى منكم كتابٌ لثمته واقررته من بعد ذاك على كبدى
فما كان من آثاركم فهو مؤثَر على العين والعِينين والعَين والنقد
فليس سواه اليوم عندى تعلّة وما غيره اُلفى لحرّى من برد
وان لم يكن تجر الدموع لما جرى وارتدّ عنه[1] كالعديم عن الرفد

[1] ١٨٥٥: عند.

But I hope that time will gladden me
With them soon, and this is the dearest of my wishes.
They tell me, "Be patient!" but how can I be patient
When to the light of insight I am not guided?
I swear, the authority of love is overwhelming. From its pitfalls
The right-thinking man is not saved, nor the rightly guided.[357]
Would that my tears had run to where they were standing
And arisen like a barrier at their feet,
To prevent them from moving on and growing more distant
For I have had enough of moving on and of distance.
O you whom we love, is your affection still sound 4.20.52
And do you, like me, still maintain the pledge?
I see the world through you yet see you not in it.[358]
My state today is that of the wise man perplexed.
The Feast brought its joys to all the people
But naught visited me then except care and woe.
How can I not complain when the distance to you is so long,
And what is between cannot be covered with the longest of strides?
And what do I have to hope for after your departure
When ease and toil to me are as one?
How excellent would be the feast of my setting off toward you
Like a thirsty bird being sent off to the water source!
And should your phantom visit me before we meet
And were I to embrace it by night, it would be my fortune.
When my eye spots the mail, my heart
Flutters with apprehension like a banner,
And if I receive a letter from you, I kiss it
And settle it thereafter next to my liver.
Whatever bears with it some trace of you is preferred by me
To eye and to al-ʿĪnayn[359] and to kind and cash
For I have nothing but it today to distract me
And naught else than it do I find to cool my burning heat,
And if there is none, my tears run for what has happened
And I turn from it like the poor man who takes nothing from charity's feast.

وقال

٥٣،٢٠،٤

اوَ ما كفانى اليوم تنآء   عمّن احبّ ولاتَ حين لقاء
يا راحلين وفى الفواد مقامهم   كم ذا اقول سكنتم احشآى
ولكم اعاتب سوء حظى فيكم   لكن دهرى لا يجيب ندآى
سافرتم للبرء مما نالكم   فمتى يكون بقربكم ابرآى
ومتى يتيح لى الزمان لقاكم   ويكفّ كفّ البين عن ايذاى
شرّقتم فانا بغُصّة غربتى   فى الغرب ذو شَرَقٍ وذو اشجآء
يامن يزقّ لذى جراحٍ مدنفٍ   انا ذو الجراح ملازم الادوآء
فَصِفَنَّ لى ما انت واصفه لمن   اشفى وكن فطنا الى الاشفآء
لا يغررنّك ما ترى من بِزّتى   تحت القشيب طهاملُ الاعضآ   الطَهْمَل الذى لا يوجد له حجم اذا مُسّ
انا والذى يحيى ويفنى لست فى الهَلكَى أُعَدّ ولا مع الاحيآء
انا ان سلت عنى الاحبّة لم اكن   اسلوهم فى البؤس والضرآ   ٥٤،٢٠،٤
انى على ما بى ارقُّ لعاشقٍ   مثلى وان هوكان من اعدآى
ما البعد يخمد نار شوقى انما   بُعد الغزالة علّة الإحمآء
ما ان يحلّ حشاشتى من بعدهم   حبٌّ وليس يحلّ نسخ وفآى
حال الورى طُرًّا تحول وحالتى   هى ما ترَى فى غدوتى ومسآى
الدمع موقوف على جَريانه   والعين مُعفاةٌ من الاغفآء
وارى الذى مثلى بكى من فرقة   مع من مناه بُعده ببكآء

And he wrote: 4.20.53

Have I not today had enough of separation
From those I love and whom it is now too late to meet?
O you who have departed when your place was in my heart
How often I say that you reside now in my guts!
How often I bemoan my bad luck with you
Though my fate does not heed my call!
You departed to be cured of what ailed you;[360]
When shall I, through your closeness, be cured?
And when will the days grant me that I meet with you
And the hand of destiny unhand me and stop hurting me?
You went east, and I, through the agony of my exile
In the west am choked and filled with anxiety.
O You who have pity on the wounded and sickly,
I am wounded, and must constantly take medicine.
Prescribe then for me what you prescribe for those who
Recover and be cunning in your treatment.
Let not what you see of my clothes deceive you:
Beneath the clean clothes the limbs are hollow (*ṭahāmil*).
By Him who grants life and annihilates, I cannot be classed
Either among the perished or among those who are alive!
I, though the ones I love may have forgotten me, 4.20.54
Do not forget them even in misery and bad times.
Despite my state, I feel pity for any lover
Like me, even though he be an enemy of mine.
Distance does not extinguish the fire of my love, rather
Separation from the gazelle causes me to grow hot.
No love after theirs can occupy my heart
Nor is an abrogation of my fidelity lawful.
Change is the condition of all mankind yet my case
Is as you see, morning and evening.
My tears can do nothing but run
And the eye is exempted from slumber
Yet I see those who, like me, once wept at separation
Now rejoined with the one whose distance afflicted him with weeping.

ṭahmal [sing. of *ṭahāmil*] is "that which, when touched, is found to have no mass."

عجبا لدهرى لم يزل بى مُبْصرا　　وضناى وارانى عن الرقبآء

عجبا لدمعى مدنفى استجمامُهُ　　وللناس يشفيهم حميم المآء

عجبا لعمرى كيف طال من النوى　　والارض ضاقت عن مدار رجآى

عجبا لليل الناس ينسرع صبحه　　وصباح ليلى دائم الابطآ

٤،٢٠،٥٥ تبنى الرجآء خواطرى فيه على　　اسّ المحال فبئس اسّ بنآء

ويخيّل الشوق المقيم باضلعى　　لى اننى مُغْف وهم ضجعآى

حتى اذا اصبحتُ بانَ انها　　لى لم تكن الّا حبالَ هبآء

يااهل ودّى ليس من دآى لكم　　عَدْوَى فعودوا وأْمنوا من دآى

سقمى من الطرف السقيم ومنحلى الخصر النحيل عَداكم اِعدآى

ما ان اكلّفكم سوى ذكر اسم مَن　　اهوى فحسبى ذاك عن اِسمآء

لوكان يجدى الفال كنتُ اليوم من　　احظى الانام واسعد السعدآ

اذ كل غاد باسمهم متفوّهٌ　　ام ذاك وسواس الهوى الغوّا

ام بعض ماذا الوجدُ يوجد انّه　　يُلْهى بمعدوم من الاشيآ

ياليت قلب الناس لى او جَدَّهم　　ان عزّ ظعنٌ فالتزام عزآء

او ليت احبابى بما بى قد دروا　　فيسارعوا شَفَقا الى انجآى

٤،٢٠،٥٦ حاشاهم ان يهجروا كَلِفًا بهم　　يكفيه ما يلقى من الاقصآء

ومع النوىّ يُرَى النوَى سهلا كما　　ان الدنوّ مع الجفوّ تنآء

How strange my fate—it never ceases to keep me under observation
  Yet my emaciation makes me invisible to any watcher!
How strange my tears—in bathing me they sicken me
  While hot water cures all others!
How strange my life—how it grows longer with separation
  While the Earth shrinks too much to hold my hopes!
How strange the night of others—how its morning comes quickly
  When my night's morning is always slow in coming!
My thoughts during it build hope upon 4.20.55
  A foundation of the impossible, and what worse foundation could there be?
And the longing that dwells within my ribs
  Makes me imagine that I am sleeping and they're my bedfellows
Until such time as I awake, when it becomes clear that they were
  But ropes of floating dust.
O you whom I hold in affection, in my malady
  There is nothing that can infect you so return and fear not my disease.
My languor is from the languid eye and that which makes me thin
  Is the slim waist, may what has infected me pass you by!
I shall burden you with naught but the mention of the name of the one
  I love—enough for me is such naming!
If my high hopes were good for anything I would today
  Be the most fortunate of mankind, the happiest of the happy
For every morning bird utters their name—
  Or is that but the deceitful whispering of the air?
Or is it part of what longing creates that it
  Should distract me with things that do not exist from those that do?
Would that people's hearts, or effort, were with me—
  Should a departure prove painful, they would be committed to commiseration!
Or would that the ones I love might be aware of how I feel
  And hasten, out of pity, to rescue me!
God forbid that they should abandon one so fond of them— 4.20.56
  Enough for him the deprival that he has known!
With a sympathetic friend, distance seems easy, just as
  With unkindness, proximity seems to recede.

لهفى على زمن تولّى وانقضى   معه السرور لديهم وهنآى
فلاىّ بثّ بعدها ورزيئة   ابقتنى الايام شرّ بقآء
كيف التصبّر للفراق وما ترى   عينى شبيههم من الارنآء
ان اشكُ لم اجدِ امراً لى مشكيا   وشماتة المشكين شرّ بلآ
واذا سكتّ توهّم السلوان بى الرآى وذلك دون فعل الرآى
ياليت شعرى ما امال احبّتى   عنى من التحذير والاغرآء
بَخِلوا علىّ بنفحة من فيهم   تاتى الصبا نحوى بها لشفآى
٥٧،٢٠،٤ انّى استمر حديد قلبهم على   نار الهوى بى لم يَلِنْ لدعآى
العلّهم وجدوا علىّ ملامة   فارتهم الحسنى من الاَسْوآ
هبنى اسات فها انا مستغفر   والعفو مامول من الكرمآء
بُرِّئ عليهم هيّن وهو الرضى   سيّان فيه من دنا والنآى
ان لم يصرِّح فيه قول فليتب   اضمار ذكر عنه فهو كفآى
انّى بحسن القصد منكم قانع   ولئن يكن قد فاتنى ارضآى

٥٨،٢٠،٤ وقال فى المعنى

اتانى كتاب من خليل منمّقُ   على كل حرف منه حسن ورونقُ
تنشّيْتُ وجدا اذ تنشّيت عَرْفه   ولِمْ لا ومنه عاطر الورد يعبق
فيا حبّذا ذاك العبير وحبذا   نسيم به نحوى التباشير يسبق

Alas, I cry, for a time that has passed and with it
The pleasure I knew with them and my happiness!
For what great sorrow now and disaster
Have the days preserved me—and how evil a preservation!
How can I patiently bear separation when my eye
After so much gazing, sees none that resembles them?
If I complain, I find no one to hear my complaint—
And the gloating of those who hear complaints is the worst of tribulations—
And if I hold my tongue, the thinker will think I am consoled,
Which is something no thinker could reasonably think.
Would that those I love had not turned
From me under pressure of warnings and seduction!
They were too miserly to spare me a fragrant breath from their mouth
That the east wind might have brought me to cure me.
How is it that their hearts have remained like iron 4.20.57
Despite the fire of my love and have not softened to my prayers?
Did they perhaps find some reason to blame me
That allowed them to distinguish the good from the bad?
Even if I did wrong, I now hereby ask forgiveness
And pardon is to be hoped for from the noble.
My cure—their approval—would cost them little,
The near and the far being as one in this.
If it may not be spoken openly, then let
A private thought take its place; that is enough for me.
I am content with your good intentions
Even if what would make me happy has passed me by.

On the same topic he wrote 4.20.58

A letter reached me from a friend—elegantly written,
Each character inscribed with beauty and flair.
I swooned with passion when I sniffed its perfume
And why not, when attar of roses wafted from it?
How lovely that scent and how lovely
A breeze that brings it to me, outpacing the good tidings!

الى الله اشكو ما لقيت من النوى   وحرّ جوى كادت به النفس تزهق
اقمت واحبابى ابرّوا وابحروا   على غير ما اهوى وشملى مفرّق
فما زلت مذ بانوا حليف صبابة   اذا حان سَبحٌ كدت بالدمع اغرق
ففى قلبى الماسور ادّخر الهوى   ومن طرفى المسجور دمعى انفق
كئيب نحيل واجدٌ متشوّف   غرب عليل فاقد متشوّق
ولست بذى صبر فيُؤمَل اجرُه   ولست بذى سلوى اليه موفق
وليس بمأمون زمانى على اللقا   وهل يؤخذنْ يوما على الدهر موثق
احنّ الى لقياهم متلهّفا   اذا ما سميرى النجم لاح واقلق ٥٩،٢٠،٤
وان ذرّ قرن الشمس اُوهِمتُ انها   تبلّغنى عنهم سلاما وتنطق
فانى ارى فيها علامات حسنهم   وفى كل حسن ذكرُ ما القلب يعشق
اعلّل قلبا بالامانى هائما   ولم يبقَ فيه للمتمنّى مصدَّق
يطير اشتياقا بى اليهم واننى   اسير هوى فيهم ببينى موثق
ويخفق من ذكر اسمهم فكانما   يخيّل لى ان مضجعى منه يخفق
واسكب دمعا كان يجرى بقربهم   فكيف وباب الوصل دونى مغلق
متى يجمع الله المحبّين ساعة   ويجب النوى بعد الوصال تمزق
وربّ بعاد كان منه دوام ما   يومّل من قرب الاحبّة شيّق
فلله اسرار يعزّ بيانها   وللدهر اطوار تسوء وتونق

هذا المعنى مسروق من الفارياقية وقد تقدمت الاشارة اليه

To God I complain of the separation I have suffered
And of a heat of ardent love at which I almost gave up the ghost.
I stayed, and my darlings departed by land and by sea
Against my desire and my family was dispersed.
Since they left, I have not ceased to swear my passion.
When it is time to take action, I almost drown in tears
For in my captive heart I store up love
And from my overflowing eye I expend tears.
Melancholy, wasted, pining, longing,
Alone, sick, lost, and yearning,
I am neither possessed of patience, that I should expect its reward,
Nor consoled and reconciled.
There is no guarantee that my fate will permit a meeting—
Has any firm commitment ever been taken from fate?
I yearn, panting, to meet them, 4.20.59
When my night companions, the stars, appear, and I am restless,
And if the rim of the sun should appear over the horizon, I am deluded
Into thinking that it brings me a greeting from them and will speak
For in it I see the marks of their beauty,
And in all beauty is a reminder to the heart of what it loves.

This trope is stolen from the Fāriyāqiyyah and was alluded to earlier.[361]

I distract a love-maddened heart with hopes
Though there is nothing left there for the hopeful to believe in.
It flies me, in longing, to them and I
Am captive to a love for them that is linked to my destiny.
It quivers at the mention of their name
And it seems to me that my bed quivers at its mention
And I pour out the very tears that I used to when I was close to them
Though how can that be when the door to union is closed?
When will God unite the lovers for an hour
And the veils of distance be ripped apart
(Though many a craving distance has resulted in the permanence that was
Hoped for from the lovers' proximity!)?
God possesses secrets whose discovery is painful,
And fate has phases that both displease and please.

٤،٢٠،٦٠

وقال

اموِّدعي والدمع كاد يحولُ ما بيننا ولظى الغرام تهولُ
كيف التصبّر بعد بُعدك موحشا وبقيتُ لا اربٌ ولا مامول
قد كان يشجيني غيابك ساعةً واخال ان قد عزّ منك قفول
والآن غبتَ على حساب صبابتي دهرًا فليل المبتلينَ طويل
اِن تنسَني اذكرْك او ان تشجني اشكرك لست الدهرَ عنك احول
ياليت طيفك في الكرى يعتادني او كان يغفي الطرف حين اُلِيل
فلَزورةٌ منه احبُّ الىّ من لذّات وصلٍ من سواك يطول
اُذهِلتُ في حُبّيك عن اَلَم النوى ولقد يريح العاشقين ذهول
انسانُ عيني انت جيَرٍ ومهجةٌ للقلب ما لهما لدىً بديل
لو في رضاك بذلتُ كل جوارحي كنتُ الضنينَ وما بذلتُ قليل
القاك في كل الجمال مصوّرًا فيطول فيه منى التأميل ٤،٢٠،٦١
واذا سمعتُ بمفرد في حسنه ايقنتُ في هذا لك التاويل
واَبيتُ اسأل عنك سيّار الدُجَى لوكان ينفع سائلا مسئول
يافاتني بدلالهِ لم يبقَ لي في العيش بعدك بَتّةً تعليل
ما كان غيرك مالكًا طرفي ولا اعتقدَ الضميرُ باَنْ سواك جميل
واذا الورى شغلتهم دنياهُمُ فانا الذي بك دائما مشغول
فيك الدليل على توحّد مبدعٍ ان عزّ عند الفلسفيّ دليل

And he wrote 4.20.60

O you who bid me farewell, the tears near parting us,
Passion's blaze striking terror,
How can there be patience after you, already missed, have departed
And I remain, neither an object of desire nor a hoped-for goal?
Your absence, even for an hour, used to grieve me
And I would imagine that it was unlikely that you would return.
Now you have been absent, at a high price to my passion,
For an age, and long is the night of the afflicted.
If you forget me, I shall remember you, or should you grieve for me,
I shall thank you; never shall I turn from you as long as time shall last.
Would that your phantom would come to me as I sleep
Or my eye close when I am overcome by night,
For a single visit by it would be dearer to me than
Love's pleasures with another enjoyed at length.
I was distracted by my twofold love for you[362] from the pain of separation,
And distraction may bring comfort to suitors.
The pupil of my eye you are—yes indeed!—and blood
Of my heart, and for these two I have no alternative.
Should I use up all my limbs in making you content,
I would still be niggardly and what I have used up would be little.
I find you pictured in everything that is beautiful 4.20.61
So I gaze at it at length in contemplation
And if I hear of one unique in beauty
I remain convinced that you have precedence in that.
I pass the night asking the planets of darkness about you
(If such an object of questioning can be of use to such a questioner).
O you who have bewitched me with your winsomeness, no
Distraction whatsoever remains to me in life after you.
No other than you has pleased me and my innermost mind
Has believed no other to be beautiful.
If man's preoccupation is this world,
Then I am the one who is forever preoccupied with you.
In you may be found proof for the oneness of a Creator,
Should the philosopher find it hard to come up with such a proof.

ارسلتُ دمعى مع كتابى عالمًا   ان لا ينوب عن الحبيب رسول

ياعاذلين على الهوى لا تعذلوا   فبلاىَ هذا اصله التعجيل

سبق الفوادُ الطرفَ منى فى الهوى   فهويت فيه فعاذلى معذول ٦٢،٢٠،٤

اسفاً على وقت الوصال فياتُرَى   للبين يغدو مثله تاجيل

لولا ادّكار نعيمه لقضيتُ من   وجدٍ فكم بالوجد طُلّ قتيل

ساعُ التعانق ليس يُنسى ذكرُها   وخطورُها[1] بالبال قطُّ حؤول

ولربَّ يوم مسرَّةٍ يغنيك عن   عمر باكدار البعاد يطول

فَلاَفطمنَّ النفس عن لذّاتها   وليشجنى بعد الغناء عويل

يامنكراً لحقيقة الغول اعتقدْ   انَّ النوى هى فى الحقيقة غول

من لم يَذُقْ اَلَمَ الفراق فما له   يوماً الى عتب الزمان سبيل

فلكل رزءٍ غيره سلوى لذى   رشد وطبٌّ بالعزآء كفيل

يالوعةَ الشوق اسكنى فى مهجتى   ما فاتنى ممَّن احبُّ وصول

خفقانُ قلبى من سكونكِ دائم   ولعلّ عن كَثَبٍ بلاىَ يزول

هذا ما انتهى الينا من اخبار الفارياق * مما اقتضى الان ايداعه ٦٣،٢٠،٤
بطون الاوراق * فمن شآء ان يدعو له او عليه فجزآوه يوم تلتف الساق
بالساق * ويقال الى ربك يؤمئذ المساق * فامّا من دعا له بعود زواجه

هذه المرّة وفى الحياة ارماق * فانى اضمن له ان يدعوه الى مادبة

حولها وفيها كل ما شاق وراق * مما ذكر فى

هذا الكتاب بالانتساق

على سرر واطباق

*

---

١ ١٨٥٥: ذكرَها وخطورَها.

I sent my tears with my letter, knowing full well
That no messenger can take the place of the beloved.
You who condemn love, be not reproachful
For this decrepitude of mine may be attributed to haste.
My heart preceded my eye in love, 4.20.62
And through it I fell; let my reproacher then be blamed.
Alas for the days of loving union! I wonder,
Can parting, like them, also suffer postponement?
Had I not had their felicity to recall, I would have died
Of passion, and how many a one slain by passion has gone unavenged!
Transformation will never cause me to forget the hours of embracing
Or ever prevent them from recurring to my mind.
Many a day of pleasure will compensate one
For a life made long by the vexations of separation.
Let me then wean the soul from its pleasures
And let wailing sadden me after song!
O denier of the reality of ghouls, know well
That distance is in truth a ghoul!
He who has not tasted the pain of separation
Has no right ever to reproach fate:
Every burden other than this has for the man of good sense
Its consolation and, in mourning, its cure.
O agony of longing, dwell in my heart
So long as contact with the ones I love is missing!
The trembling of my heart at your silence is continuous
Yet mayhap soon my wearing cares will disappear.

This is the last news we have of the Fāriyāq that must be placed at this 4.20.63
time within these *pages*, and any who wishes to bless him or curse him shall, when "leg is intertwined with leg" and it is said, "unto thy Lord that day shall be the driving,"[363] receive his *wages*. As for he who prays for the restoration of his marriage before he breathes his last, I guarantee he'll invite you to a banquet around and upon whose table will be set out, in proper order, everything this book mentions

that the appetite may *stimulate* or the eye *captivate*,
be it presented on couch
or on *dinner plate*.

الخاتمة

تم الجزء الاول من كتاب الساق على الساق فى ما هو ١،٢١،٤
الفارياق ويتلوه الجزء الثانى بعد رجم المولف او صلبه بمن الله
وكرمه امين

*

Conclusion

Part One of the Book 4.21.1
Leg over Leg
Regarding the Fāriyāq
ends here
and will be followed by
Part Two
once the author
through God's favor and generosity
has been stoned and crucified.[364]
Amen

٠،١،٥ بسم الله الرحمن الرحيم

١،١،٥ ياسيدى الشيخ ياسيدنا المطران بطرس ياابونا حنا ياابونا منقريوس ياصير ابراهام
يامستر نكتن ياهرشميط ياسنيور جوزبّى هادينى انا عملت الكتّاب دى يعنى الّفته
لا طبعته ولا جلّدته وحطّيته بين اياديكم انا اعرف طيّب ان سيدى الشيخ محمد
يضحك منه اذا كان يقراه لانه يعرف من روحه انه يقدر يعمل احسن منه ولانه
يعتقد انه شى فارغ وان كنت مليته بالحروف لكن سيدنا وابونا وصيرنا ما يقدروش
بل ما يقدروش يفهموه وعلى شان دى اطلب منهم انهم قبل ما يولّعوا النار حتى
يحرقوه يسالوا عن الطيّب فيه وعن غير الطيّب فان كان الطيّب اثقل يخلّوه لى والا
يحرقوه بجلده واذا كانوا يجدوا فيه بعض هفوات فما يكونش من العدل انهم يحرقوه
٢،١،٥ لان كل واحد منا فيه هفوات كثيرة والله تعالى لا يحرقنا بنار جهنم بسببها ياابونا
حنّا انا احلف لك انى ما ابغضكش ولكن ابغض تكبّرك وجهلك لانى لما اسلّم
عليك تلقمنى ايدك حتى ابوسها فكيف ابوسها وانت جاهل وعمرك كله ما عملت
كتّاب ولا موّال روحى ياسيدى الشيخ محمد انا اعرف ان كتب الفقه والنحو اجلّ
من كتّابى دى لان الواحد لما يقرا كتّاب من دول يقطّب وجهه ويعبّس حتى يقدر
يفهم معناه ومعلومك ان الهيبة والجلالة ما تكونش الا فى التعبيس ولكن كتب
الفقه ما تقولش ان الضحك حرام او مكروه وانت ما شا الله كيّس لبيب قريت من
كتب الادب اكثر مما اكل سيدنا المطران بطرس من الفراخ المقمّرة وفى كل كتّاب
ادب ترى باب مخصوص للمجون فلو كان المجون ضدّ الادب ما كانوا دخّلوه فيها

In the Name of God the Merciful, the Compassionate[365] 5.1.0

Sīdi[366] Shaykh Muḥammad, *Sayyidna* Metropolitan Buṭrus, *Abūna* Ḥanna, *Abūna* Manqariyūs, *Ṣirna* Abraham, Mister Necton [?], Herr Schmidt, Signor Giuseppe,[367] as you can see I've now made (that is to say written and not printed or bound) this book and placed it before you. I know well that *Sīdi* Shaykh Muḥammad will be laughing at it, if he's read it, because he knows without anyone having to tell him that he could do better and thinks it's a foolish thing even if I have filled it with letters. *Sayyidna*, *Abūna*, and *Ṣirna*, though, could not. In fact, they won't even understand it, and I therefore ask of them that, before they light a fire to burn it, they ask about what's good in it and what's not. If the good outweighs the bad, they should let me keep it; if not, they can burn it with its binding. If, though, they find in it only a few shortcomings, they shouldn't burn it, for we all have many shortcomings and God won't burn us in hellfire just because of them. 5.1.1

Father Ḥanna, I swear to you I don't hate you. I hate only your arrogance and your ignorance: when I greet you you give me your hand to kiss, but how can I kiss it when you're an ignoramus and haven't written a book, or even a hymn, in your life? My dearest Shaykh Muḥammad, I know that books of jurisprudence and grammar are more sublime than this book of mine because when one reads one of those books, one screws up one's face and frowns as one tries to understand what it's about, and you believe that venerability and sublimity are to be found only in frowning. However, the books of jurisprudence don't say that laughter is a sin or is reprehensible, and you—God protect you from envy!—are quick and intelligent. You've read more books of literature than *Sayyidna* Metropolitan Buṭrus has eaten braised chickens and in every book of literature you'll find a chapter devoted to licentiousness, which they wouldn't have included if licentiousness were against literature. 5.1.2

واهون ما يكون عليّ ان اقول فى آخر كتابى دى زىّ ما قال غيرى ومن ٣،١،٥
الله استغفر عما طغى به القلم وزلّت به القدم فنحن دى الوقت والحمد
لله صلح فاما مسيو ومستر وهر وسنيور فما همّاش ملزومين ان
يطبعوا كتابى لان كلامى ما هوش على البقر والحمير والاسود
والنمور بل هو على الناس بنى ادم ولكن
هذا هو والله اعلم سبب
غيظكم منى

تم الكتاب

The easiest of my duties is to say at the end of this book of mine, as others have done, "and I seek God's forgiveness for any excesses of the pen and slips on the path." We are now, God be thanked, at peace with one another. Monsieur, Mister, Herr, and Signor are not obliged 5.1.3

to print my book as my words aren't addressed to
cattle, donkeys, lions, and tigers[368]
but to people
—offspring of Adam—
and this may be why
(though God alone knows)
you're angry with me.

End of the Letter

بيان ما فى هذا الكتاب من الالفاظ المترادفة والمتجانسة

A List of the Synonymous and Lexically Associated Words in This Book[369]

Volume One — **Section** 5.2.1

Base sense: "Be silent!" [1.1.1]

Base sense: "priest" [1.1.3]

Base sense: "threatening" [1.1.3]

Base sense: "making mistakes and mispronouncing" [1.1.4]

"pudendum" and associated words [1.1.6]

Doublets,[370] continuing to page 63 [1.1.13–21]

"the ten head wounds" [1.2.2]

"dotty" [1.3.10]

Sounds [1.4.6]

"she made herself up," to which should be added *za'nafah* ("to 5.2.2
dress the bride"), *tazayyuq* ("to attire oneself, or to apply collyrium"), *tashannuq* ("to attire oneself"), *tamarrī* (ditto), and *taztīt* (ditto). [1.5.1]

Bad table manners, continued on page 185 [1.6.3] + [1.12.10]

Stages and varieties of love [1.10.9]

Obscure words not explained in the text [1.11.5]

The recluse [1.14.6]

"assiduous" [1.14.7]

[المجلّد الأوّل] صفحة

Volume One	**Section**
Gambling and associated words, to which should be added *mukhāḍarah*, meaning "the selling of fruits before their quality is known"	[1.16.5]
Base sense: "to take an omen or an augury"	[1.16.7]
Magic and amulets, to which should be added *ra‘b*, meaning "a charm, magic or otherwise" and *‘unnah*, the noun from *‘unna l-rajul*, said if "a man is prevented from having intercourse with his wife by magic" or "because the judge made such an order" and *al-sahm al-aswad* ("the black arrow"), i.e., the blessed arrow from which good omens are taken (as though it had been blackened by frequently being touched by the hand) and *tafyīd,* meaning "taking auguries from the call of the *fayyād*" (the male owl)	"
Glue	[1.18.4]
Names of parts of the body	"
Places in Hell, names of devils and jinn, sounds made by jinn, and so on, up to page 265, to which should be added, to the part on jinn, *quṭrub*, meaning "their young"	[1.18.5–11]
Base sense: bad dream	[1.18.12]

Volume Two

Stars and their conditions	[2.1.3] 5.2.3
Some synonyms of "crowding"	[2.1.4]
Instruments of war	[2.1.7–10]
Names of idols, to which should be added *al-Jalsad*, "the name of an idol," *Awāl*, on the pattern of *saḥāb*, an idol of the tribes of Bakr and Taghlib, and *Balj*, "a certain idol, or a name"	[2.1.11–16]
Some star names	[2.1.16]
Some synonyms of "pushing" and "pressing"	[2.1.23]

[المجلّد الثاني] صفحة

Volume Two	**Section**	
Turbans and hosiery, to which should be added *fidām* ["something the non-Arabs and Magians attach over their mouths when drinking"]	[2.2.1–2]	5.2.4
Women's movements and ways of walking	[2.2.4]	
Base sense: "contracted," to which should be added *iqʿansasa* ["to fall behind, or to withdraw to the back"]	[2.2.5]	
Land conveyances	[2.2.6–7]	
Pulses	[2.2.10]	
Seagoing vessels, to which should be added the *thurtumī* [?][371] and the like	[2.3.6–8]	
Facial characteristics	[2.4.6]	
Facial states, to page 99	[2.4.7–12]	
Describing the city	[2.5.1]	
Phrases related to divorce	[2.13.6]	
Types of beauty, to page 219, continued in Volume Four, page 235	[2.14.8–29] + [4.16.5–12]	5.2.5
Meadows	[2.14.32]	
Names of places, to which should be added *al-Ubullah*, "a place[372] in Basra, one of the paradises of this world"	[2.14.33–42]	
Places in Heaven	[2.14.43]	

[المجلّد الثاني] صفحة

Volume Two **Section**

Wonders, to which should be added *Hinda Mandu*, "a river in Sijistān into which a thousand rivers empty producing no increase in its waters and from which a thousand rivers branch producing no decrease in its waters," and *al-Jazāʾir al-khālidāt* ["the Immortal Isles"], also called *Jazāʾir al-saʿādah* ["the Happy Isles"]—"six islands in the ocean over toward where the sun sets from which astrologers begin their measurements of the longitudes of the lands and on which grow every sort of fruit, eastern and western, and every kind of aromatic plant and every flower and grain, without being planted or cultivated" [2.14.44–47]

Games of the Arabs, to which should be added *midād Qays*, "a game" [2.14.48–56]

Musical instruments [2.14.57–58]

Kinds of food, to page 267 [2.14.59–68]

Fungi and kinds of fish [2.14.69–73]

Bread, to which should be added *qizmāz*, which is "bread one prepares and turns in order to place in the ashes" [2.14.74]

Milk [2.14.75]

Sweets [2.14.76–77]

Fruit [2.14.78–81] 5.2.6

Drinks [2.14.82–84]

Base sense: "erectile dysfunction" [2.14.86]

The wife [2.14.88]

Kinds of gems and precious metals [2.16.8–11]

Jewelry and ornaments, to which should be added *sikhāb*, which is "a necklace made of *sukk*[373] and *maḥlab*[374] without gems or precious metals" [2.16.12–19]

Perfumes and aromatic pastes [2.16.20–28]

[المجلّد الثاني] صفحة

[المجلّد الثالث]

Volume Two **Section**

Vessels, household articles, and furnishings, to which should be added *ʿālah*, which is "a shade used for protection against the rain" [2.16.29–35]

Trees and minerals [2.16.36–38]

Clothes, mantles, and wraps, to page 363 [2.16.39–63]

Base sense: "to yearn," with words associated with "to turn head over heels," meaning "to strike the heart of" [2.16.71]

Aphrodisiacs [2.19.4]

Volume Three

Sicknesses and defects, to which should be added *qawas*, meaning 5.2.7
"curvature of the back," *ṣarʿ* ["epilepsy"] "a malady too well-known to require definition," *ḥajaz*, a sickness of the stomach, namely rancidness, *qudād*, "a pain in the belly," *saktah*, ["apoplexy"] "a malady too well-known to require definition," and others scarcely worth mentioning [3.1.4–30]

Base sense: "bustle" [3.5.8]

Base sense: "big-buttocked (fem.)" [3.5.17]

Base sense: "fat (fem.)" [3.5.18–21]

Base sense: "kissing" [3.6.3]

Charms of the body [3.6.7]

States and characteristics of the breasts [3.6.8]

Base sense: "hard and strong" and words of similar meaning [3.6.11]

"Alas for Zayd!"[375] [3.12.6]

Base sense: "cosseted" [3.12.6] 5.2.8

Base sense: "the racing of the pulse" [3.12.8]

Base sense: "groping and grasping" [3.12.8]

Volume Three	**Section**	
Kinds of wrestling	[3.12.12]	
Base sense: "servants and attendants"	[3.12.18]	
Names of singers, male and female	[3.12.20]	
Acts and motions specific to the small child	[3.12.21–23]	
What a woman does with her child	[3.13.14]	
Women's postpartum sicknesses	[3.13.15]	
Some synonyms of "wind"	[3.18.7]	**5.2.9**
Rotten smells	[3.18.7]	
Hapax legomena and the like	[3.18.7]	
Some synonyms of "huffing and puffing"	[3.18.9]	
Base sense: "slave" and "captive"	[3.18.9]	
Defects in a wife	[3.18.10]	
Traits desirable in a wife	[3.18.13]	
Base sense: "small-buttocked woman"	[3.19.2]	**5.2.10**
Base sense: "short woman"	[3.19.3]	
Base sense: "black (fem.)," including makeup and face paint[376] (meaning "things women use to improve their faces")	[3.19.4]	
Base sense: "old woman"	[3.19.5]	
Characteristics of the comely woman	[3.19.6]	
Maladies of the neck	[3.19.12]	
Despicable traits of the dissolute woman	[3.19.13]	
Base sense: "iteration" and "occasion"	[3.19.14]	
Base sense: "underachievement" and "falling short" and synonyms	[3.19.16]	
Base sense: "mirror"	[3.19.17]	

Volume Three	**Section**	
Base sense: "delusion" and "suspicion"	[3.20.1]	
Volume Four		
Base sense: "prating" and "raving"	[4.1.12]	**5.2.11**
Base sense: "stretching the limbs"	[4.1.13]	
Base sense: "habit"	[4.3.1]	
Base sense: "riposting" and "jesting"	[4.3.1]	
Base sense: "policeman" and "guard"	[4.3.6]	
The "preoccupied," the "disdainful," and their like	[4.4.7]	
Base sense: "shaking, shuddering," and "dizzy-headedness"	[4.4.7]	
Base sense: "lady's man"	[4.8.6]	
Base sense: "straw basket" and "palm-leaf basket"	[4.9.4]	
The *furuj* or "the woman who wears a single shift"	[4.9.6]	
Base sense: "the woman's spouse" and a list of words of the pattern *faʿīl*	[4.9.8]	
"Painting the eyelids with antimony" and associated words relating to things used by women	[4.10.4]	**5.2.12**
Base sense: "celebrated"	[4.10.5]	
Base sense: "tepid titters"	[4.11.5]	
Base sense: "tasting" and "sipping"	[4.11.6]	
Base sense: "reticence," "wariness," and "caution"	[4.11.6]	
Base sense: "certainly!" and "understanding"	[4.11.7]	
Base sense: "chortling"	[4.12.10]	
"Looking" and its various forms	[4.15.1]	
Praiseworthy traits of women and the various types of the latter	[4.16.5–12]	

[المجلّد الرابع] صفحة

ذنب للكتاب

ينتظم به لآلى اغلاط الرؤس العظام الاساتيذ الكرام مدرّسى اللغات العربية فى مدارس باريس

١،٣،٥ قال الكسندر شُذْزكُو (Alexandre Chodzko) فى فاتحة كتاب الّفه فى نحو اللغة الفارسية سنة ١٨٥٢ ما ترجمته «حصلت بلاد اوربا منذ زمن طويل «على كل ما يلزم لعلم اللغات الشرقية اذ فيها خزائن كتب ومدارس وعلمآ جديرون «بادارتها حتى انه باعتبار فن ادب لغات اسية وما يلحق بها من الفلسفة والتاريخ «اصبح استاذ الفرس ومعلّم العرب وبراهمىّ الهند وبهم افتقار الى ان يتعلموا من اساتيذنا كثيرا» (انتهى) وانا اقول ان هذه الدعوى كذب ومين وافك وافترآء وترّهة وتزوير وبهتان وإبعاط وشحط وشطط وفُرُط وهِتر وعضيهة واختلاق وزغف وتزهّف وتصلّف وتزبّب * وان قائلها ينبغى ان يدمج مع من جهلوا انفسهم فى فصل حذنبدى لانه جهل نفسه بل حمل غيره ايضا على الجهل بنفسه *

٢،٣،٥ اما اوّلا فلانه اى قائل هذه المقالة لا يعرف اللغات الشرقية ولا يعرف مقدار ما نتف منها هولآء الاساتيذ حتى يشهد لهم بالفضل والبراعة * وانه فى نقله للرسائل الفارسية التى اثبتها فى كتابه ارتكب اغلاطا كثيرة فاضحة سوآء فى النقل والترجمة * فمن ذلك قوله فى صحفة ١٩٨ قانع صفصف وهى فى الاصل قاع

Appendix to the Book

In Which Are Strung Together the Pearl-like Errors Made by the Great Masters among the Teachers of Arabic Languages[378] in the Schools of Paris

In the opening passage of a book on Persian grammar that he wrote in 1853, Alexandre Chodźko[379] states, "The countries of Europe have long been possessed of everything needed for the study of oriental languages, as they are of libraries and schools and scholars well-qualified to direct them. With regard to the literature of the languages of Asia and their associated philosophy and history, the professors of the Persians, the teachers of the Arabs, and the Brahmans of India now have much to learn from our professors." I declare this claim to be lies, chicanery, mendacity, fakery, falsehood, forgery, slander, empty boasting, implausibility, injustice, farfetchedness, fallacy, fibbing, fabrication, blarney, hyperbole, hokum, and humbuggery and that its author ought to be listed in the chapter on marvels[380] among those who delude themselves, for not only does he delude himself but he leads others to do likewise. 5.3.1

Firstly, he—that is, the writer of the essay in question—does not have the knowledge of oriental languages that would justify the witness he bears to the excellence and mastery of these professors and is unaware of the shallowness of their knowledge, for in transferring the letters[381] in Persian that he has put into his book, he makes many gross mistakes both of copying and of translation. Among these, on page 198, he writes *qāniʿ ṣafṣaf* when the original reads *qāʿ ṣafṣaf*, the quotation being from the words of the Almighty *wa-yasʾalūnaka ʿani l-jibāli qul yansifuhā rabbī nasfan fa-yadharuhā qāʿan* 5.3.2

صفصف اقتباسا من قوله تعالى وَيَسۡأَلُونَكَ عَنِ ٱلۡجِبَالِ فقُلۡ[1] يَنسِفُهَا رَبِّي نَسۡفٗا فَيَذَرُهَا قَاعٗا صَفۡصَفٗا * فلما جهل المعنى بدّل قاع بقانع وترجمه باللغة الفرنساوية بقوله ويُقنع نفسه برمل البرّية * فكيف استحلّ هذا العالم ان يملأ الكلام بالرمل واستكبر ان يسال احدا من اهل العلم عن المعنى * لكنها عادة له ولاسلافه ولاساتيذه فى انهم حين يشتبه عليهم المعنى يعمدون الى الترقيع والترميق والتلفيق *

٣،٣،٥ والثانى ان هولآء الاساتيذ لم ياخذوا العلم عن شيوخه اى عن الشيخ محمد والملّا حسن والاستاذ سعدى وانما تطفلوا عليه تطفلا وتوثبوا توثّبا * ومَن تخرّج فيه بشى فانما تخرج على القس حنا والراهب توما والخورى متّى * ثم ادخل راسه فى اضغاث احلام او ادخل اضغاث احلام فى راسه وتوهم انه يعرف شيا وهو يجهله * وكلّ منهم اذا درّس فى احدى لغات الشرق او ترجم شيا منها تراه يخبط فيها خبط عشوآ * فما اشتبه عليه منها رقّعه من عنده بما شآء * وما كان بين الشبهة واليقين حدّس فيه وخمّن فرجّح منه المرجوح وفضّل المفضول * وذلك لانه لم يوجد عندهم من تصدّى لتخطئتهم وتسوئتهم * وقد قال ابو الطيب

واذا ما خلا الجبان بارض   طلب الحرب وحده والنزالا

٤،٣،٥ ولانهم انما اعتمدوا على اتصافهم بنعت مدرسين فاجتزأوا بالاسم عن الفعل وعن حقيقة ما يراد من التدريس * فان المتصدى لهذه الرتبة الجليلة ينبغى ان يكون صادق النقل متثبتا فى الرواية * متحرّجا من التهافت على ترجيح ما استحسنه هو دون مراد المولف * مترويا فى سياق الحديث وسباقه وقرائنه وعلائقه * مضطلعا باللغة والنحو والصرف والادب * فاين هذه الصفات كلها من هولا

---

[1] ١٨٥٥: قُل.

ṣafṣafan ("They ask you about the mountains. Say, 'My lord will scatter them as dust and leave the earth level and bare. . . .'")[382]; being ignorant of the meaning, he has changed *qāʿ* ("low-lying land") to *qāniʿ* ("content") and translated it into French by saying, in his words, "and he satisfies himself with the sands of the plain."[383] How could this scholar permit himself to fill the book with sand and be too proud to ask someone knowledgeable what it meant? Such, however, is his custom and that of his predecessors and professors: when they are in doubt as to the meaning, they resort to patching, botching, and concocting.

Secondly, these professors do not get their knowledge from those who are masters of it, such as Shaykh Muḥammad, Molla Ḥasan, or Üstad Saʿdī.[384] They acquire it parasitically and pounce upon it randomly. Those who graduate with some knowledge of the subject do so at the hands of Priest Ḥanna, Monk Tūmā, and Parson Mattā and then stick their heads into confused dreams, or stick confused dreams into their heads, and imagine that they understand things that they do not. Any of them who teaches an oriental language or translates from one you will find flailing around blindly. Anything they are in doubt about they patch up any way they please and anything that lies between doubt and certainty they conjecture or guess at, giving greater weight to the less weighty and preferring the less preferred. This is because there is nobody at hand to take on the task of pointing out their mistakes and helping them to improve. As Abū l-Ṭayyib[385] says 5.3.3

If a coward finds himself alone in a land
He calls for war on his own, and for battle.

Because they have invested all their dignity in having people call them by the title of "teacher," they are content to have the name without the doing and without undertaking what is properly meant by being a teacher. He who occupies this sublime position must be truthful in his transmission, cautious in his narration, careful not to give too much credence to the likelihood of what he favors at the expense of what the author intended, thoughtful as to the material's context, to the text that precedes it, and to any delimiting attributes or relevant issues connected to it, and he must be steeped in the lexicon, as also in the grammar, syntax, and literature. Where are such qualities among these professors, who distort the author's manner of expression 5.3.4

الاساتيذ الذين يفسدون عبارة المولف ويحمّلونها معانی بعيدة ياباها الطبع والذوق *
ويوردون ما يوردون من شرحها مزابنة ومجازفة * ولعمری لو انهم كانوا من ذوی
التورّع لما تصدّروا فی هذه المراتب ولما اقدموا علی ترجمة شی مرقّع مزوَّر * فان
كان كلامك ايها الشيخ الرملیّ فی حق هولا الاساتيذ كلام ذی جدّ فقد وجب
عليك بعد قراة جدول اغلاطهم الفاضحة ان ترجع عمّا تبهلقت فيه وتزبّبت من
دون علم * وان تكذّب نفسك فی طالعة كتاب آخر تولّفه فی نحو اللغة العربية ان
٥،٣،٥ شا الله * والّا فان اثم انجاسك هذا فی عنقك * فاما ان كان مزاحا واردت
به السخرية من هولآء الاساتيذ المشاهير والاساطين المذاكير فهم اولی بان
يجيبوك * غير انی اراهم قد سكتوا عنك * فكانَّ دغدغة هرفك هذا لهم قد
اعجبتهم * فما مَثَلك ومثلهم الا مَثَل ذلك الابله الذی عشق امراة ولم يقدر علی
وصالها حتی ادنفه عشقها وهيّمه فلم يستطع بعده حراكا * فعاده رجل داهٍ مثلك
واخذ يهنّئه علی قضآ وطره منها * فقال له الابله كيف وانا مغرم بها وكلما زدت
شوقا اليها ووجدا زادت اعراضا عنّی وصدّا * قال قد رايتك بعينی تعانقها بالامس
ثم خرجت من دارها وانت مبتهج متهلل * وراك غيری ايضا وهم كثيرون * فان
انكرت فها هم كلهم يشهدون لی * وما زال به حتی اقنعه وحمله علی ان يسلوها
فافاق من مرضه * الا ان بينك وبين هذا الداهی فرقا عظيما * وذلك انه انما
استعمل دهآه للاصلاح * وانت انما استعملته للافساد * لان كتابك هذا ربما
يقع فی يد بعض ارباب السياسة الذين يجهلون الفارسية والعربية * ولغفلته
يظن ان مشايخ مصر واساتيذ الفرس محتاجون الان الی اخذ العلم عن اصحابك *
٦،٣،٥ ومتی تهوّر احد هولآء الوجوه فی ضلال تهوّرت معه الرعية باسرها * فاما
قولك ان فی البلاد الافرنجية خزائن كتب كثيرة * كانك تقول انه يوجد فيها من

and impose on it strange meanings unacceptable to both nature and taste, importing, speculatively and recklessly, whatever personal interpretations they fancy? I swear, if they had any shame, they would not occupy these prominent posts and would not make so bold as to produce such patched and faked translations! If, my sandy shaykh,[386] your words concerning these professors were intended seriously, it would be your duty, after reading the list of their appalling mistakes, to retract your ignorant hogwash and hokum and confess your mendacity in the preamble to some other book you may one day write—on Arabic grammar, God willing! If not, the sin of taking pride in a falsehood will be upon your head.

Or if it was said in jest and you intended to poke fun at those prominent 5.3.5
professors and celebrated stars, it would be better if they were to answer you, though I notice that they have said nothing to refute you, and it seems that this ill-judged praise of yours has tickled their fancies. You and they are like that fool who fell in love with a woman and was unable to have her and continued thus until his love for her made him sick and crazed, at which point he became incapable of movement. He was then visited by a crafty man such as you who kept congratulating him on having achieved what he wanted from her. "How can this be," asked the fool, "when I am besotted with love for her and the more I long and yearn for her, the more she shuns and rejects me?" Said the other, "With my own eyes I saw you embracing her yesterday, after which you left her house, radiant with joy. Many others saw you too, and if you deny it, they are all ready to bear witness against you," and he stuck to this version of events until he had persuaded him and convinced him to forget about her, and the man recovered from his sickness. Though there is a great difference between you and that crafty man: he used his cunning to do good, while you used yours to do evil. That book of yours may fall into the hands of a statesman who knows nothing of Persian and Arabic and in his ignorance he may think that the shaykhs of Egypt and the professors of Persia need to acquire knowledge from your friends—and when one of those bigwigs nonchalantly grasps the wrong end of the stick, the hoi polloi, as one, nonchalantly grasp it along with him.

Your statement that the Frankish countries have many libraries seems to 5.3.6
imply that these contain books that are not to be found in ours, but this is

الكتب ما لا يوجد فى بلادنا * لان نوّاب الدول لا يزالون يشترون من بلادنا انفس الكتب * فهو ليس بدليل على وجود العلم عند وجود الكتب * فاين حمل الاسفار هداك الله من العلم * لان العلم فى الصدور لا فى السطور * ولكن افدنى ما بال هولآء الاساتيذ لم يولّفوا فى اللغات الشرقية شيا قطّ * فغاية ما صنعوا انما هو ان احدهم ترجم من لغتنا لغة الاطيار والازهار فخمّن فيها وحدس ما شآ * واخر ترجم محاورة يهودى سمسار واحمق من التجار * وآخر مسخ امثال لقمن الحكيم الى الكلام الركيك المتعارف فى الجزائر * وآخر تعنّى لطبع اقوال سخيفة من رعاع العامة فى مصر والشام * وترك ما فيها من اللحن والفساد كما هو استذراعا بقوله كذا رايتها فى الاصل * فيظن بذلك انه تنصل من تبعة اللوم والتفنيد * فما سبب هذا التهافت على ترجمة مثل هذه الكتب وطبع مثل هذه الاقوال من لغتنا الى اللغة الفرنساوية سوى توخّم ملفقّيها على الانخراط فى سلك المولفين * ولمَ لم يعتنَّ احد منهم لترجمة شى من الكتب الفرنساوية الى العربية ليظهر براعته فى هذه حالة كونه شيخ طلبتها وإمام آميها * على ان فى اللغة الفرنساوية كتبا جليلة القدر فى كل فن * واعجب من ذلك انه لم يخطر ببال احد منهم قطّ ان يترجم نحو لغتهم الى لغتنا * فهل من سبب اخر غير التحذّر من ان يعرّضوا انفسهم للتحميق والتفنيد والتحمير * فان عبارة النحاة والمعرّبين لا بدّ من ان تكون محرَّرة صحيحة ولا عذر لهم معها ان يقولوا كذا وجدناه فى الاصل * ويا ليت شعرى ما الفائدة فى كون احد هولآء الاساتيذ يولّف كلاما معسلطا فاسدا فى لغة اهل حلب ويسمّيه نحوا * ثم يذكر فيه انجق بيكفى وايشلون كيفك خيّو وهلكتّاب وقوى طيب * وفى كون آخر يكتب بلسان اهل الجزائر كان فى واحد الدار طوبات بالزاف الطوبات كشافوا وكيناكل وراهى وانتينا وانتيّا ونجّم وخمّم باش وواسيت شغل المهابل

because the representatives of various nations are buying up the most valuable books from our countries. The presence of books is not, however, evidence of the presence of knowledge. Carrying books around does not make one, God guide you, a scholar, for knowledge is in the mind not in the lines. But tell me: how is it that these professors never write a word in the oriental languages? The extent of their production is that one of them translated from our language *Lughat al-aṭyār wa-l-azhār* (*The Language of the Birds and the Flowers*),[387] filling it with guesses and conjectures. Another translated the correspondence of a Jewish broker with an imbecilic merchant.[388] Another transmogrified the proverbs of Luqmān the Wise into the feeble language used in Algeria[389] and another labored to have printed silly sayings taken from the rabble in Egypt and the Levant,[390] leaving whatever incorrect and corrupt language he found therein as is and seeking to make excuses for himself by saying "*sic*," which he thought would allow him to evade any blame or refutation. What lies behind the craze for translating such books and printing such sayings from our language into French if not the craving of their compilers to join the ranks of authors? And why has none of them gone to the trouble of translating any French books into Arabic to show off his mastery in this area, given that he is supposedly the shaykh of those who study the language and the imam of its imams and when there are very estimable books in French in every field? Even more amazing is the fact that it has occurred to none of them to translate the grammar of their language into ours. Can there be any reason other than their reluctance to expose themselves to verification, refutation, and excoriation? The words of the grammarians and the Arabists would have to be rendered exactly, and it would be no excuse for them in this case to say "*sic*." I wish I knew what was the point of one of these professors writing a book in corrupt, mixed style, on the speech of the people of Aleppo,[391] calling it a "grammar," and recording in it words such as *anjaq* ("barely, scarcely"),[392] *biykaffi* ("it's enough"), *ishlōn* ("what?"), *kēfak* ("how are you?"), *khayyu* ("little brother"), *ha l-kitāb* ("this book"), and *awi ṭayyib* ("very good"). Or of another writing in the dialect of the people of Algeria[393] *kān fī wāḥid il-dār ṭūbāt bi-z-zāf il-ṭūbāt kishāfū* and *kīnākul* and *rāhī* and *antīnā* and *antiyyā* and *naqjam* and *khammim bāsh* and *wāsīt shughl il-mahābil* and *yiwālim* (i.e., *yulā'im*, "it suits")

ویوالم ای یلائم وماجی ای جآء وکلّی ای کانه وحرامی ای بستانی والستّاش ای
السادس والدجاجة ترجع تولّد زوج عظمات وما اشبه ذلك من المشوّ * فما بالکم ٧،٣،٥
یا اساتیذ لا تولّفون کتبا بکلامکم الفاسد الذی تسمونه پتوی * وهل تشیرون علی عربیّ
اقام بمرسیلیة مثلا ان یتعلم کلام اهلها او کلام اهل باریس * ولوکان فعلکم هذا
فعل رشید لوجب ان تقیدوا جمیع الاختلافات والفروق الموجودة عند المتکلمین
بالعربیة * فان اهل الشام یستعملون الفاظا لا یستعملها اهل مصر * وقس علی
ذلك سائر البلاد الاسلامیة * بل ان لاهل صقع واحد اصطلاحات شتی *
فکلام اهل بیروت مثلا مخالف لکلام اهل جبل لبنان * وکلام هولآء مخالف
لکلام اهل دمشق * وذلك یفضی بکم الی الهوس والی افساد هذه اللغة الشریفة
التی من بعض خصائصها انها بقیت ثابتة القواعد قارّة الاسالیب علی انقراض
جمیع ما عداها من اللغات القدیمة * وان المولفین فیها یومنا هذا لا یقصّرون عن
اسلافهم الذین انقرضوا مذ الف ومایتی سنة * فهل حسدتمونا علی ذلك وحاولتم
ان تحیلوها وتلحقوها بلغتکم التی لا تفهمون ما الّف فیها مذ ثلثمائة سنة * ویالیت ٨،٣،٥
شعری هل تاذن ارباب السیاسة عندکم لرجل اراد ان یفتح مکتبا یعلّم فیه الصبیان
فی ان یتعاطی ذلك من دون ان یُمتَحن اوّلا * فمن الذی امتحنکم انتم ووجدکم اهلا
لهذه الرتبة التی هی ارفع من رتبة معلم کتّاب * ومن ذا الذی عارض ما ترجمتم
ولفّقتم ورمّقتم بالمترجم منه * وکیف رُخّص لکم فی ان تطبعوا ذلك من دون الوقوف
علی صحته * ولعمری ان مدرسا لا یحسن ان یکتب سطرا واحدا صحیحا باللغة التی
یعلّمها لجدیر بان یرجع الی المکتب من ذی اُنُف * علی ان من هولآ الاساتیذ
من لا یفهم اذا خوطب فضلا عن جهل التالیف * ولا یفهم اذا قرا * ولا یقوّم
الالفاظ في القرآة * وقد سمعت مرة بعض التلامذة یقرا علی شیخه فی مقامات

and *mājī* (i.e., *jā'in*, "coming") and *killi* (i.e., *ka'annī*, "as though I") and *ḥirāmi* (i.e., *bustānī*, "my garden") and *is-sittāsh* (i.e., *al-sādis*, "the sixth")[394] and *id-dajājah tirja' twallid zūj 'aẓmāt* and similar kinds of laxative.

How is it, my dear professors, that you do not write books in that corrupt language of your own that you call *patois*, and would you advise an Arab who has taken residence in Marseilles, for example, to talk like the people there or like the people of Paris? If you were to be rational about this activity of yours, you would have to record all the differences and variations present among Arabic speakers, for the people of Damascus use words that the people of Cairo do not and you may extrapolate from that to the rest of the Islamic countries. Indeed, the people of one area may use a variety of different terms. The speech of the Beirutis, for example, is different from that of the people of Mount Lebanon and the speech of the latter is different from that of the people of Damascus. This would lead you into folly and the corruption of this noble language of ours, one of whose distinguishing characteristics is that its rules have remained unchanged and its style fixed in the face of the extinction of all other ancient languages and whose writers of today are in no way inferior to their predecessors who passed away one thousand two hundred years ago. Is it that you envy us this and have been trying to transform the language and bring it into line with your own, in which you cannot understand what was written three hundred years ago? 5.3.7

I would like to know if your authorities would give permission to a man who wanted to open a school for teaching children to do that without taking an examination first. Who, then, examined you and found you qualified for this rank, which is higher than that of a schoolteacher, and who compared what you translated and concocted and botched together with the original? And how did you obtain a license to print it without it first having been checked for correctness? I swear, a teacher who cannot write a single line correctly in the language that he is teaching ought to be sent back to school immediately, despite which some of these professors cannot understand if spoken to, never mind their ignorance of writing, and cannot understand if they read and cannot form the words properly when doing so. I once heard a student reading to his teacher from the *Maqāmāt* of al-Ḥarīrī, and he was barely able to enunciate clearly a single one of the letters that their 5.3.8

الحريرى ولا يكاد ينطق بحرف واحد نطقا بيّنا من هذه الحروف التى خلت منها
لغتهم * وهى الثآ والحآ والخآ والذال والصاد والضاد والطا والظا والعين والغين
والقاف والهآ * وشيخه ساكت لما انه يعلم ان تصحيحه له لا يكون الّا فاسدا *
فكيف يمكن لمن لم يسمع اللغة من اهلها ان يحسن النطق بها * كيف لا وان
من الّف منهم في نحو لغتنا شيا فانما بنى نحوه كله على فساد * فانهم يترجمون عن
الجيم بلساننا بحرفى الدال والجيم بلسانهم * وقد جهلوا انه ليس عندنا فى العربية
حروف مركبة كما فى اليونانية * فان الابتدآء بالساكن مرفوض عند العرب اذا لم
نقل انه ممتنع * ويترجمون عن الثآء بالتآ والسين وعن الذال بالتآ والزاى وكذا عن
الظآء * فاما سائر الحروف فالعين والهآ والحآء عندهم همزة والخا كاف والصاد
سين والضاد دال والطآء تآء والقاف كاف * وينطقون بالسين اذا تقدمتها حركة
كالزاى وعلى ذلك قول ذلك المطران الخطيب اقطعوا الازباب كما مرّ * فاما
الهمزة فانها وان وقعت عندهم فى اوائل الالفاظ فلا تقع متوسطة ولا متطرفة
ولا يمكنهم النطق بها الا ملينة * بل اعظم مولفيهم لا يدرى ان الالف فى اول
الكلام لا تكون الا همزة * وليس الغرض هنا تعليمهم الهمز فانهم همّازون * وانما ٩،٣،٥
الغرض ان ابيّن لهذا الرملىّ الهارف المتملّق مناضلة عن شيوخى الذين اخذت
عنهم من العلم ما اخذت ان شيوخه لا يُحسَبون فى عداد العلمآء * وانه ليس
من علمآء مصر وتونس والغرب والشام والحجاز وبغداد مَن هو محتاج لاخذ حرف
واحد عنهم * نعم انّ لهم باعًا طويلا فى التاريخ فيعرفون مثلا ان ابا تمام والبحترى
كانا متعاصرين * وان الثانى اخذ عن الاول * وان المتنبى كان متاخّرا عنهما *
وان الحريرى الّف خمسين مقامة حذا بها حذو البديع وما اشبه ذلك * الا انهم
لا يفهمون كتبهم * ولا يدرون جزل الكلام من ركيكه * وثبته من مصنوعه *

language is without—*th*, *ḥ*, *kh*, *dh*, *ṣ*, *ṭ*, *ẓ*, *ʿ*, *gh*, *q*, and *h*—and his teacher said nothing because he knew that any correction he might make would be wrong. How can anyone who has not heard the language from its native speakers pronounce it well? How can it not be so when any of them who has written anything on the grammar of our language has based it entirely on false ideas? Thus, they transcribe the letter *j* of our tongue with the two letters *d* and *j* of theirs,[395] ignoring the fact that there are no compound letters in Arabic such as exist in Greek, since for a word to begin with a double consonant is unacceptable, if not indeed inadmissible, among the Arabs. Likewise, they transcribe *th* as *ts*, and *dh* and *ẓ* as *tz*. As for the rest of the letters, *ʿ*, *h*, and *ḥ* are all glottal stops to them, *kh* is *k*, *ṣ* is *s*, *ḍ* is *d*, *ṭ* is *t*, and *q* is *k*, and they pronounce *s* preceded by a vowel as *z*. The preaching metropolitan's "cut off *azbābakum*" mentioned earlier is an example.[396] The glottal stop may occur in their language at the beginnings of words but not in the middle or at the end, and they can only pronounce it as a glide; indeed, most of their writers are unaware that an *alif* at the start of a word has to be pronounced as a stop.

It is not my intention here to teach them how to pronounce the glottal 5.3.9
stop with the proper bite—they are already (back) biters enough—but to demonstrate to this ingratiating, toadying sandman,[397] in defense of those shaykhs of mine to whom I owe whatever knowledge I may have acquired, that his shaykhs are not to be considered scholars and that not one of the scholars of Cairo, Tunis, the Maghreb, Damascus, the Hejaz, or Baghdad has need of a single letter from them. True, they have a deep knowledge of literary history. They know, for example, that Abū Tammām and al-Buḥturī were contemporaries and that the second took from the first, and that al-Mutanabbī came after them and that al-Ḥarīrī wrote fifty *maqāmah*s that advanced the *badīʿ* style and so on. They do not, however, understand the books these people wrote and cannot tell fine language from lame or established usage from invention, or recognize well-executed ideational and verbal devices or fine lexical differences or literary or grammatical jokes or poetical terminology. The most that can be said is that they have acquired a shallow knowledge of the scholarship of the Arabs via books written in French—and would they grant that an Arab who had learned their language

ولا المحسنات اللفظية والمعنوية * ولا الدقائق اللغوية * ولا النكات الادبية ولا
النحوية * ولا الاصطلاحات الشعرية * فغاية ما يقال انهم نتفوا نتفة من علوم
العرب بواسطة كتب الّفت بالفرنساوية * فهل يسلّمون لعربىّ تعلّم لغتهم من كتب
١٠،٣،٥ لغته بانه كعلمائهم وانهم محتاجون الى التخرّج عنه * ثم لا ينكر ايضا ان مسيو
دساسى (De Sacy) حصّل بقوة اجتهاده ما اقدره على فهم كثير من كتبنا بل
على الانشآء فى لغتنا ايضا * ولكن ما كلّ بيضآء شحمة * على انه رحمه الله لا يُنظَم
فى سلك العلمآء المحرّرين * فقد فاته اشيآء كثيرة فى الادب واللغة والعروض *
وانى طالما والله اثنيت على براعته واعظمت علمه وفضله * الا انه لما صارت
مهارته وبراعته هذه سببا للفساد فانها هى التى جرّات غيره على التصدّر للتدريس
بلغتنا وسوّت لهذا المفترى ان يتطاول على اهل العلم * كان من الواجب علىّ رعايةً
لحقّ العلم واهله ان اُسطر اسمه من بين اسمآء الشيوخ فى البلاد الاسلامية كافّة *
قدعا لمن تترس باسمه واستذرع بعلمه عن الدعوى والانتحال * ولولا فحش قول
هذا النقّاع المتحذلق وكذب دعواه لما تعرّضت لتخطئة احد منهم * فانى اعلم انهم لن
يرعووا عن غيّهم وما يزيدهم كلامى هذا الا غرورا * بل الشيوخ الذين قضوا عمرهم
فى طلب العلم يتورّعون من ان يقولوا مقالته * لان الانسان كلما زاد علمه زادت
معرفته بجهله * ولعل كتابى هذا يقع فى يد استاذ فارسىّ او هندى فيكون باعثا لهما
على الانتداب لتخطئتهم ايضا فى هاتين اللغتين * لانى اعلم عين اليقين انهم فيهما
اشد جهلا * لان الذين سافروا منهم الى بلاد العرب اكثر من الذين سافروا الى
١١،٣،٥ غيرها * ومع ذلك فلم يتعلّموا منها سوى الركاكة والخطل * واعلم ايها القارى العربى
انى لم اجد من بين جميع ما طبعوا بلغتنا جديرا بالانتقاد سوى مقامات الحريرى *
وانى لضيق وقتى حالة كونى على جناح السفر لم يمكن لى النظر الا فى ابيات الشرح

from books in his own was the equal of their own scholars, or that they needed to be educated by him?

At the same time, it cannot be denied that Monsieur de Sacy acquired 5.3.10
through his own efforts enough skill to be able to understand many of our books and even indeed to write in our language. However, "not everything white is a truffle."[398] Despite all of the foregoing he should not, God rest his soul, be placed among the ranks of the most reliable scholars, for he failed to grasp numerous matters in the areas of literature, lexicon, and prosody and I have, I swear, praised his command of the field and lauded his scholarship and merit time and time again. However, when this skill and command of his became a cause of evil—for they it was that emboldened others to take a leading role in teaching our language and seduced this liar into adopting an insolent attitude toward our scholars—I felt it my duty, out of concern for the rights of scholarship and scholars, to delete his name from among those of the shaykhs of the Islamic countries in their entirety as a slap in the face to those who have sheltered behind it and used his scholarship as a cover for false claims and arrogations. Were it not for the monstrous words of this pseudo-erudite blusterer, I would never have taken the time to point out the faults of any of them, as I know that they will never abandon their error and that these words of mine will only make them more arrogant. In contrast, those shaykhs who devote their lives to the pursuit of knowledge hesitate to say what it is that they have achieved, for the more a person's knowledge increases, the more he becomes cognizant of how little he knows. This book of mine may fall into the hands of a Persian or Indian professor and motivate them to take on the task of pointing out their faults in those two languages too, for I am absolutely certain that they are even more ignorant where those are concerned, since more of them have traveled to the Arab lands than to any others (despite which they have learned nothing from them but lame language and nonsense).

Know, my dear Arab reader, that the only work among all those that they 5.3.11
have printed in our language that I have found worthy of close consideration is the *Maqāmāt* of al-Ḥarīrī[399] and, given the limited time available due to my being about to travel, I was able to look only at the verses in the commentary; I have entrusted to others the task of critiquing the rest just as certain

فقط * وقد وكلت غيرى فى نقد الباقى كما وكلنى العلمآء فى نقد الابيات * ثم عثرت بعد ذلك برحلة العالم الاديب الشيخ محمد بن[1] السيد عمر التونسى مطبوعة على الحجر عن خط مسيو پيرون وقد شحنها كلها بالتحريف والغلط مما لا تصح نسبته الى ادنى تلامذة الشيخ المذكور * ايمكن لاحد من الطلبة فضلا عن العالم ان يقول جوده ناسخ لكل الوجود اى لكل الجود- وان يكتب العصا باليآء غير مرة - واعلى افعل التفضيل بالالف نحو عشرين مرة - ونجا باليا- واتعمى المعالمون عن الضيآ اى ايعمى العالمون- وامنين مطمئنين حالة كونهما مرفوعين- وفلاحين مصر- ومحمودين السيرة- واستوزر الفقيهَ مالك- ولا يعصا- ولا ارى سوء رايك اى لا ارا سوى رايك - ويتعدّا رايه- واثنى عشر ملك - ومن حيث ان اباديما والتكنياوى متعادلين لَم اى متعادلان فلَم- وتجد الرجال والنسآ حسان - ودَعَى لنا- وعجوبة- وصواحبتها وصواحباتها- ولغة فيها حماس- وانهما متقاربتى المعنى- وحتى تاتى ارباب الماشية فيقبضون- فهل احدى منكم- ويرفعون اصواتهم بذلك حتى يدخلون- وماشيِيْن- والمسمّيين- وحتى يشقون- ومنخيون- وانهم يكونوا- ولا اعتاض اى لأعْتاض * او انه يجهل بحور الشعر فيجعل الكامل هزجا والطويل
مديدا وما اشبه ذلك * ومن العجب ان الشيخ الموما اليه اورد هذين البيتين وهما ١٢،٣،٥

ابرك الايام يوم قيل لى   هذه طيبة هذى الكُتُبُ
هذه روضة طٰه المصطفى   هذه الزرقا لديكم فاشربوا

قال واليآء فى هذى بدل عن الهآء * فلما قراهما بعض التلامذة على مسير كُتان دُ پرسُفال (Caussin De Perceval) احد المدرّسين العظام اصلح

١ ١٨٥٥: ابن.

scholars entrusted me with that of critiquing the verses. Subsequently, I came across the travels of the scholar and writer Shaykh Muḥammad ibn al-Sayyid ʿUmar al-Tūnusī[400] in the form of a lithograph based on a copy in the hand of Monsieur Perron,[401] who had freighted the whole book with misspellings and mistakes of a sort for which it would be unreasonable to hold even the least of the aforesaid shaykh's students responsible. Is it possible that any student, let alone scholar, could say *jūduhu nāsikhun li-kulli l-wujūd* in place of *li-kulli l-jūd* or write, more than once, *al-ʿaṣā* with a *y*,[402] or, more than twenty times, *aʿlā* as an elative with an *alif*[403] or *najā* with a *yā'*[404] or *ataʿmā l-muʿālimūna ʿani l-ḍiyā'* for *ayaʿmā l-ʿālimūna* or *āminīna muṭma'innīna* when these words occur in the nominative[405] or *fallāḥīna Miṣr*[406] or *maḥmūdīna l-sīrah*[407] or *istawzara l-faqīha Mālik*[408] or *lā yaʿṣā*[409] or *lā arā sū'a ra'yak* for *lā arā siwā ra'yaka* or *yataʿaddā ra'yahu*[410] or *ithnay ʿashara malik*[411] or *min ḥaythu inna abādīmā wa-l-takaniyāwī mutāʿadilayni lam* for *min ḥaythu inna abādīmā wa-l-takaniyāwī mutāʿadilayni*[412] *fa-lam* or *tajidu l-rijāla wa-l-nisā'a ḥisān*[413] or *daʿā lanā*[414] or *ʿujūbah*[415] or *ṣawāḥibatuhā* and *ṣawāḥibātuhā*[416] or *lughatun fīhā ḥamās*[417] or *innahumā mutaqāribayi l-maʿnā*[418] or *ḥattā ta'tiya arbābu l-māshiyati fa-yaqbiḍūn*[419] or *fa-hal iḥdā minkum*[420] or *yarfaʿūna aṣwātahum bi-dhālika ḥattā yadkhulūn*[421] or *māshiyīn*[422] or *al-musammayayn*[423] or *ḥattā yashuqqūn*[424] or *munḥaniyūn*[425] or *innahum yakūnū*[426] or *lā-ʿtāḍa*[427] or not know the poetic meters, so that he takes *kāmil* for *hazaj*, *ṭawīl* for *madīd*, and so on?

It is amazing that the aforementioned shaykh quotes the following lines[428] 5.3.12

abraku l-ayyāmi yawmun qīla lī
hādhihi Ṭībatu hādhī l-Kuthubū
hādhihi rawḍatu Ṭāhā l-muṣṭafā
hādhihi l-Zarqā'u ladaykum fa-shrabū

(The most blessed of days was that on which it was said to me
"This is Thebes! This is al-Kuthub![429]
This is the garden of Ṭāhā the Chosen![430]
This, before you, is the Bright One,[431] so drink!")

explaining in his commentary that "the *yā'* in *hādhī* is in place of the [second] *hā'*"[432] and yet when a student read them to Monsieur Caussin de Perceval, one of the mighty teachers in question, the latter corrected his pronunciation of Ṭāhā to *waṭ'* ("treading"), explaining it as meaning "the treading of

قوله طه بوَطًا وفسرها بوَطْ الرِجْل * وابدل الهآء من قوله هذه الزرقا يآء وذلك لقول الشيخ واليآء فى هذى بدل عن الهآء فانكسر الوزن * وترك لفظة الزرقا غير مصحّحة فان مسيو پيرون وضع بعد الالف همزة فانكسر بها الوزن ايضا * وحق وط ان تكتب بغير الف * فانظر الى الناقل والمصحّح والى هذا التخليط وتعجّب *

the foot," and changed the [second] *hā'* in the words *hādhihi l-Zarqā'u* to *yā'* because of the words of the shaykh "the *yā'* in *hādhī* is in place of the *hā'*,"[433] throwing the meter off in the process. He also left *al-Zarqā'u* uncorrected (Monsieur Perron having put a *hamzah* after the *alif*),[434] which again broke the meter. *Waṭ'* should properly be written without an *alif*.[435] Observe, then, the copyist and the correcter, and all this confusion, and wonder!

بيان ما وجدته من تحريف الالفاظ العربية فى نقل الرسائل الفارسية فى كتاب الشيخ الكسندر شدزكو الرملى (Alexandre Chodzko[1])

١،٤،٥

صفحة	سطر		
١٩٢	ا	فى ما	صوابه فيما كما هو باصله *
-	٤	التيام	صوابه التئام كما فى الاصل *
١٩٢	٩	شخامت	صوابه شهامت كما فى الاصل *
-	٢٢	به مملكت	صوابه بمملكت كما فى الاصل *
١٩٣	٠٦	عظّام	صوابه عظام كما فى الاصل *
-	١٧	استخضار	صوابه استحضار كما فى الاصل *
١٩٦	٢٣	جناب اقدسى الهى	صوابه جناب اقدس الهى كما فى الاصل
-	٢٦	خلافا الاخفش	صوابه خلافا للاخفش كما فى الاصل *
١٩٧	٤	براءُ الساعة	صوابه برءُ الساعة كما فى الاصل *
١٩٨	-	قانع صفصف	صوابه قاع صفصف وقد تقدم ذكر ذلك *
٢٠٠	-	(اول الرسالة) ومبارك سلطانه	صوابه وتبارك ليقابل قوله اوّلاً تعالى شانه *
٢٠١	١٨	مولات	صوابه موالات *

على انى لم اتقصّ معارضة هذه الرسائل كلها بالاصل اذ الغرض اظهار كذب هذا المدّعى وفيما اوردته كفاية *

---

١ ١٨٥٥: Chodozko

List of Misspelled Arabic Words that I Discovered in the Transcriptions of Letters in Persian in the Book by "the Sandy Shaykh," Alexandre Chodźko

Page	Line	Misspelling	Correct spelling	5.4.1
192	1	*fī mā*	*fīmā* (as in the original)	
"	4	*iltiyām*	*ilti'ām* (as in the original)	
192	9	*shakhāmat*	*shahāmat* (as in the original)	
"	22	*bih mamlakat*	*bi-mamlakat* (as in the original)	
193	6	*ʿaẓẓām*	*ʿiẓām* (as in the original)	
"	17	*istikhḍār*	*istiḥḍār* (as in the original)	
196	23	*janāb aqdasī ilāhī*	*janāb aqdas ilāhī* (as in the original)	
"	26	*khilāfan al-Akhfash*	*khilāfan li-l-Akhfash* (as in the original)	
197	4	*barā'u l-sāʿah*	*bar'u l-sāʿah* (as in the original)	
198	"	*qāniʿ ṣafṣaf*	*qāʿ ṣafṣaf* (mentioned above)[436]	
200	" (Opening of the epistle) *wa-mubārakun sulṭānuhu*		*wa-tabāraka* etc. to match *awwalan taʿālā sha'nuhu*	
201	18	*mawlāt*	*mawālāt*	

and this despite the fact that I have not gone to the lengths of comparing every one of these epistles with the original, the point being simply to demonstrate the mendacity of his claim, what I have cited being sufficient for that purpose.

جدول اغلاط ابيات الشواهد فى مقامات الحريرى التى طبعت ثانية بعد وفاة دساسى (De Sacy) بتصحيح الشيخين الجليلين رينو ودرنبورغ (Reineaud et Darenbourg) وذلك سنة ١٨٤٧ فاما غلط الشرح فاكثر من ان يعدّ

صفحة	سطر			
				١،٥،٥
ه	١	تَرب فى موضعين	والصواب بالضم *	
–	٤	المجلَس	وصوابه بالكسر *	
–	١٠	غضاباً	صوابه بغير تنوين لانه وقع قافية *	
ح	٤	قالوا العواذل	الوجه قال العواذل فان العواذل جمع عاذلة *	
–	٩	خَدَرَت	والوجه خَدِرَت *	
–	١٣	فى النثر ذميما	والصواب دميما *	
	١٠	فى صفحة العنوان	تكتب والاعرف نكتب *	
٦	..	وان اصدق بيت	الاظهر احسن بيت *	
١١	١٧	الكرا	والوجه الكَرَى لانه يآىّ *	
١٨	..	ثنًى	الاعرف ثَنَى *	
٤١	..	فُيظلمونى	حقه فيَظلمونى *	٢،٥،٥
٤٩	١٧	ياطلحَ اكرمُ من	والوجه اكرمَ من	
٥١	١٥	فانه بنَثٍّ[1]	والوجه يُنَثُّ *	
٥٢	..	اقترحتُ العشآءَ عليه يوما	وصوابه اقترحت العشآء يوما عليه *	

---

١ ١٨٥٥: بَنثٍ.

Table Showing the Mistakes in the Probative Verses in the *Maqāmāt* of al-Ḥarīrī which appeared in a second edition, with corrections by the two eminent shaykhs Reinaud and Derenbourg,[437] in 1847 following the death of de Sacy; the mistakes in the commentary itself are too numerous to count[438]

Page	Line	[Incorrect]	[Correct]	
				5.5.1
ه	1	تَرب[439] (twice)	تُرب	
"	4	المجلَس	المجِلس	
"	10	غضاباً	Should be without *tanwīn*, for the rhyme.	
ح	4	قالواالعواذل	قال العواذل, as العواذل is the plural of عاذل.[440]	
"	9	خَدَرَت	خَدِرَت	
"	13	(in the prose) ذميما	دميما	
Title page 10		تكتب	نكتب is the more common reading.	
6	[17][441]	وان اصدق بيت	The more obvious reading would be احسن بيت.	
11	17	الكرا	الكرى because the root is with ى	
18	[10]	ثنَّى	ثَنَى is the more common reading.	
41	[24]	فيُظلمونى	فيَظلمونى	
49	17	ياطلحَ اكرمُ من	اكرمَ من	5.5.2
51	15	فانه بنَثٍّ	يُنَثُّ	
52	[26]	اقترحتُ العشآءَ عليه يوما	اقترحت العشآء يوما عليه	

صفحة	سطر			
–	..	قال لِىَ ٱلعشا	والوجه لى ٱلعشا لانه اخرج مخرج الامثال فلا تتغير كقوله الصيفَ ضيّعتِ اللبن *	
٦٩[١]	..	مبرّاءً	وصوابه مُبرَّءًا *	
٧٠	..	نراه	وحقه تراه *	
٧١	..	احسنُ من	وصوابه احسنَ لانه خبر ليس *	
٧٥	١٣	نيلِ المنا	وصوابه المُنَى لانه جمع مُنية *	٣،٥،٥
٧٦	١٠	الأَفلاس	وصوابه الإِفلاس *	
–	١٢	فى عُسْر وفى يُسَر	وصوابه ويُسُر *	
٧٨	٢١	سُلَّماً	صوابه سُلَّما بغير تنوين لوقوعه قافية *	
٨٠	٨	فى ما	الوجه فيما *	
–	–	سبيلٌ	صوابه سبيلُ ومثله دليل فى البيت الثانى *	
٨٢	..	رَكِدَ	صوابه رَكَدَ *	
٨٤	..	وكونٌ	حقه بغير تنوين *	
٨٦	١٠	جُمَّةَ	صوابه جَمَّةَ *	
–	–	امرءَ	الوجه امرأ *	
–	١٧	فانياً	صوابه فانيا بلا تنوين *	

١ ١٨٥٥: ٢٩.

Page	Line	[Incorrect]	[Correct]	
"	[27]	قال لِيَ ٱلعشا	لى ٱلعشا because he uses the word [and what follows] with the force of a proverb,[442] in which case it does not change, as when one says الصيفَ ضيّعتِ اللبن.[443]	
69	[12]	مبَرّاءً	مُبرّاءٍ ا	
70	[9]	نراه	تراه	
71	[23]	احسنُ من	احسنَ because it is the predicate of ليس.	
75	13	نيل المنا	المُنَى because it is the plural of مُنية.	5.5.3
76	10	الأَفلاس	الإِفلاس	
"	12	فى عَسْرو فى يُسَر	يُسُر	
78	21	سُلَمًا	سلَمًا without *tanwīn* as it is the rhyme word.	
80	8	فى ما	فيما	
"	"	سبيلٌ	سبيلُ, and likewise دليل in the second line of verse.	
82	[11]	رَكَدٌ	رَكَدَ	
84	[26]	وكونٌ	Without *tanwīn*.	
86	10	جُمّةً	جَمّةَ	
"	"	امرءَ	امرأ	
"	17	فانيًا	فانيا without *tanwīn*.	

صفحة	سطر		
٨٩		ومن يلقَ ما لاقيت لا بد يارقُ ارقتُ فلم تخدع بعيني نعسةٌ ٤،٥،٥	والصواب تقديم المصراع الثانى وتاخير الاول والعجب ان هذه النعسة اغمضت عين كل من دساسى ومن هذين الشيخين الجليلين فهل سمعتم يامعاشر العرب وياامة الثقلين ان الفعل المضارع يقع عروضا من غير تصريع وان التنوين فى نعسة وامثالها نحو تعسة وحقة وحبقة وسلحة وفحة يقع قافية اليس قوله ومن يلقَ مفرّعا على المصراع الاول ومخرجا مخرج المثل *
٩٢	١٩	البلاقعَ	صوابه البلاقعا بالاطلاق لكونه قافية *
٩٣	١٣	بدنًا	صوابه بدنا بغير تنوين وهلّا انتبه المدرسون لذلك بقوله فى العروض اَنا *
٩٧	٢٢	اليهُم	ما سبب هذا التبلتع *
١١٠	١٨	يغدوا	صوابه يَغْدو وفيه مهمومٍ ومهدومٍ وكلثومٍ والصواب حذف التنوين منها *
١١١	٧	ارءَف	حقه اَرْأَف *
-	٩	بَنةُ	صوابه اَبْنة *
-	١١	مجذب	صوابه مجدب *
١١٣	١٧	مراحًا - مفاحًا	صوابه بغير تنوين *

Page	Line	[Incorrect]	[Correct]

89 ومن يلقَ ما لاقيت لا بد يارقُ ارقتُ فلم تخدع بعينى نعسةٌ (“And he who meets with what I have met with must surely spend the night unsleeping / I spent the night unsleeping, and never a wink of sleep seduced my eye”) 5.5.4

The hemistichs should be reversed. The strange thing is that this *naʿsah* (“wink of sleep”) closed the eyes of both de Sacy and the other two eminent shaykhs. Did you ever—you Arabs and you nation of men-and-jinn!—hear of a rhyme word (here an imperfect verb) occurring as the last foot of an initial hemistich unless both hemistich-final words are rhymed or of the tanwīn in *naʿsah* or similar words such as *taʿsah* (“an instance of wretchedness”), *ḥamqah* (“an instance of stupidity”), *ḥabqah* (“a fart”), *salḥah* (“a turd”), or *faqḥah* (“an anal orifice”) occurring as the rhyming syllable?[444] Do not the words *wa-man yalqa* (“And he who meets with”) follow naturally from the first hemistich and are they not proclaimed as having the force of a proverb?

Page	Line	[Incorrect]	[Correct]
92	19	البلاقعَ	البلاقعا with prolongation of the vowel for the rhyme.[445]
93	13	بدناً	بدنا without tanwīn. How could these “teachers” not have noticed this, given that the last word of the first hemistich is أَنا?[446]
97	22	اليهُم	What could be the cause of such contortedness?[447]
110	18	يغدوا	يَغْدو; in the same line مهمومِ and مهدومِ and كلثومِ also occur, all of which should properly be without *tanwīn*.
111	7	اريف	آرَأَف
"	9	بنةٌ	آبِنة
"	11	مجذب	مجدب
113	17	مراحاً . . . مفاحاً	Without *tanwīn*.

صفحة	سطر			
١١٥	..	متيّمٌ اثرُها	صوابه اثرَها اذكيف يصح نسبة التتيّم للاثر واعجب من ذلك تنوين متبول ومكبول فكيف تفعلون يااساتيذ بالغول ارايتم كيف يُوقع التحذلق فى المخازى مع ان قصيدة كعب اشهر من نار على علم *	
١٢٣	١١	شيًا	والصواب شيّا ليوافق قوله يديًا وحيّا *	٥،٥،٥
١٢٤	..	الآدِبُ	والصواب الادبَ لانه مفعول لقوله لا ترى *	
١٢٥	..		جميع قوافى القصيدة المسمَّطة ينبغى ان تكون مقيدة	
١٣٢	..	دَنى	الوجه دنا لكونه واويًا *	
١٣٤	٥	كتمانى	صوابه كتمانِ *	
١٣٧	..	ناصبٍ	صوابه ناصبِ *	
١٤٦	١٦	نُثنى	صوابه نَثنى *	
١٤٧	..	اَسْفار	صوابه اَشْفار فما للاَسفار هنا وللعين ياايها المبصرون *	
١٥٢	..	حسرانًا	صوابه حسرانا بغير تنوين *	
١٥٨	١٦	صَناعة	صوابه بالكسر *	
–	٢٥	مظهرًا	صوابه بغير تنوين *	
١٥٩	٢٦	سَنّا	صوابه سَنًّى *	٦،٥،٥
١٦٩	١٢	ورُبَّتَ	حقه وربَّتْ *	
١٧٤	١٣	خُمَسَ كفّك	صوابه خَمْس *	

Page	Line	[Incorrect]	[Correct]	
115	[20]	متيّمٌ اثرُها	اثرَها since how can *tatayyum* ("enslavement to love") be attributed to *ithr* ("after")?[448] Even stranger are the *tanwīn* on متبول and مكبول! How would you deal, my dear professors, with a غول?[449] Do you not observe how such affected erudition draws people into shameful situations? Not to mention that Kaʿb's poem[450] is known to all.	
123	11	شيًا	شيّا, to agree with يديّا and حيّا.	5.5.5
124	[16]	الآدِبُ	الادبَ because it is the object of لا ترى.	
125	[1–11]		All the rhyming syllables of the *qaṣīdah muṣammaṭah*[451] should be "fettered."[452]	
132	[11]	دَنى	دنا, because it is from the root *d-n-w*.	
134	5	كتمانى	كتمانِ	
137	[24]	ناصبٍ	ناصبِ	
146	16	نُثنى	نَثنى	
147	[20]	أسْفار	أشْفار ("outer edge of the eyelid"), and what have اسفار ("books") to do with the eye, O you who see well?	
152	[15]	حسرانًا	حسرانا without *tanwīn*.	
158	16	صَناعة	صِناعة	
"	25	مظهرًا	Without *tanwīn*.	
159	26	سَنا	سَنًى	5.5.6
169	12	ورُبَّتْ	ورُبَّتَ	
174	13	خُمُسَ كفّك	خَمْس	

صفحة	سطر			
١٧٧	..	بَكور	صوابه بالضم وفيه ايضا تشميتاً وصوابه بغير تنوين	
١٧٩	..	فى الدعوةِ – الى الجفوةِ	والصواب الوقوف على الهآء *	
١٨٣	١٧	خَيارهم	صوابه بالكسر *	
–	١٨	تَسْئَلْ فَسَلْ	الوجه تسأَلْ وَسَلْ *	
١٨٣	٢١	وصُحبه	صوابه بالفتح *	
١٨٥	١٣	المنطَق	صوابه بالكسر *	
–	١٦	عنه	الوجه منه *	
١٨٩	..	البَصْرِ	الوجه البَصَرْ *	٧،٥،٥
–	..	نجئ مكررة مرتين	صوابه تجئ *	
–	..	فطورا	صوابه وطورا *	
–	–	بحميئة	صوابه بحماة *	
١٩٥	١٣	دنى	صوابه دنا *	
١٩٩	..	المِشتاة	صوابه الفتح *	
–	..	ينتقرُ	صوابه ينتقرَ *	
٢٠٤	٧	جُمَّة	صوابه جَمَّة *	
–	..	غمامٍ- زنامٍ	صوابه بغير تنوين *	
٢١	١٢	لاقِى الاحبَّةِ	الوجه لاقَى الاحبَّةَ *	
–	١٥	أَبغِض	صوابه أُبغض *	٨،٥،٥
–	١٨	اليهِمُ	هى من التبلتع بمكان *	
٢١٥	..	إن	الوجه أن *	
٢١٨	٢٤	صروفه	الوجه صروفها الا اذا كان الضمير يرجع الى مذكور قبله	

Page	Line	[Incorrect]	[Correct]	
177	[18]	بَكور	بُكور, and in the same line تشميتاً, which is correctly without *tanwīn*.	
179	[15]	فى الدعوةِ _ الى الجفوةِ	The pausal form is required.[453]	
183	17	خَيارهم	خِيارهم	
"	18	تَسْئَلْ فَسَلْ	تَسْأَلْ وَسَلْ	
"	21	وصُحبه	وصَحبه	
185	13	المنطَق	المنطِق	
"	16	عنه	منه	
189	[6]	البَصْرِ	البَصَرْ	5.5.7
"	[23]	نجئ (twice)	تجئ	
"	["]	فطورا	وطورا	
"	"	بحمِئة	بحماة	
195	13	دنى	دنا	
199	[19]	المِشتاة	المَشتاة	
"	["]	ينتقِرُ	ينتقِرْ	
204	7	جُمَّة	جَمَّة	
"	[22–23]	غمامٍ _ زنامٍ	Without *tanwīn*.	
212	12	لاقِى الاحبَّةِ	لاقَى الاحبَّةَ	
"	15	أَبْغِض	أُبْغِض	5.5.8
"	18	اليهمُ	Strangely contorted.[454]	
215	[18]	إن	اَن	
218	24	صروفه	صروفها unless the pronominal suffix refers to something mentioned earlier.[455]	

صفحة	سطر		
٢٢١		قُنبُرة	الاولى قُبَّرة * البيت فى اخر الصفحة *
٢٢٢	١٨	يمنعَ- فترتعَ	صوابه يمنعُ فترتعُ *
٢٣٢	١٧	يصنعُ	حقه يصنعِ *
–	١٨	بدوُه	صوابه بدؤُه *
٢٣٦		اَرْبِهِ - اَدْبِهِ	صوابه اَرَبِهْ اَدَبِهْ *
٢٣٧	..	وانَّ منّى لَوّا	الوجه وان لَوّا عَناءُ وكانه ظن ان عناء هنا جار ومجرور وان تاخيرها عن لوّا يكسر وزن البيت فابدلها بمنّى وجعل الضمير مفردا *
٢٣٩	١٣	ياعابِثَ الفقر	حقه ياعائب الفقرمع ان لفظة العيب المذكورة فى المصراع الثانى تهدى الاعمى الى فهم البيت ولكن اساتيذنا يحبّون العبث * ٩،٥،٥
٢٤٥	٢٣	اِنَّما	حقه اَنَّما *
٢٤٧	١٤	قوسَا	حقه قوساً *
٢٤٨	١٢	منَ آبن	حقه منِ آبن *
–	–	مامةَ كعبٍ	حقه مامةِ للاضافة *
٢٥٢	..	وَلِهًا	صوابه وَلَها اى ولها عليه رنين *
٢٥٥	..	المقانعَ	صوابه المقانعا *
٢٥٨	١٩	تَسَلَمْ مِنْ أَنْ	صوابه تَسْلَمْ مِنَ آن بحذف الهمزة للوزن

Page	Line	[Incorrect]	[Correct]	
221	[26]	قُنبُرة	قُبَّرة is preferable (line of verse at the end of the page).	
222	18	يمنعَ _فترتعَ	يمنعُ فترتعُ	
232	17	يصنعُ	يصنعِ	
"	18	بدوُه	بدؤُه	
236	[17–18]	اَرْبِهِ _اَدْبِهِ	اَرَبِهْ اَدَبِهْ	
237	[9]	واَنَّ منّى لَوًّا	وان لَوًّا عَنآءُ; he seems to have thought that عنآء here has the function of a preposition followed by its object and that putting it after لوّا would upset the meter, so he changed it to منّى and made the suffix singular.	
239	13	ياعابِثَ الفقر	اعائب الفقر, though the word عيب in the second hemistich ought to be enough to guide a blind man to the meaning of the line; our good professors, however, are fond of foolishness.[456]	5.5.9
245	23	اِنَّما	اَنَّما	
247	14	قوسَا	قوساً	
248	12	منَ آبن	منِ آبن	
"	"	مامةَ كعبٍ	مامةِ because in construct.	
252	[27]	وَلِهًا	وَلَها, i.e., ولها عليه رنين.	
255	11	المقانعَ	المقانعا	
258	19	تَسَلْمْ مِنْ أَنْ	تَسَلَّمْ مِنَ آنْ, the *hamzah* being deleted for the meter.	

صفحة	سطر			
–	٢٣	تَجَرَّبْ سبيل القصد	حقه تَحَرَّ فتصحفت الكلمة على الجميع والذى اوقعهم فى ذلك قول الشاعر فى البيت الثانى لم تجرِبْ * وقوله ولا تُسِىء الظنا حقه تسَيّئ فينكسر الوزن وقوله لدى الخَبر حقه الخُبْر اى الاختبار	
٢٦٠	..		ضَلَّتْ صوابه ضَلَّتِ *	
–	..	بَرغوثا	صوابه بُرغوثا- لولَّتْ صوابه لَوَلَّتِ فليراجعها الاساتيذ فى محلّها فاما فتح البرغوث فهو عجيب من امثالهم اذ ليس فى الكلام فَعْلول الّا صَعْفوق *	
٢٦٢	..	تَهامة	صوابه تِهامة بالكسر *	١٠،٥،٥
٢٦٣	٧	الكاسِ	صوابه الكاسِى *	
–	٨	فانك انت الآكل اللابسُ	صوابه اللاَّسِى من لسا اى اكل اكلا شديدا فكيف يمكن ايها المدرسون العظام ان تكون اللابسُ قافية مع الكاسى مع انهما بمعنى واحد فان الكاسى هنا من كَسِيَ لازماً ولو كان من كسا المتعدى لكان مدحا وهو غير مراد افلا تشعرون *	
–	٢٤	يحفِظ	صوابه يحفَظ *	
٢٦٤	١٨	ممِكّنا	صوابه ممكَّنا *	
٢٦٧	١٨	وهنُ	صوابه بالفتح *	

Page	Line	[Incorrect]	[Correct]	
258	23	تَجَرَّبْ سبيل القصد	تَجَرَّ [سبيل القصد], the word having been misread by everybody, the reason for their error being the poet's use in the following line of the words لم تجرّبْ; the words ولا تُسئ الظنا are properly [ولا] تسيء [الظنا]: the former breaks the meter. Also, the words لدى الخَبر should properly be [لدى] الخُبْر, i.e., "on being tested."	
260	[21]	ضَلَّتْ	ضَلَّتِ	
"	[22]	بَرغوثا	بُرغوثا; لولّت ought to be لَوَلَّتِ; the professors should review the rule. As for *barghūth* with *fatḥah*, it's one of the oddities their like come up with, for there are no words in the language of the pattern *faʿlūl* with the sole exception of *ṣaʿfūq*.	
262	[23]	تَهامة	تِهامة	5.5.10
263	7	الكاسِ	الكاسى	
"	8	فانك انت الآكل اللابسُ	[فانك الآكل] اللاّسِى from لسا meaning "to eat voraciously"; how, mighty teachers, can اللابسُ rhyme with الكاسى, even if they have the same meaning? الكاسى here is from كَسِىَ, which is intransitive; if it were from transitive كسا it would constitute praise, which is not what is required ("Will you not then understand?").[457]	
"	24	يحفِظ	يحفَظ	
264	18	ممكِنا	ممكَنا	
2	18	وهنُ	وهنَ	

صفحة	سطر			
٢٦٩	٢٣	قُلِبَ	حقه قِلْبا *	
٢٧١	١٥	شَتّانِ	حقه شتانَ *	
٢٧٦	٢٠	اللهُ	صوابه اللهَ *	
٢٧٩	٢١	قبلُنا	صوابه قبلَنا *	
٢٨٠	٢٣	لا يستقيم البيت بقوله وتُنقَب فلا بد من ان تكون وتنتقب *		١١،٥،٥
٢٨٧	١٩	وعَمرى	الاولى بالضم فان الشاعر غير متنطّع *	
٢٩٣	٢٢	وشُرب	صوابه بالفتح *	
–	٢٤	لجهنَّمَ	صوابه فى جهنَّمٍ فليراجع *	
٢٩٥	١٦[١]	المُغْزَل	صوابه المِغْزَل *	
–	١٧[٢]	ويَعرِى استُه	الاولى ويُعرى استَه *	
٣٠١	–	فانكَ الطاعم	صوابه فانك انت الطاعم *	
٣٠٣	١٩	والدَرَّ	صوابه والدُرَّ *	
٣١٢	..	ضَبارم	صوابه بالضم *	
٣١٦	..	قبلُهُ- بَعُدُهُ	صوابه قبلَهُ- بَعْدَهُ البيت بآخر الصفحة *	
٣١٩	..	دُرْنا دُرْنَى	الاولى الاقتصار على احداهما *	
٣٢٣	٢٧	جلاجلَ	صوابه جلاجلٍ فان ذا الرمة لم يكن من المتبلتعين	١٢،٥،٥
٣٢٤	١٢	جلاجلَ	عين ما تقدم من اللهوقة وفى البيت الاول نظر	
٣٢٦	١٦	ويُسهِرُ	صوابه ويَسْهَرُ وحَرّاها الظاهر انه جَرّاها *	

١ ١٨٥٥: ١٤. ٢ ١٨٥٥: ١٥.

Page	Line	[Incorrect]	[Correct]	
269	23	قُلبَ	قُلبا	
271	15	شَتّانِ	شتّانَ	
276	20	اللهُ	اللهَ	
279	21	قبلُنا	قبلَنا	
280	23	The line cannot be scanned properly if one reads وتُنَقَّب and it must therefore be وتنتقب.		5.5.11
287	19	وعَمرى	Should be وعُمرى as the poet was not being wordy.[458]	
293	22	وشُرب	وشَرب[459]	
"	24	لجهنَّمَ	فى جهنَّمٍ; the whole thing should be checked.	
295	16	المُغْزَل	المِغزَل	
"	1	ويَعرى استَه	Better, ويُعرى استَه.	
301	"	فانك الطاعم	فانك انت الطاعم	
303	19	والدَرَّ	والدُرَّ	
312	[22]	ضَبارم	ضُبارم	
316	[28]	قبلُهُ _ بَعْدُهُ	قبلَهْ _ بَعْدَهْ (line of verse at the bottom of the page).	
319	[12]	دُرْنا دُرْنى	It would be better to stick with one or the other.[460]	5.5.12
323	27	جلاجلَ	جلاجلٍ, as Dhū l-Rummah was not one to use contorted language.[461]	
324	12	جلاجلَ	The same botched job as before; a parallel form occurs in the first line.[462]	
326	16	ويُسهِرُ	ويَسْهَرُ; and حَرّاها should apparently be جَرّاها	

صفحة	سطر			
٣٢٩	١٧	صئيلة	صوابه ضئيلة *	
٣٣٢	١٩	مَنْجا	صوابه منْجَى *	
٣٣٨	١٢	حُنانَيْك	صوابه بالفتح *	
٣٣٩	..	الى خيبرا	لا يستقيم به البيت فلا بد من ترقيعه بلفظة سوق او نحو ذلك *	
٣٤٢	١٨	مرتهِن	صوابه مرتهَن بالفتح *	
٣٤٣	١٨	عَرَب	صوابه عُرُب *	
٣٤٤	٢٠	فآخَر	صوابه فآخِر بالكسر *	١٣،٥،٥
٣٤٦	٨	ظفَرت	صوابه ظفِرت بالكسر *	
–	٩	القرونُ	الوجه بالفتح وقوله مَنآئِيا ملفوت *	
٣٤٧	..	فى ابيات المتنبى لهوقة كثيرة *		
٣٤٨	..	وقبلُك	صوابه وقبلَك قد تكرر ذلك غير مرة ولا ادرى كيف يصح رفع الظرف عند الاساتيذ *	
٣٤٩	..	ايُّما	صوابه ايّما وقوله الرِزّ لعله بالفتح وهو صوت السمآء	
٣٥٠	٥	اَوّ اَشْرَخ	حقه اَوَ آشْرَخ *	
٣٥٣	..	عُنِيّت فى الخدر عُشرا	الظاهر غُيّبت فى الخدر عَشْرا *	
٣٥٣		والأُنس	صوابه والإِنس بالكسر *	
–	..	عنه	حقه منه *	
٣٥٨	٢١	يغشون حتى ما تهرَّ	صوابه تهرُّ *	١٤،٥،٥
–	–	السُّواد	صوابه بالفتح *	
٣٦١	١٣	اِنَّ	صوابه اَنّ *	

Page	Line	[Incorrect]	[Correct]	
329	17	صئيلة	ضئيلة	
332	19	مَنْجا	منجًى	
338	12	حُنانَيك	حَنانَيك	
339	[20]	الى خبيرا	The line cannot be scanned properly thus; it has to be made right with some word such as سوق.	
342	18	مرتهِن	مرتهَن	
343	18	عَرَب	عُرُب	
344	20	فَآخَر	فَآخِر	5.5.13
346	8	ظفَرت	ظِفرت	
"	9	القرونُ	القرونَ; also, the word مَنآيا is twisted.[463]	
347	[16–26]	Much botched work in the verses of al-Mutanabbī.		
348	[12]	وقبلُك	وقبلَك and this occurs frequently; I have no idea how the good professors think that an adverb can end in *-u*.	
349	[26]	ايُما	ايَّما; also the word الرِزّ should perhaps be الرَزّ (it is the sound of the rain).	
350	5	اَوْ اَشْرَخَ	اَوَ اَشْرَخ	
353	[25]	عُنِيّت فى الخدر عُشرا	Apparently, غُنِيّت فى الخدر عَشْرا.	
353	["]	والأُنس	والإنس	
"	[26]	عنه	منه	
358	21	يغشون حتى ما تهرَّ	[يغشون حتى ما] تهرُّ	5.5.14
"	"	السُّواد	السَّواد	
361	13	اِنَّ	اَنَّ	

صفحة	سطر		
٣٦٦	..	امن تذكر جِيْرانَ	صوابه جيْرانٍ *
٣٦٨	..	النُعْما	صوابه النعْمى *
٣٧٠	١٨	يسلِمِ	صوابه بفتح اللام *
–	٢٥	اِنى	الوجه اَنى *
٣٧٣	٩	رَكِبت	صوابه رِكبت *
٣٧٨	..	سريعةُ	حقه سريعةِ البيت بآخر الصفحة *
٣٨٧	٣	محتِقرا	صوابه محتقرا اسم مفعول *
–	٥	اِنَّ العزّ	صوابه اَنَّ * ١٥،٥،٥
–	٦	بلوغُ	صوابه بالفتح اسم انَّ *
٤٢٥	٢١	اغيدَ	صوابه اَغْيدٍ للوزن وكان ينبغى للاساتيذ ان يفطنوا لذلك لقول الشاعر فى القافية احورِ *
٤٣٣	١٢	ظفرِكَ-امرِكَ-بقدرِكَ	والصواب فيها كلها الوقف بالسكون على الكاف *
–	٢٣	فالنَعْشُ ادنى لها من ان اقول لَعا	والصواب فالتعس فان مراده اَنْ اقول لها تعساً اولى من قولى لَعا وانما تهور الاساتيذ فى ذلك لذكر النعش قبله حيث قال ويقال لا لعا لفلان اى لا اقامه الله من عثرته ولا نعشه غير ان العبارة صريحة فى ان لعا ونعشا بمعنى واحد فكيف يتخرج قوله اذا فالنعش ادنى لها من اقول لعا *
٤٣٨	١٥	نَسبتى	صوابه بالضمّ او بالكسرة *

Page	Line	[Incorrect]	[Correct]	
366	[19]	امن تذكر جِيْرانَ	[امن تذكر] جيْرانٍ	
368	[25]	النُّعْما	النعْمى	
370	18	يسلِمِ	يسلَمِ	
"	25	اِنى	اَنى	
373	9	رَكِبت	رِكبت	
378	[24]	سريعةُ	سريعةِ (line at the bottom of the page).[464]	
387	3	محتِقِرا	محتقَرا	
"	5	اِنَّ العزّ	اَنَّ [العزّ]	5.5.15
"	6	بلوغُ	بلوغَ (following *anna*).	
425	21	اغيدَ	اَغْيدِ, for the meter, and the good professors should have realized that in view of the poet's using احورِ for the rhyme.	
433	12	ظفرِكَ . . . امرِكَ . . . بقدرِكَ	All should have sukūn on the *kāf*.	
"	23	فالنَّعْشُ ادنى لها من ان اقول لَعا	[فالتَّعْسُ [ادنى لها من ان اقول لَعا is the correct reading. The poet means "It is better for me to say *ta*ʿ*s* to her than to say *la*ʿ*ā*." However, the good professors rushed to write what they did because of the earlier occurrence of *na*ʿ*sh*, when he says "and one says, 'May there be no *la*ʿ*ā* to so-and-so,' meaning 'May God not raise so-and-so after stumbling or from his bier!'" Despite this, it is clear enough from the way the verses are written that *la*ʿ*ā* and *na*ʿ*sh* have the same meaning, so how then could he come up with فالنَّعْشُ ادنى لها من ان اقول لَعا?	
438	15	نَسبتى	نِسبتى or نُسبتى	

صفحة	سطر			
٤٥٢	١٣	وحُبَّ بها مقتولةٍ	صوابه مقتولةً *	
–	٢٥	فَأُظهِرَ فى الالوان مِنْ أَلْدَمِ الدَّمُ	وهى عبارة مختلة لا يستقيم بها وزن البيت فلا بد من ترقيعه بلفظة ذا بعد قوله مِن او نحو ذلك والا فكيف يسوغ تسكين نون من وبعدها اداة التعريف *	
–	٢٧	آدَمَ	صوابه آدمٍ للوزن وفى المصراع الثانى نظر *	
٤٥٥	٥	أُغلى السَّبآءَ	صوابه بالكسر *	١٦،٥،٥
–	–	خَتامها	صوابه خِتامها *	
٤٥٩	١٩	كَلّاً	حقه كلًّا *	
٤٦٣	١٨	زُبرقان	والصواب بالكسر *	
–	..	قبلُك	والصواب بالفتح وهذه خامس مرّة فهل تتورّكون على الطبّاع كما هو شانكم اليوم وفى قوله عَوَلَ[١] نظر *	
٤٧٧	١١	تعاقَبَ	صوابه تعاقِبَ *	
–	١٩	الأُنثى	حقه التليين للوزن *	
٤٨٠	٢٥	ضُوء	الوجه بالفتح *	
٤٨٤	٢٤	البُسَيْطة	صوابه البَسِيْطة فاما المصغَّرة فلا يدخلها ال *	
–	٢٥	زَجاج	الوجه بالضم وكذا قوله سابقا الضَرّ *	

١ ١٨٥٥: عَوْلُ.

Page	Line	[Incorrect]	[Correct]	
452	31	وحُبَّ بها مقتولةٍ	[وحُبَّ بها] مقتولةً	
"	25	فأُظهِرَ فى الالوان مِنْ أَلدَّمِ الدَّمُ	The expression is grammatically disordered and it is impossible to scan the line as it stands. It must be repaired by inserting the word *dhā* or something of the sort [between *min* and *al-dami*]. Otherwise, how can the *sukūn* on the *nūn* of *min* be accepted, when it is followed by the definite article?	
"	27	آدَمَ	آدَمِ, <u>for the meter</u>; cf. the second hemistich.	
455	5	أُغلى السَّبآءَ	اِغلى [السَّبآءَ]	5.5.16
"	"	خَتامها	خِتامها	
459	19	كَلاًّ	كَلاَّ	
463	18	زُبرقان	زِبرقان	
"	[19]	قبلُك	قبلَك, this being the fifth time; are you going to put the blame on the printer as is your wont these days? Compare عَوْلَ.[465]	
477	11	تعاقَبْ	تعاقِبْ	
"	19	الأُنثى	With elision [*al-unthā* instead of *al-ʾunthā*] for the meter.	
480	25	ضُوء	ضَوء	
484	24	البُسَيْطة	البَسِيْطة, the diminutive not being allowed to take the definite article.[466]	
"	25	زَجاج	زُجاج, and the same goes for الضَرّ occurring earlier.	

صفحة	سطر			
–	٢٨	قبلُه	صوابه بالفتح لكونه ظرفا لكونه ظرفا لكونه ظرفا فهل تورّكون على الطبّاع *	١٧،٥،٥
٤٨٧	١٩	يبدو محاسنه	حقه تبدو	
٤٩٣	١٩	مناهِلُ	صوابه مناهلٌ لكونه وقع عروضا فليراجع *	
–	..	وفى البيتين الاخرين تلهوق وخروج عن الفصيح *		
٤٩٤	..	فى بيت المتنبى تنطّع * ويالكِ من خداسيل فى البيت الاخر صوابه ويالكَ *		
٥٠١	..	اشتوا	صوابه شَتَوا وقوله مثلَ حقه بالرفع *	
٥٠٣	١٣	جَنائِى وخَياره	صوابه جناىَ وخِياره *	
٥٠٨	٢٢	لِذُوى الالباب وذى	صوابه لذَوى الالباب او ذى *	
٥٠٩	١٢	والنَّجِ	صوابه بالضم *	
–	١٣	تُقاذف	صوابه بالفتح اصله تتقاذف حذفت التآ الاولى للتخفيف *	
–	١٩	وكلُّ يوم	صوابه وكلَّ منصوب بحذف الخافض *	١٨،٥،٥
٥١٥	..	خِندَف	صوابه خِندِف البيت بآخر الصحفة *	
٥١٦	٦	يُفنى	صوابه يَفنَى *	
–	١١	معتَب	صوابه معتِب *	
–	٢٢	كِثرة	صوابه كَثرة *	
٥١٧	١٥	بنُ	حقه بنَ *	
٥٢٠	٢٢	فُنّ	صوابه فَنّ *	

Page	Line	[Incorrect]	[Correct]	
"	28	قبلُه	قبلَه because it's an adverb, because it's an adverb, because it's an adverb! Are you going to put the blame on the printer?	5.5.17
487	19	يبدو محاسنه	تبدو [محاسنه]	
493	"	مناهِلُ	مناهلٌ because it occurs as the rhyme word of the first hemistich; they should review the rule .	
"	[22–23] The last two lines of verse are botched and seriously contravene the rules of the classical language.			
494	[11]	The verse by al-Mutanabbī contains unwieldy wording;[467] also وِيالكِ من خداسيل in the other line of verse should read ويالكَ.		
501	[9]	اشتوا	شَتَوا; also مثل should be مثلُ.	
503	13	جَنائِي وخَياره	جناىَ وخِياره	
508	22	لِذُوى الالباب وذى	لذَوى الالباب اوذى	
509	12	والنَّجَ	والنُّجُ	
"	13	تُقاذف	تَقاذف; originally تتقاذف, with the first *tā'* being dropped to make it lighter.[468]	
"	19	وكلُّ يوم	وكلَّ يوم, in the accusative in the absence of a genitive agent.	5.5.18
515	[29]	خِنذَف	خِندِف (line of verse at the bottom of the page).	
516	6	يُفِنى	يَفنىَ	
"	11	معتَب	معتِب	
"	22	كِثْرة	كَثْرة	
517	15	بنُ.	بنَ.	
520	22	فُنّ	فَنّ	

صفحة	سطر			
–	٢٩	نُفذت	حقه نَفذت *	
٥٣٢	٥	خَدَع	الوجه خُدَع *	
–	١٠	وعصرُه	صوابه وعصرِه *	
٥٣٥	٩	تَساق	صوابه تُساق *	١٩،٥،٥
–	١٠	مِثَل فِيْءِ	صوابه مثْل فَيْءِ *	
٥٣٥	١٤	قنَعوا	صوابه قنِعوا *	
٥٣٨	..	عَرَى	صوابه عُرْىِ *	
–	..	الشَّرك تعلِمه	صوابه الشِرك تعلَمُه *	
–	..	عِماها	صوابه عَماها العَمَى بالفتح يااساتيذ *	
٥٣٩	..	تُجهَل	صوابه تَجهل *	
٥٤١	١٩	كانوا الاكارمُ	صوابه الاكارمَ * وفى البيت الثانى لهوقة *	
٥٤٢	..	المغيظ المحنَق	حقه المحنِق بمعنى الحاقد فاما المحنَق فانه بمعنى المغضَب فيكون بمعنى المغِيظ*	
٥٤٨	..	فُمى	صوابه فَمى البيت بآخر الصفحة *	٢٠،٥،٥
٥٤٩	٩	تَنكَر	صوابه تُنكِر *	
–	–	ابتَلَيْت	صوابه ابتُلِيتَ *	
–	١٩	غدتْ بنتُ	الوجه بنتَ *	
–	٢٤	قَبلُ	صوابه قبلَ لكونه ظرفا لكونه ظرفا لكونه ظرفا وهذه سابع مرة فهل تتوركون على الطبّاع *	

Page	Line	[Incorrect]	[Correct]	
"	29	نُفذت	نَفذت	
532	5	خَدَع	خُدَع	
"	10	وعصرهُ	وعصرهِ	
535	9	تَساق	تُساق	5.5.19
"	10	مِثلَ فِيءِ	مثلُ فَيْءِ	
535	14	قنَعوا	قنِعوا	
538	[23]	عَرَى	عُرْيِ	
"	[24]	الشَّرك تعلِمُه	الشِرك تعلَمُه	
"	["]	عِماها	عَماها; العَمَى is with *a*, you professors![469]	
539	[17]	تُجهَل	تَجهل	
541	19	كانواالاكارمُ	كانوا الاكارمَ; also the second line of verse is botched.	
542	[24]	المغيظ المحنَق	المغيظالمحِنق, the second word here meaning *al-ḥāqid* ("the resentful"); *muḥnaq* means the same as *mughḍab* ("vexed") and would therefore have the same sense as *maghīẓ*.	
548	[25]	فُمِى	فَمِى (the line of verse is at the bottom of the page).	5.5.20
549	9	تَنْكَر	تُنكِر	
"	"	ابتَلَيْت	ابتُلِيْت	
"	19	غدتْ بنتُ	[غدتْ] بنتَ	
"	24	قَبلُ	قبلَ because it's an adverb, because it's an adverb, because it's an adverb! This is the seventh time. Are you going to put the blame on the printer?	

صفحة	سطر			
–	٢٥	الزَّنْد	صوابه الزُنْد وقوله ياعقارُ فيه نظر *	
٥٥٥	..	أُنْس	صوابه اِنْس *	
–	..	يَحُدُ	صوابه يحَدُ وقوله خِمسا قبله فليراجع *	
٥٦١	..	فوق رؤسِهِمُ	حقه رُوْسِهِم ومثله كثير فى هذا الكتاب *	
–	..	جلاّل	حقه اِجلال *	
٥٦٦	..	لم يَلُذَّ	صوابه يَلِذّ لان المضاعف اذا جآء لازما تكون عينه مكسورة الا فى احرف نادرة *	
٥٦٨	..	لاَسَقِيهِمْ	صوابه لَاسَقِيَهُمْ[1] البيت بآخر الصفحة *	٢١،٥،٥
٥٦٩	..	فيعرُض	حقه فيعرِض *	
٥٧٠	٢٣	كِلامَ	صوابه كَلام *	
٥٧٥	١٤	وزَهَدُ	صوابه وزُهْد *	
–	..	يساوِى	صوابه يساوَى *	
–	..	نحو مبرّد	حقه المبّرد *	
–	..	هاكِها	صوابه هاكَها *	
–	..	تُطِنّ	الوجه تطِنّ *	
٥٩٠	..	تفهِموا	صوابه تفهَموا *	
–	..	ذُوو	صوابه ذَوو وكانَّ الاساتيذ قاسوا الجمع على المفرد	
–	..	بالِ	حقه بالْ فان الوافي كلها مقيّدة *	٢٢،٥،٥

١ ١٨٥٥: لأسقِيَهُم.

Page	**Line**	**[Incorrect]**	**[Correct]**	
"	25	الزَّنْد	الزُّنْد; cf. ياعقارُ	
555	[23]	أُنْس	إِنْس	
"	[24]	يجُدُ	يجَدُ; also the word خِمسا in the previous line [is dubious], so it should be checked against the original.	
561	[16]	فوق رؤسِهِمُ	فوق رُؤسِهِمِ; the book abounds in examples of this sort.	
"	["]	جلّال	اِجلال	
566	[6]	لم يَلُذَّ	يَلِذّ, because intransitive geminate verbs have the middle consonant with *i* except in rare cases.	
568	[28]	لَا سَقِيهِمْ	لَا سَقِيَهُمْ (the line of verse at the bottom of the page).	5.5.21
569	,,	فيعرُض	فيعرِض	
570	23	كِلامَ	كَلام	
575	14	وزَهَدُ	وزُهَد	
"	[15]	يساوِى	يساوَى	
"	[17]	نحو مبرّد	[نحو] المبرّد	
"	[20]	هاكِها	هاكَها	
"	["]	تطُنّ	تطِنّ	
590	[7]	تفهموا	تفهَموا	
"	["]	ذُوو	ذَوو; the good professors seem to have formed the plural by analogy with the singular.	
"	[21]	بالِ	بالْ, the rhyme being with an unvoweled consonant throughout.	5.5.22

صفحة	سطر			
٥٩١	١٣	تعلِم	صوابه تعلَم *	
٥٩٧	..	بالمُشرفىّ	صوابه بالفتح *	
٦٠٨	٢٣	اَرْحَمْ	صوابه اِرْحم *	
٦١٠	٢٢	وِيُحسَنُ دلّها	صوابه وِيَحْسُنُ دَلُّها *	
٦١١	..	اكارعَه	حقه اكارعُه *	
٦١٤	١١	قبلَ الاَجَلْ	صوابه من قبلِ الاجل ليستقيم الوزن *	
–	١٣	لَيْلاً	الوجه لَيْلَى *	
٦٢٦	..	جُعِلنا عوارضُ	صوابه عوارضَ البيت باخر الصفحة *	
٦٢٧	..	يُنْصَحان	صوابه يَنْصَحان *	
–	..	واصبرُ	صوابه واصبِرْ وكذا فى الثانية *	٢٣،٥،٥
٦٢٨	..	يجئ	صوابه يجى مليّنة للوزن *	
٦٣٣	١٠	جَسْم مكررة مرتين	والصواب جِسْم *	
–	..	فى الابيات الاخيرة منع مسلم من الصرف اولى من كسر البيت		
٦٣٣	٢٢[1]	وقوله باردِ	صوابه بالتنوين والطَّهور بالفتح لا بالضمّ *	
٦٣٥	١٥	الاشقِينَ	حقه الاشقَينَ *	
–	..	مطبُخَهَ	صوابه مَطْبُخُهُ وساباطَ حقه بالكسر او بالالف *	
٦٣٩	..	نائلكَ	حقه نائلكم لانه واقع عروضا *	

١ ١٨٥٥: ١٠.

Page	Line	[Incorrect]	[Correct]
591	13	تعلِم	تعلَم
597	[20]	بالمُشرفي	بالمَشرفي
608	23	اَزحَمْ	اِزحم
610	22	ويُحْسَنُ دَلُّها	ويَحْسُنُ دَلُّها
611	[24]	اكارعَه	اكارعُه
614	11	قبلَ الاَجَلْ	من قبلِ الاجل to allow the verse to scan correctly.
"	13	لَيْلاً	لَيْلَى
626	[24]	جُعِلنا عوارِضُ	[جُعِلنا] عوارِضَ (the line of verse at the bottom of the page).
627	[11]	يُنْصَحان	يَنْصَحان
"	[12]	واصبُرْ	واصبِرْ and the same in the second [hemistich]. 5.5.23
628	[25]	يجئْ	يجِي, with elision of the glottal stop for the meter.
633	10	جَسَم (twice)	جِسْم
"	[10]	In the final verses, it would be better to treat مسلم as diptote than to break the meter.	
633	22	باردِ	With *tanwīn*; also الطَّهور not الطُّهور.[470]
635	15	الاشقِينَ	الاشقَينَ
"	[26]	مطبخَة	مَطْبَخُهُ; also ساباطَ should be either ساباطِ or ساباطا.
639	[12]	نائلَكَ	نائلكم because it comes as the last word of the first hemistich.

صفحة	سطر			
٦٤١	..	سعادٌ	صوابه سعادُ واثرُها صوابه بالفتح وهذه ثانى مرّة	
٦٤٥	١٠	ضَرغام	صوابه بالكسر *	٢٤،٥،٥
–	١٣	ومصابحُ	صوابه مصروفا لوقوعه عروضا *	
–	١٩	ودارَ وفارَ	حقهما السكون للقافية *	
٦٤٦	..	السِعلات	حقه السعلاةِ وعمرُو بنُ مسعود شرارُ الوجه فيها كلها النصب *	
٦٤٩	١٥	اربعةٌ	صہ اربعةً وفى جبرِئِلِ تلهوق ونَصّل حقه فَصّل *	
٦٥٠	..	تزوَّجَ ابنُ	الرواية نزوّجُ ابنَ *	
٦٥٣	..	مُعاذَ الله	صوابه مَعاذ *	
٦٥٨	..	شديدُ	الوجه بسكون الاخر *	
٦٦٠	..	ترِينَ	صوابه ترَيْنَ واعلِمِ صوابه واعلَمَ *	
–	..	من الحرفةِ	الوجه من الحِرفَهْ *	
٦٦٢	..	وطيّاً	حقه وطيئاً *	
–	..	فقَصِّرَكما	صوابه فقَصْرُكما اى غايتكما ومصيركما	٢٥،٥،٥
–	..	وتَلِدَ	صوابه تَلِدا *	
٦٦٢	..	فتًى هوأَحيا	الرواية كان احيا *	
٦٦٤	..	لعلَّ اللهُ	صوابه اللهَ البيت باخر الصفحة *	
٦٦٨	..	يَخزنى	صوابه يُخزنى *	
٦٦٩	..	مزيدَ	صوابه مزيدٍ لوقوعه عروضا *	

Page	Line	[Incorrect]	[Correct]	
641	[22]	سعادٌ	سعادُ, and اثرُها should be اثرَها, which is the second time this mistake has been made.	
645	10	ضَرغام	ضِرغام	
"	[13]	مصابحُ	مصابحٍ as it comes as the last word of the first hemistich.	5.5.24
"	19	دارَ وفارَ	دارْ وفارْ for the rhyme.	
646	[18]	السِعلات	السعلاةِ; also وعمرُو بنُ مسعود شرارُ should be with final *fatḥah* throughout.	
649	15	اربعةٌ	Corr.[471] اربعةً; also فى جبرئِلِ is botched and نَصْل should be فَصْل.	
650	[12]	تزوّجَ ابنُ	In the authoritative reading, تزوّجُ ابنَ.	
653	[18]	مُعاذَ الله	مَعاذ [الله]	
658	[16]	شديدُ	شديدْ	
660	[21]	تزِينَ	تزيَّنْ; also واعلمِ should be واعلمَ.	
"	[26]	من الحرفةِ	من الحِرَفَةْ	
662	[9]	وطيّاً	وطيئاً	
"	["]	فقصَرَكا	فقصْرُكا meaning "your objective" or "your destiny."	5.5.25
"	["]	وتَلِدَ	وتَلِدا	
662	[21]	فتى هو اَحيا	In the authoritative reading, كان احيا.	
664	[26]	لعلَّ الله	[لعلَّ] اللهَ (the line of verse at the bottom of the page).	
668	[11]	يَحزنى	يُحزنى	
669	[23]	مزيدَ	مزيدٍ because it occurs as the last word of the first hemistich.	

صفحة	سطر		
٦٧٢	..	اَحَبُّ	صوابه اُحِبُّ *
٦٧٤	..	شوامش	صوابه شوامس وشوامس الثانية ينبغى ان تكون مجرورة بالكسرة او بالف الاطلاق *
٦٧٨	..	خَبْزُه	صوابه خُبزه *
٦٧٩	١٤	شيا تُجَرّ	حقه يُجَر *
–	٢٢	اخفُّ	صوابه اخفَّ *
–	٢٣	وابصرُ	صوابه وابصرَ *

وما زال الشيخان ماشيين على هذه الطريقة الى آخر المقامات ولوتقصيت كل ما وقع من الغلط والتحريف فى المتن والشرح لكان مقدارا عظيما وكفى بما اوردته شاهدا على علميّة المشار اليهما وكذب دعوى صاحبهما فاما ما انتخبه الاستاذ الاعظم مسيو كُسّان دُ پرسُفال من قصة عنتر وما الّفه فى كلام اهل حلب وما نقله غيره ايضا من الحكايات السخيفة الركيكة فغير جدير بان يضاع فى نقده الوقت اذكله فاسد *

تم الذنب

Page	Line	[Incorrect]	[Correct]
672	[17]	اَحَبُّ	أُحِبُّ
674	[19]	شوامش	شوامس; the second شوامس should be the object of the preposition, with *-i,* or with *alif* to mark the prolongation of the vowel.
678	[20]	خَبْزه	خُبزه
679	14	شيا تُجَرّ	[شيا] يجَرُّ
"	22	اخفُّ	اخفَّ
"	23	وابصرُ	وابصرَ

and the two shaykhs keep on in the same vein to the end of the *maqāmāt*. If one were to investigate every example of error and misspelling in both the text and the commentary, it would amount to a very great quantity, so let what I provide here be sufficient testimony as to the scholarship of the two aforementioned persons and give the lie to their friend's claim. The selections of Monsieur Caussin de Perceval from *Qiṣṣat ʿAntar* (*The Story of ʿAntar*),[472] his writings on the speech of the people of Aleppo, and the transcriptions by others of silly stories in lame language are not worth the time one would waste on them, for they are all bad.

End of the Appendix

تنبيه من عادة الاساتيذ المزبورين ومن اشبههم ممن الّف فى العربية شيا ان ١،٦،٥
يعتذروا عن اغلاطهم الفاضحة بالتورّك على الطبّاع او على صفّاف الحروف بان يقولوا ان وقوع الغلط انما ينشأ عن جهلهما باللغة كما ذكر لى ذلك الكنت الكس دكُرانج (Alix Desgrange) نقلا عن الاستاذ كسان دُ پرسفال وهو عذر اقبح من ذنب فان الصفّاف كيفما وجّهته اتجه ومهما ترسم له يمتثله الَاَ ترى ان مسيو پيرو (M. Perrault, rue de Castellane, 15, Paris) مع كونه لم يعرف من اللغة العربية شيا فقد امتثل كل ما رسمنا له فى كتابنا هذا من التصحيح والتبديل بغاية التانّى وبذل مجهوده فى صف الحروف وجودة الطبع حتى جآ بحمد الله احسن ما طبع بلغتنا فى البلاد الافرنجية فلهذا ننوّه باسمه عند كل من شآء ان يطبع شيا بالعربية ولا شك انهم يحمدون سعيه ويرضون عن صنعه وان لم يكن فى المطبعة السلطانية وكفى بحسن العمل وصاة *

5.6.1 Notice: it is the habit of the abovementioned professors and those like them who have written something in Arabic to excuse their terrible mistakes by putting the blame on the printer and typesetter, saying that the mistakes are due to the latter's ignorance of the language, or so I was told by Conte Alix Desgranges,[473] who was reporting the words of Professor Caussin de Perceval. This is an excuse worse than the offense, for the typesetter does exactly what you ask of him and whatever rules you lay down he obeys. Do you not observe that M. Perrault, of Rue de Castellane, 15, Paris, even though he knows nothing about the Arabic language, has followed with the utmost care our instructions in terms of corrections and changes and gone to great lengths to compose the letters correctly and produce an excellent piece of printing, so much so that he has come up, praise God, with the best thing ever printed in our language in Europe? We commend him, therefore, to any who wish to print anything in Arabic; there can be no doubt that they will praise his efforts and be happy with his work, even if he is not with the Imprimerie Nationale, the excellence of the work being its own recommendation.

[End]

Translator's Afterword

This is the first translation into English of Aḥmad Fāris al-Shidyāq's *al-Sāq ʿalā l-sāq*,[474] a work published in Arabic in 1855 and celebrated thereafter both for its importance to the history of Arabic literature and as a "difficult" text. The book's literary and historical significance is the subject of the Foreword (Volume One, ix–xxx). This Afterword deals only with translational issues.

The first element of the work's title is itself often cited as representative of the book's difficulties. The words *al-sāq ʿalā l-sāq* are ambiguous and clearly meant to be so. The common meaning of *sāq* is "shank" and thus by metonymy the leg as a whole; less well-known are the senses "male turtle dove" and "trunk (of a tree)." What it means for a leg to be "over" or "upon" (*ʿalā*) another leg is for the reader to decide. Paul Starkey reminds us that Henri Pérès proposed that the phrase should be understood as "[sitting] cross-legged" and thus evokes "the familiar attitude adopted by a storyteller who, comfortably installed in an armchair, is about to narrate a long story of wonderful adventures."[475] This bland interpretation cannot be entirely excluded, if only on principle: if the title is intended to be ambiguous, more than one possible interpretation is, by definition, required. Pérès's definition is not, however, explicitly reflected in the text; rather, as Starkey also points out, the phrase *al-sāq ʿalā l-sāq* occurs there with sexual innuendo, as when the author writes of a woman's suitor speaking to her of "the bed, of drawing her close, of embracing, of leg over leg, of kissing, of kissing tongue to tongue, of intercourse, and the like" (Volume Three, 3.4.1); similar is the earlier use, during a discussion that exploits the sexual suggestiveness of Arabic grammatical terminology (Volume One, 1.11.9), of the phrase *alladhī yarfaʿu l-sāq* ("the one who raises his leg"). In this translation, therefore, the title has been tilted towards the erotic by the use of the perhaps more suggestive "over" in preference to "upon."

The second element of the English title—"or the Turtle in the Tree"— which builds on the two less common senses of *sāq*, has been introduced to provide a rhyme (an essential element of the title, though achieved differently in the original) and to sensitize the English reader to the ludic nature of the text as a whole.

Turning to the text, it should perhaps be made clear that *al-Sāq ʿalā l-sāq*, despite its reputation, is not always "difficult." As Pierre Cachia has written, the author is capable of expressing himself "with a simplicity and directness that a writer a century later would be pleased to claim for himself."[476] At the same time, however, his writing is characterized by two general features and two specific practices of prose organization that do pose challenges for the translator.

The two general features are a fondness for arcane vocabulary and a verbal playfulness that expresses itself through punning, word games, and humorous allusion. Both are so widely distributed throughout the text as to be numbered among its most fundamental characteristics.

To "give prominence to the oddities of the language, including its rare words" (Volume One, 0.2.1.) is the author's first stated goal for the work. Rare words are present in huge numbers either in the form of lists, which sometimes proclaim their presence with headings such as "Here are the meanings of the rare words mentioned above" (Volume One, 1.16.9) or "An Explanation of the Obscure Words in the Preceding *Maqāmah* and Their Meanings" (Volume Two, 2.14), or else embedded in the general narrative. In the latter case, the author will, on occasion, call attention to the lists by glossing them in the margin (see, e.g., the note on *izāʾ* at 1.4.2 in Volume One). The main challenge posed by such words is the time needed to research them; I must, therefore, acknowledge the help provided by online dictionary sites, without which this translation would have been too time-consuming to be feasible. The sites I used most were www.baheth.info (for, among others, al-Fīrūzābādī's *al-Qāmūs al-muḥīṭ* and Ibn Manẓūr's *Lisān al-ʿArab*) and both www.tyndalearchive.com and http://www.perseus.tufts.edu for Lane's *Lexicon*. Rare words pose a major obstacle to the translator, however, only when they fail to appear, in an appropriate sense, in any dictionary; fortunately, the number of such items is small.

Puns and allusions pose a greater challenge, partly because they may go unnoticed and partly because, even when they are recognized, native readers themselves may differ as to their meaning. Inevitably, therefore, interpretation sometimes remains speculative. The reference to *al-kāfayn* (Volume One, 1.16.5 and note 235 there)—literally "the two ks"—is a case in point: two widely differing understandings of the phrase were put forward by two scholars I consulted; my own, third, interpretation may or may not be correct.

The prose organization practice perhaps most likely to give the translator pause in this work is the use of *sajʿ* (rhymed, rhythmic prose that often involves semantic or syntactic parallelism and that is typically associated with heightened drama or emotion in the text).[477] In *al-Sāq*, *sajʿ* is employed throughout, both over the span of entire chapters and in passages within a chapter that range from a phrase or two to several pages. Patently, Arabic, with its productive morphological classes all of whose members possess, or end in, the same pattern of vowels and consonants, lends itself to this practice. It is enough, in Arabic, to choose as one's rhyme word a Form III verbal noun of the pattern *mufāʿalah*, for example, to access hundreds more words of that pattern, or to deploy, say, the third person masculine plural imperfect verb to have at one's disposal thousands of words ending in *–ūna*. The capacity of English to generate rhymes is more limited and the translator is therefore faced with a "rhyme deficit." Not surprisingly, it has often been the practice of translators faced with *sajʿ* to ignore it, even though this be at the expense of a prominent aesthetic dimension of the original.

This is not an option, however, in the case of *al-Sāq*, if only because the author's use of *sajʿ* is self-conscious and his references to the problems it creates numerous. Thus at one point the author remarks that "Rhymed prose is to the writer as a wooden leg to the walker" (Volume One, 1.10.1), following this observation with a disquisition on the dangers of its overuse and the differences between it and verse (which he claims to be less demanding). Likewise, the difficulty of writing *maqāmah*s, a genre to which *sajʿ* is intrinsic, is a favorite topic of the author's (e.g., Volume One, 1.14.1). Even his tendency, when subjected to the appropriate stimulus, to break into *sajʿ* in the midst of unrhymed prose may elicit an explicit comment from him on his own writing, as when he exclaims, "God be praised—the mere thought of women produces the urge to write in rhymed prose!" (Volume One, 1.16.2).

The translator is therefore obliged to do the best he can. Given the limitations of English, some latitude is essential. In additional to full rhyme, near rhyme, rime riche, alliteration, and assonance have all been used; occasionally, the order of the Arabic periods has been changed. Likewise, it has not always been possible in the English to rhyme the same words that are rhymed in the Arabic, which has meant a reduction in the "linking and correspondence" that the author regards as an intrinsic element of the technique (Volume One, 1.10.1).[478] It has not always even been possible to produce the same number of rhyming words in any given passage: the number of rhymes in the translation is fewer than in the original. I hope, nevertheless, that at least something of the force and humor of al-Shidyāq's *sajʿ* has been carried over.

What applies to *saj*ʿ applies equally, of course, to verse, which in the Arabic of this period is entirely monorhymed. In this translation, shorter poems have mainly been rendered into rhymed couplets.[479] Most of the longer poems, such as the Proem (Volume One, 0.4) and the poems at the end of the work (Volume Four, 4.20) have been left unrhymed.

The other challenging fundamental practice in *al-Sāq* is the presentation of large numbers of words, usually rare, in the form of lists. Studies have stressed the "sound effect of the accumulated words"[480] and the "*fonction incantatoire*"[481] of such lists, and to these aspects may be added the distancing effect (amounting, in Peled's view, to a "sense of terror")[482] created by the obscurity (i.e., the quality of their being unknown to and unknowable by the ordinary reader) of the words and, often, their phonetic exoticism. The impact of many of these lists is increased by their great length; one series of interlinked lists (Volume Two, 2.14.8–84) extends, in the original, over more than forty-two pages.

Such lists fall into two categories: those with definitions and those without. Each category calls for a different approach from the translator.

As a preliminary point of reference, the hitherto perhaps under-recognized fact that the words that constitute these lists are taken, largely and perhaps even exclusively, from al-Fīrūzābādī's renowned fifteenth-century dictionary *al-Qāmūs al-muḥīṭ* should be noted. Similarly, the definitions given for these words, where definitions are given, are verbatim transcriptions of the definitions in the same dictionary and they are not of the author's own making or drawn from any other source. Indeed, al-Shidyāq makes this explicit in the Proem when he says, "To me and to the author of the *Qāmūs* must go the credit / Since it is from his fathomless sea that my words have been scooped" (Volume One, 0.4.6) and again when he claims that the *Qāmūs* was "the only book in Arabic I had to refer to or depend on" (Volume One, 1.1.7) during the writing of *al-Sāq*; on occasion too he states that he is "copying" a particular list (*nāqilan lahu*), i.e., copying it from the *Qāmūs* (Volume Two, 2.4.12). He also refers explicitly to the *Qāmūs* in the comments that he occasionally includes within the lists (see, e.g., the entry for *ṭurmūth* in Volume Two at 2.14.74 and for *mumarjal* in Volume Two at 2.16.47).

So thoroughgoing indeed is the author's reliance on the *Qāmūs* that I am tempted to believe that my occasional failure to locate a definition in the *Qāmūs* is more likely to be due to the item's occurring in some entry other than that in which it should, on the basis of root, be found, or to a discrepancy of editions, than to its not in fact occurring there. In the translation, verbatim quotes from the *Qāmūs* occurring in the lists have been placed in quotation marks, while material that could not be found there, and author's comments, are given without quotation marks.

These facts have the important implication that these lists are lexicologically driven and bear only a tenuous and opportunistic relationship to reality. The list of headwear worn in Alexandria (Volume Two, 2.2.1), for example, tells us little about what men actually wore at that time and place; even the few items that may indeed have been present—e.g., "tall pointed hats (*ṭarāṭīr*) and tarbushes (*ṭarābīsh*)"—are included, I would argue, because they, like the other, more obscure, terms, occur in the *Qāmūs*, not because they were worn in Alexandria in the third decade of the nineteenth century. Similarly, a list of foods supposedly eaten in Alexandria (see Volume Two, 2.2.10) and consisting largely of edible vetches but containing few words for whose use in Egypt there is any evidence, tells us nothing about the diet of the inhabitants of that city at that time beyond, perhaps, the fact that it included a lot of pulses. Such lists are not intended to convey information about the world but to impress the reader—firstly, with the inexhaustible resources of the classical Arabic language and secondly, with the author's mastery thereof; perhaps they also simply reflect the author's fascination with words per se, irrespective of any intention to edify or impress.

The lists with definitions, most of which occur in the first half of the work and which can run to over forty pages, do not pose any particular methodological problem for the translator. They are, for the most part, presented by the author in the form of tables, with headwords in one column and definitions in the next.[483] The headwords in these tables must be transcribed, the definitions translated; any other approach results in the nonsense of an English translation of an Arabic word followed by an English translation of its Arabic definition.

The lists without definitions form at least as large a part of the work as the tabular lists but pose a greater challenge. The work opens with one such list—eleven synonyms or near-synonyms for "Be quiet!" (Volume One, 1.1.1)—and they continue to occur throughout. They vary in length from half a dozen to close to three hundred words (e.g., the list of women's ways of looking and walking in Volume Two at 2.2.4). Items in such lists are all synonyms, near-synonyms, or semantically associated words, and are often grouped into rhymed pairs, or series of pairs, which are sometimes also metatheses of each other. These lists pose three main problems: how to circumvent the limitations of English in terms of translational equivalents for the list items; how to deal with the under-specificity of some definitions in the *Qāmūs* (and other dictionaries), which further reduces the options available to the translator; and how to render their "incantatory," recondite, and exotic aspects.

As far as availability of equivalents is concerned, shorter lists may not pose a problem: English may furnish a sufficient number of appropriate synonyms. Even medium-length lists may be susceptible to one-to-one, or near one-to-one, translation (see, e.g., the list of the sounds made by the organ in Volume One at 1.4.6), especially when the author's use of onomatopoeia and other forms of playfulness opens the door for a degree of inventiveness in the English (see e.g., the list of types of metaphor and their fanciful subdivisions in Volume One at 1.11.5). In the case of longer lists, however, English may refuse to yield enough words within a given semantic field, while what words it does possess in that field may fail to match, even approximately, the Arabic items.

A case in point is the list of words describing women's ways of looking and moving referred to above (Volume Two, 2.2.4). It is doubtful that English possesses 288 words in this semantic field and a virtual certainty that what words it does possess will not map exactly onto the words in the text. Further examples are the list of 255 words denoting genitalia and sexual activities occurring near the beginning of the book (Volume One, 1.1.6) and the 65-word list of activities associated with gambling and risk-taking (Volume One, 1.16.5); numerous others could be adduced. In such cases, the translator is faced with a choice between presenting the "untranslatable" words in transcription—in other words, not translating them—and resorting to multi-word glosses (e.g., "her stepping out manfully and her walking proudly in her clothes, her swaggering and her swinging along, her stepping like a pouting pigeon and her rolling gait," etc.). The transcriptional approach would yield nonsense (a "translation" consisting of words in the original language); the use of multi-word glosses, while preferable, would nevertheless threaten one of these lists' most important characteristics, namely their obscurity. Sonority may perhaps be retained through the use of rhyme, alliteration, and so on in the English, but the resources are, again, more limited.

In some cases, the problem is compounded by the under-specificity of definitions in the *Qāmūs*. For example, several of the different kinds of headwear worn in Alexandria (Volume Two, 2.2.1) referred to above are defined in the Qāmūs either by the single word *ʿimāmah* (any cloth worn around the head, or "turban") or by the single word *qalansuwah* (any shaped covering for the head, or "cap"). With nothing but these generic definitions to go on, the translator is faced with the possibility of renditions along the lines of "in [Alexandria] you see some people whose heads are covered with . . . turbans . . . some with [other kinds of] turbans . . . some with [further kinds of] turbans . . . and others with [even more kinds of] turbans," etc. The solution in this case, inadequate though it may be, was to associate the Arabic word with the appropriate generic English term: "in [Alexandria] you see some people whose heads are covered with *maqāʿiṭ* turbans . . . some with *aṣnāʿ*-turbans . . . some with *madāmīj* turbans . . . some with the turban under the name *mishmadh* and others with the turban under the name *mishwadh*," etc.

Such phrasal glosses and/or the use of generic terminology, while perhaps justifiable in terms of highlighting the lexically driven nature of these lists, may also produce a numbing repetitiveness or a kind of off-list intrusiveness—"turbans . . . turbans . . . turbans . . . " or "some other way of simply walking, the same with a difference of one letter . . . and another way of simply walking with yet another letter changed" or "the vulva said four other ways"—that is very different in impact from the original list.

The translator's strategies for such lists have developed during the course of the work.

In Volumes One and Two, lists without definitions were mainly dealt with by "direct" translation (i.e., by using one-word equivalents conveying, in principle, the exact meaning of the Arabic word, such as "her strutting, her galloping"). When such equivalents proved impossible to find (as was often the case), I resorted to phrases ("her walking with her thighs far apart kicking up her feet"). Such phrasal equivalents, however, while perhaps accurately conveying the meaning of the word, betray the nature of the original text by making the translation wordier.

Starting in Volume Two, therefore, with this in mind, I also used some indirect strategies. For example, the list of forty-eight monosyllabic rhyming words (*al-azz wa-l-baḥz wa-l-bakhz* etc.) denoting a blow resulting in implicit or explicit injury (Volume Two, 2.1.23) reproduces all the monosyllabic words in the same semantic field found in *Roget's Thesaurus*, without regard for one-to-one correspondence between the Arabic and the English; the result is closer to my mind to the effect of the Arabic than a translation that sacrifices percussive sound in a search for semantically accurate correspondence. Similarly, the series of notes relating to ugliness in women (which are themselves lists) that interrupt the tabular lists on women's charms (Volume Two, 2.14.12–29) were translated using various tools: the first (2.14.13) uses mainly medical, or pseudo-medical, terms gleaned from the Internet ("nanoid, endomorphic, adipose," etc.); the second (2.14.18: "dirty crockadillapigs, shorties, runts," etc.) was compiled from http://onlineslangdictionary.com/thesaurus; the third (2.14.26: "women who have dilated dugs or deflated bellies, who are blubber-lipped," etc.) depends on *Roget's Thesaurus* and other nonspecialized lexical lists; and the fourth (2.14.29: "brevo-turpicular, magno-pinguicular, vasto-oricular," etc.) uses Google's Latin translation facility to create nonexistent terms imitative of the orotund Arabic. Again, the goal of such translations is to escape one-to-one equivalence in favor of similarity of effect.

In Volumes Three and Four, a thesaurus-based method of translating all lists too long or too generic to allow for one-to-one lexical equivalence was applied systematically. Each of the items in the given list was looked up in the *Qāmūs* and the definitions found there were assembled into a working list; the definitions were then grouped by semantic subfield based on the critical term used in the definition in the *Qāmūs*. A list of words relating to insincerity, for example, might contain twenty-four items, a number of which are defined in terms of glibness,[484] a number in terms of fickleness, and others in terms of hypocrisy. "Glibness," etc. were then looked up in Roget's Thesaurus and their synonyms organized into a new list, attention being given where possible to reproduction of nonlexical elements such as rhyme, alliteration, and rhythm as well as rarity or reconditeness. The resulting English list is thus a representation and not a translation of the original Arabic list. Since this approach violates the reader's presumed expectations of translation as a system of (more or less) one-to-one equivalency, I give notice of such "representations" in the endnotes, in a spirit of transparency.

Theoretically, this method of "representation" rather than "translation" could be extended further. If, for example, the works of Rabelais—another list maker and lover of recondite words—or of Thomas Burton, or of any other writer with a sensibility similar to al-Shidyāq's, had been found to contain word lists resembling those in *al-Sāq* and if these were culturally plausible (i.e., did not produce distractingly European resonances), it might have been appropriate or even desirable to transfer these, lock, stock, and barrel, into the English text. In the event, no lists that matched the Arabic sufficiently closely were found.

Finally, a word on chapter titles. The use of *fī* ("on, concerning") in the title of each chapter of *al-Sāq* has been said to embody an intentionally created "gap between the titular imperative . . . and its claim to an exposition of the subject that follows, and the narrative, that has nothing at all to do with the title."[485] This insight, if accepted, would call for retention of "on" in the translated chapter titles. We have, however, decided not to apply this principle for two reasons. The first is that the use of "on" in English risks distorting the meaning of most chapter titles: to translate *Fī nawādir mukhtalifah* (Volume One, 1.3), for example, as "On Various Amusing Anecdotes" would be to imply that the chapter consisted of a discussion or study of such anecdotes, whereas in reality it consists of anecdotes tout court; the same applies to many other chapters, such as "The Priest's Tale" (Volume One, 1.15), which is a tale told by a priest rather than a discussion of a tale, or "A Description of Cairo" (Volume Two, 2.5, 2.7), likewise. The second is that the use of *fī* to introduce chapter titles is a common feature of older works in the Arabic belles lettres tradition and not specific to *al-Sāq*. Thus one finds *fī* used in the title of every chapter of (by way of random example) the *Thimār al-qulūb* of al-Thaʿālibī (died 429/1038) and the *Ḥalabat al-kumayt* of al-Nawājī (died 859/1455). I have preferred, therefore, to regard *fī* as a conventional element of Arabic title headings requiring no equivalent in English.

Wahiduddin Khan's translation of the Qur'ān is that mostly used in the text and endnotes, in accordance with series policy, but Arberry's and Yusuf Ali's translations were preferred in a few cases for a better fit with the context; all these were accessed via the Tanzil website (http://tanzil.net). The King James (Authorized) version is that used for translations from the Bible, in the version available at the University of Michigan's site (http://quod.lib.umich.edu).

This translation is exploratory, an attempt to map the highly varied terrain of al-Shidyāq's masterpiece and not only to reveal something of its many pleasing landscapes but also to mark where the figurative dragons are to be found. It may also be true that the presence of the text side by side with the translation and the awareness that some readers will be comparing the two word for word may have made the translation more conservative (outside, at least, the realm of rhymed prose and the lists without definitions) than the translator would otherwise have preferred; this is especially true of the long poems. In any case, others may wish to suggest different strategies for addressing general problems, such as that of the lists without definitions, for filling in gaps with regard to historical detail (such as the real names of figures who are referred to in code), or for reinterpreting some of the author's teasingly gnomic allusions. Others too may prove more talented at the conversion of rhymed prose and long monorhymed poems into English. I hope, nevertheless, that the appearance of *al-Sāq* in English will serve to alert a wider audience to its importance and its many rewards.

It remains for me to acknowledge the generous help of Mohammed Alwan, Ahmed Alwishah, Julia Bray, Phillippe Chevrant, Robert Dankoff, Hugh Davies, Madiha Doss, Ekmeleddin Ihsanoglu, the Research Centre for Islamic History, Art, and Culture (IRCICA), Ahmet T. Karamustafa, Matthew Keegan, Jerôme Lentin, Joseph Lowry, Ussama Makdisi, Ulrich Marzolph, Simon Mercieca, James Montgomery, Mansur Mustarih, Everett Rowson, Ahmed Shawket, Adam Talib, Yassine Temlali, Shawkat Toorawa, Geert Jan van Gelder, Emmanuel Varlet, and, especially, Geoffrey Roper. Thanks are due too to the Project Committee and staff of the Library of Arabic Literature for their support and flexibility, and particularly to my Project Editor, Michael Cooperson, for his careful review of both text and translation and his numerous helpful comments and suggestions, to Chip Rossetti, Managing Editor, for his incisive direction, and to Stuart Brown, the typesetter, for his skill and meticulousness in finding solutions to the multiple challenges posed by the layout. Above all, however, thanks are due to my Cairo-based colleague Ahmed Seddik for the many hours he spent with me discussing details of the text and offering always-plausible solutions to many of its knottier problems.

Chronology: al-Shidyāq, the Fāriyāq, and *Leg over Leg*

Though it is not suggested that *Leg over Leg* should be read primarily as autobiography, it may be of interest to readers to know at what points the Fāriyāq's life as described in the work coincide with what is known of al-Shidyāq's; the following table therefore attempts to correlate the two. Much about al-Shidyāq's life (especially his earliest years) is the subject of debate, and the work itself is studiously unspecific where dates, for example, are concerned, just as it obfuscates the identity of individuals by using coded names. The following table relies to a great extent on information kindly supplied by Geoffrey Roper, who has studied contemporary primary sources, including those of the missionary organizations for which al-Shidyāq worked.[486] I have also consulted the work of Muḥammad al-Hādī al-Maṭwī[487] and of Simon Mercieca.[488] Material not in square brackets derives from the work itself; the material in square brackets comes from other sources, as do the dates. Numbers in the format (1.1.13) refer to the numbered sections of the text and translation.

Event	**Year**
Volume One	
The Fāriyāq [Fāris al-Shidyāq] is born [probably in his ancestral village of ʿAshqūt in the Kasrawān district of Mount Lebanon] (1.1.13).	1805 or 1806[489]
He attends school (1.1.13 (end), 1.1.14, 1.1.20) [probably in the village of al-Ḥadath, near Beirut, to which the family is said to have moved in 1809].	Second decade of the 19th century
His father joins a revolt against the ruler of Mount Lebanon [Bashīr II ibn Qāsim al-Shihābī, reigned 1788 to 1842] which is crushed, leading to the father's flight to Damascus; his house, where Fāris and his mother are living, is looted [by troops under the command of Ḥaydar ibn Aḥmad al-Shihābī, the ruler's cousin] (1.4.4).	1820

Event	Year
His father dies in Damascus (1.4.8).	1821
He works mainly as a copyist, both at home (1.4.8) and for an emir (1.5.2) [the same Emir Ḥaydar whose troops looted his home], but also [seeking employment] visits one of his brothers [presumably the eldest, Ṭannūs], who is working for a Druze emir (1.6), and later, with a partner, tries his hand first at selling cloth as an itinerant merchant among the villages of Mount Lebanon (1.7), then at innkeeping (1.8). Subsequently, he becomes tutor to an emir's daughter (1.10) but later resumes work as copyist for an emir (1.11); he also tries, and fails, to make money by writing a eulogy for an emir (1.18.15).	ca. 1820—25
He meets his first "Bag-man" [an American Protestant missionary working for the Board of Commissioners of Foreign Missions, in Beirut, referred to in the text as a "peddler . . . [who had] hot-footed it over bringing with him a large saddlebag"] (1.18.19) and eventually declares his adherence to Protestantism (1.19.5). [His elder brother Asʿad, a convert to Protestantism, is arrested and eventually imprisoned by the Maronite Patriarch at his residence at Qannūbīn; Asʿad will die there in 1830 (cf. 1.19.11–14).]	1826
He leaves Lebanon for Alexandria (1.19.6) [embarking at Tyre, from which he is smuggled by the missionaries amid fears for his safety.]	December 2, 1826
Volume Two	
First stay in Alexandria (2.2).	December 1826 to early 1827
He moves from Egypt to Malta (2.3) where he works for [American and subsequently British] missionaries [in the latter case, those of the Church Missionary Society (CMS)].	Early 1827
He returns from Malta to Alexandria (2.3.19), where he stays with a missionary (2.4.1).	Mid-October 1828

Event	Year
Subsequently he moves to Cairo (2.4.2) [where he is employed by the CMS].	November or December 1828
He quarrels with the missionaries (2.4.16) and decides to find other employment (2.8.1). He is directed (2.8.2) to a Christian poet [Naṣr al-Dīn al-Ṭarābulusī] (2.8.3), whom he eventually meets and who suggests he work for the "Panegyricon" [Egypt's official gazette, *al-Waqa'iʿ al-Miṣriyyah*] as a translator of eulogies in praise of a "rich prince" [the viceroy, Muḥammad ʿAlī] (2.11.5).	December 1828
He leaves the employ of the missionaries (2.12.1) and enters that of the "Panegyricon" (2.12).	January 1829
[He continues to lodge with a German missionary, Theodor Müller, and presumably continues to work for *al-Waqāʾiʿ al-Miṣriyyah*; in May 1829 he approaches the CMS with a proposal to reenter its employ at a higher salary but is refused; finally he is evicted by Müller.]	1829 to October 1830
During this period, he studies the linguistic sciences with Egyptian scholars in order to better perform his duties at the Panegyricon (2.18.1) and suffers a series of illnesses (2.18.1–7) [including tuberculosis, contracted in Malta, and a venereal disease (the latter the reason for his eviction by Müller)]. Eventually he takes a job teaching Arabic to the son of a French physician in return for treatment (2.18.7 and 2.19.8). [It is unclear whether this last is in parallel to or replaces his employment by *al-Waqāʾiʿ al-Miṣriyyah*.]	1829 to April or May 1832
He resumes work with the missionaries [being employed at the CMS seminary] (2.19.9).	April or May 1832
Volume Three	
He courts the daughter [Wardah al-Ṣūlī] of a Syrian Roman Catholic merchant (3.2.1–6); during this process, he is inspired to write verses in a "strange new style" (3.2.9–10; also 3.2.27–48).	1832–35

Event	**Year**
He is invited [by the CMS] to return to Malta and teach Arabic there and to work as a "dream interpreter" [translator] in the "Oneiromancer's Chamber" [the premises of the CMS translation project] (3.4.4). [*Leg over Leg* presents some of the events outlined in this and the following segment in reverse order.]	November 1835[491]
Eventually, the courtship of Fāris and Wardah is discovered and, despite attempts by the family to thwart their union, the couple marries, after he agrees to convert to Roman Catholicism for one day (3.2.24–26). After a brief stay in Alexandria (3.5.1), they leave on a steamship for Malta, where, on arrival, and after thirty days in quarantine, they find lodgings [in Marsamxett in Valletta] (3.5.22).	December 1835[492]
The Fāriyāq works as an interpreter of the dreams of the master of the Oneiromancer's Chamber (3.8–10). [i.e., translates texts in collaboration with the head of the CMS office in Malta, Christoph Schlienz. Starting in 1838, Schlienz employs the author principally on the project for the translation of the Bible, though at times the work is suspended due to Schlienz's intermittent bouts of mental illness due to having been hit on the head by a bargepole in Egypt in 1838.[493]]	1836–May 1842[494]
In tandem with his work for the CMS, the Fāriyāq is hired by the island's ruler [the British Governor] to "physic the foul of breath" [to teach Arabic to Maltese students at the University of Malta, at the Lyceum, and at a primary school] (3.11.1-2).	1836–38[495]
The master of the Oneiromancer's Chamber [Schlienz] invites the Fāriyāq to accompany him and his wife on a trip to Syria, he obtains permission from the university to do so (3.12.1), and they set sail for Beirut.	April 1840[496]

Event	Year
The travelers arrive in Beirut, which is in a state of upheaval due to an uprising against Egyptian rule [which began in 1831 when Ibrāhīm Pasha invaded the Levant as part of his campaign against the Ottoman Empire] (3.12.14). From there, the Fāriyāq makes a visit to his family in Mount Lebanon (3.12.14–25) [either in the village of ʿAshqūt or al-Ḥadath[497]].	After April 1840
Later, the party leaves Beirut to stay in a Greek Orthodox monastery [probably that of Mār Ilyās at El Qraye] (3.14.1). Against a background of danger and starvation caused by the presence of Egyptian troops and in the face of his wife's infidelity, the master starts to show renewed signs of insanity (3.14.5).	October 1840[498]
Following the withdrawal of the Egyptian troops, the master recovers and decides to set off for Damascus via Baalbek (3.14.5). Between Damascus and Baalbek, the Fāriyāq is injured in a riding accident (3.15.1). In Damascus, he convalesces, staying at a caravanserai (3.15.3). Recovered, he travels with an unnamed companion to Beirut and thence to Jaffa, Alexandria, and finally Malta (3.15.6) [where he resumes his work on the translation of the Bible].	October 1840?[499]
During the university's summer vacation, the author makes a trip to Tunis (3.18.3–5). [*Leg over Leg* presents the events outlined in this and the following segment in reverse order.]	Summer 1841[500]
The master [Schlienz] has a particularly bad relapse into madness, during which he incites his fellows to discard their clothes (3.17.2).	December 1841[501]
On February 5, 1842, he writes a eulogy in praise of the ruler of Tunis (3.18.6; the letter is dated in the text). Machinations by Metropolitan Atānāsiyūs al-Tutūnjī result in the latter's taking over the Bible translation project; this leads to the closure of the CMS office in Malta, leaving the Fāriyāq with	February to June 1842[504]

Event	Year
no income apart from that from his "physicking" [Arabic teaching] (3.18.1). [Representations to the Committee in London by Metropolitan Atānāsiyūs al-Tutūnjī, a Greek Melkite bishop, in early 1842, to the effect that the Fāriyāq's translation style is "too high" result in him being dismissed from the Bible translation project and the work being assigned to al-Tutūnjī instead.[502] He is assigned to translate another work. In May 1842, the CMS closes its operations in Malta due to a financial crisis and in June the author is dismissed.[503]]	
The author complains to the Society for the Promotion of Christian Knowledge (SPCK) (3.18.7). He renews contact with Sāmī Pasha, an Ottoman official and former head of *al-Waqāʾiʿ al-Miṣriyyah*, who visits the island (3.18.8) and takes him on a trip to Italy (3.18.17).	1844[505]
Eventually, the Fāriyāq's complaints to the SPCK bear fruit, al-Tutūnjī is exposed, and the Fāriyāq is invited by the SPCK to go to England to work on the translation of the *Book of Common Prayer* there [the date given is that of the minutes of the SPCK meeting at which this decision is taken]. He prepares to travel and his wife rejoins him in Malta (3.20.6).	January 28, 1845
Volume Four	
Leaving his wife in Malta, the Fāriyāq travels via Italy, Marseilles, and Paris to London, and thence to a village [Barley, in Hertfordshire, close to Cambridge, where Samuel Lee, the author's collaborator, is rector; the work is carried out at the rectory[506]] (4.3.9–11). After two months,[507] the Fāriyāq moves to Cambridge (4.4.2). During his stay there, he visits London for a month (4.5.7). He returns from London, via Paris and Marseilles, to Malta (4.6.1) and resumes, unhappily, his "physicking" of "the foul of breath" [his teaching Arabic to Maltese].	January to November 1845[508]

Event	Year
The Fāriyāq is invited by the ruler of Tunis to visit that country (4.8.1) with his family (4.8.2) [in response to a second eulogy of its ruler, written on the occasion of the latter's visit to France (November 5 to December 31, 1846)]. They go, are entertained generously by the ruler (4.8.3), and return to Malta (4.8.11).	January or February 1847[509]
The Fāriyāq plans to return to Tunis (4.9.1), but is forestalled by an invitation from "the Committee" [of the SPCK] to return, this time with his family, to England [to work on the translation of the Bible] (4.9.15). They travel to London via Leghorn, Genoa, Marseilles, and Paris, where the Fāriyāq meets Lamartine (4.10.1). After a day in London, they move to the countryside [the village of Barley, as before]. During their stay in that village, they lose their two-year-old son [Asʿad] to illness (4.14.4–5). To escape the memory of this tragedy, they move to Cambridge (4.15.1). The Fāriyāq finishes the translation of the Bible, (4.16.1). Loath to return to Malta, he seeks employment at the University of Oxford (4.16.2) [and other institutions] but is unsuccessful and returns to London, from where he resigns his post in Malta (4.16.3).	September 1848 to December 1850[510]
The Fāriyāq and his wife, both of whom have succumbed to illness in England, move to Paris for the sake of their health (4.16.4). In Paris, the author [works primarily on the correction of the proofs of his translation of the Bible though he also] establishes a language exchange arrangement with a French student and writes a poem in praise of Paris at the behest of an unnamed French scholar (4.18.11).	December 1850 to June 1853[511]
Eventually, the Fāriyāqiyyah is ordered by her doctors to leave Paris for Marseilles (4.18.15). Al-Tutūnjī, however, who is visiting Paris, once again attempts to blacken the Fāriyāq's reputation with the SPCK and is once again foiled (4.19.2). The Fāriyāqiyyah leaves for Marseilles and	Same time period

Event	Year
from there goes to Constantinople (Istanbul) where she is welcomed and hosted by Ṣubḥī Bayk, Sāmī Pasha's son (4.19.3). The Fāriyāq moves into a room on his own in Paris, meets 'Abd al-Qādir al-Jazā'irī, makes the acquaintance of leading French Orientalists, and becomes involved in gambling (4.19.4); he may also have worked as a cook (see the fifth and sixth poems in 4.20.46). [During this period, al-Shidyāq's wife apparently died.]	
[Having visited London on several occasions during the preceding period, he becomes a permanent resident there starting in June 1853.] The author ends by describing how a poem of his dedicated to the Ottoman sultan and expressing his support in the face of the looming war with Russia [the Crimean War] finds favor in the sultan's eyes and how the author is then offered a post with the Imperial Translation Bureau in Istanbul (4.20.2). He delays his departure, however, to oversee the last stages of the production of *Leg over Leg* and makes a trip to Paris, where the book is being printed; due to the machinations of a selfish acquaintance he returns to London prematurely, resulting in a delay in the book's publication. As the book ends, he prepares to leave on a steamer for Turkey (4.20.3). [In the event, his departure for Turkey is thwarted by the outbreak of the Crimean War (1854-1856) and he remains in London (until June 1857, when he departs with his family for Tunis).]	June 1853 to summer 1857[512]

As an appendage to the above, we note that the date of 1857 or 1858 that is sometimes given for al-Shidyāq's conversion to Islam[513] appears to be contradicted by language used in *Leg over Leg*, such as the author's comment regarding a Christian woman, that "she had converted to Islam, praise be to God, Lord of the Worlds" (Volume Two, 2.4.16) (unless this is meant ironically, which seems unlikely: nowhere else does the author use language in any way derogatory of Islam).

Notes

1 Mr. Drummond: unidentified but likely a member of the gentry of the village in which the Fāriyāq was "fated to reside" (see further n55).

2 "amber": i.e., such as that used to make mouthpieces for pipes.

3 "for whose typeface I take no responsibility": elsewhere, the author describes the font used in the first edition, which was made in Paris by the printer, as being "of alien form" (see "A Note on the Arabic Text," Volume One, p.xxxiii n78).

4 "turnips": the author uses the word *qulqās*, which means "taro" or "elephant's ear" (an edible tuber); since the latter is not grown widely in England, it seems likely that he had in mind turnips, which somewhat resemble taro.

5 "a quarter of a language": a reference to the supposed propensity of the author's countrymen for learning only the rude words in any language (see 4.1.3).

6 The narrative of the Fāriyāq's travels now resumes at the point where we left it at the end of the previous volume (Volume Three, 3.20.6), while the repartee that follows is in essence a continuation of that between him and his wife that preceded her own departure earlier for Cairo (Volume Three, 3.20.1–4).

7 "Half the latter and half the former" (*niṣfun min hādhā wa-niṣfun min dhāk*): the Fāriyāqiyyah probably means no more than "a bit of both" but the Fāriyāq takes her words literally (see what follows).

8 "Application of *naḥt* brings us back to the first" (*yurjiʿunā l-naḥtu ilā l-awwal*): *naḥt* means taking parts of two words and creating from them a third; here, the Fāriyāq takes the first half of the first word in his question (*nākir*) and the second half of the second (*shākir*) and finds himself (since the second half of each word is identical) back at the first, i.e., *nākir* ("hatefully").

9 "or the first brings us back to another meaning of *naḥt*" (*aw yurjiʿunā l-awwalu ilā n-naḥt*): the *Qāmūs* gives "intercourse" as one of the meanings of *naḥt*, and the first half of the first word in the Fāriyāq's question, i.e., *nākir*, is *nāk*, which means "to fuck."

10 "Which first did you have in mind?" (*ayyu awwalin aḍmarti*): i.e., "were you thinking of the first part of *nākir* (see preceding note) or of *shākir*," the first part of *shākir* being interpretable as *shākk*, i.e., "doubting."

11 "You forbade me before to deal with you on the basis of suspicion" (*innaki kunti nahaytinī ʿani l-muʿāmalah bi-l-qasm*): here, as in an earlier passage (Volume Three,

3.20.1: "dealing . . . on a basis of conjecture and suspicion"), the author puns on two senses of *qasm*, namely "doubt" and "definition by division" or "logic chopping."

12 "I'm the one sinned against" (*huwa ya'tīnī*): because her husband's questions imply doubt.

13 "Does the word 'no' have no place in your mouth?" (*a-mā fī fīki lafẓatu lā*): presumably meaning, "I would have preferred it if you had simply said, 'No, I won't' in answer to my request that you explain what you meant."

14 "It used to be pronounced 'yes'" (*kānat naʿam*): perhaps meaning, "When we were first married, I never said no to you."

15 "A no from a woman is a boon" (*inna lā mina l-mar'ati ilan*): perhaps implying that the Fāriyāq found his wife's demands exhausting

16 "If a woman doesn't fit properly she'll never give birth" (*wa-lā talidu man lā talīq*): the verb *yalīq* means "to be proper, fitting" (as in the Fāriyāq's statement) and also "to stick, to cling, to fit tightly," as in the Fāriyāqiyyah's.

17 "the same Matter . . . different Forms" (*māddah . . . ikhtilāf al-ṣuwar*): the banter now draws on the terminology of Aristotelian logic, as in an earlier passage (see Volume One, 1.6.4.). In their Aristotelian senses the *māddah* (literally, "matter") is the substratum of which any entity consists and the *ṣūrah* ("picture, shape") is the form in which it is manifested; here, the Fāriyāq argues that the Matter (i.e., sexual intercourse) is the same in essence under all circumstances (and a woman should not therefore need more than one lover) while the Fāriyāqiyyah exploits the Aristotelian idea that Matter must possess a certain degree of consistency to manifest itself to argue that if the Matter is not "copious and inseparable" (*ziyādah muttaṣilah*), it will manifest itself in a variety of Forms, i.e., if a woman does not enjoy sufficient and regular intercourse she will seek a variety of lovers.

18 "in certain circumstances . . . where the circumstances of certain people are concerned" (*fī baʿḍi l-aḥwāl . . . aḥwāli l-baʿḍ*): the Fāriyāqiyyah seems to imply that the Fāriyāq makes an exception, in the case of certain women he knows, from the preference for monogamy that he has just expressed.

19 "*ghāniyah*": literally, "she who dispenses (with something)"; see further Volume One, 1.1.11n105.

20 "*ʿawānī*": plural active participle of the verb *ʿanā* ("to be subservient; to be taken by force"); the Fāriyāqiyyah is reminded of the word because of its resemblance to *ghawānī*, plural of *ghāniyah*, from which it differs, as she goes on to say, by a single dot.

21 "though the dot on the one ought to put in a good word for the other" (*hādhihi n-nuqṭatu shafaʿat fī tilk*): i.e., the dot that produces a word (*ghawānī*) meaning women ought to

intercede to prevent those referred to by an otherwise identical word (*ʿawānī*) from being taken captive.

22 "dotting" (*al-tanqīṭ*): the word may be taken to mean either "placing dots over letters" or "dripping, spotting."

23 "scripting" (*al-taḥrīf*): in the surface context of the discussion of writing, the word may be taken to mean "creating written characters," in that of the sexual subtext as "rubbing against the edge (*ḥarf*)," and in the broader context of men's disingenuousness regarding women as "distorting the meaning (of a word)."

24 "and the woman who chases men ends up unchased" (*wa-l-ṭālibatu taʿūdu ghayra maṭlūbah*): i.e., undesired by her husband because she has entertained a suitor and undesired by her suitor because she has not acceded to his wishes.

25 "*martyrs . . . medulla oblongarters*" (*al-aḥwāl . . . al-abwāl*): the Fāriyāqiyyah means to say, "were it not for the necessity of circumstances, they wouldn't worry their heads about such things"; however, knowing that the singular of *aḥwāl* (literally, "state, condition") is *ḥāl*, she assumes that the plural of *bāl* ("mind, intellect") is *abwāl*, which, in fact, is the plural of *bawl* ("urine"). The translation substitutes a different distortion.

26 "no conformity between male and female or between female and male" (*lam takun munāsabatun bayna l-dhakari wa-l-unthā wa-bayna l-unthā wa-l-dhakar*): perhaps meaning that there would be no words such as *qafā* ("back of the neck") and *kabid* ("liver") that may be treated as either masculine or feminine (for a list see Hava, *al-Farāʾid*, v [unnumbered in the original]).

27 "the masculinization of the true feminine" (*tadhkīr ḥaqīqat al-taʾnīth*): perhaps meaning the formation of words such as *ʿajūz* ("old woman") and *ḥāmil* ("pregnant") that are masculine in form but feminine in meaning (for a list see Hava, *al-Farāʾid*, v [unnumbered in the original]).

28 "the feminization of words that have no equivalent" (*wa-taʾnīthi mā huwa ghayru muqābilin bi-mithlihi*): perhaps meaning that assignment of feminine gender to certain words such as *shams* ("sun") and *kaʾs* ("cup") that are often described as being feminine simply by usage is in fact due to their lack of any formally feminine equivalent (i.e., there is no *shamsah* or *kaʾsah*).

29 "the Syrians" (*al-shāmiyyīn*): a term that here would signify Levantines in general.

30 "Would that I had . . . two hearts to devote to these concerns of ours" (*layta lī qalbayni fī shughlinā*): meaning perhaps, "Would that I could deal with the world (or perhaps specifically the world as it affects 'us,' i.e. , us women) as both a woman and (in the terms described in the preceding passage) a man."

31 "in part by design and in part through preference and predilection" (*baʿḍuhu bi-l-takhṣīṣi wa-baʿḍuhu bi-l-tafḍīli wa-l-īthār*): meaning perhaps that some things (e.g., feminine charms) belong to women by divine design while others (e.g., wealth) do so because men cede them to them.

32 "Judges, chapter 19": the chapter relates how a man, staying overnight in the village of Gibeah, is forced to hand over his concubine to local men and how "they knew her, and abused her all the night until the morning. . . . Then came the woman in the dawning of the day, and fell down at the door of the man's house where her lord was. . . . And her lord rose up in the morning, and opened the doors of the house, and went out to go his way: and, behold, the woman his concubine was fallen down at the door of the house, and her hands were upon the threshold. And he said unto her, Up, and let us be going. But none answered." (Judges 19:25–28)

33 The following definitions in quotation marks are taken by the author directly from the *Qāmūs*.

34 "the sworn virgin, who 'abstains completely from intercourse'" (*al-shafīratu wa-hiya l-qāniʿatu mina l-biʿāli bi-aysarihi*): the author ignores, either carelessly or teasingly, the second and more contextually appropriate meaning of *shafīrah* given in the *Qāmūs*, which is "she who finds her pleasure in the edges of her vagina and therefore comes quickly."

35 4.2.13–16: as in an earlier passage (see 4.2.2), many of the terms used in this debate are taken from the vocabulary of theology (*kalām*) and philosophy (*falsafah*); of note here are *ziyādah* ("increase"), *nuqṣān* ("diminution"), *ṣifah* ("distinguishing characteristic"), *ʿāmm* ("general, universal"), *khāṣṣ* ("particular"), and *q-s-m* "definition by division."

36 "the two last characteristic abilities" (*al-ṣifatān al-madhkūratān*): reference appears to be to keeping going longer, penetrating more deeply, and maintaining a harder erection, with the author either regarding one of these three as subsidiary to one of the others or miscounting.

37 The term *taṣawwur*, meaning how the mind perceives things outside of the soul, is typically translated as "conceptualization" in philosophical contexts such as this. However, given the emphasis on the visual aspect of what is conceptualized elsewhere in the work (see 4.2.8, 4.4.5, 4.6.5, and 4.9.8), "visualization" has sometimes also been used.

38 Yaʿqūb: the reference is perhaps to Yaʿqūb (Jacob) sleeping with Leah when he supposed he was sleeping with Rachel (Gen. 29:23–25).

39 I.e., a woman will "visualize" various men in the hope of selecting from each some physical characteristic that will be passed on to her children.

40 I.e., a man's infidelities, unlike a woman's, do not serve the useful purpose of making their children better-looking since if a woman is unfaithful then her children will be better-looking than if they were fathered by her husband (it being assumed here that husbands are ugly), whereas if her husband is unfaithful his infidelity will (obviously) have no impact upon the looks of her children.

41 "the different ways in which the father and the mother visualize": the implication appears to be that men have no impact on the form of their offspring because they visualize women purely in terms of their sexual traits, while women do have such an impact because they think of men in terms of discrete and not directly sexual attributes; as a rider, it is added that proof that men do not affect the form of their offspring lies in the fact that, if they did, given their narrow obsession with sexual attributes, all their children would be females, etc.

42 "frontward is better" (*al-ṭardu awlā*): the translation reflects the meaning of *al-ṭard* when it occurs in context with *al-ʿaks* ("backward"); alone, however, *al-ṭard* has the also relevant sense of "ejection/ejaculation."

43 "Unitarians . . ." (*al-muwaḥḥidūn* . . .): the Fāriyāqiyyah, in inventing words to describe those who perform once, etc., has hit on the names of various religious sects, for which the Fāriyāq makes fun of her by invoking further real sects whose names can be similarly interpreted; thus the Muʿtazilites were practitioners of speculative dogmatism but the word can be taken to mean "those who withdraw," while the Muʿaṭṭilites were deniers of the divine attributes but the word can be taken as meaning "those who go on strike."

44 "without redeeming qualities" etc.: the Fāriyāqiyyah, being ignorant of the specialized meaning of the word (see preceding note), takes it in its literal sense of "strikers" (i.e., men who down tools).

45 "'My sense of feeling,' I said, 'is in my head'" (*ḥissī fī raʾsī*): though the author appears at first to be alluding to the opposition of heart vs. head, it emerges that by "head" he means "tip" (of the male member).

46 "Try then to break it" (*ḥāwil idhan fakkahu*): the surface meaning seems to be an appeal to the Fāriyāq to break the closed circle of their argument; however, it may also be read as a request to restore their amicable relationship by initiating sexual intercourse.

47 "I reject such a characterization" (*lā arḍā bi-hādhihi ṣ-ṣifah*): the Fāriyāq (presumably willfully) mishears *al-ʿaqd* ("contract") as *al-ʿaqid*, which can mean (of a dog) "[having its] penis . . . *compressus in coitu, et extremitate turgens*" (Lane, *Lexicon*).

48 "Was the contract over the condition?" (*hal kāna al-ʿaqdu fī l-sharṭ*): meaning either, "Was the contract (between us) dependent on the condition (*sharṭ*) (that we remain

faithful to one another)?" or "Was the contract between us dependent on the slit (also *sharṭ*)?"

49 "And was the condition without a contract?" (*wa-hal kāna l-sharṭu bi-lā ʿaqd*): or "and was the slit without a contract?", i.e., "and could you have [access to] the slit without a [marriage] contract?"

50 "that lunatic": i.e., the Bag-man who went insane and stripped off his clothes (see Volume Three, 3.17.2).

51 "utmost goal" (*muhwaʾannahā*): defined in the *Lisān* as "distant place" (*makān baʿīd*) and "broad desert" (*ṣaḥrāʾ wāsiʿ*) , the word is not found in the *Qāmūs* and seems out of place here; the translation is speculative.

52 "The king's heart is in the hand of the Lord": not in fact Psalms but Proverbs 21:1.

53 "he was 'rubbing' him" (*yatamassaḥu bihi*): on the practice of drawing the hands over the accoutrements of venerated persons, see Volume One, 1.16.7n245.

54 "the Sublime State" (*al-dawlah al-ʿaliyyah*): the Ottoman Empire.

55 "that village": i.e., Barley in Hertfordshire, where the Reverend Samuel Lee, professor of Hebrew and formerly of Arabic at Cambridge and with whom the author was engaged in the translation of the Bible, was rector; the work was carried out at the rectory (see Roper, "Aḥmad Fāris" 236).

56 "the book referred to earlier": i.e., the Bible; see Volume Three, 3.18.1n198.

57 "the *ḥadanbadā* chapter": i.e. Volume Three, chapter 19, of which *ḥadanbadā* ("marvel") is the second word.

58 "the element of discussion" (*rukn al-dhikr*): see 4.2.16.

59 "for the pressing . . ." (*lil-nabrah . . .*): in the first item of each of the following pairs, the word in question is used in its nontechnical sense, while in the second it is used in its technical sense according to the lexicon of phonetics and/or Qur'anic recitation; thus *nabrah,* as the second term, means stress or accent, *hamzah* means a glottal stop, *ḥarakah* a vowel (because a consonant followed by a vowel is said to be "in motion"), *sukūn* a consonant not followed by a vowel (because such letters are said to be "inert"), *madd* the prolongation of *a* to *ā* in a variety of vocalic contexts (see Wright: *Grammar* I/24–25), *hadhdh* a rapid quickening of pace in the recitation of the Qurʾān (considered inappropriate), *tarkhīm* the omission of one or more of the final letters of a noun in the vocative indicating a low level of energy in the uttering of the word, *tarassul* a slowing of the pace of a reading.

60 "doubling of the letter *dhāl*" (*al-tashdīd ʿalā l-dhāl*): perhaps meaning specifically in the word *al-dhakar* ("the penis"). As a "sun" letter, *dhāl* (/*dh*/) is assimilated to the *lām* (/*l*/)

of the definite article; thus *al-dhakar* is pronounced *adh-dhakar*, providing the speaker, in this case, with an opportunity to give extra prominence to the word.

61 "The best way to mend a slit is to sew it up" (*inna dawāʾa l-shaqqi an taḥūṣahu*): proverbial (see the *Qāmūs* s.v. *ḥ-w-ṣ*).

62 Ibn Alghaz: the name of a man of whom it is said that he was "much given to copulation and intercourse; he would lie down and get an erection, and the young camels would come and rub themselves against his penis, taking it for a scratching post" (*Qāmūs*).

63 the Banū Adhlagh: a tribe "characterized by intercourse" (*Qāmūs*).

64 "If at first you don't succeed . . . " (*al-ʿawdu aḥmad*): a proverb; literally, "A second, or subsequent, attempt (after a failure) is more likely to succeed because of the experience gained" (al-Maydānī, *Majmaʿ* I:324).

65 "Always count twice" (*man ʿadda ʿād*): the proverb has not been found in the sources and the relevance in this context is not obvious.

66 "Come early as the crow" (*bakkir bukūra l-ghurāb*): the crow being, proverbially, the first bird to wake (al-Maydānī, *Majmaʿ* I:79).

67 "turning disdainfully to one side . . . like a mirage dissipating" (*al-ṣufūḥ . . . muzlaʾimmah*): the following list of words related to shying and fleeing is shorter than that in the original and is intended as a representation, not a one-to-one translation, of the latter, using words from the same semantic areas drawn from thesauri, dictionaries, and other lexical resources; see further Volume Four, Translator's Afterword.

68 "an agitation . . . a rattling of the jaw" (*al-qushaʿrīrah . . . al-qafqufah*): the list of thirty-seven words in the original relating to *riʿdah* ("shaking"), *qushaʿrīrah* ("shivering"), and *ḥāʾir bāʾir* ("dizzy-headedness") (see 5.2.11) is represented here by twenty-nine English words or phrases selected from *Roget's Thesaurus* (see Translator's Afterword); *ʿusūm* is, according to the *Qāmūs*, the verbal noun of *ʿasama* "to gain," but the author appears to use it as the verbal noun of *ʿasima* "to suffer stiffness of the wrist or ankle joint," for which the correct form, according to the *Qāmūs*, is *ʿasam*.

69 "the four humors . . . each mix" (*al-akhlāṭu l-arbaʿatu . . . kullu khilṭ*): according to the Galenic system, varying combinations of the four humors (blood, black bile, yellow bile, and phlegm) in the body result in different moods (sanguine, melancholic, choleric, and phlegmatic).

70 "euphorbia fruit" (*qurmūṭah*): the comparison of euphorbia fruit, or red scrub berries, to women's breasts is conventional; see Volume Three, 3.6.8.

71 "Joshua would not have been able to enter the Promised Land": the reference is to Rahab the harlot (Josh. 2).

72 "Abraham would not have found favor with the King of Egypt": the reference is to Sarai, wife of Abram (i.e., Sarah, wife of Abraham), see Gen. 12:14–16.

73 "David . . . an image in his bed": "Saul also sent messengers unto David's house, to watch him, and to slay him in the morning: and Michal David's wife told him, saying, If thou save not thy life to night, to morrow thou shalt be slain. So Michal let David down through a window: and he went, and fled, and escaped. And Michal took an image, and laid it in the bed, and put a pillow of goats' hair for his bolster, and covered it with a cloth" (1 Sam. 19:11–13).

74 "the wife of Nabal": i.e., Abigail (1 Sam. 25).

75 "Bathsheba's stratagem against David": 1 Kings 1:11–14.

76 "the Anglican sect" (*madhhab al-inkilīz*): referring, presumably, to Queen Elizabeth I (cf. Volume Two, 2.14.89).

77 "the *ḍād* . . . the *ḍa'd*": the letter *ḍād* is supposedly unique to Arabic, which is often referred to as *lughat al-ḍād* ("the language of the *ḍād*"); *ḍa'd*, a variant of *ḍād*, also means "the vagina," probably because of the shape of the letter (ض), as is the case with the letter *ṣād* (ص), from which it differs only in having a dot (see similarly Volume Two, 2.4.15n79).

78 "the *mīm*": i.e., the letter *mīm* (م), which stands for the anus (see similarly Volume Two, 2.4.15n79).

79 "because the more bitter cold required that" (*li-kawni ziyādati qarṣati l-bardi awjaba dhālik*): meaning, presumably, that the women had been forced to put on thicker clothing.

80 "for everything that falls there's something to pick it up" (*li-kulli sāqiṭah lāqiṭah*): i.e., approx. "every Jack has his Jill," it being noted that *sāqiṭah* may also be understood to mean "fallen woman."

81 "When you enter the land of al-Ḥuṣayb, run" (*idhā ji'ta arḍa l-Ḥuṣaybi fa-harwil*): according to the *Qāmūs*, al-Ḥuṣayb is a place in Yemen "whose women are of surpassing beauty."

82 "Londra": the author alternates throughout the text between this Italian- (or possibly French-) derived form, which was that used at the time in Lebanon, and "London."

83 "hips": in the Arabic, "forearms" (*al-sā'idayn*).

84 "with undoing, dresses" (*wa-mina l-ḥalli ḥulal*): presumably meaning that a woman's acquiescence to a man's demands leads to her acquisition of dresses.

85 "with this trait" (*bi-hādhihi l-ḥilyah*): i.e., with the trait of contrariness and refusal to compromise.

86 "'A woman's eyes,' she declared . . . the situation I have described will come about" (*qālat inna ʿaynay al-marʾah . . . fa-waqaʿa mā qult*): i.e., if a woman does not keep track of how distant or close she and her husband are, the balance between the two will be disturbed (to her disadvantage).

87 "O delight of my eye!" (*yā qurrata l-ʿayn*): i.e., why do people use this phrase that implies that the eye is given to content rather than discontent?

88 "Prevention of your neighbor from visiting your house": to be taken in the context of his later reference to a handsome young neighbor who is always dropping by (4.7.4).

89 "the hair on the lower sprouts before the hair on the upper" (*shaʿru l-aʿlā yanbitu qabla l-asfal*): apparently "the hair on the upper" means the facial hair, even though the Fāriyāqiyyah subsequently talks of head hair.

90 "the first category": i.e., to the physical rather than the moral difference between men and women.

91 "trenches . . . firestones, campsites . . . women in camel litters" (*nuʾy . . . athāfī . . . dawāris . . . ẓawāʿin*): all these items are frequently referred to in pre-Islamic poetry; *nuʾy* are trenches dug around a tent pitched in the desert to take runoff from rain water; the *athāfī* are the three stones placed under a cooking pot as trivets; *dawaris* are the traces of a campsite (such as that formerly containing the beloved); *ẓawāʿin* are covered camel litters in which women ride.

92 "in origin they mean 'of unpleasant appearance'": the *Qāmūs* says: "*al-basl* [sic] means . . . the man who is of unpleasant appearance."

93 "All good things come to those who wait. . . . And every good thing should make love" (*kullu ātin qarīb . . . wa-kullu qarībin ātin*): the first phrase (literally, "everything that is near is coming") is a proverb, which the Fāriyāqiyyah then twists by taking *ātin*, active participle of *atā* "to come," in another of its senses, namely, "to have intercourse with" (cf. Q Shuʿarāʾ 26:165).

94 "such a 'universal' statement" (*bi-hādhihi l-kulliyyah*): as earlier (see Volume Two, 2.18.4n280), Aristotelian logic is invoked.

95 "all" (*jamīʿan*): i.e., the Fāriyāq, the Fāriyāqiyyah, and their child.

96 "the greatest of their poets": from the *muʿallaqah*, or "suspended ode," of Imruʾ al-Qays (translation: Arberry, *Seven Odes*, 63).

97 "the quintessence and best part of blood is of that color" (*khulāṣata l-dami wa-ṣafwatahu huwa fī dhālika l-lawn*): according to Aristotle, semen is formed from blood.

98 "So that's the reason!" (*fa-hādhā huwa l-sababu idhan*): i.e., the people of London like the color white because it is the color of semen.

99 "Now the truth has come to light" (*al-āna qad ḥaṣḥaṣa l-ḥaqq*): Q Yūsuf 12:51.

100 "the red" (*al-aḥmar*): presumably meaning, in light of the preceding, "semen."

101 "Great indeed / is women's guile" (*īnna kayda l-nisāʾi kāna ʿaẓīman*): reminiscent of Q Yūsuf 12:28.

102 "even if their promenading is leading them at that very moment to trial and litigation before His Honor the Judge": i.e., "even if they are in the process of taking one another to court."

103 "seeking to 'mix the rough with the smooth'" (*ṭalaban li-l-murāzamah*): perhaps to be taken in the sense of the saying of ʿUmar ibn al-Khaṭṭāb *idhā akaltum rāzimū* ("When ye eat . . . mix ye, in your eating, what is soft with what is hard") (Lane, *Lexicon*), the emphasis here being not on texture, however, but on variety.

104 "food for two will satisfy three" (*ṭaʿāma thnayni yushbiʿu thalāthah*): reminiscent of the hadith *ṭaʿāmu thnayni kāfī thalāthah wa-ṭaʿāmu l-thalāthati kāfī l-arbaʿah* ("the food of two is enough for three and the food of three for four").

105 "and give him hope" (*wa-tumannīhi*): or, punningly, "make him produce semen."

106 I.e., "When the husband hears that his neighbor devours his (i.e., his neighbor's) wife's lips and lies with her under her shift, so that she (the husband's wife) neither dreams of the neighbor nor he (the neighbor) of her (the husband's wife)."

107 "the swooning prude" (*al-rabūkh*): "the woman who faints during intercourse" (*Qāmūs*).

108 "back-passage bleeder" (*al-salaqlaq*): "the woman who menstruates through her anus" (*Qāmūs*).

109 "the single-barreled bawd" (*al-sharīm*): "the woman who has had so much intercourse that her two passages [the vagina and the rectum] have become one" (*Qāmūs*).

110 "play the mooning she-camel that lives its false calf to lick, for I see curly shavings on the fire stick" (*fa-ttakhidhī mudhi l-yawmi ẓīrā fa-ʾinnī arā fī l-zan(a)di īrā*): a *ẓīr* is "one [esp. a she-camel] *that inclines to*, or *affects, the young one of another, and suckles* [or *fosters*] *it*" (Lane, *Lexicon*, quoting the *Qāmūs*); *zand* ("fire stick") may also be read as *zanad* ("a stone wrapped up in pieces of rag . . . which is stuffed into a she-camel's vulva, when she is made to take a liking to the young one of another" [Lane, *Lexicon*, quoting the *Qāmūs*]); *īr* "shavings" may also be read as *ayr* ("penis"), in which case the second clause may be taken to mean "for I see a penis in [place of] the stone wrapped in rags that takes the place, etc."

111 In 1850 the author sent Queen Victoria an ode in her praise which he also had translated into English and published at his own expense as a broadsheet; however, he received neither acknowledgment nor reward for his pains (see Arberry, "Fresh Light" and *Arabic Poetry*, 136ff, both of which reproduce the Arabic text and Arberry's translation).

112 "the Austrians of Schiller": Schiller was born and died in states that were part of the Holy Roman Empire and he might be better described as German; perhaps the author was influenced by the fact that during the period covered by this book, the Austrian Empire (1804–67) was the largest and strongest member of the German Confederation, ergo the most prominent German-speaking state.

113 "rhyme-consonants and rhymes" (*al-rawīy wa-l-qāfiyah*): the *rawīy* is the final consonant at the end of a line of verse and thus "the essential part of the rhyme" (Wright: *Grammar* II:352); the *qāfiyah* is the combination of consonants and vowels that constitute the sonic effect. Both are governed by complex rules.

114 The author appears to have in mind the license required (in England, for instance, from the Lord Chamberlain) before writers such as Shakespeare could perform their works.

115 From the *muʿallaqah* ("suspended ode") of Imruʾ al-Qays (mid-sixth century AD; translation Arberry, *Seven Odes*, 62); the reference is to a woman who tends to her baby while having intercourse with the poet.

116 From the *muʿallaqah* ("suspended ode") of ʿAntarah ibn Shaddād (mid-sixth century AD; translation Arberry, *Seven Odes*, 182).

117 "the August Master": i.e., the ruler of Tunis.

118 "my eulogy of Our Lord the Emir": i.e., of the ruler of Tunis (this eulogy is not reproduced in the book).

119 "One of those ancient delusions of yours" (*min ḍalālika l-qadīm*): cf. Q Ṭā Hā 20:95 *qālū ta-llāhi innaka la-fī ḍalālika l-qadīm* ("They said, 'By God, you still persist in your old delusions!'"), said by the sons of Yaʿqūb (Jacob) to the latter when he persisted in believing that Yūsuf (Joseph) would return.

120 "the three": i.e., sensual pleasure, this world, and the next.

121 "*hakhakah*": "copiousness of intercourse" (*Qāmūs*).

122 "a reduplicative formed from *hakka hakka*" (*muḍāʿif hakka hakka*): Arabic allows the formation of new, quadriliteral, verbs from simple geminate verbs such as *hakka* ("to have sexual intercourse with a woman with force or with frequency") (*Qāmūs*) with intensifying effect; the other verbs that follow all mean "to have sexual intercourse with" (though *hanā* has not been found in the lexica, it presumably derives from *han(ah)*, "thing" or "vagina").

123 "the ones that preceded it": i.e., the verbs meaning "(plain, one-go-per-session) intercourse" (*biʿāl, mubāʿalah*) cited above.

124 "corruption" (*khamaj*): or, punningly, "lassitude."

125 "those things the Franks wear down to their waists" (*hādhihi llatī talbisuhā l-ifrinju ʿilā khuṣurihim*): i.e., jackets.

126 "a bin . . . platter" (*al-quffah . . . al-ṣaffūt*): the following list is shorter than that of words meaning kinds of basket or other containers (see 5.2.11) in the original and is intended as a representation, not a one-to-one translation, of the latter using words from the same semantic areas drawn from thesauri, dictionaries, and other lexical resources; see further Volume Four, Translator's Afterword.

127 "though not in terms of his specific attributes but as an example of the attributes of the absolute" (*lā bi-l-ṣifati l-ʿayyinati bal bi-l-ṣifati l-muṭlaqah*): i.e., as a representative of his sex in general, not because of his individual traits.

128 "her bedmate . . . her intimate" (*kamīʿahā . . . wa-khalīlahā*): the following list is shorter than that of words of the highly productive *faʿīl* pattern (see 5.2.12) in the original and is intended as a representation, not a one-to-one translation, of the latter using words from the same semantic areas drawn from thesauri, dictionaries, and other lexical resources; see further Volume Four, Translator's Afterword..

129 "clapper-board" (*nāqūs*): a wooden board or plank functioning, when struck with a mallet, as a gong.

130 Cf. the *Qāmūs*, III:377.

131 "Your friend" (*ṣāḥibuka*): the Fāriyāqiyyah picks up on the Fāriyāq's earlier reference to "the author of the *Qāmūs*" as *ṣāḥib al-Qāmūs* but understands the word in its more vernacular meaning of "friend."

132 "language is a female" (*al-lughatu unthā*): the Fāriyāqiyyah appears to be unaware that the word for "feminine" as a grammatical gender category is *muʾannath* while *unthā* refers to sexual gender.

133 "which are neither voweled nor unvoweled" (*wa-hiya laysat mina l-ḥarakati wa-lā l-sukūn*): meaning perhaps, "which are free of the male-constructed constraints of language."

134 "Conversation's carpet . . . reach its end . . . End of Days" (*fa-ʾinnamā huwa bisāṭ ḥadīth qad nushira fa-lā yuṭwā ḥattā naṣila ilā ākhirihā*): in the Arabic, the pun turns on the two meanings of the verb *nashara*: "to unroll" and "to resurrect."

135 "desert rose" (*jarāz*): a plant (Adenium obesum) distinguished by its "stout, swollen basal caudex" (http://en.wikipedia.org/wiki/Adenium_obesum).

136 "removing facial hair using a thread" (*al-taḥaffuf*): probably meaning the use of a doubled thread, looped around the fingers, whose ends are held between the beautician's teeth and which is worked by moving the head back and forth, causing the threads to revolve and thus catch and pluck out the hairs, as practiced in Egypt today.

137 "the pelvic egg" (*bayḍat al-ʿuqr*): according to the *Lisān*, an egg laid by a cockerel, used, because of its softness and delicacy, to test the virginity of slave girls.

138 “such things not being considered speech by the grammarians” (*wa-hwa ʿinda l-nuḥāti laysa bi-kalām*): in grammatical theory, the term *kalām* (“speech”) is properly bestowed only on statements that are *mufīdah* (“information-bearing”), i.e., that convey a complete thought and are thus meaningful; the author misrepresents this concept to include within it statements such as his earlier ones concerning women that are, according to his assertion, too banal and obvious to be regarded as information-bearing, and which fail, therefore, to qualify as true speech.

139 “[having] a clean-plucked beard and a pocket with a hole in it” (*mantūf al-liḥyah mukharraq al-jayb*): perhaps meaning “destitute, taken to the cleaners” (by his wife).

140 “our friend” (*ṣāḥibinā*): i.e., his future employer, for whom they are bound.

141 “Perhaps . . . excitement” (*laʿalla . . . al-tashwīq*): meaning perhaps that the thought of finding men (even mad ones) out on the streets in England and not closeted in their houses is responsible for her excitement at being there.

142 “ a city thronging with men”: i.e., Cambridge (cf. 4.4.2 and 4.5.7).

143 “the village for which they were bound”: see 4.10.7n55.

144 “Man is a creature of haste” (*khuliqa l-inṣanu min ʿajal*): Q Anbiyāʾ 21:37.

145 “Would you be kind enough to explain them to me?” (*fa-hal laka an tuwaqqifanī ʿalayh*): in his response, the Fāriyāq pretends to understand these words in an alternative sense: “Would you be kind enough to stick me on it?”

146 “cheap girls who laugh till they’re fit to bust . . . the unjust” (*al-tāghiyāt . . . al-ṭāghiyāt*): the Fāriyāqiyyah mishears the *t* of *tāghiyāt* (“slave girls who try to hide their laughter but are overcome by it”) as the *ṭ* of *ṭāghiyāt* (“[female] oppressors”).

147 “snacking . . . unenthusiastically” (*naʾj . . . tamaṣṣuṣ*): the following list of words referring to “tasting” and “sipping” (see 5.2.12) is shorter than that in the original and is intended as a representation, not a one-to-one translation, of the latter using words from the same semantic areas drawn from thesauri, dictionaries, and other lexical resources; see further Volume Four, Translator’s Afterword.

148 “sedateness . . . sanctimony” (*al-tarazzun . . . al-tanaẓẓuf*): the following list of words referring to “reticence,” “wariness,” and “caution” (see 5.2.12) is shorter than that in the original and is intended as a representation, not a one-to-one translation, of the latter using words from the same semantic areas drawn from thesauri, dictionaries, and other lexical resources; see further Volume Four, Translator’s Afterword.

149 “expose their backsides to warm them up” (*kashf adbārihim li-l-iṣṭilāʾ*): the image evoked is that of a man standing in front of a fireplace and raising his coattails.

150 “my armpit when he stretched out his body” (*rufghī idhā mā sbaṭarrā*): or, “my cunny when he lay down flat” (see the *Qāmūs*: *al-rufgh* “the armpit, or the area around a

woman's vulva" and *isbaṭarrā* "he laid down, or extended himself" and *sibaṭr* "the lion when it extends its body on leaping").

151 "their hands concealed / In skins" (*wa-l-rāḥu minhunna bi-l-jildi mustatirātun*): i.e., "wearing gloves."

152 "she spears" (*wa-ta'khudhu . . . bi-l-mishakkah*): presumably meaning the old woman referred to at the start of the poem, the abruptness of the shift of subject being attributable to the missing lines.

153 "privacy . . . wife" (*ḥurmatahu*): *ḥurmah* means both "sanctity, inviolability" and "wife."

154 "our friends": i.e., the English.

155 The Fāriyāq's translation appears to assume that the verses are addressed by a woman to a man, though the switch from first person (*su'lī ʿindak*) to third (*wa-blugh . . . minhā*) is problematic; some elements of the equally baffling English are missing from the Fāriyāq's translation.

156 "he's complaining of himself" (*huwa yashkū min nafsih*): apparently meaning that the poet is implying that he is incapable of satisfying the woman.

157 "turnips" (*qulqās*): see 4.1.10n4.

158 Cf. Deut. 7:13 "And he will love thee, and bless thee, and multiply thee: he will also bless the fruit of thy womb, and the fruit of thy land, thy corn, and thy wine, and thine oil, the increase of thy kine, and the flocks of thy sheep, in the land which he sware unto thy fathers to give thee."

159 Jephthah the Gileadite: see Judg. 11:1 "Now Jephthah the Gileadite was a mighty man of valor, and he was the son of an harlot" and 11:29ff.

160 "or so the theologians assert" (*kamā afādahu l-mutakallimūn*): the allusion is to the discussion among theologians of who—God or man—is responsible for evil, the Muʿtazilites, for example, claiming that man is responsible, the Ashʿarites, God, although the author appears to have either forgotten that the standard terms are *ḥasan* (rather than *jamīl*) for "good" and *qabīḥ* for "evil," or else has adapted the argument to his ongoing concern with the physically beautiful (*jamīl*) and the ugly (*qabīḥ*).

161 "well-endowed in both senses" (*al-jihāzān*): *jihāz* means both "dowry" and "genitalia."

162 "nothing of that greenness brings a flush of good cheer" (*lā shay'a min hādhihi l-khuḍrati yubayyiḍu l-wajh*): literally, "nothing of that greenness whitens the face," "whitening of the face" being a familiar trope.

163 See Volume One, 1.13.2n219.

164 "confines himself to 'the little nest'" (*yuḥaffishu*): the author appears to be reading the laconic definition of *taḥfīsh* that he quotes (from the *Qāmūs*) in the light of another found in the same entry there, namely, *ḥifsh*, meaning "vagina."

165 "a fastness . . . dry" (*manzahan . . . al-mā'*): a basic meaning of the root *n-z-h* is "to be distant" and especially "to be distant from anything unpleasant"; however, the *Qāmūs* highlights certain collocations in which the sense is specifically "to be distant from water."

166 "viceroy to the Creator of Nations" (*khalīfat bārī l-umam*): i.e., the Ottoman caliph.

167 "hands free, his cuffs unsoiled" (*yaduhu khafīfah rānifatuhu naẓīfah*): probably meaning that he can go home without passing by the market first to burden himself with food items demanded by his wife and getting his cuffs dirty.

168 "like a bad penny" (*sayra l-'ajāj fī kulli fujāj*): literally, "like flying dust in every mountain pass."

169 The poem that follows only gets around to comparing the married state with bachelorhood in its last lines (4.13.8), perhaps not surprisingly given that it was not written as a response to al-Hāwif ibn Hifām's question; earlier lines seem to reflect the Fāriyāq's anxieties about the pressures to which his own marriage was subject in foreign environments.

170 "his money" (*filsihi*): or, colloquially and punningly, "his anus."

171 "his spine, / His resuscitator from misery": alluding to the belief that semen is generated in the spine.

172 "The stranger . . . folk" (*inna l-gharība . . . jinsihi*): the "stranger" is presumably the one, referred to above, who marries in a small village, i.e., not in his hometown, but the wider meaning remains elusive.

173 "So long as the advantages of starting over at it / Do not damage the ending of what was good" (*mā in yaḍurra khitāma mā / qad ṭāba nāfi'u rassihi*): perhaps meaning "Do not become so attracted to the pleasures of initiating new marriages that you end earlier ones badly."

174 "And many a mother and child . . ." (*wa-rubba ummin wa-ṭiflin . . .*): the quotation is from an elegy for al-Andalus written by Abū l-Baqā' al-Rundī (601/1204 to 684/1285).

175 Num. 31:15–17: "And Moses said unto them . . . Now therefore kill every male among the little ones."

176 "Death's rule on Man's imposed. . . . This world for permanence can furnish no abode" (*ḥukmu l-maniyyati fī l-barriyyati jārī. . . . mā hādhihi l-dunyā bi-dāri qarārī*): these two hemistichs, here separated from each other and used as the second half of each of two verses, are taken from and together originally form the first verse of a poem by Abū l-Ḥasan al-Tihāmī al-Ḥasanī (d. 416/1025) composed to mourn the death of the poet's son at the age of fourteen; al-Shidyāq goes on to quote another well-known verse from the same poem below ("I kept company with my neighbors, he with His Lord— / And how different his neighbors from mine!"—see 4.14.8).

177 “the Fāriyāq had no choice but to live close to that ill-fated village”: because it was where he was working; see 4.4.1n55.

178 “Two weak things will conquer a stronger” (*wa-ḍaʿīfāni yaghlibāni qawiyyan*): the words are by Ṣafī al-Dīn al-Ḥillī (667/1278 to ca. 750/1349) (in the original *fa-ḍaʿīfāni*); the preceding hemistich runs *lā tuḥārib bi-nāẓirayka fuʾādī* (“Do not wage war with your eyes on my heart”).

179 “to peer . . . meditate” (*al-ṣaʾṣaʾah . . . al-tarannī*): the following list of words relating to “looking and its various forms” (see 5.2.12) is shorter than that in the original and is intended as a representation, not a one-to-one translation, of the latter using words from the same semantic areas drawn from thesauri, dictionaries, and other lexical resources; see further Volume Four, Translator’s Afterword.

180 “from a drop of mingled fluid” (*min nuṭfatin amshājin*): cf. Q Insān 76:2.

181 Ashʿab: i.e., Ashʿab ibn Jubayr (born 9/630–31, died during the reign of al-Mahdī, 158/775 to 169/785), whose greed became the subject of many anecdotes.

182 *qalb* (“heart”) is from the same root as the verbs meaning “to turn, transmute,” etc., a fact of which the author has already made full use in this passage, as have numerous poets and writers before him.

183 Hind and Daʿd: stereotypical names of the beloved woman.

184 “The Fāriyāq resumed”: the author appears to have forgotten that the Fāriyāq has not been described earlier as speaking.

185 “*aḥaddahā* or *ḥaddadahā . . . taḥiddu*”: these words are taken from the *Qāmūs*.

186 “and you know better than I the full sense of that word” (*wa-nta bi-tamāmi l-maʿnā adrā*): *sabd* (which is the voweling in the Arabic text) may mean, in addition to the meanings already noted by the author, “wolf” and “calamity”; however, it seems likely that he has in mind the form *subad* (indistinguishable from the former when short vowels are not written), meaning “the pubes” (*al-ʿānah*).

187 “a large musical instrument” (*ālatu ṭarabin ʿaẓīmah*): *ālah* (“instrument, tool”) is frequently used in a sexual sense.

188 “to vie with me in quoting poetry” (*tushāʿiranī*): or, punningly, “to sleep under the same blanket with me.”

189 “for I possess the very source from which relief (*faraj*) is derived” (*fa-inna ʿindī maṣdara shtiqāqi l-faraj*): the author plays with the fact that the verbal noun (*maṣdar*, lit. “source”) of *faraja* (“to provide relief to someone [of God]”) is *farj*, which also has the sense of “vagina.”

190 “if he hadn’t at first succeeded, he wouldn’t if he tried again” (*inna l-ʿawda ilayhā ghayru aḥmad*): a play on the proverb *al-ʿawdu aḥmad* (see 4.4.6n64).

191 "no metropolitan or monk": presumably another dig at Metropolitan Atanāsiyūs al-Tutūnjī (see Volume Two, 2.3.5n66 and 2.9.3 and, in this volume, 4.19).

192 "William Scoltock": matriculated at Christ Church, Oxford in 1842 aged 19, became an inspector of schools, and died 1886. "Williams" in the Arabic is the author's error.

193 "mature horses run ever longer heats" (*jaryu l-mudhakkiyāti ghilā'*): see al-Maydānī 1:106 (s.v. *jaryu . . . ghilāb*).

194 "swan-necked" (*al-jūd*): in view of the context, this may be a misprint for *al-ḥūr* ("having eyes like those of gazelles and of cows") (Lane, *Lexicon*).

195 "the scrubbers" (*al-ḥakkākāt*): the true significance of this word becomes clear only at the end of this list (4.16.5).

196 "vibrating . . . scudding" (*tatadhabdhabu . . . taṣrā*): the following list of words meaning "she moves" and/or "she oscillates" (see 5.2.12) is shorter than that in the original and is intended as a representation, not a one-to-one translation, of the latter using words from the same semantic areas drawn from thesauri, dictionaries, and other lexical resources; see further Volume Four, Translator's Afterword.

197 "What a monstrous thing to say!" (*laqad kabura qawlan*): an echo of the Qur'ān's *kaburat kalimatan takhruju min afwāhihim* ("What they say is monstrous; they are merely uttering falsehoods!" (Q Kahf 18:5).

198 "panderation . . . cuckoldism" (*daybūbiyyah . . . arfaḥiyyah*): the following list of words related to "the condition of being a pander or a wittol" (see 5.2.12) is shorter than that in the original and is intended as a representation, not a one-to-one translation, of the latter using words from the same semantic areas drawn from thesauri, dictionaries, and other lexical resources; see further Volume Four, Translator's Afterword.

199 "as it does in this noble language of ours": according to the *Lisān*, the (ancient) Arabs used the word *'atabah* ("doorstep") as an epithet for a woman.

200 "sprinkle white ashes on their heads": i.e., wear powdered wigs.

201 "slipways . . . hides" (*al-mazālij . . . al-maṣālī*): the following list of words related to "traps, snares, and associated words" (see 5.2.13) is shorter than that in the original and is intended as a representation, not a one-to-one translation, of the latter using words from the same semantic areas drawn from thesauri, dictionaries, and other lexical resources; see further Volume Four, Translator's Afterword.

202 "liquid account" (*sayyāl*): defined by the *Qāmūs* simply as "a kind of account/calculation" and not found elsewhere; the translation derives from the base sense of the root.

203 "precautionary blank-filling" (*al-tarqīm wa-l-tarqīn*): Lane, *Lexicon*: "A certain sign, or mark, of the keepers of the register of the [tax . . .] conventionally used by them, put

upon . . . accounts, or reckonings, lest it should be imagined that a blank has been left [to be afterwards filled up], in order that no account be put down therein."

204 "under the letter *yā'*" (*fī bāb al-yā'*): the primary organizing element of the *Qāmūs* is the final root consonant; thus words of the root *j-dh-y*, such as *judhā'*, ought to appear there under *yā'*.

205 "nasality . . . movingly" (*bi-l-ghunnah . . . wa-l-tarniyah*): the following list of words relating to "qualities of voice and setting to music" (see 5.2.13) is shorter than that in the original and is intended as a representation, not a one-to-one translation, of the latter using words from the same semantic areas drawn from thesauri, dictionaries, and other lexical resources; see further Volume Four, Translator's Afterword. The list includes a number of technical terms from Arabic phonetics and prosody and the science of Qur'anic recitation that by definition have no equivalents in English.

206 "the curling of the hair, its . . . rumpling" (*taqṣību l-sha'r . . . wa-taghbiyatuhu*): the following list of words relating to "hair dressing and its styles" (see 5.2.13) is shorter than that in the original and is intended as a representation, not a one-to-one translation, of the latter using words from the same semantic areas drawn from thesauri, dictionaries, and other lexical resources; see further Volume Four, Translator's Afterword.

207 "the *ku'kubbah* and the *muqaddimah*": the *ku'kubbah* is a way of wearing braids (see Volume Three, 3.9.1n106); the *muqaddimah* is defined in the *Qāmūs* as "a way of combing the hair."

208 "*rigadoon*" (*rīdūqā*): the identification is tentative.

209 "in abject submission" (*qalbuhu bayna rijlayhā*): the literal meaning of the phrase is "with his heart between her legs" and both reverses the standard expression *bayna yaday* . . . (lit. "between the hands of . . ." meaning "in front of . . . , before . . .") and allows an obvious sexual reading.

210 "they drop the ends of all the masculine words and pronounce them in the feminine" (*yaḥdhifūna fī l-lafẓi awākhira jamī'i l-alfāẓi l-mudhakkari wa-yanṭuqūna bi-hā fī l-mu'annath*): the author was perhaps thinking of a situation such as *épicier* ("male grocer") versus *épicière* ("female grocer"), where the "r" is heard only in the second.

211 "the masculine should take precedence over the feminine" (*taghlīb al-mudhakkar 'alā l-mu'annath*): probably a reference to the rule that in any plural group, if even one masculine element is introduced, the entire group is treated as masculine plural (example: *les filles et les garçons sont venus* ["the girls and boys have come"]), where *venus* has the masculine form.

212 "languorousness . . . litheness" (*al-wanā . . . al-inthiṭā'*): the following list of words relating to "limpness and rigidity" (see 5.2.13) is shorter than that in the original and is

intended as a representation, not a one-to-one translation, of the latter using words from the same semantic areas drawn from thesauri, dictionaries, and other lexical resources; see further Volume Four, Translator's Afterword.

213 "that other quality mentioned by Abū Nuwās in his poem rhyming in the glottal stop": the poet has several poems with this rhyme letter; a likely candidate is the one that begins *daʿ ʿanka lawmī fa-l-lawmu ighrāʾu / wa-dāwinī bi-llatī kānat hiya l-dāʾu* ("Leave off your blaming of me, for blame is itself an incitement / And treat me with that which was the very disease [of which you accuse me]!"); in this case, the quality attributed to some of the women of Paris would be, presumably, a willingness to engage in anal intercourse as, in line 3 of this poem, Abū Nuwās speaks of receiving wine *min kaffi dhāti ḥirin fī ziyyi dhī dhakarin / lahā muḥibbāni lūṭiyyun wa-zannāʾū* ("from the hand of one with a vagina in the dress of one with a penis, who has two lovers, one a sodomite, the other an adulterer") (Abū Nuwās, *Dīwān*, 7).

214 "is no insult" (*laysa mina l-sabbi fī say'*): an acquaintance seems to be assumed with the following entry in the *Qamūs* under *b-ẓ-r*: *huwa yumiṣṣuhu wa-yubaẓẓiruhu ay qāla lahu umṣuṣ baẓrata fulānah* ("*yumiṣṣuhu* and *yubaẓẓiruhu* mean, 'He tells him, "Suck such and such a woman's clitoris!"'"), in which *umṣuṣ* etc. seems to have the force of an insult; the point here, of course, is that it is no insult to say this in Paris because its "old experienced men" do indeed practice cunnilingus.

215 See the deuterocanonical Book of Baruch (Epistle of Jeremiah) 6:43: "The women also with cords about them, sitting in the ways, burn bran for perfume: but if any of them, drawn by some that passeth by, lie with him, she reproacheth her fellow, that she was not thought as worthy as herself, nor her cord broken."

216 "thou art among those thankful to her" (*wa-nta lahā mina l-shākirīn*): echoes a Qur'anic phrase (without *lahā*) (Q Anʿām 6:63, Aʿrāf 7:144).

217 "Yet how can a man agree to protect his dependents / With both hanger and horn?" (*wa-kayfa yarḍā mraʾun yaḥmī . . . bi-l-qirni wa-l-qarni*): i.e., how can a husband be expected to protect his dependents with his hanger (a type of sword) if his wife's conduct has rendered him a cuckold with a horn?

218 Umm Khārijah: lit., "the Mother of Khārijah," a woman from whom many tribes descended and of whom it is said that if any man said to her, "Marry me?" she replied, "Done!" The identity of the father of her son Khārijah, which means "One Who Goes Out Much," was unknown. The wit of the Arabic comes from its exploitation of the contrasts between *dākhilat al-insān* ("man's *inner* state"), *Umm Khārijah* ("Mother of Him Who Goes *Out*"), *wa-yakhruju ʿanhu l-ḥilm* ("[and] all sense of proportion will leave him [lit., '*go out* from him']"), and *wālijah* ("where she's *gone in*" or "is being *entered*").

219 “Paris is heaven for women, purgatory for men, and hell for horses”: Louis-Sébastien Mercier (1749–1814), French dramatist and commentator, attributes the description of Paris as being *le paradis des femmes, le purgatoire des hommes, et l’enfer des chevaux* to “the common people” (*le petit peuple*) (Mercier, *Tableau de Paris*).

220 “here . . . they’re forever being touched” (*sha’nahunna dawāmu l-ṭamth*): echoes the Qur’ān’s *ḥūrun maqṣūrātun fī l-khiyāmi . . . lam yaṭmithhunna insun . . . wa-lā jānn* (“[in Paradise are] pure companions sheltered in pavilions . . . whom neither a man nor a jinn . . . has ever touched” (Q Raḥmān 55:72/Muddaththir 74:72).

221 “squint-eyed . . . pinguecula” (*aḥwal . . . mudanqishan*): the following list of words relating to “persons with defective vision” (see 5.2.13) is shorter than that in the original and is intended as a representation, not a one-to-one translation, of the latter using words from the same semantic areas drawn from thesauri, dictionaries, and other lexical resources; see further Volume Four, Translator’s Afterword.

222 “skin flap” (*zanamah*): the author returns to a figurative conceit used in Volume Two (see 2.9.1).

223 “A Complaint and Complaints” (*Fī shakāh wa-shakwā*): the two words derive from the same root and are essentially synonymous, but the first must be used here in a medical sense and refer to the Fāriyāqiyyah’s sore feet (4.18.1) and the second to her complaints about Paris (4.18.2ff).

224 “and what shall teach thee what is ‘the Maid’?” (*wa-mā adrāka mā l-khādimah*): an ironic play on a rhetorical device occurring in passages in the Qur’ān such as *wa-ma adrāk mā l-ḥāqqah* (“And what shall teach thee what is the Indubitable?”) (Q Ḥāqqah 69:3; trans. Arberry, *Koran*) in which a term deemed significant but little known is highlighted.

225 “Cremorne, Vauxhall . . . Rosherville”: Cremorne Gardens, a proprietary place of entertainment on the Thames in Chelsea, opened in 1845 and closed in 1877; Vauxhall Gardens, on the south bank of the Thames at Vauxhall, opened before 1660 and closed in 1859 and was the best-known pleasure garden in London; Rosherville Gardens, at Gravesend, Kent, on the Thames, opened in 1837 and closed in 1911.

226 “the woman with lupus” (*al-dha’bah*): the word is problematic: as spelled in the Arabic text, it does not appear in the lexica; however, the term *al-dhi’bah* is used in modern medicine (but only since the early twentieth century, according to Arabic Wikipedia) in the sense of “lupus” (an autoimmune connective tissue disease that affects women more than men and leaves disfiguring scars, often on the face). I have read it tentatively as *al-dha’ibah* meaning, by analogy, “the woman with lupus.”

227 "*pissoirs* . . . tent pegs" (*al-manāṣiʿ . . . al-manādif*): the *mindaf* referred to in the Arabic is a "cotton-carder's bow," i.e., a device resembling a single-stringed harp, about a meter in length and held between the carder's thighs.

228 the Société Asiatique: established in 1822, the society publishes the *Journal asiatique.*

229 Étienne Marc Quatremère (1782–1857), student of Silvestre de Sacy, philologist and prolific translator and editor of Arabic texts, and frequent contributor to the Journal asiatique.

230 Armand-Pierre Caussin de Perceval (1795–1871) became professor of modern Arabic at the École spéciale des langues orientales in 1821 and professor of Arabic at the Collège de France in 1833. Earlier, he had worked as a dragoman in Aleppo; in 1828, he published a *Grammaire arabe vulgaire* based on the dialect of that city.

231 Joseph Toussaint Reinaud (not *Reineaud* as in the Arabic) (1795–1867) succeeded to Silvestre de Sacy's chair at the École spéciale des langues orientales on the latter's death in 1838; see also 5.5 below.

232 "like the definite article in the sentence 'Go to the market and buy meat'" (*ka-adāti l-taʿrīfi fī qawlika idhhab ilā l-sūqi wa-shtiri l-laḥm*): i.e., his acquaintance with these French scholars was nonspecific, or impersonal, just as the definite articles preceding *sūq* and *laḥm* serve to indicate that the following noun is generic (i.e., "Go to any market and buy any meat").

233 "with virtue furnished . . . a vaginal furnace" (*bi-l-khayri qamīnuna ḥariyyūn . . . qamīnun ḥiriyy*): the phrases *qamīnun bi-* and *ḥariyyun bi-* both mean "capable of" while *qamīn* means "a bathhouse furnace" and *ḥiriyy* is an adjective derived from *ḥir* ("vagina"); the consonantal ductus is the same in both senses.

234 "the women" (*al-nisā'*): "women" has to be understood as "public women" (see below).

235 "of whatever kind" (*min takhālufi anwāʿihā*): meaning apparently "whether private houses or brothels."

236 "firetraps" (*balw al-nār*): the translation is tentative.

237 "full of artifice . . . treacherous" (*al-mallādhūn . . . al-badhlākhiyyūn*): the following list of words relating to "insincere friends," "false flatterers," and "those whose friendship cannot be relied upon" (see 5.2.13) is shorter than that in the original and is intended as a representation, not a one-to-one translation, of the latter using words from the same semantic areas drawn from thesauri, dictionaries, and other lexical resources; see further Volume Four, Translator's Afterword.

238 ʿUrqūb: a giant, ʿUrqūb ibn Maʿbad ibn Asad, who was known as the biggest liar of his day; according to the *Qāmūs*, "Once a man came to him for alms and he said, 'When my palm trees grow,' and when the palm trees grew, he said, 'When they put forth dates,'

and when they put forth dates, he said, 'When they flower,' and when they flowered, he said, 'When they soften,' and when they softened, he said, 'When they dry,' and when they dried, he cut them at night and gave the man nothing."

239 "sucking their fingers after eating, and licking off what is on them" (*yamṣuṣna aṣābiʿahunna baʿda l-akli wa-yalḥasna mā ʿahayhā*): the definition is quoted from the *Qāmūs* (s.v. *rajul laṭṭāʿ*).

240 "men with heavy loads" (*aṣḥāb al-athqāl*): this apparently contradictory statement should perhaps be understood as sexual innuendo.

241 Syria (*al-Shām*): the word may denote either the city of Damascus or the surrounding lands over which it traditionally has held sway.

242 "the most generous of the Arab nation" (*akram al-ʿarab*): an allusion to the ruler of Tunis, Aḥmad Bāy, who had earlier, in response to poems written in his praise by the Fāriyāq (i.e., the author), sent him a gift of diamonds (Volume Three, 3.18.6) and subsequently hosted him and his family in Tunis (4.8.1–7).

243 "When the Christians of Aleppo suffered their calamity" (*lammā nukibat naṣārā Ḥalab*): in October of 1850, a Muslim mob turned on the Christian quarters of Aleppo and up to seventy persons died; a further five thousand Aleppines died as a result of bombardment by Ottoman forces seeking to retake the city.

244 Fatḥallāh Marrāsh: presumably the father of Faransīs Fatḥallāh Marrāsh (1836–73), who was a leading intellectual and writer of his day and whom the author later met (see Volume One, Foreword, p. xv).

245 Metropolitan Atanāsiyūs al-Tutūnjī: see further Volume Two, 2.3.5n66, 2.9.3.

246 "some town belonging to Austria—Bologna, I think" (*baladun min bilādi ūstiriyā wa-hwa fī-mā aẓunnu Būlūniyā*): Bologna, though at this time a Papal Legation, was garrisoned by Austrian soldiers.

247 "the Sassanian trade" (*al-ḥirfah al-Sāsāniyyah*): i.e., the trade of the Banū Sāsān ("Sons of Sāsān"), a name applied in medieval Islam to charlatans, vagabonds, and thieves, supposedly because of their original allegiance to a mythical "Shaykh Sāsān."

248 Islāmbūl: literally, "Find Islam," a folk-etymological adaptation of Istanbul introduced following the Muslim conquest of the city in 1453 to emphasize the centrality of the city, in its rulers' eyes, to the Islamic nation.

249 Ṣubḥī Bayk: later to hold, as Ṣubḥī Pasha, the posts of minister of education and governor of Syria; the author benefited from this contact when he himself settled in Istanbul (al-Maṭwī, *Aḥmad*, II:902).

250 For the poem in praise of Ṣubḥī Bayk, see 4.20.29–32; for those describing his longing for his wife, see 4.20.50–62.

251 "those decorated pieces of paper" (*hādhihi l-awrāq al-muzawwaqah*): i.e., playing cards; from the references to gambling and a partner that follow (and that are elaborated in his later poem on the subject, see 4.20.39–43), he likely played whist, a popular game with gamblers in Paris at the time (see, e.g., Balzac's *Le Père Goriot*, first published in 1835).

252 "the gamblers' record keeper" (*amīn al-muqāmirīn*): the definition is from the *Qāmūs.*

253 I.e., 1853, the year of the outbreak of the Crimean War, which began in October.

254 See 4.9.10.

255 "the aforementioned poem": i.e., that presented by the author to Prince Musurus (see 4.20.2).

256 "Sweden . . . some latter-day Peter": in the Great Northern War (1700–21), Peter the Great of Russia successfully contested the hegemony of the Swedish Empire in northern Europe.

257 "Muslims, check well . . ." (*yā muslimūna tathabbatū . . .*): cf Q Ḥujurāt 49:6 *yā ayyuhā lladhīna āmanū in jā'akum fāsiqun bi-naba'in fa-tabayyanū* ("Believers, if an evildoer brings you news, ascertain the correctness of the report fully").

258 "You will not attain piety until you expend / Of what you love" (*lan tanālū l-birra ḥattā tunfiqū / mimma tuḥibbūn*): Q Āl ʿImrān 3:92 (trans. Arberry, *Koran*, 57).

259 "the most firm handle" (*al-ʿurwah al-wuthqā*): "So whosoever disbelieves in idols and believes in God has laid hold of the most firm handle" (Q Baqarah 2:256; similarly Luqmān 31:22).

260 "and peck the feathers off their eagle" (*wa-nisrahumu nsurū*): an allusion to the double eagle of the imperial Russian insignia.

261 "Were you but a small band of soldiers, / They would not be overcome" (*law lam yakun minkum siwā nafarin lamā / ghulibū*): cf Q Anfāl 8:65 *wa-in yakun minkum mi'atun yaghlibū alfan* ("and if there are a hundred of you, they will overcome a thousand").

262 "the Portioned Narration" (*al-dhikr al-mufaṣṣal*): "an appellation of *The portion of the Kur-án from [the chapter entitled]* الحُجُرات *[i. e. ch. xlix.] to the end; according to the most correct opinion* . . . ; this portion is thus called because of its many divisions between its chapters . . . or because of the few abrogations therein" (Lane, *Lexicon*, s.v. *mufaṣṣal*).

263 "It was ever a duty upon us to help them" (*haqqan ʿalaynā naṣruhum*): cf. *wa-kāna haqqan ʿalaynā naṣru l-mu'minīn* ("And it was ever a duty upon us, to help the believers") (Q Rūm 30:47).

264 "and they cannot / Advance that day or delay it" (*fa-lan / yastaqdimū ʿanhu wa-lan yasta'khirū*): cf. Q Naḥl 16:61 *fa-idhā jā'ahum ajaluhum lā yasta'khirūna sāʿatan wa-lā yastaqdimūn* ("when their time [i.e., the time of living creatures] comes they cannot delay it for an hour, nor can they bring it forward").

265 "A manifest victory" (*fatḥan mubīnan*): Q Fatḥ 48:1.

266 "Gardens of Eternity" (*jannātu ʿadan*): Q Tawbah 9:72 and passim.

267 Badr: site of a battle (2/624) between the Muslim forces and the much larger army of the Prophet's opponents; the Muslims' victory was a turning point in their fortunes and is often attributed to divine intervention.

268 "their circling eagle" (*nisruhum al-mudawwimu*): see 4.20.6n260.

269 "the crescent moon" (*al-hilāl*): an allusion to the crescent of the imperial Ottoman insignia.

270 "birds in flights" (*al-ṭayr al-abābīl*): the reference is to God's destruction of an Ethiopian army that sought to take Mecca in the days before Islam (Q Fīl 105:3).

271 "You we worship" (*iyyāka naʿbudu*): the words are taken from the opening *sūrah* ("chapter") of the Qur'ān, often recited at the initiation of an enterprise.

272 "And any spiteful gelding who hates you" (*wa-shāni'uka l-baghīḍu l-abtarū*): echoes Q Kawthar 108:3.

273 "Farūq . . . the Furqān": the epithet Farūq probably means "sharply dividing" (by analogy with other intensive adjectives of this form such as *laʿūb* ["very playful"] and *ḥasūd* ["very envious"]), though the dictionaries do not give it this sense, and reflects the idea that, previous to its conquest by the Ottomans, the city represented the divide between the Christian and Muslim worlds; the author appears to share this view as he derives it from al-Furqān, an epithet of the Qur'ān, so called because it "makes a separation . . . between truth and falsity" (Lane, *Lexicon*).

274 "The stringing of the pearls . . . your palm" (*mā in yafī naẓmu l-la'āli'i . . . tuntharū*): i.e., using conventional imagery, "The arrangement of lines of verses into a eulogy for you cannot match the gifts that are dispensed from your hand's generous supply."

275 "two Hijri dates" (*tārīkhayni hijriyyayni*): i.e., the author has used the system known as *ḥisāb al-jummal*, which allots a numerical value to each letter of the alphabet, to construct the final line of the poem, each of whose hemistichs consists of letters whose values add up to 1270 (the Hijri year that began on 4 October 1853), as follows: *ʿAbd* (70 + 2 + 4 = 76) + *al-Majīd* (1 + 30 + 40 + 3 + 10 + 4=88) + *Allāh* (1 + 30 + 30 + 5 = 66) + *arkā* (1 + 200 + 20 + 10 = 231) + *ḍiddahu* (800 + 9 = 809) = 1270 and so on for the remaining hemistich; *hisāb al-jummal* values may be found in Hava, *al-Farā'id*, 4 (unnumbered).

276 "The Presumptive Poem . . . The Prescriptive Poem" (*al-Qaṣīdah al-Harfiyyah . . . al-Qaṣīdah al-Ḥarfiyyah*): see 4.18.6 above.

277 "litters" (*hawādij*): throughout these two poems, the author presses words from the early Arabic lexicon, including Qur'anic terms, into the service of contemporary purposes; here, presumably, the women's camel litter stands for the enclosed carriage.

278 "a 'Illiyyūn": a word used in the Qur'ān (Q Muṭaffifīn 83:19) and said to mean "a place in the Seventh Heaven, to which ascend the souls of the believers" (*Qāmūs*).

279 "raised couches" (*surur marfū'ah*): cf. Q Ghāshiyah 88:13.

280 "cotton mattresses" (*a'ārīs*): the translation is tentative; the word appears not to be attested in the lexica but may be an invented plural of the plural *'arānīs* (a word which according to Ibn 'Abbād has no singular) meaning something like "things made by women out of cotton" and associated with beds: see al-'Ubāb al-Zākhir in http://www.baheth.info, s.v. *'irnās* (*'irnās al-mar'ah mawḍi'u sabā'ikh quṭnihā*) and Lane, *Lexicon*, s.v. *sabīkh*, at end.

281 "the Uplifted Ones" (*al-simākayn*): Arcturus and Spica, two unusually bright stars.

282 "be delighted . . . Tunis" (*fa-tu'nasu minhā wa-hiya Tūnusu ghibṭatan*): a pun based on the identical forms of the words *tu'nasu* ("may you be delighted") and *Tūnusu* ("Tunis") when written without vowels.

283 "the Destroyer of All Pleasures" (*hādim al-ladhdhāt*): i.e., death.

284 "even should you travel so far that Jupiter lies behind you in the sky" (*wa-law amsā warā'aka Birjīsū*): perhaps an allusion to the use of Jupiter as a reference point in celestial navigation.

285 "a geomancer's spell" (*inkīs*): literally, a certain sign used by geomancers (see Volume One, 1.16.9).

286 "For if you add a zero to it, even an odd number becomes divisible by five" (*fa-fī ṣ-ṣifri li-l-fardi l-'aqīmi takhāmīsū*): perhaps meaning "so too an hour in Paris will make your life longer (for better or for worse) by orders of magnitude."

287 "oceans" (*qawāmīs*): and, punningly, "dictionaries."

288 "though it is studied" (*wa-hwa madrūsū*): or, punningly, "and has been erased."

289 The poem is referred to earlier as having been written on the occasion of a visit by Emir 'Abd al-Qādir to Paris, when the author "was honored by being invited to attend a gathering in his presence" (4.19.4); however, from references within the poem, it would seem that the relationship was more extended and included the emir's standing the author up on at least one occasion.

290 "drowsiness . . . lukewarm" (*bi-fātir . . . bil-fātir*): seductive faces are conventionally described as having "drowsy" eyes or eyelids, using the same word as for "lukewarm, neither hot nor cold."

291 "my creator" (*fāṭirī*): an apparent reference to the Qur'anic verses "then we split the earth in fissures / and therein made the grass to grow" (*thumma shaqaqna l-arḍa shaqqan / fa-nbatnā fīhā ḥabban*), Q 'Abasa 80:26–27, which is preceded by references to God's role as creator, e.g., "Of a sperm-drop He created him" (*min nutfatin khalaqahu*), 80:19.

292 "night phantom" (*ṭayf*): the appearance of the beloved as a shimmering figure in the lover's dreams is a standard trope.

293 "the Assembler" (*al-ḥāshir*): i.e., God, who will assemble men for judgment on the Last Day.

294 "word . . . consonant . . . sword-edge" (*ḥarf . . . ḥarf . . . ḥarf*): a triple pun.

295 "the emir became still" (*sakana l-amīr*): by the time the author met Emir ʿAbd al-Qādir, the latter had abandoned his struggle against the French colonization of Algeria and was living in exile.

296 "the Tablet" (*al-lawḥ*): "the Preserved Tablet" (*al-lawḥ al-maḥfūẓ*), on which God has written divine destiny.

297 "from Ṣubḥī" (*min Ṣubḥī*): or, punningly, "from my [rising in the] morning."

298 Ḥassān: i.e., Ḥassān ibn Thābit al-Anṣārī (d. probably before 40/661), the poet most associated with the Prophet Muḥammad, on whom he wrote eulogies.

299 "what I owe is [written] at the top of the board and cannot be erased" (*alladhī ʿalay-ya bi-aʿlā l-lawḥi mā huwa bi-l-mamḥī*): perhaps meaning "the sins (of eulogizing unworthy persons) for which I must pay expiation are plain for all to see."

300 "Sāmī of the Summits" (*Sāmī al-dhurā*): a reference to Ṣubḥī Bayk's father, Sāmī Pasha; however, since *sāmī* means "elevated," the phrase may also be read as "high-peaked."

301 "a cave of strength" (*kahfa ʿizzin*): the image, conventional in poetry, echoes references in the Qurʾān to God's protection of believing young men in a cave, e.g., *fa-ʾwū ilā l-kahfi yanshur lakum rabbukum min raḥmatihi wa-yuhayyiʾ min amrikum mirfaqan* ("Take refuge in the cave; your Lord will extend his mercy to you and will make fitting provision for you in your situation") (Q Kahf 18:16).

302 "Halt" (*qif*): the poem uses the conventions of the pre-Islamic ode in opening by apostrophizing an unnamed companion, who is asked to halt his camel at the abandoned campsite, identifiable by the "orts" (*al-ṭulūl*) (the remains of the eating, drinking, and sleeping places) of the poet's beloved's clan; thereafter, the poet shifts his attention from his companion to himself, which explains the shift of subject from second to first person ("Halt . . . I knew . . . I dragged" etc.).

303 "the Crown" (*al-iklīlā*): defined in the *Qāmūs* as "a mansion of the moon—four aligned stars."

304 "after a tear of mine had wetted it" (*wa-qad ballathu minnī ʿabratun*): the poet appears to picture himself peering through his tears and finding the campsite "borne upon the reins of the wind."

305 "as dry brushwood" (*ka-l-jazl*): i.e., of no importance.

306 "The mending of broken hearts may be requested of any Jubārah" (*jabru l-khawāṭiri min jubāratin yurtajā*): i.e., anyone called Jubārah (or anyone of the Jubārah family) may be asked to mend hearts because the root consonants of his name, i.e., *j-b-r*, are associated with "restoring, bringing things back to normal, helping back on one's feet, setting (broken bones)."

307 "A Poem on Gambling" (*al-qaṣīdah al-qimāriyyah*): the poem seemingly alludes to events referred to earlier (4.19.4). Its vocabulary and syntax are unusually difficult and the translation is in places tentative; choices made in the translation have therefore been more thoroughly endnoted here than elsewhere.

308 "It brought us . . . together" (*jamaʿatnā*): it is assumed here that the unexpressed subject of the verb is *al-luʿbah* ("the game") or a similar word.

309 "'the Ace,' Cavell, and Farshakh" (*al-Āṣ wa-Kawall (?) wa-Farshakh*): *āṣ* presumably means "ace," from the French, and is so used in line 4 of the poem, but here must be a nickname; *Kawall* is credible as the French/British surname "Cavell"; *Farshakh* appears to exist as a family name in Lebanon.

310 "One of us" (*baʿḍunā*): i.e., we were a pair, consisting of a practiced cardplayer and a greenhorn (the poet).

311 "a bit of a dog" (*ibn baʿṣī*): for *baʿṣ* the *Qāmūs* gives the meanings "leanness of body" and "disturbance"; however, usage on the Internet indicates that it has the same meaning as (Egyptian) colloquial *baʿbaṣah* "goosing." The translation is contextual.

312 "louis d'ors" (*mulūk*): literally "kings" but perhaps here "coins with a king's head on them," i.e., "sovereigns," or, given the French setting, as translated above.

313 "he owed" (*yudīnuhā*): i.e., perhaps, winning back debts he'd incurred.

314 "the pack" (*al-muzawwaq*): literally, "the decorated thing," cf. *al-awrāq al-muzawwaqah* ("[decorated] playing cards") above (4.19.4).

315 "his hand" (*taʾlīfu*): literally, "his blend, his mixture."

316 "In part a seal ring, in part a bezel" (*baʿḍuhu khātaman baʿḍuhu ka-faṣṣī*): meaning perhaps "part flat but engraved (like an inscribed seal ring; i.e., etched with anger), part bulging (like a curved stone set in a ring; i.e., bulging with fury)."

317 "him" (*minhu*): reference apparently switches from "the wizard of the pack" to the poet's overenthusiastic partner on his winning streak.

318 "a true friend" (*khilṣī*): i.e., his partner, the poet, who would need "covering for" if he is the "greenhorn" referred to at the start of the poem.

319 "stinging" (*yaqruṣu*): punning on the meanings "to sting" (like an insect) and hence "to speak bitingly," and "to pinch" (with the fingers).

320 "After forty-six" (*baʿda sittin wa-arbaʿīn*): i.e., presumably, "after reaching the age of forty-six," an age that, given his likely birth date of 1805 or 1806 (see Chronology, n488), accords with his stay in Paris between December 1850 and June 1853 (al-Maṭwī, *Aḥmad*, I:116); thus the meaning may be that the poet viewed unenthusiastically the prospect of living the rest of his life in poverty as a result of gambling.

321 "he'd not served him in writing notice of any protest" (*wa-lam yublighhu ʿan bandati ḥtijājin bi-naṣṣī*): the meaning of *bandah* is not obvious; *iḥtijāj* is taken here in the sense of "protest regarding nonpayment of a bill"; it is assumed that the subject of "served" is the player who failed to cover for the poet, who therefore by implication involved the pair in losses; the whole may mean that while the poet, though not a skilled player, had joined in the game, he had not expected to become liable for any debts that he and his partner might incur.

322 "All he thought about . . . whitewash" (*fikruhu fī . . . bi-jiṣṣī*): i.e., he was completely preoccupied with the writing of eulogies for persons of elevated station who paid him too little even to allow him to whitewash his room.

323 "gullibility . . . person" (*rubbamā . . . hirṣī*): i.e., perhaps the actual order of the world will be reversed one day and naïve but cautious persons, such as the poet, will in fact benefit from their virtues (but, it is implied, this is not likely to happen soon).

324 "Whenever he tried to write poetry with hairs from his mustache" (*wa-bi-shaʿrin min shāribayhi idhā ḥā/wala shiʿran*): the image of the poet twisting his mustache when deep in thought was used earlier in the work (see Volume Three, 3.8.5: "he set about playing with his mustache, as was his custom . . . until he was guided to an understanding of its meaning"). The subsequent use of the feminine pronoun apparently in reference to the hairs of the mustache (*yunḥī ʿalayhā . . . atāhā*) is problematic; perhaps the poet is evoking an unstated plural (*ashʿār*).

325 "soon . . . yellow" (*ʿan qarībin . . . ḥurṣī*): i.e., soon the white hairs in his mustache will be colored black with ink or yellow with nicotine.

326 "A partner of his" (*wa-sharīkun lahu*): presumably "Farshakh" (see the opening line of the poem); this and the following lines appear to picture the author's partner calculating the pair's winnings and losses.

327 "the game" (*al-dast*): or, punningly, "the gathering place, the divan."

328 "spitters" (*bassāqīna*): the reference is unclear.

329 "cloven hoofs" (*dhāt ẓilf*): Jewish dietary law permits the eating of animals that have cloven hoofs (and chew the cud).

330 "No great critic . . . my room" (*mā ʿābahā jihbidhun . . . ghurfatī*): meaning perhaps that the occurrence of the game anywhere but inside his room would be considered by the

critics so unlikely as to constitute a challenge to the readers' credulity and hence a literary flaw.

331 "Its shape" (*shakluhā*): i.e., the shape of the room.

332 "Room Poems" (*al-Ghurfiyyāt*): the name refers to the author's habit of writing poems on the door of the room he rented while in Paris (see above 4.19.4).

333 Saturn (*Zuḥal*): associated elsewhere by the author with bad luck (Volume Two, 2.9.5).

334 "repose . . . quiescent . . . cunt" (*farajan . . . bi-sukūnin . . . al-farj*): the author exploits the fact that *faraj* ("relief") differs from *farj* ("vagina") only by a single additional vowel and that *sukūn* means both "inactivity" and "quiescence (i.e., vowellessness)" of a consonant.

335 "Against the onslaught of grammar" (*min ḍarbi Zaydin wa-ʿAmr*): literally, "against the beatings of Zayd and ʿAmr," the latter being generic names used in teaching the rules of grammar through exemplary sentences such as *ḍaraba Zaydun ʿAmran* ("Zayd beat ʿAmr").

336 "People have fire without smoke" (*li-l-nāsi nārun bi-lā dukhānī*): perhaps meaning, "People (such as those who come and sponge off me) have matches but no tobacco," i.e., expect me to supply the latter.

337 "chew the cud when I retire" (*wa-abītu qārī*): i.e., in the absence of a friend with matches, the poet is forced, at the end of the evening, to chew his tobacco.

338 "the lowest of the low" (*bi-asfali sāfilīna*): cf. Q Tīn 95:5 "then we cast him down as the lowest of the low."

339 "of exalted standing" (*rafīʿ al-darajāt*): or, punningly, "elevated in terms of stairs."

340 "distribute a predicate" (*murāʿāt al-naẓīr*): in rhetoric, applying to each member of a series a predication appropriate to it.

341 "my fire" (*nārī*): *nār* ("fire") is feminine in gender.

342 "liar" (*mayyān*): here and often elsewhere in the author's verse, references to lying and liars are to be taken in the context of his reference to "the lies of panegyric" above (4.20.44, second poem).

343 "This, the infection of your hand . . . has infected you not" (*fa-hādhihi ʿadwā kaffikum . . . muṭlaqan*): perhaps meaning that though the door is sick of being opened by visitors, the visitors have never grown sick of opening it.

344 "what's been scratched through the wrinkled paint by the scraping of nails" (*tanqīru aẓfārihi fī-naqri aẓfārī*): the translation is tentative and depends on understanding the first *aẓfār* as meaning "the creased parts of a skin" (see Lane, *Lexicon*, s.v. *ẓufr*).

345 "thus saith the owl" (*qālahu l-būmū*): the owl is popularly considered a harbinger of bad luck.

346 "a peen" (*al-shīqā*): in the Arabic, "a mountaintop" or, punningly, "the head of a penis."

347 "*Sammū* before entering my home" (*sammū ʿalā manzilī qabla l-dukhūlī*): i.e., "Invoke the name (*sammū*) of God (using some conventional formula)," as it is normal for a man not of the family to do before entering a house so as to warn its female inhabitants of his presence.

348 "*Sammū . . . samm*": the author exploits the coincidental identicality of ductus of *sammū* ("invoke the name of God!") (*s-m-w*) and *summū* ("poison!") (*s-m-m*).

349 "I live in my room in a state of commotion" (*anā sākinun fī ghurfatī mutaḥarrikun*): or, punningly, "I am both 'quiet' (*sākinun*) in my room and 'in motion' (*mutaḥarrikun*)" with a further resonance of "I am a quiescent (i.e., vowelless) letter (*sākinun*) that is also voweled (*mutaḥarrikun*)."

350 "trying to screw it" (*yuḥāwilu naḥtahā*): *naḥt* means "to exhaust" as well as "to have intercourse with."

351 "Except that beneath it run no rivers" (*siwā an laysa tajrī taḥtahā l-anhārū*): cf. the phrase *tajrī taḥtahā l-anhārū* ("beneath it run rivers") much used in the Qurʾān to describe Paradise (e.g., Q Baqarah 2:25, 266, Āl ʿImrān 3:15, etc.).

352 "the very moons" (*al-aqmārū*): "moon" is a conventional trope for a beautiful person.

353 "Poems of Separation" (*al-Firāqiyyāt*): i.e., of separation from his wife and children when they left him in Paris and went to Istanbul.

354 "My past felicity had no like" (*fa-māḍī naʿīmī lam yakun min muḍāriʿin lahu*): or, punningly, "The perfect tense of my felicity had no imperfect," i.e., "was destined not to last."

355 "Why, what would it have harmed . . . to the end?" (*wa-mādhā ʿalā . . . ṭūlahā*): the author asks why the ill fortune of his earlier days should have been allowed to affect his later, happily married, life.

356 Hind . . . Mayyah . . . Daʿd: women's names often used nonspecifically in poetry.

357 "The right-thinking man . . . the rightly guided" (*al-rashīd . . . al-mahdī*): or, punningly, the caliphs (Hārūn) al-Rashīd and Muḥammad al-Mahdī.

358 "do not see you in it" (*wa-lastu arākumu/bi-hā*): meant either literally (because the poet is in Paris while his family is in Istanbul) or in the sense that "I do not see you as worldly creatures."

359 al-ʿĪnayn: a mountain at Uḥud near Mecca (site of a battle between the first Muslims and the idolaters of the city) from whose summit the devil is said to have proclaimed, falsely, that the Prophet Muḥammad had been killed (*Qāmūs*); presumably, it is the value of its association with the Prophet that makes it something to be cherished in the poet's eyes, along with the assonance between this and the preceding and following words (*al-ʿayn, al-ʿayn*).

360 "You departed to be cured of what ailed you" (*sāfartum li-l-bar'i mimmā nālakum*): a reference to his wife's illness and subsequent departure (see 4.18.15).

361 See 4.9.7: "for everything pulchritudinous reminds [a woman] of a handsome man" (*wa-kullu ḥusnin innamā yudhakkiru bi-l-ḥasan*).

362 "my twofold love for you" (*ḥubbayka*): perhaps meaning his love for the beloved both before separation and after it.

363 "when 'leg is intertwined with leg . . . unto thy Lord that day shall be the driving'" (*yawma taltaffu l-sāqu bi-l-sāq . . . ilā rabbika yawma'idhin al-masāq*): i.e., the Day of Judgment (Q Qiyāmah 75:29–30; trans. Arberry, *Koran*, 620).

364 "Part One . . . Part Two" (*al-juz' al-awwal . . . al-juz' al-thānī*): according to the translator's first reading of the text, this statement would indicate a humorously lopsided (709 pages in Part One versus 33 in Part Two in the 1855 edition) division of the work into two parts (see Volume One, xxxi-xxxii); it now seems more likely to him that "Part Two of the work will follow after the author has been stoned and crucified" should be understood to mean "once the critics have had their say." That the author gave at least half-serious thought to writing a continuation of *Leg Over Leg* is indicated by his earlier statement, "My friendship for you [the Fāriyāq] will not prevent me, should I examine your situation at some later time, from writing another book about you" (4.20.1).

365 The letter that follows is written in Egyptian dialect, an unusual choice at that date (for context, see Davies and Doss, *al-ʿĀmmiyyah*) and one for which the author gives no explanation; Michael Cooperson suggests that the author may have chosen colloquial to make the point that the addressees ("Shaykh Muḥammad" presumably excepted) were likely to be ignorant of literary Arabic.

366 "*Sīdi*" etc.: in keeping with the colloquial nature of the letter, titles (*Sīdi*, etc.) have been given in their colloquial forms; *Sīdi* means literally "My Master" and *Sayyidna* "Our Master," while *Ṣirna* ("Our Sir") is a humorous adaptation of "Sir" to Egyptian titling norms.

367 "*Sīdi* Shaykh Muḥammad, *Sayyidna* Metropolitan Buṭrus," etc.: attempts have been made to identify at least some of these persons (see, e.g., al-Maṭwī, *Aḥmad*, I:80); however, it seems more likely that they represent categories of person, i.e., the Muslim scholar ("Shaykh Muḥammad"), Christian clergymen ("Metropolitan Buṭrus," etc.), and Europeans of various nationalities. For further examples of "Shaykh Muḥammad" used generically, see Volume Two (2.18.1n272) and 5.2.4 below, and for a similar roll call of European titles, see Volume Three, 3.12.25.

368 "my words aren't addressed to / cattle, donkeys, lions, and tigers" (*kalāmī mā hūsh ʿala l-baqar wi-l-ḥimīr wi-l-usūd wi-l-numūr*): Rastegar suggests that "the animals . . . are

perhaps a reference to the orientalists, religious scholars, colonial officials, and others with whom Shidyaq was compelled to work (and who, outside the small exilic Arab population, were the only possible audience for an Arabic text published in Europe)" (Rastegar, *Literary Modernity*, 118).

369 Long as this list of lists is, it is not complete. To cite but one example, the list of "despicable traits of the dissolute woman" in Volume Three, at 3.19.13, is succeeded in the same paragraph by a brief list of words for types of city streets, followed by another long list of words relating to sexual intercourse, which is itself followed by a brief list of words relating to inappropriate behavior by women; the last three are not listed here. In addition, the semantic range covered in the text is sometimes wider than that suggested by the particular word or words the author has chosen to represent it in this list.

370 "Doublets": i.e., two-part exclamations such as *marḥā marḥā* ("Bravo! Bravo!").

371 "*thurtumī* [?]": the meaning of *thurtum* is "food or condiments left in the dish" (*Qāmūs*), in which sense it occurs a few lines before this list of vessels (Volume Two, 2.3.5).

372 "a place": the Arabic text, quoting the *Qāmūs*, uses the abbreviation ع for موضع (*mawḍiʿ*, "place, locality").

373 "*sukk*": discs made from an aromatic, musk-based substance called *rāmik* (see Volume Two, 2.16.25n252) that are strung on a string of hemp and left for a year and of which the *Qāmūs* says "the older they get, the better they smell."

374 "*maḥlab*": a kind of plum (*Prunus mahaleb*); presumably the stones are what are used.

375 "Alas for Zayd" (*wayḥan li-Zayd*): the passage cited contains a list of six words meaning "Alas!"; the words "for Zayd" seem to be added to situate the phrases within a spuriously scholastic context, "Zayd" being a name conventionally used in examples by teachers of grammar.

376 "makeup and face paint" (*al-khumrah wa-l-ghumrah*): the relationship between the two words as used here is ambiguous: the *Qāmūs* defines *khumrah* as above and defines *ghumrah* simply as "saffron," which is one of the substances listed among those used as makeup in Volume Three, at 3.19.4; to the *Lisān*, *khumrah* is a variant of (*lughatun fī-*) *ghumrah*.

377 "Things peculiar to women " (*ashyāʾun khāṣṣatun bi-l-nisāʾ*): in fact, the text refers only to the women of Paris.

378 "Arabic languages" (*al-lughāt al-ʿarabiyyah*): meaning, perhaps, Arabic in all its literary and dialectal varieties; note the discussion of diversity in Arabic at 5.3.7.

379 In his *Grammaire Persane, ou, Principes de l'Iranien Moderne* (Imprimerie Nationale, Paris, 1852), Chodźko writes, "L'Europe est depuis longtemps en possession de tout ce qui est nécessaire pour l'étude des langues orientales; elle a des bibliothèques, des écoles

et des savants parfaitement en état de les diriger: aussi, sous le rapport de la philologie, de la philosophie et de l'histoire des langues d'Asie, un ustad persan, un muéllim arabe ou un brahmane hindou auraient beaucoup à apprendre de nos professeurs" (p.i).

380 "the chapter on marvels" (*faṣl ḥadanbadā*): Volume Three, chapter 19.

381 "the letters" (*al-rasā'il*): the *Grammaire Persane* contains a number of letters as exemplars of epistolary style.

382 Q Ṭā Hā 20:106.

383 "and he satisfies himself with the sands of the plain": in the French (p. 201) *Ils se contentent du sable des déserts* [*sic*; the French uses the plural ("they satisfy themselves")].

384 "Shaykh Muḥammad, Molla Ḥasan, or Üstad Saʿdī": i.e., from an Arab, a Persian, or a Turkish scholar.

385 Abū l-Ṭayyib: i.e., Abū l-Ṭayyib al-Mutanabbī; see Glossary.

386 "my sandy shaykh" (*ayyuhā l-shaykhu l-ramlī*): see 5.3.2n383.

387 *Lughat al-aṭyār wa-l-azhār* (*The Language of the Birds and the Flowers*): the Sufi work *Kashf al-asrār ʿan ḥikam al-ṭuyūr wa-l-azhār* (*The Uncovering of the Secrets Concerning the Wise Sayings of the Birds and the Flowers*) by ʿIzz al-Dīn ʿAbd al-Salām ibn Aḥmad ibn Ghanim al-Maqdisī (d. 678/1279) was published in Arabic in 1821 along with a translation by Joseph-Héliodore-Sagesse-Virtu Garcin de Tassy (1794–1878) under the French title *Les oiseaux et les fleurs: allégories morales* (Paris, Imprimerie Royale).

388 "the correspondence of a Jewish broker with an imbecilic merchant" (*muḥāwarat simsār yahūdī wa-aḥmaq mina l-tujjār*): the reference may be to Louis Jacques Bresnier's *Cours pratique et théorique de langue arabe . . . accompagné d'un traité du langage arabe usual et de ses divers dialectes en Algérie*, Alger, Bastide, 1855 (second edition), which includes (pp. 465, 467) an example of Jewish Arabic in the form of a letter from a Jewish businessman to a cloth merchant. According to Bresnier (p. xi), "Nous publiâmes . . . en 1846 la première édition de cet ouvrage, que l'insuffisance des resources typographiques nous contraignait à autographier nous-même" and it may be that this was the edition that the author saw. However, the second, more formal, edition was published in Paris in the same year as *al-Sāq ʿalā l-sāq* and by the same publisher (Benjamin Duprat) and he may have seen it then.

389 "the proverbs of Luqmān the Wise [in] the feeble language used in Algeria" (*amthāl Luqmān al-ḥakīm [fī] al-kalām al-rakīk al-mutʿāraf fī l-Jazā'ir*): in all likelihood, *Fables de Lokman, adaptées à l'idiome arabe en usage dans la régence d'Alger; suivies du mot à mot et de la prononciation interlinéaire* by J. H. Delaporte fils ("secrétaire interprète de l'intendance civile"), Algiers, Imprimerie du Gouvernement, 1835 (see Chauvin, *Bibliographie*, III:16 [21]).

390 "silly sayings taken from the rabble in Egypt and the Levant" (*aqwāl sakhīfah min raʿāʿ al-ʿāmmah fī Miṣr wa-l-Shām*): if *aqwāl* ("sayings") here is to be taken to mean "utterances," a possible candidate would be Berggren, *Guide français-arabe vulgaire des voyageurs et des francs en Syrie et en Égypte: avec carte physique et géographique de la Syrie et plan géométrique de Jérusalem ancien et moderne, comme supplément aux Voyages en Orient* (Uppsala, 1844), which is a French-Arabic dictionary of the dialects in question with an appended grammar; if the author intended "proverbs," the choice is less clear: many collections of Arabic proverbs were compiled by French writers during the late eighteenth and early nineteenth centuries (see Chauvin, *Bibliographie*, I) but none apparently cover both Egypt and the Levant. It may seem unlikely that the author would direct his criticism in this passage at a Swedish writer, albeit one writing in French, but Berggren was a corresponding member of the Société Asiatique (personal communication from Geoffrey Roper) and al-Shidyāq may have seen his book there.

391 "a book . . . on the speech of the people of Aleppo": presumably Caussin de Perceval's *Grammaire arabe vulgaire* (see 4.18.11n230).

392 "*anjaq*": see further Volume Three, 3.15.5.

393 "the dialect of the people of Algeria" (*lisān ahl al-jazāʾir*): *kān fī wāḥid il-dār ṭūbāt bi-z-zāf il-ṭūbāt kishāfū* "In a house there were many rats (*ṭubbāt*, sing. *ṭubbah*). The rats, when they saw . . . ." and *kīnākul* "When I eat" and *rāhī* "She is (now) . . ." and *antīnā* (= *ntīna*) "you (fem. sing.)" and *antiyyā* (= *ntiyya*) "ditto" and *naqjam* "I joke" and *khammim bāsh* "he thought he would . . ." and *wāsīt shughl il-mahābil* "I did something crazy" . . . and *il-dajājah tirjaʿ tiwallid* [= *tūld*] *zūj ʿaẓmāt* "the hen now lays two eggs." Some of the preceding is open to more than one interpretation and the sectioning sometimes results in incomplete utterances; different Algerian regional dialects may also be represented. Though one might expect al-Shidyāq to have taken this material from Bresnier's grammar (see 5.3.6n388), only some of the individual words occur there.

394 "(i.e., *al-sādis*, 'the sixth')": an error for "the sixteenth."

395 "they transcribe *j* . . . with . . . *d* and *j*": the Arabic letter *jīm* is pronounced in literary usage like the *j* in *Jack*. As in French orthography *j* is not pronounced like this, but like the *s* in *measure*, traditional French transcription employs *dj* for *jīm* (e.g., *Djerba*) to avoid misrepresentation of that letter by French *j*.

396 "The preaching metropolitan's 'cut off *azbābakum*'": see Volume Two (2.3.3, last sentence, Arabic), where the preacher (who is not, as here, identified as a metropolitan) says *azbābakum* ("your pricks") for *asbābakum* ("your ties to this world").

397 "this . . . sandman" (*hādhā l-ramlī*): see above 5.3.2n383.

398 "not everything white is a truffle" (*mā kullu bayḍā'a shaḥmah*): i.e., "appearances can be deceptive" (see al-Maydānī, *Majma'*, II:156).

399 "the *Maqāmāt* of al-Ḥarīrī": Silvestre de Sacy's edition was first published in 1822; the author critiques aspects of the second edition (1847) below (5.5).

400 "the travels of the scholar and writer Shaykh Muḥammad ibn al-Sayyid 'Umar al-Tūnusī": the title page of this work reads *Hādhā kitāb tashḥīdh al-adhhān bi-sīrat bilād al-'Arab wa-l-Sūdān* ("This is the Book of the Honing of Minds through an Account of the History of the Lands of the Arabs and the Blacks") *li-mu'allifihi l-akh al-ṣadīq Muḥammad ibn al-Sayyid 'Umar al-Tūnusī ibn Sulaymān* ("by our brother and friend Muḥammad ibn al-Sayyid 'Umar al-Tūnusī ibn Sulaymān"); no indication of place of publication, publisher, or date is given in the work but the catalog of the Institut Français d'Archéologie Orientale in Cairo, where a copy was examined, contains the information (in Arabic) "Paris: Kīblīn [?], 1850."

401 During his tenure as director of the medical school at Abū Za'bal, Perron collaborated with Muḥammad al-Tūnusī (see preceding note) to produce a French translation of the latter's account of his 1845 journey to Darfur and to edit and publish the same in Arabic (Pouillon, *Dictionnaire*, 750–51, where the date of publication is given as 1851 rather than 1850 [see preceding note]). The justification for al-Shidyāq's statement that the lithograph edition is "based on a copy in the hand of Monsieur Perron" is unclear: the only reference to Perron occurs in the prologue, where the author says that Perron "urged me to adorn the face of the notebook (*wajh al-daftar*) with a clear account of the wonders that I had seen there and to report to him the strange events that had befallen me on these travels—a command that I obeyed"(pages 5–6). The reference to "our brother and friend" on the title page (see preceding note) does indicate that the copyist was not the author, but the elegance and clarity of the hand argue for a native pen.

402 "*al-'aṣā* with a *y*": i.e., عصى for عصا, as though the root were *'-ṣ-y* rather than *'-ṣ-w*.

403 "*a'lā* as an elative with an *alif*": i.e., اعلا for اعلى.

404 "*najā* with a *yā'*": i.e., نجى for نجا, as though the root were *n-j-y* rather than *n-j-w*.

405 I.e., when they should be written *āminūna muṭma'innūna*.

406 "*fallāḥīna Miṣr*": for *fallāḥī Miṣr* ("the peasants of Egypt," *iḍāfah*).

407 *maḥmūdīna l-sīrah*: for *maḥmūdī l-sīrah* ("those of praiseworthy conduct," *iḍāfah*).

408 "*istawzara l-faqīha Mālik*": for *istawzara l-faqīha Mālikan* ("he appointed the jurisprudent Mālik as minister," Mālik being in the accusative and triptote).

409 "*lā ya'ṣā*": for *lā ya'ṣī* ("he does not disobey").

410 I.e., يتعدا for يتعدى.

411 "*ithnay 'ashara malik*": for *ithnay 'ashara malikan*.

412 "*abādīmā wa-l-takaniyāwī muta'ādilayni*": the error lies in writing *muta'ādilayni* for *muta'ādilāni*; *al-takaniyāwī* is the title of the holder of a certain office in the Darfur sultanate (al-Tūnusī, *Tashḥīdh*, 91 by the translator's count: the pages are unnumbered); *abādīmā* was not identified.

413 "*tajidu l-rijāla wa-l-nisā'a ḥisān*": for *tajidu l-rijāla wa-l-nisā'a ḥisānan.*

414 "*da'ā lanā*": i.e., دعى لنا for دعالنا.

415 "*'ujūbah*": i.e., for *u'jūbah.*

416 "*ṣawāḥibatuhā* and *ṣawāḥibātuhā*": the feminine endings *–at* (singular) and *–āt* (plural) cannot be added to a broken plural.

417 "*lughatun fīhā ḥamās*": the phrase as it stands is not ungrammatical; perhaps the original (which was not found in the text) read *lughatun fī ḥamās* ("a dialectal variant of [the word] *ḥamās*").

418 "*innahumā mutaqāribayi l-ma'nā*": for *innahumā mutaqāribā l-ma'nā.*

419 "*ḥattā ta'tiya arbābu l-māshiyati fa-yaqbiḍūn*": for *ḥattā ta'tiya arbābu l-māshiyati fa-yaqbiḍū.*

420 "*fa-hal iḥdā minkum*": for *fa-hal aḥadun minkum.*

421 "*yarfa'ūna aṣwātahum bi-dhālika ḥattā yadkhulūn*": for *yarfa'ūna aṣwātahum bi-dhālika ḥattā yadkhulū.*

422 "*māshiyīn*": for *māshīn.*

423 "*al-musammayayn*": for *al-musammayn.*

424 "*ḥattā yashuqqūn*": for *ḥattā yashhuqqū.*

425 "*munḥaniyūn*": for *munḥanūn.*

426 "*innahum yakūnū*": for *innahum yakūnūn.*

427 "*lā-'tāḍa*": for *la-'tāḍa.*

428 al-Tūnusī, *Tashḥīdh*, 11.

429 "al-Kuthub" (literally, "the sand dunes"): thus clearly in the original work, but perhaps an error for "al-Kushub," the name of a mountain (*Qāmūs*).

430 Ṭāhā: a name given to the Prophet Muḥammad; the contracted spelling—Ṭh—explains the mistake made by de Perceval (see further down in 5.3.12).

431 "the Bright One" (*al-Zarqā'*): literally, "the Blue One," meaning here both the city of that name (today in Jordan) and "wine" (because, according to the dictionaries, of its clearness).

432 "the *yā'* in *hādhī* is in place of the [second] *hā'*": i.e., the poet used the form *hādhī*, a variant of *hādhihi* (see Wright, *Grammar*, I:268B).

433 “He also changed the [second] *hā’* . . .”: i.e., he generalized from the shaykh’s use of the variant, thus changing the scansion from a long syllable followed by two short syllables (*hādhihi*) to two long syllables (*hādhī*) and throwing off the meter (*al-ramal*).

434 “He also left *al-Zarqā’u* uncorrected (Monsieur Perron having put a *hamzah* after the *alif*)”: i.e., though al-Zarqā’ is so pronounced in prose, the meter here calls for omission of the *hamzah* for the sake of the meter, a subtlety the copyist failed to notice.

435 “*Waṭ’* should properly be written without an *alif*”: i.e., should be written وَطْء and not, as de Perceval presumably had it, وطأ.

436 See 5.3.3.

437 Derenbourg: not Darenbourg as in the Arabic.

438 The commentary was written by de Sacy based on the best-regarded Arabic commentaries. The verses analyzed here occur in both the primary text and the commentary.

439 Though Arabic words normally have been transcribed in this translation, the Arabic is retained here since a number of the items cited involve orthographic issues.

440 “قال العواذل” etc.: i.e., *‘awādhil*, as a plural noun, cannot be preceded by a plural verb of which it is the subject; additionally, as *‘awādhil* is the plural of a feminine noun, the words cannot be understood as an appositional phrase (“they said, the censurers”) which should rather be قلن العواذل.

441 “[17]”: the two dots that appear here and frequently elsewhere in the second column of the original table (as well as the occasional blank) are assumed to be the equivalent of an ellipsis, marking references that the author had not recorded in full and was unable to supply later; the relevant line number is therefore supplied here in square brackets.

442 “with the force of a proverb” (*makhraja l-amthāl*): i.e., and therefore as a self-standing utterance unaffected by the phonetic context.

443 “الصيفَ ضيّعتِ اللبن” (*’al-ṣayfa ḍayya‘ti l-laban*): “in the summer you wasted the milk”—a proverb about an opportunity willfully wasted or a good foregone; the grammatical point is presumably that the first word is pronounced with an initial glottal stop for the same reason as that of the preceding example.

444 “the *tanwīn* . . . occurring as the rhyming syllable” (*al-tanwīna . . . yaqa‘u qāfiyah*): for the rule see Wright, *Grammar*, II:352B.

445 “with prolongation of the vowel for the rhyme” (*bi-l-iṭlāq li-l-qāfiyah*): for the rule see Wright, *Grammar*, II:352D Rem.a.

446 “ بدنا without *tanwīn* . . . آنا”: the main rule involved is that *tanwīn* (“nunation”) is never used in rhyme; additionally, the editors should have been alerted to the need to read بدنا rather than بدنًا by the occurrence of انا as the last word of the first hemistich, which

should rhyme with the last word of the second hemistich when the line is the first in a poem (Wright, *Grammar*, II:351 C).

447 The correct form is, of course, *ilayhim* rather than, as de Sacy etc. have it, *ilayhum*, which breaks a fundamental rule of the harmonization of the front vowel in this situation.

448 "how can *tatayyum* ("enslavement to love") be attributed to *ithr*": de Sacy's reading (*ithruhā*) would require that the word be read as a noun ("mark, trace"), yielding "her mark is enslaved to love"; in fact it is here used as a preposition, thus "(my heart) is enslaved to love. After her . . . ."

449 "How would you deal, my dear professors, with a غول?" (*wa-kayfa tafʿalūna yā asātīdhu bi-l-ghūl*): a sarcastic jab, exploiting the rhymes *makbūl*, *matbūl*, and *ghūl*, the last meaning "ghoul"; the sense is thus something like "How would you deal, my dear professors, with something really scary (i.e. difficult)?"

450 "Kaʿb's poem": i.e., the ode by Kaʿb ibn Zuhayr (first/seventh century) in which he apologizes to the Prophet Muḥammad for having satirized Islam and which became "one of the most famous Arabic poems" (Meisami and Starkey, *Encyclopedia*, 1:421).

451 *qaṣīdah musammaṭah*: a poem in which the two hemistichs of each line rhyme but each line has a different rhyme.

452 "fettered" (*muqayyadah*): i.e., the rhyming syllables should all end in a vowelless consonant.

453 "The pausal form is required" (*al-ṣawābu l-wuqūfu ʿalā l-hā'*): i.e., دعوهْ . . . جفوهْ.

454 "Strangely contorted" (*hiya mina l-tabaltuʿi bi-makān*): apparently meaning that the writing of the *kasrah* and the *ḍammah* is superfluous.

455 "unless the pronominal suffix refers to something mentioned earlier" (*illā idhā kāna l-ḍamīru yarjiʿu ilā madhkūrin qablahu*): the hemistich in question runs *ʿadhīrī mina l-ayyāmi maddat ṣurūfuhu* but it is more natural to read *ṣurūfuhā* ("days whose vicissitudes have passed") than "my advocate (*ʿadhīrī*) whose vicissitudes have passed."

456 "are fond of foolishness" (*yuḥibbūna l-ʿabath*): the author exploits the meaning of the mistakenly written *ʿābith*.

457 "Will you not then understand?" (*a-fa-lā tashʿurūn*): reminiscent of Qur'an *law tashʿurūn* ("if only you could understand") (Q Shuʿarā' 26:113) and similar phrases.

458 "Should be وعُمري as the poet was not being wordy" (*al-ūlā bi-l-ḍammi fa-inna l-shāʿira ghayru mutanaṭṭiʿ*): i.e., the poet says "and my life . . . " and is not using the oath *la-ʿumrī*, which might be considered unnecessary and thus "wordy."

459 وشُرب: the author has misread de Sacy's edition, which does in fact read وشَرِبَ.

460 "It would be better to stick with one or the other" (*al-awlā l-iqtiṣāru ʿalā iḥdāhumā*): de Sacy says in his commentary that *durnā*, with upright *alif*, is a noun of place (de Sacy,

Maqāmāt, I:319 line 13), then quotes a verse in support of this in which he uses the same word with *alif*-in-the-form-of-*yā'*.

461 "Dhū l-Rummah was not one to use contorted language": i.e., the meter requires a long syllable in this position, and the normally diptote form *jalājila*, ending in a short vowel, has to be read as triptote.

462 "a parallel form occurs in the first line" (*wa-fī l-bayt al-awwal naẓar*): the final word of the first hemistich of the first line of the probative verse quoted here is *bi-qafratin*, also with *tanwīn*, which should have alerted the editors.

463 "the word مَنَآئِيا is twisted": the reference is to the line above, where مَنَآئِيا is an error for امانيا.

464 "line at the bottom of the page": in fact, the line before the line at the bottom of the page.

465 "compare عَوْلَ": according to some lexicographers, this word is invariable (see Lane, *Lexicon*).

466 "the diminutive not being allowed to take the definite article": the words *al-basīṭah* and *busayṭah* (diminutive of the former) both mean "the earth" but the latter is always without the definite article, being treated as a proper name.

467 "unwieldy wording" (*al-tanaṭṭu'*): de Sacy's version of the second hemistich of the verse runs *wa-bi-nafsī rtafa'tu lā bi-judūdī*; more authoritative versions have the shorter *fakhartu* for *irtafa'tu*.

468 "the first *tā'* being dropped to make it lighter" (*ḥudhifat al-tā'u l-ūlā li-l-takhfīf*): on omission of *ta-* from the imperfect of Form V and VI verbs, see Wright, *Grammar*, I:65B.

469 "العمى is with *a*, you professors!" (*al-'amā bi-l-fatḥ yā asātīdh*): also, punningly, "Damn that *a*, you professors!" from the Lebanese colloquial expression *il-'ama* ("Damn!").

470 "also الطَّهور not الطُّهور": الطهور appears in the last line on p. 633.

471 "Corr.": in the Arabic ص (*ṣ*) is used apparently as an abbreviation of صوابه (*ṣawābuhu*), meaning "the correct form being . . ."

472 "*Qiṣṣat 'Antar* (*The Story of 'Antar*)": a popular romance relating a mythologized version of the life of the pre-Islamic poet 'Antarah ibn Shaddād al-'Absī; dating to the eleventh or twelth century AD, it employs a language with oral features and "drew the interest of nineteenth-century Orientalists, who saw 'Antar as the paramount Bedouin hero" (Meisami and Starkey, *Encyclopedia*, I:93). Caussin de Perceval's *Notice et extrait du roman d'Antar* was published at the Imprimerie Royale in Paris in 1833.

473 Conte Alix Desgranges: not "Desgrange" as in the Arabic.

474 The only other translation of which I am aware is René Khawam's into French (Faris Chidyaq, *La jambe sur la jambe*). This does not, however, pretend to be complete, since the translator asserts, without offering evidence, that much of the Arabic text

was originally written separately and included in *al-Sāq* simply to take advantage of the availability of funds for publication; the translator has omitted this extraneous material and thus, according to his claim, presents the book, for the first time, "dans toute son originalité" (Chidyaq, Jambe, 19). Khawam does not specify exactly what he has omitted, but examples include the "Memorandum from the Writer of These Characters" in its entirety (Volume One, 1.19.11–23) and, more surprising in its selectivity, many but not all items of certain lexical lists (e.g., forty-three items omitted out of an original fifty-six between *Shiʿb Bawwān* (Volume Two, 2.14.42) and *bint ṭabaq* (Volume Two, 2.14.46) in the list of things incapable of preventing a man from shrieking "I want a woman!"; see Chidyaq, *Jambe*, 311). Khawam also omits the Appendix (Volume Four, 5.3.1 to 5.3.12). The result is a radical shortening of the text that appears to run counter to the author's wishes as expressed in the warning in the Proem (also omitted by Khawam), "Beware, though, lest you add to it or / Think of using it in abbreviated form, / For no place in it is susceptible / To abbreviation, or to addition, to make it better." (Volume One, 0.4.12.).

475 Starkey, "Fact," 32.

476 Cachia, "Development," 68.

477 On *sajʿ* in general, see Meisami and Starkey, *Encyclopedia*; for a discussion of *sajʿ* in *al-Sāq ʿalā l-Sāq*, see *Jubran*, "Function."

478 This loss of "linking and correspondence"—by which I take the author to mean strict parallelism—would probably have particularly upset him: in a eulogy of *sajʿ* written later he writes, "And what shall teach thee what is *sajʿ*? Well-matched words to which man cleaves by *disposition* and to whose sound his heart must yield in passionate *submission*, so that they become impressed upon his memory, and how effective that *impression*—especially when adorned with some of those beauties of the elaborate rhetorical *style* that employ orthographic and morphological *guile*. . . . This is the miracle with which no non-Arab can vie or to whose peaks draw *nigh*!" (al-Shidyāq, *Sirr*, 3–4).

479 Again, the author would not have been best pleased at the sacrifice of monorhyme: "As for the poetry of foreign languages, it consists of no more than farfetched figures and convoluted exaggerations and it is impossible to write a whole poem in them with a single rhyme throughout. You find them varying the rhyme and introducing little-used and uncouth words; and despite that, because of their inability to follow this system [of monorhyme], they say that a poem with only one rhyme is to be regarded as ugly. What hideous words and what appalling ignorance!" (al-Shidyāq, *Sirr*, 4).

480 Peled, "Enumerative," 129.

481 Zakharia, "Aḥmad," 510.

482 Peled, "Enumerative," 139.

483 The author appears to have developed the preferred format for the presentation of such lists in stages. Thus, at the occurrence of the first such list (104 words related to augury and superstition, Volume One, 1.16.7), he first provides the list of words without definitions, then some lines later repeats all but fifteen items (those omitted being presumably the most familiar and thus the least in need of definition) in the form of a table, with headwords in one column and definitions in another (Volume One, 1.16.9), in effect rendering the first list redundant; to avoid reproducing two identical lists in the translation, the first iteration is reproduced there in transcription, resulting in the spectacle, possibly bizarre in a translation, of a block of text consisting entirely of Arabic. Thereafter the two-column table format prevails. Further, this first tabular list is not integrated syntactically into the narrative while most of those that follow are (exceptions include the "five work groups," Volume Two, 2.16.8–63). The alphabetical principle applied to the tables also varies, with some arranged by first letter (e.g., Volume One, 1.16.9–18) and others by last letter (e.g., Volume Two, 2.1.11–16), with occasional anomalies. Even after arriving at the two-column table format, the author continues to ring changes on it. Thus, after a short table of words and definitions relating to attractiveness of the face (Volume Two, 2.4.6), he switches to a non-tabular format (Volume Two, 2.4.7 to 2.4.12), which allows him to group together words with the same root or that are metatheses of one another, while continuing to provide definitions, e.g., "and her *ladīds* have a *ladūd* (the *ladīds* are 'the sides of the neck below the ears' and the *ladūd* is 'a pain that affects the mouth and throat')" (Volume Two, 2.4.11). Later, he interrupts tables with "notes" (see, e.g., Volume Two, 2.14.13), a technique that allows him to enrich the lexical mix by introducing antonyms to the words in the tables.

484 The *Historical Thesaurus of the Oxford English Dictionary*, of which I became aware, unfortunately, only very late in the translation process, was also used to a limited degree. It has the benefit of offering a selection of words many of which are as rare and recondite as those in *al-Sāq* and might provide the best starting point for any future renditions of these lists.

485 Rastegar, "On Nothing," 108. On the relationship between title and contents, the author himself says, "Every one of these chapters, I declare, has a title that points to its contents as unambiguously as smoke does to fire; anyone who knows what the title is knows what the whole chapter is about" (Volume One, 1.17.3.). Though the author may be teasing the reader a little here, the majority of titles do in fact reflect the topic dealth with ("The Priest's Tale," Volume One, 1.15; "A Description of Cairo," Volume Two, 2.5, 2.7; etc.), while others either allude to the governing concept of the chapter (e.g., "Raising a Storm," Volume One, 1.1) or—and this is especially true when the chapter ranges over

a variety of topics—consist of or contain a word that is to be found within the chapter (e.g., "Snow," Volume One, 1.17, or "Throne" in "A Throne to Gain Which Man Must Make Moan," Volume Two, 2.4) in a manner reminiscent of the names of certain *sūrah*s of the Qur'ān.

486 Relying largely on Geoffrey Roper, "Fāris al-Shidyāq as Translator and Editor," in *A Life in Praise of Words: Aḥmad Fāris al-Shidyāq and the Nineteenth Century*, edited by Nadia al-Baghdadi, Fawwaz Traboulsi, and Barbara Winkler. Wiesbaden: Reichert (Litkon 37) (forthcoming; details are provisional) and personal communications.

487 Muḥammad al-Hādi al-Maṭwī, *Aḥmad Fāris al-Shidyāq 1801–1887: ḥayātuhu wa-āthāruhu wa-ārā'uhu fī l-nahḍah al-ʿarabiyyah al-ḥadīthah*. 2 vols. Beirut: Dār al-Gharb al-Islāmī, 1989.

488 Simon Mercieca, "An Italian Connection? Malta, the Italian Risorgimento and Al-Shidyaq's Political Thought." Unpublished paper.

489 The birth date 1805 or 1806 (rather than, as in many sources, 1801 or 1804) is based on a declaration in the author's hand dated 6 August 1851 accompanying his application for British nationality in which he gives his age as 45 (National Archives, Kew, ref. HO1/41/1278A) (Roper, personal communication). The plausibility of this date is reinforced by the statement of a visitor to Malta in 1828, who met "Pharez . . . a most interesting youth, about 22 years of age" (Woodruff, *Journal*, 47).

490 Roper, "Translator," 5.

491 Roper, "Translator," 5.

492 Roper, "Translator," 5.

493 Roper, personal communication.

494 Roper, "Translator," 5, 8.

495 Mercieca, "Italian Connection," 13.

496 Roper, "Translator," 7.

497 al-Maṭwī, *Aḥmad*, 91.

498 al-Maṭwī, *Aḥmad*, 92.

499 Egypt did not finally withdraw from Lebanon until February 1841. If al-Maṭwī is correct in believing that al-Shidyāq returned to Malta in October 1840 (for the start of the academic year at the University of Malta) (al-Maṭwī, *Aḥmad*, 92), the author's words *fa-sārat al-ʿasākir mina l-bilād* ("and the soldiers left the country") (3.14.5) would have to be understood as meaning that they withdrew from Mount Lebanon to the coast. Al-Maṭwī's timetable would also require the author to have left Qraye after 10 October (the date of the defeat of the Egyptian fleet), traveled to Damascus, stayed there long

enough to recover from his accident, go on to Jaffa, and return to Malta all in twenty days, which, while not perhaps impossible, seems unlikely.

500 al-Maṭwī, *Aḥmad*, 125.

501 Roper, personal communication.

502 Roper, "Translator," 8.

503 Roper, "Translator," 8.

504 Roper, "Translator," 8.

505 The author wrote at least twice to the joint committee of the SPCK and CMS complaining of his treatment; the letter referred to in the text is probably that send by al-Shidyāq in March 1844 (Roper, Translator, 8), which resulted in his eventual reinstatement (*idem* 9).

506 Roper, personal communication.

507 al-Maṭwī, *Aḥmad*, 103

508 al-Maṭwī, *Aḥmad*, 103.

509 al-Maṭwī, *Aḥmad*, 126.

510 al-Maṭwī, *Aḥmad*, 105.

511 al-Maṭwī, *Aḥmad*, 109.

512 al-Maṭwī, *Aḥmad*, 110.

513 al-Maṭwī, *Aḥmad*, 137–38.

Glossary

ʿAbd al-Majīd, Sultan thirty-first Ottoman sultan, reigned 1839–61.

ʿAbd al-Qādir (ibn Muḥyī l-Dīn al-Jazāʾirī), Emir (1808–83) from 1834 the most successful leader of resistance to French rule in Algeria; exiled to France in 1847.

Abū l-Ḥasan al-Tihāmī al-Ḥasanī a poet of Arabian origin who died (416/1025) in Cairo.

Abū Tammām Abū Tammām Ḥabīb ibn Aws al-Ṭāʾī (ca. 189/805 to ca. 232/845), Abbasid court poet and anthologist, teacher and rival of al-Buḥturī.

Andalus (al-) those parts of the Iberian Peninsula that were under Islamic rule from the seventh to the fifteenth centuries.

badīʿ an innovative style appearing in poetry starting in the third/ninth centuries featuring complex wordplay; eventually, the term evolved to mean "rhetorical figures" collectively.

Bilqīs Queen of Sabaʾ (Sheba) in Yemen, the story of whose visit to Sulaymān (Solomon) is told in the Qurʾān (Q Naml 27:22–44).

Buḥturī (al-) Abū ʿUbādah al-Walīd ibn ʿUbayd (Allāh) al-Buḥturī (206/821 to 284/897), Abbasid court poet, student and rival of Abū Tammām.

Chodźko, Alexandre Aleksander Borejko Chodźko (1804–91), Polish poet, Slavist, and Iranologist, who worked for the French ministry of foreign affairs from 1852 to 1855 and was later appointed to the chair of Slavic languages at the Collège de France.

Committee, the the Society for the Promotion of Christian Knowledge, which oversaw many of the translation projects, including that of the Bible, in which al-Shidyāq was involved.

Derenbourg, Joseph (1811–95) a Hebraist and Arabist.

de Sacy see Silvestre de Sacy.

Desgranges, Conte Alix Desgranges (d. 1854) held the post of *secrétaire interprète* to the French state, in addition to being, as of 1833, professor of Turkish at the Collège de France; in his former capacity "he welcomes and escorts all Orientals who pass through Paris" (Pouillon, *Dictionnaire*, 292).

dhikr the repetition of the name of God as an exercise intended to bring the one who pronounces it closer to Him.

Dhū l-Rummah nickname ("He of the Frayed Cord") of Abū Ḥārith Ghaylān ibn ʿUqba, an Umayyad poet (d. 117/735?).

Ḥalq al-Wād the port of Tunis, also known as La Goulette.

Ḥarīrī (al-) Abū Muḥammad al-Qāsim ibn ʿAli al-Ḥarīrī (446/1054 to 516/1122), Iraqi poet, man of letters, and official, best known for his collection of fifty *maqāmāt* (see *maqāmah*).

Ḥimṣ Homs, a city between Damascus and Aleppo.

Ibn Abī ʿAtīq Muḥammad ibn ʿAbd al-Raḥmān ibn Abī Bakr (first/seventh century to second/eighth century), usually referred to as Ibn Abī ʿAtīq, was the great-grandson of the caliph Abū Bakr al-Ṣiddīq and "a friend of many poets and singers, who appears in many stories and anecdotes as a kind of wit" (Van Gelder, *Classical*, 379, 460); it is not obvious why the author brackets him with Ibn Ḥajjāj (q.v.), as unlike the latter he was irreverent rather than foulmouthed.

Ibn Ḥajjāj al-Ḥusayn ibn Aḥmad Ibn (al-)Ḥajjāj (ca. 333/941 to 391/1000): a Baghdadi poet known for his obscene poetry.

Ibn Nubātah Jamāl al-Dīn Muḥammad ibn Shams al-Dīn (686/1287 to 768/1366), an Egyptian poet.

Ibn Ṣarīʿ al-Dilāʾ Abū l-Ḥasan ʿAlī ibn ʿAbd al-Wāhid (d. 412/1021), a poet of Baghdadi origin whose later life was spent in Cairo. Ibn Khallikān refers to him as a poet of *mujūn* ("license").

Imruʾ al-Qays Imruʾ al-Qays ibn Ḥujr (sixth century AD), a pre-Islamic poet, author of one of the *muʿallaqāt* ("suspended odes").

ʿĪsā Jesus.

Islāmbūl Istanbul.

Jubārah, Ghubrāʾīl one of a group of Levantines who supported the author financially and morally during his years in Paris and London; on May 1, 1851 he took the author with him from Paris to London for the opening of the Great Exhibition as a translator and guide.

jubbah an open-fronted mantle with wide sleeves.

Kaḥlā, Rāfāʾīl litterateur and collaborator of al-Shidyāq's in Paris, who paid for the publication of *Al-Sāq ʿalā l-sāq* and contributed to it a publisher's introduction (Volume One, 0.3).

Khawājā a title of reference and address afforded Christians of substance.

maqāmah, plural *maqāmāt* "short independent prose narrations written in ornamented rhymed prose (*sajʿ*) with verse insertions which share a common plot-scheme and two constant protagonists: the narrator and the hero" (Meisami and Starkey, *Encyclopedia*, 2/507).

Mikhallaʿ (al-), Mikhāʾīl one of the group of Levantines who assisted the author financially and morally during his years in Paris and London, and an early convert to Protestantism.

Mūsā Moses.

Musurus, Prince Kostaki Musurus (1814 or 1815 to 1891) served as Ottoman ambassador to London without interruption from 1851 until 1885; he translated Dante's *Divine Comedy* into Turkish and Greek.

Mutanabbī (al-) Abū l-Ṭayyib Aḥmad ibn Ḥusayn al-Mutanabbī (ca. 303/915 to 354/965), a poet renowned for his virtuosity and innovation, which he deployed in praise of a series of the rulers of the day.

Perron, Nicolas (1798–1876) French physician, Arabist, and Saint-Simonist. Perron studied medicine and also took courses at the École des langues orientales, especially those given by Caussin de Perceval. Later he became director of the hospital of Abū Zaʿbal, near Cairo, Egypt's first health facility based on a Western model.

Rashīd Pasha, Muṣṭafā (ca. 1800–58) Ottoman politician, diplomat, reformer, litterateur, and traveler. Ambassador to Paris and London, then foreign minister and later chief minister, he met al-Shidyāq during his second tenure as ambassador to Paris and was later instrumental in bringing him to Constantinople.

Reinaud, Joseph Toussaint (1795–1867) French Orientalist; Toussaint succeeded to Silvestre de Sacy's chair at the École des langues orientales on the latter's death.

Sāmī Pasha, ʿAbd al-Raḥmān an Ottoman reformer, born in the Peloponnese. He entered Egyptian service in 1821, was appointed director in 1828 of the official gazette, *al-Waqāʾiʿ al-Miṣriyyah* (where al-Shidyāq may have made his acquaintance), and became the Ottoman Empire's first minister of education in 1856. He wrote prose and verse in Turkish (al-Maṭwī, *Aḥmad*, 898–99).

Silvestre de Sacy, Antoine Isaac (1758–1838) prominent French philologist who wrote grammars of Arabic and edited a number of Arabic texts, including al-Ḥarīrī's *Maqāmāt*.

Ṣubḥī Bayk son of ʿAbd al-Raḥmān Sāmī Pasha (q.v.) and later himself also Ottoman minister of education and then governor of Syria (al-Maṭwī, *Aḥmad*, 902).

Sublime State, the the Ottoman Empire.

Sulaymān Solomon.

tanwīn pronunciation of word-final short vowels followed by *-n*, thus *-un*, *-an*, *-in*; also called "nunation."

Tūnusī (al-), Muḥammad ibn al-Sayyid ʿUmar (ibn Sulaymān) an interpreter at the Abū Zaʿbal medical school who wrote an account of his travels in Darfur in the early nineteenth century.

wird a section of the Qurʾān specified for recitation at a certain time of day or night or for use in private prayer.

zaqqūm tree a tree mentioned in the Qurʾān as growing in hell and bearing exceedingly bitter fruit.

Bibliography

Abū Nuwās, al-Ḥasan ibn Hāni'. *Dīwān*. Beirut: Dār Ṣādir and Dār Bayrūt, 1962.

Alwan, Mohammed Bakir. *Aḥmad Fāris ash-Shidyāq and the West*. Unpublished PhD Dissertation. Indiana University, 1970.

Amīn, Aḥmad. *Qāmūs al-ʿādāt wa-l-taqālīd wa-l-taʿābīr al-miṣriyyah*. Cairo: Lajnat al-Ta'līf wa-l-Tarjamah wa-l-Nashr, 1953.

Arberry, Arthur J. *Arabic Poetry: A primer for students*. Cambridge: Cambridge University Press, 1965.

Arberry, Arthur J. "Fresh Light on Ahmad Faris al-Shidyaq." *Islamic Culture*, 26 (1952), 155–68.

Arberry, Arthur J. *The Koran Interpreted*. Oxford World's Classics. Oxford: Oxford University Press, 1982.

Arberry, Arthur J. *The Seven Odes: The first chapter in Arabic literature*. London: George Allen and Unwin, 1957.

ʿĀshūr, Raḍwā. *Al-ḥadāthah al-mumkinah, al-Shidyāq wa-l-sāq ʿalā l-sāq, al-riwāyah al-ūlā fī-l-adab al-ʿarabī al-ḥadīth*. Cairo: Dār al-Shurūq, 2009.

Badawi, El-Said and Martin Hinds. *A Dictionary of Egyptian Arabic, Arabic–English*. Beirut: Librairie du Liban, 1986.

Baghdādī, ʿAbd al-Laṭīf al-. *Al-ifādah wa-l-iʿtibār fī-l-umūr wa-l-ḥawādith al-muʿāyanah bi-arḍ Miṣr*, edited by Salāma Mūsā. Cairo: Maṭbaʿat al-Majallah al-Jadīdah, n.d.

Brincat, Joseph F. *Maltese and Other Languages: A linguistic history of Malta*. Santa Venera: Midsea Books, 2011.

Brustad, Kristen. "Jirmānūs Jibrīl Farḥāt." In *Essays in Arabic Literary Biography* 1350–1850, edited by Joseph Lowry and Devin J. Stewart, 242–51. Wiesbaden: Harrassowitz Verlag, 2009.

Cachia, Pierre. "The Development of a Modern Prose Style in Arabic Literature." *Bulletin of the School of Oriental and African Studies*, University of London 52, no. 1 (1989):65–76.

Chateaubriand, François-René. *Oeuvres complètes de Chateaubriand*. Vol. VI: *Voyages en Amérique, en Italie, au Mont Blanc. Mélanges littéraires*. Paris: Garnier, [1861].

Chauvin, Victor. *Bibliographie des ouvrages arabes ou relatifs aux arabes publiés dans l'Europe chrétienne de 1810 à 1885*. 3 vols. Liège: H. Vaillant-Carmanne and Leipzig, O. Harrassowitz, 1882–85.

Dankoff, Robert. "Ayıp değil! (No Disgrace!)." *Journal of Turkish Literature* 5 (2008):77–90.

Dozy, R.P.A. *Dictionnaire détaillé des noms des vêtements chez les arabes.* Amsterdam: Jean Müller, 1843 (offset, Beirut: Librairie du Liban, n.d.).

——— *Supplément aux dictionnaires arabes.* 2 Vols. Leiden: E.J. Brill, 1881 (offset, Beirut: Librairie du Liban, 1968)

EI2 = *Encyclopaedia of Islam,* edited by P.J. Bearman, Th. Bianquis, C.E. Bosworth, E. van Donzel and W.P. Heinrichs et al., 2nd Edition., 12 vols. with indexes and etc., Leiden: E. J. Brill, 1960–2005.

El Mouelhy, Ibrahim. "Le Qirmeh en Égypte." Bulletin de l'Institut d'Égypte, 24 (1946–47): 51–82.

Ewald, Ferdinand Christian. *Journal of Missionary Labours in the City of Jerusalem during the Years 1841-2-3.* 1st edition. London: B. Wertheim, 1845.

Fīrūzābādhī [=Fīrūzābadī] (al-), Muḥammad ibn Ya'qūb. *Al-Qāmūs al-muḥīṭ.* 4 volumes. 2nd edition. Cairo: al-Maṭba'ah al-Ḥusayniyyah, 1344 H, also accessed at http://www.baheth.info/.

Flaubert, Gustave. *Flaubert in Egypt,* translated and edited by Francis Steemuller. 2nd edition. Chicago: Academy Chicago, 1987.

Graf, Georg. *Geschichte der christlichen arabischen Literatur.* 5 vols. Vatican: Biblioteca apostolica vaticana, 1944–53.

Hava, J. G. *Al-Farā'id al-durriyyah fī l-lughatayn al-'arabiyyah wa-l-inkilīziyyah.* Beirut: Catholic Press, n.d.

Ḥillī, Ṣafī al-Dīn al-. *Sharḥ al-kāfiyyah al-badī'iyyah,* edited by Nasīb Nashāwī. Damascus, 1983.

Ibn al-Athīr, Majd al-Dīn Abū l-Sa'ādāt al-Mubārak ibn Muḥammad. *Kitāb al-nihāyah fī gharīb al-ḥadīth wa-l-athar.* 4 vols. Cairo: al-Maṭba'ah al-'Uthmāniyyah, 1311 H.

Ibn al-Fāriḍ, 'Umar ibn 'Alī. *Dīwān.* Cairo: Maktabat al-Qāhirah, 1951.

Ibn Khālawayh, al-Ḥusayn ibn Aḥmad. *Laysa fī kalām al-'Arab,* edited by Aḥmad 'Abd al-Ghafūr 'Aṭṭār. 2nd edition. Mecca, 1399/1979 .

Ibn Manẓūr, Jamāl al-Dīn Muḥammad ibn Mukarram al-'Ifrīqī. *Lisān al-'Arab.* Accessed at http://www. baheth.info/.

Jubran, Suleiman. "The Function of Rhyming Prose in 'Al-Sāq 'alā al-Sāq'." *Journal of Arabic Literature,* 20, no. 2 (Sep. 1989): 148–58.

Karamustafa, Ahmet T. *God's Unruly Friends: Dervish Groups in the Islamic Later Middle Period 1200–1550.* Salt Lake City: University of Utah Press, 1994.

Kayat, Assaad Y. [= Khayyāṭ, As'ad Ya'qūb]. *A Voice from Lebanon.* London: Madden & Co., 1847.

Khawam, René. *La Jambe sur la jambe*. Paris: Phébus, 1991.

Lamartine, Alphonse de. *Oeuvres de A. de Lamartine: Méditations poétiques*. Paris: Charles Gosselin, 1838.

Lane, Edward. *An Arabic-English Lexicon*. 8 vols. London: Williams and Norgate, 1863 (offset edition Beirut: Librairie du Liban, 1968).

———. *Manners and Customs of the Modern Egyptians*. 5th edition. Cairo: American University in Cairo Press, 2003.

Levey, Martin. "Medieval Arabic Toxicology: The Book on Poisons of ibn Wahshīya and its relation to early Indian and Greek texts." Transactions of the *American Philosophical Society*, New Series, 56, no. 7 (1966): 1–130.

Lisān see Ibn Manẓūr.

Makdisi, Ussama. *The Artillery of Heaven: American missionaries and the failed conversion of the Middle East*. Ithaca, NY/London: Cornell University Press, 2008.

Maṭwī, Muḥammad al-Hādi al-. *Aḥmad Fāris al-Shidyāq 1801–1887: ḥayātuhu wa-āthāruhu wa-ārāʾuhu fī l-nahḍah al-ʿarabiyyah al-ḥadīthah*. 2 vols. Beirut: Dār al-Gharb al-Islāmī, 1989.

Maydānī, Aḥmad ibn Muḥammad al-. *Majmaʿ al-amthāl*. 2 vols. Cairo: al-Maṭbaʿah al-Khayriyyah, 1310 H .

Meisami, Julie Scott & Paul Starkey (eds.). *Encyclopedia of Arabic Literature*, 2 vols. London and New York: Routledge, 1998.

Mercieca, Simon. "An Italian Connection? Malta, the Italian Risorgimento and Al-Shidyaq's Political Thought." Unpublished paper.

Mutanabbī, Abū l-Ṭayyib al-. *Dīwān Abī l-Ṭayyib al-Mutanabbī*, edited by ʿAbd al-Wahhāb ʿAzzām. *Al-Dhakhāʾir* 1. Cairo: al-Hayʾah al-ʿĀmmah li-Quṣūr al-Thaqāfah, n.d.

Muʿāmilī, Shawqī Muḥammad al-. *Al-ittijāh al-sākhir fī adab al-Shidyāq*. Cairo: Maktabat al-Nahḍah al-Miṣriyyah, n.d. [1988].

Nelson, Kristina. *The Art of Reciting the Qurʾan*. Cairo/New York: American University in Cairo Press, 2001.

Nīsābūrī, al-Ḥasan ibn Muḥammad ibn Ḥabīb al-. *ʿUqalāʾ al-majānīn*, edited by Fāris al-Kīlānī. Cairo: al-Maṭbaʿah al-ʿArabiyyah, 1924.

Patel, Abdulrazzak. *The Arab Nahdah: The Making of the Intellectual and Humanist Movement*. Edinburgh: Edinburgh University Press, 2013.

Peled, Mattityahu. "The Enumerative Style in ʿAl-Sāq ʿalā al-sāqʾ." *Journal of Arabic Literature*, 22, no. 2 (Sep. 1991): 127–45.

Qāmūs see Fīrūzābādhī al-.

Rastegar, Kamran. *Literary Modernity between the Middle East and Europe: Textual transactions in nineteenth-century Arabic, English, and Persian literatures*. London and New York: Routledge, 2007.

Roget, Peter Mark. *Roget's International Thesaurus*, 4th edition, revised by Robert L. Chapman. New York: Thomas Y. Crowell, 1977.

Roper, Geoffrey. "Aḥmad Fāris al-Shidyāq and the libraries of Europe and the Ottoman Empire." In *Libraries and Culture*, 33, no. 3 (1998): 233–48.

———. "Faris al-Shidyaq (d. 1887) and the transition from scribal to print culture." In *The Book in the Islamic World*, edited by G.N. Atiyeh, 209–32. Albany, NY: SUNY Press, 1995.

———. "Fāris al-Shidyāq as translator and editor." In *A Life in Praise of Words: Aḥmad Fāris al-Shidyāq and the nineteenth century*, edited by Nadia al-Baghdadi, Fawwaz Traboulsi, and Barbara Winkler. Wiesbaden: Reichert (Litkon 37) (forthcoming).

Rosenthal, Franz. *Humor in Early Islam*. Leiden/Boston: Brill, 2011.

Rowson, Everett. "The Effeminates of Early Medina." *Journal of the American Oriental Society* 111 (1991): 671–93.

Sale, George. *The Koran: Commonly called the Alcoran of Mohammed*. London: William Tegg, 1850.

Sayyid (al-) al-Raḍī. *Dīwān*. Baghdad (?): *Maṭbaʿat Nukhbat al-Akhyār*, 1306/1888–89.

Sharīf (al-) al-Raḍī, Muḥammad ibn Abū Ṭāhir al-Ḥusayn ibn Mūsā see al-Sayyid al-Raḍī .

Shidyāq (al-), Aḥmad Fāris al-. *Kitāb al-jāsūs ʿalā l-qāmūs*. 2nd edition. Constantinople: Maṭbaʿat al-Jawāʾib, 1299 [1860-61]; reprinted, Beirut: al-Muʾassasah al-ʿArabiyyah li-l-Dirāsāt wa-l-Nashr, 2004.

———. *Kitāb sirr al-layāl fī l-qalb wa-l-ibdāl*. Al-Āsitānah [Istanbul]: al-Maṭbaʿah al-ʿĀmirah al-Sulṭāniyyah, 1284 [1867].

[Shidyāq (al-)], Aḥmad Fāris Afandī. *Al-Wāsiṭah fī maʿrifat aḥwāl Māliṭah*. 2nd revised edition (in the same volume: *Kashf al-mukhabbā ʿan funūn Urubbā*). Constantinople: Maṭbaʿat al-Jawāʿib, 1299/1881.

Spiro, Socrates. *An Arabic-English Vocabulary of the Colloquial Arabic of Egypt*. Cairo: al-Mokattam Printing Office, 1895. [Offset with title changed to *An Arabic-English Dictionary* etc., Beirut: Librairie du Liban, 1973.]

Starkey, Paul. "Fact and Fiction in al-Sāq ʿalā l-Sāq." In *Writing the Self: Autobiographical Writing in Modern Arabic Literature*, edited by Robin Ostle, Ed de Moor and Stephan Wild, 30–38. London: Saqi Books, 1998.

Sterne, Laurence. *The Life and Opinions of Tristram Shandy, Gentleman*. Mineola: Dover Publications, 2007 .

Stewart, Devin. "The Maqāma." In *Arabic Literature in the Post-Classical Period* (The Cambridge History of Arabic Literature, Vol. 6.), edited by Roger Allen and D. S. Richards, 145–58. Cambridge, New York: Cambridge University Press, 2008.

Ṣulḥ (al-), ʿImād. *Iʿtirāfāt al-Shidyāq fī kitāb al-Sāq ʿalā l-sāq*. Dār al-Rāʾid al-ʿArabī: Beirut, 1982.

Täckholm, Vivi. *A Students' Flora of Egypt*. Beirut: Cooperative Printing Co., 1974.

Tāj see Zabīdī (al-).

Tūnusī (al-), Muḥammad ibn al-Sayyid ʿUmar (ibn Sulaymān). *Tashḥīdh al-adhhān bi-sīrat bilād al-ʿArab wa-l-Sūdān*. Paris: Kīblīn [?], 1850.

Van Gelder, Geert Jan. *Classical Arabic Literature: A Library of Arabic Literature Anthology*. New York: New York University Press, 2013.

Watt, W. M. Bell's *Introduction to the Qurʾān*. Edinburgh: Edinburgh University Press, 1970.

Woodruff, Samuel. *Journal of a Tour to Malta . . . in 1828*. Hartford: Cooke & Co., 1831.

Wright, W. A. *Grammar of the Arabic Language*. 3rd edition, revised by W. Robertson Smith and M. J. de Goeje. 2 vols. Cambridge: Cambridge University Press, 1951.

Zabīdī (al-), al-Sayyid Abū l-Fayḍ Muḥammad ibn Muḥammad ibn ʿAbd al-Razzāq al-Murtaḍā. *Tāj al-ʿarūs min jawāhir al-qāmūs*. Accessed at http://www.shamela.ws.

Zakharia, Katia. "Aḥmad Fāris al-Šidyāq, auteur de 'Maqāmāt'." *Arabica*, T. 52, Fasc. 4 (Oct. 2005): 496–521.

Further Reading

ʿAbbūd, Mārūn. "ʿĀlim an-nahḍah al-ḥadīth: Aḥmad Fāris al-Shidyāq 1804–1887." *Al-kitab* 2 (1946): 587–606.

———. *Ṣaqr Lubnān, baḥth fī l-nahḍah al-ʿarabiyyah al-ḥadīthah wa-rajuliha al-awwal Aḥmad Fāris al-Shidyāq*. Beirut: Dar al-Makshūf, 1950.

Agius, Dionysius. "Arabic under Shidyaq in Malta 1833–1848." *Journal of Maltese Studies* 19–20 (1989–90): 52–57.

ʿAkkāwī, Riḥāb. *Al-Fāryāq, Aḥmad Fāris al-Shidyāq*. Beirut: Dār al-Fikr al-ʿArabī, 2003.

Alwan, Mohammed. "The History and Publications of Al-Jawa'ib Press." *MELA Notes* 11 (1977), pp. 4–7.

Āṣāf, Yūsuf. *Huwa l-bāqī*. Cairo: Maṭbaʿat al-Qāhirah al-Ḥurrah, 1305/1885.

ʿĀshūr, Raḍwā. *Al-ḥadāthah al-mumkinah, al-Shidyāq wa-l-sāq ʿalā l-sāq, al-riwāyah al-ūlā fī-l-adab al-ʿarabī al-ḥadīth*. Cairo, Dār al-Shurūq, 2009.

Abu-Lughod, Ibrahim. *The Arab Rediscovery of Europe: A Study in Cultural Encounters*. Princeton, NJ: Princeton University Press, 1963.

Al-Bagdadi, Nadia. "The Cultural Function of Fiction: From the Bible to Libertine Literature: Historical Criticism and Social Critique in Aḥmad Fāris al-Šidyāq." *Arabica*, T. 46, Fasc. 3 (1999): 375–401.

Arberry, A. J. "Fresh Light on Ahmad Faris al-Shidyaq." *Islamic Culture* 26 (1952): 155–68.

Bayham, Muḥammad Jamāl. "Aʿlām al-lughah: Aḥmad Fāris al-Shidyāq." *Al-lisān al-ʿarabī* (Rabāṭ), 8/1, January 1975.

Bustānī, Fu'ad Ifrām al-. "Fī l-Nahḍah al-adabiyyah: Nāṣif al-Yāzijī wa-Fāris al-Shidyāq." *Al-mashriq* 34, 1936: 443–47.

Cachia, Pierre. "An Arab's View of XIXth Century Malta: Shidyaq's *ʿAl-Wasitah fi ma`rifat ahwal Malitah*.'" *Maltese Folklore Review* 1 (1962–66), pp. 62–69, 110–16, and 232–43.

———. "The Development of a Modern Prose Style in Arabic Literature." *Bulletin of the School of Oriental and African Studies, University of London*, Vol. 52, No. 1 (1989): 65–76.

Cassar, Francis Xavier, trans. *Al-Wāsiṭah fī maʿrifat aḥwāl Mālitā. El-Wasita. Tagħrif dwar Malta tas-Seklu 19*. Paola: Centru Kulturali Islamiku F'Malta, 1988.

Ḍāwī, Aḥmad ʿArafāt. *Dirāsah fī adab: Aḥmad Fāris al-Shidyāq wa-ṣūrat al-gharb fīh*. Amman: Wizārat al-Thaqāfah, 1994.

Dāyah, Jān. "Aḥmad Fāris al-Shidyāq fī l-qiṣṣah al-qaṣīrah." *Fikr* (Beirut), Issues 27–28, December 1978–January 1979.

El-Ariss, Tarek. *Trials of Arab modernity: literary affects and the new political.* New York: Fordham University Press, 2013.

Hajrasī, Maḥmūd. "Al-Sāq ʿalā l-Sāq." *Majmūʿat turāth al-insāniyyah* (Egypt), 5, n.d.

Hārūn, Jiyurj. "Al-Shidyāq rāʾid al-ḥurriyyāt fī fikrina al-ḥadīth." *Ḥiwār* (Beirut), 1 September–October 1963, 79–87.

Ḥasan, Muḥammad ʿAbd al-Ghanī. *Aḥmad Fāris al-Shidyāq.* Cairo: al-Dār al-Miṣriyyah li-l-Taʾlīf wa-l-Tarjamah, n.d.

Ibn ʿĀshūr, Muḥammad al-Fāḍil. "Athar Tūnus fī ḥayāt Fāris al-Shidyāq." *Al-Zamān* (Tunis), Year 10, Issue 462, 12 January 1979.

Ibn Maḥmūd, Nūr al-Dīn. "Fāris al-Shidyāq fī Tūnus." *Al-nahḍah* (Tunis), 2, May 1937.

Jabrī, Shafīq. "Sukhriyyat al-Shidyāq." *Majallat al-majmaʿ al-ʿilmī al-ʿarabī bi-Dimashq,* 2/34, April 1959.

———. "Lughat al-Shidyāq." *Al-mawrid,* 4/3, 1974.

Jubran, Sulaiman. "The Function of Rhyming Prose in 'Al-Sāq ʿalā al-Sāq'." *Journal of Arabic Literature,* Vol. 20, No. 2, September 1989: 148–58.

Jubrān, Sulaymān. *Al-mabnā wa-l-uslūb wa-l-sukhriyyah fī kitāb al-sāq ʿalā l-sāq fī-mā huwa l-Fāryāq li-Aḥmad Fāris al-Shidyāq.* Cairo: Qaḍāyā Fikriyyah li-l-Nashr wa-l-Tawzīʿ, 1993.

Karam, A. G. "Faris al-Shidyak," in *The Encyclopaedia of Islam,* vol. II: 800–2. 2nd edition. Edited by B. Lewis, C. Pellat, and J. Schacht. Leiden: Brill, 1965.

Khalaf Allāh, Muḥammad Aḥmad. *Aḥmad Fāris al-Shidyāq wa-ārāʾuh al-lughawiyyah wa-l-adabiyyah.* Cairo: Maṭbaʿat al-Risālah, 1955.

Khayr al-Dīn, Tāhir. "Ḥawla Fāris al-Shidyāq fī Tūnis" *Al-nahḍah* (Tunis), 16 May 1937.

Khūrshīd, Fārūq. "Miṣr fī adab al-Shidyāq." *Al-hilāl,* February 1979.

Maʿlūf, Amīn al-. "Khamsūna sanah ʿalā wafāt al-Shidyāq." *Majallat al-muqtaṭaf,* 3/91, October 1937.

Maṭwī, Muḥammad al-Hādi al-. *Aḥmad Fāris al-Shidyāq 1801–1887: ḥayātuhu wa-āthāruhu wa-ārāʾuhu fī l-nahḍah al-ʿarabiyyah al-ḥadīthah.* 2 vols. Beirut: Dār al-Gharb al-Islāmī, 1989.

Muʿāmilī, Shawqī Muḥammad al-. *Al-ittijāh al-sākhir fī adab al-Shidyāq.* Cairo: Maktabat al-Nahḍah al-Miṣriyyah, 1988.

Musʿad, Būlus. *Fāris al-Shidyāq.* Cairo: Maṭbaʿat al-Ikhāʾ, 1934.

Najārī, ʿAlī Ḥaydar al-. "Aḥmad Fāris al-Shidyāq wa-qaṣīdatān makhṭūtatān la-hu." *Al-adīb* (Beirut), Year 27, February 1978.

Naṣṣār, ʿIṣmat. *Aḥmad Fāris al-Shidyāq: qirāʾah fī ṣafāʾiḥ al-muqāwamah.* [Cairo]: Dar al-Hidāyah, [2005].

Paniconi, Maria Elena. "La Thématisation de depart et la (trans)formation du personage fictionnel dans Al-sāq ʿalā l-sāq d'Aḥmad Fāris al-Šidyāq." *Annali di Ca' Foscari: Rivisti della Facoltà di Lingue e Letterature Straniere dell'Università Ca' Foscari di Venezia*, 48 iii (Serie 40), 2009 (2010): 241–59.

Peled, Mattityahu. "al-Sāq ʿAlā al-Sāq: A Generic Definition." *Arabica*, T. 32, Fasc. 1 (Mar., 1985): 31–46.

———. "The Enumerative Style in ʿAl-Sāq ʿalā al-sāqʾ." *Journal of Arabic Literature*, Vol. 22, No. 2 (Sep., 1991): 127–45.

Pérès, Henri. "Les Premières manifestations de la renaissance littéraire arabe en Orient au XIXe siècle. Nasif al-Yazigi et Faris ash-Shidyak." *Annales de l'Institut d'Études Orientales* 1 (1934–35): 232–56.

———. "Voyageurs musulmans en Europe aux XIXe et XXe siècles," in *Melanges Maspero*, Vol. III: 185–95. Cairo: Impriméríe de l'Institut Français d'Archéologie Orientale, 1940.

Qāsimī, Ẓāfir al-. "Musṭalaḥāt Shidyāqiyyah." *Majallat al-majmaʿ al-ʿilmī al-ʿarabī bi-Dimashq*, 2/40, April 1965: 431–51.

Rastegar, Kamran. *Literary Modernity between the Middle East and Europe: Textual transactions in nineteenth-century Arabic, English, and Persian literatures.* London and New York: Routledge, 2007.

Roper, Geoffrey. "Aḥmad Fāris al-Shidyāq and the Libraries of Europe and the Ottoman Empire." *Libraries & Culture* 33/3 (Summer 1998): 233–48.

———. "Arabic printing in Malta 1825–1845: Its history and its place in the development of print culture in the Arab Middle East. " Doctoral thesis, Durham University, 1988.

———. "Faris al-Shidyaq and the Transition from Scribal to Print Culture in the Middle East." In *The Book in the Islamic World: the written word and communication in the Middle East.* Edited by George N. Atiyeh. Albany, State University of New York Press, 1995.

———. "Fāris al-Shidyāq as Translator and Editor." In *A Life in Praise of Words: Aḥmad Fāris al-Shidyāq and the nineteenth century.* Edited by Nadia al-Baghdadi, Fawwaz Traboulsi, and Barbara Winkler. Wiesbaden: Reichert (Litkon 37) (forthcoming).

———. "National Awareness, Civic Rights and the Role of the Printing Press in the 19th Century: The Careers and Opinions of Faris al-Shidyaq, His Colleagues and Patrons." In *Democracy in the Middle East. Proceedings of the Annual Conference of the British Society for Middle Eastern Studies.* St. Andrews: University of St. Andrews [for the British Society for Middle Eastern Studies], 1992.

Ṣawāyā, Mīkhā'īl. *Aḥmad Fāris al-Shidyāq, ḥayātuhu, āthāruhu*. Beirut: Dar al-Sharq al-Jadīd, 1962.

Starkey, Paul. "Fact and Fiction in al-Sāq 'alā l-Sāq." In *Writing the Self: Autobiographical Writing in Modern Arabic Literature*, 30–38. Edited by Robin Ostle, Ed de Moor and Stephan Wild. London: Saqi Books, 1998.

———. "Voyages of Self-definition: The Case of [Ahmad] Faris al-Shidyaq." In *Sensibilities of the Islamic Mediterranean: Self-Expression in a Muslim Culture from Post-Classical Times to the Present Day*, 118–32. Edited by Robin Ostle. London, I.B. Tauris, 2008.

Ṣulḥ, 'Imād al-. *Aḥmad Fāris al-Shidyāq: āthāruhu wa-'aṣruhu*. Beirut: Dār al-Nahār li-l-Nashr, 1980.

———. "Shakhṣiyyāt Tūnusiyyah fī-ḥayāt al-Shidyāq." *Majallat al-Fayṣal*, 31, December 1979.

Traboulsi, Fawwaz. "Ahmad Fâris al-Chidyâq (1804-1887)". In *Liban: figures comtemporaines. Essais rassemblées et présentées par Farouk Mardam-Bey*, 11–24. Paris: Institut du Monde Arabe/Circé, 1999.

Yāghī, Hāshim. "Jawānib min Aḥmad Fāris al-Shidyāq al-nāqid." *Majallat al-afkār* (Jordan), 1/1. June 1966.

Zakharia, Katia. "Aḥmad Fāris al-Šidyāq, auteur de 'Maqāmāt'." *Arabica*, T. 52, Fasc. 4 (Oct. 2005): 496–521.

Zaydān, Jurjī. "Aḥmad Fāris." *Al-hilāl*, 14 (15 March 1894) and 15 (1 April 1894).

Index

About the NYU Abu Dhabi Institute

The Library of Arabic Literature is supported by a grant from The NYU Abu Dhabi Institute, a major hub of intellectual and creative activity and advanced research. The Institute hosts academic conferences, workshops, lectures, film series, performances, and other public programs directed both to audiences within the UAE and to the worldwide academic and research community. It is a center of the scholarly community for Abu Dhabi, bringing together faculty and researchers from institutions of higher learning throughout the region.

NYU Abu Dhabi, through the NYU Abu Dhabi Institute, is a world-class center of cutting-edge research, scholarship, and cultural activity. The Institute creates singular opportunities for leading researchers from across the arts, humanities, social sciences, sciences, engineering, and the professions to carry out creative scholarship and conduct research on issues of major disciplinary, multidisciplinary, and global significance.

About the Typefaces

The Arabic body text is set in DecoType Naskh, designed by Thomas Milo and Mirjam Somers, based on an analysis of five centuries of Ottoman manuscript practice. The exceptionally legible result is the first and only typeface in a style that fully implements the principles of script grammar (*qawāʿid al-khaṭṭ*).

The Arabic text in the footnotes and margin notes is set in DecoType Emiri, drawn by Mirjam Somers, based on the metal typeface in the naskh style that was cut for the 1924 Cairo edition of the Qur'an.

Both Arabic typefaces in this series are controlled by a dedicated font layout engine. ACE, the Arabic Calligraphic Engine, invented by Peter Somers, Thomas Milo, and Mirjam Somers of DecoType, first operational in 1985, pioneered the principle followed by later smart font layout technologies such as OpenType, which is used for all other typefaces in this series.

The Arabic text was set with WinSoft Tasmeem, a sophisticated user interface for DecoType ACE inside Adobe InDesign. Tasmeem was conceived and created by Thomas Milo (DecoType) and Pascal Rubini (WinSoft) in 2005.

The English text is set in Adobe Text, a new and versatile text typeface family designed by Robert Slimbach for Western (Latin, Greek, Cyrillic) typesetting. Its workhorse qualities make it perfect for a wide variety of applications, especially for longer passages of text where legibility and economy are important. Adobe Text bridges the gap between calligraphic Renaissance types of the 15th and 16th centuries and high-contrast Modern styles of the 18th century, taking many of its design cues from early post-Renaissance Baroque transitional types cut by designers such as Christoffel van Dijck, Nicolaus Kis, and William Caslon. While grounded in classical form, Adobe Text is also a statement of contemporary utilitarian design, well suited to a wide variety of print and on-screen applications.

About the Editor-Translator

Humphrey Davies is an award-winning translator of some twenty works of modern Arabic literature, among them Alaa Al-Aswany's *The Yacoubian Building* and Elias Khoury's *The Gate of the Sun*. He has also made a critical edition, translation, and lexicon of the Ottoman-period *Hazz al-quḥūf bi-sharḥ qaṣīd Abī Shādūf* (*Brains Confounded by the Ode of Abū Shādūf Expounded*) by Yūsuf al-Shirbīnī and compiled with a colleague an anthology entitled *Al-ʿāmmiyyah al-miṣriyyah al-maktūbah: mukhtārāt min 1400 ilā 2009* (*Egyptian Colloquial Writing: selections from 1400 to 2009*). He read Arabic at the University of Cambridge, received his Ph.D. from the University of California at Berkeley, and, previous to undertaking his first translation in 2003, worked for social development and research organizations in Egypt, Tunisia, Palestine, and Sudan. He is affiliated with the American University in Cairo, where he lives.